0009101

Fifth Edition

TODAY'S MATHEMATICS

Concepts and Methods in Elementary School Mathematics

JAMES W. HEDDENS

Kent State University

SRA® SCIENCE RESEARCH ASSOCIATES, INC.
Chicago, Henley-on-Thames, Sydney, Toronto

An IBM Company

Library of Congress Cataloging in Publication Data

Heddens, James W., 1925–
  Today's Mathematics.

  Includes bibliographies and index.
  1. Mathematics—Study and teaching (Elementary)
I. Title.
QA135.5.H42   1984   372.7'3044   84-1290
ISBN 0-574-23110-2

Printed in the United States of America.

10 9 8 7 6 5 4 3

Contents

Preface

This edition of *Today's Mathematics* is the fifth edition of this successful book. Each succeeding edition has been updated to reflect constant changes in the elementary school mathematics curriculum. This edition reflects the recommendations of the National Assessment of Educational Progress in Mathematics, as published by the National Council of Teachers of Mathematics in *An Agenda for Action*. This edition also attempts to reflect the emphasis that is now being placed upon hand-held calculators and microcomputers in both industry and the classroom. We must help teachers to feel comfortable using this technology in their classrooms.

Today's Mathematics has always emphasized the need for a good foundation in the basics. Using the calculator, we can accomplish the mechanics of an exercise much more quickly. However, the basics must include developing an understanding of concepts, emphasizing the thought processes, and teaching logical step-by-step procedures.

This edition of the text follows a format similar to previous editions, but we have augmented each unit to include suggestions for using hand-held calculators and microcomputers at each grade level. A checklist for a complete mathematics program has been included in the appendices. Teachers can easily use this checklist to develop a strong mathematics program to meet the needs of the particular children in each classroom.

The value of a mathematics program at any grade level is determined by how thoroughly the teacher understands what is being taught and how each child can learn in the most effective way. Certainly no text or course of instruction can give all the answers, but this text is designed to help you

1. Understand mathematical concepts in respect to structures of mathematics and number systems
2. Present these concepts to the learner
3. Comprehend how a given concept is developed at a given grade level and how it is expanded and reinforced at each successive level.

This text is structured to help you accomplish these goals quickly and easily. Each of the 17 units in this edition is organized into a carefully designed learning package:

1. The behavioral objectives are stated for each unit so that you can plan an effective learning program.
2. A set of related mathematical concepts (indicated by the unit title) is thoroughly developed with numerous examples.
3. Opportunity is provided for you to apply these concepts in solving examples; many such examples are provided.
4. Activities and materials are provided illustrating how the concepts presented in each chapter can be molded into a spiral curriculum.
5. Illustrative examples are provided to suggest the inclusion of calculator and microcomputer exercises in the elementary school mathematics program.
6. A bibliography of suggested readings is provided for each unit.

The author expresses gratitude to all the reviewers who have contributed invaluable suggestions and comments. I am thankful for this input and have incorporated their suggestions whenever possible. I am particularly indebted to Dr. William Speer of Bowling Green State University for his detailed analysis of the fourth edition of *Today's Mathematics*, including rewritten versions of units 1 and 17.

J.W.H

1 Teaching Mathematics

Teaching Competencies

Upon completing this unit, you will be able to:

Describe the characteristics of a contemporary elementary school mathematics program

Contrast the characteristics of a contemporary mathematics program with those of a more traditional program

Relate the advantages and disadvantages of a contemporary mathematics program

Describe the basic philosophy of teaching mathematics to children in a manner that promotes effective learning

Discussion

Society is in constant change, and the elementary program must keep pace with the changing society. For too many years the elementary mathematics program was static. The introduction of "modern mathematics" during the 1960s was an attempt to incorporate new content, learning theory, and research into school mathematics programs.

Our contemporary world demands a kind of mathematical knowledge that is very different from that required in the past. In previous generations people needed to be able to calculate efficiently and accurately. But now much of the task of calculation is being taken over by the machine. Hand calculators are now very inexpensive, compact, and easily obtainable. Many people in the business world carry their hand calculators with them for immediate use. Since machines are replacing clerks, people need to redefine their roles in our technological society. Today, and even more in the future, the need is for individuals who can, through disciplined imagination, define significant problems and discover creative ways to solve them.

Today an effective elementary school mathematics program must consider a wider range of objectives than just computational skill. Certainly, *skills* necessary for daily life must be taught but these are neither more nor less important than the development of *understandings* that free children from rote memorization. A contemporary mathematics program should also attempt to provide a satisfactory foundation for further study and exposure to a cultural and historical perspective of the role of mathematics in our society.

During the past 30 years, substantial changes have occurred in both teaching strategies and curricula of elementary mathematics programs. Learning theories—particularly the work of Robert Gagné, Catherine Stern, Jerome Bruner, Jean Piaget, and Zoltan Dienes—have greatly influenced how mathematics is taught. The content of elementary mathematics programs is constantly being evaluated and revised, and such phenomena as the "back-to-basics" approach, "new math," and curricular projects of the 1950s and 1960s have greatly changed the content of mathematics programs. More recently, the National Council of Supervisors of Mathematics issued a position describing 10 basic mathematics skills that should be incorporated in all mathematics programs. These skill areas, which are not intended to be mutually exclusive, include problem solving; estimation and approximation; alertness to reasonableness of responses; applying mathematics to everyday life; measurement; geometry; reading and interpreting graphs, tables, and charts; using mathematics to predict; computer literacy; *and* computational skill. It is important to note that computational skill represents only *one*, albeit important, basic skill area; of course, it is also an integral part of the other basic skill areas. Since computational skill is listed separately, this indicates that an overemphasis on computation to the exclusion of other skills should be avoided in a contemporary program.

The person is still the key. Machines are capable of fantastic computations, but constructing computer programs, programming them, and interpreting the vast amounts of data they produce are tasks for well-trained, analytical minds. The calculating capacity of computers has released us from the necessity for time-consuming computation and has given us the time for creative thinking—and for discovering and expressing the complex problems to be solved by machines. This necessity for abstract thought demands critical and analytical ability—and creative imagination—to discover new questions.

As we begin to explore what a good elementary school mathematics program consists of, three basic questions must be asked: What is mathematics? How do children learn mathematics? What mathematics should children learn?

At one time mathematics was thought to be the process of making calculations; mathematics programs were usually based upon computational drill and memorization of facts. Contemporary programs stress understanding basic mathematics and the interrelationships among different number systems. Does this mean that students must no longer memorize basic facts and no longer practice to develop computational skills? *Definitely not!* The point is that memorization and drill must be preceded by an understanding of why basic facts are true and why computational procedures (algorithms) work. Without this understanding, the pupil has little chance of progressing very far in mathematics or applying the mathematics he or she knows to significant practical problems or applications. An effective elementary school mathematics program emphasizes both understanding mathematical concepts and developing skills to provide the child with real ability in mathematics.

The second question to which we want to address ourselves is how children learn mathematics. If elementary mathematics instruction is to develop creative and imaginative mathematical minds, then the methods of presentation and instruction must be examined. For generations, the technique of instruction in mathematics was a two-step process:

1. The teacher used examples to *show* how to solve a particular type of example, or problem.
2. Students routinely imitated the given procedure mechanically to find answers to a great number of similar examples.

It is very easy for this method of instruction to degenerate into a mindless application of the deductive process. This "show-and-tell" approach to teaching mathematics promotes mainly imitation and drill of seemingly meaningless facts and rules. This method of instruction reveals little or nothing of the meaning behind the process that the student is imitating. Thousands of people solve problems daily; they "borrow" and "carry" numbers, wonder what to do with a remainder, or try to remember which of two fractions is the right one to "invert and multiply." Such confusion is the natural outcome of learning mathematics by imitation and rote memorization.

Rather than such a passive method of mathematics instruction, a contemporary program promotes an *active* learning process—active mentally, physically, and emotionally. In this active, guided discovery method, a skilled teacher places children into situations where each child's behavior reveals the extent of his or her reasoning and comprehension of the techniques and processes being presented. Pupils who "think through" mathematics in this way gain more confidence by their own discoveries than by trying to recall memorized rules. They comprehend the reasoning behind mathematical operations and processes and can apply them in new situations.

Using this interpretation of teaching, children *still* need to memorize basic facts or fundamental algorithms for calculating. Also, children still need practice and drill. Systematic reinforcement must be built into a good mathematics program. Such reinforcement must be based on the notion that the child has developed sufficient understanding of the concept to avoid the mechanical application of rules and procedures.

The guided discovery approach relies heavily on inductive (rather than deductive) methods. Children are asked to solve some examples using previously learned techniques and then make a general statement for solving examples of this particular type. In effect, children find their own rules or generalizations (with the teacher's guidance) and then use the generalizations to solve other examples. The teacher is providing a focus for the children's active discussion, rather than simply showing them the procedure to use in a given situation.

If you were visited by a creature from another planet and you wanted to convey the notion of what a tree is, you would hardly succeed by writing the word TREE on a slip of paper. Your success might improve if you tried to draw a picture of a tree. The stranger would then have a better chance of gaining some idea of what a tree is, but that understanding would be severely limited by your ability to draw. In any case, even a photograph would leave some misunderstandings about the nature of trees. If you want to give the stranger a foundation for understanding what a tree is, then it would be better to take the stranger outside to see one.

This is a good analogy for the teaching of mathematics. If you want to teach children about division, you would have little success simply stating a rote rule or procedure. A picture of what takes place when you divide would certainly be more beneficial, but it would still be less effective than using physical objects to illustrate the process of dividing a set or collection into equivalent groups. Students are not prepared to learn a concept at the abstract or symbolic level until they have had sufficient experiences with the concept at the concrete or manipulative level or, at the very least, at the representative or pictorial level.

One great advantage of the inductive approach is the freedom children experience in looking for ways to solve mathematical examples. Without set rules to condition their thinking, children are free to find that a given example can be solved in various ways. Thus pupils discover through their own experience one of the major features of contemporary mathematics: there is often more than one way to arrive at a solution. When children are allowed this freedom and are encouraged to use their imaginations without being tied to arbitrary rules and rigid patterns, they will learn to seek the best way to solve any problem. Even slower students, guided by a careful and patient teacher, can appreciate the fact that a problem doesn't necessarily have just one way of being solved. This may, in fact, be a great encouragement to the slower, less imaginative student, who no longer must be baffled and discouraged by trying to remember half-understood rules.

In most cases a child's approach will be conditioned by his own experience. He may not choose the best or quickest method to solve a problem if his experience has not included relevant knowledge. For example, if a child does not understand place value and is called on to complete an addition sentence such as $23 + 41 = \square$, his best approach would probably be to use counters as a model: to count out 23 counters, count out 41 counters, then scoop the two sets up together and count to determine that he has a total of 64 counters. Another child might recognize that he has 23 counters and, beginning with 23, count out 41 more counters to arrive at a total of 64. The second method is slightly more sophisticated than the first. A third child might recognize 23 on the number line and begin counting from that point. Beginning at 23, he would count 41 units and arrive at a point named 64. Another child, familiar with place value, might react in this fashion: "Add the tens: $40 + 20 = 60$; add the ones: $1 + 3 = 4$; $60 + 4 = 64$; therefore my answer is 64." Still another child might arrange the addends vertically. He might think "$3 + 1 = 4$" and write the 4; "$20 + 40 = 60$" and write 60 under the 4; and "$4 + 60 = 64$" and write 64 for the answer.

$$
\begin{array}{rcr}
23 & & 23 \\
+41 & & +41 \\
\hline
4 & \text{or} & 60 \\
+60 & & +\ 4 \\
\hline
64 & & 64
\end{array}
$$

So we have at least five different methods for completing the addition sentence $23 + 41 = \square$. In each case the child has had the opportunity to think according to his own level of ability. In this example each student had used the same basic concepts but at different levels of comprehension and abstraction. The purpose is certainly not to keep children operating at a primitive level but to move them as quickly as possible through appropriate experiences to more efficient levels of operation.

Problem-solving activities should be varied and taken from real-life situations so that students do not get the idea that mathematics problems exist only in textbooks. Research in learning theory suggests that the frequent use of physical objects that children can manipulate and experiment with is essential for developing abstract concepts. It is likewise an important part of developing skill in solving practical mathematical problems. Thus it is no surprise that there is increasing interest in laboratory activities and manipulative materials for the mathematics classroom.

Laboratory activities can be used for a variety of purposes—to build readiness for abstract concepts, to provide motivation, to develop problem-solving skills, and to present significant applications of mathematics to practical problems. Children at all levels of ability can profit from laboratory experiences, and a folder of activities can be a valuable resource for the classroom teacher.

Children should not be allowed to get the idea that problem solving is simply a matter of thrashing around aimlessly until one happens to find a solution. An orderly and well-thought-out approach

should be stressed. The approach used should be selected with reasoning and understanding. Children should realize, however, that even with careful selection one does not always choose the best method the first time, and they should be encouraged to take various approaches to a given problem when a solution is not readily apparent. Today teachers and pupils may spend time together seeking solutions to problems. Children should be aware that even capable scientists and mathematicians do not have a magical "instant" solution to every problem. It is good for them to know that mathematicians may solve problems, check them, and then go back and look for other approaches when their results indicate that something is wrong. The very nature of the word "problem" indicates that often a solution is not readily apparent.

Let us examine briefly some of the learning theories and experimental projects that are influencing elementary school mathematics programs.

One influential theory in mathematical learning has been that of Jean Piaget, noted Swiss psychologist. Piaget has identified four stages of child development: *sensory-motor, preoperational, concrete operational,* and *formal operational.* The sensory-motor stage occurs from birth to about age two, a preverbal and presymbolic stage in which intelligence is defined as the ability to accomplish some task (for instance, to obtain a toy on a blanket by pulling the blanket). At this stage, the child solves problematic situations by experimentation and action rather than by a mental process. In the preoperational stage, which begins at about the age of two and continues until about age seven, language is acquired and the child begins to understand signs and symbols as representations of the real world. However, the child still does not develop knowledge of conservation, the concept that essential properties of things do not change when superficial properties are changed. A classical example of conservation involves two rows of counters, spaced differently; a child is asked if the rows contain the same number of objects, fewer objects, or more objects. (See top of page 6.)

In the first example, the child at the preoperational stage will say there are the same number of counters; in the second, he or she will say there are more white counters; in the third, the response will be that there are more black ones. The child will display the same kind of reasoning when confronted with other conservation tasks.

In stage three of Piaget's theory of development, the concrete operational stage, the child develops logico-mathematical thought. This stage begins at approximately age seven (sometimes earlier, sometimes as late as age nine or ten). At this stage, children can manipulate objects and show logical

Begin with

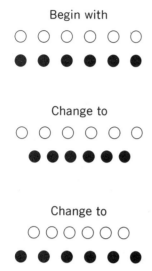

Change to

Change to

thinking—they understand conservation and other logical processes. (For activities to see if a child is functioning at these various stages, see Richard Copeland's *Math Activities for Children: A Diagnostic and Developmental Approach*.) Finally, at stage four, the formal operational stage, children develop the ability to think abstractly, to make hypotheses. This stage begins at around age eleven or twelve.

Considerable research is still needed to verify Piaget's work—there is still some question about whether the rate of progress through the four stages can be accelerated or impeded and, if so, how. But one assumption that we can make is that teachers should do everything possible to provide a stimulating environment for children and encourage them to experiment, discover mathematical patterns themselves, and question how processes of mathematics work.

Another theory of learning that is receiving a great deal of attention today is Jerome Bruner's idea that a child passes through three levels of understanding: *enactive, iconic,* and *symbolic.* At the enactive level, the child manipulates objects and in the process develops the ability to conceptualize; at the iconic level, the child can think without manipulating objects; at the symbolic level, the child becomes capable of manipulating symbols and translating experience into language. Bruner's theory suggests that children should begin by manipulating concrete, or tangible, objects, then generalize a concept or idea based on the manipulating of these materials, then move to expressing the concept in symbolic form. The discovery method of teaching is based on Bruner's theory—process is more important than product. For more information, consult Bruner's book, *Toward a Theory of Instruction.*

Another step forward in mathematics education is due to Zoltan P. Dienes, British educator and creator of the Dienes Multibase Arithmetic Blocks. Dienes identifies four basic principles upon which he structured the multibase blocks:

1. According to *dynamic principle,* children should be given undirected free play with the blocks before they are given structured activities.

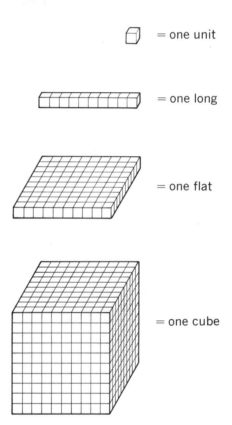

2. According to the *constructive principle,* children develop constructive thinking intuitively before analytical thinking (before they can make logical judgments). For instance, the children see what a place-value system is by manipulating the base-ten blocks.

The children should realize that it takes ten units to have as much wood as one long, that it takes ten longs to have as much wood as one flat, and that it takes ten flats to have as much wood as one cube. This requires constructive thinking but not analytical thinking (which according to Dienes is not usually developed before the age of twelve).

For example, the following figure represents the number 134.

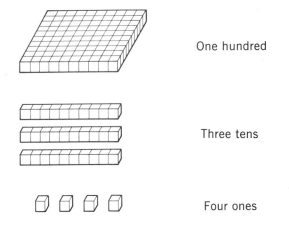

One hundred

Three tens

Four ones

3. According to the *mathematical variability principle* the relationship among variables can remain constant although the variables are changed. Using the place-value concept exemplified with Dienes Blocks, it can be seen that ten longs contain as much wood as one flat and ten units have as much wood as one long. For example, look at the following arrangement:

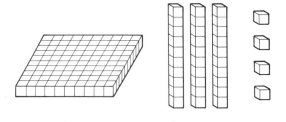

One long may be exchanged for ten units; then we have:

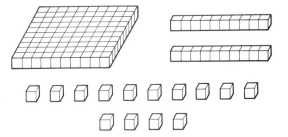

4. According to the *perceptual variability principle*, a conceptual structure can remain unchanged when precepts are changed. With Dienes Blocks we can use the same conceptual

structure of base-ten blocks and then substitute the base-five or base-three blocks. The place-value concept is exactly the same but the blocks are grouped by fives or by threes.

Dienes recommends that the children have free play with the blocks and then move to structured activities from which they can abstract basic mathematical concepts; these concepts should then be examined in many different contexts.

In the second edition of Robert Gagné's book, *The Conditions of Learning*, he discusses what he calls the internal and external conditions of learning. Internal conditions are those the learner already possesses that are needed for a successful learning experience. External conditions are those over which the learner has no control—for instance, instructions for activities or exercises.

Gagné describes a hierarchy of learning in which he identifies eight steps in the learning process. Each step is discussed in respect to the internal and external conditions of learning. Beginning with the least complex form of learning, the eight steps or *types* are:

Type 1 Signal learning
Type 2 Stimulus-response learning
Type 3 Chaining
Type 4 Verbal association
Type 5 Multiple discrimination learning
Type 6 Concept learning
Type 7 Principle learning
Type 8 Problem solving

The child is guided step-by-step through a learning experience. The step the child is operating on is determined by a pretest; then, when the subject matter is determined, a sequential program is developed and presented to the learner. The learner moves from the lower levels of learning systematically through concepts and principles to the highest level of problem solving. A great deal of emphasis is placed upon prerequisite learning *and* prerequisite experiences—previous knowledge and activities that are necessary to comprehend the new material.

Catherine Stern has developed a "structural arithmetic" program based on a unique set of materials. Using a set of blocks (which are scored blocks) and a variety of containers, the learner is to "see" and develop the basic relationships among numbers from 1 to 10. The number system can be presented through 100 with these materials. The learner is taken through the materials three times, but each time a different purpose is to be accomplished. The first time through the materials concepts of relationships between numbers are developed, the second time through the materials concepts of numbers are developed, and the third time the use of numerals is developed. The program continues through the primary grades. Catherine Stern's book *Helping Children Discover Arithmetic* is a must for primary teachers.

Cuisenaire rods are a color-coded set of rods that have received some attention in mathematics in American schools. Color is a significant attribute of the rods that helps learners develop concepts of numbers. A significant characteristic is the flexibility that Cuisenaire rods can introduce into an elementary school mathematics program. You may want to examine the rods and other materials available from the Cuisenaire Company of America.

Many different manipulative and pictorial aids can be effectively used to illustrate mathematical concepts typically found in a contemporary elementary school mathematics program. Geoboards, balances, counting blocks or sticks, pattern or attribute blocks, and many everyday items such as spoons or milk cartons can be used to model concepts and processes. Remember it is important to begin at the concrete—manipulative level, when introducing concepts, and work toward more efficient methods and processes once the foundation is firm.

In this unit we have attempted to introduce you to mathematics as it is taught today. Mathematics education is bringing together new learning theories and new materials for creative teachers to use in developing exciting classroom environments.

Terminology, Symbols, and Procedures

Algorithm   The form in which mathematical computations are written and solved, showing the steps necessary to solve them, is an algorithm. For example:

$$
\begin{array}{r}
\left.\begin{array}{r} 2 \\ 30 \\ 200 \end{array}\right\}232 \\
23\overline{)5349} \\
4600 \\ \hline
749 \\
690 \\ \hline
59 \\
46 \\ \hline
\textcircled{13}
\end{array}
\qquad \text{or} \qquad
\begin{array}{r}
232 \\
23\overline{)5349} \\
46 \\ \hline
74 \\
69 \\ \hline
59 \\
46 \\ \hline
\textcircled{13}
\end{array}
$$

Deductive Method   The process of examining a general rule or set of rules and applying the rules to a specific situation is called deductive reasoning (for example, applying the general rule, "the product of two negative numbers is always positive," to the specific exercise: $(-5) \times (-7) = \square$).

Inductive Method   The process of examining several specific situations and formulating a general rule that applies to each case is called inductive reasoning. The processes of inductive reasoning and guided discovery teaching are used when searching for patterns, comparisons, and similarities in mathematics.

Level of Abstraction   Mathematics can be presented at several levels of abstraction—for example, *symbolically* (using abstract symbols and words), *representatively* (using pictures and visual aids), and *concretely* (using manipulatable physical objects). When

introducing a concept, it is best to begin with a concrete model that aids understanding of the concept. After the child has attached some meaning to the concept
through manipulative and pictorial experiences, then symbols may be introduced.

Rote Memorization   The process of memorizing information or rules without an understanding of the principles or meaning underlying the information or rules is called rote
memorization.

Discussion Questions

1. Describe the characteristics of a good elementary mathematics program.

2. Give some examples that will contrast inductive and deductive teaching of
mathematics.

3. Select two theories of learning; compare and contrast them as they relate to the
teaching of elementary school mathematics.

4. Select a topic from elementary school mathematics, and describe activities for that
topic at the concrete—manipulative, representative—pictorial, and abstract—symbolic
levels.

5. Describe the importance of having children work with proper materials so they can
discover and generalize about mathematical concepts. (Locate and examine the materials
mentioned in this chapter.)

Suggested Readings

Ashlock, Robert B., and others *Guiding Each Child's Learning of Mathematics: A Diagnostic Approach to Instruction.* Columbus, Ohio: Merrill, 1983.

Begle, Edward, ed. *Mathematics Education.* The Sixty-Ninth Yearbook of the National Society for the
Study of Education, Part I. Chicago, Ill.: University of Chicago Press, 1970.

Billstein, Rick, and Lott, Johnny W. "More Reflections on Teaching Mathematics for Elementary
School Teachers." *The Arithmetic Teacher,* vol. 29, no. 5, January 1982.

Brown, Sue D., and Brown, Donald E. "A Look at the Past." *The Arithmetic Teacher*, vol. 27, no. 5,
January 1980.

Dienes, Zoltan P. *Building Up Mathematics.* London: Hutchinson Educational, 1960.

Fey, James T. "Mathematics Teaching Today: Perspectives from Three National Surveys." *The Arithmetic Teacher*, vol. 27, no. 2, October 1979.

Fowler, Mary Anne. "Diagnostic Teaching of Elementary School Mathematics." *The Arithmetic
Teacher*, vol. 27, no. 7, March 1980.

Gagné, Robert M. *The Conditions of Learning.* New York: Holt, Rinehart & Winston, 1965.

Gibb, E. Glenadine. "One Point of View: Teaching Effectively and Efficiently." *The Arithmetic Teacher*, vol. 29, no. 7, March 1982.

Glenn, John A., ed. *Teaching Primary Mathematics*. New York: Harper & Row, 1977.

Hamrick, Kathy B. "Are We Introducing Mathematical Symbols Too Soon?" *The Arithmetic Teacher*, vol. 28, no. 3, November 1980.

Leake, Lowell. "Some Reflections on Teaching Mathematics for Elementary School Teachers." *The Arithmetic Teacher*, vol. 28, no. 3, November 1980.

Lindquist, Mary Montgomery, ed. *Selected Issues in Mathematics Education*. 1981 Yearbook of the National Society for the Study of Education. Berkeley, Calif.: McCutchan, 1980.

Long, Calvin T. "A Modern Mathematics Fable." *School Science and Mathematics Association*, vol. 83, no. 2, February 1983.

Mendell, Robert L. "Children Can Understand Mathematics." *The Arithmetic Teacher*, vol. 29, no. 5, January 1982.

National Council of Teachers of Mathematics. *Priorities in School Mathematics*. Reston, Va.: NCTM, 1981.

Oberlin, Lynn. "How to Teach Children to Hate Mathematics." *School Science and Mathematics Association*, vol. 82, no. 3, March 1982.

Piaget, Jean. *The Child's Conception of Number.* New York: Norton, 1965.

Schaefer, Sister M. Geralda. "Motivational Activities in Elementary Mathematics." *The Arithmetic Teacher*, vol. 28, no. 9, May 1981.

Shufelt, Gwendolyn, ed. *The Agenda in Action*. Reston, Va.: National Council of Teachers of Mathematics, 1983.

Silvey, Linda, ed. *Mathematics for the Middle Grades (5–9)*. Reston, Va.: National Council of Teachers of Mathematics, 1982.

Speer, William R. "'Do You See What I Hear?' A Look at Individual Learning Styles." *The Arithmetic Teacher*, vol. 27, no. 3, November 1979.

Stern, Catherine, and Stern, Margaret B. *Helping Children Discover Arithmetic: An Introduction to Structural Arithmetic.* New York: Harper & Row, 1971.

Virginia Council of Teachers of Mathematics. *Practical Ways to Teach the Basic Mathematical Skills*. Richmond, Va.: VCTM, 1978.

Whitaker, Donald R. "Contemporary Goals for Mathematics Instruction." *School Science and Mathematics Association*, vol. 82, no.7, October 1982.

2 Technology, Teaching, and Learning

Teaching Competencies

Upon completing this unit, you will be able to:

State uses for the hand-held calculator and the microcomputer in a good mathematics program

Determine whether a microcomputer is appropriate to use with children in specific situations

Explain the uses for microcomputers in a mathematics classroom

State the difference between hardware and software

List the advantages and limitations of a microcomputer in a classroom

Use some beginning BASIC language in an appropriate manner and context

Discussion

The popularity of low-cost, hand-held calculators and low-cost microcomputers is raising serious questions concerning the teaching of mathematics. Obviously, technology has had a major impact *outside* the classroom. However, is the use of technology appropriate *inside* the classroom? Preparing children to function successfully in the real world is a primary goal of mathematics instruction. Thus, since technology is part of the real world, school systems and teachers have an obligation to teach children how to use that technology. Society is now becoming aware that children need computer literacy just as much as they need reading and writing.

The responsibility for teaching children to understand and use computers rests almost entirely on the administrators and teachers in our school systems. Most educators feel that the mathematics program is the instructional area that must accept this challenge. Unfortunately, some elementary school teachers are entirely unprepared to handle the curriculum planning and teaching computer literacy to children. Some elementary school teachers have never even touched a microcomputer, let alone program or use the computer in their teaching. David Moursand, a well-known computer education expert, has stated that "we are asking computer-illiterate teachers to help students become computer-literate at a functional level."

The growing placement of microcomputers in classrooms is supported by school administrators, teachers, and parents. Schools usually begin to plan how to use the computers after they are installed. If we make the assumption that technology is a viable tool of mathematics instruction, when should computers be introduced into the instructional program? Should technology be introduced in the primary grades, or should we hold off until students have mastered basic mathematics concepts and skills? Should microcomputers be an integral part of classroom instruction, or should they be reserved for special uses? The range of opinion concerning these and other related questions is indeed broad.

Hand-Held Calculators

Calculators have for some time been the focus of considerable discussion among mathematics educators. Of course, extreme viewpoints have been represented along with the more common moderate opinions. Some have argued that the calculator should never be used in an elementary school classroom until the basic facts have already been mastered. Others believe that the calculator does not pose a threat to skill mastery so there is no harm introducing it at any point.

The aggressiveness of this debate has subsided in recent years. Now, the commonly accepted position is that, when used appropriately, the calculator can be effective at all levels of instruction, including the primary grades. The phrase "used appropriately" usually implies that the calculator is used for more than simply checking answers to seatwork or homework papers. The calculator can be used so that it serves as an aid to understanding concepts.

For example, how can we find the square root of a given number, and what does *square root* mean?

To develop an understanding of square root, *do not use the square root key* on the calculator. Let's locate an approximate square root value for 13. Since we understand what squaring a number means, let's use this concept as the starting point. What square numbers are located on each side of 13? We know that $3 \times 3 = 9$ and that $4 \times 4 = 16$: 13 is located between 9 and 16. So the square root of 13 must be between 3 and 4. Now let's locate the number in the tens place. The number 13 is closer to the number 16 than it is to 9. So we will select a number a little greater than 3.5. Now try 3.6, and square it. Using the calculator, we find that $3.6 \times 3.6 = 12.96$. Now let's try $3.7 \times 3.7 = 13.69$. Since 12.96 is closer to 13 than 13.69, we should try a number a little greater than 3.6. Using the calculator to multiply 3.61×3.61, we find that the square is 13.0321. Continue this estimating process until the square root of 13 is estimated to the number places needed.

The calculator can also be a *self-checking* device, as illustrated in the addition example described here. Round the following numbers to the nearest hundred. After rounding each one, enter the result in the calculator, and press the + key. When you finish, the number in the display should match the following boxed number.

$$6137$$
$$13490$$
$$2856$$
$$9720$$
$$\underline{26882}$$
$$\underline{59100}$$

In this example, the objective is to round numbers to the nearest hundred. The student, not the calculator, must satisfy this objective. That is, the calculator does not perform the task; it merely serves as a self-checking device. If the student does not get a result of 59100 at the end of this exercise, then an error must have occurred and the student will be made aware of this. Note, however, that the calculator does not provide information about *where* the error occurred. This is beneficial in this case; since the number of exercises is not large, the student who has not mastered the objective must now check each exercise, rather than simply go to the one "marked wrong."

Remember, as we begin to explore hand-held calculators, most capabilities of calculators are shared by microcomputers used in the immediate mode.

The purpose of this section is to explore the arguments for and against the use of calculators in the classroom and to help develop competence using the calculator. Since the hand-held calculator has appeared on the market, it has enjoyed tremendous popularity. It is estimated that in 1980 there were nearly 80 million calculators in use in the United States. As the price of calculators continues to decline, many more children will have access to them. Obviously, the calculator boom is a phenomenon that the school cannot afford to ignore. Calculators are here to stay, and education must accept that fact and provide for the instruction of mathematics with calculators.

Effective use of the hand-held calculator in the classroom will depend largely upon the skill, knowledge, and ingenuity of the classroom teacher. The calculator should be an integral part of the mathematics curriculum and not just an appendage for checking calculations already performed. The calculator is especially useful in developing understanding of place value, reversibility, relationships among numbers, operations, decimals, metric measure, prime factoring, composites, changing fractions to decimals, and in percentages, as well as for making mathematical estimates. Other uses will become apparent as we develop the curriculum for calculator instruction.

For elementary school use, a calculator should be based upon algebraic logic. The calculator should be inexpensive, durable, accessible to the children, and have multiple uses. The keyboard should be of reasonable size with spring-loaded keys that click when they are depressed. The display should be bright, easily readable, and visible from a reasonable angle. The most desirable power source will depend upon the facilities available to the teacher. If many electrical sockets are available, then rechargeable batteries with AC adapters are superior. If rechargeable facilities are limited, then long-life replaceable batteries are preferable. Solar-powered calculators are becoming very popular; they are cheaper than many other models.

There are basically two types of calculators: LED (light-emitting diode) or LCD (liquid crystal display). The LCD uses less energy and has a brighter display screen than the LED. The brighter screen is easier to read in sunlight or from an angle. Many newer calculators have automatic shut-off features.

For effective use of the hand-held calculator in the classroom, it is recommended that teachers have available preservice and inservice workshops.

Right from the beginning develop good techniques for using the hand-held calculator. Do not watch the keys as you calculate. Watch the display panel and assess the reasonableness of the values that appear on it. When batteries are weak or the calculator is broken, wrong answers can appear on the display panel. Learn to operate the calculator with the opposite hand from the one you use to write. Thus you can hold a pencil, and record the results of the calculation with one hand while using the calculator with the other. Begin each calculator example by pressing the **clear key** ©. This will always prevent any extraneous numbers from interfering with the results.

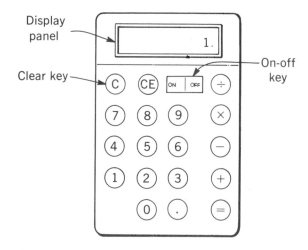

The calculator will have an on-off switch, a **display panel,** and 18 keys or more. In this text, a number or a letter with a ring around it indicates a key that should be pressed on the calculator. For example, Ⓒ ① would mean to push the clear key followed by pushing the one key; and a 1 should appear in the display panel. Note that the numeric keys on a hand-held calculator are located in the same place as the number pads on a microcomputer.

A musician plays a musical instrument without looking at the keys; a typist types without watching the keyboard. Similarly, an individual should become familiar with the hand-held calculator keyboard so that it is not necessary to look at the keys as one calculates. Cut a small hole in the bottom of a medium-sized paper sack and place the keyboard inside it so that only the display is observable.

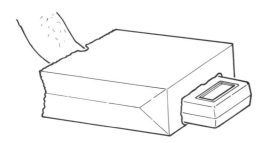

Practice by pushing a predetermined key on the calculator and then check the display to make sure that the correct key was depressed. Now push the clear key Ⓒ without looking and try another example. Practice until you are accurate. Remember to use the hand that you do *not* use to write.

After the digits keys have been located correctly, begin to incorporate additional keys one at a time. The addition key ⊕ might be the next logical key to select. Use the paper sack and practice simple addition examples such as $1 + 2 = 3$. By watching the display you will observe the 1 after you have pushed the ① key. If the addition key ⊕ is pushed next the 1 should still appear on the display. Now push the ② key and a 2 should appear on the display. Next hit the ⊜ key and a 3 should appear on the display. Press the clear key Ⓒ and you are ready to use the calculator for the next example. The key marked Ⓒᴱ can be used to correct an entry. If a key is accidentally pushed, depress the Ⓒᴱ key and it will remove the incorrect number from the calculator so that you may enter the correct number.

Let us examine several more addition examples using the calculator. For example, $34 + 51 = \square$. One would start with the ③ key and read from left to right.

Push Key   Ⓒ ③ ④ ⊕ ⑤ ① ⊜

Display   0   3   34   34   5   51   85

Now try this example: $123 + 78 + 6 + 37 = \square$

Push Key

Ⓒ ① ② ③ ⊕ ⑦ ⑧ ⊕ ⑥ ⊕ ③ ⑦ ⊜

Display

0   1   12   123   123   7   78   78   6   6   3   37   244

If the sequence in which we push the keys is written in vertical form we get what we call a **program.** It is a great deal like a computer program. The program for the example above would be:

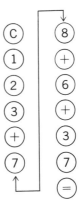

Long programs like the preceding one can be shortened into steps; each step is called an **instruction. Input** is used to indicate what numbers should be put into the calculator. The preceding program can be written:

Instruction
Ⓒ
Input 123
⊕
Input 78
⊕
Input 6
⊕
Input 37
⊜

Instruction refers to a step in a program. *Input* means to push the keys to enter the proper numbers.

Solve an addition example that has decimals such as: $6.78 + 34.8 = \Box$.

Press
⑥ ⊙ ⑦ ⑧

Press
③ ④ ⊙ ⑧

Instructions	Display
ⓒ	0
Input	6.78
⊕	6.78
Input 34.8	34.8
⊜	41.58

To solve any addition example with a hand-held calculator, use the following program:

Instructions
ⓒ
Input A
⊕
Input B
⊕
Input C
⋮

Program for any addition example

Now let us look at the inverse operation of subtraction, then solve examples. We will use the key marked ⊖. Our first example will be: $9 - 5 = \Box$.

Instructions	Display
ⓒ	0
⑨	9
⊖	9
⑤	5
⊜	4

Try a subtraction example that involves decimals: $3.78 - .46 = \Box$.

③ ⊙ ⑦ ⑧

⊙ ④ ⑥

Instructions	Display
ⓒ	0
Input 3.78	3.78
⊖	3.78
Input .46	.46
⊜	3.32

Try a subtraction example in which the addend is greater than the sum: $56 - 74 = \Box$.

⑤ ⑥

⑦ ④

Instructions	Display
ⓒ	0
Input 56	56
⊖	56
Input 74	74
⊜	⁻18

The inverse operation of subtraction can be generalized into a program with the following set of instructions: $A - B = \Box$.

Instructions
ⓒ
Input A
⊖
Input B
⊜

The two operations of addition and subtraction can be put into one example. However you may encounter some difficulties in these examples, particularly if parentheses are involved. Begin with the example: $8 + 7 - 6 = \Box$.

Instructions	Display
ⓒ	0
Input 8	8
⊕	8
Input 7	7
⊖	15
Input 6	6
⩵	9

The example $9 - 4 + 3$ can be interpreted two different ways.

$$9 - (4 + 3) = \square \quad \text{or} \quad (9 - 4) + 3 = \square$$
$$9 - 7 = 2 \qquad\qquad\quad 5 + 3 = 8$$

Instructions	Display
ⓒ	0
Input 4	4
⊕	4
Input 3	3
⩵	7
ⓒ	0
Input 9	9
⊖	9
Input 7	7
⩵	2

Instructions	Display
ⓒ	0
Input 9	9
⊖	9
Input 4	4
⊕	5
Input 3	3
⩵	8

Always do the calculations within the parentheses first. Sometimes it will be necessary to do

a calculation, clear the calculator, and enter the next part of the example. This will be necessary when the parentheses appear first in the mathematics statement.

Let us experiment with the multiplication key. As a beginning example, consider: $7 \times 8 = \square$.

Instructions	Display
ⓒ	0
Input 7	7
⊗	7
Input 8	8
⩵	56

Since no parentheses appear in this example, the operation can be performed in normal order, from left to right.

Now let's experiment with an example that involves decimals: $23.5 \times 7.89 = \square$.

Instructions	Display
ⓒ	0
Input 23.5	23.5
⊗	23.5
Input 7.89	7.89
⩵	185.415

Note that again the information is entered into the calculator from left to right in order. An example with three factors can be solved in any order. This is permissible because the associative property is applicable to multiplication. Multiply $3 \times 4 \times 5 = \square$, then multiply $4 \times 5 \times 3 = \square$, then try $3 \times 5 \times 4 = \square$.

Instructions	Display
ⓒ	0
Input 3	3
⊗	3
Input 4	4
⊗	12
Input 5	5
⩵	60

Instructions	Display
Ⓒ	0
Input 4	4
⊗	4
Input 5	5
⊗	20
Input 3	3
⊜	60

Instructions	Display
Ⓒ	0
Input 3	3
⊗	3
Input 5	5
⊗	15
Input 4	4
⊜	60

In all three examples, the same factors are multiplied, the order of the factors is changed, yet the product is the same.

Let us now try a division example: $24 \div 4 = \Box$.

Instructions	Display
Ⓒ	0
Input 24	24
⊘	24
Input 4	4
⊜	6

Try a division example with decimals: $26.352 \div 8 = \Box$.

Instructions	Display
Ⓒ	0
Input 26.3522	26.352
⊘	26.352
Input 8	8
⊜	3.294

We have learned that division is not associative: therefore we know that the order in which a division example is calculated makes a difference in the answer. Consider the example: $24 \div 4 \div 2 = \Box$. Does $24 \div (4 \div 2)$ give the same answer as $(24 \div 4) \div 2$?

$$24 \div (4 \div 2) = 24 \div 2 = 12$$

$$(24 \div 4) \div 2 = 6 \div 2 = 3$$

We can see that it *does* make a difference in what order we proceed with a division example.

After you have become familiar with your calculator and you have solved many examples on it, you will want to study and work with the other keys on the calculator. Calculators are useful tools and you will want to work continually to extend your understanding of their use.

Encourage children to learn how to operate the hand-held calculator and understand when it would be beneficial and when it would not. The calculator will only do what it is told to do—students must learn to decide what kinds of situation require a calculator and how to use the calculator in those situations.

Microcomputers in the Immediate Mode

Hand-held calculators have moved into the school setting, and now the invasion of microcomputers has also begun. It has been estimated that 49,000 microcomputers were installed in schools during 1981.* The rise in installations of microcomputers in educational settings is predicted to continue throughout the 1980s, so that by 1987 more than 2.5 million microcomputers will be installed in the schools. The rapid growth in the number of computers in the schools has placed pressure upon teachers to become knowledgeable about computers. Some teacher education programs require all education majors to become computer literate.

The microcomputer, when used in the immediate mode, functions much like the hand-held calculator. Statements are used to provide instructions to the microcomputer; statements given to the computer in the immediate mode are executed immediately.

When a microcomputer is powered up (turned on), it will display a word such as READY with a flashing cursor on the video screen. The machine is now in the immediate mode and ready to be used. Input from the typewriter-like keyboard will appear at the point where the cursor is positioned. The cursor will move one space to the right, as each key is depressed. Most computers have a key for erasing something from a particular location on the screen.

Each statement in the immediate mode must be preceded by a question mark. After a statement has been typed into the computer by pressing the RETURN or ENTER key, the computer will execute that statement. Here are some samples of immediate-mode computer statements for practice:

Immediate Mode Statement	Strike either	Screen Display
?3+4	RETURN or ENTER key	?3+4 7
?8−5		?8−5 3
?4*5		?4*5 20
?8/2		?8/2 4
?"HELLO"		?"HELLO" HELLO

*David Rosenwald. "Commodore Meets the Challenge of a Growing Education Market." *The Commodore Microcomputer Magazine*, vol. 4, no. 2, May 1983.

If you make an error in the immediate mode, the computer will display ?SYNTAX ERROR on the video screen. Note the symbols used for the arithmetic operations:

Symbol	Meaning
+	Add
−	Subtract
*	Multiply
/	Divide

Parentheses are used to indicate the order of operations, as with ordinary mathematical computations; parentheses are interpreted to mean "do me first." Study these examples:

a) (3+4)/(2*3) means add 3 and 4, then divide the 7 by 6, which equals 1.16666667.
b) 7−(1+4) means add 1 and 4, then subtract that sum from 7, which equals 2.
c) (3*4)+(7−5)/3 which means 3 times 4, added to the number 7 − 5 divided by 3, which equals 12 + .6666667 for a total of 12.6666667.
d) ((3*4)+(7−5))/3 which means 3 times 4, add 7 subtract 5 (which is 12 add 2) then divide by 3, which is 4.66666667.

All these examples can be solved on a hand-held calculator or a microcomputer in the immediate mode. The microcomputer can be used to print words as well as to solve arithmetic examples. The procedure is to begin the statement with a question mark, then type what is to be printed within quotation marks. For example:

Immediate mode Statement	Strike ENTER or RETURN key	Screen Display
?"Saturday"		?"Saturday" Saturday
?"January"		?"January" January

You will want to experiment with the microcomputer and create many statements in the immediate mode. After an example is entered into the computer, study the example, solve it, then press the ENTER or RETURN key and check to make sure you are correct. If you are having difficulty, consult the manual that accompanies your computer.

Microcomputers in the Program Mode

The focus of the debate over technology in the classroom has recently switched from the calculator to the microcomputer. Many of the same arguments are presented although the opposition is considerably reduced. In fact, most schools are actively seeking ways to incorporate the microcomputer into their curriculum in all subject areas. The remaining debate centers on the educational uses of the microcomputer.

Various types of software programs have been developed and are available to teachers for classroom use. These include but are not limited to the following categories:

> Drill and practice
> Educational games
> Simulations
> Tutorial
> Problem solving
> Records management
> Material generation

These uses are not mutually exclusive but the majority of available computer programs focus mostly on one particular area. It is important for teachers to distinguish between these uses, in order to judge the effectiveness and efficiency of a given program. For example, we might examine a program dealing with basic multiplication facts couched in an arcade-like setting and easily categorize this as an educational game. Actually, such a program would be better classified as drill and practice, since the concepts involved are to be memorized and/or subject to immediate recall.

Similarly, a program that involves estimating various lengths and angles (couched in a golf or artillery game) could be classified as drill and practice, although it should really be considered an educational game. In this instance, the game format is not used to drill knowledge-level material, but rather to assist the students to develop estimation skills not subject to immediate recall.

Teachers must become effective software evaluators. Software evaluation techniques and forms are available in the literature. Research the literature, and locate available criteria for evaluating software. First isolate the purpose of the program. Then compare the purpose with the features of the program, in respect to grade level, validity of content, correlation with curriculum, and instructional design features.

Drill and practice seem to be the major uses of microcomputers in the classroom. The computer is thus a rather expensive electronic worksheet for children. However more computer-assisted instruction (CAI) programs are becoming available for classroom use. CAI is an instructional situation between learner and computer that presents material in an interactive mode, with systematic evaluation as an integral part of the program.

Teachers are also using computers for computer-managed instruction (CMI). CMI provides the classroom teacher with computer technology to keep records, store test information, and provide prescriptive information to meet individual student needs.

Now let's look at the teacher's capability for using programming techniques within the classroom. Many languages are available to be used on a microcomputer. Because of the popularity of BASIC (Beginners All-purpose Symbolic Instruction Code), we will deal only with this language. Primary teachers might want to become familiar with LOGO, however. Other languages available for elementary-school teachers include PILOT and COMAL. The COMAL language is more popular in Europe than in the United States.

Operating a microcomputer in the program mode using BASIC requires each statement to begin with a line number. After each statement is typed into the computer, it must be placed into memory by pressing the ENTER or RETURN key. Using line numbers changes the computer from the immediate to the program mode. A program consists of several program lines each beginning with a statement number. When executed in order, these statements will cause certain tasks to be performed. The program can be executed by typing the word RUN without a statement number, followed by pressing the ENTER or RETURN key.

Programs may be entered into the computer either by typing on the keyboard, or by loading the program from a cassette or diskette. Most computers have specific loading procedures; therefore, it is recommended that you study the procedure presented in your computer manual.

Now let's examine a simple, short mathematics computer program. Before we begin entering the program into the computer, we will type the word NEW. Note that we did not use a statement number. The word NEW is thus entered on the computer screen. By pressing the ENTER or RETURN key, we caused the computer to remove all material previously stored in memory. Now we have cleared the computer's memory and we are ready to type the following program.

```
10   REM—A SHORT ADDITION PROGRAM—
20   ?"I WILL GIVE YOU A SUM IF YOU GIVE ME
     TWO ADDENDS."
30   ?"WHAT IS YOUR FIRST ADDEND";
40   INPUT A
50   ?"WHAT IS YOUR SECOND ADDEND";
60   INPUT B
70   S=A+B
80   ?"THE SUM OF ";A;" AND ";B;" IS ";S
```

We will help you to learn some simple BASIC programming commands and techniques so you can read the microcomputer activities at the end of each chapter in this book. This portion of the text is not intended to teach you all you need to know about computers or even how to program. Our purpose here is to introduce you to the ways that computers might be integrated into a mathematics program. We recommend that all elementary school mathematics teachers become computer literate, by studying computers and their functioning. We further recommend that all teachers receive instruction in the language appropriate for the computers available in their schools and for the children they will be teaching. Computer terms and symbols appropriate to mathematics teaching can be found in Appendix C.

Since each line of this sample program begins with a number, we know that we are in the program mode. Note that the numbers selected for the program statements are multiples of ten. This will be convenient if we ever want to edit the program, because there is room between statements for additional statement numbers.

It is a good idea to provide adequate documentation (written information about a program) within the program itself. The first statement of the sample program is a REM statement (which is an abbreviation for REMARK). REM statements are ignored by the computer, but they serve as communication with a user looking at the program. This can help a programmer to locate specific sections of a program for editing purposes.

The next two statements in the program are PRINT statements used to provide information to the computer user. These statements start with a question mark (?); the question mark is a shortcut for the word PRINT. The computer will print all information following the question mark that appears within quotation marks. The semicolon at the end of line 30 instructs the computer to place a question mark at the end of this line. Line number 40 is an INPUT statement, so the computer will wait until the user provides some information. In this case, a number has been requested; the computer will store the number in a storage spot labeled A.

Line 50 asks another question, so we have told the computer to print what appears inside the quotation marks. We have not placed a question mark at

the end of this statement, since the computer will automatically provide a question mark. Line 60 is another INPUT statement, so again the computer will wait until the user provides a number.

The computer needs to know what the relationship will be between the value of A and the value of B and the sum, which we will assign the symbol S. Remember that + is the symbol that tells the computer to add the values for A and B.

The results of this program must now be reported to the user; statement 80 is a report of the results. Note the structure of the statement and where the quotation marks are placed. Remember that the computer will print everything appearing inside the quotation marks. The letters A, B, and S outside the quotation marks tell the computer to print the value that has been stored for each of these variables.

Teachers can begin using microcomputers in the mathematics program by reading the manuals that accompany the computer and then providing commercial software packages. A microcomputer work area should become an important learning center in every elementary school classroom. Do not encourage games for their own sake. Use the classroom microcomputer for educational purposes. Encourage children to become familiar with the immediate mode and to solve mathematics examples on the computer. Permit different children the opportunity to complete a limited number of mathematics assignments on the computer.

Teachers should avail themselves of every opportunity to learn how to write simple programs appropriate for the children they are teaching. Often simple programs can easily be changed to accommodate the needs of different children. For instance, an addition program could be revised by changing the data in the READ—DATA statements. An addition program can also be changed to a subtraction or multiplication program. Once programs are developed, they can be stored on diskettes or cassettes and are then readily accessible for student use or revision.

Develop a good filing system to allow easy access to programs needed for particular purposes. Individualizing mathematics will become easier as teachers learn how to change and create programs addressed to specific student needs. The microcomputer can become a record keeper for each child and free the teacher from the tedium of paperwork. Each teacher needs to experiment with the microcomputer and its use in the mathematics program, in order to develop more effective and efficient techniques. The computer has great educational potential, but we must first learn to use the unique characteristics of the computer to increase the efficiency of mathematics teaching.

Terminology, Symbols, and Procedures

BASIC   (Beginners All-purpose Symbolic Instruction Code)   BASIC is a computer language that converses with the user in English words.

Computer-assisted instruction (CAI)   CAI is an instructional situation between learner and computer that presents material in an interactive mode, using systematic evaluation as an integral part of the program.

Computer-managed instruction (CMI)   CMI is computer technology used to keep records, store test information, and provide information to meet individual needs.

Command   A statement that indicates a request or an instruction to the computer is called a command.

Courseware   Courseware includes programs designed to be similar to instructional techniques used in a classroom.

Cursor   A cursor is a light spot on the display screen indicating where the next character will be displayed.

Data   Any kind of information is called data.

Debug   To debug a program means to change or correct the program so it will accomplish what the programmer intended.

Disk operating system (DOS)   DOS is a program that allows a computer to use a disk system.

Diskette   A floppy disk used to store computer programs is called a diskette.

Display screen   A video screen used to show computer information or programs is known as a display screen.

Display panel   The screen that displays the numbers on a hand-held calculator is a display panel.

Documentation   Documentation is written information about a computer program. The information is intended to aid programmers or operators using the program. Documentation can be either internal or external.

Floppy disk   A floppy disk is a soft disk in a paper jacket, usually about $5\frac{1}{4}$ inches in diameter, used for storing microcomputer programs.

Hardware The physical components of a computer system are called hardware.

Input Information or data entered into a microcomputer is called input.

Immediate mode A computer instruction that is to be executed immediately is considered to be in the immediate mode.

Instruction Each step in the program for a hand-held calculator is an instruction.

Interactive A user and microcomputer communicating with each other are considered interactive.

Keyboard A keyboard is a set of typewriter-like keys used to enter information or data into a microcomputer.

Light-emitting diode (LED) A hand-held calculator uses a diode to energize the display screen.

Liquid crystal display (LCD) An LCD is a hand-held calculator display screen energized by liquid crystals.

Load To load is to enter information into computer memory, usually from a disk or cassette.

LOGO LOGO is a language using words designed for young children to communicate with a computer.

Memory The part of a computer that stores information is called its memory.

Microcomputer A small computer is called a microcomputer.

Output Any information coming out of a computer is considered output. Examples of computer output include programs, program results, and information placed on a diskette or printed out on a printer.

Program A series of instructions written in a computer language to accomplish a certain task comprises a program.

Programmer A person who writes, debugs, and documents computer programs is a programmer.

Program mode A series of sequenced statements executed by the computer on command are in the program mode.

Random-access memory (RAM)   RAM is the portion of a computer's memory that is immediately available for the user to manipulate. RAM is erased when the power is turned off.

Read-only memory (ROM)   ROM is the portion of a computer's memory that is permanently stored on a memory chip. It cannot be altered by a user or affected by power loss.

Solar-powered calculator   This is a hand-held calculator powered by solar energy.

Software   The programs that indicate what operations the computer must perform are called software.

Statement   An instruction to a computer is called a statement.

Subroutine   A subroutine is a portion of a computer program designed to accomplish a specific task and to be repeated numerous times.

Practice Exercises

1. Use a hand-held calculator to solve each example.

a) $576 + 831 =$ d) $257 - 497 =$
b) $984 - 695 =$ e) $853 - 34 =$
c) $753 \times 432 =$ f) $89 \times -23 =$

2. Set up the hand-held calculator so that the calculator will display the circumference of another circle for every two keys that are pushed. Use the calculator to find the circumference of circles with these diameters:

a) 17   b) 47   c) 23   d) 89   e) 4.3

3. Enter this simple microcomputer program and run it.

```
10   REM—MULTIPLES FOR ANY NUMBER—
20   PRINT"FOR WHAT NUMBER DO YOU WANT MULTIPLES"
30   INPUT A
40   PRINT"HOW MANY MULTIPLES DO YOU WANT"
50   INPUT B
60   FOR X=1 TO B
70   C=X*A
80   PRINT C
90   NEXT X
100 PRINT"THESE ARE THE ";B;" MULTIPLES FOR ";A
```

4. Press the keys indicated in the first column, and write your estimated answer in the second column. Use your hand-held calculator to solve the exercise, and write the calculated answer in the last column. Then compare your estimated answer with the calculator display screen.

	Estimate	Answer
a) C 3 + = = =	_____	_____
b) C . 4 + = = = =	_____	_____
c) C 1 2 + = = =	_____	_____
d) C 2 7 – 3 = = = =	_____	_____
e) C 2 . 8 – . 3 = = =	_____	_____
f) C 1 3 × 7 = = =	_____	_____
g) C 7 9 ÷ = =	_____	_____
h) C 3 7 × 4 = = =	_____	_____
i) C 7 . 1 ÷ 4 = =	_____	_____

5. Set up the hand-held calculator as indicated for using a constant. Write your estimated answer for each example; then use your calculator, and compare your estimate with the calculator display. Set up $1 + 7 =$

Enter	Estimate	Answer
a) 5 =	_____	_____
b) 9 =	_____	_____
c) 1 7 =	_____	_____
d) 7 9 3 =	_____	_____

6. Estimate the answers to the following examples. Use the hand-held calculator to check your answers. Explain why you got the answers you received.

a) $9 \div 0 =$
b) $789654 \times 764 =$

7. Use a constant to solve these examples. Solve the first three examples; then estimate the answers to the remaining examples, and check them on the calculator.

	Estimate	Answer
a) $1 \times 9109 =$	_____	_____
b) $2 \times 9109 =$	_____	_____
c) $3 \times 9109 =$	_____	_____
d) $4 \times 9109 =$	_____	_____
e) $5 \times 9109 =$	_____	_____
f) $6 \times 9109 =$	_____	_____
g) $7 \times 9109 =$	_____	_____
h) $8 \times 9109 =$	_____	_____
i) $9 \times 9109 =$	_____	_____

8. Use the microcomputer in the immediate mode to solve Example 4.

9. Can a constant, as set up on the hand-held calculator, also be set up on the microcomputer in the immediate mode? Try Exercise 5 on the microcomputer. Did the microcomputer in the immediate mode function the same as the hand-held calculator in this example? When do the microcomputer and calculator function the same, and when do they function differently?

10. Compare the results of this simple program with those shown on the hand-held calculator and the set-up for Exercise 5. You might want to use a line number 15 for clearing the screen; if so, line 60 should be changed to read: 60 GOTO 15.

```
10 REM—THIS PROGRAM WILL ADD 7 TO ANY NUMBER—
20 PRINT "WHAT NUMBER DO YOU WANT TO ADD 7 TO"
30 INPUT A
40 X=7+A
50 PRINT A;"ADDED WITH 7 IS ";X
60 GOTO 20
```

11. Change the previous computer program (Exercise 10) to add 73 to a given number. Run your new program.

12. Change this program so it will multiply any number by 9.

13. Change the program again so that it will solve the examples in Exercise 7. You might want to write several programs.

Discussion Questions

1. Should computer literacy be taught in the mathematics class or in a separate class?

2. What effects do hand-held calculators have on computational skills and learning?

3. At what grade level should microcomputer programming be introduced and taught to children?

4. Why should children be taught to use microcomputers?

5. How can hand-held calculators be used to help children understand the concept of place value?

6. How should estimating techniques be used in conjunction with hand-held calculators or microcomputers?

7. Study and discuss the recommendations for classroom use of the calculator and microcomputer, given by the National Council of Teachers of Mathematics in *An Agenda for Action.*

8. What is the role of the hand-held calculator in a beginning mathematics program?

9. How can microcomputers be used in other ways than for practice and drill?

10. How could microcomputers be used in a mathematics program? How should they be used?

Hand-Held Calculator Activities for the Primary Grades

1. Have the children display a given number on the calculator screen:

    a) stated orally and simultaneously shown on a flash card.
    b) shown only on a flash card.
    c) stated orally only.

2. Help the children set up the calculator so that it will count (by ones) to ten. Use 1 + = . . .

3. Extend the preceding activity to numbers beyond ten.

4. Set up the calculator to count by twos; use this set-up: 0 + 2 = = ... The children can use the "walk-on number line" and compare the numbers on the display screen with the number under the right (or left) foot. Compare this with walking up the stairs two at a time.

5. Set up the calculator to count by twos; start with the number 1.

6. Make the display read a given number, using only the 1 key and the operation keys.

7. Use only the 1 and 2 keys, along with the operation keys, and place a given number on the display screen using the least number of punches.

8. Check arithmetic worksheets, using the hand-held calculator.

9. Count backward on the calculator, by pressing 1 0 − 1 = = = ... How will you handle the situation when the children press the equals key more than ten times?

Microcomputer Activities for the Primary Grades

Some of the preceding hand-held calculator activities can be adapted for the microcomputer.

1. Commercial software packages are available for primary grade children; sets are displayed on the video screen, and the child must find and enter the correct number.

2. Display a flash card with a number on it; have the children look for that number on the computer and strike the proper key. Compare the number on the flash card with the number on the video screen.

3. State a number; have the primary children locate that key on the microcomputer, press the key, and observe the number as it appears on the screen.

4. Obtain a LOGO software package, and introduce the children to turtle graphics.

5. Obtain a "Big Track," and help the children learn how to program the tank. Provide ample opportunity for the children to play with Big Track during work time.

6. Write simple programs for the children. As you become more experienced, you can continually make the programs more friendly and more elegant.

7. Here is a sample program. Use of this program requires that the children be able to read four words: FIND, GOOD, TRY, and AGAIN. The numbers of the DATA statement can easily be changed. Also, the program can easily be made more elegant and friendly.

```
10   REM—RECOGNIZING NUMBERS—
20   CLS (Use appropriate clear-the-screen command)
30   READ M
40   DATA 3,6,1,8,2,5,4,9,7
50   ?:?:?:?:?"FIND ";M
60   INPUT A
70   FORT=1 TO 5000:NEXT T
80   IF A=  M THEN PRINT?"GOOD!"
90   IF A<>M THEN PRINT "TRY AGAIN":GOTO 50
95   IF M=7 THEN END
100 GOTO 20
```

Hand-Held Calculator Activities for the Intermediate Grades

Impress upon the children that a hand-held calculator is only a supplemental tool. It is still important for the children to be able to solve all mathematics problems and examples without the calculator. At this age level, all children should learn how to use the four operation keys with the number pad. They should also learn how to use a constant. Children *must* learn correct procedures for using the calculator at the outset. Proper development of a good foundation will help to avoid confusion at later grade levels.

Proper classroom management of the calculators should also be established early. They should be used in a laboratory setting. Calculators should be introduced in the primary grades, but power with calculators should be developed in the intermediate grades with mastery of the operations (addition, subtraction, multiplication, and division); study of whole numbers and decimals should be completed by the end of sixth grade.

1. Children should be taught how to round numbers, since this is an important skill when working with calculators. The following examples are representative, but children will need many similar practice examples. Use the number line as a tool as children work through the following questions.

a) Find the number 42 on the number line. What is the next smaller even ten? What is the next greater even ten? Which even ten is closest to 42: 40 or 50? The number 42 would be rounded to 40.

b) Use the same procedure with 27, 56, 64, etc. Now try the number 45. Discuss with the children that, when a number ends in 5, the number is always rounded up.

c) Using the number line and the same procedure, extend this idea to three-place numbers rounded to the nearest hundred, then round three-place numbers to the nearest ten. Use examples such as 127, 464, 812, 593, 453, 849, and 290.

d) Round four-place numbers to the nearest thousand, hundred, and ten.

2. Round each addend to the nearest hundred and estimate a sum. Use the hand-held calculator to calculate the actual sum and compare the two sums.

Example	Rounded Number
459	_____
208	_____
762	_____
+ 317	_____
Sum	

3. Round these numbers mentally to the nearest ten, and estimate the sum. Check your estimated sum with the actual sum, using the hand-held calculator.

47	52	83	78
+ 34	+ 48	+ 26	+ 41

4. Use the estimation techniques we have developed extended to the other operations. Check your estimated answers on the calculator.

5. State numbers; have the children enter the numbers into the calculator. Then write the numbers in words on the chalkboard, and have the children enter the numbers into their calculators.

6. Solve the following examples:

Add	Subtract
One hundred forty-three	Eight hundred sixty-three
Four hundred sixty-eight	Three hundred fifty-seven
One hundred seven	
Eight hundred twenty-nine	

7. Have the children check each other's mathematics papers using the hand-held calculator.

8. Provide word problems for children to solve using their hand-held calculators. For example, if the escape velocity of a rocket going to the moon is 25,000 miles per hour, how fast is that per minute? per second? Locate the distance to the moon, and calculate how long it would take for a rocket to go from the earth to the moon. (Assume that the rocket can go directly.)

9. Have children solve given examples from their mathematics assignments on their hand-held calculators.

10. Use the operation keys and digits 4, 5, and 6; place the number 23 on the display screen, using the least number of key punches.

11. Practice changing fractions to decimals by interpreting a fraction as division.

12. Add and subtract decimal numbers.

13. Study place value by multiplying and dividing by 10, 100, or 1000.

14. Factor numbers into their prime-number components.

Microcomputer Activities for the Intermediate Grades

1. Continue expanding the microcomputer activities suggested in the primary grades.

2. Encourage the children to begin simple programming such as:

```
10 REM—BASIC ADDITION PROGRAM—
20 PRINT "GIVE ME TWO ADDENDS AND I WILL GIVE YOU THE SUM."
30 PRINT:PRINT"WHAT IS THE FIRST ADDEND";
40 INPUT A
50 PRINT:PRINT"WHAT IS THE SECOND ADDEND";
60 INPUT B
70 S=A+B
80 PRINT:PRINT:PRINT"THE SUM OF ";A;" AND ";B;" IS ";S
```

3. Change the preceding addition program to a subtraction program.

4. Write a program for finding the area of a rectangle.

```
10 REM—FIND AREA OF A RECTANGLE—
20 PRINT:PRINT"I WILL FIND THE AREA OF A RECTANGLE FOR YOU."
30 PRINT:PRINT"WHAT IS THE LENGTH OF YOUR RECTANGLE IN METERS";
40 INPUT L
50 PRINT:PRINT"WHAT IS THE WIDTH OF YOUR RECTANGLE IN METERS ";W
60 INPUT W
70 A=L*W
80 PRINT:PRINT"IF YOUR RECTANGLE IS ";L;" METERS LONG AND ";W; METERS
WIDE, "
90 PRINT"THEN THE AREA IS ";S;" SQUARE METERS."
```

5. Change the preceding program so that it will calculate the perimeter of a rectangle.

6. Create a computer program to calculate the area of a triangle.

7. Create a computer program to calculate the volume of a cube.

8. Write a computer program to provide practice and drill for students in finding the area of a rectangle.

```
10   REM—PRACTICE ON AREA OF RECTANGLES—
20   CLS (Use the appropriate command for your computer)
30   READ L,W
35   IF L=999 THEN END
40   DATA 9,4,7,3,13,7,28,19,8.2,6.3,999,999
50   PRINT:PRINT"WHAT IS THE AREA OF A RECTANGLE "
60   PRINT"THAT IS ";L;" METERS LONG AND ";
70   PRINT W;" METERS WIDE ";
80   INPUT Z
90   A=L*W
100 IF Z=A THEN PRINT"CORRECT, TRY THIS ONE.":FOR T=1 TO 3000: NEXT T:
GOTO 20
110 IF Z<>A THEN PRINT "SORRY, TRY AGAIN!":GOTO 50
```

9. Change the program in Exercise 8 so practice can be provided with different rectangles. The DATA statement is the only statement that must be changed.

10. Change the program in Exercise 8 to provide practice in finding the perimeter of a rectangle.

11. Change the program in Exercise 8 to provide practice in finding the area of a triangle.

Hand-Held Calculator Activities for the Upper Elementary Grades

Activities for primary and intermediate grade children can easily be adapted for upper elementary grade children.

1. Use the hand-held calculator to explore the concept of place value. Divide a given number by 10. Using 10 as a constant, divide many different examples. Children should generalize that, every time the ⊟ key is pressed, the number is divided by ten and this moves the decimal point one place to the right. Study many examples.

2. Practice using the calculator for changing fractions to decimals to percents.

3. Gradually introduce the percent key to upper elementary grade children. What is 38% of 128?

Enter Ⓒ ① ② ⑧ ⊠ ③ ⑧ ⅋

4. We use 15,600 liters of water in our home each month. If 19% of the water is used in the bathroom, how many liters of water are used in the bathroom each day? (Use 30 days to equal one month.)

5. At the upper elementary grade level, children should learn how to use proportion. For example: Jon used 10.5 gallons of gas to drive 268 miles. How much gas will he need to drive 375 miles? The children can set up a proportion to solve the example:

$$\frac{268}{10.5} \diagdown\!\!\!\!\diagup \frac{375}{X}$$

Enter this in the calculator as follows:

Ⓒ ③ ⑦ ⑤ ⊠ ① ⓪ ⨀ ⑤ ⊟ ② ⑥ ⑧ ⊜

6. Children can calculate the average of their mathematics grades.

7. Use the hand-held calculator to find the batting averages of selected major-league baseball players.

8. Use the hand-held calculator to compute statistics during the football season.

9. Use the calculator to prepare data for graphing. For example, find percentages to use in making circle graphs. Multiply the percent by 360 degrees to find the number of degrees that each sector of the circle graph should have.

10. Using a constant, calculate the circumference of several circles.

11. Using a constant, find the area of several circles.

12. Use a sale advertisement from a newspaper to calculate the percent of savings for various sale items.

13. Have children study palindromic numbers; use the calculator to reverse the numbers and add them. Keep a record of how many times each number must be reversed and added before it again becomes a palindrome.

Microcomputer Activities for the Upper Elementary Grades

All microcomputer activities we have suggested for primary and intermediate grade children can be adapted for upper elementary grade children. Adapt as many as possible of the hand-held calculator activities to the microcomputer in the immediate mode.

1. Encourage children to write mathematics programs that are more friendly and elegant.

2. Introduce more IF—THEN statements in your programs.

3. Introduce subroutines, so that children can use the commands GOSUB—RETURN.

4. Introduce FOR—NEXT statements as counters.

5. Familiarize the children with the DOS system appropriate for the computers you have available.

6. All computers handle graphics differently, so you need to introduce the children to graphics that are appropriate for your specific computer and also appropriate for their age level.

7. Obtain some of the microcomputer program workbooks available for children, and encourage the children to study microcomputers on their own.

8. Set up a classroom microcomputer library for student use.

Suggested Readings

Banet, Bernard. "Computers and Early Learning," *Creative Computing*, vol. 4, no. 5, September—October 1978.

Bell, Max S. "Calculators in Elementary Schools? Some Tentative Guidelines and Questions Based on Classroom Experience." *The Arithmetic Teacher*, vol. 23, no. 7, November 1976.

Bitter, Gary G., and Mikesell, Jerald L. *Activities Handbook for Teaching with the Hand-Held Calculator.* Boston: Allyn & Bacon, 1980.

Caldwell, Robert M. "Considerations and Guidelines for Developing Basic Skills Curriculum for Use with Microcomputer Technology." *National Educational Computing Conference Proceedings*, Norfolk, Va.: 1980.

Caravella, Joseph R. *Minicalculators in the Classroom*, Washington, D. C.: National Education Association of the United States, 1977.

Dennis, J. Richard. "Stages of Development in Introducing Computing to Teachers." *National Education Computing Conference Proceedings*, Iowa City: 1979.

Gawronski, Jane D., and Coblentz, Dwight. "Calculators and the Mathematics Curriculum." *The Arithmetic Teacher*, vol. 23, no. 7, November 1976.

Guthrie, Larry F., and Wiles, Clyde A. "Why Not Have a Calculator Tournament?" *The Arithmetic Teacher*, vol. 23, no. 7, November 1976.

Hill, Shirley A. "The Microcomputer in the Instructional Program." *The Arithmetic Teacher*, vol. 23, no. 7, November 1983.

Manji, Jamal F. "Birth of the Microcomputer Age in the Classroom." *School Product News*, August 1980.

Milner, Stuart D. "Analysis of Computer Education Needs for K–12 Teachers." *National Education Computing Conference Proceedings*, Iowa City: 1979.

Molnar, Andrew R. "The Next Great Crisis in American Education: Computer Literacy." *Association for Educational Data Systems Journal*, vol. 12, no. 1, Fall 1978.

Moursand, David. "ACM Elementary and Secondary Schools Subcommittee Progress Report." *National Educational Computing Conference Proceedings*, Norfolk, Va.: 1980.

Perlman, R. *Using Computer Technology to Provide a Creative Learning Environment for Preschool Children* (LOGO Memo No. 4). Cambridge, Mass.: Artificial Intelligence Laboratory, May 1976.

Taylor, Robert P., and others. "Computing Competencies for School Teachers." *National Educational Computing Conference Proceedings*, Norfolk, Va.: 1980.

3 Beginning Mathematics

Teaching Competencies

Upon completing this unit, you will be able to:

State the anticipated mathematics knowledge that children have when they enter school

Evaluate children's mental and physical development in terms necessary for beginning mathematics concepts

Conceptualize and state appropriate learning experiences for children in a beginning mathematics program

Describe the development of number concepts, beginning on the concrete level and moving through the semi-concrete, semiabstract, and abstract levels

Suggest activities for children, using concrete materials to develop specific beginning mathematics concepts

Describe the relationship between real-world experiences and basic mathematics concepts

Discussion

A good beginning mathematics program for children is developed upon the mathematics knowledge with which children enter school. The mathematics experiences of entering children vary tremendously, depending on the education of their parents, the amount of time the parents devote to their children, attendance at preschools, travel experiences, play materials and opportunities, family relationships (older brothers and sisters), television viewing habits, exposure to books, and listening to reading by others. This defines the first mathematical task of the classroom teacher: assess the mathematics experiences of the students. Knowledge of each child's past will provide valuable information for the beginning program, but it will also provide a basis upon which the teacher can group the children for beginning experiences.

Beginning mathematics programs traditionally focus on counting, addition, and subtraction. Today, however, schools are placing more emphasis on the research and development of learning theorists, such as Piaget, Skemp, Bruner, and Gagné. These learning theories provide a different perspective from which to assess the mathematics background of young children. Let's now review Piaget's learning theory. Recall that Piaget defined four levels of cognitive development:

1. Sensorimotor stage (birth to about two years of age)—During this stage, the child masters many motor activities. The child can move at will: walk, run, reach food, pick up objects, and perform other physical activities.
2. Preoperational stage (two to about six or seven years of age)—During this stage, the child observes from his point of view only; focuses on one attribute at a time; and begins to use symbols, to draw, and to imitate.
3. Concrete operational stage (six or seven to about eleven or twelve years of age)—During this stage, the child begins to develop a system of thought but still functions on the concrete level, gaining reversibility, developing conservation, and learning sequentially.
4. Formal operational stage (begins at about eleven or twelve years of age)—During this stage, the child develops a growing ability to reason, beginning with a hypothesis and ending with all of its logical conclusions. Experiences on the concrete level are still advantageous, but the child can operate using thoughts and theories.

Most children will be in the preoperational stage upon entering school; thus they are ready to begin developing a systematic thought process. Since this thought process has not yet been developed, the teacher must begin to teach all mathematics concepts from a concrete base and develop the thought process as mathematical concepts are developed. Before beginning instruction, the teacher must consider each child's preschool experiences and capabilities. The most effective mathematics program probably should be taught in conjunction with other content areas.

Children who enter school with counting ability do not necessarily exhibit readiness for mathematics. The child could have memorized a series of word names but have little or no concept of the numberness involved. Teachers need to isolate the types of mathematical experiences that the children have had before entering school. Children could have had any of the following experiences:

Dialing the telephone
Earning and spending their own money
Buying their own tickets to the theater
Recognizing their house numbers
Turning the television dial to a designated channel
Playing with a hand-held calculator
Playing video games
Loading software into a home computer
Using a microcomputer keyboard

The preschool experiences of the children dictates the foundation of the mathematics program. This is the basis for grouping children, setting up work stations, and developing the beginning mathematics program.

A theoretical base for the mathematics program can be built upon Piaget's learning theory, as well as learning theories by Bruner, Skemp, Gagné, and others. However, each theorist seems to support the idea that all mathematics should begin in the real world with concrete materials. Children learn by doing and need many firsthand experiences manipulating, examining, discussing, and sharing mathematical ideas.

A beginning primary mathematics program should start with the unique mathematics experiences young children have had prior to school. Situations that develop from the real world should be set up in the classroom. Easily recognizable, familiar materials—such as plastic spoons, forks, knives, paper cups, napkins, and so forth—should be the principal teaching materials. Some specialized educational materials, such as attribute blocks, Cuisenaire rods, Dienes Blocks, Stern rods, and people pieces, can also be used to provide a sound base for development in mathematics. People pieces are blocks with pictures of people with different characteristics: blue, red, or green; tall or short; fat or thin; male or female.

At one time mathematics focused on the ability to juggle numbers rapidly and accurately. Today's mathematics places equal, if not greater, emphasis on the recognition and the study of patterns. A beginning mathematics program must therefore establish the kind of foundation upon which a solid contemporary mathematics program can be developed.

Children are entering school from a real world in which they have handled real objects. This is the place a mathematics program must begin—the concrete level. Giving children tasks based upon Piaget's experiments can help determine their developmental level.

Four activities that seem vital for helping children understand numbers are:

1. Sorting or classifying items into sets
2. Recognition of the cardinal number of a set
3. One-to-one correspondence, which will help with counting
4. Ordering of ideas

Sorting is a natural activity. Children sort toys when they place cars in garages, dishes in cupboards, dolls in doll beds. At a more advanced level children must sort through information in order to select appropriate sets. In mathematics we sort for numbers, lowest common denominators, prime numbers, factors, and so on. At the beginning levels, sorting leads to the development of the concept of numbers. A child experiences many sets with three elements—three cups, three napkins, three forks, three spoons, three toys. Ultimately he or she needs to conceptualize and abstract the common property of "threeness." A child might be shown a red triangle-shaped attribute block and be asked to find three more triangles or to locate three more red blocks. As time progresses children can be asked to sort out orally described sets—for example, to locate all of the red triangles or locate all of the small thin squares.

Attribute blocks provide opportunities for children to sort, classify, and search for and develop patterns that are basic to all mathematical thinking. Attribute blocks are a set of blocks that have varying identifying characteristics. A typical set of attribute blocks might vary in *color, shape, size,* and *thickness.*

Color	Shape	Size	Thickness
red	square	large	thick
blue	rectangle	small	thin
yellow	triangle		
	circle		

The first level of activity might be referred to as a free play period. During such beginning activities, sets of attribute blocks are randomly distributed to groups of children. They are given no instructions or structuring during this period. After they have familiarized themselves with the blocks, ask them to classify the blocks. Usually they will select *color* and make three piles—for example, one pile of yellow blocks, one pile of blue blocks, and one pile of red blocks. Challenge them to try to classify the blocks in other ways. *Shape* is very often selected as a second way to classify the blocks. Children will probably need to be encouraged to try other less obvious attributes such as *size* or *thickness.*

On the next level, start a pattern with the blocks and allow a child to select the next block. For example, lay out the following blocks and ask the child to place the next block.

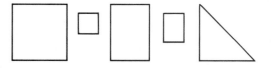

Thus the child must carefully examine the pattern presentation and then decide what attribute block must be placed next to extend the pattern. The activities at the end of this unit contain more developmental activities.

Cuisenaire rods are a set of rods based on the centimeter and varying in length and color. The rods are *not* scored. Cuisenaire rods can be used to sort, classify, develop patterns, and develop numberness. (The color names in the accompanying manual may vary.)

Color	Size of rod (in cubic centimeters)
Natural wood	$1 \times 1 \times 1$
Red	$1 \times 1 \times 2$
Light green	$1 \times 1 \times 3$
Purple	$1 \times 1 \times 4$
Yellow	$1 \times 1 \times 5$
Dark green	$1 \times 1 \times 6$
Black	$1 \times 1 \times 7$
Brown	$1 \times 1 \times 8$
Blue	$1 \times 1 \times 9$
Orange	$1 \times 1 \times 10$

The first activities with Cuisenaire rods should be free play, during which neither structure nor instruction are provided. After the children have become familiar with the rods, then instruction can begin. Rods may first be organized by separating the rods by color or by length. The same classification will result in either case. Children need many experiences with relationships between the rods. How many red rods equal one purple rod?

How many different ways can we show a dark green rod?

Children will soon learn that the length of every rod can be shown using other rods. Note that, in their beginning experiences, the chidren are developing relationships and do not associate numbers with the rods. Number concepts are associated later with each rod. Because of the nature of the rods, *one* can be defined many different ways. In one case, the natural wood rod could be defined as one; yet at another time, the red rod could be defined as one. As soon as a base is established, this automatically assigns a number to all other rods. Children should understand the interrelationships among the rods before numberness is associated with the rods. Relationships are developed first, followed by numberness and counting.

For additional information about using Cuisenaire rods in a beginning mathematics program, research the literature and locate teachers' manuals specifically designed to direct such a program.

Stern rods are another set of materials using scored rods. The rods are consistent in their color patterns, but color is not an important characteristic of the rods. A set of Stern materials also includes number trays, a number track, a number rack, pattern boards, and other materials. Primary teachers should read Catherine Stern's book, *Helping Children Discover Arithmetic*, for detailed instructions for using Stern rods.

Materials such as attribute blocks, Stern rods, Cuisenaire rods, Dienes Blocks, people pieces, and Piaget tasks provide a firm foundation upon which children can build and develop mathematical thinking. Using sets is a sound and logical way to develop the concept of numbers in gradual stages.

Most contemporary mathematics programs at the elementary school level include the concepts of sets. There is less emphasis on sets today than during the "modern mathematics" era, and this emphasis seems to be declining each year. Nevertheless, some people feel that set concepts should be introduced early, that they help young children form proper number concepts, and that the formation of proper number concepts will make advanced mathematics concepts easier to grasp at subsequent grade levels. Sets are not taught for their own sake but to provide techniques for introducing fundamental ideas of mathematics. By using set concepts, we are able to describe mathematical ideas and operations more clearly and more simply than with previous methods alone. Sets are used with children to develop the concept of numbers as well as classifying, sorting, and ordering.

What would you take with you to play golf? What would you buy if you needed dishes to serve eight people? Yes, you would play golf with a **set** of clubs, and you would buy a set of dishes. Using these two examples, we can discuss the nature of a set. Although not formally defined in mathematics, a set can be regarded as any collection or group of things or ideas that are precisely described. The things or ideas that compose a given set are called the **elements** (or **members**) of the set. A group or collection considered as a set may be composed of ideas, numbers, people, shapes—anything at all. Objects and ideas do not, by themselves, form sets; but they do form sets whenever we choose to think of them as such. We have often used other words to indicate a set—words such as team, flock, herd, club, family. These terms indicate that the members of such a set have some common characteristic. A herd would suggest that all the members are elephants (or cattle, or bison, or the like); a team indicates two or more persons playing or working together. However, a set could be made up of elements that have almost nothing in common—a tree, a house, and a car, for example. A set, in mathematics, can be composed of any elements we choose to include. The only thing the elements must have in common is membership in the set. It is not necessary for the items to be related.

We can describe a set in several different ways. We can describe a set by taking the real objects and putting them together. For example, a class party requires a decoration committee; the members appointed to that committee are Betty, Jean, and Mary. This set is seen to be composed of real elements. When we work with real or tangible items, we call this a **concrete** situation. Using real items on the concrete level will help children relate the mathematics they are about to learn to the real world. For instance, children have had experiences with sets of cookies, toys, and playmates.

A second way to describe a set is by drawing pictures of the members of the set. A set of three chairs could then be represented this way:

Instead of working with real chairs, we use drawings of the chairs to represent the real objects. We call this a **semiconcrete** situation. The semiconcrete level is a representation of a real situation but presents pictures of the real items rather than the items themselves.

A **semiabstract** representation uses tallies to represent elements. A common example of such a representation is ⫼⫽ . The semiabstract level involves a symbolic representation of a concrete item, but the symbols or pictures do not look like the objects they stand for. A set can also be described by using abstract symbols. We might use the letters *a, b,* and *c* to stand for the chairs. We can also describe a set by using words—for example, "the set of all 1985 Fords." Are words and symbols as precise as the other means of describing sets? Yes, words and symbols can be just as precise; however, they are more abstract.

In each case we have clearly and precisely described the members of the given set.

Children reach the **abstract** level when they can understand and use numbers and numerals.

It is extremely important that our sets consist of **distinguishable, well-defined** objects. A set is well defined when we can readily tell exactly what the elements of the set are. Consider this example: "all the good-looking girls in Brownsville School." Would this set be clear to everyone? No, because "good-looking" is not precise. One person's idea of what "good-looking" means will not always be another person's idea. Another example might be "all the tall trees in Sherwood Forest." Again, this is not a well-defined set; "tall" does not have a precise meaning. Is a five-foot tree tall? a twelve-foot tree? a sixty-foot tree? We must describe the elements of a set precisely in order to have a well-defined set. Thus the set of all trees in Sherwood Forest that are over forty feet tall is a well-defined set. The set of all daisies in Mrs. Smith's yard today is well defined; the set of all pretty flowers in Mrs. Smith's yard is not well defined.

Let's see how sets are used for a progressive development of number concepts.

The first level might be called the **concrete** level. In kindergarten and first grade the idea of set is developed with real objects. A pack of crayons, a box of pencils, or a dozen apples can be presented as a

set. This idea can then be extended to present any collection of different real objects as a set. For example, a pencil, a ball, and a book could be placed together and described as a set.

On the next level, such a set of physical objects can be represented by drawings (on chalkboard or paper). The use of drawings is more abstract than the use of the objects themselves, so we might call this the **semiconcrete** level. The real objects presented at the concrete level would now be drawn:

At the third level, the child is able to match tallies (tally marks or objects such as ice cream sticks) with the elements of a given set. On this **semiabstract** level we are drawing his attention away from irrelevant properties of individual elements of the given set and directing it toward the question "how many?"

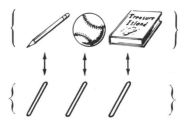

When the child performs such a matching, he is discovering whether one set has as many elements as another, although he is still not using numbers as such.

On the fourth level, the **abstract** level, the child matches the elements of a given set with numbers, starting with 1.

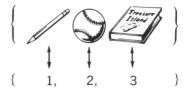

The child comes to understand that the last counting number used in such a matching can be used to tell how many objects are in the given set. Thus he can speak and write an abstract symbol (a **numeral**) to tell how many objects are in the given set.

We can now consider the **cardinal numbers** of given sets; for example, Set A:

Having matched the elements of the set with the set of counting numbers, we can write

$$n(A) = 3$$

When working with young children we often ask, "What is the number of the set?" Usually we just write 3 under the set. At one time considerable emphasis was placed upon distinguishing between *number* and *numeral*, but most elementary programs today do not emphasize the difference. In this textbook we will use the word *number* rather then expect young children to distinguish between *number* and *numeral*.

The cardinal number of the set above, represented by the numeral 3, is an expression of the **number property** of the set—in this case, the property of "threeness." This idea of "numberness" enables children to discuss sets in terms of number and provides a means by which they can understand the meaning of number. The property of threeness is amplified through comparison of sets. Children are now able to look at sets such as those below in a new way.

It is evident that all these sets have something in common: the property of "threeness."

Sets can now be compared by comparing their cardinal numbers.

Sometimes we may have a set that has no elements. For instance, suppose you were asked to list the members of a Set D composed of all rabbits with wheels. Since rabbits do not have wheels, we would have the **empty set.**

$$D = \{ \ \}$$

A set that does not have any elements is called the empty set or the null set. Another symbol used to designate the empty set is ϕ, the Greek letter phi. Note the distinction between the empty set and the set whose only element is zero.

$$E = \{0\}$$

Set E is the set whose only element is zero. This set has one element, whereas the empty set has *no* elements. Note also that we refer to "*the* empty set." There is only one empty set. Whether we are describing the set of all giraffes in the classroom or the set of all Martians in Congress, we are describing *the* empty set.

Sometimes we are interested not in the elements that compose a set but in only one particular property of the set. One such property that we might want to consider is the **cardinal number** of the set. (Note that as soon as we use the cardinal number of a set we are functioning on the abstract level.) The cardinal number of a given set is the number that indicates how many elements the set has.

The set of counting numbers can be written

$$\{1, 2, 3, 4, 5, \ldots\}$$

When there is no final element, the ellipsis indicates that the sequence of elements continues in the same way endlessly.

When we count a set, we are essentially putting it into one-to-one correspondence with a set of counting numbers that has the form

$$\{1, 2, 3, \ldots, n\}$$

where n is a counting number. In other words, we match the elements of the set with successive counting numbers, starting with 1. Any set that is empty or that can be counted in this fashion is called a **finite** set. Sets which are not empty and which are not finite are called **infinite** sets. You are probably familiar already with these mathematical examples of infinite sets:

(1) The set of counting numbers:

$$\{1, 2, 3, 4, 5, \ldots\}$$

(2) The set of whole numbers:

$$\{0, 1, 2, 3, 4, \ldots\}$$

(3) The set of even (whole) numbers:

$$\{0, 2, 4, 6, \ldots\}$$

(4) The set of odd (whole) numbers:

$$\{1, 3, 5, 7, \ldots\}$$

Each of these sets continues on and on without end.

In the physical world, most sets are finite—in fact, it could be that there are no examples of infinite sets in the physical world. The number of grains of sand on the earth's surface is a staggeringly large number, but these grains form a finite set.

A **one-to-one correspondence** between two sets means that each element in the first set is matched with exactly one element in the second set, and each element in the second set is matched with exactly one element in the first set. In a one-to-one correspondence between two sets there are no elements left over, or left unmatched, in either set. Consider the set of fingers on your left hand and the set of fingers on your right hand. Can these two sets be placed in one-to-one correspondence? Yes. Each finger (element) in one set can be matched with exactly one finger in the other set, and there are no fingers in one set left over, or unmatched with fingers in the other set.

Two sets that can be placed in one-to-one correspondence are called **equivalent sets.**

$$A = \{a, e, i, o, u\}$$
$$\updownarrow \ \updownarrow \ \updownarrow \ \updownarrow \ \updownarrow$$
$$B = \{1, 2, 3, 4, 5\}$$

Sets A and B are equivalent sets, because each element in A is matched with exactly one element in B, and no element in either set is left unmatched. Since they have the same number of elements in one-to-one correspondence, equivalent sets have the same cardinal number. Are the sets pictured below equivalent?

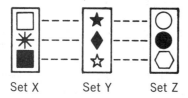

Set X   Set Y   Set Z

Yes. Each element in Set X is matched with one element in Set Y, and each element in Set Y is matched with one element in Set Z.

Let D represent the set of letters in the word "face" and let E represent the set of letters in the word "cafe." Sets D and E can easily be placed in one-to-one correspondence:

$$D = \{f, a, c, e\}$$
$$\updownarrow \ \updownarrow \ \updownarrow \ \updownarrow$$
$$E = \{c, a, f, e\}$$

This shows that Sets D and E are equivalent sets. But even more can be said: Sets D and E consist of exactly the same letters. We can therefore say that Set D *is equal to* Set E. To express the equality in symbols, we write D = E. If two sets are *equal*, they contain exactly the same elements.

Imagine that you have a bowlful of pennies and that you take from the bowl a set of four pennies. Suppose you drop the pennies back in the bowl and again take out four pennies. Are the two sets of four pennies equal? The answer is "yes" only if the second set contained exactly the same coins that you took out the first time. Of course, in both cases the value of the set of coins you took from the bowl would be 4 cents. But the sets are equal only if the coins were exactly the same coins.

Compare Set X with Set Z:

$$X = \{Mary, Betty, Jane\}$$
$$Z = \{Mary, Jean, Joan\}$$

The elements of Set X are not the same as the elements of Set Z—Betty and Jane are not identical with Jean and Joan. Set X is not equal to Set Z. We write this relation as X ≠ Z, which is read "Set X is not equal to Set Z." Although the elements of Sets X and Z are not the same, they can nevertheless be placed in one-to-one correspondence. Therefore Set X is equivalent to Set Z. We can write this as X ↔ Z, which is read "Set X is equivalent to Set Z." Since equivalent sets can be placed in one-to-one correspondence, they have the same cardinal number.

We are usually interested in one-to-one correspondence when we compare sets. Sometimes, however, we may wish to consider a **one-to-many** correspondence or a many-to-one correspondence. If we compared Set G (a set of 3 girls) and Set M (a set of mittens for the 3 girls), we would illustrate a one-to-many correspondence. Each element of Set G is matched with more than one element of Set M.

Set G = { 👧 👧 👧 }
Set M = { 🧤🧤 🧤🧤 🧤🧤 }

Set B is a set of 12 cookies, and Set C is a set of 3 boys. Several elements of Set B are matched with each element of Set C.

Set B = { 🍪🍪🍪🍪 🍪🍪🍪🍪 🍪🍪🍪🍪 }
Set C = { 👦 👦 👦 }

The relation between Set B and Set C can be expressed as a four-to-one correspondence, a **many-to-one** correspondence. This can help to develop the background for introduction of multiplication and division.

Another aspect of basic set concepts involves parts of sets:

Set F = { 🪑🛋🪑🪑🛋🪑 }

Set F, a set of furniture, includes six elements. Suppose we want to talk only about the chairs, or only about the tables. Mathematically, if we want to talk about only part of a set, we use the term **subset.**

Then we say that the set of chairs is a subset of the set of furniture, or that the set of tables is a subset of the set of furniture. What is a subset of a set? Set A is a subset of Set B if every element of Set A is also an element of Set B. Consider Set V:

$$V = \{a, e, i\}$$

What subsets can be formed from Set V?

$\{a\}, \{e\}, \{i\}, \{a, e\}, \{a, i\}, \{e, i\}, \{a, e, i\} \{\quad\}$

Let's summarize this information about subsets.

1. The empty set is a subset of every set.
2. Every set is a subset of itself.
3. A finite set that is a subset of itself and can be placed in one-to-one correspondence with itself is an equal set.

A special symbol is used in mathematics to indicate the relation between a given set and subsets of the given set.

$$A = \{1, 2, 3\} \qquad B = \{5, 4, 3, 2, 1\}$$

Set A is a subset of Set B. This relation is written as $A \subset B$, which is read "A is a subset of B" or "A is contained in B." If a set is not a subset of a given set, this is indicated by the symbol $\not\subset$. Thus we might write

$$A = \{1, 2, 3, 4, 5\}$$
$$B = \{6, 7, 8\}$$
$$B \not\subset A \text{ (read "B is not a subset of A")}$$

Do not present the symbols $\subset$ and $\not\subset$ to children; we present this here only for your knowledge. Do *not* require children to use more symbolization than necessary.

Can we predict the number of subsets that could be made from any given set? Complete the first table below, and make a generalization that tells how the number of elements in a set is related to the number of subsets.

Set	Number of Elements	Subsets	Number of Subsets
{ }	0	{ }	1
{☆}	1	{☆} { }	2
{☆ ○}	2	{☆ ○} {☆} {○} { }	
{☆ ○ □}	3		
{☆ ○ □ △}	4		

Careful examination of the preceding table indicates that the number of subsets of any set is the number found by raising 2 to a power equal to the number of elements in the given set. This pattern is shown in greater detail in the following table.

Number of Elements	Number of Subsets	Generalization Applied
0	1	2^0
1	2	2^1
2	4	2^2
3	8	2^3
4	16	2^4
5	32	2^5
.	.	.
.	.	.
.	.	.
10	1024 and so on	2^{10}

Note: We have used exponents here to extend the idea. For understanding of exponents, see Unit 5.

The table shows that if a set has five elements, the number of subsets can be determined by taking 2 to the fifth power. Two to the fifth power is 32 ($2^5 = 2 \times 2 \times 2 \times 2 \times 2 = 32$).

Besides being interested in the various subsets of a particular set, we are often interested in all the possible sets to which a given set may belong. That is, any given set may be considered a subset of other sets. For example, in thinking about the set of all 1985 Fords, we might consider the set of all 1985 Fords a subset of the set of all Fords produced by the Ford Motor Company. In this case we would refer to the set of all Fords produced by the Ford Motor Company as the **universal set.** All the elements in our given set are also elements of our universal set. (The universal set is often referred to as the **universe** for a particular situation.) The symbol for the universal set is the capital letter *U*.

Consider Set M:

$$M = \{1, 2, 3, 4, 5, 6\}$$

Set M can be considered a subset of the universal set of all whole numbers, $U = \{0, 1, 2, 3, \ldots\}$. Let's examine this idea more closely. Imagine Mrs. Watson's fourth-grade mathematics class at Lakewood School in Northville. Now consider the set of boys in Mrs. Watson's class. Let's call this Set B:

B = Set of all boys in Mrs. Watson's math class

What are some possible sets in which Set B could be contained?

Set of all children in Mrs. Watson's class
Set of all boys in Lakewood School
Set of children in Lakewood School
Set of all boys in Northville
Set of all children in Northville
Set of all fourth-grade children
Set of all children from eight to twelve years old

There are many possibilities, and each represents a possible universal set. For this reason we usually define the universal set for a given problem.

This discussion should have given us a clearer idea of what the universal set in fact is. What is the universal set? It is the set of all elements that can be discussed in a given situation.

Now let us consider another aspect of sets. In working with numbers we use two fundamental operations: addition and multiplication, and their inverse, subtraction and division. We can also perform operations on sets. Two of the simpler and more important operations on sets are the operation of **set union** and the operation of **set intersection.** The operations of addition, subtraction, multiplication, and division are called **binary operations,** because they involve working with two numbers at a time. For example, in adding $2 + 3 + 4 = \Box$, we first add 2 and 3 to obtain the sum of 5; then to that 5 we add 4 to obtain the final sum of 9. All of the fundamental operations on numbers are binary operations.

The set operations we will examine are also binary operations, because we operate on only two sets at a time. Consider these two sets:

$$A = \{\text{Harry, Bob, Nick, Ted}\}$$
$$B = \{\text{Phil, Henry, Nick, Ted}\}$$

Suppose Set A represents the Newspaper Club and Set B represents the Hiking Club. If the two clubs held a joint meeting, what would be the elements of the set of boys at the meeting? The set of boys at the meeting would be {Harry, Bob, Nick, Ted, Phil, Henry}. Nick and Ted are not repeated in the combined listing because they are elements common to the two sets. The operation of joining two sets in this way is called the union operation. If we join two sets so that all members of the first set and all members of the second set form a new set containing only the members of the two sets, we have performed the operation of union on the two sets.

The operation of union on Sets A and B is written A ∪ B. This is read "the union of Set A and Set B." After children are familiar with sets, they can use the more common reading, "A union B."

$$A \cup B = \{\text{Harry, Bob, Nick, Ted, Phil, Henry}\}$$

The equal sign can be used because A ∪ B is another name for the set {Harry, Bob, Nick, Ted, Phil, Henry}.

Now apply the operation of set union to equal sets.

$$C = \{1, 2, 3, 4\}$$
$$D = \{2, 1, 4, 3\}$$

Since C and D are different names for the same set (or C = D), we can write

$$C \cup D = \{1, 2, 3, 4\}$$

Two sets may have some common elements, or they may have no common elements. If the operation of set union is applied to sets that have common elements, the new set formed is a combination of the elements of both sets in which the elements common to the two sets are not repeated.

$$A = \{a, b, c, d\}$$
$$B = \{c, d, e, f, g\}$$
$$A \cup B = \{a, b, c, d, e, f, g\}$$

Two or more sets that have no elements in common are called **disjoint** sets. If the operation of set union is applied to disjoint sets, the new set formed is a combination of all the elements from both sets.

$$A = \{a, b, c\}$$
$$B = \{d, f, g, h\}$$
$$A \cup B = \{a, b, c, d, f, g, h\}$$

The operation of set union on equal, equivalent, and disjoint sets will be discussed further in Unit 6, when addition of whole numbers is considered.

The next operation on sets that we will consider is intersection of sets.

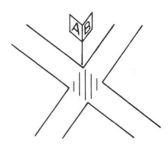

To help us define intersection of sets, consider Avenue A and Avenue B in the drawing above. What do we call the part of the road where Avenue A crosses Avenue B? This is the intersection of Avenue A and Avenue B. The distinctive feature of the intersection is the fact that it is common to the two avenues.

The intersection of two or more sets is the set that consists of the common elements of the sets, just as the intersection of two streets is the area the streets have in common.

$$A = \{a, b, c, d, e\}$$
$$B = \{d, e, f, g\}$$

If we compare Set A with Set B, we see that the sets have two elements in common: d and e. The symbol for intersection of sets is ∩ (read simply "intersection"). Using symbols to show the intersection of Set A and Set B, we would write

$$A \cap B = \{d, e\}$$

This is read "Set A intersection Set B is equal to the set whose elements are *d* and *e*."

Now let's apply the operation of set intersection to disjoint sets. Remember that disjoint sets are defined as two or more sets with no common elements.

$$D = \{1, 2, 3\}$$
$$E = \{4, 5, 6\}$$

Set D and Set E are disjoint sets. Applying the operation of set intersection, we write

$$D \cap E = \{ \ \} \text{ or } D \cap E = \phi$$

This is read "D intersection E is equal to the empty set."

After working through other examples of intersection of disjoint sets, we should be able to make the generalization that the operation of set intersection on disjoint sets always results in the empty set.

What generalization can be made about equal sets under the operation of set intersection?

$$F = \{1, 2, 3\}$$
$$G = \{1, 2, 3\}$$
$$F \cap G = \{1, 2, 3\}$$

The operation of set intersection on equal sets always results in the set itself. What about the union of equal sets? This operation, too, results in the set itself.

$$F = \{1, 2, 3\}$$
$$G = \{1, 2, 3\}$$
$$F \cup G = \{1, 2, 3\}$$

Then, in the case of two or more equal sets, we can say that both the union and the intersection of **equal** sets will result in the same (equal) set.

$$F \cup G = \{1, 2, 3\}$$
$$F \cap G = \{1, 2, 3\}$$

Sets are used in classifying, describing, comparing, and ordering, to develop numberness. Mathematical concepts should be developed before mathematical notation. The ability to count evolves out of manipulating, observing, and conceptualizing numbers. After a strong base is established, children might then be ready to begin writing numerals. Children are usually asked to write numerals under displayed sets.

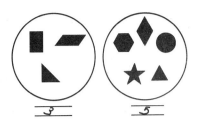

It must be emphasized here that you should *not* rush children into writing numerals. Muscular development of children varies a great deal. Some five-year-old children will be developed well enough to begin writing numerals, but others will need to wait until they are six or even seven years of age. Do *not* request a child to write numerals before he or she has had many opportunities to observe them. A child needs to have a mental image of what a numeral looks like in order to write it. Children who have not developed an accurate mental image of the numerals will often write a 3 as Ɛ.

Begin teaching children to visualize numerals by using cards with numerals written on them and matching them with sets. Hold the cards in your hand and with a finger trace the numeral as if you were writing it. You may want to put a small *x* on the numeral showing children where to begin. The numerals should look like these.

$$1\ 2\ 3\ 4\ 5\ 6\ 7\ 8\ 9\ 0$$

Next have the children trace each numeral with a finger. When you feel the children have the numeral configurations well in mind, they are ready to begin writing. Give the children large sheets of paper without lines. Provide a model of the numeral to be drawn and ask the child to draw one like the model.

Primary paper with one-inch lines and half-inch guide lines should then be used. Make little *x*'s so the child knows where to begin each numeral. Provide models so that children never write numerals backwards. Preventative instruction is much better than corrective instruction.

Remember that the cardinal number of a finite set is found by matching the elements of the set with the counting numbers, each element with a separate counting number. The last counting number in such a matching is the cardinal number of the set. As children begin to compare the cardinal numbers of sets, they are ready to expand their idea of number to discover the relations between numbers.

$$A = \{\square \triangle \bigcirc \bigstar \blacklozenge\} \qquad B = \{a, b, c, d, e\}$$
$$\updownarrow \; \updownarrow \; \updownarrow \; \updownarrow \; \updownarrow \qquad\qquad \updownarrow \; \updownarrow \; \updownarrow \; \updownarrow \; \updownarrow$$
$$\{1, 2, 3, 4, 5\} \qquad\quad \{1, 2, 3, 4, 5\}$$
$$n(A) = 5 \qquad\qquad n(B) = 5$$
$$5 = 5$$

The cardinal numbers of Sets A and B above are equal, but observe that the sets are not equal; they are equivalent.

Now consider Sets M and N:

$$M = \{m, n, o, p\} \qquad N = \{a, b, c\}$$
$$\updownarrow \; \updownarrow \; \updownarrow \; \updownarrow \qquad\qquad \updownarrow \; \updownarrow \; \updownarrow$$
$$\{1, 2, 3, 4\} \qquad\quad \{1, 2, 3\}$$
$$n(M) = 4 \qquad\qquad n(N) = 3$$

The cardinal numbers of Sets M and N are not equal. This can be expressed in mathematical symbols as

$$M \neq N$$

The symbol $\neq$ means "is not equal to." From the fact that $M \neq N$ we can conclude that Sets M and N are nonequivalent sets.

If two numbers are not equal to each other, we know that one of the numbers is either **greater than** or **less than** the other number. Look again at M and N.

$$n(M) = 4 \qquad\qquad n(N) = 3$$

We can say that four is greater than three. Using symbols, we write

$$4 > 3$$

The symbol $>$ means "is greater than." What other relation exists between the two numbers? Clearly, three is less than four. This is written

$$3 < 4$$

The symbol $<$ means "is less than." What does $3 < 4$ tell us about the given Sets M and N? Since the cardinal number of Set N is less than the cardinal number of Set M, Set N is equivalent to a proper subset of Set M.

For the cardinal numbers of any two Sets A and B, only three relations are possible:

1. A = B
    The cardinal number of set A is equal to the cardinal number of Set B.
2. A > B
    The cardinal number of Set A is greater than the cardinal number of Set B.
3. A < B
    The cardinal number of Set A is less than the cardinal number of Set B.

Cardinal numbers of finite sets are usually referred to as **whole numbers.** Let's review briefly one of the stages in the development of the concept of whole numbers.

1. We begin with groups of physical objects, considered as sets.
2. Next we use pictures of physical objects to represent the elements of sets. Eventually we can use sets whose elements are geometric shapes or symbols such as letters:

$$\{a, b, c, d, e\}$$

3. We can name a set with a single letter. For example, we can refer to $\{a, b, c, d, e\}$ as Set A:

$$A = \{a, b, c, d, e\}$$

4. We can match the elements of two sets one-to-one. In particular, we can match the elements of any given finite set with counting numbers to determine the cardinal number of the set.

$$A = \{a, b, c, d, e\}$$
$$\updownarrow \; \updownarrow \; \updownarrow \; \updownarrow \; \updownarrow$$
$$\{1, 2, 3, 4, 5\}$$

5. The cardinal number of Set A (the last counting number in the matching) can be expressed by a numeral.

$$n(A) = 5$$

6. The number named by the numeral can then be compared with any other number. Between any two numbers a and b, one and only one of the following relations will hold true:

$$a = b$$
$$a > b$$
$$a < b$$

This fact is sometimes called the **law of trichotomy.** "Trichotomy" comes from the Greek word for "threefold."

The empty set is an important part of this number development. The empty set has *no* elements and is therefore not matched with any counting number. The cardinal number of the empty set is zero.

$$A = \{ \; \} \text{ or } A = \phi$$
$$n(A) = 0$$

Note particularly the relation of the empty set to this set:

$$B = \{0\}$$

Set B is the set whose only element is 0. This set can be matched with a counting number:

$$B = \{0\}$$
$$\updownarrow$$
$$\{1\}$$

Therefore $n(B) = 1$. What about the relation between these two sets, then?

$$A = \{ \} \text{ or } A = \phi$$
$$B = \{0\}$$
$$n(A) = 0$$
$$n(B) = 1$$
$$n(B) > n(A) \quad \text{or} \quad n(A) < n(B)$$
$$1 > 0 \qquad\qquad 0 < 1$$

This idea may be difficult for some children. On the physical (concrete) level, it might be demonstrated by means of two small boxes and a felt (or cardboard) 0 symbol. The empty set is represented by the empty box: the empty set has no elements. But the box with the cardboard 0 inside represents a set with one element, that element being the 0.

We have presented a logical development beginning with concrete representation of sets and leading to awareness of the possible relations between any two numbers. It is hoped that children will be able to follow through this development rapidly and arrive at a proper understanding of the concept of "number."

Children arrive at school with different backgrounds in number concept development. The task of the teacher is to determine at what level each child is functioning. Some children will be operating on a rote-counting level, others will have some comprehension of sets, others will have a well-developed concept of numbers. Differing backgrounds raise problems that the teacher must solve by individualizing the mathematics program.

Once children understand the concept of numbers, there are several devices that can be used to reinforce their understanding of relations between numbers. One useful device is the **number line.** A number line is a representation of a geometric line with an arrowhead at each end to indicate that the line continues in both directions.

We mark two points on the line. The first point we label 0, and the second point we label 1:

Now we have marked a line segment of one **unit length** on the number line. We can now mark off other congruent line segments (segments having the same measurement) on the number line and label their end points:

We can establish a unit length on our number line to be any convenient length, provided that on any given number line all unit lengths are congruent. Also, we can select any portion of the number line that we wish to use. For example:

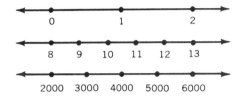

In using the number line, we agree that numbers of greater value are represented to the right of numbers of lesser value. Children can use the number line as another means of examining relations between numbers. For example, on the following number line

some of the evident relations are $2 > 1$, $3 > 2$, $1 < 3$, $0 < 2$, $3 > 1$, and so on.

Remember that the number line is used at the semiabstract level of development. So before you introduce the number line, children should have had experiences on the concrete and semiconcrete levels of development.

Number lines will prove useful for much of a child's mathematical development. In the first and second grades the number line can be used to suggest the concept of **ordinal number.** Here are two ways of representing a set that consists of a star, a square, a circle, a diamond, and a hexagon.

In the representation on the left, the elements are jumbled up. In the one on the right they are listed in a certain order: the star is first, the square is second, the diamond is third, and so on. The numbers we use to tell what position the elements occupy are ordinal numbers. To attach an ordinal number to an element of a set, the elements must be arranged in a definite order, one after another, starting with a certain element.

Terminology, Symbols, and Procedures

Attribute blocks   Attribute blocks are a set of blocks that have different characteristics, such as color, shape, size, and thickness.

Cardinal number   The cardinal number is used to answer the question "How many?" In set language a cardinal number is a property of any set, since it answers the question "How many elements are in the set?" In counting the elements of a finite set, we match them one to one with elements of the set of counting numbers, and the last (or terminal) counting number named is the cardinal number of the set. For example

$$L = \{m,\ n,\ o,\ p,\ q\}$$
$$\updownarrow\ \updownarrow\ \updownarrow\ \updownarrow\ \updownarrow$$
$$\{1,\ 2,\ 3,\ 4,\ 5\}$$

The cardinal number of Set L is 5. Whole numbers are used to designate the cardinal numbers of finite sets. The cardinal number of the empty set is 0 (zero).

Counting numbers   The set of counting numbers is the set $\{1,\ 2,\ 3,\ \ldots\}$.

Cuisenaire rods   Cuisenaire rods are a set of non-scored rods related by color and length. Color is a very important attribute of these rods.

Dienes Multi-base Blocks   Dienes Blocks are a set of scored, natural-wood blocks based on metric measure and composed of cubes, longs, flats, and blocks. The materials are made for several number bases.

Elements (or members) of a set   The individual things or ideas that compose a set are the elements of the set. These items may be related or unrelated. Any collection can form a set if we describe the members precisely and call them a set. For example, Set A is made up of the elements *a, b,* and *c.* We would write this as A = $\{a, b, c\}$. When we write a set by listing or tabulating its elements, we use braces, { }, to enclose the elements.

Empty set (or null set)   The empty set is the set that has no elements. For example, the set of all kings of the United States has no elements. We would write this as

$$K = \{\ \}$$

or

$$K = \phi$$

Equal sets   Equal sets are sets having the same elements. All equal sets are in one-to-one correspondence. For example

$$\text{Set A} = \{\text{Tom, Dick, Harry}\}$$
$$\updownarrow\quad\updownarrow\quad\updownarrow$$
$$\text{Set B} = \{\text{Tom, Dick, Harry}\}$$
$$\text{Set A} = \text{Set B}$$

The symbol = means "is equal to."

Equivalent sets   If two sets have the same cardinal number (that is, the same number of elements) even though the elements are not the same, the sets are equivalent. All equal sets are also equivalent sets, but not all equivalent sets are equal sets. For example

$$A = \{\text{Billy, Joe, Ned}\}$$
$$\updownarrow\quad\updownarrow\quad\updownarrow$$
$$B = \{\text{Billy, Tom, Don}\}$$
$$A \leftrightarrow B \text{ but } A \neq B$$

The symbol $\leftrightarrow$ means "is equivalent to."

Finite set   A finite set is an empty set or one that can be put into one-to-one correspondence with a set of the form

$$\{1, 2, 3, \ldots, n\}$$

Intersection of sets   The intersection of two sets is the set that contains the elements common to the two sets. For example

$$Set\ A = \{a, b, c, d, e\}$$
$$Set\ B = \{d, e, f, g\}$$
$$A \cap B = \{d, e\}$$

$A \cap B$ is read "Set A intersection Set B."

Law of trichotomy   For any two numbers a and b, one and only one of the following relations holds true:

$$a = b$$
$$a > b$$
$$a < b$$

Levels of abstraction in relation to number   *Concrete level:* set of actual objects; for example, a pencil and a ball. *Semiconcrete level:* pictures of objects; for example

Semiabstract level: matching elements of a set one-to-one with a set of tallies. *Abstract level:* matching the elements of a set with counting numbers to determine the cardinal number of the set.

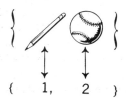

Many-to-one correspondence   Suppose that each element of one set is matched with exactly one element of a second set and that each element of the second set is matched with two or more elements of the first set. Suppose also that each element of the second set is matched with the same number of elements of the first set. Then the first set is in many-to-one correspondence with the second set.

$$D = \{p, q, r, s, t, u, v, w, x\}$$

$$E = \{\ a,\quad b,\quad c\ \}$$

Number   A number is a concept or idea that indicates *how many*.

Number line   A number line is a representation of a geometric line with an arrowhead at each end to indicate that the line continues endlessly in both directions. Points are marked to divide the line into sections of equal length, and each point is matched with a whole number. For example

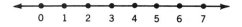

Number property   The number property of a set indicates the number of elements in that set.

Numeral   A written symbol representing a number is a numeral.

One-to-many correspondence   Suppose that each element of one set is matched with two or more separate elements of a second set and that each element of the second set is matched with exactly one element of the first set. Suppose also that each element of the first set is matched with the same number of elements in the second set. Then the first set is in one-to-many correspondence with the second set. The definition is long and wordy, but the idea is simple, as the following example shows:

Set B = 3 girls
Set C = 12 balloons

Set B is in one-to-many correspondence with Set C. (In this case Set B is in one-to-four correspondence with Set C.)

One-to-one correspondence   If each element in a first set is matched with exactly one element in a second set, and if each element in the second set is matched with exactly one element in the first set (so that no element in either set is left over or unmatched), the two sets are in one-to-one correspondence. For example

A = {Tom, Dick, Harry}
$\updownarrow$ $\updownarrow$ $\updownarrow$
B = {Ed, Louis, Bob}

Set A is in one-to-one correspondence with Set B.

Ordinal number   A number that indicates which position a certain object occupies in a given set is called an ordinal number.

Set   A set can be thought of as a group of things or ideas that are precisely described.

Stern rods   Stern rods are a set of scored rods and cubes used with number trays, pattern boards, a number rack, a number track, and other materials.

Subset   A subset of a given set is a set that contains all, some, or none of the elements of the given set, and contains only elements of the given set. Two subsets of every given set are the set itself and the empty set. For example, if

A = {a, b, c}

the possible subsets of Set A are

{ }, {a}, {b}, {c}, {a, b}, {a, c}, {b, c}, {a, b, c}

Union of sets   The union of two sets is the set containing all the elements of both sets, with no element repeated. For example

A = {Harry, Bob, Nick, Ted}
B = {Phil, Henry, Nick, Ted}
A ∪ B = {Harry, Bob, Nick, Ted, Phil, Henry}

A ∪ B is read "Set A union Set B."

Universal set (universe) All the elements that can be discussed in a given situation compose the universal set for that situation. For example, the set {*a, e, i*} is a subset of the set of all vowels in the English alphabet, a subset of all letters in the English alphabet, and a subset of all written letters. Any of these three sets contains the set under discussion, {*a, e, i*}, and could serve as the universe in this particular situation.
The universal set is generally represented by the capital letter *U*.

Whole numbers The cardinal numbers of finite sets are called whole numbers. The set of whole numbers is the set {0, 1, 2, 3, . . .}.

Practice Exercises

1. Tell at which level the child is operating in each situation—concrete, semiconcrete, semiabstract, or abstract.

   a) One child walks around the room and counts the children present by touching each on the head.
   b) A child holds up five fingers when he is asked how many members are in his family.
   c) A child cuts pictures of shoes out of a catalog and pastes them on a sheet of construction paper for a set of shoes.
   d) A child makes a set using a ball, a mitt, and a bat.
   e) A child keeps score of a spelling bee by placing tallies on the chalkboard.
   f) A child is asked how many dolls she has and responds by saying, "five."

2. Using sets and one-to-one correspondence, show that seven is less than nine.

3. Write the cardinal number for each set.

   a) A = {*a, b, c, d*}   d) D = {0}
   b) B = {2, 3, 4}   e) E = {1, 2, 3, . . ., 70}
   c) C = { }   f) F = {4, 6, 8, 10, 12}

4. Construct a number line and mark the first eight counting numbers.

5. The following patterns were made using attribute blocks. Extend each pattern by drawing the next three blocks.

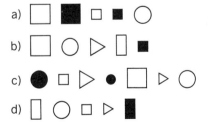

6. Use Cuisenaire rods to answer the following:

   a) How many red rods equal a brown rod?
   b) How many white rods equal a black rod?
   c) How many light green rods equal a blue rod?
   d) How many red rods equal a black rod?
   e) How many red rods equal an orange rod?

7. Name four sets of manipulable materials that can be used to develop patterning.

8. Create a sequence using Dienes Blocks, by drawing a picture. (Answers will vary. Draw enough elements to establish a pattern.)

9. Use Dienes Blocks to continue drawing the established pattern.

10. Place $>$, $<$, or $=$ in the ◯ to make each sentence true.

   a) 4 ◯ 9
   b) 8 ◯ 4 + 4
   c) 7 ◯ 5

11. Fill in the blanks with the correct symbol ($\subset$ or $\not\subset$) to indicate whether the set in Column I *is* or *is not* a subset of the corresponding set in Column II.

I	II	
a) A = {a, b, c}	B = {a, b, c, d}	A __ B
b) R = {△ □}	S = {☆ △ ●}	R __ S
c) M = { }	N = {x, y, z}	M __ N
d) D = {1, 2, 3}	E = {2, 1, 3}	D __ E
e) T = {1, 3, 5}	V = {a, b, c, d, e}	T __ V

12. Write *f* for each set that is finite and *i* for each set that is infinite.

   a) {1, 2, 3, 4, . . . , 19}   d) Counting numbers greater than 5
   b) {9, 99, 999, . . .}   e) Seconds in time
   c) All plants that are animals   f) Molecules in the earth

13. Suppose the universal set U is {1, 2, 3, 4, 5, 10, 11, 13, 14}. Write the following in set notation.

   a) The set of even numbers
   b) The set of odd numbers
   c) The set of numbers greater then 4
   d) The set of numbers greater then 5 but less than 10

14. Suppose M = {w, x, y, z}.

   a) Write all subsets of M.
   b) How many subsets of M have 3 as their cardinal number?

15. A = {a, b, c, d}   B = {c, d, e}

   a) The elements of Set A are ___, ___, ___, and ___.
   b) The elements of Set B are ___, ___, and ___.
   c) A ∪ B =
   d) A ∩ B =

16. Tabulate each of the following in set notation.

   a) The set of even numbers between 6 and 18
   b) The set of odd numbers between 7 and 9
   c) The set of elements that are in {2, 4, 6, 8, 10} but not in {1, 2, 3, 4, 5}
   d) The set of counting numbers less than 9

17. The symbol ϕ stands for the ___ ___.

18. Describe each of the following sets in words.

    a) D = {Monday, Tuesday, Wednesday, Thursday, Friday, Saturday, Sunday}
    b) Z = {6, 8, 10, 12}
    c) K = {w, x, y, z}
    d) M = {0, 1, 2, 3, 4, 5}

Discussion Questions

1. How are Dienes Blocks and Stern rods alike? How are they different?

2. Discuss and describe activities that can be used to help children develop an understanding of number conservation.

3. Research and then discuss the importance of using patterns in the introductory stages of learning mathematics.

4. Describe the process of characterizing an object by its attributes.

5. Discuss the importance of searching, describing, and extending patterns in a beginning mathematics program.

6. Discuss the advantages and disadvantages of a structured mathematics program, as compared with an incidental mathematics program in kindergarten.

7. Discuss the types of activities that are beneficial for children in developing number readiness.

8. What types of activities can be used with children to help them associate a set with a number and with a numeral?

9. After children have developed the concept of numberness to ten, describe the role of counting in the mathematics program.

10. Discuss the use of the number line to help children comprehend the law of trichotomy.

11. Study the learning theory of a particular theorist (such as Piaget, Bruner, or Gagné) and describe the implications for the teaching of mathematics.

12. Suggest evaluation activities that can be used with young children to determine whether they are ready to begin a formal mathematics program.

13. Describe activities for the concrete, semiconcrete, semiabstract, and abstract levels of developing numberness.

14. Discuss the importance of developing the concept of one-to-one correspondence in a beginning mathematics program.

15. How does a teacher know when a child is ready to begin writing numerals?

16. Discuss the role of sets in a beginning mathematics program.

17. Discuss how a hand-held calculator could be used to help young children recognize and discriminate among the basic numerals.

18. Research and then discuss how a microcomputer might be used in a kindergarten mathematics program.

Activities for the Primary Grades

If our educational system is to prepare children for success, we must teach them to recognize mathematics in the real world. Beginning with attribute blocks, sets, and materials from the real world provides a valuable vehicle for relating mathematics to the real world. It is best to begin with concrete materials and then move gradually to the abstract world of mathematics. The children first need to understand the concepts of sets and one-to-one correspondence and learn to write numerals as a solid base for developing mathematical concepts.

Teaching children to identify, describe, and classify objects and abstract ideas is generally considered sound educational practice. Children need numerous experiences observing, identifying, and verbalizing ideas to others. As ideas become more abstract and thus harder to identify, children can use the concept of sets to help understand and use proper symbolism, as prerequisites for classifying and identifying.

Children will usually find the set approach to numberness and operations a simple, enjoyable, and logical approach to mathematics. While basic mathematics concepts are being developed, the children are also developing logical thought processes in mathematics.

DESCRIBING SETS

1. Have sets of materials available for children to manipulate and describe. Every first-grade room has the basic equipment for this task: boxes of crayons, books, pencils, chairs, desks, and, of course, children.

2. Obtain materials from the local drive-in such as disposable plastic spoons, forks, or cups and use them as mathematics equipment. Do *not* use items that some children may not be familiar with, such as beads.

3. Some children will probably have collections of small toys such as cars, dolls, dishes, or furniture. Permit them to bring their collections to school and let other children describe the sets.

4. Obtain pictures of items (semiconcrete level) for children to separate into sets. Pictures can be cut from old magazines, newspapers, or catalogs and placed in a large brown

envelope. Use four old stationery boxes and paste a picture of the elements to be placed in each set inside the bottom of each box.

Box I   A set of furniture
Box II A set of dishes
Box III A set of shoes
Box IV A set of clothing

The child takes a picture from the envelope and places it in the proper box. After all the pictures have been separated, the boxes can be placed on the teacher's desk for checking. The pictures can then be mixed up and put back into the large brown envelope for a different child to separate at another time. Four or five different sets of pictures can be made.

5. Use the chalkboard to draw pictures of items and loop the items to be placed together for a set. Permit the children to describe each set orally.

6. A flannel board with felt cutouts and yarn can be used to make sets on a semiconcrete level. Have children take turns making sets and have another child orally describe the set. Three or four different groups of children can do this activity simultaneously.

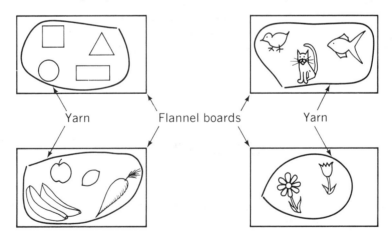

Yarn   Flannel boards   Yarn

7. Use an overhead projector to project sets of items made from different colored plastic objects encircled in yarn. Let one child at a time assemble a set on the projector while the rest of the children take turns orally describing the sets.

A set of red
geometric shapes

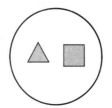

A set of blue
geometric shapes

8. Dictating statements to encourage response from pupils is very useful. Some examples of the type of statements that might be used in first grade are

  a) the set of all children wearing shoes (the children could stand up so that the real objects—concrete level—composing the set would be seen by all the pupils)
  b) the set of all girls in the room
  c) the set of all boys in the room (be sure to sit down if you are a female teacher)
  d) the set of all children who are wearing glasses

Ask the children to think of statements to dictate for group response; then ask other children to describe the sets.

Note: Many first-grade children are not physically able to draw pictures of sets.

THE EMPTY SET

1. Have several covered containers available, such as one-pound coffee cans, one or two large cardboard boxes, and some small balls, small dolls, or wooden blocks.

   In one container place three items, in another two items, one item in another, and no items in the last container. Give the four containers to four different children and have each one describe the set of items he sees in his container. Discuss how we would describe the set with no members.

   Use this approach to guide the children into understanding the idea of an empty set.

2. Discussing questions such as the following can help build a concept of the empty set. Discuss these and then encourage the children to think of similar ones.

  a) How many children in the room are taller than the teacher?
  b) How many purple zebras do we have in the classroom?
  c) How many pieces of chalk are there in the empty chalk box?

CARDINAL NUMBER OF SETS

1. Let children make sets of cards with various numbers of pictures of items pasted on them. Have another set of cards with a numeral written on each card. Begin with numbers less than four and ask the children to match the set card with the proper numeral card. Continue the activity, using more cards, until ten has been reached.

2. After the children have learned how to match the set cards with the numeral cards, they can play Concentration. Turn all the set and numeral cards face down on a table. Two to four children may play by turning over any two cards during a turn. If the cards are a set and its corresponding numeral card, the child may keep the pair. If the cards do not match, they must again be turned face down. The child with the most pairs of cards after all the cards have been matched wins the game.

3. Mark an X on each set of 1.

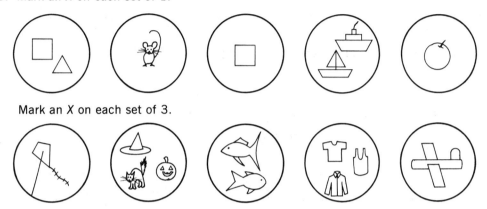

Mark an X on each set of 3.

4. After the children can recognize sets and numerals through 9, practice can be provided through games. Make bingo cards with numerals on the cards; make markers large enough to cover a numeral. Play by showing set cards one by one. If a child has the numeral on the set card on his bingo card he can cover it. Only one numeral may be covered in any one turn. The first child to cover five numerals in a row wins the game.

Bingo			
9	3	2	7
5	8	4	1
2	4	7	5
8	1	3	6

Bingo			
1	5	3	6
8	4	2	9
7	8	5	4
6	9	4	7

Bingo			
6	1	9	7
4	8	5	1
6	3	4	7
1	5	9	2

Bingo cards — one for each child

Place at least three set cards for each number face down on the desk. Pick the cards at random and show them to the class.

5. Draw a ring around the numeral that represents the cardinal number of each set.

1 2 3	3 4 2	1 3 2	4 6 7	6 7 8 9	4 5 6
3 2 0 1	2 4 6 8	5 6 7 8	9 8 7 6	5 6 7	2 3 4 5

6. Draw a ring around a set that has as many objects as the numeral names.

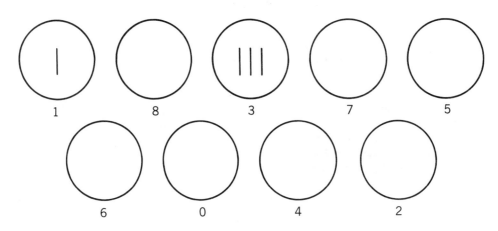

○□△ ◇☆○	△□○ □○◇	□○○ ▽□△	◇□○ ▽△▽	△□○ ☆□◇	△□▽ ○□□
1	5	4	2	6	3

7. Make as many marks (I) in the set as the number under each circle.

(|)   ( )   (|||)   ( )   ( )
1   8   3   7   5

( )   ( )   ( )   ( )
6   0   4   2

8. Tape a roll of shelf paper to the floor. Mark off spaces about equal to one child's pace. Write the numerals so the child views the numeral correctly as he walks on the number line.

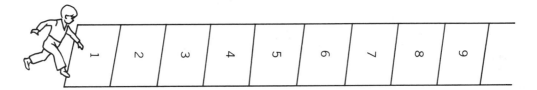

9. If stairs are available, make squares of cardboard the size of the width of a stairstep. Write a numeral on each square and tape it on the proper step. As a child says a number, have another child go to the step with the corresponding numeral on it.

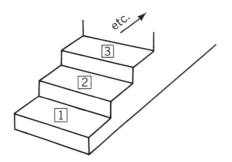

EQUIVALENT SETS

As a rule it is helpful, especially for primary-school children, to show objects and shapes that differ in appearance in a set. Doing so reinforces the idea that all the elements of a given set are different. However, it is difficult and often distracting to do this if a set contains many elements. Therefore to facilitate visual comparisons, elements of sets in the following activities have the same shape. We will consider these elements "distinguishable" if they occupy different positions.

1. Draw line segments to connect the sets with the same number of elements.

2. Draw sets to complete this table.

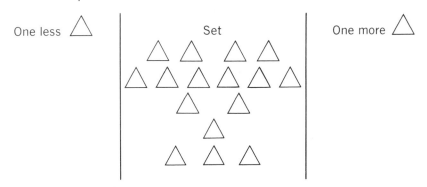

3. Write the numeral for each set. Then mark the set that has the greater number of elements with an *X*.

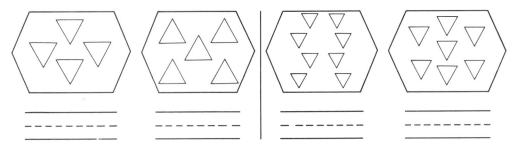

4. Write the numeral for each set. Then mark the set that has the lesser number of elements with an *X*.

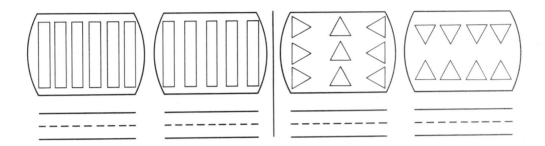

—————————   ————————— | —————————   —————————
- - - - - - - - -   - - - - - - - - - | - - - - - - - - -   - - - - - - - - -

5. Draw **a** loop around the numeral naming the greater number.

(3 or 4)   (2 or 1)   (0 or 1)   (7 or 6)

6. Draw a ring around the numeral naming the lesser number.

(6 or 5)   (1 or 3)   (7 or 9)   (3 or 0)   (4 or 2)

7. Draw a loop around the numeral naming the lesser number.

(39 or 29)   (123 or 321)   (46 or 36)   (60 or 66)   (345 or 435)

8. Draw a ring around the numeral naming the greater number.

(15 or 51)   (213 or 123)   (49 or 51)   (17 or 71)   (69 or 96)

UNION OF SETS

At the primary level, operations on sets are largely confined to union of disjoint sets. The union of sets is the basic model that leads to understanding the addition of whole numbers. Use many concrete experiences illustrating the joining of two sets to create a third set. In joining two disjoint sets to form a new set, guide children to discover that the original sets are subsets of the new one. By manipulating sets, children should discover that two sets can be joined in two ways.

1. For primary children who have not learned to read, the rebus may be used. In example *a*, the children can read that three triangles and four discs make seven triangles and discs. How would you read example *b*?

a.   How many?

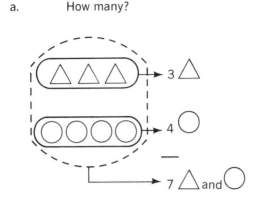

b.   How many?

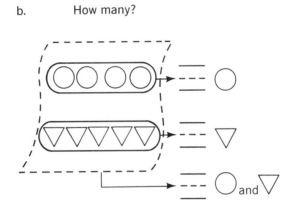

In these examples, children are not adding. They are merely counting the number of triangles, the number of discs, and the number of triangles and discs. This is a readiness activity using sets as a model for addition.

2. Numerals may be used to relate number ideas to the two disjoint sets and to the new set created by putting the two sets together. Addition is not used, but counting the elements in each set provides readiness for addition.

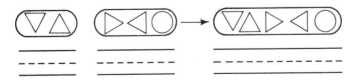

3. Let the children complete examples by drawing the elements of the union in the empty figure on the right. Do not use elements that are beyond their psychomotor development level.

4. Extend the idea by relating numberness to each set and have the children write a numeral for each set.

5. Loop the number of elements shown and complete the table below the sets.

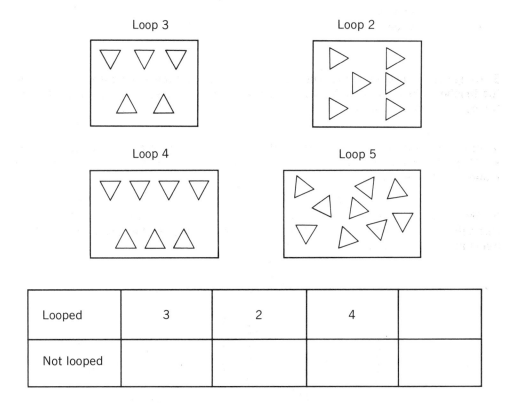

Loop 3   Loop 2

Loop 4   Loop 5

Looped	3	2	4	
Not looped				

WHOLE-NUMBER RELATIONS

1. Make a set of numeral cards by cutting numerals from materials of different textures (such as sandpaper and velvet). Have each child place a finger at the point where one would begin drawing the numeral and then trace the entire numeral. Children can also trace numerals in the air.

2. Make a number line on the floor with masking tape. Have the children walk along the number line, stopping at a particular number.

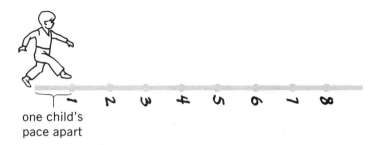

one child's
pace apart

3. Assign each child a number. The class is arranged in a circle around the teacher. When the teacher calls out a number, the student who has been assigned that number taps out the correct number and runs around the circle.

4. Assign each child a number, which the children keep as secrets. The students then knock on the door a number of times corresponding to their assigned numbers. The class responds, "Come in number 7 (number 12, etc.)."

5. Give each child an egg carton in which a numeral has been written in each indention. Use pebbles or small pieces of drinking straws and have the children place that number of items in each compartment.

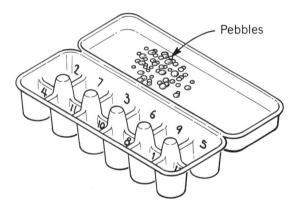

Pebbles

6. Draw a ring around the numeral for each set.

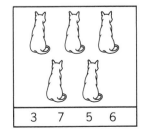
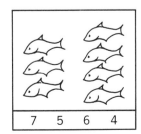

7. Write a numeral for each set.

(Children should always have guidelines for writing numerals. The size to be used should vary with the level of the child's development.)

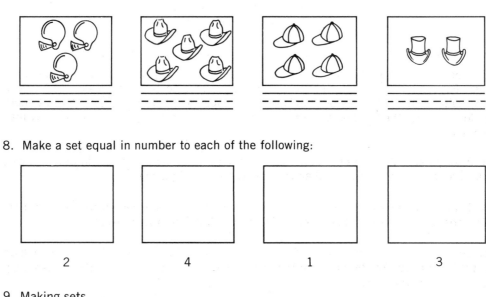

8. Make a set equal in number to each of the following:

2	4	1	3

9. Making sets.

ONE LESS	SET	ONE MORE

10. Write a numeral for each set. Then place $<$, $>$, or $=$ in the $\bigcirc$.

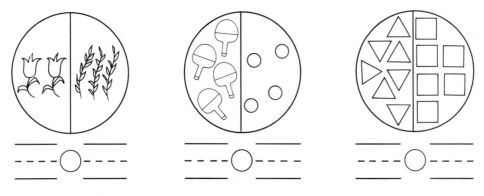

11. Mark the third element X
Mark the first element △
Mark the second element ☐

12. Request that the children take objects out of their desks and place them in a stated order. For instance, "Place your eraser first, a pencil second, a red crayon third, and a paper clip fourth." After the objects have been placed in order, you may ask them to hold up, for example, the third object. You can check the children very easily. The activity may continue.

13. Assign each child an ordinal number and have the children line up in proper order. This can be done at recess or when the children are being dismissed.

14. Call children by their "ordinal names" rather than by their given names: for instance, "first one, second row," "third one, first row," or "fifth one, fourth row."

15. Children enjoy drawing dot pictures. They will readily understand what has to be done with this exercise. Ask them where they think they should begin. When they finish, they should identify the picture.

16. Cut pieces of cardboard 4 cm by 8 cm for dominoes. Make a set of dominoes with sets on one end and numerals on the other end. At first, use sets and numbers the children understand. Continually add new dominoes as the children develop concepts of numbers. Play the game using the standard rules for the game of dominoes.

  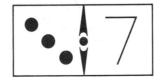

17. Use the number line to help you decide which symbol (<, =, >) you will put inside each circle to make the sentence true.

```
←——•——•——•——•——•——•——•——•——•——•——•——•——•——•——→
    0   1   2   3   4   5   6   7   8   9  10  11  12  13
```

a) 6 ◯ 5   d) 9 ◯ 9   g) 9 ◯ 7

b) 7 ◯ 8   e) 7 ◯ 3   h) 2 ◯ 12

c) 2 ◯ 1   f) 2 ◯ 11   i) 0 ◯ 4

18. Children need many experiences with patterns on the concrete, semiconcrete, and semiabstract levels before you should attempt to introduce patterns on the abstract level. Discover the pattern and fill in the blank for each of the following:

a) 1, 2, 3, 4, —, 6, —, —, —, 10
b) 7, 8, 9, —, —, 12, —, —, 15
c) 2, 4, 6, —, —, —, —, —, —
d) 17, 16, 15, —, —, —, —, 10

19. This activity is very rich. It has many possibilities for being used in many places in the mathematics program. The number of patterns that can be discovered in this table are innumerable and include even numbers, odd numbers, place value, prime numbers, and addition and subtraction patterns.

Mark a large square piece of cardboard into 100 squares (10 by 10). Make a set of numeral cards from 1 to 99 so that the cards will fit on the board. Have a child begin putting the numeral cards on the board and ask others to complete the entire board. Have them study the cards on the board and look for number patterns.

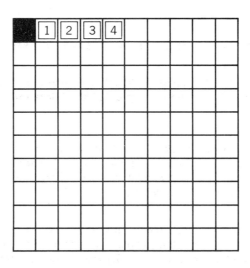

20. Mark with an X each one that names a number less than 37.

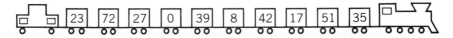

21. Mark with an X each one that names a number greater than 27 and less than 45.

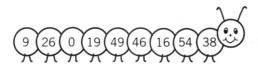

Hand-Held Calculator Activities for the Primary Grades

1. Teach the children how to turn on the hand-held calculator. Some calculators will have an off/on switch; other calculators will have a key. Children must first identify the on/off switch or key. Children must then understand that, if a zero does not show up on the display screen when the calculator is turned on, something is wrong with the calculator.

2. The hand-held calculator can be used to help the children identify the numbers 1 through 10. Write a 2 on the chalkboard, and ask each child to place a finger on the 2 on the number line taped to the front of each child's desk. Request the children to locate 2 on a key on the calculator and then press that key. A 2 should appear on the display screen. Compare the 2 on the number line with the 2 on the keyboard and the 2 on the display screen. Do all the twos look alike? Use a similar procedure with all the numbers up to 10.

3. State a number, and have the children press that particular key on the calculator. Children can hold up their calculators with the display screen facing the teacher, and she can quickly check to make sure that all children are correct. Now children do not have a model to use as a comparison. They must recognize the correct numeral and press the key without looking at a model.

4. Help the children set up the calculators to count. Turn on the calculator, press the + key, the 1 key, and then press the = key ten consecutive times. The display screen should count from 0 through 10.

5. Teach the children to clear the display by using the clear key.

6. Primary children need to have hand-held calculators available for work sessions or free play periods. These sessions should be unstructured. Children will discover many ideas by themselves.

7. Start a pattern on a display screen for a child and request that the child continue the pattern. For instance, turn on the calculator and press 1, then 2, then 1; then hand the calculator to the child and ask her to extend the same pattern. The child should press 2, 1, 2, 1, 2, etc. The display screen should show 12121212.

8. Try a pattern that repeats itself using three numbers. For instance, turn on the calculator and enter 1, 2, 3, 1. Hand the calculator to a child. He should enter 2, 3, 1, 2, and the display screen should show 12312312. Try many other patterns, and ask the children to continue the patterns. This will require the children to analyze and then continue a given pattern.

9. Start a pattern of 1, 2, 3, 4, and ask a child to complete the pattern. The child should press 5, 6, 7, and 8. The display screen should then show 12345678. Press 2 and ask a child to show a counting pattern beginning with 2. The child should then press 3, 4, 5, 6, 7, 8, and 9 in order. The display screen should show 23456789.

10. Have the children work in pairs. Ask one child to start a pattern and a second child to continue the pattern. Check to make sure that a pattern is apparent on the display screen.

Microcomputer Activities for the Primary Grades

All hand-held calculator activities can be used on a microcomputer in the immediate mode. The microcomputer offers some advantages over the hand-held calculator. Display screens on hand-held calculators are limited to eight places; microcomputer display screens have 20, 40, or 80 character spaces per line. Longer character lines provide a much greater opportunity for observing, analyzing, and extending numerical patterns. Remember that, to use the computer in the immediate mode, each statement must be preceded with the word "PRINT"; a question mark can be used as an abbreviation for the word PRINT. Do not use the equals sign in a mathematical sentence.

Microcomputers should be used in unique ways to accomplish educational tasks that cannot be achieved with normal classroom procedures. However, at the primary level, children must first become familiar with computers. Activities that require drill and practice may be the best techniques for introducing children to computers. LOGO and BASIC are the two most prevalent languages in the primary grades.

From the beginning, children should be taught to use a microcomputer properly. Do *not* allow children to abuse the computers. Children should learn how to turn on the microcomputer properly and how to load software. Children who cannot handle a computer properly should be denied the privilege until they have shown that they can behave responsibly.

1. Microcomputers can be used to help young children learn to recognize the numbers 1 through 9. The following program, prepared specifically for a Commodore Vic-20, can be typed into the microcomputer and placed in one of the work stations that children might select. Alterations can easily be made in this program, so it can be adapted for another computer. Remind children to press the return key after pressing a number key.

```
10   REM RECOGNIZE NUMBERS 1—9
20   N=INT(RND(1)*9)+1
30   ?"⊡":REM—CLEARS SCREEN)
40   ?:?:?"        FIND ";N
50   INPUT A
60   IF A=N THEN GOTO 190
70   IF A<>N THEN 75
75   Z=0
80   ?N,
90   Z=Z+1
100  IF Z=20 THEN 30
110  FOR T=1 TO 1000:NEXT T
120  GOTO 75
190  X=0
200  L=INT(RND(1)*500)+1
210  C=INT(RND(1)*8)+1
220  POKE 7680+L,160
230  POKE 38400+L,C
240  X=X+1
250  IF Z=100 THEN 20
260  GOTO 200
```

2. Begin patterning with simple patterns and continually increase the difficulty. Pattern difficulty can vary to meet the development levels of individual children. Remember that patterns can either be constant or systematically change. The following set of patterns

might be considered as examples. You will want to provide more than one example of each type of pattern.

a) 121212. . . .   g) 12112111211112. . . .
b) #*#*#*. . . .   h) 505500555000. . . .
c) abcabca. . . .   i) #-##--###---. . . .
d) 24624. . . .   j) &-----&&----&&&. . . .
e) 2482482. . . .   k) 1121221222. . . .
f) #'/#'/#'/. . . .

3. The microcomputer can be used to help children associate numerals with sets. The following program was specifically written for a TRS-80 model II but can easily be adapted for other microcomputers.

```
10  REM—ASSOCIATING NUMBER WITH SETS—
20  ?@290,"HOW MANY #"
30  ?:?"# # # #"
40  INPUT A
50  IF A=4 THEN ?"GOOD":FOR T=1 TO 1500:NEXT T:GOTO 80
60  IF A<>4 THEN ?"WRONG":FOR T=1 TO 1500:NEXT T:GOTO 20
80  ?@290,"HOW MANY *"
90  ?:?"* * * * * *"
100 INPUT B
110 IF B=6 THEN ?"GOOD":FOR T=1 TO 1500:NEXT T:GOTO 140
120 IF B<>6 THEN ?"WRONG":FOR T=1 TO 1500:NEXT T:GOTO 80
```

This program can be continued to provide as many examples as the children need. As the teacher becomes more familiar with programming, the programs can be made to be more friendly. By this we mean that a greeting could be used in the beginning, children could be asked to enter their names, and names could be incorporated into the program. A personalized ending could also be included.

Activities for the Intermediate Grades

DESCRIBING SETS

1. Describe each set in words.

January February March April	Monday Tuesday Wednesday Thursday Friday

CARDINAL NUMBER OF SETS

For obvious reasons, elements that occupy different spaces will be considered "distinguishable" in this and subsequent exercises.

1. Write a numeral showing the number of elements in each set.

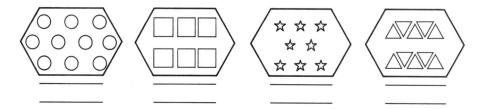

_____   _____   _____   _____

2. Write a numeral for the number of elements.

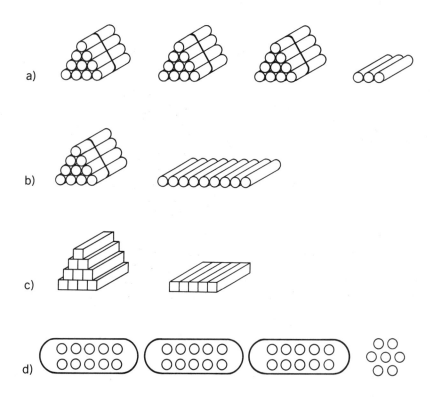

3. Write a numeral for the set and each of _its subsets._

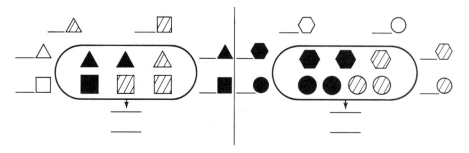

4. Draw a ring around each set of ten. Then write a numeral in each blank that shows how many sets of ten are in that box.

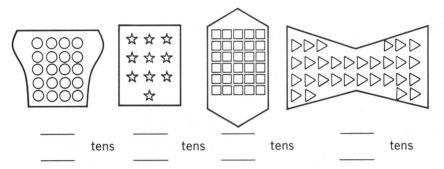

_____   _____   _____   _____
    tens   tens   tens   tens
_____   _____   _____   _____

5. Make a set of playing cards. Half the deck should show sets of tens and ones; the other half should be made up of matching cards that show the numeral for each set card. Make one card that is different, such as the "old maid." Use the cards to play Old Maid. The child that ends the game with the odd card loses.

UNION OF SETS

1. Union of sets is one model that can be used to help the child understand addition.

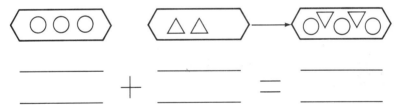

_____ + _____ = _____

2. Symbolization becomes more abstract as sets depicted with objects now can be notated with letters or numerals.

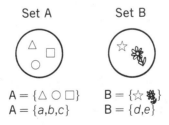

$$A = \{\triangle \bigcirc \square\} \quad B = \{\star \, \text{❀}\}$$
$$A = \{a, b, c\} \quad B = \{d, e\}$$

3. A = {a, b, c}   D = {a, c, e, g}
    B = {d, e, f}   E = {x, y, z}
    C = {d, o, g}   F = {b, o, y}

Consider the sets above and list all pairs of sets that are disjoint.

4. A = {a, b}   B = {c, d, e}
   {a, b} joined with {c, d, e} = {a, b, c, d, e}

   _____   +   _____ = _____

5. A = {a, e, i, o, u}   C = {c, a, f, e}
   B = {b, c, d, f}   D = {g, a, m, e}

Consider the sets above and list all pairs of

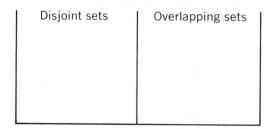

Disjoint sets	Overlapping sets

You will note that these exercises are somewhat more abstract and should only be used after a concrete approach to sets. The exercises can be accomplished at any grade level, depending on the amount of background the children have.

6. Use { } and tabulate each set described below.

   a) The set of school days in each week
   b) The set of numbers greater than five and less than seventeen
   c) The set of teachers you have this year in school
   d) The set of months in a year
   e) The set of days in a week that begin with the letter D

7. Describe each set in words.

   a) A = {a, e, i, o, u}
   b) B = {2, 4, 6, 8, . . .}
   c) C = {4, 5, 6, 7, 8, 9}
   d) D = {3, 5, 7, 9, 11}

8. Find the number for each set.

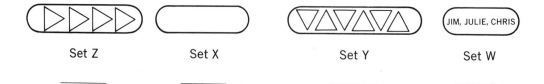

Set Z   Set X   Set Y   Set W

_____   _____   _____   _____

9. Make a deck of cards with a set pictured on each card. Place all cards face down on a table and play Concentration. If the two cards turned over are equivalent, the player keeps the pair. If the two cards are nonequivalent, they must be replaced face down on the table. The player with the most pairs wins. The number of players may vary from two to four, depending on how many cards are in the deck.

10. Use the set of cards described above and make a card for the "old maid." Play Old Maid, making pairs of equivalent sets.

11. Write all of the subsets for each of the given sets.

   a) A = {a, b, c}
   b) B = {1, 2, 3, 4, 5}
   c) C = {1, 3, 5, 7}

WHOLE-NUMBER RELATIONS

1. Children need to learn to recognize the number of items in a set without counting. To help children recognize numbers without counting, make two sets of cards with dots. One set has domino patterns, and the other has randomly placed dots. These cards can be flashed at the children, who then tell how many dots are on each card. Children can check their responses by counting, if necessary.

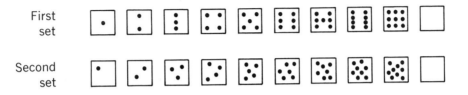

First set

Second set

2. A card with dots (like those described in Question 1) is given to each student. The teacher writes a numeral on the board, then the students with the cards just preceding and following the number stand on each side of the written numeral.

3. Complete the table on the right and mark the sets as indicated in the table.

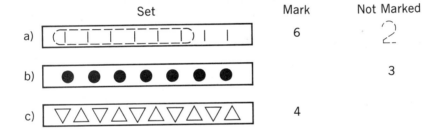

	Set	Mark	Not Marked
a)		6	2
b)			3
c)		4	

4. Find the pattern and fill in the blanks.

a) 10, 12, 14, ___, ___, ___, ___, ___, ___, ___.
b) 68, 69, ___, ___, ___, ___, ___, ___, ___, ___.
c) 10, 20, 30, ___, ___, ___, ___, ___, ___, ___.
d) ___, ___, ___, ___, 58, 59, ___, ___, ___, ___.
e) 10, 9, 8, ___, ___, ___, ___, ___, ___, ___.
f) ___, ___, ___, 18, ___, 22, ___, ___, ___.
g) 239, ___, ___, 242, ___, ___, ___, ___, ___.
h) 147, ___, 151, ___, ___, ___, ___, ___, 163.
i) 17, ___, ___, ___, ___, ___, ___, ___, 35.

5. Place <, >, or = in the circle to make each statement true.

a) 28 ○ 29
b) 46 ○ 64
c) 327 ○ 327
d) 104 ○ 14
e) 434 ○ 344
f) 237 ○ 327
g) 51 ○ 15
h) 81 ○ 79

6. Place the following numerals in order from the least to the greatest.

a) 19, 22, 17, 20, 18, 21.
b) 43, 34, 25, 52, 24, 42, 30.
c) 127, 230, 226, 130, 187, 198, 203.
d) 78, 76, 68, 85, 87, 67, 58, 65, 57, 86, 75.

7. Connect each boat with its ordinal number.

ninth, third, seventh, fourth, eighth, first, fifth, second, tenth, sixth

8. Make a set of cards with two-place numerals written on them. Have a child arrange the cards in order on his desk from the least value to the greatest. For example:

WHOLE-NUMBER RELATIONS

1. Given a set of cards with numerals on one side and letters on the opposite side, have the students place the cards in order from least to greatest. The student can check the answer by turning the cards over to see if the message is correct.

When students
turn cards
over:

| 78 | 79 | 80 | 81 | 82 | 83 | 84 | 85 |

| H | A | P | P | Y | D | A | Y |

2. Study the patterns and fill in the blanks.

    a) 19, 24, 29, ___, ___, ___, ___, ___, ___, 64.
    b) 91, 84, 77, ___, ___, ___, ___, ___, ___.
    c) ___, ___, ___, 136, 150, 164, ___, ___, ___, ___.
    d) 323, 333, ___, ___, ___, ___, ___, ___, 403.
    e) ___, ___, ___, ___, ___, ___, 473, 485, 497.
    f) 42, ___, ___, 51, ___, ___, 60, ___, ___, 69.
    g) ___, 184, ___, 170, ___, ___, ___, ___, ___, 128.

3. Mark the number that has greater value.

a)	43	34
b)	8	23
c)	19	18
d)	85	59
e)	79	89
f)	61	19
g)	26	41

4. Mark the number that has less value.

a)	43	34
b)	19	23
c)	56	65
d)	123	231
e)	85	58
f)	49	51
g)	197	179

5. Complete the table.

100 Less	10 Less	1 Less		1 Greater	10 Greater	100 Greater
			278			
			142			
			369			
			520			
			401			

Hand-Held Calculator Activities for the Intermediate Grades

Hand-held calculator activities for primary children can be easily adapted for intermediate grade children. However, at this age level, all children should be able to identify the numbers 1 through 9. Number identification should now be extended into more decimal places. (Check the activities for Unit 5.) Children should observe and discover the patterns that exist in our place-value system.

1. In the primary grades, as children are learning to count, use numbers only in ascending order. Young children find it difficult to count in descending order. At the intermediate level, patterns such as 987 . . . may be introduced.

2. Children should understand how to use constants with the hand-held calculator and how to use the calculator to count by numbers other than one. (See the calculator activities for Unit 6.) Place emphasis on patterns developed counting by numbers other than one.

3. Introduce the students to more difficult patterns. Following are some suggested patterns; teachers will also want to create patterns of their own.

a) 97397. . .   d) 9173 . . .
b) 9897. . .   e) 8062 . . .
c) 9182 . . .   f) 5432 . . .

In the last case, the pattern will terminate with zero, if each digit is placed in the calculator. If a student generates a pattern using subtract one as a constant, the calculator will move into negative numbers. Be prepared for this.

Microcomputer Activities for the Intermediate Grades

Computer activities listed for the primary grades can also be used at the intermediate level. LOGO or BASIC or both languages can be used at the intermediate grade level.

1. Have the children type in the following program and then state what each statement will cause the computer to do.

```
20 X=0
30 X=X+1
40 ?X
50 IF X>20 THEN END
60 GOTO 30
```

2. Change line 30 to each of the following. How will this change the program?

    a) X=X+2
    b) X=X+3
    c) X=X+X

Why did X=X+X print only 0? What other statement must be changed in the program?

3. Change line 20 to X=1. How did this change the program? Why?

Hand-Held Calculator Activities for the Upper Elementary Grades

Hand-held calculator activities that involve patterning and numbers can be selected from the primary and intermediate activities or from other units within the text.

Microcomputer Activities for the Upper Elementary Grades

Some upper elementary children enjoy creating microcomputer programs to develop simple numeric patterns on the screen. The sample programs presented here can be used on any computer that accepts BASIC. One adjustment must be made to the statements that involve clearing the screen.

1. Create a computer program to make a pattern counting by one.

```
10 REM—COUNTING PROGRAM—
20 CLS
30 FOR X=1 TO 100
40 ?X
50 NEXT X
```

2. Create a computer program to make a pattern counting by two.

```
10 REM—COUNTING BY TWOS—
20 CLS
30 FOR X=1 TO 100 STEP 2
40 ?X
50 NEXT X
```

3. Create a computer program to count by even numbers to 50.

4. Create a computer program to count by five; begin with five and count to 100.

5. Create a unique program for counting.

6. Study each of these number sequences; then write a program to create the pattern and continue the pattern, ending at 40.

    a) 0, 1, 3, 6, 10, 15, 21, . . .
    b) 1, 2, 4, 7, 11, . . .
    c) 0, 2, 6, 12, 20, 30, . . .

```
10   REM—PROGRAM FOR ADDING A VARIABLE—
20   CLS
30   X=0
40   Y=1
50   ?X
60   ?X+Y
70   X=X+Y
80   Y=Y+1
90   IF Y=9 THEN END
100 GOTO 60
```

Suggested Readings

Alberti, Del; Davitt, Robert J.; and others. *Attribute Games and Problems—Teacher's Guide*. New York: McGraw-Hill, 1974.

Andrews, E. E., and Nelson, Doyal L. "Beginning Number Experiences and Structured Materials." *The Arithmetic Teacher*, vol. 10, no. 6, February 1963.

Bitter, Gary G., and Mikesell, Jerald L. *Activities Handbook for Teaching with the Hand-held Calculator*. Boston: Allyn & Bacon, 1980.

Copeland, Richard W. *Mathematics Activities for Children: A Diagnostic and Developmental Approach*. Columbus, Ohio: Merrill, 1979.

Davidson, Jessica. *Using the Cuisenaire Rods*. New Rochelle, N.Y.: Cuisenaire Company of America, 1969.

Dawes, Cynthia G. *Early Maths*. Longman Early Childhood Education Series. New York: Longman, 1977.

Dienes, Zoltan P. *Modern Mathematics for Young Children*. Essex, England: The Educational Supply Association Limited, 1965.

Hendrickson, Dean A. "A Psychological Sound Primary School Mathematics Curriculum." *The Arithmetic Teacher*, vol. 30, no. 5, January 1983.

Holt, Michael, and Dienes, Zoltan. *Let's Play Math*. New York: Walker & Company, 1973.

Lorton, Mary. *Workjobs*. Menlo Park, Calif.: Addison-Wesley, 1972.

Marolda, Maria. *Attribute Games and Activities*. Palo Alto, Calif.: Creative Publications, 1976.

National Council of Teachers of Mathematics. *Mathematics Learning in Early Childhood*. 37th Yearbook. Reston, Va.: NCTM, 1975.

O'Brien, Thomas C., and Richards, June V. "Interviews to Assess Number Knowledge." *The Arithmetic Teacher*, vol. 18, no. 5, January 1968.

Piaget, Jean. *The Child's Conception of Number*. New York: Norton, 1965.

Skemp, Richard R. *The Psychology of Learning Mathematics*. New York: Penguin Books, 1979.

Stern, Catherine, and Stern, Margaret B. *Helping Children Discover Arithmetic*. New York: Harper & Row, 1971.

Yvon, Bernard R., and Spooner, Eunice B. "Variations in Kindergarten Mathematics Programs and What a Teacher Can Do About It." *The Arithmetic Teacher*, vol. 29, no. 5, January 1982.

4 Problem Solving in Mathematics

Teaching Competencies

Upon completing this unit, you will be able to:

Classify the components of a mathematical sentence

Describe mathematical sentences

Define problem solving

State and use many different strategies in solving problems

Write mathematical sentences for solving problems

Discussion

The results of The National Assessment of Educational Progress indicate that the problem-solving abilities of children have deteriorated over the past decade. The National Council of Teachers of Mathematics has emphasized problem solving in their recommendations for the 1980s, *An Agenda for Action*. It is a common belief among researchers that problem solving is the most important activity of mathematics and that more emphasis must be placed upon developing mathematics problem-solving strategies with children. Most teachers seem to feel inadequate when teaching problem-solving techniques to children. Thus this unit on problem solving is perhaps the most critical unit in the text. Problem-solving activities will also be incorporated into the activity sections of each unit.

What is problem solving? **Problem solving** describes the processes an individual uses to reach a solution when a method of solution is not immediately obvious. A person's ability to solve a problem depends upon many factors, such as conceptual style, organizational ability, techniques of processing information, mathematical background, desire for a solution, and confidence. Students who are oriented toward answers and key words rather than techniques or strategies for solving problems will not gain power in problem solving.

An analysis of problem solving as presented in elementary school textbooks indicates that present teaching is inadequate. Some shortcomings common to elementary school mathematics textbooks are:

1. An overemphasis on one specific type of word problem: for example, providing only subtraction word problems that deal with "take away" subtraction and few, if any, word problems dealing with "comparison" or "how many more are needed?" subtraction. Most division word problems presented use measurement division with little emphasis on partition division.
2. Most mathematics word problems present the question at the end of the problem. In life we usually start with a question and from the question the word problem evolves.

3. Elementary mathematics word problems present little if any extraneous data or information. In life we must sort out data relevant to the problem.
4. Similar types of word problems are grouped together. For instance, in the addition chapter all word problems are solved by adding; in the subtraction chapter all examples are solved by subtraction, and so forth.
5. Usually the solution to an example presented at the top of a mathematics textbook page is the same procedure used to solve all word problems on that particular page. The only apparent difference is that different numbers are substituted.

Now let us carefully examine the strategies being taught to children to help then develop problem-solving techniques. Traditionally, a four-step process was taught: read the problem, find what is given, decide what is to be found, and then solve and check. These four steps do not really help children solve word problems.

What problem-solving strategies can we teach children? Children who have a good background in using attribute blocks, classifying, looking for patterns, and extending patterns are definitely ready for solving word problems with patterns. This word-problem strategy can begin in kindergarten and can be extended to all other grade levels.

If we charge 25 cents for a ticket for our play, how much should we charge for 2 or 3 tickets? A pattern is developed: if 1 costs 25 cents, then 2 will cost 25 cents add 25 cents. Three tickets will sell for $25 + 25 + 25$. This is a pattern. Now we can put the data into a table.

Now we are beginning to bring the strategy of looking for patterns together with the next strategy to be developed: creating tables.

Learning to organize data into tables is a problem-solving technique that can help children solve word problems. Consider this problem: I want to build a pen for my dog. I would like the dog to have as much play area as possible. In the garage is a roll of fencing that I will use; it is 36 meters long.

Number of tickets	1	2	3	4	5	6
Price to charge	25	50	75	1.00	1.25	1.50

What should be the dimensions of the playpen for the dog? Children should think about the data involved in the problem and organize the information into a table. The pertinent facts involved are perimeter, length, width, and area. Let us make a table for the problem by systematically entering data into the table. (Other types of tables would also be acceptable.)

Perimeter (in meters)	Length (in meters)	Width (in meters)	Area (in square meters)
36	17	1	17
36	16	2	32
36	15	3	45
36	14	4	56
36	13	5	65
36	12	6	72
36	11	7	77
36	10	8	80
36	9	9	81
36	8	10	80

After the children have made a table, discuss it with them. You will want to discuss such questions as: Why does the area start to increase? At what point will the area begin to increase? The children should discover that the greatest area is obtained when the length and width are the same. The children should generalize that a square will have more area than the related rectangles with the same perimeter.

Note that at this point the teacher is discussing with the students the existing concepts and relationships rather than the answer to the problem. Organizing data and using tables are important mathematics problem-solving strategies. The problem begins with a question and then a technique for solving the problem is developed by using a table. Many examples of this type should be used so children will learn the problem-solving strategy. Use problems that will require the use of many different operations.

For many years, dramatization has been used to help children understand reading lessons. Dramatization is another technique that can be applied to problem solving. How many apples are in Tom's sack if Mary put in 3 apples and George put in 4 apples? Using dramatization, have children take the part of Tom, Mary, and George and act out the problem.

Ask the children to write a mathematical sentence for what they observed: $3 + 4 = \square$. What number belongs in the box? What is the answer to the word problem? Remember that it is important to answer word problems with complete sentences: Tom now has 7 apples in his sack. Make the problems gradually more complicated. Have the children dramatize a problem in which four children put apples into a sack.

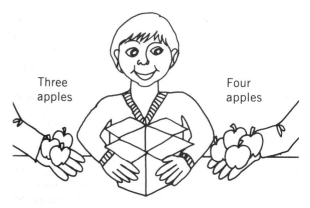

Three apples

Four apples

All children could participate at once; provide the children with money and challenge them to manipulate coins to find how many different ways they can make 10 cents.

One dime

Two nickels

One nickel
Five pennies

Ten pennies

Again two problem-solving strategies have been brought together: dramatization and writing mathematical sentences. Children should always be encouraged to write mathematical sentences to express a problem-solving situation.

Another effective word-problem strategy that can be taught to children is to guess and check. Children should be encouraged to make reasonable guesses and not just select a random number. For instance, ask them what number can be used to make $4 \times \square + \square = 30$? What number belongs in the box? Take a guess and then check it.

Will the number 4 make the sentence true? Check $4 \times 4 + 4 = 20$. Discuss with the children what they have learned. Why doesn't 4 make the sentence true? 4 is too small. Then what should we try? Do you want to try 5? $4 \times 5 + 5 = 25$. Discuss the guess again. Is the value 5 closer to the correct number? How do you know? What number do you want to try now? Should we try 6? $4 \times 6 + 6 = 30$. Six checks out so 6 is the number that fits into the box.

Another technique to help children solve mathematical problems is to make a diagram. Encourage children to make sketches to help them visualize spatial relationships. How many tiles will be needed to place a new floor in a given room? Draw a sketch of the room and then draw squares to represent the tiles. This will help the children to comprehend the concept and develop a technique for solving area problems. Of course this technique should be used to develop understanding of the concept of area for figures of all shapes.

Children need experiences with word-problem situations where only approximations may be used to estimate an answer. For example, how many beans are in a gallon container? Children could count the number of beans they can place into a half-pint jar and then multiply to approximate the number of beans in a gallon container. If a half-pint container is not available, any small container may be used; count the number of beans in one small full container and then count the number of times that the container must be filled to fill the gallon container. Similar estimating techniques can be used to estimate the number of blades of grass on a football field, the number of windows in a skyscraper, or the area of a playground.

From the literature on problem solving we can derive certain general maxims that can help children learn to solve mathematical word problems. Children must be taught problem-solving techniques, and practice must be provided continuously throughout the elementary school mathematics program. Many different problem-solving strategies must be taught. Children must analyze and synthesize solutions to word problems and not just practice computational

skills. They must learn how to write mathematical sentences that will help them solve word problems. Let us now compare English and mathematical sentences.

One of the most important ways in which we communicate with each other is through language. In language arts classes children learn to construct complete, meaningful English sentences. We learn that, to be complete, a sentence must express at least one complete idea. To convey ideas, we learn to use particular patterns of words to form complete sentences.

Mathematics, too, is concerned with expressing complete mathematical ideas in particular patterns called **mathematical sentences.** The child learns to translate verbal sentences into mathematical sentences and mathematical sentences into verbal sentences. The techniques of translation are the basis for successful word-problem solving.

Mathematics is a language, and in some respects can be compared with the English language. In English we express ideas by symbols called words, which are arranged in patterns to form sentences. In mathematics we express ideas by mathematical symbols, arranged in meaningful patterns called mathematical sentences. Just as in English we observe certain conventions in writing sentences, in mathematics, too, we follow certain rules in constructing mathematical sentences.

In general, the language of mathematics uses four categories of symbols: symbols for **ideas** (numbers and elements), symbols for **relations** (which indicate how ideas are connected or related to one another), symbols for **operations** (which indicate what is done with the ideas), and symbols for **punctuation** (which indicate the order in which the mathematics is to be completed). Some of these symbols are listed in the following table.

NUMBER SYMBOLS	NUMBER-OPERATION SYMBOLS			PUNCTUATION SYMBOLS		
Digits	Symbol	Meaning	Example	Symbol	Meaning	Example
0	+	addition	$1 + 2 = 3$	.	decimal point	$\pi = 3.1416$
1						
2	−	subtraction	$3 - 2 = 1$	,	comma	$A = \{3, 4, 5\}$
3						
4				( )	parentheses	$2 + (3 + 1) = 6$
5						
6	×	multiplication	$2 \times 3 = 6$			
7				[ ]	brackets	$2 + [1 + (3 + 1)] = 7$
8						
9	÷	division	$6 \div 3 = 2$	{ }	braces	$\{1, 2\} = \{2, 1\}$

In order to express a complete thought, a declarative English sentence requires, as a minimum, a noun phrase and a verb phrase. Consider the sentence "The girl is running." This sentence has both a noun phrase (The girl) and a verb phrase (is running). If we had just said "The girl," this would not have been a complete sentence, since we would not have been expressing a complete thought (no verb phrase). Similarly, "is running" is not a complete sentence, since these words by themselves do not express a complete thought (no noun phrase).

Mathematical sentences, too, require a particular structure. An examination of various mathematical sentences should suggest ideas about the structure of mathematical sentences in general. Examine the following mathematical sentences carefully.

$$2 + 4 > 5$$
$$\square \div 7 = 2$$
$$\frac{1}{2} + \frac{1}{4} = \frac{3}{4}$$
$$3 \times (n + 4) = (3 \times n) + (3 \times 4)$$

Let us first examine how these mathematical sentences should be read; then we will study the common characteristics of mathematical sentences.

$2 + 4 > 5$ is read "Two add four is greater than five."

$\square \div 7 = 2$ is read "What number divided by seven is equal to two?"

$\frac{1}{2} + \frac{1}{4} = \frac{3}{4}$ is read "One-half add one-fourth is equal to three-fourths."

$3 \times (N + 4) = (3 \times N) + (3 \times 4)$ is read "Three times the quantity N add 4 is equal to three times N added to three times four."

Is there some common characteristic of these sentences? It should become clear through comparison that each sentence has a particular pattern. **Each sentence consists of two or more names for numbers joined together by a relation symbol.** In general, a mathematical sentence must follow this pattern:

symbol(s) for number(s) — relation symbol — symbol(s) for number(s)

Consider $2 + 4 = 6$. This is a mathematical sentence, since it has the form we have described. The sentence "$2 + 4 = 6$" contains number symbols on the left (an expression composed of two number symbols and an operation symbol) and a number symbol on the right (6), joined by a relation symbol (=). But none of these three symbols or expressions

forms a sentence by itself, just as neither "John" nor "runs" forms a sentence by itself. However, the expression "$2 + 4 = 6$" is a mathematical sentence, just as "John runs" is an English sentence, because it expresses a complete thought. Unlike an expression (such as "$2 + 4$"), a complete sentence can be examined for truth or falsity. We are able to judge "$2 + 4 = 6$" to be true or false because it contains enough information to convey a complete idea.

The English sentence "There are seven days in a week" would be classified as true. The sentence "There are 29 days in a week" would be classified as false. In the same way, mathematical sentences can be classified as true or false. The mathematical sentence "$7 < 3$" would be called false. The sentence "$4 = 3 + 1$" would be called true. (All examples are in base ten.)

NUMBER-RELATION SYMBOLS		
Symbol	Meaning	Example
$=$	is equal to	$2 + 3 = 5$
$\neq$	is not equal to	$8 + 1 \neq 7$
$<$	is less than	$3 < 4$
$\not<$	is not less than	$3 \not< 2$
$>$	is greater than	$9 > 7$
$\not>$	is not greater than	$7 \not> 9$
$\leq$	is less than or equal to	$4 \leq 4$
$\not\leq$	is not less than or equal to	$4 \not\leq 3$
$\geq$	is greater than or equal to	$6 \geq 5$
$\not\geq$	is not greater than or equal to	$5 \not\geq 6$

Suppose someone wrote, "He was a president of the United States." This is a complete sentence, but we cannot judge it to be true or false until we know who "he" is. What about the following sentences?

   a) Theodore Roosevelt was a president of the United States.
   b) J. Fred Muggs was a president of the United States.

Both are complete sentences, and both contain enough information to be judged true or false, since in both sentences a name has been substituted for "he." Thus sentence A we can judge to be true, and sentence B we can judge to be false.

Now look at these mathematical sentences (all in base ten):

$$\text{a) } \square + 7 = 13$$
$$\text{b) } 6 + 7 = 13$$
$$\text{c) } 14 + 7 = 13$$

Sentence A is a complete mathematical sentence —two number expressions joined by a relation symbol. But we cannot judge the sentence to be true or false until we know what numeral the placeholder represents. In sentence B the numeral 6 has replaced the placeholder. Thus we have enough information to judge B to be true. Sentence C is clearly false.

Mathematical sentences that cannot be judged true or false, such as $\square + 7 = 13$, are called **open sentences.** Sentences such as B or C, which contain enough information to be judged true or false, are called **mathematical statements** (or **closed sentences**). Sentence B, then, is a true statement, and sentence C is a false statement.

Relation symbols must be observed carefully as children examine sentences for truth or falsity. It is easy for children to become confused by relation symbols in a sentence such as $7 + 2 + 5 \neq 12$. This is a true statement, of course, because the sum of 7, 2, and 5 is not equal ($\neq$) to 12. Now consider the following sentences:

$11 + 3 = 14$	(true statement)
$11 + 3 \neq 10$	(true statement)
$11 + 3 \neq 14$	(false statement)
$11 + 3 = 10$	(false statement)

Children should work to master relation symbols and thus come to understand sentences such as these.

When we write an open mathematical sentence, it is necessary to indicate in some way that a numeral is missing. Very often a frame or placeholder is used to show that one or more numerals are missing. A box is a geometric figure, $\square$, that holds the place

of a missing numeral. The following are some typical placeholders used in elementary programs:

The idea of using figures such as these to hold the place of missing symbols in mathematical sentences is developed early in the primary grades. As an introduction to this idea, the teacher can write a simple sentence on a sheet of construction paper:

$$2 + 3 = 5$$

After children have seen this sentence, the teacher cuts out one of the numerals, leaving a box-shaped opening:

$$2 + \square = 5$$

Children can see that numerals (on box-shaped pieces of paper) can be placed in the box to complete the sentence. Sentences such as the following can provide computational drill and familiarize children with placeholders in mathematical sentences.

$\square + 3 = 8$	$7 - 3 = \triangle$
$\bigcirc + 5 = 12$	$8 \div \bigcirc = 4$
$3 + \square = 10$	$3 \times \pentagon = 27$

Later children can examine sentences with missing relation symbols and supply the missing symbols:

$3 + 2 \bigcirc 4 + 1$	$\not\gtr$ or $=$ or $\not\lt$
$14 \div 7 \bigcirc 10 \div 1$	$\neq$ or $<$ or $>$
$3 \times 7 \bigcirc 2 \times 9$	$\neq$ or $>$ or $\not\lt$

Missing operation signs can be supplied in the same way:

$$8 \bigcirc 2 = 10 \qquad \boxed{+}$$
$$9 - 7 = 10 \triangle 5 \qquad \boxed{\div}$$
$$6 = 9 \triangle 3 \qquad \boxed{-}$$
$$18 \triangle 2 = 12 \triangle 3 \qquad \boxed{\times}$$

Such exercises provide vital reinforcement of computational skills while teaching the meaning of operations and relations.

As children become familiar with sentences that contain frames, they can be led to see that letters can also be used as placeholders. Letters that are used in this way are called **variables.** For example, $3 + n = 8$. What numeral can replace n to make the sentence a true statement? (5) As children develop a more sophisticated concept of place-holders, they should understand that when a particular placeholder is used more than once in the same sentence, it represents the same value each time. For example, the open sentence

$$\boxed{} + \boxed{} = 8$$

indicates that the same numeral is to be used in both boxes:

$$\boxed{4} + \boxed{4} = 8$$

This same concept is also valid in algebra. A given letter represents the same value wherever it occurs in any one problem.

It is interesting to note at this point that traditional elementary arithmetic programs disregarded all mathematical sentences except those using the relation symbol =, "is equal to." Consider, for example, a typical simple story problem.

"If John is 45 inches tall and Jim is 48 inches tall, how much taller is Jim than John?"

This problem would usually be solved in the following way:

$$\begin{array}{r} 48 \\ -\,45 \\ \hline 3 \end{array}$$

"Jim is 3 inches taller than John." This problem, as traditionally introduced, merely involves the translation of an English sentence into a simple subtraction problem. In a traditional elementary arithmetic class, the variety of ways of expressing the relations involved are usually not stressed. The following are some examples of true statements that can be made from the information given in the story problem.

$48 - 45 = 3$	Jim is three inches taller than John.
$45 + 3 = 48$	John's height plus three inches equals Jim's height.
$48 > 45$	Jim is taller than John.
$45 < 48$	John is shorter than Jim.
$45 \neq 48$	John is not the same height as Jim.

At this point we can begin to classify mathematical sentences according to the relation symbols in the sentences. We have seen sentences of

the type called equations. An **equation** is a mathematical sentence in which two expressions are joined by an equals sign.

$$8 - 3 = 4 + 1$$

The equals sign indicates that the expression on the left of the sign names the same number as the expression on the right. In the sentence above, $8 - 3$ names the same number as $4 + 1$.

If the expression on the left names a number different from the one on the right, we can use the symbol $\neq$ to make a true mathematical sentence. For example, $9 \div 3$ is 3 and 3×4 is 12. Therefore $9 \div 3$ and 3×4 are two different numbers, and we can write

$$9 \div 3 \neq 3 \times 4$$

We can use the relations symbol $>$ (which means "is greater than") and the symbol $<$ (which means "is less than") to express the relationship with greater precision:

$$9 \div 3 < 3 \times 4$$
$$3 \times 4 > 9 \div 3$$

Sentences of this kind are examples of **inequalities.** We call $9 \div 3 \neq 3 \times 4$ an **inequality.**

There is an inequality symbol ($\geq$) to express "is greater than or equal to" and an inequality symbol ($\leq$) to express "is less than or equal to."

$n \geq 5$	n is greater than or equal to five.
$m \leq 10 + 15$	m is less than or equal to ten plus fifteen.

Other inequality symbols are the following:

$\not>$	is not greater than
$\not<$	is not less than
$\not\geq$	is not greater than or equal to
$\not\leq$	is not less than or equal to

Here are some sentences that use these symbols:

$4 \not> 5$	Four is not greater than five.
$p \not< 10$	p is not less than ten.
$q \not\geq 5$	q is not greater than or equal to five.
$10 \not\leq 4 + 5$	Ten is not less than or equal to four plus five.

The child begins at a very early age to make comparisons using terms such as "larger," "smaller," "more," "less," and so on. Even though a child may not yet be able to count, he can make decisions regarding the size of two sets by matching the elements one to one. By doing this, he can say that one set has more elements than another set. Let's recall the kind of thing that children can do by matching sets. If a child is presented with two sets of lollipops:

$$A = \left\{ \begin{array}{cccc} \varphi & \varphi & \varphi & \varphi \end{array} \right\}$$

$$B = \left\{ \begin{array}{ccc} \varphi & \varphi & \varphi \end{array} \right\}$$

he will probably choose the set that has more lollipops. By trying to match each element in Set B with only one element in Set A, he sees that there is one lollipop unmatched, or left over, in Set A. His matching might be done mentally, but on paper it would look like this:

$$A = \left\{ \begin{array}{cccc} \varphi & \varphi & \varphi & \varphi \end{array} \right\}$$

$$\updownarrow \quad \updownarrow \quad \updownarrow$$

$$B = \left\{ \begin{array}{ccc} \varphi & \varphi & \varphi \end{array} \right\}$$

In situations such as this we realize that children have a background of real experiences in dealing intuitively with nonequivalent sets. It seems only natural to make use of this experience to further their mathematical knowledge to include unequal as well as equal sets.

A brief review of terminology at this point will help to clarify our discussion. We have shown that certain symbols are used in mathematical sentences to indicate the ways in which numbers (disregarding sets for the time being) are connected, or related to one another. These are the symbols of relation:

$$\begin{array}{cc} = & \neq \\ > & \not> \\ < & \not< \\ \geq & \not\geq \\ \leq & \not\leq \end{array}$$

The symbols for the two fundamental operations of arithmetic and their inverse operations are also part of the grammar of mathematics:

$$+ \quad \text{(addition)}$$
$$- \quad \text{(subtraction)}$$
$$\times \quad \text{(multiplication)}$$
$$\div \quad \text{(division)}$$

These symbols indicate operations to be performed but do not by themselves form mathematical sen-

tences. They indicate operations to be performed on numbers, not relations between numbers. For example, the expression

$$(4 + 3) - (6 \div 2)$$

indicates several operations to be performed. If these operations are performed, giving $7 - 3$, or 4, we see that we have renamed the original expression. Another name for $(4 + 3) - (6 \div 2)$ is thus 4.

When several operations are to be performed but no symbols are included to indicate the order in which the operations should be accomplished, multiplication is always first, followed by division, then addition, and then subtraction last. Children should learn the order of operations. Consider this example: $2 + 3 \times 4$. If 2 is added to 3 and then multiplied by 4, the answer is 20. If 3 and 4 are multiplied first and then 2 is added, the answer becomes 14. Following the mathematical order of operations, 14 is the correct answer. So that there can be no mistake in the order of operations, we should use parentheses and write $2 + (3 \times 4)$. However, if we really want to add 2 and 3 first and then multiply the sum by 4, we should write $(2 + 3) \times 4$; then the answer would be 20.

If we wish to indicate a relation, or connection, between numbers, we must use one of the relation symbols and construct a mathematical sentence. For example

$$(4 + 3) - (6 \div 2) = \square$$

Now we have made an open mathematical sentence. It is a complete mathematical sentence because one expression, $4 + 3 - (6 \div 2)$, is joined (or related) to another expression, $\square$, by the equal sign (=), a symbol of relation. It is an open sentence because we cannot judge it to be true or false. We can perform the indicated operations as follows:

$$\begin{aligned} (4 + 3) - (6 \div 2) &= \square \\ 7 - 3 &= \square \\ 4 &= \square \\ \therefore (4 + 3) - (6 \div 2) &= 4 \end{aligned}$$

The last sentence is a mathematical statement. A mathematical statement is a mathematical sentence that can be judged true or false. It contains no placeholders or unknowns. It is sometimes called a closed mathematical sentence. In this case we have made a true mathematical statement, because $(4 + 3) - (6 \div 2)$ is another name for 4. If we had said $(4 + 3) - (6 \div 2) = 9$, we would have made a false mathematical statement.

As work with mathematical sentences becomes more complex, another kind of symbolism must be considered. When a mathematical sentence contains several numbers and several operations to be performed, it is often necessary to indicate the order in which the operations are to be performed. To indicate this order, we use punctuation or grouping symbols — parentheses, brackets, and braces. Consider this mathematical sentence:

$$7 - 4 - 1 = \square$$

How are we to interpret this open sentence? Does it mean that we are to subtract 4 from 7 and then subtract 1 from that difference? In that case our solution is 2: $7 - 4 = 3$; $3 - 1 = 2$. Or does this sentence mean that we are to subtract 1 from 4 and then subtract that difference from 7? ($4 - 1 = 3$; $7 - 3 = 4$). We obtain two different answers, 4 and 2, depending on our interpretation of the order in which we perform the indicated operations. However, the language of mathematics has a standard method for indicating the order of operations. **Parentheses** are grouping symbols used to indicate which operations are to be performed first. You might interpret parentheses to mean "do me first." Some teachers prefer to use this expression with children. In the example $7 - 4 - 1 = \square$, we might write $(7 - 4) - 1 = \square$, which means that we are to subtract 4 from 7 first and then subtract 1 from that difference:

$$(7 - 4) - 1 = \square$$
$$3 - 1 = \square$$
$$2 = \square$$

Or we might write $7 - (4 - 1) = \square$, which means that we are to subtract 1 from 4 first and then subtract that difference (3) from 7;

$$7 - (4 - 1) = \square$$
$$7 - 3 = \square$$
$$4 = \square$$

In either case the operation to be performed first is indicated within the parentheses.

More than one set of parentheses can be used in the same equation, as in $(7 + 2) - (2 + 3) = \square$. Again, the operations indicated within the parentheses are to be performed first. The sum of $2 + 3$ is to be subtracted from the sum of $7 + 2$:

$$(7 + 2) - (2 + 3) = \square$$
$$9 - 5 = \square$$
$$4 = \square$$

Later, children will be introduced to another grouping symbol, square **brackets,** usually printed [ ]. These are used when one or more pairs of parentheses have already been used and another pair might result in confusion. For example, this sentence is a bit confusing to the eye:

$$\left(\frac{1}{4} \times \left(\frac{2}{3} \times 24 \right) \right) \div \frac{2}{3} = \square$$

It is more clearly written as

$$\left[\frac{1}{4} \times \left(\frac{2}{3} \times 24 \right) \right] \div \frac{2}{3} = \square$$

The grouping symbols still indicate the order in which operations are to be performed. The operation within the parentheses is usually performed first, then the operation within the brackets.

In exceedingly complicated expressions we may use parentheses, brackets, and **braces** as punctuation symbols. For example

$$500 - (50 \div (2 \times (3 + 5))) = \square$$

is not nearly as easy to read as

$$500 - \{ 50 \div [2 \times (3 + 5)] \} = \square$$

Braces are written as { }. They are used in punctuating number expressions and in naming sets. Context always makes it clear how they are being used in any given situation.

An open sentence that contains a placeholder is neither true nor false. It becomes true or false if we replace the placeholder with a numeral. For example, if we replace the $\square$ in the sentence $\square < 5$ with 0, 1, 2, 3, or 4, we get true statements:

$$0 < 5$$
$$1 < 5 \qquad \text{TRUE}$$
$$2 < 5 \qquad \text{STATEMENTS}$$
$$3 < 5$$
$$4 < 5$$

If we replace the $\square$ with 5, 6, 7, 8, and so on, we get false statements:

$$5 < 5$$
$$6 < 5 \qquad \text{FALSE}$$
$$7 < 5 \qquad \text{STATEMENTS}$$
$$8 < 5$$
$$\vdots$$

In this example we have used whole numbers as replacements for the placeholder. We say that the set of whole numbers is the **replacement set** in this situation. The set of all numbers that make a sentence true is the **solution set.** In the example $\square < 5$, the solution set is {0, 1, 2, 3, 4}.

The importance of acquiring skill in translating English words into mathematical expressions and sentences will become apparent as children learn to solve word problems as discussed earlier in this unit.

As children develop problem-solving ability, the teacher must constantly remind them to apply basic ideas in the process of solving word problems, as follows:

1. Read the word problem several times to make sure you understand it.

2. Think about the relation between the information given in the problem and what is being asked for.
3. Translate the word problem into a mathematical sentence that expresses this relation.
4. Check the mathematical sentence with the original problem.
5. Find the solution set of the mathematical sentence.
6. Write an English sentence that translates the mathematics back into English.

For children to develop successful problem-solving techniques, instruction must begin early and constantly be nurtured as each new mathematical concept is introduced and developed. Problem-solving techniques should begin in the primary grades: first, discuss everyday situations that require mathematics, such as, "How many cups will be needed for the children at two tables if there are four children at one table and five at another?" This way children will begin to relate mathematics to real-life situations.

As children begin to learn to read, they can be given word problems using rebuses. A rebus is a picture that is substituted for a word. Study this example:

I have 2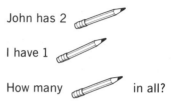

You have 1

How many   in all?

This example should be answered in a complete sentence. A child might print and use a rebus such as:

There are 3   in all.

Make sure that the picture used for a rebus can easily be drawn by children. Do not use animals or other things difficult for children to draw. Stickers may also be used as rebuses.

Before beginning word problems with a class, have one child read the examples aloud as the other children follow along silently. The children will need to reread each example before they attempt to solve it. A child who is still having difficulty in reading the examples may want to use a cassette recorder with the examples taped as an aid.

In these first steps to solving word problems, have the children develop good habits right from the beginning. Children should read and reread an example before beginning work on paper. Insist upon having an equation written for each example even if the word problem is easily solved, and do not accept incomplete answers. You are teaching a technique as well as how to obtain correct answers. For instance, consider this example:

John has 2

I have 1

How many   in all?

Do not accept a written 3 for the solution to this example. The equation $2 + 1 = \square$ should be written and the answer should be, "There are 3   in all." Using this procedure forces children to think about the reasonableness of their answers. Each answer is a complete sentence that must make sense in response to the question they are trying to answer.

The following examples suggest how mathematical sentences may be written for other word problems:

> Bob has 32 marbles. He wins 17 more marbles in a game. How many marbles does Bob have now?

We can translate the problem into a mathematical sentence this way:

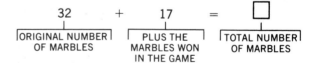

32	+	17	=	$\square$
ORIGINAL NUMBER OF MARBLES		PLUS THE MARBLES WON IN THE GAME		TOTAL NUMBER OF MARBLES

To solve the problem we must find a solution set — in this case another way to say $32 + 17$, since our mathematical sentence is an equation.

$$32 + 17 = 49$$

Bob has 49 marbles.

Now look at another example:

> Bob has a certain number of marbles. He won 23 marbles in a game today. He now has 47 marbles. How many marbles did Bob have before?

What kind of mathematical sentence can we use to translate this story problem? Some pupils might write addition sentences, and others might write subtraction sentences.

$$\Box + 23 = 47$$
$$47 - 23 = \Box$$
$$\Box = 47 - 23$$
$$23 + \Box = 47$$

Is each of these mathematical sentences a correct translation of the story problem? Examples such as this show the flexibility of thinking and interpretation and the variety of approaches to any problem that contemporary mathematics emphasizes. Any one of the sentences above is acceptable. Here are two more problems:

How many eggs are there in 3 dozen? How many different mathematical sentences can you write for this problem?

$$3 \times 12 = \Box$$
$$12 \times 3 = \Box$$

If each of 32 children in a class has a desk and they are arranged in rows with eight children in each row, how many rows of desks are there in the classroom?

How many different mathematical sentences may be written for this problem?

$$32 \div 8 = \Box$$
$$32 \div \Box = 8$$
$$8 \times \Box = 32$$
$$\Box \times 8 = 32$$

As children learn to translate story problems into mathematical sentences, the teacher should check their work carefully. Sometimes children have difficulties reading and comprehending the stories and these difficulties are assumed to be a lack of mathematical ability.

There are many different types of problems for which we must learn to write mathematical sentences. Let's look at more examples:

1. Jon has three football cards. Lila gave Jon her four football cards. How many football cards does Jon have in all?

   Mathematical sentence: $3 + 4 = \triangle$

   Answer: Jon has seven football cards in all.
2. Bonnie collects sea shells. After Sally gave Bonnie two shells, she then had eight shells. How many shells did Bonnie have to begin with?

   Mathematical sentence: $\Box + 2 = 8$

   Answer: Bonnie had six shells to begin with.

3. Joy has three pencils. George gave Joy the pencils he owed her and now Joy has eight pencils. How many pencils did George owe Joy?

   Mathematical sentence: $3 + \Box = 8$

   Answer: George owed Joy five pencils.
4. Millie had five rings. She gave three of the rings to Sue. How many rings does Millie have left?

   Mathematical sentence: $5 - 3 = \Box$

   Answer: Millie has two rings left.
5. Karen had seven pictures made of their teacher. Karen gave some of the pictures to other classmates. When Karen counted the number of pictures she had left she found three. How many pictures did Karen give away?

   Mathematical sentence: $7 - \Box = 3$

   Answer: Karen gave away four pictures of their teacher.
6. Mike had some Matchbox cars. He gave five of the cars to Jon. Mike had four Matchbox cars left. How many Matchbox cars did Mike have to begin with?

   Mathematical sentence: $\Box - 5 = 4$

   Answer: Mike had nine Matchbox cars to begin with.
7. How many eggs are in 4 dozen eggs?

   Mathematical sentence: $4 \times 12 = \Box$

   Answer: There are forty-eight eggs in 4 dozen.
8. Ted will need twenty-four balloons for his birthday party. If eight balloons are in a package, how many packages of balloons will Ted need to buy?

   Mathematical sentence: $24 = \Box \times 8$

   Answer: Ted will need to buy three packages of balloons.
9. There are thirty-six chairs set up for a play in our classroom. There are four rows of chairs. How many chairs are in each row?

   Mathematical sentence: $36 = 4 \times \Box$

   Answer: There are nine chairs in each row.
10. Hank's mother gave him twelve cookies. If Hank shares the cookies equally with two other friends, how many cookies will each of the three boys have?

    Mathematical sentence: $12 \div 3 = \Box$

    Answer: Hank and each of his friends will receive four cookies each.

There are still other types of word problems that children must learn to solve. Provide the children with word problems each day so that they will begin to develop techniques in solving word problems and maintain those skills.

Another technique that has proven successful is to write a story at the top of a page and then to ask a series of questions about the story at the bottom of the page. For example:

Martha is planning her twelfth birthday party. She will be 15 years old that day. She wants to invite nine of her friends to share the party with her. Of course she will want to include her three younger brothers, her mother, and her father. Martha would like to give each child three balloons. They will play games at the party. Two teams will be formed to play the peanut relay game, and there will be four teams formed to play Twister. Help Martha plan her birthday party by answering the following questions. Remember to write a mathematical sentence for each example and to write a complete sentence to answer each question.

1. If all of those invited attend the birthday party, how many will be at the party?
2. How many children will attend the party?
3. How many balloons will Martha need?
4. How many children will be on each team when they play the peanut relay game?
5. How many children will be on each team when Twister is played?
6. How many years did Martha not have a birthday party?
7. How tall will Martha be on her fifteenth birthday?
8. How many boys will be at the birthday party?

Note there is not sufficient data for the children to answer all of the questions; questions 7 and 8 could not be answered from the information given.

Terminology, Symbols, and Procedures

Inequality An inequality is a mathematical sentence in which two number expressions are joined by one of the following relation symbols

$$> \qquad \not> \qquad \leq$$
$$< \qquad \not< \qquad \not\geq$$
$$\neq \qquad \geq \qquad \not\leq$$

Examples of inequalities are

$$2 < 5 + 1 \qquad 20 - 3 \geq 14$$
$$6 \not> 9 \qquad\qquad 8 + 1 \neq 3$$

Mathematical sentence A mathematical sentence is a sentence that follows a pattern such as the following

symbol(s) for number(s) — relation symbol — symbol(s) for number(s)

In a mathematical sentence, one number is joined by a relation symbol to another number. For example

$$3 + 4 = 7$$

$$6 + 13 > 5$$

Mathematical statement (or closed mathematical sentence)   A mathematical statement is a mathematical sentence that contains enough information to be judged true or false. It does not have a placeholder or unknown. It is sometimes called a closed mathematical sentence. For example

$$5 + 4 = 9$$

Open mathematical sentence   An open mathematical sentence is a mathematical sentence that does not contain enough information to be judged true or false. For example

$$5 + 4 = \square$$

Equation   An equation is a mathematical sentence in which two or more expressions are joined by an equals sign (=). For example

$$7 = 2 + 5$$
$$3 + 6 = (2 - 1) + 8$$

Problem solving   Problem solving describes the processes an individual uses to reach a solution when a method of solution is not immediately obvious; it must involve more than just applying an algorithm.

Punctuation or grouping symbols   Parentheses, ( ), brackets, [ ], and braces, { }, are grouping symbols used to indicate the order in which the operations in a mathematical expression or sentence are to be performed.

Replacement set   The replacement set is the set of all numbers that must be tested to determine the set of numbers that make a particular mathematical sentence a true statement. For example, given the sentence $3 + \triangle < 10$, we can define the replacement set as the set of all whole numbers, which means that we will consider only whole numbers as possible values of $\triangle$.

Solution set   The set of all numbers that make a mathematical sentence a true statement is called the solution set.

Practice Exercises

1. Decide which of the suggested problem-solving strategies would be most appropriate and then use that technique to solve this problem: A candy factory has a warehouse full of cardboard cut into rectangles eight and one-half inches by eleven inches (the size of a regular sheet of paper). You have been asked to design a box (a bottom and four sides) that will hold the most candy by cutting a square in each corner, folding, and gluing. What should the size of the box be so that it will have the most volume for holding candy?

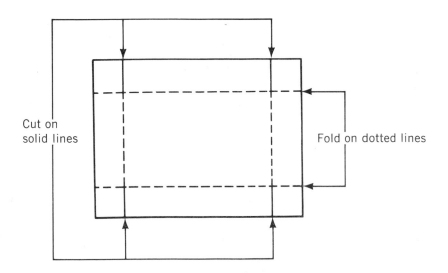

2. Find all rectangles having the same numerical value for their area and perimeter. Use only whole numbers for measurements.

$$A + A + B + B = A \times B$$

3. How many ways can six squares be drawn on a sheet of paper so that, when it is cut out, it can be folded into a rectangle? For example:

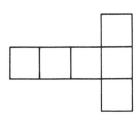

4. Label each of the following "true statement," "false statement," "open sentence," or "not a sentence."

a) $3 \times 4 = 7$

b) $t^2 < 1 +$

c) $2 + \square > 6$

d) $n = 3n + 2$

e) $x + y > 14$

f) $\square + \triangle \neq 8$

g) $3^2 > 1 + 2^2$

h) $7 + 9 \neq 8 - 4$

i) $12 = [(2 \times 5) - 3] + 1$

j) $18 \div 2 \neq 3^2$

k) $a^2 + 1 > 2$

l) $6 + (3 + 7) = (6 + 3) + 7$

m) $9 \times y \not< 7$

n) $[\bigcirc \times 2] \div 4 > 5$

5. Tabulate the solution set of each sentence. Use the set $\{0, 1, 2, 3, \ldots, 99, 100\}$ as the replacement set.

a) $\square + 1 = 8$

b) $x \geq 96$

c) $1 + k \neq 1$

d) $3 + \square < 10$

e) $n \times n < 25$

f) $200 - \triangle < 100$

6. Translate each word problem below into a mathematical sentence. Notice that each story problem can be translated in more than one way. If necessary, use the table of symbols.

    a) Bobby weighs fourteen pounds more than Edward. Edward weighs fifty-nine pounds. How much does Bobby weigh?

    b) Last year there were forty-two children playing at the school playground. This year thirteen more children are playing there. How many children are playing at the school playground this year?

    c) Bill has twice as many football trading cards as John. Bill has 234 football trading cards. How many football trading cards does John have?

    d) Tommy Tuna weighs 130 kilograms and Barry Barracuda weighs twenty kilograms. How much more does Tommy Tuna weigh than Barry Barracuda?

7. Solve each equation.

    a) $(3 + 4) \times 2 = \square$ e) $(3 - 2) + (7 - 1) = \square$

    b) $3 + (4 \times 2) = \square$ f) $(\square \times 2) + 3 = 15$

    c) $(6 + 2) \div 2 = \square$ g) $(2 + 3) + (\square + 7) = 12$

    d) $6 + (2 \div 2) = \square$ h) $(2 \times \square) + (3 \times \square) = 20$

8. Solve the following verbal problem. Be sure to write an appropriate mathematical sentence. Remember to translate the mathematics back into an English sentence.
Mike is three years older than Lila. The sum of their ages is twenty-nine. How old is each?

9. Find the solution set for the open sentence $2x > x + 2$, where the replacement set is the set of whole numbers.

10. Solve the following verbal problem. Mary is one year older than four times Tammy's age. Kelly is three times as old as Mary. If Kelly is twenty-seven, how old are Mary and Tammy?

11. Indicate which operation should be used to solve each of the following problems:

    a) What will two bicycles cost if one sells for $49.95?

    b) If I buy a new suit, coat, and hat, how much will all three items cost?

    c) How much change will I get back from $10.00 if I buy a pair of gloves?

    d) How many balloons will go to each of seven people at my birthday party if I have 28 balloons to distribute?

12. Write a dozen mathematical sentences for the number 43, using each operation at least once.

13. Write numerical sentences for each example. Do not compute the answers.

    a) If each of the 32 students in our classroom brings a quarter for the March of Dimes, how much money will our room contribute?

    b) Our classroom has a perimeter of 40 meters. How many centimeters is that?

    c) If we distribute six dozen cookies equally to the 29 members of our class, how many cookies will each person get?

    d) How much change will I receive from a dollar if I buy an ice cream cone for 47 cents?

Discussion Questions

1. Discuss how the problem-solving strategies presented in this unit are different from the techniques you learned for solving word problems.

2. Discuss the merits and difficulties of each of the word problem strategies suggested in this unit.

3. Locate the results of the National Assessment of Educational Progress and present the findings on word problem-solving to your class.

4. Research the relationship between reading and problem-solving ability, and present your findings to the class.

5. Discuss the relationship that should exist between problem solving in the mathematics program and the entire mathematics curriculum.

6. Discuss the roles of the hand-held calculator and the microcomputer in developing problem-solving skills.

7. Report to the class on Marilyn Suydam's article in the February 1982 issue of *The Arithmetic Teacher*, "Update on Research on Problem Solving: Implications for Classroom Teaching."

8. Make a report to your class on the article by Frank Lester, Jr., "Research on Mathematical Problem Solving," Chapter 10 in the book *Research in Mathematics Education* published by the National Council of Teachers of Mathematics.

9. Discuss the pros and cons of developing a card file of good word problems. How should such a file be organized? How should it be used in the classroom?

10. Obtain copies of Steve Meiring's publication "Problem Solving . . . a basic mathematics goal" (Books 1 and 2) from the Ohio Department of Education in Columbus, Ohio. Present a report to the class on the strategies that he suggests for a good problem-solving curriculum.

Activities for the Primary Grades

Problem solving should begin in kindergarten and be expanded at every grade level. Problem-solving techniques can be developed before children learn to read. Problem-solving situations should be set up for student participation; then the teacher discusses the mathematics with the children. Children need to recognize mathematics in life and learn how to deal with it. For example, the teacher might place four chairs at a table and ask a group of five children to sit at the table. The children are now involved in a real mathematics problem, because there are not enough chairs for all students to be seated. The teacher should discuss the situation with the children and then obtain another chair for the extra student.

In many elementary mathematics programs in the past it was assumed that children at the primary level cannot write and solve mathematical sentences. This assumption had the character of a self-fulfilling prophecy, with the result that children entered Grades 7 and 8 very poorly prepared for their first encounters with "solving equations."

However, experience shows that children in kindergarten and first grade have no trouble working with simple mathematical sentences if the teacher is careful to use correct mathematical language and symbolism.

Writing mathematical sentences in the horizontal form is one more way for the first-grade teacher to make use of the "left to right" pattern that is so important in beginning reading, writing, and now—mathematics! Anything that helps to develop this pattern is advisable. At the same time, children should be exposed to open sentences in the vertical form so that they do not think the horizontal form is the only way to write a mathematical sentence.

The use of the mathematical sentence from the very beginning of the child's mathematical experience is part of a consistent approach to problem solving. It makes it possible for the child to realize there may be more than one way to set up the format for a problem. Moreover, there may be several ways to solve it—although one way may be more efficient than another. We are discouraging the "one-way" approach and encouraging the discovery approach based on logical thinking.

1. Activities in primary grades should begin with sets of real objects, flannel board and chalkboard demonstrations, number-line demonstrations, and discussion of these activities. For example, all these activities might be combined in this way: Give three or four children sets of nine objects. Have two or three more children at the chalkboard, one at the flannel board, and one at the number line. Ask the children with the objects to form two sets—one set of five and one set of four. Ask the children at the chalkboard to draw a simple diagram or picture of a set of five and a set of four. Have the child at the flannel board create a set of five and a set of four. Then ask the child at the number line to demonstrate what he would do to show that he had a set of five and a set of four.

Let each child verbalize the situation to illustrate possible variety in the thinking process. The children with the concrete objects might indicate variations such as these:

"I had nine blocks and I took five of them away and that left four."

"I took four blocks and made one set and counted the other set to see if I had a set of five."

The child at the flannel board might select five felt shapes of one type and four of another. Chalkboard diagrams will vary the same way—some indicating the complete set of nine with a line to separate, others indicating separate sets. The child at the number line has the responsibility for illustrating the numerical symbolism involved.

After this verbalization, ask the children what new set is formed when they combine a set of five and a set of four. When they reply "nine," ask them how they could write this using numerals so that anyone would know what they mean. If a child indicates that he knows how this could be done, ask him to write his answer on the chalkboard. If not, write "$5 + 4 = 9$" on the chalkboard yourself and ask if anyone can explain what it means. This is the time to explain the use of the operation and relation symbols. It is also the time to reinforce the idea that $5 + 4$ is just another way of naming 9 (assuming that we are presenting this idea to children just beginning the operation of addition).

2. Today most elementary mathematics programs give practice from the start in writing addition facts and subtraction facts in vertical and horizontal form.

Vertical	Horizontal	Vertical	Horizontal
5	$5 + 3 = 8$	7	$7 - 4 = 3$
$+\,3$		$-\,4$	
8		3	

When children write basic number facts in horizontal form, they are writing mathematical sentences. Encourage frequent practice with basic facts written in both horizontal and vertical form.

3. Write the missing numerals in the frames.

a) $3 + 2 = \square$ c) $7 + 1 = \square$ e) $4 + \square = 6$

b) $\square + 1 = 3$ d) $\square + 4 = 5$ f) $1 + \square = 7$

4. Children enjoy making up stories. Write a simple sentence such as $2 + \square = 5$ on the chalkboard. Ask the children to make up a story to go with the sentence. [Possible response: I have two marbles in my hand, and I've got more in my pocket. I have five in all. How many marbles do I have in my pocket?] Let several of the children tell the stories they make up. Repeat this activity, using a different sentence each time.

5. Children in first grade who are having reading difficulties may continue to develop mathematically if the rebus is often used in story problem development.

6. Children can develop facility in forming open sentences by the following game called Peekaboo. A group of children can play this game with the teacher. A child is given a box containing two blocks with numerals on their faces. He then shakes the box and calls out the two numerals on the top of each cube. For example, the pupil may call out 4 and 8. The first person who can form an accurate open sentence with those two numerals gets to be the leader. Thus the box is passed to the successful constructor of a number sentence. For the example presented, acceptable responses may be $8 - 4 = \square$, $4 + \square = 8$, or $4 + 8 = \square$, among others.

7. Cards marked with numerals and operation symbols can be a useful vehicle for developing open sentences. Children may form several open sentences at their desks and then compare them. A count may be made of how many open sentences the class formed. Also, pupils may be asked to complete an open sentence that you have written on the chalkboard. Some examples are:

a) $82 \bigcirc 21 = 61$ c) $4 \bigcirc 4 < 9$

b) $5 \bigcirc 3 = 15$ d) $3 \bigcirc 3 < 6$

8. Jean and Joan together have fifteen dolls. This is seven more than Jane has. How many dolls does Jane have? Write a number sentence for this problem.

Possible answers: $\square + 7 = 15$ $15 = 7 + \square$ $15 - 7 = \square$ $15 - \square = 7$

Children frequently give the erroneous translation $15 + 7 = \square$. Discussion of the various ways of writing the sentence—why this particular sentence would be incorrect, why one way may be a better interpretation than another—is extremely important. Encourage the children to explain why. It will be difficult for you to squelch the urge to tell them too much —but squelch it anyway.

Jim bought twenty new marbles for his collection. When he counted all of the marbles in his collection, he discovered he had seventy-four. How many marbles did he have before he bought the new ones? How could we write a number sentence for this problem?

Possibilities: $20 + \square = 74$ $74 - 20 = \square$ $\square + 20 = 74$ $74 - \square = 20$

Give the children ample opportunity to explain their thinking processes as they present different ways of writing these sentences.

Many problems of this type can be presented orally as well as on worksheets. Encourage children to think of similar problems to present to the group orally. Since many children at this level have a speaking vocabulary that is more extensive than their reading and writing vocabulary, it is important to provide this type of "thinking" activity rather than constantly restrict problem solving to the current reading level. You can act as a recorder, when necessary, to write the dictated story on the chalkboard.

9. True or false?

a) $4 + 8 = 10$ c) $1 < 6$ e) $4 > 3$ g) $5 < 2$
b) $7 + 2 > 8$ d) $10 - 3 < 5$ f) $6 = 3 + 4$ h) $17 - 7 = 10$

10. Styrofoam cubes can be effectively used to develop awareness of relations occurring within number sentences. For example, suppose a child rolls three cubes and comes up with the numerals 4, 5, and 7 on the respective faces. He may be asked to form a number sentence. One possibility might be $4 + 5 > 7$; another could be $4 < 5 + 7$. What other number sentences can you form? (An advantage in using styrofoam is that children can work quietly in a corner of the room.)

11. List all the whole numbers you can think of that will make these sentences true.

a) $\square < 4$ c) $2 + \square = 9$ e) $\square < 10$ g) $\square = 13$
b) $15 - 5 = \square$ d) $10 - \square = 3$ f) $2 \times 3 = \square$ h) $\square \times 2 = 8$

Hand-Held Calculator Activities for the Primary Grades

1. Children will naturally be curious about the various keys on the calculator. During work time allow a group of children to play with hand-held calculators. Discuss with the children what they discover. When a key is pushed, its symbol will appear on the display screen.

2. Have the children place certain numbers on the display screen. Ask the children to display:

a) Their ages
b) The day that was marked on the calendar that morning
c) Their addresses (If the children have not memorized their addresses, show their house numbers on the display screen. Clear the screen and have the children copy their own addresses from a paper prepared by the teacher.)
d) Their telephone numbers (If the children have not memorized their phone numbers, show each child's telephone number on the display screen. The teacher can prepare sheets of paper with one child's telephone number printed on each.)

3. Dramatize word-problem situations; have the children use their calculators to solve the problems and orally give their answers. For example, place seven chairs in a reading circle. Ask the children: "If two more chairs are needed in the library area and are taken from the reading circle, how many chairs will be left in the reading circle?" The teacher should actually move two chairs from the reading circle to the library area.
    Ask the children to use their hand-held calculators to solve this problem, using complete sentences to state their answers to the problem.

Microcomputer Activities for the Primary Grades

1. All activities suggested for the hand-held calculator can also be used by primary children on a microcomputer in the immediate mode.

2. Have children play with the computer keyboard and note what appears on the display screen.

3. First- and second-grade children can learn to solve simple addition and subtraction examples, using the microcomputer in the immediate mode. The children must remember to use a question mark before entering the mathematics and not to use equals signs.

4. Have some children use a hand-held calculator and some a microcomputer to solve the same examples.

5. State a mathematics situation orally, and have the children solve it, using the micro-computer in the immediate mode. The teacher should evaluate the children's input and the computer response. For example, place three books on Tom's desk and four books on Robin's desk. State the problem situation. Ask the children to use the microcomputer to show how many books are on Tom's and Robin's desks together. Set up real-life situations, and have the children enter the mathematics into the computer to obtain a reasonable answer. Always spend time discussing the reasonableness of the answers obtained. Require the children to state the results of each problem in a complete sentence.

6. Second-grade children should be able to write simple programs in BASIC to solve mathematics examples. Using good programming procedures, they might write:

```
10 REM ADD ONE
20 CLS (Use appropriate method for clearing the screen)
30 PRINT "WHAT NUMBER DO YOU WANT TO ADD ONE WITH"
40 INPUT N
50 X=N+1
60 PRINT N;" + 1 = ";X
70 FOR T=1 TO 2000 : NEXT T
80 GOTO 20
```

The teacher might need to insert the timer for the children. In teaching children problem-solving techniques, the teacher should first state the problem; after the children solve the example, they should give the proper oral response.

7. Move systematically from completely oral to written examples. Children should be able to answer problem-solving situations orally and in writing.

8. As mathematics is taught, at least one real-life problem situation should be solved every day, using the mathematics concepts being taught. Much dramatizing and verbalizing should be involved. Have the children take turns using the microcomputer to solve the mathematics problems.

Activities for the Intermediate Grades

1. A useful activity that allows children to practice formulating questions and open sentences is the Question Game. Pupils are given "answers" like 639, 69 meters, 756 hours and are asked to form open sentences with those numbers as answers. Some children may be able to develop a story problem related to the answers that they are given.

2. Write the correct relation symbol ($<$, $>$, or $=$) in each $\bigcirc$.

   a) $2 \times 3 \bigcirc \ 8 - 5$ b) $20 \div 5 \bigcirc 7 - 3$ c) $9 \div 9 \bigcirc 9 \times 0$

3. Solve for the unknown in each of the following open sentences.

a) $500 + \square = 561$

b) $270 - 80 = 260 - \square$

c) $8 \times 3 = \square$

d) $3 \times (4 \times 0) = \square$

e) $\square + 39 = 139$

f) $\square \times 5 = 15$

g) $25 \div 5 = \square$

h) $4 \times \square \times 9 = 0$

i) $90 + 50 = 170 - \square$

j) $\square \times \square = 25$

k) $24 \div 3 = \square$

l) $2 \times \square = 18$

4. Place the correct sign $(+, -, \times, \text{ or } \div)$ in each $\triangle$ and $\triangledown$. There may be more than one possibility. See how many true statements you can make.

a) $10 \triangle 2 = 15 \triangledown 3$

b) $2 \triangle 5 = 10 \triangledown 3$

c) $9 \triangle 3 = 3 \triangledown 1$

d) $8 \triangle 4 = 4 \triangledown 2$

5. Write mathematical sentences for each puzzle.

a) I'm thinking of a number. If you add 5 to it, you get 14. What is the number? $(n + 5 = 14; n = 9)$

b) I'm thinking of a number. If you add 4 to it and then add 3, you get 15. What is the number?

c) I'm thinking of a number. If you subtract 9 from it, you get 11. What is the number?

d) If I subtract 4 from a number and then subtract 8, I get 4. What is the number?

e) I'm thinking of a number. If you add the number to itself and then add 4, you get 12. What is the number?

6. Rewrite each sentence. Replace each letter with a numeral to make true statements.

a) $n + 21 = 83$

b) $4 \times n = 356$

c) $34 + n = 99$

d) $0 + n = 795$

e) $107 + 257 = n$

f) $n + 5 = 115$

7. Which of the following are true statements?

a) $15 - 9 = 25 - 19$

b) $96 - 53 \neq 69 - 35$

c) $439 - 439 \neq 528 - 528$

d) $241 - 37 \neq 200 - 4$

8. Place the correct relation symbol $(<, >, \text{ or } =)$ in each $\bigcirc$.

a) $13 + 26 \bigcirc 31 - 15$

b) $86 - 53 \bigcirc 68 - 35$

c) $321 + 123 \bigcirc 231 + 213$

d) $741 \times 8 \bigcirc 7000 - 1072$

e) $2\frac{1}{3} + \frac{1}{3} \bigcirc \frac{10}{3} + \frac{2}{3}$

f) $6\frac{1}{3} - 2\frac{1}{6} \bigcirc \frac{19}{3} - \frac{6}{3}$

9. Find the greatest number that will make each sentence true.

a) $n \times 5 < 47$ b) $n \times 8 < 43$ c) $n \times 3 < 60$ d) $n \times 9 < 66$ e) $n \times 7 < 189$

10. Write a number sentence for each puzzle. What's my number?

a) When I add 5 to it, I get 13. $(n + 5 = 13)$

b) When I subtract 3 from it, I get 7.

c) When I multiply it by 8, I get 24.

d) I get 19 when my number is subtracted from 26.

e) When I divide it by 4, I get 12.

f) When I divide it by 2 and then multiply by 2, I get 34.

11. A helpful technique for developing problem-solving abilities is a technique involving a picture or drawing. Show the class a picture of an athletic contest (or a picture of another activity). For permanence, pictures may be dry mounted and covered with clear plastic.

Ask the class to study the picture and to use their creative powers to write a story problem about the characters in it. Have the pupils solve the story problems they create and then share them with the class. An amazing number of creative problems may be formulated this way.

12. Invent your own problem for the following given information. Use any units you care to and write an open sentence describing the problem you have invented.

    a) Bill has 18 ....
        Steve has 12 ....
        ....
    b) Mary bought 16 ....
        Phyllis bought 26 ....
        ....

13. Write an equation for each sentence. Find the solution.

    a) In 4 years John will be 13 years old. How old is he now?
    b) Peter grew 4 inches during the past year. If he is now 52 inches tall, how tall was he last year at this time?

14. Ask the class to calculate the average number of chews that a student can get from one small Tootsie Roll candy. Provide each student with one small candy and have each child count the number of chews until the candy is all gone. Collect the data, organize the data into a table or graph, and calculate the average number of chews.

15. George holds his dog as he steps on the scale to weigh himself. Then George weighs himself without the dog. How can George find the weight of his dog?

16. Bring a grocery store ad from the local newspaper into the classroom. Have the children create a week's shopping list from the ad, calculate the bill, and figure the sales tax.

17. Ask the local bank to furnish banking material and have the children create their own bank accounts, learn to write checks, and balance their checkbook at the end of the month. Children can create their bank statements for the month.

Hand-Held Calculator Activities for the Intermediate Grades

The hand-held calculator can provide computing capabilities for the students, so that they can concentrate on the mathematics involved in solving word problems. Using hand-held calculators in solving problems is part of functioning in society today, so children need to know how to use this device in real-life situations. The calculator cannot make decisions about when to add, subtract, multiply, or divide. Students must organize the data themselves and learn to use the calculator as a tool.

1. Count your pulse for one minute to determine the number of heartbeats per minute. Calculate the approximate number of heartbeats you have had since your birth.

2. A plumber earns $15.00 per hour and receives time and a half for overtime. What is the plumber's weekly wages if he worked the normal 40-hour week with five hours of overtime?

3. If you earn one dollar every minute, how long would it take you to earn one thousand dollars, one million dollars, and one billion dollars?

4. Provide the children with a shoe box. Have the children calculate the number of shoe boxes that could be placed in the classroom. Remember that this cannot be calculated by volume, because you cannot use half of a shoe box.

5. If a million one dollar bills were piled one on top of another, how tall would the pile be?

6. You have one kilometer of fencing and you want to enclose a field containing the most area. Describe the shape of the figure and indicate in square meters the total area that your figure will enclose. (If children do not include a circle, suggest that they find the area of a circle with a circumference of one kilometer.)

7. Calculate the number of minutes in each of the following:

    a) one hour
    b) one day
    c) one week
    d) one month of May
    e) one month of April

    f) one regular year
    g) one leap year
    h) one decade
    i) one century

8. How long have you lived? Calculate the number of days, hours, minutes, and weeks. Calculate the number of years in decimals to the nearest thousandth.

9. Get menus from local restaurants. Have the children collect orders and prepare bills.

Microcomputer Activities for the Intermediate Grades

All the activities suggested for the hand-held calculator can be used on a microcomputer in the immediate mode. Remember to use the PRINT command, and do not use the equals sign.

1. Intermediate level students can learn to write simple programs to accomplish a specific task. Suggest that the children write a simple microcomputer program in BASIC to calculate the area of a rectangle. A simple program might look like this:

```
10 REM—AREA OF A RECTANGLE—
20 CLS
30 ?"WHAT IS THE LENGTH OF YOUR RECTANGLE";
40 INPUT A
50 ?"WHAT IS THE WIDTH OF YOUR RECTANGLE";
60 INPUT B
70 C=A*B
80 ?"THE AREA OF YOUR RECTANGLE IS ";C;" SQUARE UNITS."
```

2. Ask the children to change their area program so it will compute the perimeter of a rectangle. The new program might look like this:

```
10 REM—PERIMETER OF RECTANGLE—
20 CLS
30 ?"WHAT IS THE LENGTH OF YOUR RECTANGLE";
40 INPUT A
50 ?"WHAT IS THE WIDTH OF YOUR RECTANGLE";
60 INPUT B
70 P=2*A+2*B
80 ?"THE PERIMETER OF YOUR RECTANGLE IS ";P;" UNITS."
```

3. Ask the children to combine these two programs so that both the area and perimeter are calculated for a rectangle. The combined program might look like this:

```
10 REM*AREA AND PERIMETER OF RECTANGLE*
20 CLS
30 ?"WHAT IS THE LENGTH OF YOUR RECTANGLE";
40 INPUT A
50 ?"WHAT IS THE WIDTH OF YOUR RECTANGLE";
60 INPUT B
70 C=A*B:P=2A+2B
80 ?"THE AREA OF YOUR RECTANGLE IS ";C;" SQUARE UNITS AND THE PERIMETER
   OF YOUR RECTANGLE IS ";P;" UNITS."
```

4. Children should be able to change the above programs to include loops with a timer. Add the following statements to the previous programs:

```
90  FOR T=1 TO 2000:NEXT T
100 GOTO 30
```

5. Encourage the children to enhance these programs with some introductory statements to the user. For instance, the following statement could be added to the program in exercise 3.

```
25 ?"THIS PROGRAM WILL CALCULATE THE AREA AND PERIMETER OF YOUR
   RECTANGLE."
27 ?:?:?"YOU MUST TELL US THE LENGTH AND WIDTH OF YOUR RECTANGLE."
```

6. Encourage the children to make their programs friendly by including names in their programs. Children will need instruction in string variables and how to use string variables. They can also begin to learn about spacing by using PRINT statements. For instance, the following statements might also be added to the program in exercise 3:

```
12 CLS
14 ?"WHAT IS YOUR NAME";
16 INPUT N$
18 CLS
20 ?"HELLO, ";N$;" NICE TO MEET YOU."
22 ?:?:?:?
```

7. Give the children the opportunity to solve mathematics assignments on a microcomputer, if they can program the mathematics examples into the computer. Children must have a good understanding of mathematics to program the computer.

Activities for the Upper Elementary Grades

1. Write a story problem to fit each equation.

   a) $5\frac{1}{2} + n = 10\frac{1}{4}$ b) $\frac{n-3}{3} = 3$ c) $(4 \times n) + 6 = 26$

2. Write an equation for each problem.

   a) The Glen Park School bus has enough room for 34 children. If the driver started with a full load, stopped at North School to let off 18 children, and picked up 9 more children going to South School, how many children were then on the bus?

b) Jerry came home from a school baseball game and was hungry, as usual. He found a note from his mother telling him to help himself to a piece of pie and a glass of milk. Someone else had already eaten part of the pie, because only $\frac{2}{3}$ of it was left in the pan. After Jerry cut a piece for himself, only $\frac{1}{2}$ of the pie remained. What part of the whole pie did Jerry eat?

3. Present a variety of simple equations using frames or letters as placeholders for missing numerals. Encourage the students to check their solutions by testing to see whether the numbers they obtain actually make the sentence true.

a) $2 \times n = 24$ c) $n - 4 = 83$ e) $n \div 7 = 2 \times 14$
b) $4 \div n = 4$ d) $(5 \times n) + 5 = 20$ f) $(8 + 6) \div 2 = n$

4. Find the solution set for each of the following open sentences. Use only the set of counting numbers between 0 and 25.

a) $\Box + 2 = 7$ b) $\triangle - 2 > 15$ c) $3 \times \Box < 21$ d) $\Box + (3 \times \Box) = 8$

It is important to remember at this point that many of these situations involving mathematical sentences can be used at Grades 4, 5, or 6, depending on the ability of the children.

5. Problem solving in the elementary school can be approached by the use of task cards. These can be constructed by the teacher and often contain a problem for which many strategies and solutions may be obtained. For example, a card with the following questions can be constructed.

How long is a minute?
How many times do you breathe in a minute?
Estimate; then find out.
Do you always breathe the same number of times each minute?
Can you prove your hypothesis?

6. If the universal set is the set of counting numbers, find the solution set for each of the following sentences.

a) $(\Box \times \Box) - (12 \times \Box) + 27 = 0$ d) $\Box + 3 > 6$
b) $\Box + \Box - 10 = 12$ e) $(2 \times \Box) + (3 \times \Box) + 5 = 20$
c) $\Box + \Box = 10^2$ f) $\Box + 5 < 30$

7. If the universal set is the set of integers, find the solution set for each of the following sentences. (Integers will be discussed further in Unit 13.)

a) $^-15 + n = 13$ c) $4 + n = ^-3$ e) $n + (^-3) = 6$
b) $n + 7 = ^-81$ d) $^-20 + n = ^-90$ f) $n + (^-4) = 16$

8. Write the correct relation symbol ($<$, $>$, or $=$) in each $\bigcirc$.

a) $(^-3) + (^-6) \bigcirc (^-6) + (^-3)$ b) $(^-2) + (^-7) \bigcirc 2 + 7$

9. Write an equation for each of the following. Find the solution.

a) Jean is 5 years older than Jane. Sue is 2 years younger than Jean. How much older than Jane is Sue?
b) There are 30 pupils in Roy's class: 16 boys and 14 girls. If $\frac{3}{4}$ of the boys are in the sixth-grade mathematics club and $\frac{1}{2}$ of the girls are in the sixth-grade music club, how many members of the class do not take part in either of these activities?

10. This problem can be posed to the class: "If you had $10.00 to plan a party for the class, what would you buy?" This problem can offer several directions. Children can estimate costs for the party and then check them with actual prices appearing in stores and newpapers.

11. Compare the height from which a rubber ball is dropped to the height of its first bounce. Then check the height of its subsequent bounces. Show your findings on a graph. Can you form an open sentence that describes the results you obtained?

12. Have a child write his name on a piece of paper and then determine how long a piece of paper and how much time she/he would need to write the name one million times.

13. If snow falls at the rate of .3 of an inch per hour, how much snow will fall in 8.5 hours?

14. Connie has 4 pennies, 3 nickels, 2 dimes, and 3 quarters. How many different amounts of money can Connie make by using all the possible combinations of coins?

15. Select a specific pine tree, and have the children calculate the number of needles on the tree. Discuss with the children how the best estimate can be made.

16. All the word problem ideas in the intermediate activities can be applied to the upper elementary grades by using decimals or fractions for numerical amounts.

Hand-Held Calculator Activities for the Upper Elementary Grades

All intermediate level activities for the hand-held calculator can also be used at the upper elementary level.

1. Locate the population and land area for 5 states. Calculate the population per square mile. Which of the 5 states you chose has the most people per square mile?

2. Calculate the difference in population per square mile among the five states you selected.

3. Have each child in the class count the number of breaths taken per minute. What is the average number of breaths per minute for the children in your classroom? How many combined breaths are taken by all the children in your classroom in one day?

4. A person who lifts 100 pounds on earth could lift 600 pounds on the moon. How much could a person lift on the moon who can lift 135 pounds on earth?

5. Find the median number between 17 and 29.

6. Use data from the sports page of your local newspaper, and (for example) calculate batting averages for each player.

7. Calculate the percent of your state's population located in each of the larger cities.

8. Use a local newspaper sale advertisement for tires and calculate the percent of savings on each tire on sale.

Microcomputer Activities for the Upper Elementary Grades

All microcomputer activities listed for intermediate grades may also be used in the upper elementary grades. All activities suggested for the hand-held calculator may also be used on the microcomputer in the immediate mode.

1. Write a simple program in the BASIC language that will ask you the name of two of your friends and then print their names.

2. Write a simple program in BASIC that will print your name on the screen continuously.

3. Write a simple program using BASIC language to multiply two numbers and print the product.

4. Write a simple microcomputer program using BASIC language to add three numbers and print the sum on the monitor.

5. Use BASIC language and write a simple microcomputer program to print the greater of two numbers.

6. Describe what each statement of this microcomputer program will do.

```
10 CLS
20 LET A=5
30 LET B=8
40 C=A+B
50 ? "THE SUM OF ";A;" AND ";B;" IS ";C
```

Suggested Readings

Biggs, Edith E., and MacLean, James R. *Freedom to Learn: An Active Learning Approach to Mathematics*. Don Mills, Ontario, Canada: Addison-Wesley, 1969.

Carpenter, T. P.; Coburn, T. C.; and others. "Notes from National Assessment: Word Problems." *The Arithmetic Teacher*, vol. 23, no. 4, April 1976.

Earp, Wesley N. "Procedure for Teaching Reading in Mathematics." *The Arithmetic Teacher*, vol. 17, no. 8, November 1970.

Grossman, R. "Problem-Solving Activities Observed in the British Primary School." *The Arithmetic Teacher*, vol. 16, no. 1, January 1969.

Henney, M. "Improving Mathematics Verbal Problem-Solving Ability Through Reading Instruction." *The Arithmetic Teacher*, vol. 18, no. 4, April 1971.

Kantowski, E. L. "Processes Involved in Mathematical Problem Solving." *Journal for Research in Mathematics Education*, vol. 8, no. 3, 1977.

Lester, Frank K. "Research on Mathematical Problem Solving." *Research in Mathematics Education*, Reston, Va.: National Council of Teachers of Mathematics, 1980.

———. "Ideas About Problem Solving: A Look at Some Psychological Research." *The Arithmetic Teacher*, vol. 25, no. 2, November 1977.

Meiring, Steven P. *Problem Solving . . . a basic mathematics goal*. Book 1 and Book 2. Columbus, Ohio: Ohio Department of Education.

Orans, S. "Go Shopping! Problem-Solving Activities for the Primary Grades with Provision for Individualization." *The Arithmetic Teacher*, vol. 17, no. 7, November 1970.

5 Numeration and Place Value

Teaching Competencies

Upon completing this unit, you will be able to:

Identify the basic features of a place-value numeration system

Describe several ancient numeration systems

Use standard notation, expanded notation, and exponential notation to express a given number

Identify the characteristics of any place-value system

Name, read, and write numbers with multi-place values

Model numbers using a place-value box and numeral expanders

Discussion

The concept of decimal place value is an important concept that is basic to the set of whole numbers, integers, and rational numbers expressed as decimals. Understanding the concept of place value is essential to comprehending the algorithms we teach; in general, many teachers do not adequately emphasize place value in their teaching. The principles of place value make our numeration system far superior to any other system. Zero as we use it in our numeration system is another concept that makes our system unique. Now let us carefully examine place value.

Any place-value numeration system has a scheme of grouping that is basic to that system. The number of symbols necessary in a particular numeration system is directly related to this basic grouping. For example, in the base-ten system there are ten symbols or **digits:**

$$0, 1, 2, 3, 4, 5, 6, 7, 8, 9$$

With various combinations of these ten digits, any number, no matter how great or small, can be expressed. This is possible because the **decimal system** (or base-ten system) uses **place value** and has a special symbol, the **zero,** for indicating "not any."

When we agree that ten is to be the base of a numeration system, we are saying that ten is the basis for grouping in that system. We can count from 1 to 9 and record this count in the ones column (the first column to the left of the decimal point in the base-ten system) with a single digit; when we reach a count of ten, we group the set of ten and express it by a 1 in the next (tens) column to the left. A count greater than nine but less than one hundred must be expressed as a set or sets of ten, and any ones left over are recorded in the ones column.

A single symbol, 1, would not be sufficient to express one set of ten, because the single symbol is understood to express one set of one. For this reason we employ the special symbol 0 to indicate that the ones column (or units column) has no sets of one. Thus, in base ten, the numeral 10 indicates

And 14, for example, indicates

Grouping by tens in the tens column is done in the same way. Again, we cannot record more than nine sets of ten; ten sets of ten must be grouped into one set of one hundred.

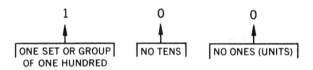

Zero is a number. It indicates that there are no sets of one and no sets of ten in 100. The importance of zero, then, lies in its function as a number expressing "not any" in a place-value system.

The decimal system, with its orderly grouping by sets of ten and multiples of ten, produces regular and logical patterns. Besides contributing to the ease of using the decimal system, these patterns possess a symmetry and beauty that any child should easily notice and appreciate.

Children need many experiences grouping and regrouping objects into sets of ones and tens. Place two sheets of paper in front of the children. On one sheet print the word *ones* and on the second sheet print the word *tens.*

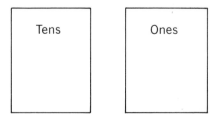

Have the children place plastic forks on the sheet marked ones. Instruct children that whenever ten

items (forks in this case) are on the ones sheet they must be regrouped into one ten.

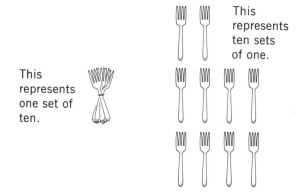

This represents one set of ten.

This represents ten sets of one.

A place-value box may also be used. A place-value box is any box that has compartments labeled corresponding to decimal places. For example,

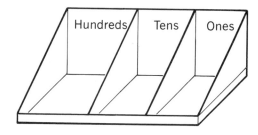

The number 23 can be shown with two sets of tens and three ones. In the place-value box we would place three single forks in the compartment labeled "ones," and we would place two packages of ten forks each into the compartment labeled "tens." The number 23 can be shown by placing three single forks on a sheet of paper marked "ones" and placing to the left two packages of ten forks each on a sheet labeled "tens."

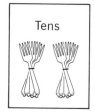

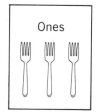

Have the children select numeral cards and place them on the place-value sheets.

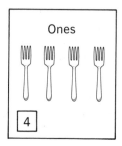

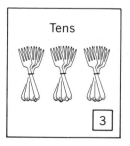

We have already said that ten is the basis for grouping in the decimal system. Now let's examine the regular patterns inherent in this grouping. A set of ten ones becomes 1 ten and 0 ones; a set of ten tens becomes 1 hundred, 0 tens, and 0 ones; a set of ten hundreds becomes 1 thousand, 0 hundreds, 0 tens, and 0 ones. This can be shown in a grid. A large grid can be made for the children and they can manipulate sets of objects bundled in ones, tens, or hundreds right on the grid. A small grid like the following may be used by the children by placing numeral cards on the grid or using a marking pencil on a grid covered with a clear plastic film.

Thousands	Hundreds	Tens	Ones	
		1	0	Ten ones or one ten
	1	0	0	Ten tens or one hundred
1	0	0	0	Ten hundreds or one thousand

It is evident that whenever we have ten in any set we move one place to the left and record a one in that column (for one set of ten, one set of one hundred, and so on). Thus a numeral in any column has ten times the value of that same numeral in the column to its right. For example, the numeral 1 in the thousands column has ten times the value of the numeral 1 in the hundreds column. We can rearrange the information in our grid to express this another way:

$10 \times 10 \times 10$	10×10	10	1
Thousands	Hundreds	Tens	Ones

This is an abstract idea, very difficult for children to comprehend. Provide a great deal of material for children to manipulate, and systematically teach, apply, and have children practice the concept. By noting the number of times 10 is used as a factor, we see that each column represents 10 times the value of the column to its right. By the use of exponential notation, we can write this in simpler fashion. We write a numeral (called an **exponent**) above and to the right of the 10 to tell how many times 10 is used as a factor. We can abbreviate $10 \times 10 \times 10$ by writing 10^3 and 10×10 by writing 10^2. We can read 10^3 as "ten to the third power" and we can read 10^2 as "ten to the second power." The number 10 can be written as 10^1 (ten to the first power), since 10 occurs only once. Study the following list of **powers** of 10.

Do you see a pattern that indicates how 1 can be written as a power of 10?

$$1000 = 10^3$$
$$100 = 10^2$$
$$10 = 10^1$$
$$1 = 10^?$$

The exponents are decreasing by one as we go down the list, so the exponent that we want is 0. 1 is equal to 10 to the zero power: $1 = 10^0$. We can show the values for each column in the grid by using **exponential notation:**

10^3	10^2	10^1	10^0
Thousands	Hundreds	Tens	Ones

In this chart 10 is called the base and 3, 2, 1 and 0 are called exponents. A positive exponent on a numeral indicates the number of times that the base is to be used as a factor.

Base $\rightarrow 10^2 \leftarrow$ Exponent

A number with an exponent is said to be raised to a power; the power is named by the exponent. The powers of 10 in the last grid are as follows:

10^0 means 10 to the zero power (except for zero, any number raised to the zero power is equal to 1)

10^1 means 10 to the first power (any number raised to the first power is the number itself; so $10^1 = 10$)

10^2 means 10 to the second power (10^2 means 10 used as a factor two times; $10 \times 10 = 100$)

10^3 means 10 to the third power (1000), and so on

To illustrate how exponential notation and place value are related, consider the number 1314. Arrange the numerals in a grid as we did earlier:

10^3	10^2	10^1	10^0
1	3	1	4

In this grid the place value of each digit is indicated by the power of ten at the top of the column.

$$1314 = (1 \times 10^3) + (3 \times 10^2) + (1 \times 10^1) + (4 \times 10^0)$$
$$= (1 \times 10 \times 10 \times 10) + (3 \times 10 \times 10) + (1 \times 10) + (4 \times 1)$$
$$= (1 \times 1000) + (3 \times 100) + (1 \times 10) + (4 \times 1)$$
$$= 1000 + 300 + 10 + 4$$
$$= 1314$$

Thus we see the relation in our decimal system between place value and exponential notation.

The operations that children perform on numbers are understood more easily through the use of **expanded notation,** in which numbers are thought of in particular component parts before operations are performed. These component parts show the place values of the digits in the numerals. A numeral written in expanded notation is called an **expanded numeral.**

Consider the number 2146 written in expanded notation.

a) $2000 + 100 + 40 + 6$

By naming a number in this way, children see at a glance the makeup of the number in terms of sets of ones, tens, hundreds, thousands, and so on. The expanded notation above can also be written as

b) $(2 \times 1000) + (1 \times 100) + (4 \times 10) + (6 \times 1)$

c) 2 thousands   1 hundred   4 tens   6 ones

d) $(2 \times 10 \times 10 \times 10) + (1 \times 10 \times 10) + (4 \times 10) + (6 \times 1)$

or, as we showed using exponential notation:

e) $(2 \times 10^3) + (1 \times 10^2) + (4 \times 10^1) + (6 \times 10^0)$

Forms a and b are sufficient for the elementary school child; forms d and e tend to be too abstract at this level. However, form c is probably the most meaningful for the elementary child. Expanded notation helps the child understand grouping and to see clearly the set of numbers that are being regrouped.

$$2146 = 2000 + 100 + 40 + 6$$
$$= (2 \times 1000) + (1 \times 100) + (4 \times 10) + (6 \times 1)$$
$$= (2 \times 10 \times 10 \times 10) + (1 \times 10 \times 10) + (4 \times 10) + (6 \times 1)$$
$$= (2 \times 10^3) + (1 \times 10^2) + (4 \times 10^1) + (6 + 10^0)$$

Often it is less confusing for children if words are used instead of numerals. This is particularly true for subtraction. Study this example written with numerals alone and with words and numerals.

$$\begin{array}{r} 46 = \\ -23 = \\ \hline \end{array} \begin{array}{r} \text{4 tens 6 ones} \\ -\text{2 tens 3 ones} \\ \hline \text{2 tens 3 ones} = 23 \end{array} \qquad \begin{array}{r} 46 = \\ -23 = \\ \hline \end{array} \begin{array}{r} (40 + 6) \\ -(20 + 3) \\ \hline 20 + 3 = 23 \end{array}$$

hundreds	tens	ones	hundreds	tens	ones	hundreds	tens	ones	hundreds	tens	ones	hundreds	tens	ones	hundreds	tens	ones	hundreds	tens	ones	hundreds	tens	ones	hundreds	tens	ones	hundreds	tens	ones	hundreds	tens	ones	hundreds	tens	ones

{1 2 3}, {4 5 6}, {7 8 9}, {1 2 3}, {4 5 6}, {7 8 9}, {1 2 3}, {4 5 6}, {7 8 9}, {1 2 3}, {4 5 6}, {7 8 9}

Period names (left to right): Decillions, Nonillions, Octillions, Septillions, Sextillions, Quintillions, Quadrillions, Trillions, Billions, Millions, Thousands, Units

Period Name

Children often add the numbers in the ones place and subtract the numbers in the tens place (in this case, obtaining an answer of 29).

Place value can be expressed in general terms that are applicable to any base. Let b stand for any base; then place value can be expressed in exponential notation as indicated in the grid below.

b^4	b^3	b^2	b^1	b^0
$b \times b \times b \times b$	$b \times b \times b$	$b \times b$	b	1

Let us examine the organization of our base-ten number system. The places of this system are separated by commas into periods. Each period has three places; they are named, right to left, *ones*, *tens*, and *hundreds*. The names *ones*, *tens*, and *hundreds* are repeated in each period. Each period has its own name and is used every time we read a number.

Since commas are not used in the metric system, computers, or hand-held calculators to separate periods within a number, children must be able to read numbers separated by spaces as well as those separated by commas.

Now let us consider the number above. (We introduce this so you can become familiar with place-value names. It is not necessary for children to learn all these places.)

Each period has a name and a ones, tens, and hundreds place. Study this pattern. To read a decimal number, read the three digits in a period; then give the period name. Continue this process from left to right. Thus the number would be read: one hundred twenty-three decillion; four hundred fifty-six nonillion, seven hundred eighty-nine octillion, one hundred twenty-three septillion, four hundred fifty-six sextillion, seven hundred eighty-nine quintillion, one hundred twenty-three quadrillion, four hundred fifty-six trillion, seven hundred eighty-nine billion, one hundred twenty-three million, four hundred fifty-six thousand, seven hundred eighty-nine.

Dienes Blocks or multi-base blocks are excellent materials to use when teaching place value. For more information about using Dienes Blocks, we recommend Zoltan Dienes' book *Modern Mathematics for Young Children*. Now let us examine Dienes Blocks or multi-base blocks. The materials for a base-ten place-value system are composed of:

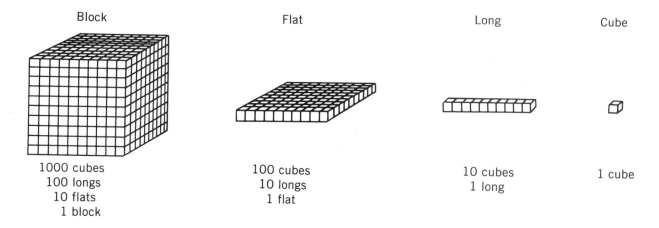

Block	Flat	Long	Cube
1000 cubes 100 longs 10 flats 1 block	100 cubes 10 longs 1 flat	10 cubes 1 long	1 cube

Study the relationship that exists among these materials—cube, long, flat, and block.

Children would benefit from manipulating and exchanging blocks so they have the same amount of wood. For example: if a child has 123 cubes, what is the least number of pieces of wood he or she could have? In this case the child would have 1 flat, 2 longs, and 3 cubes. Have the child go to the bank and exchange one of the pieces for an equivalent amount of wood. The child might change one long for ten cubes. Then he would have 1 flat, 1 long and 13 cubes. If the child now exchanges 1 long at the bank so that the amount of wood remains constant, then the child would have 1 flat, 0 longs and 23 cubes. This same process can be used so that the amount of wood is always the same but the number and types of pieces vary. A child should see all possible combinations. All possible combinations for 123 cubes are:

		123 cubes
	1 long,	113 cubes
	2 longs,	103 cubes
	3 longs,	93 cubes
	4 longs,	83 cubes
	5 longs,	73 cubes
	6 longs,	63 cubes
	7 longs,	53 cubes
	8 longs,	43 cubes
	9 longs,	33 cubes
	10 longs,	23 cubes
	11 longs,	13 cubes
	12 longs,	3 cubes
1 flat,	2 longs,	3 cubes
1 flat,	1 long,	13 cubes
1 flat,	0 longs,	23 cubes

Children should now begin to realize that in each case there is exactly the same amount of wood. The only differences are the type and the number of pieces.

The block, flat, long, and cube can be related to the base-ten, place-value system. Have the children study the relationships among the blocks and the base-ten place-value system.

Ones place	One is equivalent to a cube
Tens place	Ten is equivalent to a long
Hundreds place	Hundred is equivalent to a flat
Thousands place	Thousand is equivalent to a block

This will provide the children with many experiences on the concrete, semiconcrete, and semiabstract levels. Children could have more experiences on the semiabstract and abstract levels by using chip trading.

Once children have learned about the base-ten system, they may want to apply this knowledge to other systems. At this point, it's a good time to introduce them to some of the number systems used in the past.

As human beings mastered their environments and developed organized societies, they found that a major necessity, in addition to language, was a method of counting and recording numbers. From primitive one-to-one matching (notching a stick to keep a tally) to present-day electronic computers, people have created a bewildering variety of ways to count and record numbers. We tend to take our familiar base-ten decimal system for granted; so much so, in fact, that we usually fail to understand the full meaning of the numerals we write and of the computations we perform. A brief examination of several historical numeration systems, as well as systems using bases other than ten, may afford a fuller understanding of the features of our decimal system, such as place value, the zero symbol, and the base of ten.

Obviously we can't study all of the many different numeration systems that have been invented over the centuries. But we can look at examples of additive systems, multiplicative systems, and place-value systems. The ancient Egyptian numeration system is an example of an additive system; the Romans used a modified additive system; the ancient Chinese used a multiplicative system; and the Babylonian system is an example of a place-value system. Our base-ten (decimal) system also uses place value.

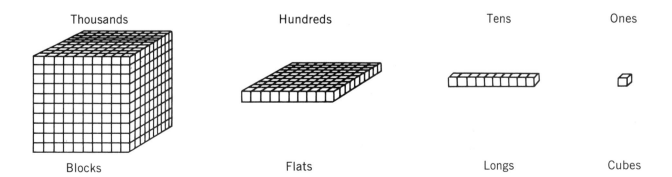

Thousands	Hundreds	Tens	Ones
Blocks	Flats	Longs	Cubes

Every **numeration system** uses a set of symbols to represent numbers. The following chart shows the symbols used by the ancient Egyptians.

Egyptian Numeral	Number Named	Meaning of Picture Symbol
|	1	stroke
∩	10	cattle hobble or oxen yoke
૧	100	coil of rope
ৗ or ૪	1000	lotus plant
₯ or ⌠	10,000	bent finger
⌐	100,000	tadpole
¥ or ¥	1,000,000	a god with arms supporting the sky

The Egyptians used an **additive system** of numeration in which the values of numerals were added together regardless of the order in which the numerals were written. For example, $10 + 1 + 1 + 1 = 13$ could be written as ∩\|\|\|, \|\|\|∩, or \|∩\|\|, and so on.

$$100 + 10 + 10 + 10 + 1 + 1 + 1 + 1 + 1 = 135$$

$$૧ \cap \cap \cap \; \text{\|\|\|\|\|} = 135$$

$$\cap \cap \cap \cap \cap \cap \cap \cap \cap \; \text{\|\|\|\|\|\|\|\|\|} = 99$$

$$⌐ (૪ ૧ ∩ \text{\|} = 111,111$$

Complete the following table.

Egyptian Numeral	Hindu-Arabic Numeral
⌐(((∩∩∩||	130,032
	2352
	1,300,123
	43,016
₯₯૪૧૧૧∩	
⌐₯૧૧∩|||	
₯₯₯₯૧૧૧|||	

The numerals for the table are:

$$\text{₮₮ ૧૧૧ } {\cap\cap \atop \cap\cap\cap} \text{\|\|} = 2352$$

$$\text{¥ ₯₯₯ ૧∩∩\|\|\|} = 1,300,123$$

$$((((₮₮₮ ∩ {\text{\|\|\|} \atop \text{\|\|\|}} = 43,016$$

$$₯₯ ₮ ૧૧૧૧ ∩ = 21,310$$

$$⌐₯ ૧૧ ∩ \text{\|\|\|} = 110,213$$

$$₯₯₯₯ ૧૧ ૧૧ \text{\|\|\|} = 30,303$$

What do you think your major difficulties would be if you had to calculate in the Egyptian system? As you study the following examples, you should begin to appreciate the advantages of calculating with a place-value system. Do not ask students to calculate in other numeration systems or in other base systems. This system is illustrated here to help students comprehend and appreciate our base-ten system. Children who are weak in mathematics or have little interest in mathematics will not profit from study of this type. It would be more advantageous to devote teaching time to the study and understanding of our base-ten system.

Addition: ૧૧∩∩∩∩∩\|\|\| + ૧∩∩∩ ${\text{\|\|\|} \atop \text{\|\|\|}}$

$$= \quad {\text{∩∩ \|\|\|\|\|} \atop \text{૧૧૧ ∩∩∩∩\|\|\|\|}}$$

Subtraction: ૧૧∩∩∩\|\|\| − ૧∩∩\|\|\|\| = ૧ ${\text{\|\|\|\|} \atop \text{\|\|\|\|\|}}$

Add the following. ${\text{∩∩∩ \;\; \|\|\|} \atop \text{૧ ∩∩∩∩}}$
${\text{\|\|\|\|} \atop +\;\; \text{૧૧ \;\; ∩∩ \;\; \|\|\|\|\|}}$

The steps in obtaining the answer might look like this:

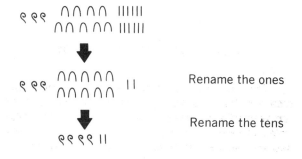

Rename the ones

Rename the tens

The Egyptian system was based on simple addition, but its symbols represented powers of ten. It did not have place value, and it did not have a symbol for zero. Such a system becomes very clumsy and difficult when greater numbers are involved.

The Roman system of numeration is probably the most familiar to us of all the older systems. We still see Roman numerals used for book chapters, clock numerals, and formal inscriptions. The Roman system was not a place-value system and did not have a symbol for zero. The most common Roman symbols are listed below.

Roman Numeral	Value of Numeral
I	1
V	5
X	10
L	50
C	100
D	500
M	1000

To find the value of a numeral the Romans added the values of numerals much as the Egyptians did.

$$XVI = 10 + 5 + 1 = 16$$
$$LXVIII = 50 + 10 + 5 + 1 + 1 + 1 = 68$$

However, the Roman numeration system was not based entirely on simple addition of number values represented by numerals in any order. Although the Roman system did not have place value, numerals of greater value were usually placed to the left of numerals of lesser value.

$$CLXVI = 100 + 50 + 10 + 5 + 1 = 166$$

A numeral of lesser value placed to the left of (or preceding) numerals of greater value indicated that the lesser value was to be subtracted from the greater value. For example

$$IX = 10 - 1 = 9$$
$$IV = 5 - 1 = 4$$
$$XCIV = (100 - 10) + (5 - 1) = 94$$

The Chinese used a **multiplicative system** to indicate number value. This system had symbols to represent the numbers from 1 through 9 and separate symbols for powers of 10. The Chinese symbols and their values are shown in the following table.

Chinese Symbol	Value
一	1
二	2
三	3
四	4
五	5
六	6
七	7
八	8
九	9
十	10
百	100

Repetition of symbols was avoided by multiplying given numbers by powers of 10. For example, 70 would be written as:

七十

$$7 \times 10 = 70$$

Greater numbers could be written this way:

四 百 五 十 六

$$(4 \times 100) + (5 \times 10) + 6 = 456$$

The ancient Babylonian civilization was one of the first to develop and use a place-value system. The basic symbol of the Babylonians was a wedge shape. Symbols were inscribed on wet clay tablets with a stylus, and the tablets were then dried. Owing to the dry climate, many of these tablets containing Babylonian cuneiform writing and mathematical symbols have been preserved. The Babylonian place-value system was based on groupings of 60 and multiples of 60; for this reason it is called a sexagesimal system. The system did not have a symbol for zero until about 200 B.C.

The symbols generally used by the Babylonians were two distinctive wedge-shaped marks, ◄ and ▼. The table below summarizes the principal values of these symbols.

| 36,000 | 3600 | 600 | 60 | 10 | 1 |

Obviously, since the same symbol could represent more than one value, there was likely to be some confusion in interpreting numerals. Apparently the Babylonians depended on the context of the numerals to indicate their values. Values from 1 through 9 were noted by simple repetition and addition:

Babylonian Symbol	Value	Babylonian Symbol	Value
▼	1	▼▼▼ / ▼▼▼	6
▼▼	2	▼▼▼▼ / ▼▼▼	7
▼▼▼	3	▼▼ ▼▼ / ▼▼▼▼	8
▼▼▼ / ▼	4	▼▼▼ / ▼▼ / ▼▼▼	9
▼▼ / ▼▼	5	◄	10

Place value was indicated by the arrangement of the numerals. In the examples below, the values of the numerals are indicated.

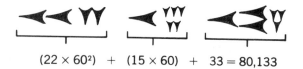

$$(22 \times 60^2) \; + \; (15 \times 60) \; + \; 33 = 80{,}133$$

Since the Babylonians did not have a symbol for zero for many centuries, their place-value system was liable to be misread. For example, ◄◄ ▼ could represent 21; or, if the first two symbols were read as $600 + 600$, it could represent either 1201 or 1260. Similarly, the number 35 could be written

$$(3 \times 10) + (5 \times 1)$$

But this could also be interpreted as 2100:

$$(3 \times 600) + (5 \times 60)$$

A symbol for zero, it seems, is a necessity in an efficient place-value system. The numeration sys-

tem that we use today was invented by the Hindus and modified by the Arabs. The Hindu-Arabic system eventually spread through Europe and developed into our modern **base-ten** or **decimal** system of numeration. The efficiency of the decimal system depends on two important features, a symbol for zero and the use of place value. These two features eliminate awkward notation and provide for ease in calculation.

Many elementary mathematics programs provide an introduction to other numeration systems, including numeration systems having bases other than ten. There are several reasons for examining numeration systems in an elementary mathematics program. They create an awareness of mathematics as part of our cultural history. They also demonstrate the possibility of using numeration systems that differ from ours in significant ways.

The basic generalizations made about the base-ten system also apply to bases other than ten. Teaching other base systems thus reinforces the meaning of the structure of our base-ten system. Children have an opportunity to apply what they have discovered about one place-value system to new situations. If we teach base five merely for its own sake or as a curiosity of numbers, and not to reinforce the children's knowledge of mathematical structure and number relations, we are wasting their time.

Throughout history, various societies have developed different types of numeration systems, or ways of counting and calculating. We have seen a few examples in this unit. But the idea of grouping probably occurred when people began to work with large quantities. The basic concept for any place-value system is some method of grouping.

Let's take an imaginary trip to a faraway country. The inhabitants of this country have, it seems to us, an odd way of recording number. In order to write a numeral to represent

they write ⑬ . To count a group, they count 1, 2, 3, 4, 5 and then draw a figure round that group, or set, and record 1. Then they count the elements not included in the set—1, 2, 3—and record 3.

The 1 and the 3 are then written and looped: ⑬. This numeral represents the set of five elements and the left-over three elements.

Using this system, how would they record the following quantity?

They would count five and draw a figure enclosing that set. They would then count five more and draw a figure round that set. They would find that four elements are left over. They would record the count as ㉔. The 2 stands for two sets of five, and the 4 stands for four ones.

These people, you discover, are grouping sets by fives. A system based on grouping by fives is called a **base-five or quinary** numeration system. When we calculate using base five, or any base other than base ten, we usually write the name of the base as a subscript to avoid any confusion. Thus we could record the two sets of five and four ones as 24_{five}. This is read, "Two-four, base five," and means two groups of five, and four ones.

Now let's examine the following table, which is written in the base-five, or quinary, system.

Base-Five Grouping	Base-Five Notation	Base-Five Name
•	1	one
••	2	two
•••	3	three
••••	4	four
•••••	10_{five}	one-zero base five
••••• •	11_{five}	one-one base five
••••• ••	12_{five}	one-two base five
••••• •••	13_{five}	one-three base five
••••• ••••	14_{five}	one-four base five
••••• •••••	20_{five}	two-zero base five
••••• ••••• •	21_{five}	two-one base five
••••• ••••• ••	22_{five}	two-two base five
••••• ••••• •••	23_{five}	two-three base five
. . .	. . .	. . .
••••• ••••• ••••• ••••• ••	42_{five}	four-two base five
••••• ••••• ••••• ••••• •••	43_{five}	four-three base five
••••• ••••• ••••• ••••• ••••	44_{five}	four-four base five

Let's use these basic ideas about grouping to develop an **octal** numeration system. An octal sys-

tem is a system in which we group by eights. Using this system, how would you count the following elements?

Since we are grouping by sets of eight, we would count 1, 2, 3, 4, 5, 6, 7, 8, draw a figure round this set, and record a 1 to represent the set of eight. There are two left over, so this number would be recorded as a 2. The completed numeral is 12_{eight}. The 1 stands for one set of eight, the 2 stands for two ones, and the subscript reminds us that we are grouping in base eight. How can we record the following items in base eight?

How many sets of eight are there? (Three.) How many ones? (Three.) The number, then, would be recorded as 33_{eight}. Now let's examine the octal numeration table that follows.

Octal Grouping	Octal Notation	Octal Name
•	1	one
••	2	two
•••	3	three
••••	4	four
•••• •	5	five
•••• ••	6	six
•••• •••	7	seven
•••• ••••	10_{eight}	one-zero base eight
•••• •••• •	11_{eight}	one-one base eight
•••• •••• ••	12_{eight}	one-two base eight
•••• •••• •••	13_{eight}	one-three base eight
•••• •••• ••••	14_{eight}	one-four base eight
•••• •••• •••• •	15_{eight}	one-five base eight
•••• •••• •••• ••	16_{eight}	one-six base eight
•••• •••• •••• •••	17_{eight}	one-seven base eight
•••• •••• •••• ••••	20_{eight}	two-zero base eight

We have developed base five and base eight for two-digit numerals. Now let's consider the third place. In base five the first column was used to record the number of ones, and the second column was used to record the number of groups, or sets, of five. What meaning does a numeral have in the third place? As soon as five ones are counted, they are recorded as 1 in the fives column, or the second place. This indicates one set of five. What happens when we count five sets of five? Five sets of five are written as 100_{five}. The third column, then, is used to record the number of sets of twenty-five.

TWENTY-FIVES	FIVES	ONES
1	0	0

$$100_{five} = 25_{ten}$$
100_{five} is 1 set of 25
no sets of 5
no sets of 1

What does 123_{five} mean? It means 1 set of 25, 2 sets of five, and 3 ones, or 38_{ten} $(25 + 10 + 3 = 38)$.

What value would the third column have in base eight? The first column is used to record the number of ones, and the second column the number of sets of eight. The third column, then, would be used to record the number of sets of eight times eight, or 64. Eight sets of eight would be written 100_{eight}. This means 1 set of 64, no sets of eight, and no ones.

SIXTY-FOURS	EIGHTS	ONES
1	0	0

$$100_{eight} = 64_{ten}$$

Actually, we use many bases other than 10 on a day-to-day basis; for instance:

2 dozen and 3 eggs are 27 eggs or $23_{twelve} = 27_{ten}$
3 weeks and 4 days are 25 days or $34_{seven} = 25_{ten}$
1 hour and 8 minutes are 68 minutes or $18_{sixty} = 68_{ten}$
2 quarters, 1 nickel, 4 pennies are 59 cents or $214_{five} = 59_{ten}$

A number system can be developed using any method of grouping. The base indicates the number of items grouped as one set. The following table indicates the notation for numeration systems based on various groupings.

Base Ten	Base Twelve	Base Eight	Base Five	Base Three	Base Two
1	1	1	1	1	1
2	2	2	2	2	10_{two}
3	3	3	3	10_{three}	11_{two}
4	4	4	4	11_{three}	100_{two}
5	5	5	10_{five}	12_{three}	101_{two}
6	6	6	11_{five}	20_{three}	110_{two}
7	7	7	12_{five}	21_{three}	111_{two}
8	8	10_{eight}	13_{five}	22_{three}	1000_{two}
9	9	11_{eight}	14_{five}	100_{three}	1001_{two}
10	T	12_{eight}	20_{five}	101_{three}	1010_{two}
11	E	13_{eight}	21_{five}	102_{three}	1011_{two}
12	10_{twelve}	14_{eight}	22_{five}	110_{three}	1100_{two}
13	11_{twelve}	15_{eight}	23_{five}	111_{three}	1101_{two}
14	12_{twelve}	16_{eight}	24_{five}	112_{three}	1110_{two}
15	13_{twelve}	17_{eight}	30_{five}	120_{three}	1111_{two}
16	14_{twelve}	20_{eight}	31_{five}	121_{three}	10000_{two}
17	15_{twelve}	21_{eight}	32_{five}	122_{three}	10001_{two}
18	16_{twelve}	22_{eight}	33_{five}	200_{three}	10010_{two}
19	17_{twelve}	23_{eight}	34_{five}	201_{three}	10011_{two}
20	18_{twelve}	24_{eight}	40_{five}	202_{three}	10100_{two}
21	19_{twelve}	25_{eight}	41_{five}	210_{three}	10101_{two}
22	$1T_{twelve}$	26_{eight}	42_{five}	211_{three}	10110_{two}
23	$1E_{twelve}$	27_{eight}	43_{five}	212_{three}	10111_{two}
24	20_{twelve}	30_{eight}	44_{five}	220_{three}	11000_{two}
25	21_{twelve}	31_{eight}	100_{five}	221_{three}	11001_{two}

Note the column for base twelve. How many numerals would be needed for a base-twelve numeration system? (Twelve.) We cannot represent all twelve by using base-ten numerals, because base ten has only ten one-digit numerals. Consequently we must invent two new symbols. In this case, we have chosen to use T and E as one-digit numerals to represent sets or groupings of ten and eleven.

Considering the previous discussion, the numeration table, and our knowledge of the base-ten system, we can make the following generalizations about the nature of place-value numeration systems using any base.

1. The first column on the right is always the ones place in any base system.
2. The second column is always used to record the groupings named by the base. In base five the second place is called the fives place. In base eight the second place is called the eights place. In base ten the second place is called the tens place.
3. The third column is always used to record the number of groupings named by the square of the base. In base five the third place is for the number of sets of twenty-five (5^2). In base eight

the third place is for the number of sets of sixty-four (8^2). In base ten the third place is for the number of sets of 100 (10^2).

4. The numeral that records the number named by the base is always 10. In base five, 10_{five} stands for one set of five. In base eight, 10_{eight} stands for one set of eight.

5. The number of symbols used in any whole-number numeration system is the same as the base of the system. Base five uses a set of five symbols, which could be {0, 1, 2, 3, 4}. Base eight uses a set of eight symbols, which could be {0, 1, 2, 3, 4, 5, 6, 7}. Base ten uses a set of ten symbols: {0, 1, 2, 3, 4, 5, 6, 7, 8, 9}.

Using these generalizations we can develop a base-two, or binary, system. We know that we will need how many symbols? (Two. We are constructing a base-two system.) We know that one of the symbols will have to be a 0. Why? (Because our binary system has place value.) Let's use the symbols 0 and 1. Let's name the following set in binary notation.

First we want to record the number of ones in the ones place, so we draw a figure round all the possible groups of two.

There is one 1 left over to record in the ones column. What will we record in the next column? (The number of sets of two.) How many sets of two are there? (Two.) But 2 is not a numeral in our base-two system. What about the third column? What is recorded there? (The number of sets grouped according to the square of the base. In this case, 2^2, or 4.) How many sets of four are there? (One.)

From this diagram, we see that we have 1 set of four, 0 sets of two, and 1 set of one. We can now write the base-two numeral as 101_{two}.

In the binary system the values of the places are shown by this diagram:

sixteen(2^4)	eight(2^3)	four(2^2)	two(2^1)	one

Note that the fourth column is used to record the number of sets of eight and the fifth column the number of sets of sixteen. Drawing on what we have just learned about the binary system, we can now draw up a table of the binary notations for the first twelve numbers.

Decimal Notation	Binary Grouping	Binary Notation
1	●	1
2	●●	10_{two}
3	●● ●	11_{two}
4	●● ●●	100_{two}
5	●● ●● ●	101_{two}
6	●● ●● ●●	110_{two}
7	●● ●● ●● ●	111_{two}
8	●● ●● ●● ●●	1000_{two}
9	●● ●● ●● ●● ●	1001_{two}
10	●● ●● ●● ●● ●●	1010_{two}
11	●● ●● ●● ●● ●● ●	1011_{two}
12	●● ●● ●● ●● ●● ●●	1100_{two}

Can we now develop a base-four system? This time let's invent four new symbols instead of borrowing Hindu-Arabic symbols.

Quantity	Symbol
	○
●	/
●●	∠
●●●	△
●●●●	/○

In our notation the first column on the right is used to record the number of ones, the second column to record the number of sets of four, and the third column to record the number of sets of sixteen.

Sixteens	Fours	Ones	Grouping
		/	●
		∠	●●
		△	●●●
	/	○	●●●●
	/	/	●●●● ●
	/	∠	●●●● ●●
	/	△	●●●● ●●●
	∠	○	●●●● ●●●●

(Table continues on next page.)

(Table continued from page 117.)

Sixteens	Fours	Ones	Grouping
	∠	/	•••• • ••••
	∠	∠	•••• •• ••••
	∠	△	•••• ••• ••••
	△	◯	•••• •••• ••••
	△	/	•••• •••• •••• •
	△	∠	•••• •••• •••• ••
	△	△	•••• •••• •••• •••
/	◯	◯	•••• •••• •••• ••••

Now let's again consider our base-ten (decimal) system. It has the same characteristics as systems in other bases. A base-ten system must have ten symbols. We use the ten Hindu-Arabic digits:

0, 1, 2, 3, 4, 5, 6, 7, 8, 9

In the first column on the right (or the first column to the left of the decimal point if the number is written as a decimal), we record the number of ones. In the second column (the tens place) we record the number of sets of ten. In the third column (the hundreds place) we record the number of sets of 100 (10×10, or 10^2).

Thus we see what "place value" means. In a place-value numeration system, the **value** a digit represents depends on the **place** of the digit within the numeral.

Terminology, Symbols, and Procedures

Additive system of numeration   In the additive system of numeration digits have definite values regardless of the order in which they are written; the value of a numeral is obtained merely by adding together the values of the individual symbols that form the numeral. For example, the Egyptian system and, to a more limited extent, the Roman were additive systems.

Base   The base of any place-value numeration system is determined by the method of grouping in that system. The **base-ten** system groups by **tens**. This means that when we reach a count of 9 ones, the next number will be recorded as 1 set of ten:

1 0

one set _____↑ ↑_____ no sets
of ten   of ones

More than 9 sets of ten is recorded as one set of 10×10, or 100:

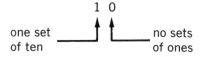

one set
of 10×10, or ———↑ ↑ ↑——— no ones
100   │
                    no tens

In a **base-five** system we group by **fives.** We can count 4 ones, and the next number is recorded as

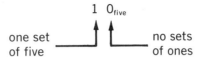

Five sets of five is recorded as

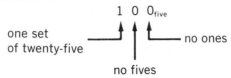

The base-two system is sometimes called the **binary** system, and the base-eight system, the **octal** system.

Decimal system A decimal system is a place-value numeration system in which 10 is the basis for grouping.

Dienes Blocks or multi-base blocks These are a set of blocks designed to represent one cube, ten cubes, one hundred cubes, and a thousand cubes. These blocks are related to the base-ten system of ones, tens, hundreds, and thousands.

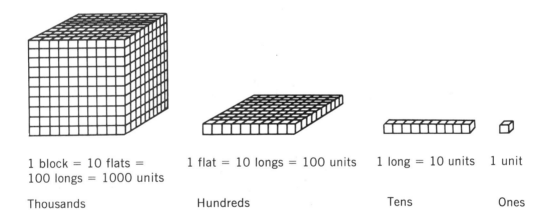

1 block = 10 flats = 100 longs = 1000 units

Thousands

1 flat = 10 longs = 100 units

Hundreds

1 long = 10 units

Tens

1 unit

Ones

(Dienes Blocks are also available in other sizes of blocks to represent bases other than ten. Blocks are available for base five, four, three, and two.)

Multiplicative system of numeration A multiplicative system of numeration represents numbers by symbols in which the values of pairs of numerals are multiplied and added. The ancient Chinese system, for example, was a multiplicative system.

Notation The three ways of expressing a number in base ten are as follows:

Standard notation: 347
Expanded notation: $(3 \times 100) + (4 \times 10) + (7 \times 1)$
Exponential notation: $(2 \times 10^2) + (4 \times 10^1) + (7 \times 10^0)$

Standard notation The conventional method that we use for writing numbers every day is called standard notation. For example, these numbers are written in standard form: $-256, -57, -1342.$

Expanded notation Numbers written in expanded notation are in a form that indicates numerical value and place value in words or by numbers such as 1, 10, 100, or 1000. For example, 275 can be written in expanded notation as 2 hundreds 7 tens 5 ones or as

$$(2 \times 100) + (7 \times 10) + (5 \times 1)$$

Exponential notation Numbers written in a form that indicates the numerical value are in exponential notation. The place value is expressed in powers of ten. For example, 358 can be written in exponential notation as

$$(3 \times 10^2) + (5 \times 10^1) + (8 \times 10^0)$$

Numeration system A system that uses a set of symbols to represent numbers is called a numeration system.

Place-value numeration system A place-value numeration system is one in which the value of a digit is determined by its place in the numeral. Examples of place-value systems include the Babylonian system and the decimal system.

Procedure for translating a numeral in a base other than ten into a base-ten numeral.
1. Set up a place-value grid for the given base.

2. Write the numeral in base ten, using exponential notation.

3. Determine the value of each term in the base-ten numeral.

4. Add the numbers obtained in step 3.

Example: Translate 231_{seven} into a base-ten numeral.

a)

7^3	7^2	7^1	7^0
343	49	7	1

b) $(2 \times 7^2) + (3 \times 7^1) + (1 \times 7^0) = (2 \times 49) + (3 \times 7) + (1 \times 1)$

c) $98 + 21 + 1$

d) 120

Procedure for translating a base-ten numeral into a numeral in some base other than ten.
1. Set up a place-value grid showing the value for each place in the grid.

2. Compare the base-ten numeral with this place-value grid to determine how many sets are to be counted in each place.

Example: Translate 120 into a base-seven numeral.

7^3	7^2	7^1	7^0
343	49	7	1

Questions to be considered:
a) If I have 120 items, can a set of 343 items be made? The answer would be no.
b) If I have 120 items, can a set of 49 items be made? The answer would be yes. The next question would be: how many sets of 49 would there be? The answer would be two: 2×7^2.
c) If two sets of 49 are made, how many items are left over? The answer would be that 22 items are left over.
d) How many sets of 7^1 can be made from the set of 22 items? The answer would be three: 3×7^1.
e) One item is left over from the 22 items. How many sets of 1 can be made from 1? The answer would be 1: 1×7^0.
f) Combining this information, we can see that:
$$120_{ten} = (2 \times 7^2) \times (3 \times 7^1) + (1 \times 7^0)$$
$$= 231_{seven}$$

Procedure for reading any number in the base-ten numeration system.
1. Begin reading the number from the left-hand side.
2. Read the number in the first period on the left; then say the period name.
3. Continue this process one period at a time from left to right until all periods have been read.

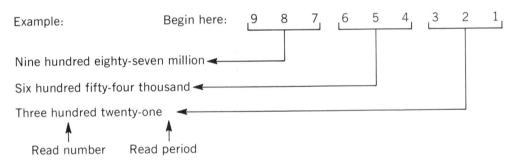

Example: Begin here:

Nine hundred eighty-seven million

Six hundred fifty-four thousand

Three hundred twenty-one

Read number   Read period

Zero power If a number other than 0 is raised to the zero power, the result is equal to 1. For example:

$$1^0 = 1 \qquad 999^0 = 1$$
$$289^0 = 1 \qquad n^0 = 1 \ (n \neq 0)$$

Practice Exercises

1. State the number of tens, hundreds, and ones for each of the following numbers:

a) 423   d) 1365
b) 79   e)   37
c) 382   f) 963

Note: Some elementary textbooks make the mistake of asking children how many tens are in 123 and then state that the answer is 2; 2 is the number in the tens place, but there are 12 tens in 123.

2. What number is in the tens place in 578? How many tens are in the number 578?

3. What number is in the hundreds place in 2481? How many hundreds are in the number 2481?

4. What number is in the ones place in 386? How many ones are in the number 386?

5. Using Dienes Blocks, state the least number of pieces necessary to represent each number. Then state the blocks that should be used.

   a)   214   d)   563
   b) 2496   e)   731
   c)   63   f) 3867

6. List four characteristics of our base-ten place-value system.

7. Write each number three ways, using expanded notation (using words, exponents, and numbers only).

   a)   197   d) 476
   b)   59   e)   38
   c) 7526   f) 314

8. State all the possible ways that Dienes Blocks can be used to represent the number 123.

9. Write the decimal equivalent of each of the following numerals.

a)   b)   c)   d) MCCLXXIX

e)   f)   g) MMDCCCXLIX

10. Tell how you would read each of the following numerals.

    a) 35_{eight} b) 87_{nine} c) 40_{five} d) 432_{ten}

11. Explain why it would not be good to read 125_{twelve} as "one hundred twenty-five, base twelve."

12. Using proper base grouping, name the number represented by the tally marks.

//////////////////////

    a) ——————— eight   c) ——————— two   e) ——————— nine
    b) ——————— twelve   d) ——————— five   f) ——————— four

13. a) If you wanted to "invent" a base-sixteen numeration system, how many basic symbols would you need?

b) Develop a numeration system with a base of sixteen; then list the first twenty counting numbers.

14. In the number 9843 the four represents a value how many times as great as the eight?

15. Make a place-value grid showing the first five places in base 2, base 3, base 4, base 5, base 6, base 7, base 8, base 9, and base 12.

Base 2

		2^2	2^1	2^0
			2	1

16. Use the symbol b for base and use exponents to write a place-value sentence that you can apply to any base system. Make the sentence for at least ten places.

17. Write the five consecutive numerals in the base indicated after each number.

a) 21_{nine}

b) 14_{five}

c) 101_{two}

d) TE_{twelve}

e) 1005_{seven}

f) 535_{eight}

g) 1088_{nine}

h) 1212_{three}

i) 233_{four}

18. Complete the table by writing each numeral in standard notation, in expanded notation, and in exponential notation.

Standard Notation	Expanded Notation	Exponential Notation
101101_{two}		
1234_{five}		
3765_{eight}		
three	$(2 \times 100)_{three} + (1 \times 10)_{three}$ $+ (2 \times 1)_{three}$	
seven	$(6 \times 1000)_{seven} + (4 \times 10)_{seven}$ $+ (5 \times 1)_{seven}$	
six		$(5 \times 10^3)_{six} + (2 \times 10^2)_{six}$ $+ (1 \times 10^1)_{six} + (4 \times 10^0)_{six}$
four		$(2 \times 10^2)_{four} + (1 \times 10^1)_{four}$ $+ (2 \times 10^0)_{four}$
$12TE_{twelve}$		
nine	$(8 \times 1000)_{nine} + (6 \times 100)_{nine}$ $+ (4 \times 10)_{nine}$	

19. Count in each base shown below by writing the numerals in the table.

Base ten	Base nine	Base eight	Base seven	Base six	Base five	Base four	Base three	Base two
0								
1								
2								
3								
4								
5								
6								
7								
8								
9								
10								
11								
12								
13								
14								
15								
16								
17								
18								
19								
20								
21								
22								
23								
24								
25								

20. a) A system for naming numbers in which a digit receives its value from where it is placed is called a _____ system.
    b) The number that indicates the number of objects that can be grouped together in a number system is called the _____.
    c) Any number (except zero) to the power zero is equal to _____.
    d) In any place-value system a numeral may be written in _____ notation, _____ notation, or _____ notation.
    e) In a base-ten system, the basic symbols used to name numbers are called _____.

21. Write in words how each of the following base-ten numbers is read.

    a) 345, 768, 231
    b) 800, 172, 438, 410
    c) 21, 478, 000
    d) 7, 000, 402, 008
    e) 403, 003, 500, 010
    f) 1, 001, 001, 001, 001, 001
    g) 73, 403, 201, 100, 907
    h) 243, 000, 000, 657, 200, 400
    i) 56, 020, 040, 060, 050, 040, 030, 020
    j) 700, 000, 000, 000, 000, 000, 700

* 22. Study these numerals written in base nine and base three.

$$578_{nine} = 122122_{three}$$
$$483_{nine} = 112210_{three}$$
$$56_{nine} = 1220_{three}$$
$$3452_{nine} = 10111202_{three}$$

Can you discover a pattern that will permit you to convert quickly from a base-nine numeration system to a base-three system without changing to base ten?

Discussion Questions

1. Analyze elementary-school mathematics textbooks, isolating all instances where place value is used; then make a list of your findings.

2. Discuss the importance of place value in the elementary-school mathematics program.

3. Discuss the relationship between patterning and place value.

4. Research an ancient numeration system not described in this book, and present your findings to the class.

5. Discuss the implications of the Piagetian theory of four levels of development on the teaching of place value. When is a child ready to learn place value, according to Piagetian theory?

6. What portion of the elementary-school mathematics program should be devoted to number systems with bases other than base ten?

7. Make a list of materials that can be used for teaching place value to children.

8. Make a list of place-value teaching procedures for each of the four levels of development: concrete, semiconcrete, semiabstract, and abstract.

9. Research the names for very large and very small numbers in our base-ten system of numeration. Name 35 places to the left and to the right of the decimal point.

10. Research the historical development of the Hindu-Arabic numeration system, and present your findings to the class.

---

*Asterisks are used throughout the text to indicate the more difficult exercises.

Activities for the Primary Grades

The development of the concept of place value is very important, beginning in the first grade with the base-ten (decimal) system. As soon as children learn two-place numbers they should be introduced to place value. Begin with two-place numbers and continually expand the number of places at each grade level until the children are able to generalize and use a place-value system. At the primary level we will be concerned with the structure of our place-value system—understanding, extending, expanding, and comparing what is discovered at each successive step.

Once they reach the intermediate level, some children may want to look beyond the base-ten system and apply the knowledge they have gained through experience to other systems. Children are often curious about the past. They are often interested in knowing what happened before and after a particular event.

We should give children an opportunity to apply some of the mathematical concepts they learn to situations that will allow them to think analytically and creatively. Ancient numeration systems provide a mental transition for children that should arouse not only curiosity about mathematics but curiosity about history as well. Ancient systems of numeration may be presented as part of a social studies unit, integrating mathematics and social studies. The geographical, social, and economic structure of particular societies may be analyzed so that children can compare these systems from a broader perspective and realize that our system isn't the "one and only," that we might well have had another system, and that we had a great deal of work done for us by ancient cultures we read about in history books.

COUNTING AND RECORDING

1. Take any length of rope or heavy cord and tie a knot in the rope for each child. The length of the rope will depend on the size of the class. Have each child hold a knot and discuss the one-to-one correspondence of children to knots in the rope. This activity can be used effectively by taking the class on a walk; variations can be done using additional rope and "leftovers."

2. Study the following chart and compare the numerals. Can you find any interesting patterns? Can you think of places or objects where you have seen these numerals used?

Hindu-Arabic	Roman	Hindu-Arabic	Roman	Hindu-Arabic	Roman
1	I	11	XI	21	XXI
2	II	12	XII	22	XXII
3	III	13	XIII	23	XXIII
4	IV	14	XIV	24	XXIV
5	V	15	XV	25	XXV
6	VI	16	XVI	26	XXVI
7	VII	17	XVII	27	XXVII
8	VIII	18	XVIII	28	XXVIII
9	IX	19	XIX	29	XXIX
10	X	20	XX	30	XXX

3. a) What Hindu-Arabic numeral do we write for the following Roman numerals?

III_____ XX_____ XV_____ IV_____ XII_____ VIII_____
XIX_____ IX_____ XXVI_____ XIX_____ XXI_____ I_____

b) Fill in the blanks.

18 = 10 + 8	→	XVIII = X + VIII
14 = 10 + _____	→	XIV = X + _____
25 = 20 + _____	→	XXV = XX + _____
37 = 30 + _____	→	XXXVII = XXX + _____
39 = 30 + _____	→	XXXIX = XXX + _____

Do you notice any similarities between the expanded form of the Hindu-Arabic numerals and the expanded form of the Roman numerals?

GROUPING AND PLACE VALUE

1. Place ten objects on a table. Have one child count the objects while another places a tally mark on the chalkboard as each object is counted. Have the children think about the various ways we could group these objects. Encourage them to express some of these ways, such as ten sets of one, two sets of five, five sets of two, and so on. Then ask them to think of these ten objects as one set of ten. Ask how a numeral could be written to record this. Discuss the meaning of the number and the identifying numeral.

Extend this kind of activity to help children understand groups of 11 through 19, 20 through 29, and so on.

2. Children beginning to work with teen numbers consider them as wholes and not as tens and ones. Each child should have three sets of small cards (2″ by 3″) with one digit written on each card. To do this exercise, children should have had experience matching a digit card with its sets.

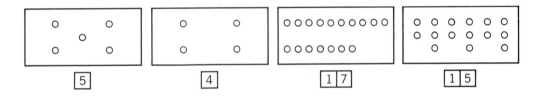

3. Lay out two sheets of paper. "ONES" should be printed on one sheet and "TENS" printed on the other. Each child should place the *ones* sheet on his right and the *tens* sheet on his left. You may use the overhead projector with a transparency showing *ones* on the right-hand side and *tens* on the left.

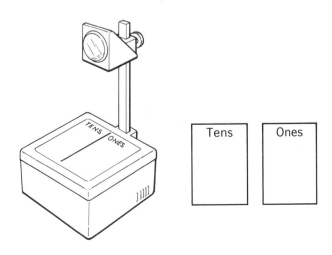

Children may also use small orange juice cans labeled as *ones* and *tens*.

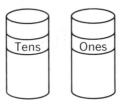

Using the labeled sheets of paper, count objects as they are laid on the *ones* sheet. Use objects that children are familiar with, such as plastic forks or spoons.

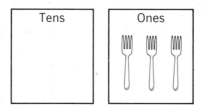

When ten forks are in the ones place, talk about one set of ten and ten sets of one. How are they different? How are they the same?

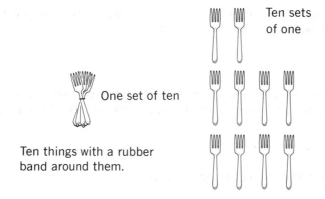

One set of ten

Ten things with a rubber band around them.

Ten sets of one

4. Now relate the numeral cards to the sets shown on the papers by having the children lay the correct numeral card on the ones and the tens sheets.

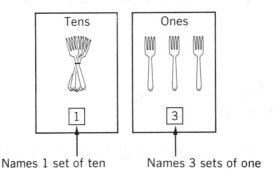

Names 1 set of ten   Names 3 sets of one

5. Show and discuss how the two numeral cards are brought together to name the number thirteen as

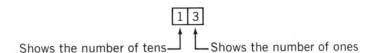

Shows the number of tens—┘   └—Shows the number of ones

6. Children need many experiences reading and seeing numbers in tens and ones.

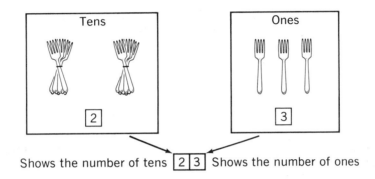

Shows the number of tens [2][3] Shows the number of ones

Do not use an abacus or one fork for a set of ten. Children should see packages of tens with rubber bands around them in the tens place.

7. Place numerals on the overhead projector and have each child lay out the correct number of packages of tens and ones on the place-value papers. The orange juice cans can also be used.

8. Instruct children to loop or ring sets of ten objects.

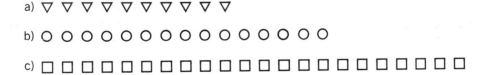

a) ▽ ▽ ▽ ▽ ▽ ▽ ▽ ▽ ▽ ▽

b) ○ ○ ○ ○ ○ ○ ○ ○ ○ ○ ○ ○ ○ ○

c) □

9. How many sets of ten?

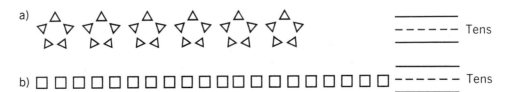

a) _____ Tens

b) _____ Tens

10. How many tens and ones? Loop the sets of ten and write how many tens and ones.

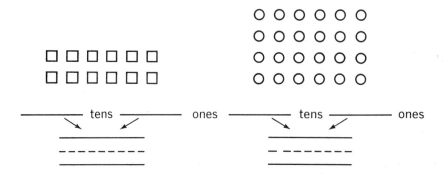

11. Numeral expanders are excellent devices for children to manipulate and for teachers to demonstrate the meaning of place value. The number 124 can be viewed in many different ways; following are two types of numeral expanders:

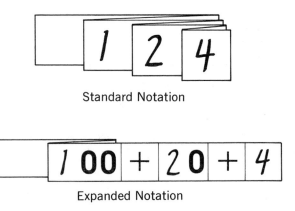

Standard Notation

$$100 + 20 + 4$$

Expanded Notation

The number 124 can be thought of in many different ways.

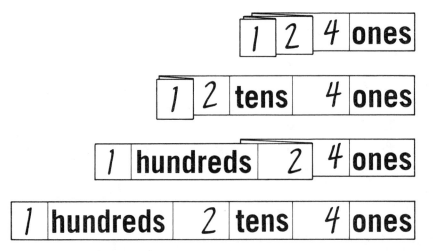

Note: Numeral expanders with a manual can be purchased directly from James Heddens, Department of Education, Kent State University, Kent, Ohio 44242.

12. Name the tens and ones for each number.

    a) 47 = _____ tens _____ ones
    b) 34 = _____ tens _____ ones
    c) 20 = _____ tens _____ ones
    d)   7 = _____ tens _____ ones

13. Write the numeral for each.

    a) 4 tens 2 ones = _____.
    b) 1 ten   9 ones = _____.
    c) 3 tens 0 ones = _____.
    d) 0 tens 8 ones = _____.

14. Have each child place the correct number of counters in orange juice cans or on the ones and tens sheets in response to an oral direction:

a) "Put out 24 counters."

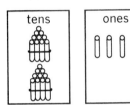

b) "Show 31 counters."

15. Place some counters on the overhead projector and have the children write the numeral.

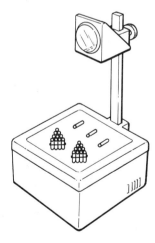

16. Loop the correct numeral for each.

    a) 3 tens 2 ones   23 32 20
    b) 4 tens 6 ones   46 64 60
    c) 1 ten 0 ones   01 10 11

Expanded notation should be used from the very beginning to help the children understand the meaning of the numerals they write. Using folding numeral expanders will help them readily comprehend the concept.

17. Write different numerals for sets.

a)

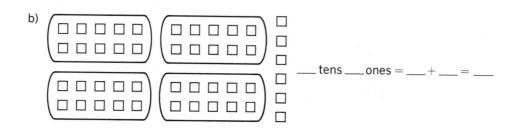

—— ten —— ones = 10 + 4 = 14

b)

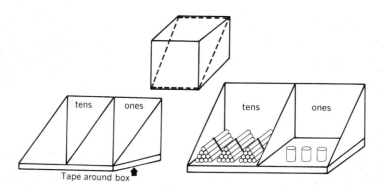

—— tens —— ones = ___ + ___ = ___

18. Children can write numerals for counters put in a place-value box. Cut a box into two along the diagonal. Tape the two half boxes together and label one bin *ones* and the other *tens*.

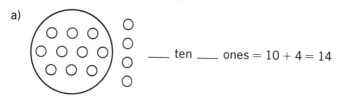

Tape around box

19. Make a set of playing cards to play Rummy. One-fourth of the cards should show sets of tens and ones; one-fourth should show standard notation for the sets; one-fourth should show expanded notation for the sets; and one-fourth should name the tens and ones. For example:

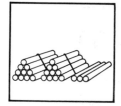

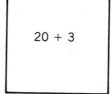

20 + 3

2 tens
3 ones

23

Make twelve sets of four cards for a deck. Play the game like regular Rummy. Remember, games are for drill and not for teaching.

20. Prepare numeral cards from 1 through 99. Allow children to place them on a hundreds board and study the board to locate patterns in the numerals.

	1	2	3	4	5	6	7	8	9
10	11	12	13	14	15	16	17	18	19
20	21	22	23	24	25	26	27	28	29
30	31	32	33	34	35	36	37	38	39
40	41	42	43	44	45	46	47	48	49
50	51	52	53	54	55	56	57	58	59
60	61	62	63	64	65	66	67	68	69
70	71	72	73	74	75	76	77	78	79
80	81	82	83	84	85	86	87	88	89
90	91	92	93	94	95	96	97	98	99

21. Children may use numeral cards to play the Greatest Number game. The cards are randomly dealt among the players. (Begin with two players; then play the game with three or four.) Cards are stacked face down on the table; each child turns over one card at a time. The child with the greatest (or least) value wins the other cards of that round. Cards that are won can be added to the bottom of the winner's pile. At the end of the playing time, the child with the greatest number of cards is the winner.

22. Have four, five, or six children select cards without seeing the numerals on them. Let two children at a time compare cards to see which represents the greatest number; then have all the children hold up their cards and line them up in order from least to greatest. Later in the year, cards can be prepared for the numerals 100 through 999 to be used in the same way.

23. Use sets of numeral cards to review basic concepts developed in Grades 1 and 2.

43	four tens and three ones	40 + 3
34	three tens and four ones	30 + 4
29	two tens and nine ones	20 + 9
92	nine tens and two ones	90 + 2

| 17 | one ten and seven ones | 10 + 7 |
| 71 | seven tens and one one | 70 + 1 |

Ask one child to display his card. Then have all the children holding cards with different names for the same number stand. Vary the activity by displaying the cards in different places around the room. Ask a child to collect all cards that name the number 43, for example. Continue the activity until all cards have been collected.

24. To extend understanding of place value and the meaning of the numbers 1000 through 9999, use prepared numeral cards again—for example, 3051, 3151, 3501, 3115, 3105, 3510, and so on—in the same way they were used for the numbers 1 through 99 and 100 through 999. Always ask for the reasoning behind the selection and comparison. This will present many opportunities to discuss why one way may be more efficient than another. It should be understood that more than one way is correct, but that one way may be the most efficient.

25. Write numerals for each number.

    a) 7 tens 3 ones = _____.
    b) 9 tens 1 one = _____.
    c) 1 hundred 6 tens 4 ones = _____.
    d) 4 hundreds 5 tens 3 ones = _____.
    e) 5 thousands 8 hundreds 6 tens 2 ones = _____.
    f) 4 thousands 5 hundreds 0 tens 0 ones = _____.

26. Fill each blank with the correct numeral.

    a)   37 = ____ tens ____ ones.
    b)   70 = ____ tens ____ ones.
    c)   387 = ____ hundreds ____ tens ____ ones.
    d)   149 = ____ hundreds ____ tens ____ ones.
    e) 9370 = ____ thousands ____ hundreds ____ tens ____ ones.
    f) 3907 = ____ thousands ____ hundreds ____ tens ____ ones.

27. In the above activity, watch for these common misunderstandings of the place-value concept:

         38 = 30 tens 8 ones.
        164 = 100 hundreds 60 tens 4 ones.
       2728 = 2000 thousands 700 hundreds 20 tens 8 ones.

28. By comparing place value, determine which relation symbol ($<, =, >$) should be placed in each $\bigcirc$. Have the children explain their reasoning for selecting the symbol.

    a) 76 $\bigcirc$ 67   c) 58 $\bigcirc$ 57   e) 357 $\bigcirc$ 357   g) 4554 $\bigcirc$ 4544

    b) 456 $\bigcirc$ 546   d) 203 $\bigcirc$ 302   f) 409 $\bigcirc$ 410   h) 3000 $\bigcirc$ 4000

29. Write several rows of numerals on the chalkboard. Then have children write them (or respond orally) in order: (1) from least to greatest (2) from greatest to least.

a) 69, 68, 70
b) 530, 503, 350
c) 354, 453, 534

d) 989, 999, 1009
e) 346, 364, 436
f) 765, 756, 675, 657

g) 1028, 1258, 342, 585, 854
h) 5021, 512, 5200, 520, 5102

30. Complete the table.

Numbers	Hundreds	Tens	Ones
306			
	6	0	3
596			
		3	2
956			
823			

31. Relate pennies and dimes to the numeral and place value of ones and tens. One dime is one ten. Ten pennies has the same value as one dime.

Hand-Held Calculator Activities for the Primary Grades

1. Discuss with the children how each number key that is pressed causes the digit on the display screen to move over one place in place value. For example, place a 1 on the display screen; discuss that this 1 is in the ones place. Strike the 0 key and now the 1 has moved over to the tens place. The 1 now means one set of ten. Demonstrate the concept with a set of plastic spoons—one spoon, ten sets of one, and one set of ten.

2. Use a felt-point pen to print numbers on childrens' finger nails indicating which finger should be used on each number key. A right-handed child should have 1, 4, and 7 written on the index finger; 3, 6, and 9 written on the ring finger; and 2, 5, and 8 written on the second finger. Help children use the proper finger on each of the keys. Children should be encouraged not to watch the key board but to watch the display instead. Have the children put 14714714 on the screen without looking at the key board. Try 25825825 and 36936936.

3. Place a 9 on the display screen and then add 1. What happens on the display screen? Discuss the place value. Place 99 on the screen and then add 1. Discuss the place value. Later you may also want to try 999 add 1.

4. Demonstrate expanded notation on the calculator. If 10 + 3 is entered into the calculator, when the equal key is struck 13 will appear on the display screen. What number is 30 + 7? Strike the equal key to verify your guess.

Microcomputer Activities for the Primary Grades

1. Use the calculator activities for primary children on a microcomputer in the immediate mode.

2. Make a walk-on keyboard for the digits on a microcomputer. Using a plasticized roll of shelf paper, mark it into rectangles to represent the keys in the top row of the computer. Have children take turns walking on the walk-on keyboard and typing on the computer.

3. Children who are typing on the computer key board can learn to keyboard. With a felt-point pen write the number on the child's finger nail that relates to that particular key. Write 1 on the left-hand little finger and continue through to 0 written on the right-hand little finger. Remember the index finger on each hand will be assigned to two keys.

4. Try this microcomputer program with children.

```
10   REM—PLACE VALUE ONES AND TENS—
20   CLS (use the clear screen command for your computer)
30   PRINT:PRINT:PRINT "THIS IS A PLACE VALUE PROGRAM."
40   PRINT:PRINT:PRINT "I WILL GIVE YOU A NUMBER LIKE 24 AND"
50   PRINT"YOU TELL ME HOW MANY ONES AND HOW MANY TENS."
60   READ A, B, C
70   IF A = 99999 THEN GOTO 1000
80   PRINT:PRINT:PRINT" HOW MANY ONES IN ";A;
90   INPUT F
100 IF F =B THEN PRINT "CORRECT"
110 IF F<>B THEN PRINT "TRY AGAIN":GOTO 80
120 PRINT:PRINT:PRINT"HOW MANY TENS IN ";A;
130 INPUT P
140 IF P = C THEN PRINT "CORRECT"
150 IF P<> C THEN PRINT "TRY AGAIN ":GOTO 120
160 FOR T = 1 TO 2000 :NEXT T
170 GOTO 60
180 DATA 24,4,2,78,8,7,46,6,4,29,9,2,53,3,5,18,8,1
190 DATA 91,1,9,37,7,3,62,2,6,97,7,9,99999,1,1
1000 PRINT "THAT IS THE END OF THE PROGRAM .": END
```

Different numbers can easily be used by changing the DATA line. More DATA lines can also be used. The program could be enhanced and made more friendly very easily.

Activities for the Intermediate Grades

COUNTING AND RECORDING

The study of systems of numeration other than our own emphasizes the structure of our decimal system and the meaning of our numerals by comparison and contrast. The study of place value and the examination of the strengths and weaknesses of several systems of numeration sharpen children's interest in the history of our Hindu-Arabic numerals and the development of decimal numeration.

1.

HINDU-ARABIC	1	10	100	1000	10,000
EGYPTIAN					

Write a Hindu-Arabic numeral for each Egyptian numeral.

a)

b)

c)

d)

e)

f)

Write an Egyptian numeral for each Hindu-Arabic numeral.

g) 123_____
h) 24_____
i) 1001_____
j) 1111_____
k) 223_____
l) 1214_____

2. Complete the table.

ROMAN NUMERALS	I		III		V		VII		IX		XI	
HINDU-ARABIC NUMERALS		2		4		6		8		10		12

3. Write three different names for these numbers. One of the three names must be a Roman numeral.

6   14   21   29   34   35

4. Write the Roman numeral for: 300 _____   92 _____   505 _____

Write the Hindu-Arabic numeral for: CI _____   CDXX _____   XCIX _____

5. Write the correct symbol (<, >, or =) in each circle to make true statements.

a) XXX ◯ III

b) 23 ◯ XXXII

c) IV ◯ IV

d) XXXIV ◯ 30 + 4

e) 20 + 6 ◯ XXIV

f) XXXIX ◯ XXXI

g) IX ◯ 10 − 1

h) XVII ◯ 7 + 10

6. Use expanded notation to help you compare each pair of numerals.

a) $10 + 7 = $ _____ $X + VII = $ _____	**c)** $23 = 20 + 3$ _____ $= $ _____ $+ III$

b) $XXX + VI = $ _____ _____ $+ 6 = $ _____	**d)** $XIX = $ _____ $+ $ _____ _____ $+ $ _____ $= 19$

7. Complete the tables.

HINDU-ARABIC NUMERAL	EXPANDED NOTATION	ROMAN NUMERAL	ROMAN NUMERAL	EXPANDED NOTATION	HINDU-ARABIC NUMERAL
13	$10 + 3$	XIII	XVII	$10 + 7$	17
49	___ $+$ ___	XLIX	XL	___ $-$ ___	40
14	_____	_____	XVIII	_____	_____
52	_____	_____	LX	_____	_____
15	_____	_____	XIX	_____	_____
28	_____	_____	XXXIX	_____	_____
16	_____	_____	XX	_____	_____
73	_____	_____	XLIV	_____	_____
21	_____	_____	XXIII	_____	_____
70	_____	_____	XLIX	_____	_____

8. Color green each balloon with a numeral representing a number less than 10; color red each balloon with numerals represented by numbers between ten and twenty; color yellow each balloon with numerals representing numbers between thirty and forty.

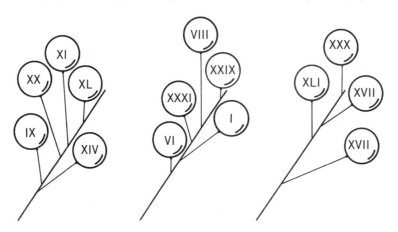

9. Suppose that a recent excavation near Rome unearthed a secret code that was "cracked" after the code-breakers found a translation from Roman numerals to Roman letters. Using English letters and Hindu-Arabic numerals for our example, can you break the code?

a-6	g-89	m-40	s-329	y-77
b-63	h-8	n-980	t-39	z-98
c-41	i-146	o-981	u-1	
d-56	j-230	p-1584	v-232	
e-23	k-240	q-78	w-800	
f-1500	l-564	r-2	x-802	

Number	DLXIV	XXIII	XXXIX	CCCXXIX	VIII	VI
Letter	___	___	___	___	___	___
	CCXXXII	XXIII	VI	LXIII	CXLVI	LXXXIX
	___	___	___	___	___	___
	MDLXXXIV	CXLVI	XCVIII	XCVIII	VI	
	___	___	___	___	___	

GROUPING AND PLACE VALUE

If a child understands place value in numerals through 9999, he should have no difficulty applying this understanding to five- and six-digit numerals and the numbers represented by these numerals. At the fourth-grade level we are concerned with evaluating and extending the understanding of place value that was developed at the primary level.

1. Make a number tray from half-gallon milk containers.

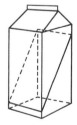

Cut three milk containers as shown. Tape them together to make a number tray. The whole tray may be covered with self-adhesive plastic.

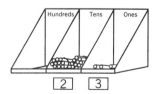

Label the sections to correspond to the place values in the base-ten system. Make three sets of numeral cards with digits from 0 through 9 on them.

a) Place numeral cards in front of each section of the number tray. Then ask a child to place single straws and bundles of ten straws in the tray to show the number indicated by the cards.

b) Place single straws and bundles of straws in the number tray and have a child locate the numeral cards and place them in front of the proper place-value section.

2. Construct several 10×10 grids, several 1×10 grids, and several 1×1 squares for children to manipulate.

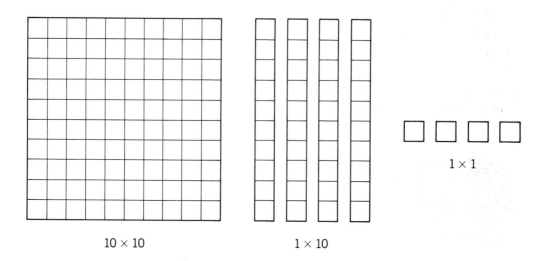

10×10 1×10 1×1

Have the children manipulate these grids to help them understand place value. If Dienes Blocks are available, they are excellent for helping children understand place value. Stern Blocks or Cuisenaire rods can also be used to develop place-value concepts.

3. Fill in the numbers to complete each sentence.

a) $2000 + 500 + 60 + 6 = $ _____

b) $1000 + 700 + 70 + 3 = $ _____

c) $4000 + 200 + 30 + 8 = $ _____

d) $7000 + 200 + 80 + 2 = $ _____

e) $5000 + 500 + 90 + 7 = $ _____

f) _____ $+ 200 + 50 + $ _____ $= 3252$

g) $5000 + $ _____ $+$ _____ $+ 8 = 5768$

h) $8000 + $ _____ $+ 0 + $ _____ $= 8108$

4. Numbers may be named many different ways. Name the number of tens two ways. Numeral expanders are an excellent device to use with this concept.

a) $347 = 3$ hundreds 4 *tens* 7 ones or 34 *tens* 7 ones

b) $732 = 7$ hundreds 3 *tens* 2 ones or 73 *tens* 2 ones

c) $1056 = 1$ thousand 5 *tens* 6 ones or 105 *tens* 6 ones

d) $4789 = 4$ thousands 7 hundreds 8 *tens* 9 ones or 4 thousand 78 *tens* 9 ones or 478 *tens* 9 ones

5. Complete the table for standard and expanded notation.

Expanded Notation for Number One Less	Number	Expanded Notation for Number One Greater
		$600 + 40 + 7$
	700	
	899	
$300 + 90 + 0$		
		$400 + 30 + 1$

6. Place the symbols $<, =, >$ in the ◯ between each pair of examples.

a) $3 + 2$ ◯ $4 + 3$ e) $123 + 2$ ◯ $130 - 7$

b) $20 + 4$ ◯ $30 + 3$ f) $300 + 40 + 7$ ◯ $300 + 70 + 4$

c) $19 + 1$ ◯ $20 - 1$ g) $50 + 2$ ◯ $60 - 9$

d) $40 - 1$ ◯ $39 + 1$ h) $100 + 40 + 6$ ◯ 146

7. Dienes Blocks or multi-base blocks should be used with intermediate-grade children. Have a student represent a number using Dienes Blocks; then have each class member write the number for the blocks. Write the number for this block representation:

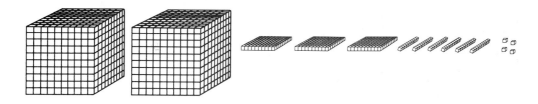

8. Provide the children with numbers written on a worksheet, and have the children model each number using Dienes Blocks. Model each of these examples with Dienes Blocks:

a) 359   b) 641   c) 47   d) 2317

9. Use as many different combinations of Dienes Blocks as you can to represent the number 107.

10. Divide the class into groups for mathematics. Provide each student with a place-value chart with ones, tens, hundreds, and thousands. Children then take turns rolling a pair of dice. At each roll of the dice the child takes from the bank blocks to represent the number that was rolled. All players must continually turn in blocks so that each always has the least number of blocks possible. The first child to obtain a block (representing 1000) is the winner.

11. Draw rings around sets of 5; then fill in the blanks.

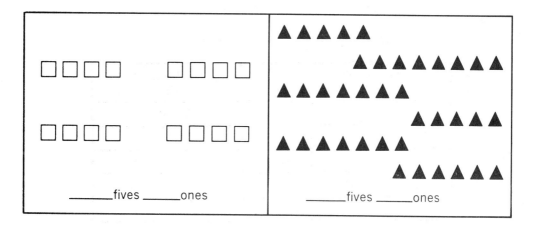

_____fives _____ones   _____fives _____ones

12. With 37 objects I can make

_____ sets of seven and _____ ones left over
_____ sets of eight and _____ ones left over
_____ sets of twelve and _____ ones left over
_____ sets of ten and _____ ones left over
_____ sets of nine and _____ ones left over

13. a) A gum manufacturer has decided to place five sticks of gum in each pack. What base system can be used to describe the packaging process?
   b) What number could be represented by the following pictures of gum?

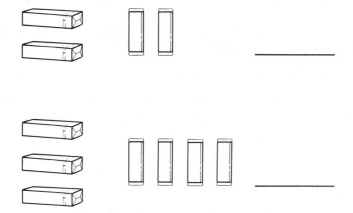

14. Have children toss four beanbags into four large cans. Label one can 125, one can 25, one can 5, and one can 1. As the children toss the beanbags into the cans, have them record the base-five numeral they score.

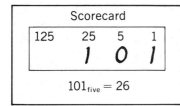

This child would receive a score of 26.

15. Draw a ring around all the numerals that could be used to make each sentence a true statement.

a) 14,621 > _____	14,261	12,421	16,124	14,612
b) 76,543 = _____	76,543	76,435	76,453	76,534
c) 80,010 < _____	81,000	80,100	80,001	80,110
d) 49,052 < _____	49,520	49,025	49,502	49,205
e) 35,093 > _____	35,039	35,930	35,390	35,309

16. a) Write the numeral for the greatest number that can be named with a two-digit numeral that has 7 as one of its digits.
   b) Write the numeral for the least number named with a two-digit numeral that has 3 as one of its digits.
   c) Write the numeral for the greatest number named with a four-digit numeral that has 3 as one of its digits.
   d) Write the numeral for the greatest number named with a four-digit numeral that has 4 as one of its digits.
   e) Write the numeral for the least number named with a three-digit numeral that has 0 as one digit.

17. a) One hundred is _____ tens.   c) One thousand is _____ hundreds.
    b) One thousand is _____ tens.   d) _____ thousands is one million.

18. In deciding what relation symbol should be used between each pair of numerals, first compare place value. Write the proper symbol in the $\bigcirc$, and then give the place value of the digit that helped you decide.
   Example: 83762 $\ominus$ 83672—hundreds place

   a) 342,432 $\bigcirc$ 345,342   d)   90,999 $\bigcirc$ 90,909
   b)   68,723 $\bigcirc$ 67,832   e) 505,525 $\bigcirc$ 502,555
   c) 234,572 $\bigcirc$ 245,372   f)   89,901 $\bigcirc$ 89,899

Hand-Held Calculator Activities for the Intermediate Grades

1. Have the children carefully observe what happens as they enter digits into the hand-held calculator. Enter the number 123 into the calculator. Push the 1 key; the 1 is placed in the ones place. Next push the 2 key; the 1 immediately moves to the tens place, and the 2 is placed in the ones place. If the 3 key is pushed next, the 1 moves to the hundreds place, the 2 moves to the tens place, and the 3 is then in the ones place. Discuss with the children how the place value changes continually as digits are entered into the calculator.

2. Have the children work in pairs with one calculator between them. One student should enter a large number into the calculator. Now hand the calculator back and forth, and request each child to remove one digit by placing a 0 in its place. As an example, suppose the number 12345 is entered into the calculator. The first child asks the second child to remove the 2. The second child must know that the 2 is in the hundreds place and, to remove the 2, 200 must be subtracted from the number. Now the number becomes 10345. The second child may now request that the first child remove a digit. The children are demonstrating their understanding of place value.

3. Provide many experiences for the children to multiply a given number by 1, 10, 100, 1000, and so on, using a hand-held calculator. Have the children discuss how the place value changes when multiplying by a number with a given number of zeros. For example, multiplying 23 by 1, 10, and 100 changes the place value of the 2 and the 3. Do *not* tell the children that you "add a zero" to the number. When you multiply by 10, the place value is changed. Children usually have a different concept of what adding a zero means.

4. Children need many experiences estimating answers and evaluating whether answers are approximately correct. Require the children to use worksheets to write their estimates, and then use the hand-held calculator to verify whether the estimate is close to the real answer.

5. Rounding numbers requires a student to have a firm grasp of place value. To round 456 to the nearest hundred, the student must know which is the hundreds place and which is the tens place. Have children solve examples using rounded numbers, and then verify that their answers are approximately correct, using the calculator.

Example	Estimated answer	Actual answer
823 + 278	1100	1101
98 × 47	5000	4606
37 × 10	370	370
283 × 100	28300	28300

6. Have children use the expanded form of a number and enter it into the calculator with the proper operations. The results in the display should be the number in standard notation. For example 2000 + 600 + 40 + 7 = 2647. Enter the 2000, the addition sign, the 600, the addition sign, the 40, the addition sign, the 7, and the equals sign. Now the display should read 2647. This will illustrate to the children that place value is used in numbers.

7. Have the children enter one million into their hand-held calculators, so that they know what the number one million looks like. Clear the calculator display. Now enter the number 1000. What number should 1000 be multiplied by to obtain one million again on the display? Have children try their guesses. Provide many such experiences with large numbers so that children begin to realize the relationship that exists among the place values of very large numbers.

8. Have two children work together with their own calculators. Roll a die and have the children enter the digit into any place value they want, in order to obtain the greatest number possible. Only one nonzero digit may be entered into any one place. Roll the die eight times. The student with the greatest number displayed on his calculator wins that round. Continue for a set number of rounds. For example, if the first roll of a die is 4, which place value should that digit be placed in so that the greatest number can be obtained? One child may place the 4 in the millions place and the other child may place the 4 in the thousands place hoping that a greater number will be rolled in the next roll. Since eight rolls are used in each round, each of the eight places on the calculator display will show a number other than zero.

Microcomputer Activities for the Intermediate Grades

Many activities suggested for the hand-held calculator may easily be adapted to the microcomputer in the immediate mode. The teacher should provide many microcomputer experiences for intermediate children in both the immediate and program modes. Place value is an important concept; it is used in every operation with whole numbers and in every operation with rational numbers expressed as decimals. Teachers do not generally devote sufficient instruction time to the concept of place value and do not emphasize place value sufficiently in application. Calculators and microcomputers are excellent ways to reinforce place-value concepts.

1. Teachers may write simple practice microcomputer programs for children. This sample BASIC program will run on most microcomputers, but a few minor adjustments may be necessary for a specific dialect of the language. If you use an Atari microcomputer, you will need to add dimension statements. You may also want to add some color and/or sound.

```
10   REM—PLACE VALUE PRACTICE—
20   CLS
30   ?"GOOD DAY, WHAT IS YOUR NAME"
40   INPUT N$
60   ?"NICE TO KNOW YOU, ";N$;", TODAY WE WILL PRACTICE PLACE VALUE."
70   ?:?:?:?"FOR EACH EXAMPLE TYPE THE PLACE VALUE FOR THE GIVEN NUMBER."
80   ?:?:?:?
90   DATA 3,234,TENS,6,6732,THOUSANDS,4,456,HUNDREDS,
100  DATA 2,832,ONES,9,1792,TENS,0,0,END
110  READ A,C,B$
120  IF A=0 THEN ?"THAT'S ALL!":END
130  ?"WHAT IS THE PLACE VALUE OF THE ";A;" IN THE NUMBER ";C
140  INPUT Z$
145  IF Z$<>B$THEN ?"SORRY, TRY AGAIN!":GOTO 130
150  IF Z$=B$ THEN ?"YOU ARE CORRECT."
160  FOR T=1 TO 2000:NEXT T:CLS:GOTO 110
```

This program is the bare minimum. You may want to enhance the program and make it more friendly. Additional data may be added by including more data statements.

2. You may want to add a counter to this program so it will tell each student how many attempts he or she has needed to complete the entire set of examples. The following statements could be added to the program:

```
25   K=0
110  IF A=0 THEN?"YOU COMPLETED 5 EXAMPLES";?"IT TOOK YOU ";K;" TRIES.":END
135  K=K+1
```

The number 5 in line 110 should correspond to the number of examples you have placed in the program.

3. Children should discuss and experiment with place-value examples. Enter example (a) into your microcomputer. After entering each example, push the RETURN or ENTER key.

   a) ?500+7+90
     The microcomputer will print examples of this type in the proper place value. It makes no difference in which order the numbers are entered. In this example, the computer will print 597.

b) ?8+7000+60+300
The microcomputer will print 7368. Discuss the place value of each digit.

c) ?700+20000+40+1+9000.
The computer will print 29741.

d) ?800000000000+7000+9000000000+5+1000000+3000000000
After the children have experimented with large numbers, you may want to initiate a study of scientific notation or the use of the letter e in a number.

Activities for the Upper Elementary Grades

COUNTING AND RECORDING

1. Make a counting chart to compare the symbols that would be used in base-two, base-five, base-eight, and base-ten systems.

BASE TEN	BASE EIGHT	BASE FIVE	BASE TWO
1	1	1	1
2	2	2	_____
3	_____	_____	_____
4	_____	_____	_____
5	_____	_____	_____
6	_____	_____	_____
7	_____	_____	_____
8	_____	_____	_____
9	_____	_____	_____
10	_____	_____	_____
11	_____	_____	_____
12	_____	_____	_____
13	_____	_____	_____
14	_____	_____	_____
15	_____	_____	_____
16	_____	_____	_____

Can you find any interesting patterns in this chart? Could you make a counting chart for other bases from what you have discovered?

PLACE VALUE

1.

10,000	1000	100	10	1	$\frac{1}{10}$	$\frac{1}{100}$

a) Each place in the grid has _____ times the value of the place to its right.

b) Each place in the grid has _____ times the value of the place to its left.

c) Make a decimal grid and fill in the following numerals.

$$473 \qquad 83,079$$
$$1006 \qquad 20,000.09$$
$$476.54 \qquad 113.27$$

d) Write each numeral in Part c in expanded notation.

e) Write the numeral for the greatest number you can name using only the digits 6, 0, 8, 1, and 2.

f) Write the numeral for the least number you can name using only the digits 9, 8, 7, 4, and 5.

g) Why is it not possible to write a five-place numeral naming a number less than 10,000?

h) Why is it not possible to write a five-place numeral naming a number greater than 99,999?

PLACE VALUE AND OTHER BASES

Place-value systems other than ten are receiving much less emphasis in mathematics programs today than they did ten years ago. A study of other place-value systems in different bases can help you understand some of the difficulties that children have in understanding the decimal system. Bases other than ten are still in some elementary school mathematics programs because of the historical value of studying them and for the children's general information.

In Grades 5 and 6, exponential notation is presented, reinforcing the concept of the decimal system and showing it in a new light.

1. Study the following place-value grid for 142_{five}.

Twenty-fives	Fives	Ones
1	4	2

Make similar place-value grids for each of the following numerals.

a) 34_{five} c) 212_{five} e) 1234_{five} g) 42_{eight}

b) 11_{two} d) 101_{two} f) 1011_{two} h) 643_{eight}

2. a) A traveler went on vacation for two weeks and three days. How many days was he on vacation?

$$23_{seven} = 17_{ten}$$

b) How is the above example related to base seven?

c) 1 week 4 days can be written _____ $_{seven}$ and 11 days can be written 11_____.

d) Complete the following table:

Vacation	Base 7	Base 10	Days
3 weeks 1 day			
	16_{seven}		
			43 days
		17_{ten}	
4 weeks 5 days			
		36_{ten}	
3 weeks 1 day	43_{seven}		
			65 days

3. a) I purchased one dozen eggs and found five eggs in the refrigerator. How many eggs were there altogether?

b) How is the above example related to base twelve?

c) Complete the following table:

Dozen	Base 12	Base 10	Eggs
2 dozen 11 eggs			
	34_{twelve}		
		26_{ten}	
			42 eggs
	19_{twelve}		
3 dozen 7 eggs			
			60 eggs
		36_{ten}	

4. a) A child wanted to buy some candy. He had 2 quarters, 1 nickel, and 4 pennies. How much money did he have?

$214_{five} = 59_{ten}$

b) How is the above example related to base five?

c) Complete the following table:

Coins	Base Five	Base 10	Total Money
1 quarter 2 nickels			
	43_{five}		
		83_{ten}	
			79 cents
	342_{five}		
		42_{ten}	
			92 cents
3 quarters 4 nickels 3 pennies			

5. A light switch in a classroom can be used as a model of the binary numeration system. Assign zero to the "off" position and one to the "on" position. Suppose the light is off and you flick the light switch 2^7 or 128 times. Would this light be on or off? Justify your answer.

6. Encourage the students to create and develop number systems of their own. Students can present their systems to the class for discussion and further exploration.

EXPONENTIAL NOTATION

With proper understanding of place value, grouping, and expanded notation, the use of exponential notation comes naturally at this level. The student is able to see the practical value of exponential notation and has reached the point where he can place it in proper perspective in his thinking.

As one example, have a child write 5,432,216 in expanded notation:

$$5,000,000 + 400,000 + 30,000 + 2000 + 200 + 10 + 6$$

The children will groan—and well they should at this point. Now write the same example in this form:

$$(5 \times 1,000,000) + (4 \times 100,000) + (3 \times 10,000) + (2 \times 1000) + (2 \times 100) + (1 \times 10) + (6 \times 1)$$

Ask the children whether they think this method is any better and why. Give them an opportunity to compare the two forms and to express any pertinent observations they may have. It is possible a child might suggest that there is a still more efficient way of writing the numeral so that the meaning can be understood. However, it is also possible that you may have to initiate the idea in some way.

Begin with 10:

$$10 \times 1 = \underline{\hspace{1cm}}$$
$$10 \times 10 = \underline{\hspace{1cm}}$$
$$10 \times 10 \times 10 = \underline{\hspace{1cm}}$$
$$10 \times 10 \times 10 \times 10 = \underline{\hspace{1cm}}$$

Children will soon see the familiar pattern. Then ask if anyone would like to express an idea about the products written in this form:

$$10^1 \qquad 10^2 \qquad 10^3 \qquad 10^4$$

When the children can make a generalization about what is happening, it will be necessary to explain to them the meanings of the words "base" and "exponent." They can then make these words a part of their vocabularies.

Check their understanding by using various numbers for the base factor and a variety of exponents. When children first begin using exponents, the tendency is to multiply the base factor by the exponent. For example, 5^3 is likely to elicit a response of 15 rather than 125. When this happens, ask the child to write the meaning of the numeral without the exponent: $5 \times 5 \times 5$.

It is also important to establish the fact that the exponent indicates the number of times the base is used as a factor.

1. Chalkboard activity: Write various numerals on the chalkboard.

26	335	4167	53,248
1207	80,933	2979	450

Have children write them in the expanded form. For example, $335 = (3 \times 100) + (3 \times 10) + 5$. See if they can generalize about renaming each numeral using exponents. Let children work examples of their own at the chalkboard, and have other members of the class explain and verify each example.

2. a) Rewrite each of the following using exponents.

   $4 \times 4 \times 4 \times 4 \times 4 \qquad\qquad 5 \times 5 \times 5 \times 5 \times 5 \times 5 \times 5$

   b) In each of the following, how many times is 5 used as a factor?

   $5^3 \qquad\qquad 5^7 \qquad\qquad 5^{10} \qquad\qquad 5^{12} \qquad\qquad 5^{20}$

   c) Rename each of the following numbers without exponents.

   $4^3 \qquad\qquad 3^4 \qquad\qquad 7^7 \qquad\qquad 175^2$

Hand-Held Calculator Activities for the Upper Elementary Grades

Activities from other grade levels may also be used in the upper elementary grades. Activities at this level should include more decimals, exponents, and scientific notation.

1. Use a hand-held calculator to multiply a given number by 1, 10, and 100. Then divide that product by 1, then by 10, 100, 1000, 10000, 100000, and so forth. Study this sequence of examples:

$9 \times 1 =$	$9000 - 1 =$	$9 - 1 =$
$9 \times 10 =$	$9000 - 10 =$	$9 - 10 =$
$9 \times 100 =$	$9000 - 100 =$	$9 - 100 =$
$9 \times 1000 =$	$9000 - 1000 =$	$9 - 1000 =$
	$9000 - 10000 =$	$9 - 10000 =$
	$9000 - 100000 =$	$9 - 100000 =$

2. Use a hand-held calculator to multiply decimal numbers by 1, 10, 100, 1000, etc., and discuss the effect on the numbers. Consider these examples:

a) 3.476 ×	1 =	b)	1 × .0931 =
3.476 ×	10 =		10 × .0931 =
3.476 ×	100 =		100 × .0931 =
3.476 ×	1000 =		1000 × .0931 =
3.476 ×	10000 =		10000 × .0931 =

3. Use a hand-held calculator to add decimal numbers expressed in expanded notation and to see how they are put together into standard notation. Add these examples.

a) .3 + .05 + .007 =
b) .08 + .9 + .001 =
c) .02000 + .00005 + .10000 + .0004 + .00300 =
d) .1 + .02 + .003 + .0004 + .00005
e) 8 + 90 + .70 + .06 =

4. Use a hand-held calculator to solve this sequence of examples. Record your answers. To begin enter the number 0.2456.

0.02456 × 10 = _____ × 10 = _____ × 10 = _____ × 10 = _____ × 10 = _____ × 10 = _____ × 10 = _____ × 10 = _____ − 10 = _____ − 10 = _____ − 10 = _____ − 10 = _____ − 10 = _____ − 10 = _____ − 10 = _____ − 10 = _____ − 10 = _____ − 10 = _____ − 10 = _____ − 10 = _____ − 10 = _____ − 10 = _____ − 10 = _____

Discuss with the children the sequence of answers to these examples. Create other similar examples.

5. Use the hand-held calculator to multiply and divide many different numbers by 10. Use both whole numbers and decimals.

Microcomputer Activities for the Upper Elementary Grades

The previous activities may be used on a microcomputer in the immediate mode. Remember that you must precede any mathematical calculation with the command PRINT; do not use the equals sign. Enter the command and the mathematics example, and then push the RETURN or ENTER key. The computer activities for the intermediate grade level may also be used at the upper elementary grade level.

1. This decimal place-value practice program is easily individualized for a specific student by merely changing the data lines. The first number in the data statement is the number to be studied, the place value is listed second, and the number in that particular place value is listed third. The program may easily be adjusted to fit the particular needs of any student.

```
10    REM—DECIMAL PLACE VALUE PRACTICE—
20    K=0
30    CLS
40    ?"WHAT IS YOUR NAME";
50    INPUT N$
60    CLS
70    ?:?:?:?:?" HI, ";N$;" !"
```

```
80    ?:?:?" ***************"
90    ?:?:?:"TODAY WE WILL PRACTICE DECIMAL PLACE VALUE"
100   GOSUB 1000
110   CLS
120   READ A,B$,C
130   DATA 23.45,TENTHS,4,56.032,TENS,5,3.89,HUNDREDTHS,9,
135   DATA 16.128,THOUSANDTHS,8,91.231,HUNDREDTHS,3,
140   DATA 3.80,TENTHS,8,7.248,ONES,7,42.61,TENS,4,0,V,0
150   ?:?" NO ERRORS PLEASE!!"
160   IF A=0 THEN GOTO 230
170   ?:?:?:?"STUDY THIS NUMBER ",A
180   ?:?"WHAT NUMBER IS IN THE ";B;" PLACE"
190   INPUT Z
200   K=K+1
210   IF Z=C THEN?"GREAT! YOU ARE CORRECT.":GOSUB 1000:GOTO 120
220   IF Z<>C THEN?"SORRY, TRY AGAIN!.":GOSUB 1000:GOTO 170
230   CLS:?"YOU HAVE SOLVED 8 EXAMPLES IN ";K;" TRIES."
240   ?"THANKS, ";N$;" SEE YOU AGAIN SOON!"
999   END
1000  FOR T=1 TO 2000:NEXT T
1010  RETURN
```

2. Teachers can write simple programs as well as provide drill and practice on a micro-computer to help teach a concept. Here is an example of a program to help teach decimal place value. The program may easily be expanded to introduce more decimal places. Additional questions might also be added for more student input.

```
10    REM—TEACHING DECIMAL PLACE VALUE—
15    CLS
20    ?"I DON'T REMEMBER YOUR NAME, PLEASE TYPE IN YOUR NAME"
30    INPUT N$
40    ?:?:?:?:?
41    ?"I WILL HELP YOU ";N$;", LEARN ABOUT DECIMAL PLACE VALUE."
42    GOSUB 5000
45    CLS
50    ?"LET'S FIRST REVIEW PLACE VALUE FOR WHOLE NUMBERS."
55    GOSUB 5000
60    ?:?:?"LOOK AT THE NUMBER 423."
70    ?:?" ***NOTE***"
80    ?:?"THE 3 IS IN THE ONES PLACE."
85    GOSUB 5000
90    ?:?"THE 2 IS IN THE TENS PLACE."
95    GOSUB 5000
100   ?:?"THE 4 IS IN THE HUNDREDS PLACE."
105   GOSUB 5000
110   ?:?"WHAT NUMBER IS IN THE TENS PLACE?"
120   INPUT A
125   IF A=2 THEN?"YOU ARE CORRECT.":GOSUB5000:CLS
126   IF A<>2 THEN?"WRONG! TRY AGAIN.":GOSUB5000:CLS: GOTO 60
130   ?:?:?"THE REFERENCE POINT IS CALLED A DECIMAL POINT. IT IS A PERIOD (.)"
135   GOSUB 5000
140   ?:?:?"LOOK AT THE NUMBER 423."
150   ?:?" ***NOTE ***"
160   ?:?:?"THE DECIMAL POINT AFTER THE 3."
170   ?:?:?"NOW EXAMINE THE NUMBER 423.6"
180   ?:?:?:?"THE NUMBER 423.6 HAS A DECIMAL POINT."
190   ?:?:?:?"THE 6 IS IN THE FIRST PLACE TO THE RIGHT OF THE DECIMAL POINT."
```

```
200  GOSUB 5000
210  ?:?:?" 423.6"
220  ?:?"WE SAY THE 6 IS IN THE TENTHS PLACE."
230  GOSUB 5000
240  ?:?:?:?" ***NOTE***"
250  ?"TENTHS IS THE WORD 'TEN' WITH 'THS' ON THE END."
260  GOSUB 5000:CLS
999  END
5000 FOR T=1 TO 5000:NEXT T
5010 RETURN
```

Suggested Readings

Calvo, Robert C. "Placo—A Number-Place Game." *The Arithmetic Teacher.* vol. 15, no. 1, May 1968.

Dienes, Zoltan P., and Golding, E. W. *Modern Mathematics for Young Children.* New York: Herder & Herder, 1970.

Easterday, Kenneth E. "Teacher-Made Aids for Teaching Place Value and Estimation." *The Arithmetic Teacher.* vol. 25, no. 1, January 1978.

Eves, Howard. *An Introduction to the History of Mathematics.* 4th ed. New York: Holt, Rinehart & Winston, 1976.

Heddens, James W. *Numeral Expanders.* Kent, Ohio: James W. Heddens, 1974.

Pennington, Mary Jane. "Base Ten Trading Game." *The Arithmetic Teacher.* vol. 26, no. 3, March 1979.

Ronshausen, Nina L. "Introducing Place Value." *The Arithmetic Teacher.* vol. 26, no. 1, January 1978.

Smith, Karl J. "Inventing a Numeration System." *The Arithmetic Teacher.* vol. 20, no. 7, November 1973.

Smith, Robert W. "Diagnosis of Pupil Performance on Place-Value Tasks." *The Arithmetic Teacher.* vol. 20, no. 5, May 1973.

Sulkowski, Toni J. "An Approach to Teaching Numeration Systems." *The Arithmetic Teacher.* vol. 25, no. 5, September 1978.

Ziesche, Shirley S. "Understanding Place Value." *The Arithmetic Teacher.* vol. 17, no. 8, December 1970.

6 Addition and Subtraction of Whole Numbers

Teaching Competencies

Upon completing this unit, you will be able to:

State and then demonstrate two different models used to develop an understanding of addition

Construct an addition table and insert the sums into the table according to structures

Model three types of subtraction examples, using sets, the number line, and inverse relationships

Observe two different sets and then write four related addition and subtraction sentences

Use a place-value box and demonstrate regrouping for both addition and subtraction

Write examples to demonstrate three basic properties of addition

Discussion

The previous units have suggested techniques for developing numberness and place value with young children. These two basic ideas form the framework for teaching the concept of addition. Consequently, when teaching addition to children, the first step is to evaluate the children's readiness. The teacher should evaluate conservation of number, seriation, one-to-one correspondence, counting, recognition of numbers, and writing basic numbers. Research supports the concept that addition should also proceed from the concrete level through the semiconcrete, semiabstract, and abstract levels. Two models are used to help children develop an understanding of addition: sets and number line. Many materials are available to use for the concrete level—for example, Cuisenaire rods, Dienes Blocks, and Stern rods. Check the manuals for each of these materials for more detailed instructions about how to use each of these materials with children. Also remember that word problems and problem solving should be included in each step of addition development. Some suggestions will be included in the activities section.

This unit on teaching addition and subtraction is organized around the five basic concepts that must be understood before an individual can solve any addition or subtraction example. These five major organizational areas are: understanding the operation, the basic facts, place value, basic structures, and regrouping. These areas serve not only as a basis for organizing the addition and subtraction program but also as the basis for review at each subsequent grade level.

Now let's begin our study by examining two sets of real objects. Using two separate sheets of paper, place two cubes on one sheet and three cubes on the second sheet.

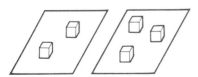

Children now have three available techniques to associate a number with each set. One technique is to count the cubes, a second technique is to use partial counting. In using partial counting, the child recognizes the number of cubes in one set and then, beginning with that number, counts the number of cubes in the second set. A third available technique

is just to associate 2 and 3 with each set, respectively. Children should be encouraged to associate a number with a set without counting. Discourage children from counting at this point. They should look, visualize, and state the number for each set (unless the sets have more than five objects). Counting is *not* adding.

Ask the children to find a card with the proper number on it to fit with each set. Place the number cards under the sets. Then place an additional sheet of paper to the right of the sets, and move the two cubes to that sheet. Move the three cubes onto the new sheet, and ask the children how many cubes there are altogether. Have a child find a card with a number that describes this new set. It is important to stress that two cubes and three cubes are put together to get five cubes. Do *not* use two cubes, three cubes, and another set of five cubes. Put the two cubes with the three cubes to get five cubes. Discourage counting. Children should begin to associate the numbers 2, 3, and 5. After they have had many similar experiences, you can begin to write 2 + 3 = 5. Generally, teachers do not provide adequate experiences before requiring children to write numbers. *Do not rush into writing.*

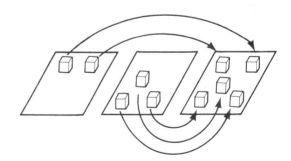

In the operation of addition, the numbers to be added are called **addends,** and the number obtained by adding the addends is called the **sum.**

$$\text{Addend} + \text{Addend} = \text{Sum}$$
or
$$\text{Sum} = \text{Addend} + \text{Addend}$$

The addition operation can be symbolized as $a + b = s$ or $\frac{+b}{s}$, where a and b are addends and s represents the sum. The addition sentence is read "addend add addend equals sum." Addition is a **binary operation** because only two numbers can be added at one time.

The sum of 5 obtained by adding 2 and 3 is **unique** because no other sum can possibly be obtained using the addends 2 and 3.

The set model for addition is on the concrete level if children are actually manipulating the materials. The set model is on the semiconcrete level if the teacher is demonstrating the set model for the children. Remember that the number-line model is on the semiabstract level of development for children.

A second model that is useful in developing understanding of addition is the number line. Recall that a number line is a representation of a geometric line, with arrows at each end to indicate that the line extends in both directions. Two points are marked on the number line, and the resulting line segment is used to mark off congruent segments. These segments determine a series of points on the line, and the points are then named by placing them in one-to-one correspondence with the set of whole numbers.

We can use the number line to model addition examples. To illustrate how this is done, let's solve the example $2 + 3 = \square$. When we use the number line with young children, remember that we always begin modeling at the reference point, zero. From zero we measure a segment two units long. From that point we measure a segment three units long and arrive at the point named 5. Thus the number-line model suggests that $2 + 3 = 5$.

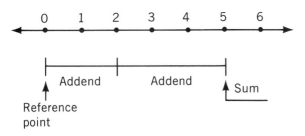

Note that we do not place arrows on the number line segments representing the addends since that indicates a direction; direction is not introduced until the set of integers is introduced.

Models of sets and number line will help children develop an understanding of addition. Remember that each is a model that achieves the same results as addition but is *not* addition. Counting is *not* addition. Partial counting is *not* addition. Putting objects together is *not* addition. Then what is addition?

> Addition is a binary operation performed on a pair of numbers called addends in order to obtain a unique sum.

Place each of the terms and symbols for addition on separate cards.

Addend + Addend = Sum

Place the cards randomly in front of the children, and have them arrange the cards in proper order for an addition sentence. Other cards containing numerals may be placed on the addend and sum cards to relate numbers with the addition sentence.

A **family of numbers** is often used in helping children extend their understanding of addition. A family of numbers includes all possible combinations of addends that will produce a given sum. A family of numbers is used for development and not for memorization of the basic addition facts.

Place a set of cubes and two sheets of paper in front of small groups of children, and ask them to make all possible combinations of two sets. The children should record each of their discoveries.

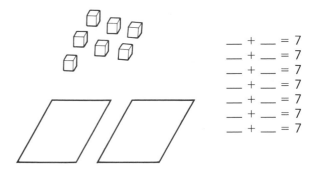

By placing all cubes into two sets, children should discover and write these mathematical relationships:

$1 + 6 = 7$	$5 + 2 = 7$
$2 + 5 = 7$	$6 + 1 = 7$
$3 + 4 = 7$	$7 + 0 = 7$
$4 + 3 = 7$	$0 + 7 = 7$

This set of examples would be called the *family of seven.*

The teacher should develop the children's understanding of addition by using sets and the number line as models. When the children are able to generate families of numbers, they are ready to begin memorizing the **basic addition facts.**

Basic addition facts include all combinations of any one-place whole number (addend) added to any one-place whole number (addend) to obtain a one- or two-place sum.

Examples will range from $0 + 0 = 0$ to $9 + 9 = 18$. Now let's consider these two sets.

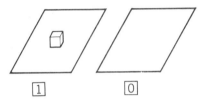

Have the children locate the number cards to place under the sets. The numbers of the two sets are 1 and 0. Under the addition operation, $1 + 0$ is another name for 1. Thus we can say that $1 + 0 = 1$. Now let's look at this example:

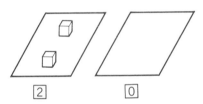

Under the addition operation, the sum of the numbers 2 and 0 is another name for 2. The sum is unique, because the sum obtained for $2 + 0 = \square$ is always 2.

Now let's consider the following set of addition examples:

2	5	0	0	7	9	0
+0	+0	+8	+3	+0	+0	+4
2	5	8	3	7	9	4

Have the children respond to these questions: How are all these examples alike? How are all the examples different? After discussing the students' discoveries, what generalization should children make about the operation of adding the number 0 to another number? The sum of 0 and any other number is always the other number. For this reason, zero is called the **identity element of addition.** Using this basic generalization, children can begin to construct an **addition table.**

An addition table is an orderly arrangement of columns and rows. Each row and column is headed by an addend, and each cell in the table contains a sum.

The following is an uncompleted addition table:

+	0	1	2	3	4	5	6	7	8	9
0										
1										
2										
3										
4					Sums					
5										
6										
7										
8										
9										

Addends (columns heading) / Addends (rows heading)

Write sums in the addition table for all basic addition facts related to the identity element of addition.

+	0	1	2	3	4	5	6	7	8	9
0	0	1	2	3	4	5	6	7	8	9
1	1									
2	2									
3	3									
4	4				Sums					
5	5									
6	6									
7	7									
8	8									
9	9									

Addends (columns heading) / Addends (rows heading)

Note that sums related to the identity element of addition will complete the first row and the first column of the addition table. Remember that learning the basic addition facts is a two-step process. The first step is to develop the basic facts in a family of numbers, and the second step is to memorize the basic facts when organized in structures. From an understanding of this one generalization, children should be able to memorize 19 basic addition facts.

Now let us carefully examine another basic structure that will help children memorize basic addition facts. We begin with another set model.

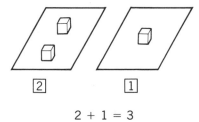

$$2 + 1 = 3$$

Now examine the same example, using the number line as a model.

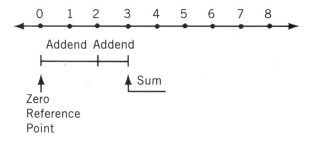

$$2 + 1 = 3$$

The expression $2 + 1$ is another name for 3. Consider this set of examples:

3	5	1	1	7	4
+1	+1	+8	+6	+1	+1
4	6	9	7	8	5

After the children have solved a number of these types of examples and studied these models, ask them: How are all these examples alike? How are the examples different? After a discussion with the children, they should be able to generalize that the sum of 1 and any other number is the next greater counting number. If children can count, they can add 1 to a number. These sums will fit into the second row and second column of the addition table.

From this generalization, children should memorize 17 basic addition facts. Using the two generalizations previously developed, the children will have memorized a total of 36 basic addition facts. Two generalizations will help the children memorize more than one third of the basic addition facts.

+	0	1	2	3	4	5	6	7	8	9
0	0	1	2	3	4	5	6	7	8	9
1	1	2	3	4	5	6	7	8	9	10
2	2	3								
3	3	4								
4	4	5								
5	5	6				Sums				
6	6	7								
7	7	8								
8	8	9								
9	9	10								

(Column header: Addends; Row header: Addends)

The application of this discovery process to the basic structure of our number system will help to explain the use of the addition table. Discovery of the **commutative property of addition** will almost cut in half the task of memorizing the basic addition facts. The basic structural property of commutativity for addition can be examined using sets.

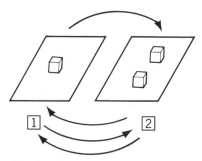

Using sets of cubes on sheets of paper, have children write the addition example $1 + 2 = 3$. Now interchange the two sheets of paper with cubes on them, and have the children write an addition sentence: $2 + 1 = 3$. Give the children experience with many similar examples, using sets and number sentences.

We can use the number-line model to demonstrate the commutative property of addition. Using the same example, we can show that $1 + 2 = 2 + 1$ with the following model. The children should model many examples.

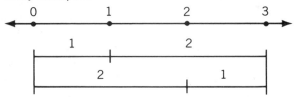

Discuss the two models shown on the number line, discuss the relationship with the set model, illustrate many different examples, and then have the children generalize the commutative property of addition.

> The commutative property of addition means that the order of two addends does not affect the sum. For example 2 + 3 = 3 + 2.

Now let us return to the organization of the basic addition facts for memorization, using basic structures. Children must be taught to count by twos long before they begin addition of whole numbers. Examine this set of basic addition facts.

3	2	6	5	2	2	8
+2	+7	+2	+2	+4	+9	+2
5	9	8	7	6	11	10

Have the children examine these examples and determine how they are alike and how they are different. Some children may want to use models to help them discover likenesses and differences. After a discussion with the children, they should generalize that adding 2 to a number is just like counting by twos. Also reinforce the commutative property of addition.

These sums will fit into the third row and the third column of the addition table.

+	0	1	2	3	4	5	6	7	8	9
0	0	1	2	3	4	5	6	7	8	9
1	1	2	3	4	5	6	7	8	9	10
2	2	3	4	5	6	7	8	9	10	11
3	3	4	5							
4	4	5	6			Sums				
5	5	6	7							
6	6	7	8							
7	7	8	9							
8	8	9	10							
9	9	10	11							

(Addends across the top; Addends down the side)

From this generalization, the children will have memorized 15 basic addition facts. With three generalizations to remember, the children will have memorized 51 basic addition facts, over half of the facts.

Children seem to have less difficulty memorizing basic facts where the two addends are the same number. We will call these the doubles, and we will discuss with the children how these examples are alike and how they are different.

This set of examples is:

3	4	5	6	7	8	9
+3	+4	+5	+6	+7	+8	+9
6	8	10	12	14	16	18

This set of sums will fit into the addition table on the diagonal; now the table will look like this.

+	0	1	2	3	4	5	6	7	8	9
0	0	1	2	3	4	5	6	7	8	9
1	1	2	3	4	5	6	7	8	9	10
2	2	3	4	5	6	7	8	9	10	11
3	3	4	5	6						
4	4	5	6		8		Sums			
5	5	6	7			10				
6	6	7	8				12			
7	7	8	9					14		
8	8	9	10						16	
9	9	10	11							18

(Addends across the top; Addends down the side)

Immediately following the doubles, we have children memorize basic addition facts called related doubles. Each double has two related doubles (except for 9 + 9).

3	4	5
+3	+4	+5

3	4	4	5	5	6
+4	+3	+5	+4	+6	+5

6	7	8	9
+6	+7	+8	+9

6	7	7	8	8	9
+7	+6	+8	+7	+9	+8

The generalizations become more abstract as we move through the basic addition facts, but the children are also becoming more sophisticated. Memorizing the seven doubles will help the children memorize the twelve related doubles. Since 3 add 4 is one more than 3 add 3, the sum of 3 add 4 will be one more than 6. The sums of all related basic facts will be one more than the corresponding double.

Following the structural approach to memorizing the basic addition facts, the students will have techniques for memorizing 70 basic facts. The addition table will now look like this:

		Addends								
+	0	1	2	3	4	5	6	7	8	9
0	0	1	2	3	4	5	6	7	8	9
1	1	2	3	4	5	6	7	8	9	10
2	2	3	4	5	6	7	8	9	10	11
Addends 3	3	4	5	6	7			Sums		
4	4	5	6	7	8	9				
5	5	6	7		9	10	11			
6	6	7	8			11	12	13		
7	7	8	9				13	14	15	
8	8	9	10					15	16	17
9	9	10	11						17	18

The next set of basic facts to be introduced for memorization are the ten facts related to "tenness." Let's examine this set of basic facts:

7	4	9	9	5
+9	+9	+6	+3	+9
16	13	15	12	14

This set of addition facts can be related to place value and tenness. As the children have been bundling and unbundling sets of ten, the tenness concept is related to this set of facts. One is taken from the set other than ten and is placed with the nine to make a set of ten. Thus the sum will be a set of ten with one less than the other addend. Now we have accounted for 80 basic addition facts.

		Addends								
+	0	1	2	3	4	5	6	7	8	9
0	0	1	2	3	4	5	6	7	8	9
1	1	2	3	4	5	6	7	8	9	10
2	2	3	4	5	6	7	8	9	10	11
Addends 3	3	4	5	6	7					12
4	4	5	6	7	8	9		Sums		13
5	5	6	7		9	10	11			14
6	6	7	8			11	12	13		15
7	7	8	9				13	14	15	16
8	8	9	10					15	16	17
9	9	10	11	12	13	14	15	16	17	18

Sums

There are 20 basic facts yet to be memorized. By using the commutative property of addition, these remaining addition facts are reduced to ten. These ten facts are:

3	3	3	3	4	4	4	5	5	6
+5	+6	+7	+8	+6	+7	+8	+7	+8	+8
8	9	10	11	10	11	12	12	13	14

These facts are the most difficult addition facts for children to memorize. Do not rush the children into memorizing these facts. Practice just one fact per week, but consider the fact and its commuted form.

Basic addition facts should be memorized *after* the children understand the concept of addition and the basic addition structures. Have the children consider only one classification at a time. For instance, study the identity element of addition for one week, and show the children how easy it is to memorize 19 basic facts.

Regular and systematic practice must be provided to help children memorize the basic addition facts. Have the children look at the facts, state the facts, listen to the facts, write the facts, visualize the facts, and classify the facts. Aids, such as flash cards, cassette tapes, hand-held calculators, microcomputers, games, and individual drill activities are valuable for helping children to memorize the basic addition facts.

As the basic facts become more difficult the children can use the **associative property of addition,** in conjunction with place value. From the beginning children have learned that numbers have many names. Use these two ideas and consider the example 6 + 7 = □:

$$6 + 7 = 6 + (6 + 1)$$
$$= (6 + 6) + 1$$
$$= 12 + 1$$
$$= 13$$

This example is given to help the reader understand the concept; do not have children write many examples this way.

In the operation of addition, the associative property allows us to combine (or associate) addends with one another in whatever way we choose. That is, we can elect to operate on any two addends at a time. For example, we can add 3 + 6 + 4 in either of two ways without changing the order of the addends:

$$(3 + 6) + 4 = 9 + 4 = 13$$
or
$$3 + (6 + 4) = 3 + 10 = 13$$

(The parentheses tell us how to group or *associate* the addends.) We can consider 3 and 6, then add 4; or we can choose to associate the 6 and 4 and then add 3 to the sum. Solving the example this way we might proceed: 6 add 4 is 10, and 10 add 3 is 13. Since 10 is an easy number to build on, it is simpler to add 3 to 10 than to approach the computation as 3 + 6 = 9 and 9 + 4 = 13.

> The associative property of addition means that, when three or more numbers are to be added, the way in which the addends are grouped does not affect the sum.

This example may be modeled on the number line.

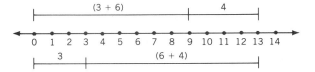

While children are memorizing the basic addition facts and developing an understanding of the associative property, column addition might be introduced. **Column addition** is the addition of three or more addends in one example. Beginning examples should include only one-place numbers, such as:

$$\begin{array}{c} 4 \\ 3 \\ +2 \end{array} \quad \text{or} \quad \begin{array}{c} 6 \\ 2 \\ +1 \end{array}$$

Since addition is a binary operation, the first two addends are added, and that sum is then added to the next addend. In the first example, 4 and 3 are addends; the sum 7 becomes the **unseen number.** The unseen number of 7 is added to the next ad-

dend, 2. Thus 7 and 2 is 9. In the second example, 8 is the unseen number, and 8 and 1 are added to obtain a sum of 9.

Children will need physical models to help them comprehend the concept of column addition. Again, sets and the number line are used as models. Sets of objects can be used on sheets of paper, flannel boards, magnetic boards, or an overhead projector. Children need to use many different materials and manipulate the concept of column addition.

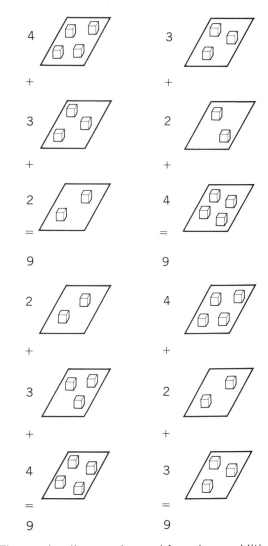

The number-line may be used for column addition.

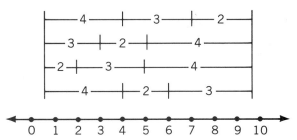

The students are now applying the associative property of addition. After several examples have been modeled and solved, the children should generalize the associative property of addition—that is, a different grouping of the addends does not change the sum. The concept must be extended into more places as children develop their understanding of place value. This provides an excellent opportunity to review the concept of place value.

A logical extension of the basic addition facts is to use multiples of ten. The basic fact of 2 + 3 can be extended into 20 + 30. Think 2 + 3 = 5, and relate the fact to 2 tens + 3 tens = 5 tens. Plastic forks or spoons can be used to model this concept. Place the two following sets on the overhead projector, and ask the children to state a mathematical sentence for placing the two sets together.

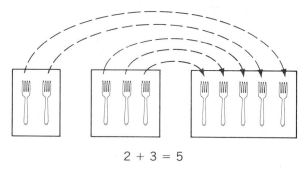

$$2 + 3 = 5$$

Hold up a package of ten plastic forks. Ask the children: "How many plastic forks?" Ask the children to watch you carefully as you exchange each plastic fork in this set with a package of ten plastic forks.

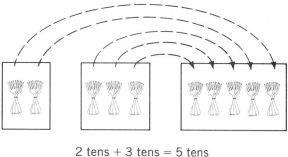

$$2 \text{ tens} + 3 \text{ tens} = 5 \text{ tens}$$
$$20 \ + \ 30 \ = \ 50$$

Children are now bringing together the concept of place value and the concept of addition. After examining many examples, children should generalize that the basic addition facts are the same regardless of their place value.

Expanded notation provides an efficient method for introducing the addition of numbers having two or more digits. In expanded notation, a number is separated into its component parts (hundreds, tens, ones, and so forth). This way children can better see the structure of the numbers and are better able to rename the numbers in a more convenient form.

$$35 = 3 \text{ tens } 5 \text{ ones}$$
$$+ 21 = 2 \text{ tens } 1 \text{ one}$$
$$5 \text{ tens } 6 \text{ ones} = 56$$

Children have studied the basic facts 2 + 3 = 5 and 1 + 5 = 6. The understanding of the basic fact 2 + 3 = 5 has been extended to 2 tens + 3 tens = 5 tens, which can be written 20 + 30 = 50.

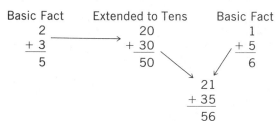

When children have memorized the basic addition facts and understand place value, these two concepts can be brought together and the children can think through examples such as 21 + 35. The same approach may be used as children move into addition examples with more decimal places. Now let's examine a three-place addition example, using expanded basic facts and place value.

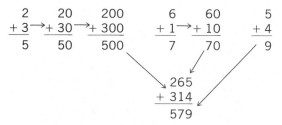

Children need to understand that the basic facts remain the same regardless of the place value. Understanding place value and memorizing the basic addition facts are the prerequisites needed to extend the addition concepts. Children with a solid foundation in the concept of addition, the basic addition facts, and place value have a great deal of power with addition.

Children are now in a position to move rapidly forward through addition, without regrouping. Instead of a worksheet with several basic addition examples, all the basic examples of addition facts can be placed together in one example. Carefully study these two sample worksheets:

Traditional Worksheet

Add each example

1. 2 + 3	2. 1 + 4	3. 6 + 0	4. 3 + 1	5. 0 + 7	6. 2 + 4
7. 8 + 1	8. 4 + 2	9. 2 + 1	10. 1 + 5	11. 3 + 3	12. 2 + 6

New Approach

```
1.  216302
   +340174


2.  842132
   +121536
```

Note that the practice with basic addition facts is the same on both worksheets. Children will have a greater feeling of accomplishment after completing the "new approach" worksheet. Children feel that having more places to add makes examples more difficult. This is not necessarily true (as illustrated above).

One major concept of addition remains to be developed: **regrouping.** If regrouping is introduced on an abstract level, children will often have difficulty with place value, when writing the sum. Consider the example

$$37$$
$$+\ 25$$

Children will often obtain a sum of 512. Presenting the example on the concrete level or requiring children to write partial sums will help prevent this difficulty. Preventative action is better than corrective action.

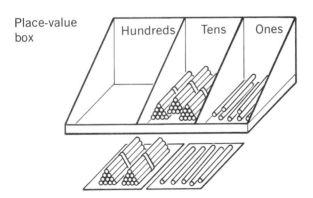

Place-value box

Using the place-value box, place seven single straws in the ones place and three packages of ten in the tens place. On a sheet of paper in front of the ones place, place five single straws; in front of the tens place (on another sheet of paper) place two packages of ten straws. Combine the five straws with the seven straws. Ask these questions: "How many straws are now in the ones place? What do you do if you have more than nine straws in the ones place?" The twelve straws are regrouped into one ten and two ones. Place the two straws into the ones place. Place a rubber band around the ten straws and make one

set of ten. Place the one set of ten straws into the tens place; this now makes four sets of ten straws in the tens place. Then place the two sets of ten straws on the sheet of paper with the set of four tens. There are now six packages of ten straws in the tens place. Thus we have 62 straws in the place-value box.

Relate the manipulation of tens and ones with recording the numbers on the chalkboard or overhead projector. Seven and five is twelve. What did we do with the twelve when we manipulated the straws? The twelve was regrouped as one ten and two ones. The two is written in the ones place.

$$37$$
$$+\ 25$$
$$\overline{2}$$

Now combine the tens: the one regrouped ten is combined with the three tens and then with the two tens, to obtain a sum of six tens.

$$37$$
$$+\ 25$$
$$\overline{62}$$

If partial sums are recorded, the example would be:

$$37$$
$$+\ 25$$
$$\overline{12}$$
$$\underline{50}$$
$$62$$

When teaching children, teachers generally do not solve enough examples using partial sums so children can really comprehend them. Provide children with much manipulating at this point, and have them record the partial sums.

The preceding example indicates the sequence of thought that a child should follow in learning the operation of regrouping. Much practice will be necessary before the children can begin to take short cuts. Mastery of the concept must come first. Once the children understand the meaning of addition, they can omit the manipulative steps and write the examples in more abbreviated forms. Do *not* rush the children. Developing this good foundation will save time in the future. Here is an abbreviated form that children can discover and use:

$$37$$
$$+\ 25$$
$$\overline{62}$$

These are the familiar forms of the **addition algorithm.** By **algorithm** we mean the form in which we write and solve the example. Children should eventually master the familiar algorithm and omit unnecessary writing of the regrouped numbers. Discourage children from writing the regrouped number above the example. The familiar short form is written:

$$\begin{array}{r} 37 \\ + 25 \\ \hline 62 \end{array}$$

The development of subtraction should stress the relationship between addition and **subtraction.** We could say that subtraction is a binary operation like addition, since it involves only two numbers at a time. Subtraction is the **inverse operation** of addition. If one operation "undoes" what another operation does, the "undoing" operation is called the inverse operation. Familiar operations and their inverse operations include lacing our shoes and then unlacing them or buttoning our shirts and then unbuttoning them. Remember we can also say that lacing our shoes is the inverse operation of unlacing our shoes. Similarly, we can add and then "unadd" or subtract.

Addend + Addend = Sum
or
Sum = Addend + Addend

becomes

Sum − Addend = Addend
or
Addend = Sum − Addend

In addition we look for a missing sum; in subtraction we look for a missing addend.

Addition	Subtraction	
$a + b = \square$	$a + \square = S$	$\square + b = S$
$\begin{array}{r} a \\ + b \\ \hline \square \end{array}$	$\begin{array}{r} S \\ - a \\ \hline \square \end{array}$	$\begin{array}{r} S \\ - b \\ \hline \square \end{array}$

Understanding addition helps prepare children for subtraction, but some elementary textbooks introduce addition and subtraction at approximately the same time. Research to indicate the optimum time to introduce subtraction has been inconclusive. However, introducing addition and subtraction simultaneously is apt to lead to confusion. On the other hand, waiting for children to master addition seems to delay subtraction concepts too long. Teachers must use their own judgment, based upon Piagetian concepts, the children in the classroom, and their own basic philosophies.

Readiness for subtraction includes numberness, conservation of number, some place value, a beginning understanding of the addition concept, and reversibility. Reversibility concepts (as defined by Piaget) are probably the most important. Children should be tested by using Piagetian tasks to determine their readiness to begin the study of subtraction.

With children, the subtraction concept must be developed from the concrete to the abstract. However, subtraction is more difficult to teach and more difficult for children to learn, because there are three different types of subtraction situations. Models used to introduce subtraction concepts include sets and the number line. The inverse relationship between addition and subtraction is also beneficial in teaching subtraction.

Remember that three types of subtraction situations must be taught. Some elementary school mathematics textbooks only teach children one type of subtraction. If the other two types of subtraction situations are not taught to children, they will experience difficulty when they encounter examples such as $4 + \square = 7$.

Now let us examine "take away" subtraction. If we have seven spoons and we take away three spoons, how many spoons will be left? If children count the four spoons that are left, they are not subtracting: they are counting! To prevent counting, the teacher might show the seven spoons on the overhead projector and then turn the projector off. Have the children watch as they see you remove the three spoons. Then ask the question: "How many spoons are still on the overhead projector?" After the children have subtracted, turn on the projector and check their response.

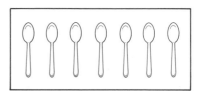

Children see the seven spoons and they see three spoons physically removed; then they must subtract. They can readily check to see whether they are correct.

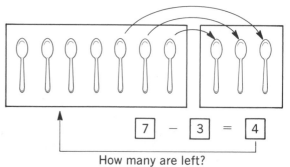

$$\boxed{7} - \boxed{3} = \boxed{4}$$

How many are left?

Children need to model many "take away" subtraction examples and record each step of the inverse operation in writing. Relate addition with subtraction by combining the two sets of objects that were separated and having children write the addition sentence. Discuss how 3, 4, and 7 are related.

Another type of subtraction is "comparison" subtraction. Consider the two following sets:

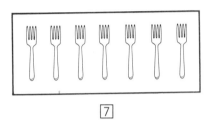

One set has seven forks, and the other has four forks. The teacher can ask either: "How many more forks does the first set have?" or "How many fewer forks does the second set have?" One-to-one correspondence can be used to compare the two sets.

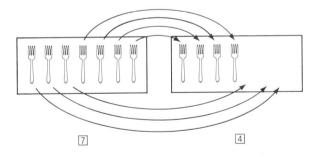

The difference between the two sets is 3, because three of the forks in one set cannot be paired with three forks in the other set. We write $7 - 4 = 3$.

Comparison subtraction is more difficult than "take away" subtraction because the student must think about two different sets at once and then compare the two sets by using one-to-one correspondence.

The third type of subtraction is called *"How many more are needed?"* Look at the following set and ask, "How many more forks are needed in order to have seven forks?"

This is difficult for children because they must think of the number 7 and compare the four forks that they see with the number 7. The missing addend can also be obtained by counting beginning with 5 and, as forks are placed, counting 6 and 7. Three forks were added: $4 + 3 = 7$ or $7 - 4 = 3$.

Children need many experiences on the concrete level with each of the three types of subtraction. Teach only one type of subtraction at a time. After children become effective with one type of subtraction, then they are ready to move on to the next type. After all three types of subtraction have been taught and the children can function with each type, the teacher may provide mixed practice with all three types.

Using these three set models for subtraction, children are then ready to understand a working definition for subtraction. Remember that subtraction is *not* counting either forward or backward. Then what is subtraction?

> Subtraction is an operation performed on a sum and one addend in order to obtain the missing addend.

The children are now ready to use the same addend and sum cards used with addition. Children need many experiences changing an addition sentence to an subtraction sentence and changing a subtraction sentence to an addition sentence.

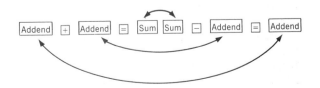

Many elementary school mathematics programs successfully use the number line as a model for developing an understanding of subtraction. Consider the example $7 - 4 = \square$. Since 7 is the sum and 4 is an addend, we can write $7 - 4 = \square$. Then subtraction is modeled just as addition was. Children know that all modeling on the number line should begin at the reference point, zero. Draw a line segment from 0 to 4 for the known addend. On the number line locate the point that corresponds to the sum, 7. Now use a dotted line and draw a line segment from 4 to 7. This dotted line segment represents the missing addend $\square$. How long is the dotted line segment? It is three units long.

This way we can see that the missing addend is 3. Therefore $4 + 3 = 7$, so $7 - 4 = 3$.

At this stage of development, children should be able to look at two sets and write four related mathematical sentences.

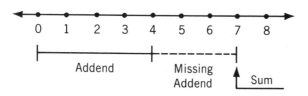

$$4 + 5 = 9 \qquad 9 - 4 = 5$$
$$5 + 4 = 9 \qquad 9 - 5 = 4$$

If children have memorized the basic addition facts, then they also know the basic subtraction facts. What is a basic subtraction fact?

> A basic subtraction fact is a one- or two-place sum subtract a one-place addend in order to obtain another one-place addend.

For example, if children have memorized $4 + 5 = 9$ and if they understand the inverse relationship between addition and subtraction, then they should see that the solution to $4 + \square = 9$ is 5. Can you discover another way to express this inverse relationship?

$$5 - 3 = \square \quad \text{or} \quad \begin{array}{r} 5 \\ -3 \\ \hline \square \end{array} \quad \text{or} \quad \begin{array}{r} 3 \\ +\square \\ \hline 5 \end{array}$$

The table of basic addition facts can be used to solve subtraction examples. Consider $7 - 4 = \square$. In this example 7 is the sum, 4 is the known addend, and the box indicates the missing addend. In the addition table, the addends are located in the top row and in the left-hand column. Locate the known addend 4 in the top row, and look down the column until you come to the sum 7. Now look along the row containing 7 until you come to the missing addend, 3, in the left-hand column. Clearly, $7 - 4 = 3$.

		Addends								
+	0	1	2	3	4	5	6	7	8	9
0	0	1	2	3	4	5	6	7	8	9
1	1	2	3	4	5	6	7	8	9	10
2	2	3	4	5	6	7	8	9	10	11
3	3	4	5	6	7	8	9	10	11	12
4	4	5	6	7	8	9	10	11	12	13
5	5	6	7	8	9	10	11	12	13	14
6	6	7	8	9	10	11	12	13	14	15
7	7	8	9	10	11	12	13	14	15	16
8	8	9	10	11	12	13	14	15	16	17
9	9	10	11	12	13	14	15	16	17	18

(Left-hand column labeled Addends)

The basic subtraction facts must be developed, organized into a table, and then memorized. This procedure for teaching subtraction is much like that for addition. Teachers report that organizing basic subtraction facts into a structural or conceptual approach much like addition is helpful for memorization of the basic subtraction facts.

Now let us begin by considering this set of basic subtraction facts:

$$\begin{array}{ccccccccc} 1 & 2 & 3 & 4 & 5 & 6 & 7 & 8 & 9 \\ -1 & -2 & -3 & -4 & -5 & -6 & -7 & -8 & -9 \\ \hline 0 & 0 & 0 & 0 & 0 & 0 & 0 & 0 & 0 \end{array}$$

Students should again look for likenesses and differences. They should generalize much as they did when learning addition and discover that, when a number is subtracted from itself, the missing addend is zero. With this concept, children will have memorized nine basic subtraction facts.

Examine this set of basic subtraction examples:

$$\begin{array}{ccccccccc} 1 & 2 & 3 & 4 & 5 & 6 & 7 & 8 & 9 \\ -0 & -0 & -0 & -0 & -0 & -0 & -0 & -0 & -0 \\ \hline 1 & 2 & 3 & 4 & 5 & 6 & 7 & 8 & 9 \end{array}$$

Following standard procedure, the children should be encouraged to examine these examples for likenesses and differences. Children should discover that, when zero is subtracted from a number, the other number is the same as the missing addend. Another nine basic facts have now been memorized; thus using only two basic ideas, children can memorize nineteen basic subtraction facts.

As numberness has been developed with the children, we have noted which number comes after a certain number and which number comes before a certain number. What number is just before 6? Children can use the number line as a model to help them. This idea will help them to memorize this set of basic subtraction facts:

2	3	4	5	6	7	8	9	10
−1	−1	−1	−1	−1	−1	−1	−1	−1
1	2	3	4	5	6	7	8	9

These examples can be considered neighbors, as the children look for likenesses and differences. When 1 is subtracted from a number, the number that precedes it is the missing addend. Nine more basic facts have been memorized, so a total of 28 basic facts have been memorized. More than one-fourth of the basic subtraction facts have now been memorized.

Extending the idea of neighbors a little further, we can consider this set of examples:

3	4	5	6	7	8	9	10
−2	−3	−4	−5	−6	−7	−8	−9
1	1	1	1	1	1	1	1

Again, after the children have studied the examples, encourage them to discover that, when a number just before a given number is subtracted, the missing addend is 1. Eight more basic subtraction facts have been memorized, making a total of 36 basic facts that have been memorized (more than one-third of all basic subtraction facts).

Now review counting by twos with the children. This concept will help them to memorize this set of basic subtraction facts:

4	5	6	7	8	9	10	11
−2	−2	−2	−2	−2	−2	−2	−2
2	3	4	5	6	7	8	9

Using the number line, the children can skip a number and relate 2 with 4. This is the third row of the subtraction and addition table. These eight examples with the 36 already memorized make a total of 44 basic subtraction facts.

Related to the previous set of subtraction facts is the following set of facts:

5	6	7	8	9	10	11
−3	−4	−5	−6	−7	−8	−9
2	2	2	2	2	2	2

These numbers are two apart on the number line, so the missing addend is 2. This will help to memorize seven more basic subtraction facts. Now a total of 51 basic subtraction facts have been memorized.

The children have studied the doubles with respect to basic addition facts. Now relate the doubles to the subtraction facts. This set of facts is:

6	8	10	12	14	16	18
−3	−4	−5	−6	−7	−8	−9
3	4	5	6	7	8	9

After careful examination, the children should discover that the given addend is the same as the missing addend. Seven more basic subtraction facts have been memorized, for a total of 58.

The next set of subtraction facts to consider is:

12	13	14	15	16	17
−9	−9	−9	−9	−9	−9
3	4	5	6	7	8

After studying these examples, the children should discover that the missing addend is one greater than the number in the ones place of the sum. This generalization will help the children to memorize six more basic facts, for a total of 64.

Consider this set of facts with a difference of nine:

12	13	14	15	16	17
−3	−4	−5	−6	−7	−8
9	9	9	9	9	9

In subtraction, when the numbers in the ones place are neighbors and the smaller number is on top, the missing addend is 9. This makes another six basic subtraction facts, so at this point the children should have 70 basic facts memorized. Encourage the children to examine carefully the last 30 basic subtraction facts that must be memorized and to use whatever they discover will help them. All children do not need the same set of rules. The basic subtraction facts remaining to be memorized are:

7	8	9	10	11	9	10	11	12
−3	−3	−3	−3	−3	−4	−4	−4	−4
4	5	6	7	8	5	6	7	8

11	12	13	13	14	15	7	8	9
−5	−5	−5	−6	−6	−7	−4	−5	−5
6	7	8	7	8	8	3	3	4

9	10	11	10	11	12	13	11	12
−6	−6	−6	−7	−7	−7	−7	−8	−8
3	4	5	3	4	5	6	3	4

13	14	15
−8	−8	−8
5	6	7

This last set of 30 basic facts are difficult for children. Give them one basic fact to memorize at a time. Teachers tend to require too much memorization too rapidly. This organization has been successful even with children suffering from severe learning difficulties.

After understanding place value, subtraction as the inverse of addition, and the basic subtraction facts, children should be ready to discover how to extend the basic subtraction facts. Help the children relate the following two examples, much as we did for addition:

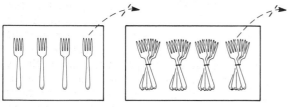

Write: $4 - 1 = 3$ Write $40 - 10 = 30$

Children should generalize that the basic subtraction facts are the same, regardless of the decimal place in which they are placed. Understanding place value and memorizing basic facts are necessary for a child to solve two-place subtraction examples successfully.

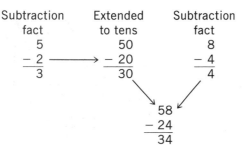

Subtraction examples can also be written in another form:

$$
\begin{array}{rl}
64 = & 6 \text{ tens } 4 \text{ ones} \\
-\,12 = & -\,1 \text{ ten } \ 2 \text{ ones} \\
\hline
& 5 \text{ tens } 2 \text{ ones} = 52
\end{array}
$$

$$
\begin{array}{rl}
57 = & 5 \text{ tens } 7 \text{ ones} \\
-\,23 = & -\,2 \text{ tens } 3 \text{ ones} \\
\hline
& 3 \text{ tens } 4 \text{ ones} = 34
\end{array}
$$

$$
\begin{array}{rl}
45 = & 4 \text{ tens } 5 \text{ ones} \\
-\,31 = & -\,3 \text{ ten } \ 2 \text{ one} \\
\hline
& 1 \text{ ten } \ 4 \text{ ones} = 14
\end{array}
$$

Do *not* write the examples like this:

$$
\begin{array}{rl}
64 = & 60 + 4 \\
-\,12 = & -\,10 + 2 \\
\hline
\end{array}
$$

Children will subtract the number in the tens place and add the number in the ones place, because they see the addition sign in the middle of the subtraction example. This is a poor teaching procedure that will start the children out with bad habits. Proceed systematically through three, four, five and more place values. The children are just applying the concepts of subtraction and place value and the basic facts to examples with more decimal places. Actually, no new teaching is necessary. Study the example at the bottom of this page.

Practice exercises for children can be placed together to make one large example, as demonstrated with addition. For instance, study the two following samples to learn how the first five basic facts are combined into one example.

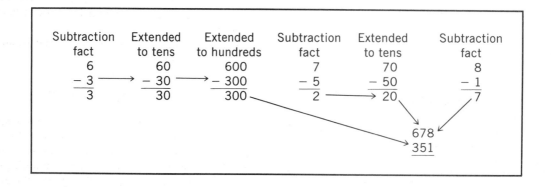

Solve each.

1. 7
  −4
	2. 5
	  −1
		3. 6
		  −2
			4. 3
			  −0
				5. 8
				  −5

6. 9
  −6
	7. 4
	  −3
		8. 1
		  −0
			9. 2
			  −2
				10. 8
				  −7

Solve each.

1. 75638
   −41205

2. 94128
   −63027

All children can proceed this way, including children who are experiencing difficulty learning mathematics. Children think that the more digits an example has, the more difficult it is, but this is not necessarily true. Children can develop a feeling of accomplishment from solving examples with more digits.

The concept of inverse operation is an important aspect of basic mathematical structure; it is essential to understanding elementary mathematics. The basic properties of subtraction must be examined. Using manipulative materials, children should examine the ideas of basic structures and they should generalize that:

1. Subtraction is not commutative:
   $8 − 6 \neq 6 − 8$
2. Subtraction is not associative:
   $(8 − 4) − 2 \neq 8 − (4 − 2)$
3. Subtraction does not have an identity element:
   $0 − 7 \neq 7 − 0$

The trend today is to use the term *regroup* rather than *borrow* or *carry*. Regroup is more descriptive of the relationship that exists. The manipulation and concept is the same for addition and subtraction; a set of ten ones is changed to one set of ten and one set of ten is changed to ten sets of one. The terminology will help to relate the two ideas, but it is only a process of regrouping. This is taught as one concept, not as two separate concepts.

Before introducing subtraction examples that require regrouping it is a good idea to review expanded notation and the concept that a number can be named in many ways. The children should use some type of counters and demonstrate each

name for a number. The number 372, for example, can be written as:

3 hundreds 7 tens   2 ones
2 hundreds 17 tens   2 ones
2 hundreds 16 tens 12 ones
2 hundreds 15 tens 22 ones
and so on

When beginning subtraction with regrouping, children will subtract the smaller number from the greater number, regardless of the position of the numbers in the example. For example, children think that $71 − 28 = 57$. Since 8 cannot be subtracted from 1, children will subtract 1 from 8. This type of reaction indicates that the children do not really understand the concept of subtraction and that the children were taught to regroup on the abstract level. If children are started on the concrete level, they will not make this type of error. It is better to anticipate the children's difficulties and prevent them from occurring than to try to correct the misconceptions later. Now let's carefully examine regrouping in subtraction:

How would a child subtract 27 from 53, beginning on the concrete level? Using a place-value box with 53 counters, have the students remove 27 counters.

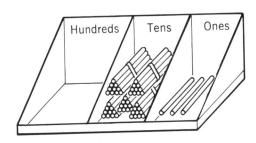

To remove seven ones, the student must regroup one package of ten. A student cannot remove seven counters from the ones place without regrouping one ten to ten ones. This is the same way a child must think in order to understand regrouping in subtraction. Children need many concrete examples before they can begin to record their ideas using the algorithm.

Next, have the students use place value to rewrite this example:

$$53 = \quad 5 \text{ tens } 3 \text{ ones}$$
$$− 27 = − 2 \text{ tens } 7 \text{ ones}$$

The children should see that they cannot subtract yet, since the number of ones in the first line of the example is less than the number of ones in the second line. Children with a weak understanding of subtraction will not recognize this difficulty and will subtract the smaller number from the larger regardless of the position of the numbers. Continually relate to the concrete model, using the place-value box as we have pictured. To overcome the difficulty, 5 tens 3 ones can be regrouped as 4 tens 13 ones:

$$
\begin{array}{rl}
53 = & 4 \text{ tens } 13 \text{ ones} \\
-27 = & -2 \text{ tens } \ \ 7 \text{ ones} \\
\hline
& 2 \text{ tens } \ \ 6 \text{ ones} = 26
\end{array}
$$

Children need to model and record the results of many examples.

Children who have been taught regrouping from the concrete level to the abstract level will be able to apply the concept to more places and manipulate counters to understand the regrouping.

$$
\begin{array}{rl}
321 = & 3 \text{ hundreds } \ \ 2 \text{ tens } \ \ 1 \text{ one} \\
-156 = & -1 \text{ hundred } \ \ 5 \text{ tens } \ \ 6 \text{ ones} \\
\hline
= & 2 \text{ hundreds } 11 \text{ tens } 11 \text{ ones} \\
= & -1 \text{ hundred } \ \ 5 \text{ tens } \ \ 6 \text{ ones} \\
\hline
\end{array}
$$

Place value and expanded notation can be used to develop an understanding of regrouping. After children understand regrouping, it should be easy for them to see the relationship of these concepts to the mental processes involved in using the short subtraction algorithm with which they are familiar:

$$
\begin{array}{r}
321 \\
-156 \\
\hline
165
\end{array}
$$

Children who have been taught this way will not need to write regrouped numbers above the examples. Children who understand the concept will not need "crutches"; children with a weak understanding will need additional help. Children who have a sound understanding of regrouping will have little difficulty with zeros in subtraction.

Consider the example 700 − 256. Traditionally, this type of example required double regrouping:

$$
\begin{array}{r}
{\scriptstyle 6 \ \ 10 \ \ 10} \\
\not{7} \ \not{0} \ \not{0} \\
-2 \ \ 5 \ \ 6 \\
\hline
4 \ \ 4 \ \ 4
\end{array}
$$

If we think of the number 700 as 70 tens and 0 ones, we need only one regrouping. Study this example. Note that no markings are placed above the example.

$$
\begin{array}{rl}
700 = & 70 \text{ tens } 0 \text{ ones} = 69 \text{ tens } 10 \text{ ones} \\
-256 = & 25 \text{ tens } 6 \text{ ones} = 25 \text{ tens } \ \ 6 \text{ ones} \\
\hline
& 44 \text{ tens } \ \ 4 \text{ ones} = 444
\end{array}
$$

It is of historical interest that other algorithms have been used for subtraction. You may be interested in doing research on the Austrian method and the method of complementary subtraction. List some probable advantages and disadvantages of these other algorithms.

In summary, there are five major concepts that a person must understand to solve any *addition* example: (1) The student must understand what addition is. (2) The student must understand the basic addition facts and have them memorized. (3) The student must understand place value and be able to relate the place-value concept to addition. This allows the student to extend the basic addition facts. (4) The student should understand the basic structures or properties (for example, the commutative property and the identity element of addition). (5) The student must understand the concept of regrouping and be able to relate the regrouping concept to addition.

There are also five major concepts that a person must comprehend to solve any *subtraction* example: (1) The student must understand the concept of subtraction. (2) The student must comprehend the

	Addition	Subtraction
Understanding the operation	A + A = S	S − A = A
Basic facts	100 basic facts	100 basic facts
Place value	Same as for subtraction	Same as for addition
Structures	Commutative property, associative property, identity element of addition, etc.	Properties do not apply to subtraction
Regrouping	Change ones to tens, etc.	Change tens to ones, etc.

basic subtraction facts and have them memorized. (3) The student must understand place value and relate the place-value concept to the inverse operation of subtraction. (4) The student must understand that the basic structures or properties do not apply to subtraction. (5) The student must understand the concept of regrouping as it applies to subtraction.

The major concepts of addition and subtraction can be organized into a convenient table. See table at bottom of page 170.

Terminology, Symbols, and Procedures

Addends   Each of the two numbers in an addition example is called an addend.

Addition   The operation of addition is a binary operation performed on a pair of numbers called addends in order to obtain a unique sum. Addition is symbolized as:

$$\text{Addend} + \text{Addend} = \text{Sum} \quad \text{or} \quad \begin{array}{r} \text{Addend} \\ + \text{Addend} \\ \hline \text{Sum} \end{array}$$

Addition is read "addend add addend equals sum" or $2 + 3 = 5$ is read "two add three equals five."

Addition table   An addition table is an orderly arrangement of columns and rows. Each row and column is headed by an addend and each cell in the table contains a sum.

Algorithm   The form in which mathematical computations are written and solved, showing the steps necessary to solve them. There can be several types of algorithms for one example, such as a short algorithm and a long algorithm. For example:

$$\begin{array}{cc} \text{Horizontal Algorithm} & \text{Vertical Algorithm} \\ 2 + 3 = 5 & \begin{array}{r} 8 \\ + 5 \\ \hline 13 \end{array} \end{array}$$

$$\begin{array}{cc} \text{Long Algorithm} & \text{Short Algorithm} \\ \begin{array}{r} 67 \\ + 48 \\ \hline 15 \\ 100 \\ \hline 115 \end{array} & \begin{array}{r} 67 \\ + 48 \\ \hline 115 \end{array} \end{array}$$

Associative property of addition   The associative property of addition means that, if three or more numbers are to be added, the way that the addends are grouped does not affect the sum. For example: $(2 + 3) + 4 = 2 + (3 + 4)$.

Basic addition facts   Basic addition facts include all combinations of one-place whole numbers (addends) added to one-place whole numbers (addends) to obtain a one- or two-place sum. There are 100 basic addition facts.

Basic subtraction facts   Basic subtraction facts include all combinations of one-place whole numbers (addends) subtracted from one- or two-place whole numbers (sum) to obtain a one-place whole number (addend). There are 100 basic subtraction facts.

Binary operation   The two fundamental operations on numbers (addition and multiplication) and their respective inverse operations (subtraction and division) are often referred to as binary operations, because computation is done with only two numbers at one time.

Commutative property of addition   The commutative property of addition means that the order of the two addends does not affect the sum. For example: $2 + 3 = 3 + 2$.

Family of numbers   All the possible combinations of whole-number addends that will produce a given sum are called a family of numbers. For example: The family of five equals $0 + 5$, $1 + 4, 2 + 3, 3 + 2, 4 + 1$, and $5 + 0$.

Identity element of addition   Zero (0) is the identity element of addition, since the sum of any number and zero is always that number. For example:

$$6 + 0 = 6, 0 + 9 = 9, 4 + 0 = 4.$$

Regrouping   Regrouping is the process used in changing a set of ten to ten sets of one or changing ten sets of one to one set of ten. For example: 47 can be regrouped from 4 tens 7 ones to 3 tens 17 ones; 2 tens 16 ones can be regrouped as 3 tens 6 ones.

Subtraction   Subtraction is defined as the inverse operation of addition. It is a binary operation performed on a sum and one addend, to obtain the missing addend. Subtraction is symbolized as:

$$\text{Sum} - \text{Addend} = \text{Addend} \quad \text{or} \quad \begin{array}{r} \text{Sum} \\ - \text{ Addend} \\ \hline \text{Addend} \end{array}$$

Sum   The result of adding a pair of addends.

Practice Exercises

These exercises are designed for the reader of this book; these examples should not necessarily be administered to children in this form.

1. Make a number-line diagram to solve these examples. Label the addends and sum for each one:

a) $5 + 4 = \square$ c) $1 + 6 = \square$
b) $3 + 2 = \square$ d) $8 + 7 = \square$

2. Make a number-line diagram to solve these examples. Label the addends and sum for each one:

   a) $9 - 4 = \square$ c) $8 - 2 = \square$
   b) $7 + \square = 11$ d) $15 - 9 = \square$

3. Use the addition operation and its inverse to write four related sentences, using each of the given numbers.

   a) 4, 7, 11   c) 6, 13, 7
   b) 9, 2, 7   d) 31, 75, 44

4. Write two subtraction sentences for each of these addition sentences:

   a) $8 + 9 = \square$ c) $\square = 53 + 39$
   b) $4 + 9 = \square$ d) $7 + 6 = \square$

5. Name the two basic facts and the expanded basic fact that will help children solve each of the following two-place addition examples.

   a) $18 + 31 = \square$ c) $73 + 15 = \square$ e) $47 + 22 = \square$
   b) $26 + 31 = \square$ d) $52 + 45 = \square$ f) $68 + 21 = \square$

6. Rewrite each example in expanded notation and solve:

   a)   18   c)   73   e)   48   g)   87
       + 41   + 25   − 17   − 64

   b)   247   d)   364   f)   765   h)   597
      + 532   + 213   − 213   − 156

7. Solve each example with regrouping and show each step of the regrouping process:

   a)   37   c)   73   e)   378   g)   346   i)   521
      + 49   + 88   + 154   − 83   − 146

   b)   61   d)   219   f)   56   h)   459   j)   832
      + 54   + 466   − 29   − 272   − 398

8. Use expanded notation to calculate each sum. Show your work in horizontal form, and name the property of addition that justifies each step. (This is to help teachers understand the mathematics. Do not ask children to solve examples like this.)

   a)   37   b)   276   c)   48
      + 28   + 49   + 75

9. Solve each subtraction example, using renaming and only one regrouping and with no marks above the example.

   a)   500   b)   802   c)   900
      − 273   − 367   − 258

10. Using the words *addend* and *sum*, write four related addition and subtraction sentences.

Discussion Questions

1. What prerequisite skills and concepts are needed for the development of the addition concept? Subtraction concept?

2. What types of materials can be used with children to develop the concepts of addition and subtraction?

3. Research the literature for alternative ways to add and subtract, and then compare and contrast the different methods (for example: low-stress algorithms, Austrian method of subtraction, and the equal additions method).

4. According to Piagetian theory, when should a child be ready to understand subtraction?

5. When should the hand-held calculator be introduced for the teaching of addition?

6. Some authors suggest that addition and subtraction should be taught simultaneously; other authors recommend that subtraction be taught after addition. Take a stand and support your position.

7. Discuss how Cuisenaire rods, Stern rods, and Dienes Blocks can be used in developing addition and subtraction concepts.

8. How do attribute blocks provide readiness for the teaching of addition?

9. Research the literature and then discuss effective techniques for encouraging children to memorize the basic addition and subtraction facts.

10. Discuss the pros and cons for each model used to develop an understanding of the addition and subtraction operations.

11. Discuss the likenesses and differences between how addition and subtraction are presented in this unit and how you remember learning these operations.

12. What can be done with a computer in the classroom that cannot be done using worksheets with the children?

Activities for the Primary Grades

Developing the operation of addition and its inverse operation, subtraction, is the prime consideration of the primary mathematics program. These two fundamental concepts are developed in the primary grades and then continuously reinforced at every grade level. We suggest starting the mathematics program for each grade level with new concepts and ideas and then reinforcing the operations when the need arises. Children become bored when each grade level is begun with addition, subtraction, multiplication, and division.

Children need much practice and drill to maintain skills and concepts that they have previously developed. Practice and drill can be obtained in many interesting and unique ways. Don't forget to use the latest technology as well as the tried and true: worksheets, hand-held calculators, microcomputers, games, and mathematics interest centers.

A systematic, cyclic approach to concept and skill development is essential. The activities for this unit follow a consistent pattern of presentation and reinforcement. As children develop and become more complex individuals, the problems that they encounter also become more complex.

The operation of addition and its inverse have always been part of the child's work in mathematics. The objective is still to find a shorter way than counting to determine a total or a part, but the child's understanding must precede the teacher's presentation of the conventional algorithms. Encourage children who can develop insight into mathematics to program the computer to solve their mathematics examples.

Experiences for children should progress from the concrete through the semiconcrete and semiabstract to the abstract. Remember that many types of materials are available and should be used in developing children's concepts of addition and subtraction. Materials that should be explored at this time include Stern rods, Dienes Blocks, Cuisenaire rods, hand-held calculators, and microcomputers. Use only materials that come from the child's real world, such as plastic spoons, plastic forks, napkins, paper cups, etc. We do not recommend using the abacus, since it is as abstract as place value itself and since the abacus is not used in our culture. However, the abacus could be used with gifted children for historical discussions.

1. Use many concrete situations in teaching the understanding of addition and its inverse, subtraction, at this level: counting sticks, plastic spoons, plastic forks, paper cups, flannel board, cutout shapes, and anything available from the child's everyday world. For example:

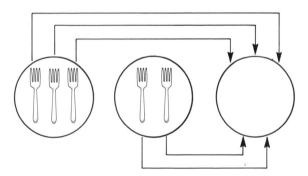

Place plastic forks on a table and encircle them with yarn to indicate sets. Use another piece of yarn to make the outline of another set. Move the three forks and the two forks into the new set. This is a model for the concept 3 + 2 = 5. A set of three elements joined with a set of two other elements forms a new set of five elements. Many of these experiences with sets should be used to teach the children what actually happens when two sets are joined. Then introduce the sign of operation (+) and the relation symbol (=) in developing mathematical sentences.

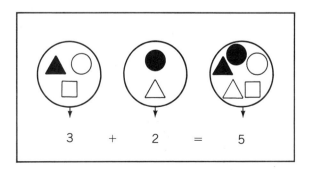

2. Make three sets of numeral cards with the numerals 0 to 9. Also make cards with the symbols +, =, and −. Have the children construct addition sentences for sets shown on the flannel board or overhead projector. For example, if you display a set of two stars and a set of five discs, the numeral-card addition sentence would look like this:

3. Make a set of cards with the words *addend, addend,* and *sum* on them. Using the symbol cards, children can show an addition sentence.

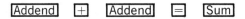

4. The cards from activities 2 and 3 above can be used for many games. You can omit the card for either the addend or for the sum and let one of the children put in the missing card. Change the sentence and repeat the activity. Children can play this game in groups of two or three.

5. On a set of cards about 2″ by 3″ write the numerals 0 through 9. Place the cards face down and draw two cards to use as addends. Model the addition example on the number line. Exercises of this type provide practice in addition facts by using number-line diagrams.

a)

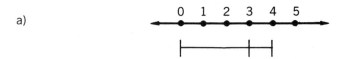

Children can label the addends and the sum. They can write the addition sentence $3 + 1 = 4$.

b) Model $1 + 4$ on the number line.

6. Make a set of dominoes with a pair of addends on one end of the domino and a sum on the other. Play the game of dominoes by using the cards in which only a sum may be matched with a pair of addends. Some of the dominoes might look like this:

| 6 | 4 + 1 | | 5 | 3 + 10 | | 3 | 6 + 1 | | 7 | 2 + 3 |

7. Make bingo cards of sums for each child in the classroom. At random, draw flash cards and have the children place markers on the sums. The first child with five in a row wins.

2	4	5	7	1
12	7	8	4	13
3	6	9	2	10
9	2	15	1	6
6	12	1	9	8

4	13	8	2	16
10	7	5	14	9
5	6	13	9	11
3	6	10	17	5
15	8	12	4	7

10	5	12	6	18
17	8	11	13	3
16	12	2	9	14
11	7	5	4	6
6	18	15	12	9

8. Help children memorize the basic addition facts by:

a) making flash cards of a set of cardboard keys that can be put on key chains

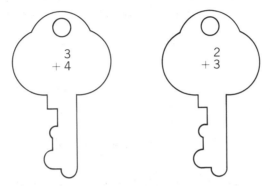

b) making flash-card necklaces with yarn and paper medallions

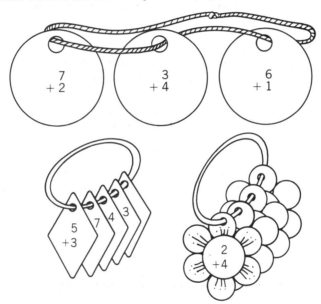

While the children memorize the basic facts, have them live with the flash cards (as designed above) all day long. Have the children wear the keys on a key chain attached to their belt loops. Have them wear necklaces of cardboard medallions. Parents, other teachers, brothers, and sisters can reinforce the flash cards when they see a child wearing them. Classroom teachers can reinforce the flash cards as children are lining up for recess, change of activities, lunch period, or dismissal. Children will enjoy seeing the packet of medallions grow as they memorize the facts.

9. Write the sums in the outer regions:

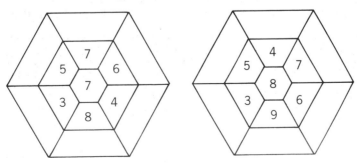

10. Use cubes or other concrete materials and place a set of objects on the overhead projector so that the entire class can observe the set. Have the children write a numeral for the cardinal number of the set. Remove some of the cubes and have them write a numeral for the cardinal number of the cubes removed. For example:

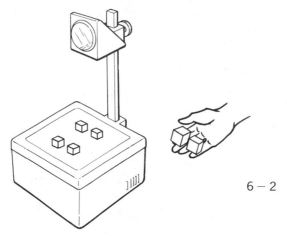

$6 - 2$

Discuss the set operation, relate it to the concept of subtraction, and introduce the subtraction symbol (−). Thus the mathematical sentence $6 - 2 = \square$ has developed. Proceed the same way with many different concrete materials.

11. Use the flannel board to display two disjoint sets with different cardinal numbers. Discuss how the two sets are different. Use yarn to connect the elements of the two disjoint sets to show one-to-one correspondence. Write a comparison subtraction sentence. Discuss the subtraction sentence that can be written. Then place a numeral for the cardinal number of the set under that set.

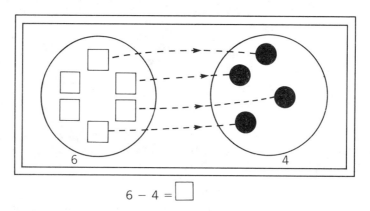

$6 - 4 = \square$

12. Present set pictures similar to the ones above. Have the children fill in the boxes with the correct numerals.

$3 - 1 = \square$ $\qquad$ $2 - 1 = \square$ $\qquad$ $3 - 2 = \square$
$\square - 1 = 2$ $\qquad$ $2 - \square = 1$ $\qquad$ $\square - 2 = 1$
$3 - \square = 2$ $\qquad$ $\square - 1 = 1$ $\qquad$ $3 - \square = 1$

13. Give each child a set of blocks. (Provide for individual differences by giving different-sized sets of blocks to different children.) Have the children separate the set of blocks into two subsets as many different ways as they can and write mathematical sentences to record their findings.

$6 - 1 = 5$ $\qquad$ $6 - 4 = 2$ $\qquad$ $6 - 0 = 6$ (This example may
$6 - 2 = 4$ $\qquad$ $6 - 5 = 1$ $\qquad\qquad\qquad$ be difficult for
$6 - 3 = 3$ $\qquad$ $6 - 6 = 0$ $\qquad\qquad\qquad$ some children.)

Eventually the children should discover all of the possible combinations for all numbers one to ten. Repeat the activity on other days so that all the basic subtraction facts can be discovered by all the children.

14. Use the word cards with *addend* and *sum* on them to develop the relation between addition and subtraction.

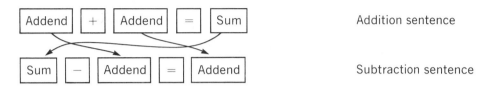

Addition sentence

Subtraction sentence

Use concrete examples in conjunction with this development.

15. With a set of objects and the word cards children should be able to write four related sentences.

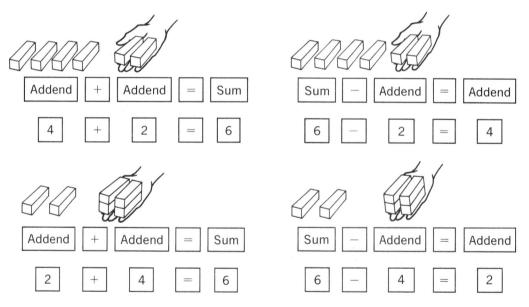

16. Solve each example.

a) 4   b) 6   c) 8   d) 9   e) □   f) 2
   +□   +□   −□   −□   + 5   +□
    9   8   5   3   10   10

g) □ + △ = 7   h) △ + □ = 8   i) □ + △ = 6

17. Make a set of cards of various basic addition facts. Have the children match these cards with numeral cards for the addition facts.

18. The preceding activity might also be done with the addends written on a disc (12″ diameter) and the sums written on pie-shaped pieces that fit on top.

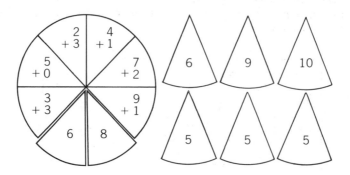

An example written on a pie-shaped piece can also be matched with a disc that has the sum written on it.

19. Write the sums.

a) $7 + 2 = \square$ d) $2 + 4 = \square$ g) $\begin{array}{r} 4 \\ +5 \\ \hline \square \end{array}$ h) $\begin{array}{r} 6 \\ +3 \\ \hline \square \end{array}$ i) $\begin{array}{r} 2 \\ +8 \\ \hline \square \end{array}$

b) $6 + 1 = \square$ e) $3 + 3 = \square$

c) $4 + 3 = \square$ f) $8 + 2 = \square$

20. Find the missing addend.

a) $7 - 2 = \square$ d) $5 - 1 = \square$ g) $\begin{array}{r} 3 \\ -2 \\ \hline \square \end{array}$ h) $\begin{array}{r} 6 \\ -4 \\ \hline \square \end{array}$ i) $\begin{array}{r} 9 \\ -6 \\ \hline \square \end{array}$ j) $\begin{array}{r} 7 \\ -6 \\ \hline \square \end{array}$

b) $8 - 3 = \square$ e) $4 - 2 = \square$

c) $6 - 3 = \square$ f) $9 - 7 = \square$

21. Practice can be made more interesting by making practice worms. Cut discs with a 3″ radius out of light-colored construction paper. Give each child a disc and have him or her draw a worm face on it. Write one practice example on each plain disc (these may be dittoed on a sheet of paper and each child may cut out his own.) The practice sheet can meet individual needs by having sheets with different examples for different children. As the children solve the examples and get them correct, they may staple the discs together to make a practice worm. The worms may be posted on the mathematics bulletin board for display.

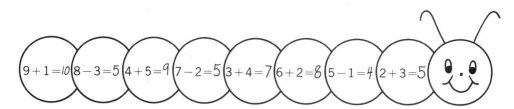

22. The procedure for making worms may also be used for making trains. The child receives an engine, a caboose, and a series of boxcars with examples to solve. As the examples are completed correctly they may be stapled together. Which child can get the longest train during mathematics period today? The trains may be posted on the bulletin board.

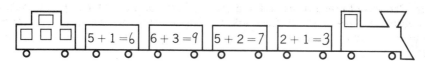

23. In the fall, a large tree branch may be placed in the corner of the classroom, perhaps in a Christmas tree stand. Worksheets of colored construction paper may be made showing examples on leaves. Have the children cut out the leaves and solve the examples. Examples with correct answers may be tied on the tree. Different shapes, such as apples or flowers, may be used the next week.

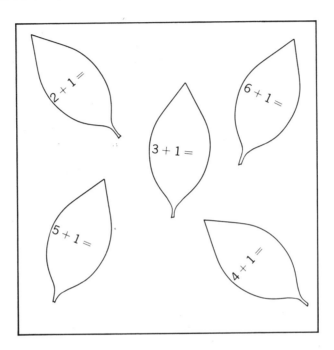

24. Obtain empty one-gallon cans from the lunchroom. Use masking tape and tape six cans together as illustrated.

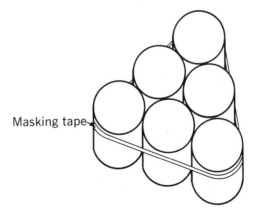

Masking tape

Place discs with large numerals drawn on them in the bottom of each can. For example

Use beanbags and a strip of masking tape for a baseline. Place the cans about three meters from the base line. Have the children toss two beanbags to obtain two addends for addition practice. Continue to take turns and add scores. Three or more beanbags may be used for column addition. Five or six of these addition games may be operating at one time. The values in the bottom of the cans may vary to meet the practice needs of a given set of children.

25. A race track may be used for addition and subtraction practice. It is easy to construct a board like the one illustrated.

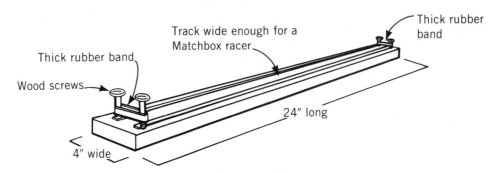

A one-inch-thick board approximately 4″ wide and 24″ long can be used to make a race track. Use 1″ wood screws at each end; place thick rubber bands around the screws at each end of the board. Glue a heavy strip of white cardboard the length of each side of the board, just wide enough for a Matchbox car to move freely. Mark off each strip of cardboard in squares and alternate the lines on each side of the track. Cover the white cardboard with clear self-adhesive plastic. Use a china marker to write addends on the plastic. The addends can be varied to meet the children's needs.

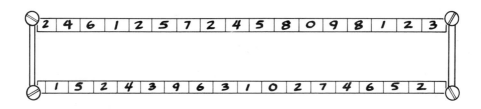

Place the car on the track and let the children push it against a rubber band and let it bounce back. Use the number in front of the car as an addend. Repeat to get a second addend. The same procedure may be used for subtraction by writing sums on one side and addends on the other. The race track may be used for multiplication, division, fractions, decimals, and in many other places in the mathematics program.

26. Introduce simple story problems. Begin on the concrete level and discuss the example. Early in the year use some words and rebuses for story problem development.

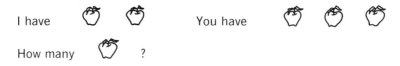

The child should write $2 + 3 = \square$.
Then he should solve the problem and write "You have 5 🍎."

"Betty has three balls. Tom has one ball. How many balls are there in all?"
The children can write $3 + 1 = \square$.
The child must answer with a complete sentence: "There are four balls in all."

Develop word problems using the words children can read and write. Integrate reading and writing with mathematics just as soon as children can handle the skills.

27. Complete the addition example that goes with each set picture.

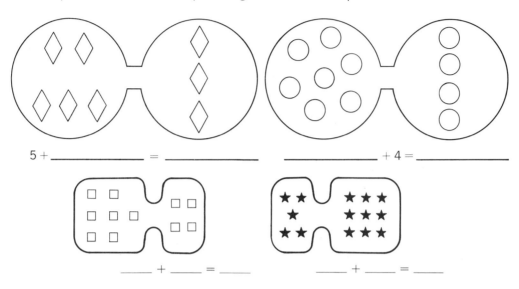

5 + _____ = _____   _____ + 4 = _____

_____ + _____ = _____   _____ + _____ = _____

28. Use flash cards of basic addition facts for review. Do not use the same set of fact cards for all the children in the classroom; each child should work only on the facts he needs. Do the same for the basic subtraction facts.

29. To find missing addends, the following activity can be used. Construct a cardboard garage from a milk carton. Ten small cars will be needed. The students are shown the ten cars and asked to close their eyes while the "mechanic" takes several cars into the garage. The students open their eyes, see how many cars are *outside* the garage, and then are requested to tell how many cars are *inside* the garage, by subtraction.

30. Prepare several sheets of paper or construction paper with an additon fact on each sheet; for example:

$$3 + 5 = 8 \qquad 4 + 2 = 6$$

Have the children close their eyes. Then say, "I'm going to cut out one of the addends. See if you can tell what addend I have cut out." With a scissor the teacher cuts three sides of one addend and then folds the piece up so that the children cannot see the missing addend. Ask the children, "What was on the piece that was cut out?"

$$3 + \square = 8 \qquad 4 + \square = 6$$

When asked to respond to $3 + \square = 8$, most children will write 11 in the box. This is a logical response from children with a weak understanding of addition: they see an addition sign and two numbers and their immediate response is to add.

31. Have the children model addition and subtraction examples on the number line. Then have them write number sentences from number line models. $9 + 5 =$ _____

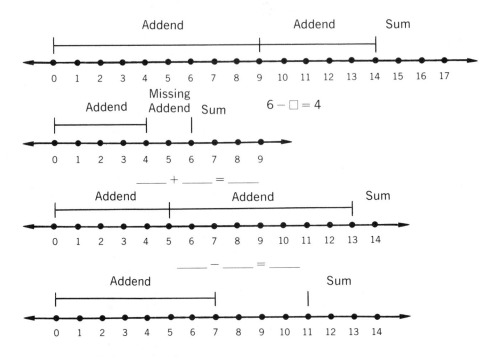

_____ + _____ = _____

_____ − _____ = _____

32. Fill in the missing numerals.

a) $\begin{array}{r} 32 = \quad 3 \text{ tens } 2 \text{ ones} \\ + 54 = + 5 \text{ tens } 4 \text{ ones} \\ \hline \rule{0pt}{0pt}\text{____} = \text{__ tens \_ ones} \end{array}$

d) $\begin{array}{r} 39 = \quad 3 \text{ tens } 9 \text{ ones} \\ - 25 = - 2 \text{ tens } 5 \text{ ones} \\ \hline \rule{0pt}{0pt}\text{____} = \text{__ tens \_ ones} \end{array}$

b) $\begin{array}{r} 27 = \quad 2 \text{ tens } 7 \text{ ones} \\ + 51 = + 5 \text{ tens } 1 \text{ one} \\ \hline \rule{0pt}{0pt}\text{____} = \text{__ tens \_ ones} \end{array}$

e) $\begin{array}{r} 63 = \quad 6 \text{ tens } 3 \text{ ones} \\ - 41 = - 4 \text{ tens } 1 \text{ one} \\ \hline \rule{0pt}{0pt}\text{____} = \text{__ tens \_ ones} \end{array}$

c) $\begin{array}{r} 42 = \quad 4 \text{ tens } 2 \text{ ones} \\ + 35 = + 3 \text{ tens } 5 \text{ ones} \\ \hline \rule{0pt}{0pt}\text{____} = \text{__ tens \_ ones} \end{array}$

f) $\begin{array}{r} 84 = \quad 8 \text{ tens } 4 \text{ ones} \\ - 32 = - 3 \text{ tens } 2 \text{ ones} \\ \hline \rule{0pt}{0pt}\text{____} = \text{__ tens \_ ones} \end{array}$

33. Complete the examples.

a) $\begin{array}{r} 73 \\ + \text{\_\_} \\ \hline 93 \end{array}$
b) $\begin{array}{r} 3\text{\_} \\ + \text{\_}2 \\ \hline 56 \end{array}$
c) $\begin{array}{r} \text{\_}9 \\ - 2\text{\_} \\ \hline 65 \end{array}$
d) $\begin{array}{r} 98 \\ - \text{\_}6 \\ \hline 72 \end{array}$
e) $\begin{array}{r} 87 \\ - \text{\_}2 \\ \hline 5\text{\_} \end{array}$

34. When the children are well grounded in the basic addition facts and the basic ideas of place value, they should be able to handle column addition with three one-place addends. The following examples can be used for practice. Observe that in several examples if you group properly you can get a sum of ten for two of the addends. This can be used to simplify the computation greatly.

a) $\begin{array}{r} 2 \\ 3 \\ + 7 \\ \hline \end{array}$
c) $\begin{array}{r} 9 \\ 1 \\ + 8 \\ \hline \end{array}$
e) $\begin{array}{r} 3 \\ 2 \\ + 6 \\ \hline \end{array}$
g) $\begin{array}{r} 4 \\ 5 \\ + 4 \\ \hline \end{array}$
i) $\begin{array}{r} 6 \\ 4 \\ + 8 \\ \hline \end{array}$

b) $\begin{array}{r} 5 \\ 2 \\ + 5 \\ \hline \end{array}$
d) $\begin{array}{r} 6 \\ 7 \\ + 9 \\ \hline \end{array}$
f) $\begin{array}{r} 8 \\ 3 \\ + 7 \\ \hline \end{array}$
h) $\begin{array}{r} 9 \\ 6 \\ + 4 \\ \hline \end{array}$
j) $\begin{array}{r} 5 \\ 8 \\ + 7 \\ \hline \end{array}$

Hand-Held Calculator Activities for the Primary Grades

1. Do not allow children to check their papers by using an answer book. Give each child a hand-held calculator when he or she is ready to check the answers; use the calculator as the means of checking papers.

2. Have children estimate answers to addition or subtraction examples, and then have them check how close their answers are, using the hand-held calculator.

Example	Estimation	Calculator	Close
21 + 38	60	59	yes
49 + 32	80	81	yes
19 + 28	40	47	no

3. Children in the primary grades can learn to add a constant using the hand-held calculator. When adding a constant, the same number can be added to many numbers without reentering the constant number. For instance: if the constant number is 3 and we want to add 3 to many different numbers, we would use the following procedure:

Any number		Enter the constant		Display reads
1	+	3	=	4

The calculator is now set up to add the constant 3 to any number that is entered. If you press the 2 key and the equals key, the display will show 5. We can now enter any number and then hit the equals key, and the calculator will add 3 to the entered number and display the new sum.

Example	Keys pushed	Display shows
7 + 3 =	7 =	10
12 + 3 =	1 2 =	15
37 + 3 =	3 7 =	40

4. The same procedure can be used to subtract a constant using the hand-held calculator. Subtracting a constant means to subtract a given number from many numbers without reentering the constant. For example: if the constant is 4 and we want to subtract 4 from many different numbers, we would use the following procedure:

Enter any number		Enter the constant		Display reads
7	−	4	=	3

The calculator is now set up to subtract 4 from any number that is entered.

Example	Keys pushed	Display shows
9 − 4 =	9 =	5
47 − 4 =	4 7 =	43
82 − 4 =	8 2 =	78

Microcomputer Activities for the Primary Grades

1. The microcomputer can be used much like a hand-held calculator, when it is used in the immediate mode. The following procedure will function on most microcomputers in the immediate mode: Turn on the microcomputer. Type on the microcomputer keyboard exactly what is underlined here: ? 2 + 3. Now strike the ENTER or RETURN key (depending on

which microcomputer you are using). The computer will print 5 on the video screen. Do *not* type an equals sign. Primary school children can learn how to solve addition examples using the microcomputer. Experiment with many different examples.

2. Primary school children can also learn to use the microcomputer to solve subtraction examples. Turn on the microcomputer, and type on the computer keyboard exactly what is underlined here: ?7 − 5. Strike the ENTER or RETURN key (depending on which microcomputer you are using). The computer will print 2 on the video screen. Do *not* type an equals sign. Have the children practice solving many subtraction examples.

3. Many software or courseware programs are available to provide drill and practice in addition and subtraction for primary school children. Many programs focus on specific basic facts or mathematical concepts. Primary school children can learn to operate software programs on microcomputers. Programs of this nature will add interest and motivation to the mathematics program. In general, microcomputers should be used for objectives that cannot be accomplished using traditional classroom methods.

Activities for the Intermediate Grades

Many of the activities that we have suggested for the primary grades may be adapted for intermediate grade children. Do not hesitate to use manipulative materials with intermediate children, when they do not comprehend a concept. Select the materials carefully so the children do not feel that they are using kindergarten material. Select new sets of materials that are real to these children (for instance: use money, ET dolls, hot wheels, sticks of gum in individual wrappers).

1. Provide practice exercises with some numbers missing. For example:

$$
\begin{array}{r}
1\square57 \\
+\ 4731 \\
\hline
5988
\end{array}
$$

$$
\begin{array}{r}
\square394 \\
+\ 5602 \\
\hline
999\square
\end{array}
$$

$$
\begin{array}{r}
3\square58 \\
+\ 26\square1 \\
\hline
5989
\end{array}
$$

2. Have the children use multi-base blocks to demonstrate the concepts of regrouping in both addition and subtraction. The children may work in small groups; one member is the banker and the children must exchange the blocks at the bank.

3. Have the children illustrate examples by manipulating concrete materials on the overhead projector. Use small sheets of colored transparent plastic to represent different sets of materials. Draw faces on the bowls of plastic spoons to add interest.

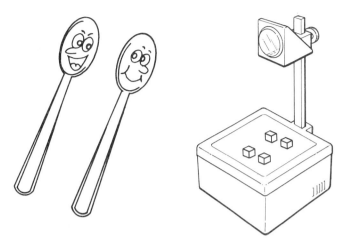

4. Use the place-value box (as described in the place-value unit) for demonstrating the regrouping process in both addition and subtraction.

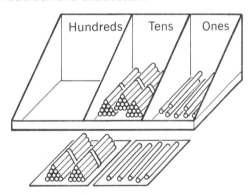

5. An elliptical adding machine can be used to practice addition with two or more addends. Construct the adding machine out of cardboard. Three or more strips of thin cardboard 2 centimeters wide should be cut. These strips can be marked off into 2-centimeter squares.

Choose appropriate addends for the student to practice: the student inserts these strips into the elliptical adding machine and manipulates the strips to arrive at various addends.

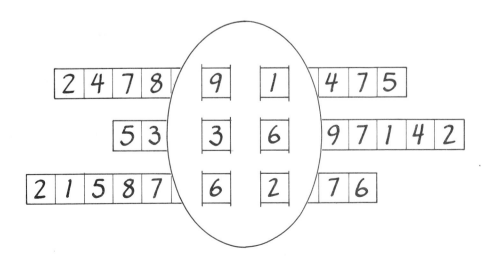

6. The "diffy board" is an excellent device to use for subtraction practice. Herbert Wills' article in the October 1971 issue of *The Arithmetic Teacher,* page 65, discusses the use of the board.

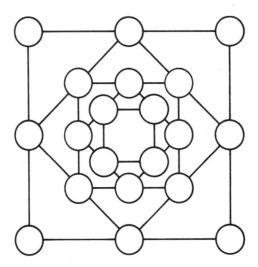

With the diffy board, place any number in each of the four corners. Subtract the smaller number from the larger on any one line, and write the difference between the two in the circle. Continue the process as you work toward the center of the square.

7. Cut a piece of cardboard of any geometric shape into puzzle pieces. On each edge place an addition or subtraction example, so that the matching edges yield the same answer.

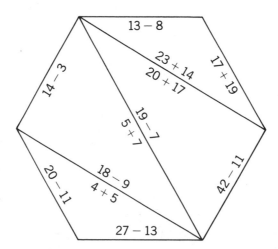

8. For the following activity, you will need a deck of cards with the face cards removed. Before the game begins, a sum is decided upon (such as 10). Each student is dealt five cards. Four cards are turned face up with the remainder of the deck placed in the middle (see illustration). The students take turns playing their cards on one of the four cards face up to obtain the predetermined sum. If a student does not have a card to play, a card is drawn from the deck to see if it can be played; this is continued until he or she can play. In the following example, proper plays would be 7, 9, 2, and 6, respectively.

Changing the sum is one of many ways of varying this activity.

9. Cards with addition and subtraction examples can be used in the game of concentration. Students must match cards that have the same difference or sum.

10. Many variations on cross-number puzzles can be used to further develop students' addition and subtraction skills. Some examples of cross-number puzzles are shown below. Place the numbers 1, 3, 5, 7, 11, 13, 15, and 17 into the table so that the sum is the same in each row, column, and diagonal.

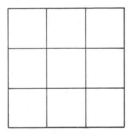

11. Place the sum of each example in the proper column or row. Only one number may be put into any one square and you may check the sum by verifying the number both horizontally and vertically.

Down
1. $9 + 6 + 9 + 8 = $ ___
2. $7 + 5 + 15 + 19 = $ ___
3. $23 + 14 + 9 + 8 = $ ___
4. $8 + 7 + 8 = $ ___
5. $54 + 63 + 15 = $ ___
6. $13 + 9 + 12 + 8 + 9 + 7 = $ ___
7. $27 + 18 + 15 + 14 = $ ___

Across
1. $8 + 3 + 7 + 5 + 9 = $ ___
2. $6 + 12 + 5 + 7 + 11 = $ ___
3. $9 + 14 + 11 + 7 + 15 = $ ___
4. $7 + 9 + 7 = $ ___
6. $19 + 15 + 12 + 7 = $ ___
7. $31 + 23 + 5 + 14 = $ ___
8. $126 + 53 + 31 + 17 + 15 = $ ___

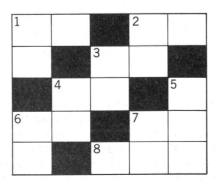

12. Palindromes are useful devices to practice addition skills. A palindrome reads left to right the same as it does right to left. Choose any two- or three-digit number, reverse the digits, and add until the sum is a palindrome. The following examples illustrate how palindromes can be used.

Some numbers will have to be manipulated many times to arrive at a palindrome; for example, try 649.

13. A student's understanding of basic subtraction facts may be checked by having him or her sort small flash cards into cups. Place a digit (0—9) on each of ten small paper drinking cups.

Cut cards large enough to fit on the bottom of the cups horizontally. Write a basic subtraction fact on each card. A child may sort the cards by placing each one in the cup that has the difference written on its side. The cups will stack because the cards all fit flat on the bottom of each cup. The cups may be put on the teacher's desk and he or she can check for accuracy at a later time.

14. In the following activity 81 cards are used, each six centimeters by three centimeters or two inches by three inches. Each set of nine cards should be composed of the numbers 1 through 9. Shuffle the entire deck and place the cards face down. A sum greater than 9 is decided upon before the beginning of the game. Each player draws 15 cards. The first puts down two or more cards to add up to the predetermined sum. The following players place their cards in such a way that the sum of the cards is equal to the predetermined sum. The play continues until one of the players is out of cards or until no other play can be made. In the latter case, the player with the lowest sum on the cards in his or her hand is declared the winner. In this case a sum of 12 is used.

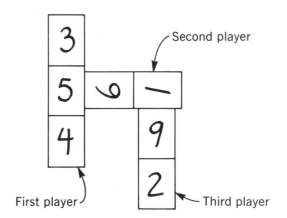

15. Construct a magic square out of cardboard. Place clear self-adhesive plastic over the board so that the student can write on the magic square with a china marker. In the magic square below, all numbers in a row, column, or diagonal must add up to 15. Many variations on the magic square can be devised.

2	9	4
7	5	3
6	1	8

Hand-Held Calculator Activities for the Intermediate Grades

1. Children should use the hand-held calculator to check addition and subtraction examples that have been completed using standard algorithms.

2. Children can examine a sequence of numbers, determine the pattern, and then complete the pattern. The hand-held calculator is a convenient device to use in checking such sequences. Use the concept of adding a constant as developed in the primary grade section, and extend these sequences. Begin using only addition sequences, try subtraction sequences, and then combine addition and subtraction sequences. Study the following examples:

   a) 1, 3, 5, 7, __, __, __, __, __, __.
   After studying this sequence, the child should clear the calculator and then enter 1. Since the student thinks that the pattern is add 2, he should push the keys in order as suggested: $1 + 2 = = = = = = = = = =$. The calculator display should show: 1, 1, 2, 3, 5, 7, 9, 11, 13, 15, 17, 19.

   b) 73, 70, 67, 64, 61, __, __, __, __, __, __.
   Study this sequence, and determine the operation and the numerical amount. Use your hand-held calculator to verify the sequence. The student should clear the calculator and then enter the following values: $7\ 3 - 3 = = = = = = = = = = = =$. The calculator will display: 7, 73, 73, 3, 70, 67, 64, 61, 58, 55, 52, 49, 46, 43.

   c) 5, 9, 6, 10, 7, 11, __, __, __, __, __
   Note that this sequence first adds 4 and then subtracts 3. The student should clear the calculator and then enter the following values: $5 + 4 = - 3 = + 4 = - 3 = + 4 = - 3 = + 4 = - 3 = + 4 = - 3 =$.

3. This is a game played by two children using one hand-held calculator. The children take turns by passing the calculator back and forth. The rules of the game define a set of one-place numbers to be used with the operation of addition. The winner of the game is the player who causes a preselected sum to appear on the display. For example: in this game, children will use addition and the digits 1, 2, 3, 4, 5, 6, and 7. The winner must display the sum of 31. Suppose that the first player enters the digit 3 and passes the calculator to the second player. The second player enters the operation + and a selected digit such as 7; 10 will appear on the display. The calculator is then passed back to the first player. For his second turn he presses + and a selected digit such 4; 14 will appear on the display. This process continues until the preselected number (31 in this case) appears on the display.

Microcomputer Activities for the Intermediate Grades

1. The activities suggested for the hand-held calculator on the intermediate level can also be used with a microcomputer in the immediate mode.

2. The suggested activities for the microcomputer on the primary level can easily be adapted to the intermediate level.

3. Software and courseware packages appropriate for intermediate grades are available on the commercial market. Most available material is practice and drill. Timed practice is excellent to help children memorize the basic facts. Children should not be competing against each other; they should compete against themselves to improve accuracy and speed. There is no substitute for memorizing the basic addition and subtraction facts.

4. At the intermediate grade level, some children can begin to write simple programs to calculate mathematics for them. A sample program is:

```
10 REM *A SIMPLE ADDITION PROGRAM*
20 LET X=6
30 LET Y=5
40 PRINT X+Y
50 END
```

5. Encourage children to revise the simple program that they wrote in the previous example. The children can change the program so it will add the values of X and Y selected by the user. For example:

```
10 REM*REVISED SIMPLE ADDITION PROGRAM*
20 PRINT "WHAT IS THE VALUE OF X"
30 INPUT X
40 PRINT "WHAT IS THE VALUE OF Y"
50 INPUT Y
60 PRINT "THE VALUE OF ";X;" + ";Y;" = ";X+Y
70 END
```

6. With just a little programming experience, teachers can write simple programs to meet the specific needs of a particular group of children. The following program was written by a group of teachers for an Atari computer, after 12 hours of microcomputer class work. It took the teachers about 40 minutes to write this program.

```
10   REM*ADDITION BASIC FACT DRILL*
20   PRINT CHR$(125)
30   PRINT"WHAT IS YOUR NAME";
40   DIMN$(10)
50   INPUT N$
60   PRINT CHR$(125)
70   PRINT"HI ";N$
80   N=0
90   PRINT"LET'S DO SOME ADDITION TODAY!"
100  X=INT(10*RND(1))
105  Y=INT(10*RND(1))
110  PRINT X;" + ";Y;" = ";
120  INPUT Z
130  IF Z=X+Y THEN PRINT"GREAT! YOU ARE CORRECT."
140  IF Z<X+Y THEN PRINT"YOUR ANSWER IS TOO SMALL, TRY AGAIN":GOTO 110
150  IF Z>X+Y THEN PRINT"YOUR ANSWER IS TOO LARGE, TRY AGAIN":GOTO 110
```

```
160 FOR X=1 TO 1000:NEXT X
170 N=N+1
180 IF N=10 THEN 500
190 GOTO 100
500 ?"DO YOU WISH TO TRY TEN MORE EXAMPLES(YES OR NO)";
510 DIMZ$(10)
520 INPUT Z$
530 IF Z$="YES" THEN 70
540 IF Z$="NO" THEN PRINT"THANKS, SEE YOU AGAIN!"
550 END
```

Activities for the Upper Elementary Grades

Many of the activities suggested for primary and intermediate grade levels may be adapted for the upper grade levels. Some children may still need experiences on the concrete level. Select materials appropriate for the ages of the children being instructed.

1. Using whole numbers for the sides of a rectangle, write the dimensions of all rectangles that could be constructed having a perimeter of 48 meters.

2. Complete the following addition table:

Addend

A	84			98
d	33	50		
d				94
e	67		52	
n		61		81
d	49			

3. Using numbers 1 through 25, place one number in each circle of the following figure, so that adding the three numbers on any one line will always produce the same sum.

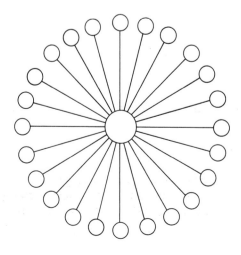

4. Use no paper or pencils until you are ready to write your answer for this activity. Begin with number 43, and continue to subtract 4 mentally until the number is in the twenties. Write your answer in large numbers, and hold it up so the teacher may check your answer. Children could check themselves by subtracting the constant 4 on their hand-held calculators.

5. At the upper grade levels, provide much mental addition and subtraction. Whenever some time is available, the teacher might say, "Follow me: ready? 7 add 9, add 5, subtract 6, add 23, the sum is □." The teacher should create examples that are appropriate for the students in the class.

Hand-Held Calculator Activities for the Upper Elementary Grades

Hand-held calculator activities for the primary and intermediate levels may also be used at the upper grade levels.

1. Have the children take turns passing the calculator back and forth. Each player subtracts 1, 2, 3, or 4 from the display number on the calculator. Begin with number 43 on the display. The first person to display 0 is the winner. Play additional games using different digits and another sum.

2. Estimate the sum of each example by rounding each number to the nearest hundred. Use your calculator to find the sum.

Example	Estimate	Example	Estimate
318	300	786	
+ 432	+ 400	+ 207	
196		578	
+ 469		+ 623	

3. Palindromes are always fun. These are numbers that read the same from left to right as they do from right to left. Here are some examples of palindromes: 12321, 242, 6357536, and 131. To find a palindrome, add to any number the digits in reverse order; continue until a palindrome is found. For instance, place 37 on your hand-held calculator display. Now add 73 to the 37. Your display should now read 110. Now reverse the digits of 110 and add again: 110 + 011. The sum is 121, and 121 is a palindrome. You can now reverse the digits of 121 and add this to 121; the sum is 242 which is also a palindrome. Children should have a great deal of fun playing with palindromes on a hand-held calculator. By adding, change these numbers into palindromes: 49, 79, 182, and 386.

Microcomputer Activities for the Upper Elementary Grades

All microcomputer activities for the primary and intermediate grades may also be used in the upper grades.

1. Children who have had experience programming in the BASIC language can write simple programs to practice specific types of addition and subtraction examples. For example:

This program could be used on a TRS-80 microcomputer. The teacher can change the practice in this type of program by changing only the data line. Thus programs can be prepared for specific students rather easily.

```
10   REM *A SIMPLE SUBTRACTION PROGRAM*
20   PRINT"WHAT IS YOUR NAME";
30   INPUT N$
40   PRINT"HERE IS SOME SUBTRACTION PRACTICE FOR YOU, ";N$
50   READ A,B
60   DATA 17,8,14,6,16,9,15,7,13,7,17,9,14,7,13,5,14,8,15,6,9999,0
70   PRINT A;" − ";B;" = ";
80   INPUT C
90   IF C=A−B THEN PRINT"YOU ARE CORRECT":GOTO 40
100 IF C<A−B THEN PRINT"SORRY, YOUR ANSWER IS TOO SMALL. TRY
     AGAIN":GOTO 70
110 IF C>A−B THEN PRINT"SORRY, YOUR ANSWER IS TOO LARGE. TRY
     AGAIN":GOTO 70
120 IF C=9999 THEN END
```

2. Teachers should continue to provide practice and drill for the students on the microcomputer, either writing simple programs themselves or using commercially prepared programs.

Suggested Readings

Ashlock, Robert B. "Teaching the Basic Facts: Three Classes of Activities." *The Arithmetic Teacher*, vol. 18, no. 6, October 1971.

Ashlock, Robert B., and Herman, Wayne L., Jr. *Current Research in Elementary School Mathematics*. London: Collier-Macmillan, 1970.

Bitter, Gary G., and Mikesell, Jerald L. *Activities Handbook for Teaching with the Hand-held Calculator*. Boston: Allyn & Bacon, 1980.

Bright, George. "Ideas." *The Arithmetic Teacher*, vol. 24, no. 3, March 1977.

Caravella, Joseph R. *Minicalculators in the Classroom*. Washington, D.C.: National Education Association, 1977.

Cox, L. S. "Diagnosing and Remediating Systematic Errors in Addition and Subtraction Computation." *The Arithmetic Teacher*, vol. 22, no. 2, February 1975.

Dumas, Enoch. *Math Activities for Child Involvement*. Boston: Allyn & Bacon, 1971.

Gibb, E. Glenadine. "Children's Thinking in the Process of Subtraction." *Journal of Experimental Education*, September 1956.

Heckman, Mary Jane. "They All Add Up." *The Arithmetic Teacher*, vol. 21, no. 4, April 1974.

Heddens, James W. "A Theoretical Study of the Organization of Basic Addition Facts for Memorization." *1981 Research Monograph*, Kent, Ohio: Research Council for Diagnostic and Prescriptive Mathematics, 1981.

Higgins, Jon L., and Sachs, Larry A. *Mathematics Laboratories: 150 Activities and Games for Elementary Schools*. Reston, Va.: National Council of Teachers of Mathematics, 1974.

Kennedy, Leonard M., and Michon, Ruth L. *Games for Individualizing Mathematics Learning*. Columbus, Ohio: Merrill, 1973.

Lazerick, Beth E. "Mastering Basic Facts of Addition: An Alternate Strategy." *The Arithmetic Teacher*, vol. 27, no. 7, March 1981.

Leutzinger, Larry P., and Nelson, Glenn. "Using Addition Facts to Learn Subtraction Facts." *The Arithmetic Teacher*, vol. 26, no. 4, December 1979.

National Council of Teachers of Mathematics. *Mathematics Learning in Early Childhood*. Reston, Va.: NCTM, 1975.

Riedesel, C. Alan. *Teaching Elementary School Mathematics*. 3d ed. Englewood Cliffs, N.J.: Prentice-Hall, 1980.

Sherrill, James M. "Subtraction: Decomposition versus Equal Additions Method." *The Arithmetic Teacher*, vol. 26, no. 1, September 1979.

Troutman, Andrea P., and Lichtenberg, Betty K. *Mathematics: A Good Beginning*. 2d ed. Monterey, Calif.: Brooks/Cole, 1982.

Underhill, Robert G. *Teaching Elementary School Mathematics*. 2d ed. Columbus, Ohio: Merrrill, 1977.

Weaver, J. Fred. "Some Factors Associated with Pupils' Performance Levels on Simple Open Addition and Subtraction Sentences." *The Arithmetic Teacher*, vol. 18, no. 7, November 1971.

Wheatley, Grayson H., and Wheatley, Charlotte L. "How Shall We Teach Column Addition? Some Evidence." *The Arithmetic Teacher*, vol. 25, no. 4, January 1978.

7 Multiplication and Division of Whole Numbers

Teaching Competencies

Upon completing this unit, you will be able to:

State and then physically demonstrate four different models that can be used to develop an understanding of multiplication

Model two types of division (measurement and partition) using four different models

Use any model illustrating multiplication or division, and then write four related mathematical sentences

Use a place-value box, and demonstrate regrouping for both multiplication and division

Write examples to demonstrate the basic properties of multiplication

Discussion

Of the basic operations (addition and multiplication) and the inverse operations (subtraction and division), we have considered addition and its inverse, subtraction (Unit 6). In this unit we will examine the operation of multiplication and its inverse operation, division. The basic format for teaching multiplication and division is similar to that used for teaching addition and subtraction.

Readiness for multiplication and division includes an understanding of numberness to at least thousands; place value of at least ones, tens, and hundreds; conservation of number; reversibility; and addition and subtraction as inverse operations. This readiness has been developed in Units 1–5, so we can now develop an understanding of the operation of multiplication and its inverse operation, division.

The first step in teaching multiplication to children is to develop your own understanding of the operation. An understanding of an operation is developed from the concrete level to the abstract level using models. We will use four models to develop an understanding of multiplication. Multiplication is a **binary operation;** that is, numbers are multiplied two at a time. When we perform multiplication on two whole numbers, we obtain a unique result. The numbers we multiply are called **factors,** and the result of the multiplication is called a **product.** For example, in the mathematics sentence

$$3 \times 4 = 12,$$

the numbers 3 and 4 are the factors, and 12 is the product.

$$\text{Factor} \times \text{Factor} = \text{Product}$$
$$3 \quad \times \quad 4 \quad = \quad 12$$

Now let's carefully examine how to introduce children to multiplication. Most elementary school mathematics programs use one or more of the following models to develop an understanding of multiplication: sets, arrays, number line, and successive addition. Let us begin to develop an understanding by examining each multiplication model as we would develop them with children. Remember that children must do the actual manipulating to function on the concrete level.

The set approach to multiplication resembles the set approach to addition. Suppose we want to find the product of 3 sets of 4. The children should be asked to make three separate sets with four items in each set. To illustrate this idea, select three sets with four elements in each. For example,

$$3 \times 4 = 12$$

The first factor (3) tells us the number of sets; the second factor (4) tells us how many elements should be in each set. The product (12) is the total number of elements. This model would be read as: "Three sets of four is twelve." The mathematical sentence $3 \times 4 = 12$ is then related to the model, and the reading of "three sets of four is twelve" is related to reading the sentence as "three times four is twelve."

Since children have already studied addition, the model of successive addition can be introduced to help the children realize why three sets of four is twelve. We can obtain the same results by placing the three sets together much as we did in addition. We can think of 3×4 in terms of addition, but remember that *repeated addition is not multiplication.* Repeated addition is only a model to help children develop an understanding of multiplication.

$$3 \times 4 = 4 + 4 + 4 = 12$$

Therefore, we can think of this example as $4 + 4 + 4 = 12$ or 3 sets of 4 is 12 or $3 \times 4 = 12$. Using multiplication, we write $3 \times 4 = 12$ (read "three times four is equal to 12").

Similarly, we can find the product of 4×5.

$$4 \times 5 = 20$$

Here we have four sets with five elements in each set. We can read this as "four sets of five equals 20." The addition sentence that helps explain that 4×5 is 20 is: $5 + 5 + 5 + 5 = 20$. Remember if a child adds four fives, he is not multiplying; he is adding. This only helps the child to realize that four sets of five is really twenty. The multiplication sentence

$$4 \times 5 = 20$$

is read "four times five equals 20."

Now let's examine another extrememly useful model for multiplication: an **array.**

> An array is an arrangement of objects or symbols into orderly rows and columns.

This array would be called a 3-by-5 array. The child should use the eye movement developed in learning to read and begin at the upper left-hand corner. The child's eye moves across, visualizing one set of 5, down to two sets of 5, and then down to three sets of 5. Thus a child would think of this array as three sets of five, and it would be read as three sets of five. The product of the number of rows and the number of columns in an array is always equal to the number of objects or symbols in the array. Thus, to discover that $3 \times 5 = 15$, the child can count the objects or symbols in a 3-by-5 array or use successive addition $(5 + 5 + 5)$ to obtain the product.

Arrays can be helpful for developing basic facts and properties for multiplication. For example, a 2-by-4 array can be turned on its end to form a 4-by-2 array. This can be done to show that $2 \times 4 = 4 \times 2$.

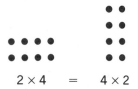

$$2 \times 4 \quad = \quad 4 \times 2$$

This illustrates that the multiplication of whole numbers is commutative. This is reasonable, since multiplication of whole numbers can be considered in terms of repeated addition (addition of equal addends).

Consider that $3 \times 2 = 6$ could mean $2 + 2 + 2 = 6$. It is easy to illustrate the commutative property of multiplication by simply turning an array on its end. In the array pictured here, the total number of objects is six in both cases.

The grouping or physical arrangement is different, but the product is the same. Whether two sets of three or three sets of two are used, the total number involved is six. This is the **commutative property of multiplication.** Many more examples of the commutative property of multiplication should be presented to children in the same fashion.

> The commutative property of multiplication means that the order of two factors does not affect the product. For example, $3 \times 2 = 2 \times 3$.

Multiplication can also be examined using the number line. Let us look again at the example $3 \times 4 = 12$ and show it by modeling on the number line, using repeated addition:

We begin to model at the reference point, 0, and mark off four units, which puts us at the place named by 4. From this point we mark off another four units; and from that point, named by 8, we mark off four more units. This puts us at the point labeled 12. Therefore, $4 + 4 + 4 = 12$ and $3 \times 4 = 12$. The same procedure can, of course, also be used to show that $4 \times 3 = 12$, thus illustrating the commutative property of multiplication.

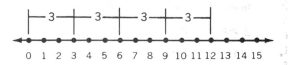

With young children, always begin modeling on the number line at the reference point 0. In this example we mark off three units, starting at zero, which puts us at the point named by 3. From that point, we mark off another three units; from that point (6) we mark off three more units; and from that point (labeled 9) we mark off another three units. Now we have arrived at a product of 12. Thus this model illustrates that four sets of three modeled on the number line shows that $4 \times 3 = 12$. Provide children many experiences modeling multiplication on the number line. This will also reinforce the commutative property of multiplication.

The **Cartesian product** can also be used as a model for multiplication; however, it is not recommended for elementary school. This model is more difficult to comprehend, so it should be reserved for more mature children (about junior high-school level).

Consider one set of two sweaters and one set of three pairs of pants. How many color combinations of sweaters and pants are possible?

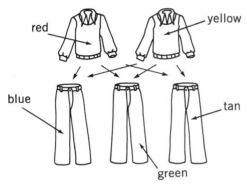

The red sweater (r) may be worn with each pair of slacks to give the following color combinations:

$$(r,b) \qquad (r,g) \qquad (r,t)$$

The yellow sweater (y) may also be worn with each pair of slacks. Thus we have three more possible combinations:

$$(y,b) \qquad (y,g) \qquad (y,t)$$

The set of all color combinations is shown in the following table:

		Sweaters red	yellow
P	blue	(r,b)	(y,b)
a			
n	green	(r,g)	(y,g)
t			
s	tan	(r,t)	(y,t)

Each time we match a sweater with pants, we obtain an ordered pair. For example, (r,t) is the ordered pair obtained by matching the red sweater with the tan pants. The set of all ordered pairs obtained by matching the elements of sweaters with the elements of pants is called the Cartesian product of sweaters and pants. This set of ordered pairs is denoted by A × B (read "the Cartesian product of A and B").

Note that, when we use a table to display the possible combinations of two sweaters and three pants, an array is generated. In this case we have a 3-by-2 array that provides six different combinations.

We have identified five models that can be used for multiplication. Four of these models can help children discover and develop an understanding of multiplication: sets, successive addition, arrays, and number line. The model of the Cartesian product should be taught later. None of these models is likely to solve all a child's difficulties in understanding multiplication. The teacher should be flexible and sensitive and must vary the models to suit the needs of the children in each class.

How are these models used to help children understand multiplication? Let's deal with sets as an example of a model. Place three sheets of paper on a desk; on each sheet of paper place two cubes, small toys, or plastic eating utensils.

These questions must be asked:

How many sets are there?
How many items are in each set?
How many items are there altogether?

In this case there are three sets with two items in each set, so there are six items altogether. Thus we can say that 3 sets of 2 is 6.

$$3 \text{ sets of } 2 = 6$$
$$3 \times 2 = 6$$

Children need to view many sets of materials and to say, discuss, and write multiplication sentences. The overhead projector is an excellent technique for presenting sets and arrays to children. Use small rectangles of colored plastic on an overhead projector for each set, and place plastic spoons or forks as items on each set. Arrays can be made on overhead transparencies by pasting circular discs in columns and rows. Gummed discs also work well.

Do *not* begin with two sets of two, because 2 add 2 gives the same result as 2 times 2. Use Dienes Blocks, Stern rods, Cuisenaire rods, attribute blocks, people pieces, and other materials. Consult the specific manual designed to help teachers use the materials.

Make multiplication arrays on sheets of paper, using gummed dots. Roll up the sheets of paper; as the students unroll each array, they can develop the **multiples** for any given number.

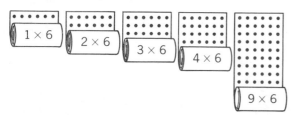

Multiples of a given number include all products obtained by multiplying the set of whole numbers by a given factor. For example, the multiples of 4 are obtained by multiplying 0, 1, 2, 3, 4, 5, . . . by 4. Thus the multiples of 4 are 0, 4, 8, 12, 16, 20, . . .

The number line is another model that should be used with children. How would the multiplication example 3×2 be modeled on the number line?

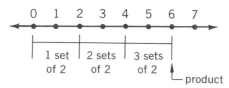

Always begin to model at the reference point 0. Mark off one set of two, then two sets of two, and then three sets of two. The number at the end of the three sets of two indicates the product which is 6. We read "3 sets of 2 is 6" or "3 times 2 is 6" and write $3 \times 2 = 6$.

Successive addition will help children to understand the relationship between addition and multiplication.

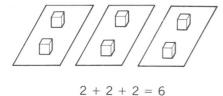

$$2 + 2 + 2 = 6$$

From these models children need to generalize that:

Multiplication is a binary operation on a pair of factors to obtain a unique product.

Factor $\times$ Factor = Product

By using appropriate models, children should be able to develop the basic facts of multiplication and organize them into a multiplication table. Ten

digits are written on the horizontal axis and on the vertical axis. Since there are 10×10 or 100 possible pairs of one-place factors, the children must memorize 100 basic multiplication facts. Two things must be done: the basic multiplication facts must be developed and memorized.

The basic multiplication facts include all one-place factors multiplied by all one-place factors to obtain a one- or two-place product.

Now let us begin with the development of the basic multiplication facts that do not involve zero as a factor. If zero is used as a factor, how can zero sets of 3 be shown on the concrete level? It may be difficult for the children to comprehend 3 sets of zero as a beginning example.

The children can use sets, successive addition, arrays, and the number line to discover facts such as $2 \times 3 = 6$, $3 \times 2 = 6$, $4 \times 2 = 8$, $2 \times 4 = 8$, $3 \times 4 = 12$, and $4 \times 3 = 12$. As the children discover basic facts, help them to become aware of basic structure (commutativity is especially helpful). Arrays, as we have already mentioned, can be very convincing models for illustrating the commutative property of multiplication.

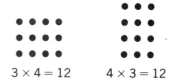

$$3 \times 4 = 12 \qquad 4 \times 3 = 12$$

Now children can begin to generate the multiples of a number by using sets as models. Generating the multiples of 2 using sets as models is illustrated here as an example:

▫	1 set of 2	$1 \times 2 = 2$
▫ ▫	2 sets of 2	$2 \times 2 = 4$
▫ ▫ ▫	3 sets of 2	$3 \times 2 = 6$
▫ ▫ ▫ ▫	4 sets of 2	$4 \times 2 = 8$
▫ ▫ ▫ ▫ ▫	5 sets of 2	$5 \times 2 = 10$
▫ ▫ ▫ ▫ ▫ ▫	6 sets of 2	$6 \times 2 = 12$
▫ ▫ ▫ ▫ ▫ ▫ ▫	7 sets of 2	$7 \times 2 = 14$
▫ ▫ ▫ ▫ ▫ ▫ ▫ ▫	8 sets of 2	$8 \times 2 = 16$
▫ ▫ ▫ ▫ ▫ ▫ ▫ ▫ ▫	9 sets of 2	$9 \times 2 = 18$

Skip counting helps children learn to generate the multiples of a number. Practice counting by 2, then by 5. Try having the children skip count by 3 while they are looking at a number line. Practice skip counting by many different numbers. Counting by 2, which children have already learned and reviewed, can be related to this model. Children need many experiences generating multiples of a given number. Remember that a multiple is a product obtained by multiplying the set of whole numbers by a given factor. Applying the definition to a given factor of 6, we multiply 0, 1, 2, 3, 4, . . . by 6. This procedure must be followed very carefully. Note that the first factor changes but the second factor remains constant. In this example, we continually add another set of 6 and generate the multiples for 6.

Whole numbers as factors	Factor	Multiples
0	6	0
1	6	6
2	6	12
3	6	18
4	6	24
5	6	30
6	6	36
7	6	42
8	6	48
9	6	54
10	6	60
.	.	.
.	.	.
.	.	.

Sets are perhaps the most useful model for introducing multiplication facts such as $2 \times 0 = 0$ and $4 \times 0 = 0$. Two empty boxes would be excellent models for two empty sets, $2 \times 0 = 0$; four boxes could model four empty sets, or $4 \times 0 = 0$.

$$4 \times 0 = 0 + 0 + 0 + 0 = 0$$

When the children have used arrays or other models to discover the commutative property of multiplication, then they can use this property to discover that

$$0 \times 2 = 0$$
$$0 \times 4 = 0$$
and so on

The children need to generalize that the product of 0 and any other factor is 0.

$$n \times 0 = 0$$
$$0 \times n = 0$$

This generalization allows the completion of one entire row and one entire column of the multiplication table.

					Factor					
×	0	1	2	3	4	5	6	7	8	9
0	0	0	0	0	0	0	0	0	0	0
1	0									
2	0									
3	0									
4	0									
5	0									
6	0									
7	0									
8	0									
9	0									

(Factor — left side: F a c t o r)

A similar approach can be used to develop the identity element for multiplication. Three sets of 1 can be modeled with three boxes and one block in each box.

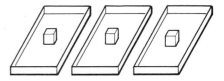

By applying the basic property of commutativity, we see that $1 \times 3 = 3$. Successive addition will also help children understand the relationship between addition and multiplication and the commutative property.

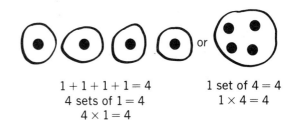

$$1 + 1 + 1 + 1 = 4 \qquad 1 \text{ set of } 4 = 4$$
$$4 \text{ sets of } 1 = 4 \qquad 1 \times 4 = 4$$
$$4 \times 1 = 4$$

Again, by applying the basic property of commutativity, we see that $1 \times 4 = 4$. The children can now make the generalization that the product of 1 and any other factor is equal to the other factor. The number 1 is thus defined as the **identity element of multiplication.** For any whole number *a*,

$$a \times 1 = a$$
$$1 \times a = a$$

×		0	1	2	3	4	5	6	7	8	9
					Factor						
	0	0	0	0	0	0	0	0	0	0	0
	1	0	1	2	3	4	5	6	7	8	9
	2	0	2								
F	3	0	3								
a	4	0	4								
c											
t	5	0	5								
o											
r	6	0	6								
	7	0	7								
	8	0	8								
	9	0	9								

The children will eventually be able to construct the entire multiplication table of basic facts. When the students have memorized 55 of the basic multiplication facts in the table, they will know the remaining 45 facts because of the commutative property of multiplication. (The symmetry resulting from the commutative property is indicated here by shading.)

×		0	1	2	3	4	5	6	7	8	9
					Factor						
	0	0	0	0	0	0	0	0	0	0	0
	1	0	1	2	3	4	5	6	7	8	9
	2	0	2	4	6	8	10	12	14	16	18
F	3	0	3	6	9	12	15	18	21	24	27
a	4	0	4	8	12	16	20	24	28	32	36
c											
t	5	0	5	10	15	20	25	30	35	40	45
o											
r	6	0	6	12	18	24	30	36	42	48	54
	7	0	7	14	21	28	35	42	49	56	63
	8	0	8	16	24	32	40	48	56	64	72
	9	0	9	18	27	36	45	54	63	72	81

As soon as children understand place value and the operation of multiplication, they can solve a great number of related examples. For example, if they understand that $3 \times 2 = 6$, then they should be able to solve these related examples by relating multiplication and place-value concepts. Two sets of 3 can be modeled as:

Now exchange each element in each set with a package of ten. The model now becomes:

Children can easily count to verify that two sets of 3 is 6 and two sets of 30 is 60. Two sets of 3 tens is 6 tens. From many of these related models, children should generalize what happens in each case. The basic fact is the same in both examples: $2 \times 3 = 6$. The only difference is the place value. This concept is known as expanding the basic facts. By using place value, the basic fact of $2 \times 3 = 6$ has been expanded into $2 \times 30 = 60$. Children should generalize that the basic facts are the same regardless of place value.

$$\begin{array}{r} 3 \\ \times 2 \\ \hline 6 \end{array} \qquad \begin{array}{r} 30 \\ \times 2 \\ \hline 60 \end{array}$$

You might want to review place value before giving this lesson.

The multiplication table could be expanded to include an indefinite number of products, but it would then become large, awkward, and difficult to use. Instead, given an understanding of the properties of multiplication and the basic multiplication facts, an algorithm can be developed for solving multiplication examples that involve greater numbers.

Before we continue the development of multiplication with children, let us examine some other properties of this operation. We have already studied the commutative property of multiplication.

The commutative property of multiplication means that the order of the two factors does not affect the product. For example $2 \times 3 = 3 \times 2$ or $A \times B = B \times A$.

Now let us consider the **associative property of multiplication.** Multiplication is a binary operation; this means that it can be performed on only two numbers at one time. This gives us the freedom to associate factors in different ways for greater ease in computation. Consider the associative property of multiplication, and note its effective application in this example:

$$(29 \times 25) \times 4 = 29 \times (25 \times 4)$$

The parentheses tell us how to associate the factors. The parentheses are saying: "Do me first." Obviously, the student who does not learn to look for shortcuts will multiply 29 × 25 and then multiply the product by 4.

$$
\begin{array}{rr}
29 & 725 \\
\times\, 25 & \times\quad 4 \\
\hline
145 & 2900 \\
58 & \\
\hline
725 &
\end{array}
$$

However, an observant student who understands the associative property of multiplication will rewrite the example (29 × 25) × 4 as 29 × (25 × 4): 25 × 4 = 100, and 29 × 100 = 2900. Using the associative property of multiplication to look at an example this way, we can see the kind of efficiency and understanding that a good mathematics program stresses.

In this example, we used a specific instance of the associative property:

$$(29 \times 25) \times 4 = 29 \times (25 \times 4)$$

In general,

> The associative property of multiplication means that, when three or more factors are to be multiplied, the grouping of the factors does not affect the product. For example: (2 × 1) × 4 = 2 × (1 × 4) or (A × B) × C = A × (B × C).

Let's look at an example that uses both the commutative and associative properties of multiplication: 60 × 21 × 5.

$$
\begin{array}{lll}
(60 \times 21) \times 5 & = 60 \times (21 \times 5) & \text{Associative property} \\
& = 60 \times (5 \times 21) & \text{Commutative property} \\
& = (60 \times 5) \times 21 & \text{Associative property} \\
& = \quad 300 \quad \times 21 & \text{Multiplication} \\
& = 6300 &
\end{array}
$$

Do not ask children to label each statement of an example; we have done this here only to illustrate the properties being used. Children should study examples before they begin to calculate. If they can see that a property will help them to simplify an example, they should use the property. In this case, the use of two properties has simplified the example.

Use of basic structural properties achieves another worthwhile objective: it keeps children from believing that there is only one way to solve a math-

ematics problem. Since mathematics uses a highly disciplined approach to problem solving and since there is frequently only one answer to a given problem, it is easy for children to believe that there is only one approach to a correct solution. This mistaken belief is one of the greatest enemies of insight, creativity, and intelligence in problem solving. Students must learn to seek from the many possible paths the best approach for a given situation. They must be released from narrowly channeled patterns of thought and allowed to develop their own critical and analytical abilities.

Another fundamental property of operations on whole numbers is the **distributive property of multiplication over addition.** This simply means that an example such as 3 × (20 + 3) can be written as (3 × 20) + (3 × 3). The steps in the calculation are then much simplified:

$$
\begin{array}{lll}
3 \times 23 = 3 \times (20 + 3) & = (3 \times 20) + (3 \times 3) \\
& = \quad 60 \quad + \quad 9 \\
& = \quad 69
\end{array}
$$

Inspection of this statement reveals that our multiplication algorithm depends on the distributive property of multiplication over addition. Every multiplication example having two or more places requires using the distributive property over addition to solve it. Essentially, in multiplication we express one of the factors as the sum of two or more addends. For instance, in the previous example, 3 × 23, we rename 23 as (20 + 3). We then find the partial products and the final product by applying the distributive property, just as we did in the previous example.

Many elementary school mathematics textbooks inappropriately introduce the distributive property of multiplication over addition with two one-place numbers. For example, 2 × 8 can be solved as: 2 × (2 + 6) = (2 × 2) + (2 × 6) = 4 + 12 = 16. The distributive property can be applied, but the children see no need for this property, since we expect them to memorize the product of 2 × 8. So do not introduce the distributive property of multiplication over addition until the children are ready to multiply a two-place number by a one-place number.

Now consider another exercise: 2 × 42 = □. In this case, we can set up our multiplication as follows:

$$
\begin{array}{rl}
42 & \\
\times\;\; 2 & \\
\hline
4 & \longrightarrow (2 \times 2) \\
+\; 80 & \longrightarrow (2 \times 40) \\
\hline
84 & \longrightarrow (2 \times 42)
\end{array}
$$

We are renaming the number 42 as sets of tens and sets of ones. Then we can state the example as 2 × (40 + 2). The distributive property allows us to express this multiplication in another form: $(2 \times 40) + (2 \times 2)$. Carrying out these operations gives us $80 + 4$, or 84. The product is the same as that obtained by using the multiplication algorithm.

Showing the multiplication step by step in expanded notation can be helpful for guiding children to a clear understanding of the operation.

Expanded notation
$$2 \times 42 = 2 \times (40 + 2)$$
$$= (2 \times 40) + (2 \times 2)$$
$$= \quad 80 \quad + \quad 4$$
$$= \quad 84$$

Vertical form

Long algorithm
```
  42
×  2
----
   4
  80
----
  84
```

Standard algorithm
```
  42
×  2
----
  84
```

Our numeration system is a place-value system. Thus the shorter algorithm (the standard algorithm) represents a brief and accurate method of performing the operation. In other words, multiplying 2 ones by 2 in the ones place gives us 4 ones, which is recorded in the ones column. Then, multiplying 4 tens by the 2 in the ones places gives 8 tens. The 8 is written in the tens column to the left of the 4 in the ones column. The alignment of the numbers in the vertical algorithm is correct because of our place-value numeration system and the distribution of multiplication over addition.

Suppose a child wants to multiply 28 by 4. Using the distributive property, she can make the example easier to solve by breaking up one of the factors into another grouping. Considering our decimal system of numeration, she might write $4 \times (20 + 8)$. This is grouped in terms of tens and ones. (This is not necessarily the most efficient arrangement, however.) The child would then think: $(4 \times 20) + (4 \times 8) = 80 + 32 = 112$. Or else she might group in this manner: $4 \times (25 + 3)$. In this case she would think: $(4 \times 25) + (4 \times 3) = 100 + 12 = 112$. Adding to the number 100 it is clearly a simple matter; it is also clear that 4×25 is 100. Familiarity with our money system (a decimal system) makes it simple for children to multiply such combinations.

The distributive property of multiplication over addition means that the product of a number and a sum can be expressed as a sum of two products, as in the following examples: $4 \times (20 + 3) = (4 \times 20) + (4 \times 3)$ or $A \times (B \times C) = (A \times B) + (A \times C)$.

Zero displays special properties when it is used in the operation of multiplication. What pattern do you notice in these examples?

$$2 \times 0 = 0 \qquad 0 \times 9 = 0$$
$$14 \times 0 = 0 \qquad 0 \times 25 = 0$$
$$6 \times 0 = 0 \qquad 0 \times 100 = 0$$

We refer to this as the **multiplication property of zero.**

The multiplication property of zero means that, when two factors are multiplied and one of the factors is zero, then the product is zero. For example: $5 \times 0 = 0$, $0 \times 7 = 0$, $A \times 0 = 0$, and $0 \times A = 0$.

Zero has special properties, and so does the number 1. The number 1 is the identity element of multiplication. Any number multiplied by 1, or 1 multiplied by any number, always results in the other number. Again, examples will clarify this for the children. Remember to use concrete examples, and then move slowly to the abstract level.

$$8 \times 1 = 8 \qquad 2 \times 1 = 2$$
$$1 \times 8 = 8 \qquad 1 \times 2 = 2$$

One (1) is the identity element for multiplication, since the product of any number and one is always that number. For example $7 \times 1 = 7$, $A \times 1 = A$, and $1 \times A = A$.

Now that we have examined some properties of multiplication, we can return to the multiplication program. For a sound understanding of multiplication involving factors with two or more digits, the children will need to be familiar with the distributive property of multiplication over addition. Arrays are excellent for helping children to discover this property:

$$3 \times 12 \qquad (3 \times 10) + (3 \times 2)$$

Two one-place factors are basic multiplication facts; children will not see the need for the distributive property over addition if 2 one-place numbers are used. Do *not* begin to study the distributive property of multiplication over addition with one-place numbers; children cannot comprehend the use of this property with one-place numbers. Introduce the distributive property of multiplication over addition as you begin to study multiplication of a two-place number by a one-place number.

Consider this example: $3 \times 13 = \square$. The number 13 can be named in many ways. In this case, let's use $(10 + 3)$ because place value is useful in the multiplication algorithm. If the distributive property is used, children can apply basic multiplication facts to find the product:

$$
\begin{aligned}
3 \times 13 &= 3 \times (10 + 3) & \text{Renaming 13} \\
&= (3 \times 10) + (3 \times 3) & \text{Distributive property} \\
&= \quad 30 \quad + \quad 9 & \text{Multiplication} \\
&= \quad 39 & \text{Addition}
\end{aligned}
$$

The solution to this example can also be written as follows:

$$
\begin{array}{c}
13 = \\
\underline{\times \quad 3} =
\end{array}
\Rightarrow
\begin{array}{r}
\times 1 \text{ ten } 3 \text{ ones} \\
\underline{\times \qquad 3} \\
3 \text{ tens } 9 \text{ ones} = 39
\end{array}
\Rightarrow
\begin{array}{r}
13 \\
\underline{\times \ 3} \\
39
\end{array}
$$

Encourage children to look for the relationships that exist within the examples. For instance, the preceding example can be examined as follows:

Basic fact		Extended basic fact		Basic fact
1		10		3
$\times 3$	$\Rightarrow$	$\times \ 3$		$\times 3$
3		30		9

$$
\begin{array}{r}
13 \\
\underline{\times \ 3} \\
39
\end{array}
$$

The children have memorized the basic multiplication facts, so they should know the basic facts in this example: 3×1 and 3×3. The basic fact 3×1 has been expanded to 3×10. The two examples 3×10 and 3×3 are put together using the concept of place value, to get the example 3×13.

Consider the example $3 \times 23 = \square$. The number 23 can also be named as $(20 + 3)$. Again the students can apply the distributive property.

$$
\begin{array}{c}
23 = \\
\underline{\times \ 3} =
\end{array}
\Rightarrow
\begin{array}{r}
2 \text{ tens } 3 \text{ ones} \\
\underline{\times \qquad 3} \\
6 \text{ tens } 9 \text{ ones} = 69
\end{array}
\Rightarrow
\begin{array}{r}
23 \\
\underline{\times \ 3} \\
69
\end{array}
$$

Renaming using expanded notation can also help to develop the concept of multiplication with three-place factors:

$$
\begin{array}{c}
124 = \\
\underline{\times \quad 2} =
\end{array}
\blacktriangleright
\begin{array}{r}
1 \text{ hundred } 2 \text{ tens } 4 \text{ ones} \\
\underline{\times \qquad\qquad 2} \\
2 \text{ hundreds } 4 \text{ tens } 8 \text{ ones} = 248
\end{array}
\blacktriangleright
\begin{array}{r}
124 \\
\underline{\times \ 2} \\
248
\end{array}
$$

Another form of algorithm can be used when an understanding of multiplication has been developed through expanded notation.

$$
\begin{array}{r}
121 \\
\underline{\times \quad 3} \\
3 \longrightarrow (3 \times \quad 1) \\
60 \longrightarrow (3 \times \quad 20) \\
\underline{300} \longrightarrow (3 \times 100) \\
363
\end{array}
$$

Use the longer forms of the multiplication algorithm to develop an understanding. When the children are ready to develop skill, use the short algorithm. Children should have the opportunity to apply their knowledge of basic structure and of the algorithm to two-place multiplication.

A good beginning example could involve an even ten (10, 20, 30, etc.). Consider the example $10 \times 12 = \square$. The identity element of multiplication has been developed:

$$
\begin{array}{r}
3 \\
\underline{\times 1}
\end{array}
\qquad
\begin{array}{r}
4 \\
\underline{\times 1}
\end{array}
$$

The basic facts have been expanded into

$$
\begin{array}{r}
30 \\
\underline{\times \ 1}
\end{array}
\qquad
\begin{array}{r}
40 \\
\underline{\times \ 1}
\end{array}
$$

Spend time with the children now to help them understand the place-value concepts involved at this point.

$$
\text{If}
\begin{array}{r}
12 \\
\underline{\times \ 1} \\
12
\end{array}
\qquad
\text{Then}
\begin{array}{r}
12 \\
\underline{\times 10} \\
120
\end{array}
$$

$$
\text{If}
\begin{array}{r}
12 \\
\underline{\times \ 2} \\
24
\end{array}
\qquad
\text{Then}
\begin{array}{r}
12 \\
\underline{\times 20} \\
240
\end{array}
$$

After the children understand the concept of multiplying by an even ten, then two examples that children can already solve may be put together. Consider the example $12 \times 14 = \square$. The two examples prerequisite to solving 12×14 are: 10×14 and 2×14. Both of these examples have been taught. Now you must help the students to bring these two ideas together into one example:

$$
\begin{array}{r}
14 \\
\underline{\times 10} \\
140
\end{array}
\qquad
\begin{array}{r}
14 \\
\underline{\times \ 2} \\
28
\end{array}
$$

$$
\begin{array}{r}
14 \\
\underline{\times 12} \\
28 \\
\underline{140} \\
168
\end{array}
$$

Note that, in each method for solving this example, the answer has been obtained by taking the sum of four different products: (2×4), (2×10), (10×4), and (10×10). This idea must then be expanded into more decimal places. Children must be able to analyze multiplication examples and see all the different multiplication examples that make up the new example.

There is still another major concept that must be developed for multiplication: **regrouping** (sometimes called *carrying*). The term *regrouping* is used here because it applies to addition, subtraction, multiplication and division; we do not need to introduce *carrying* and *borrowing* as two different concepts if we introduce *regrouping* and use it with all the operations. The term *regrouping* is used to indicate when a number is renamed from one place value to another. The following example illustrates the idea of *carrying*, which we will call regrouping:

$$\begin{array}{r} 24 \\ \times\ 3 \\ \hline \end{array}$$

A child might think and write:

$$\begin{array}{r} 24 \\ \times\ 3 \\ \hline 12 \\ 60 \\ \hline 72 \end{array}$$

The child thought 3×4 and wrote 12 and then thought 3×20 and wrote 60; there was no regrouping in this case. The two partial products are then added. Examples of this type are prerequisite to understanding the regrouping concept. Rewriting the example using tens and ones is another excellent activity:

$$\begin{array}{r} 24 \\ \times\ 3 \end{array} = \begin{array}{r} 2 \text{ tens } 4 \text{ ones} \\ \times\qquad\ 3 \\ \hline 6 \text{ tens } 12 \text{ ones} \end{array}$$

This is the beginning of readiness for regrouping:

6 tens 12 ones
6 tens (1 ten 2 ones)
7 tens 2 ones = 72

If the child thinks 3×4 is 12 and then thinks of 12 as 1 ten and 2 ones, the child is regrouping. Regrouping was used at the stage where 12 was regrouped as 1 ten and 2 ones and the 1 ten was regrouped with the tens. Regrouping is also used in the following example:

$$\begin{array}{r} 48 \\ \times\ 2 \\ \hline 96 \end{array}$$

In multiplying 2×8 to get 16, we record the 6 in the ones place and regroup 1 ten. Multiply 2×40 or 2×4 tens (we very often just say 2×4) to get 8 tens, add the regrouped number of 1 ten with 8 tens, and record the 9 in the tens place. Regrouping is also used in the following example:

$$\begin{array}{r} 268 = \\ \times\ 26 = \end{array} \begin{array}{r} 2 \text{ hundreds } 6 \text{ tens } 8 \text{ ones} \\ \times\qquad\qquad\ 2 \text{ tens } 6 \text{ ones} \\ \hline \end{array}$$

$$\begin{array}{rl} 48 & \longleftarrow (6 \times\quad 8) \\ 360 & \longleftarrow (6 \times\quad 60) \\ 1200 & \longleftarrow (6 \times 200) \\ 160 & \longleftarrow (20 \times\quad 8) \\ 1200 & \longleftarrow (20 \times\quad 60) \\ 4000 & \longleftarrow (20 \times 200) \\ \hline 6968 & \end{array}$$

When multiplying 6×8 to get 48, we record 8 in the ones column and regroup the 4 (40). When multiplying 6×60 to get 360, we record 6 in the tens column and regroup the 3 (300). The carried or regrouped numbers are written in the proper columns and added to the sum. Note that the regrouped figure is *not* written above the example. If children need to record the regrouped number as a crutch, teach them to write it below the example, *where it has real meaning*.

The familiar short algorithm, however, requires us to omit the extra steps that show how we regroup:

$$\begin{array}{r} 268 \\ \times\quad 26 \\ \hline 1608 \\ 5360 \\ \hline 6968 \end{array}$$

When the concept of regrouping is taught, a great deal of practice must be provided. The concept must be extended into more decimal places so children can multiply a many-place number by a many-place number with multiple regroupings. However, in our society today we will usually use a hand-held calculator or microcomputer to multiply many-place numbers. The consumer of mathematics must be able to understand the concept and estimate the reasonableness of the answer provided by the calculator or computer.

Most elementary school programs no longer use the term *carry*. *Regroup* seems to suggest more clearly that we are renaming a number in a particular way and using the associative property of addition.

At this level of development all the basic ideas of multiplication have been taught:

1. Understanding what multiplication is.
2. The basic multiplication facts (which have been developed and memorized).

3. Place value and multiplication of greater numbers.
4. The structures of multiplication (the commutative property of multiplication, the associative property of multiplication, the zero property, the identity element of multiplication, and the distributive property of multiplication over addition). There are other properties, but these are the properties usually taught in elementary school.
5. The concept of regrouping.

The concepts thus developed must be applied to many different examples; children should practice and review them. Electronic devices can be used with children as means to drill and practice these concepts. Microcomputer software is available, but teachers must carefully evaluate the software to make sure that the practice is appropriate for each child. Children in upper grade levels can write simple microcomputer programs to solve their mathematics exercises. Any child who can program the computer certainly knows the mathematics concepts.

Division has the same inverse relationship to multiplication that subtraction has to addition. Division "undoes" what multiplication does; we might use the term "unmultiply" to indicate division. Teaching the basic ideas of division should parallel the teaching of multiplication. The concepts of subtraction can also be used to advantage here. Traditional mathematics programs have not placed sufficient emphasis on division as the inverse operation of multiplication. The understanding of division has often been neglected, because so much emphasis has been placed on memorizing the algorithm and developing skill of computation. Also, research tells us that division is the most difficult operation to teach.

To develop children's understanding of division, instruction should begin on the concrete level. Many mathematics programs try to teach division on the abstract level; children learn only to calculate and do not learn the meaning of division. Models that might be used to introduce division include sets, arrays, successive subtraction, number lines, and the inverse relationship between multiplication and division. Let's carefully examine each of these models as we develop an understanding of division.

Consider a set of six plastic spoons:

We can ask the children: How many sets of two spoons can we make from a set of six plastic spoons?

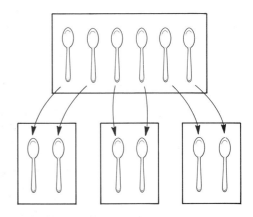

By moving the plastic spoons and making sets of two spoons, children see that they can make three sets. A set of six plastic spoons can be separated into three sets of two. We can write:

$$\begin{array}{r} 3 \\ 2\overline{)6} \\ -\,6 \\ \hline 0 \end{array}$$

We could have asked another question about the six plastic spoons: If the six plastic spoons are separated into two sets, how many spoons will be in each set? Again, children must be able to manipulate the plastic spoons into the two sets.

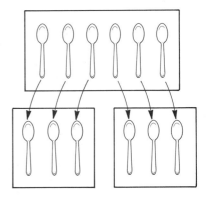

These are the two set models used to teach division to children. Now let us consider the use of arrays in division. The following array has a total of eight dots, but a sheet of paper is covering part of the array. We can ask: How many dots are in each row?

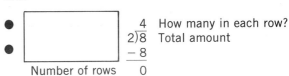

$$\begin{array}{r} 4 \\ 2\overline{)8} \\ -\,8 \\ \hline 0 \end{array}$$ How many in each row?
Total amount

Number of rows

There are four dots in each row. After the children think about the example and decide that there are four dots in each row, they can remove the sheet of paper and check to see whether this answer is correct.

An array can be used in another way. Use the same procedure as in the previous example, but this time use the sheet of paper to cover part of the columns. We can ask: How many dots are in each column? The example will be written the same, but the labels will be different. There are four dots in each column. After the children have discussed the example and reached a conclusion, the sheet of paper can be removed and the chiildren can check to make sure they are correct.

We have examined the set model and the array model to develop an understanding of division. Now let's study the number line used as a model for division. We will look again at the example $2\overline{)8}$ and model this on the number line.

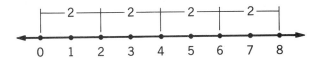

We begin at the reference point, 0, and mark off two units, which puts us at the point marked 2. From the point named 2, we mark off another two units; from that point, named 4, we mark off two more units. We continue marking off two-unit segments until we reach 8. Now we can see that there are four segments each two units long in 8. Therefore $8 - 2 = 6$, $6 - 2 = 4$, $4 - 2 = 2$, and $2 - 2 = 0$ (or $8 \div 2 = 4$), because 2 has been subtracted four times from 8. Thus, successive subtraction can also be used to model $8 \div 2 = 4$.

The children have learned that $4 \times 2 = 8$ and that 4 and 2 are factors and 8 is the product. Begin with multiplication examples written on a sheet of paper; use a pair of scissors to cut out one of the factors. Now ask the question: "What number was on the piece of paper that has been cut out?"

$$2 \times \boxed{} = 8$$

Since division is the inverse operation of multiplication, we can think of division in terms of finding a missing factor. Thus the example $12 \div 3 = \square$ can be thought of as $3 \times \square = 12$. The example $12 \div 3 = \square$ can be written in other equivalent forms; for example

$$3\overline{)12}^{\square} \quad \text{or} \quad \frac{12}{3} = \square \quad \text{or} \quad \frac{12}{\square} = 3$$

$$3 \times \square = 12 \quad \text{or} \quad \square \times 3 = 12$$
$$\text{or} \quad 12 = \square \times 3 \quad \text{or} \quad 12 = 3 \times \square$$

It is important for children to recognize division when it is written in any of its many different forms. Children should be able to rewrite any of these examples into a form that they can use to calculate the missing factor.

If a factor times a factor equals a product, then division can be thought of as an operation in which a product divided by a factor equals a factor.

$$\text{Factor} \times \text{Factor} = \text{Product}$$
$$\text{Product} \div \text{Factor} = \text{Factor}$$

Division can be written in several different ways.

$$\text{Product} \div \text{Factor} = \text{Factor}$$

$$\frac{\text{Product}}{\text{Factor}} = \text{Factor}$$

$$\text{Factor}\overline{)\text{Product}}^{\text{Factor}}$$

Two types of division must be developed with children: **measurement division** and **partitive division.**

Measurement division is more easily understood by children, so it is usually taught first. Consider the following example: If a farmer has 8 lambs and wishes to give 4 lambs to each of his children, to how many children can he give 4 lambs?

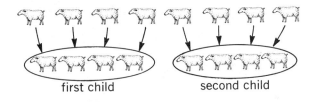

first child   second child

The student can see 8 lambs and then place 4 lambs into the first set and 4 lambs into the second set. Measurement division begins with a product and then asks the question: "How many sets of a certain number can be made?" "How many sets of 4 can be made from 8?" This can be written as

$$4\overline{)8}^{2}$$

Therefore, measurement division begins with a product and the number of elements in each set. We must find the number of sets.

Factor × Factor = Product
□ × 4 = 8

Partitive division is usually taught after measurement division. If a farmer has 8 lambs and wishes to give each of his 4 children the same number of lambs, how many lambs will each child receive?

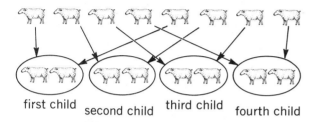

first child   second child   third child   fourth child

It would *not* make sense to use successive subtraction to solve this type of division problem. If a farmer has eight lambs, he cannot subtract two children. However, in the example of division measurement, it makes sense to begin with 8 lambs and then subtract 4 lambs, and then subtract 4 lambs again. Thus, 4 lambs can be taken away from 8 lambs and you then have two sets of 4 lambs. Therefore, partition division begins with a product and the number of sets. We must find the number of elements in each set.

Factor × Factor = Product
4 × □ = 8

Children need many experiences with models of set separation, arrays, number lines, and successive subtraction to develop an understanding of division. Both measurement and partition division must be modeled and developed. The terms **dividend, divisor,** and **quotient** also need to be developed.

$$\begin{array}{cc} \text{Factor} & \text{Quotient} \\ \text{Factor}\overline{)\text{Product}} & \text{Divisor}\overline{)\text{Dividend}} \end{array}$$

Difficulties arise if we attempt to divide by zero. Consider the sentence 5 ÷ 0 = □. If we rewrite this sentence as a multiplication sentence with a missing factor, we obtain:

$$0 \times \square = 5$$

There is no whole number we can use in the box to make the sentence true. Regardless of which whole number *n* we put in the box, the product will be 0, so the resulting sentence will be false.

$$\begin{array}{l} 0 \times \square = 5 \\ 0 \times n = 5 \\ 0 = 5 \quad \text{false} \end{array}$$

An even stranger situation results when we attempt to divide zero by itself. The sentence 0 ÷ 0 = □ could be rewritten as 0 × □ = 0. What whole number will make this sentence true? Any whole number! There is no unique number that can be considered the quotient for 0 ÷ 0 = □. Each time we attempt to divide by zero, we encounter this dilemma. *Teachers must be careful not to tell children that any number divided by itself equals 1*. Zero divided by zero is an exception to this statement. Therefore, we either leave division by zero undefined, or else we say that *division by zero is impossible*.

Basic division facts exist, just as basic subtraction facts do. However, when children thoroughly understand multiplication and the inverse relation, they already know all basic division facts.

The multiplication table should also be used for the basic division facts. Locate the given factor in the top row; then move down that column until you locate the product. Move to the left on that row; the first number is the missing factor. To use the table with the example 6 ÷ 2 = □, find the factor 2 in the top row of the table. Move down the 2 column until the product 6 is located. Now move to the left, and you will find the missing factor, 3.

				↓							Factor
×	0	1	2	3	4	5	6	7	8	9
0	0	0	0	0	0	0	0	0	0	0
1	0	1	2	3	4	5	6	7	8	9
2	0	2	4	6	8	10	12	14	16	18
3	0	3	6	9	12	15	18	21	24	27
4	0	4	8	12	16	20	24	28	32	36
5	0	5	10	15	20	25	30	35	40	45
6	0	6	12	18	24	30	36	42	48	54
7	0	7	14	21	28	35	42	49	56	63
8	0	8	16	24	32	40	48	56	64	72
9	0	9	18	27	36	45	54	63	72	81

(The left margin of the table is labeled vertically: F a c t o r)

Sometimes children need a guide to help them locate a specific example in the multiplication table. Make a guide by cutting two strips from a sheet of transparent acetate. Use rubber cement to connect the two strips at a 90-degree angle. Cut a square for the product where the two strips overlap.

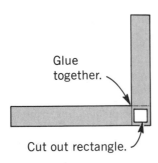

Glue together.

Cut out rectangle.

After acquiring an understanding of division, children should be given ample practice in the basic division facts, to learn to calculate efficiently. Again you might want to obtain software practice programs for your microcomputer, to provide the necessary practice of the basic division facts. Many examples similar to the following should be provided for practice:

$6 \times \square = 24$　　$2 \times \square = 4$　　$\square \times 3 = 12$
$\square \div 6 = 3$　　$8 \div 2 = \square$　　$10 \div \square = 2$
$2\overline{)6}$　　　　$5\overline{)15}$　　　$3\overline{)9}$

What is the missing factor in the example $2\overline{)7}$? Three different answers might be given, and all could be considered correct.

If the example refers to two packages of gum that sell for 7 cents, how much will one package of gum cost? This example of 7 divided by 2 has an answer of 4. At the store the child will pay four cents per package of gum. There is no remainder in this case. One-half is not a remainder because the child can't pay in half cents.

If the example refers to seven children forming two teams, with the same number of children on each team, how many children will be on each team? This example of 7 divided by 2 is 3; there will be three children on each team and one person left over to referee the game.

If the example refers to seven candy bars to be equally shared by two children, the question becomes: "How much candy will each child receive?" In this case the answer is three and one-half candy bars for each child; there is no remainder.

Children need to understand that remainders are handled in different ways, depending on the situation. We do not know what the solution to $2\overline{)7}$ is until the example has been placed in context. From the context of an example, we choose one of three ways to handle a remainder:

1. Drop the left-over part.
2. Raise the answer to the next number.

3. Place the left-over part as a fraction of the missing factor.

We do *not* recommend that children be taught to write a missing factor as 3r1. What is the meaning of "r1"? This is only a mechanical way to write a response so that the student's paper will be easier for the teacher to grade. The real meaning of a remainder is not apparent if r1 is used. Teach the three methods that have meaning in real-life situations.

After solving examples of this type, an example involving division with a remainder can be introduced, using the method of successive subtraction. For example, $19 \div 4 = \square$.

$$
\begin{array}{rl}
19 & \\
\underline{-\ 4} & \quad (1) \\
15 & \\
\underline{-\ 4} & \quad (2) \\
11 & \\
\underline{-\ 4} & \quad (3) \\
7 & \\
\underline{-\ 4} & \quad (4) \\
3 &
\end{array}
$$

We can see that there are 4 fours in 19, with a remainder of 3. This example can also be shown using the number line as a model.

Beginning at the reference point, 0, we mark off successive segments of four units each and find three units left over.

After studying the basic facts and solving a number of simple examples such as these, the children will be ready to extend the basic division facts. Using $6 \div 2$ and sets, we can think of six objects separated into sets of two. How many sets of two can we make from one set of six?

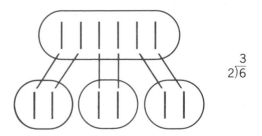

$2\overline{)6}$ with 3 above

Six elements can be separated into three sets of two.

Using the same example but substituting bundles of ten for each element, we can ask: "How many sets of two bundles each can we make from a set of six bundles?"

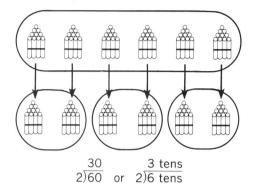

$$\frac{30}{2)\overline{60}} \quad \text{or} \quad \frac{3 \text{ tens}}{2)\overline{6 \text{ tens}}}$$

Six bundles of ten can be separated into three sets of two bundles of ten. Thus 60 elements can be separated into sets of two bundles of ten, and we find three sets of two bundles of ten. Children should be given many such examples extending the basic division facts.

After extending the basic division facts, children are ready to study division of a two-place number by a one-place number. Consider 69 divided by 3. The children have solved:

$$\frac{2}{3)\overline{6}} \\ \underline{-6} \\ 0$$

and extended the basic fact to:

$$\frac{20}{3)\overline{60}} \\ \underline{-60} \\ 0$$

They have also solved:

$$\frac{3}{3)\overline{9}} \\ \underline{-9} \\ 0$$

Now these two examples can be put together so the children can solve $3)\overline{69}$. Addition, multiplication, and subtraction examples are solved by beginning on the right-hand side; children need to know that division is begun on the left-hand side. First give them simple examples that they already know how to solve.

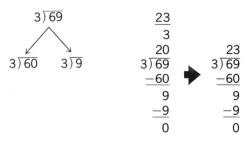

Children should then solve each of the following examples:

$$2)\overline{6} \quad 2)\overline{60} \quad 2)\overline{600} \quad 2)\overline{8} \quad 2)\overline{80} \quad 2)\overline{4}$$

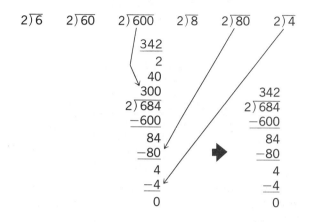

Again, children must learn to analyze division examples so they can see the simple examples that they know how to solve within the more complex examples. After solving division examples of a two-place number divided by a one-place number, the division concept must be extended into one, two, or many products divided by one-place factors. Examples with and without remainders should be considered.

The division algorithm and techniques of estimating quotients must be developed with children. Let us examine the example $7)\overline{247}$ and develop the algorithm using a place-value box.

Example	Question
$7)\overline{247}$	How many sets of 7 can be made from 247 things?
	Can one set of 7 be made? Can ten sets of 7 be made? Can one hundred sets of 7 be made?

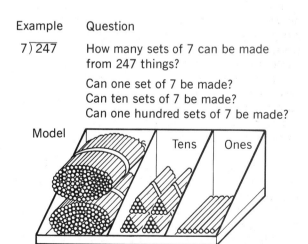

2 Hundreds   4 Tens   7 Ones

Children now need the skill of multiplying by 1, 10, and 100.

$$7\overline{)247}$$

How many sets of 7 can be made from 24 tens?

Where does the 3 belong?

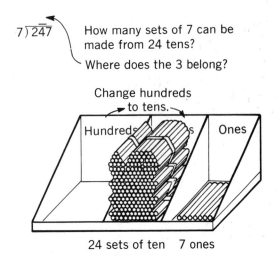

Change hundreds to tens.

24 sets of ten   7 ones

$$\begin{array}{r} 3 \\ 7\overline{)247} \\ -21 \\ \end{array}$$

If 30 sets of 7 are removed from the box, how many things are removed?

$$30 \times 7 = 210$$

$$\begin{array}{r} 3 \\ 7\overline{)247} \\ -21 \\ \hline 37 \end{array}$$

How many things are still left in the place-value box?

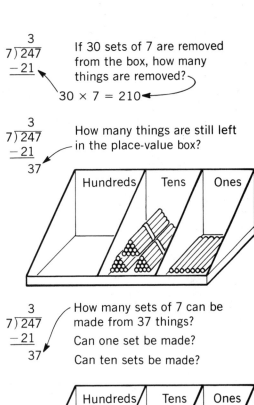

$$\begin{array}{r} 3 \\ 7\overline{)247} \\ -21 \\ \hline 37 \end{array}$$

How many sets of 7 can be made from 37 things?

Can one set be made?

Can ten sets be made?

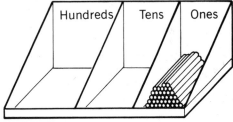

As soon as a "no" answer is received, the children have established the place value again.

$$\begin{array}{r} 35 \\ 7\overline{)247} \\ -21 \\ \hline 37 \\ -35 \\ \hline 2 \end{array}$$

How many sets of 7 can be made from 37 things?

$5 \times 7 = 35$ — How many things will be in 5 sets of 7?

How many things are left over?

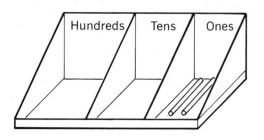

Children need a great deal of practice using tangible materials and relating them to the development of the division algorithm. Mastery of one-digit division is essential before beginning two-digit division.

Now consider this example:

$$15\overline{)349}$$

Here we need to know how many multiples of 15 can be subtracted from 349. Can 100 fifteens be subtracted from 349? No, since $100 \times 15 = 1500$, which cannot be subtracted from 349. Can 10 fifteens be subtracted from 349? Yes, since $10 \times 15 = 150$, which can be subtracted from 349. Can a greater multiple be subtracted? Yes; 20 fifteens can be subtracted: $20 \times 15 = 300$.

$$\begin{array}{r} 20 \\ 15\overline{)349} \\ -300 \\ \hline 49 \end{array} \leftarrow (20 \times 15)$$

How many fifteens can be subtracted from 49? Try 3:

$$\begin{array}{r} 23 \\ \hline 3 \\ 20 \\ 15\overline{)349} \\ -300 \\ \hline 49 \\ -45 \\ \hline 4 \end{array} \begin{array}{l} \\ \\ \\ \leftarrow(20 \times 15) \\ \\ \leftarrow(3 \times 15) \\ \end{array} \quad \text{or} \quad \begin{array}{r} 23 \\ 15\overline{)349} \\ -300 \\ \hline 49 \\ -45 \\ \hline 4 \end{array}$$

$$349 = (23 \times 15) + 4$$

Thus we see that there are 23 fifteens in 349, with a remainder of 4.

Consider another example: $34\overline{)856}$. How many sets of 34 can be made from 856 things?

Can one set be made?	$1 \times 34 = 34$
Can ten sets be made?	$10 \times 34 = 340$
Can one hundred sets be made?	$100 \times 34 = 3400$

Thus, the first estimate must be in the tens place. How many tens in 856? Compare 34 with 85. The first estimate would be 2, so that is placed in the tens place, or 20.

$$\begin{array}{r} 2 \\ 34\overline{)856} \\ -68 \\ \hline 176 \end{array}$$

How many sets of 34 can be made out of 176 things?

Can one set be made?	$1 \times 34 = 34$
Can ten sets be made?	$10 \times 34 = 340$

So this estimate must be placed in the ones place. Comparing 3 with 17, the best estimate is 5.

$$\begin{array}{r} 25 \\ 34\overline{)856} \\ -68 \\ \hline 176 \\ -170 \\ \hline 6 \end{array}$$

The more accurately a pupil estimates the trial quotient, the shorter his computation will be. For instance, inaccurate estimates make the following example unnecessarily long.

$$\begin{array}{r} 25 \\ 1 \\ 4 \\ 10 \\ 10 \\ 27\overline{)691} \\ -270 \longleftarrow (10 \times 27) \\ \hline 421 \\ -270 \longleftarrow (10 \times 27) \\ \hline 151 \\ -108 \longleftarrow (4 \times 27) \\ \hline 43 \\ -27 \longleftarrow (1 \times 27) \\ \hline 16 \end{array}$$

These examples are provided to help student teachers visualize the steps through which children progress as they learn to divide. It is *not* suggested that children write each step.

With more accurate estimates:

$$\begin{array}{r} 25 \\ 5 \\ 20 \\ 27\overline{)691} \\ -540 \longleftarrow (20 \times 27) \\ \hline 151 \\ -135 \longleftarrow (5 \times 27) \\ \hline 16 \end{array} \qquad \begin{array}{r} 25 \\ 27\overline{)691} \\ -540 \\ \hline 151 \\ -135 \\ \hline 16 \end{array}$$

Children's comprehension of division begins with real-world experiences from which we help them visualize, understand, and record. The basic facts of division must be memorized. Establishing place value, then making the estimate of a trial quotient is an aid for children in dividing. Much practice of division is necessary as children progress and learn new concepts.

Terminology, Symbols, and Procedures

Array An orderly arrangement of objects or symbols into rows and columns. An array with m rows and n columns (where m and n are whole numbers) is called an m-by-n array.

5-by-3 array   4-by-9 array

Cartesian product   If A and B are any two sets, then the Cartesian product A × B is the set of all ordered pairs (a, b) whose first elements are members of A and whose second elements are members of B. For example, if A = $\{p, q, r\}$ and B = $\{h, k\}$, then

$$A \times B = \{(p, h), (p, k), (q, h), (q, k), (r, h), (r, k)\}$$

Division algorithm   The division algorithm is the numerical process that is applied to a dividend and a divisor to obtain a quotient. Below is an application of this algorithm.

$$
\begin{array}{r}
54 \\
\hline
4 \\
\hline
50 \\
\end{array}
$$

$$
\begin{array}{r}
23\overline{)1242} \\
-1150 \longleftarrow (50 \times 23) \\
\hline
92 \\
-92 \longleftarrow (4 \times 23) \\
\hline
0 \\
\end{array}
\qquad
\begin{array}{r}
54 \\
23\overline{)1242} \\
-1150 \\
\hline
92 \\
-92 \\
\hline
0 \\
\end{array}
$$

$$(54 \times 23) = 1242$$

Division, dividend, divisor, and quotient   Division is the basic operation performed on a product and a factor to obtain the second factor. The given product in a division example is called the dividend; the known factor (the number by which we divide) is called the divisor; and the result of performing the operation is called the quotient. For example

$$
\begin{array}{lll}
5 \times \square = 15 & \text{or} & 15 \div 5 = \square \\
5 \times 3 = 15 & & 15 \div 5 = 3
\end{array}
$$

Division is the inverse operation of multiplication; that is, division "undoes" what multiplication does. If a number is first multiplied and then divided by the same quantity, the number is left unchanged. For example

$$7 \times 4 = 28 \qquad 28 \div 4 = 7$$
$$\text{or}$$
$$(7 \times 4) \div 4 = 7$$

Identity element for multiplication   The product of 1 and any other factor is always the other factor. The identity element for multiplication is 1:

$$1 \times a = a$$
$$a \times 1 = a$$

Multiple   A multiple is a product obtained by multiplying the set of whole numbers by a given factor. For example, the set of multiples of 4 is created as follows:

Set of whole numbers as factors	Given factor	Multiples
0	4	0
1	4	4
2	4	8
3	4	12
4	4	16
.	.	.
.	.	.
.	.	.

Multiplication A binary operation on whole numbers that matches with any two whole numbers (called factors) a unique whole number (called the product). The operation can be defined as follows: If a and b are any two whole numbers, and if A and B are sets such that $n(A) = a$ and $n(B) = b$, then $a \times b$ is by definition the cardinal number of the set A X B; that is, $a \times b = n(A \times B)$, where X is the Cartesian product.

The product of two whole numbers can be obtained by using many models: sets, Cartesian products, arrays, or the number line.

Multiplication algorithm The multiplication algorithm is the numerical process that is applied to two factors to obtain a product. Below is an application of this algorithm.

$$
\begin{array}{r}
54 \\
\times\,23 \\
\hline
12 \longleftarrow (3 \times 4) \\
150 \longleftarrow (3 \times 50) \\
80 \longleftarrow (20 \times 4) \\
1000 \longleftarrow (20 \times 50) \\
\hline
1242
\end{array}
$$

Properties of division Division of whole numbers has the following properties:

1. Division is not commutative; for example:

$$12 \div 3 \neq 3 \div 12$$

2. Division is not associative; for example:

$$(24 \div 4) \div 2 \neq 24 \div (4 \div 2)$$

3. Division is distributive only if the distribution is on the *left* of the division sign, not if it is on the right:

$$(20 + 8) \div 4 = (20 \div 4) + (8 \div 4)$$
$$24 \div (2 + 4) \neq (24 \div 2) + (24 \div 4)$$

Properties of multiplication The properties of multiplication discussed in this unit are:

1. Multiplication is commutative: For any whole numbers a and b,

$$a \times b = b \times a$$

2. Multiplication is associative: For any whole numbers a, b, and c,

$$(a \times b) \times c = a \times (b \times c)$$

3. Multiplication is distributive over addition: For any whole numbers a, b, and c,

$$a \times (b + c) = (a \times b) + (a \times c)$$
$$(b + c) \times a = (b \times a) + (c \times a)$$

Regroup To regroup is to convert a unit from one place value to another place value, keeping the value of the number constant but changing the grouping. For instance, the number 42 can be regrouped to 3 tens and 12 ones; the number 42 remains constant but 4 tens and 2 ones is renamed as 3 tens and 12 ones.

Zero as a factor The product of 0 and any other factor is always 0.

Practice Exercises

1. Use the multiplication example $3 \times 4 = \square$ and draw a model using

   a) sets
   b) arrays
   c) the number line
   d) ordered pairs

2. Draw an array for each example.

   a) $4 \times 2 = 8$ c) $2 \times 3 = 6$
   b) $3 \times 6 = 18$ d) $5 \times 3 = 15$

3. Draw arrays to show a model for

   $3 \times 6 = 6 \times 3$

4. Write a multiplication sentence for each array.

 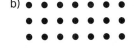 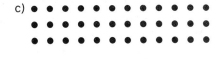

5. Model 6×4 on a number line.

6. Show how successive addition can verify that $4 \times 5 = 20$.

7. Suppose that $A = \{x, y, z\}$ and that $B = \{e, f, g, h\}$.

   a) Tabulate the set of ordered pairs for A X B.
   b) Tabulate the set of ordered pairs for B X A.
   c) Show that the sets of ordered pairs you wrote for Parts a and b are equivalent.
   d) If R and S are any finite sets, will it always be true that R X S is equivalent to S X R? What property of multiplication of whole numbers does this suggest?

8. Write a multiplication sentence for each example; then write a related inverse sentence.

   a)   b)

9. Use a number-line model to show each division example.

   a) $18 \div 3 = \square$ c) $16 \div 8 = \square$
   b) $12 \div 4 = \square$ d) $11 \div 3 = \square$

10. Write two inverse sentences for each given sentence.

    a) $7 \times 8\ =\square$ e) $12 \times 14 = 168$

    b) $72 \div 9\ =\square$ f) $108 \div 9\ = 12$

    c) $6 \times 18=\square$ g) $221 \div 17 = 13$

    d) $8 \times 23 = 184$ h) $124 \times 9\ = 1116$

11. Solve each set of examples.

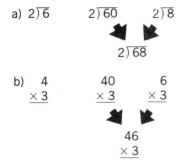

12. We have used the distributive property of multiplication over addition. We can also use the distributive property of multiplication over subtraction. Study the general statement; then solve the following examples:

$$A \times (B - C) = (A \times B) - (A \times C)$$

    a) 6×97 b) 7×48 c) 4×98 d) 3×1998

13. Show how successive subtraction can verify $48 \div 6 = 8$.

14. On a sheet of squared paper 24 squares wide and 36 squares long, demonstrate that 24×36 is 864, using the distributive property of multiplication over addition.

15. Use squared paper, and demonstrate how you can verify that $448 \div 14$ is 32.

Discussion Questions

1. Research the work of John Napier, and make a report on the use of "Napier's Bones" in teaching multiplication.

2. Discuss the prerequisite knowledge that is necessary to understand multiplication and division.

3. When multiplying a number by another number having a zero in the ones place, discuss the objections to writing the zero to the right of the ones place. For example:

$$\begin{array}{r} 23 \\ \times\ \ 40 \\ \hline \end{array}$$

4. Research three methods of estimating quotients to two-place division examples, and discuss the merits and disadvantages of each. These methods are: the apparent method, the increase-by-one method, and the round-off method.

5. Discuss the reasons that division is the most difficult operation for children to learn.

6. Create word problems to demonstrate measurement and partition division.

7. Discuss the remainder idea in division and the advantages and disadvantages of expressing the remainder in each of the possible ways.

8. Demonstrate why it is impossible to divide by zero.

9. Discuss how the hand-held calculator can be integrated into the teaching of multiplication and division.

10. Consider how children might use a microcomputer to help them learn multiplication and division.

11. Locate the results of the National Assessment of Educational Progress in Mathematics, related to multiplication and division. Discuss the implications of the National Assessment.

12. Discuss the likenesses and differences between teaching multiplication and division.

Activities for the Primary Grades

Like addition and subtraction, the concepts of multiplication and division are not new but the methods that we use to teach them to children have been updated. Manipulating concrete objects from the real world, using the number line, and studying illustrations allow children to build an understanding of the computational process, before conventional algorithms are presented. Understanding must precede skill; when understanding and skill are properly developed, children will have a great deal of power in mathematics.

The suggested activities presented here have been separated for primary, intermediate, and upper elementary children, but many activities can easily be adapted for older or younger children. Multiplication and division activities for primary children are readiness activities; abstract teaching does not take place until the intermediate grades. Through these activities, study how the concepts of multiplication and division are developed with children.

1. Many set situations that indicate multiplication can be discussed with first-grade children. For instance, if you have four tables and six children are sitting at each, the children can count to find out how many are seated at the tables. Do not refer to multiplication as such; it isn't needed at this point. Make use of occasions when children line up in pairs, or by threes, or fours, and again discuss the multiplication situation.

2. In primary grades, the number line provides a natural readiness activity for children. Run a strip of masking tape the length of the classroom. About one step apart, place small strips of masking tape perpendicular to the strip. Write numerals on the cross strips to make a number line. Have the children walk on the number line and say the number that the right foot steps on—2, 4, 6, 8, 10, etc. These numbers are the multiples of two.

3. Ask children to add a series of addends in which all addends have the same value, such as $3 + 3 = 6$, $6 + 3 = 9$, $9 + 3 = 12$, and so forth.

4. Place sets of plastic forks on small cards (5"-by-8" or 15 cm-by-25 cm). Put two forks on each card.

Ask questions such as:

a) How many sets?   3
b) How many forks in each set?   2
c) How many all together?   6

Then state, "We have 3 sets of 2, or 6 in all."
After many experiences like the example above, the × symbol for multiplication may be introduced.

5. Plastic clothespins may also be put on cards to model sets for multiplication.

How many sets?   2
How many pins in each set?   3
How many in all?_____

Then state, "We have 2 sets of 3, or we have 6 in all."

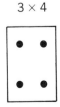

How many pairs of shoes?   _____
How many shoes in a pair?   _____
How many shoes?   _____

7. Give the children a set of counters and 15 cm-by-25 cm (or 5"-by-8") cards. Have the children model many multiplication facts.

3 × 4

8. Using checkers on construction paper, have the child model two rows of 3. Discuss this with the child. Rotate the paper 90 degrees. Discuss the result of three rows of 2.

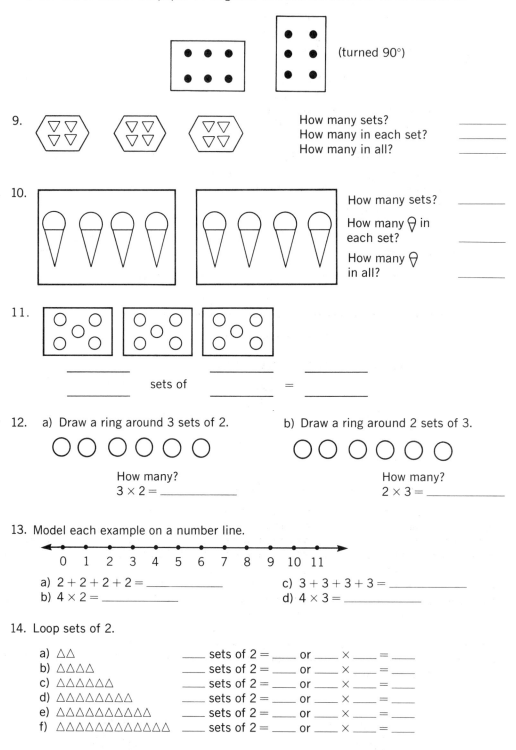

(turned 90°)

9. How many sets? _____
How many in each set? _____
How many in all? _____

10. How many sets? _____

How many ⊖ in each set? _____

How many ⊖ in all? _____

11. _____   _____   _____

_____ sets of _____ = _____

12. a) Draw a ring around 3 sets of 2.

How many?
3 × 2 = _____

b) Draw a ring around 2 sets of 3.

How many?
2 × 3 = _____

13. Model each example on a number line.

0 1 2 3 4 5 6 7 8 9 10 11

a) 2 + 2 + 2 + 2 = _____
b) 4 × 2 = _____

c) 3 + 3 + 3 + 3 = _____
d) 4 × 3 = _____

14. Loop sets of 2.

a) △△ ____ sets of 2 = ____ or ____ × ____ = ____
b) △△△△ ____ sets of 2 = ____ or ____ × ____ = ____
c) △△△△△△ ____ sets of 2 = ____ or ____ × ____ = ____
d) △△△△△△△△ ____ sets of 2 = ____ or ____ × ____ = ____
e) △△△△△△△△△△ ____ sets of 2 = ____ or ____ × ____ = ____
f) △△△△△△△△△△△△ ____ sets of 2 = ____ or ____ × ____ = ____

15. Fill in the missing numerals in each sequence.

a) 2, 4, 6, 8, ____, ____, ____, ____, ____, ____
b) 5, 10, 15, ____, ____, ____, ____, ____, ____, ____
c) 3, 6, 9, ____, ____, ____, ____, ____, ____, ____

16. Fill in each blank.

   a) $3 + 3 + 3 + 3$ $=$ ____ or $4 \times 3 =$ ____
   b) $2 + 2 + 2 + 2 + 2 =$ ____ or $5 \times 2 =$ ____
   c) $1 + 1 + 1$ $=$ ____ or $3 \times 1 =$ ____

17. Write $+$, $-$, or $\times$, in each $\triangle$.

   a) $5 \triangle 6 = 11$ e) $3 \triangle 4 = 12$
   b) $7 \triangle 4 = 3$ f) $7 \triangle 3 = 10$
   c) $2 \triangle 3 = 6$ g) $8 \triangle 5 = 3$
   d) $9 \triangle 4 = 5$ h) $5 \triangle 4 = 20$

18. Write a multiplication sentence for each number-line model.

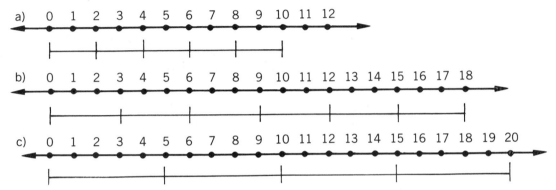

19. Write a multiplication sentence for each array.

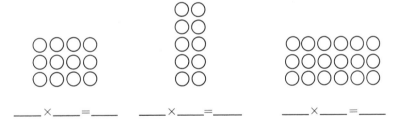

____ $\times$ ____ $=$ ____   ____ $\times$ ____ $=$ ____   ____ $\times$ ____ $=$ ____

20. Cut two octagons about six inches across out of heavy cardboard. With a felt-tip marker draw all the diagonals and print a different numeral on each sector of the octagon. Place a short sharpened pencil through the center of each octagon. When the pencil is spun the octagon will come to rest on one of the numbered sides. Two children can play by each spinning his octagon on a pencil and using the numbers on the side they land on as the factors. The children can take turns saying the product. If the octagons are covered with clear self-adhesive plastic, a china marker may be used to change the numerals so that each child can practice on the multiplication facts he needs. For example, to begin one could use numbers 1, 2, 3, 4, 5, 6, 7, and 8 on one octagon and numbers 1, 2, 3, 1, 2, 3, 1, 2 on the other. More advanced students might use numbers 2, 3, 4, 5, 6, 7, 8, 9 on one octagon and 7, 8, 9, 7, 8, 9, 6, 9 on the other. Vary the examples to provide the practice that a given pair of children might need.

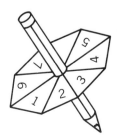
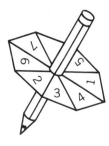

21. Make a pair of cubes out of wood or sponges and write numerals on each side to be used as factors. The children can take turns rolling the dice, saying the products, and checking each other. If the product is correct they may place a card with a O or an X on a tic-tac-toe board.

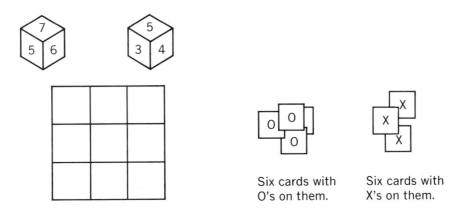

Six cards with O's on them.   Six cards with X's on them.

Children have difficulty learning division for two major reasons. First, most teachers begin teaching division on an abstract level. Remember, when introducing a new concept, teaching should begin on the concrete level. Also, some mathematics programs begin teaching division concepts much too early. Piaget's theory suggests that children must be in the formal operational level of development before beginning to study division. Some mathematics programs introduce division in the second grade but most wait until the third grade.

22. String twelve wheel macaroni on a string about one meter long (about four feet long). Tie the string between two chairs.

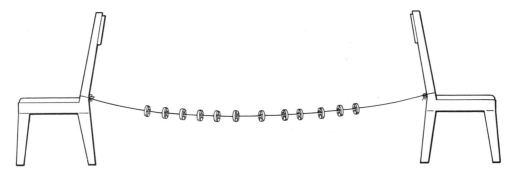

Say, "There are twelve macaroni on the string. How many sets of four can we make?" Begin by having a child count a set of four and clip on a clothespin; then count another set of four and place another clothespin. This shows there are three sets of four in twelve.

23. Give the children 15 cm-by-25 cm (or 5"-by-8") cards on which to place sets.

How many sets?

Here are six forks:

If we separate the six forks into three equivalent sets, how many forks will be in each set? After the children discuss the problem, distribute the forks. Now the children can see that six forks placed into three sets makes two forks in each set. Thus 6 ÷ 3 = 2.

Hand-Held Calculator Activities for the Primary Grades

Hand-held calculators should have very limited use with multiplication and division at the primary level.

Microcomputer Activities for the Primary Grades

Microcomputers should have very limited use with multiplication and division at the primary level.

Activities for the Intermediate Grades

Students should be reintroduced to multiplication and division with concrete materials from the real world. They should see many different models to help them think about the meaning of multiplication and division. Children should memorize the basic multiplication facts and become acquainted with the distributive property of multiplication over addition and its use in solving multiplication examples. At the intermediate level, the meaning of division should be developed and the children should memorize many division facts. The study of division is completed in the upper elementary grade levels.

1. Use the overhead projector and objects such as pennies, checkers, or quarters to make arrays. Have the children write a multiplication sentence on a transparency; then turn the transparency 90° and have them write another multiplication sentence.

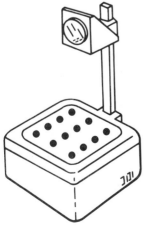
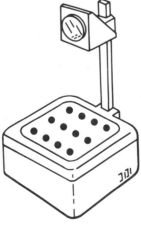

The children would write   Transparency turned 90°
4 × 3 = 12   3 × 4 = 12

Discuss the two different sentences made from the one array and relate them to the commutative property of multiplication.

Have different children make arrays for class members to write multiplication sentences.

2. Write the multiplication sentence suggested by each number-line diagram.

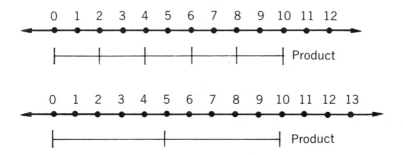

Compare the two multiplication sentences. Note how the products are the same but the factors are interchanged.

$$5 \times 2 = 10 \text{ and } 2 \times 5 = 10$$
$$\therefore 5 \times 2 = 2 \times 5$$

Again discuss the commutative property of multiplication.

3. To help establish the basic idea of a multiplication sentence, introduce and teach the words *factor* and *product* in the same way as you would teach new words in reading. Make cards of the words and symbols for a multiplication sentence and manipulate the cards to show a multiplication sentence. Have each child make his own set of cards to manipulate.

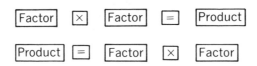

Relate the multiplication sentence to the models for multiplication.

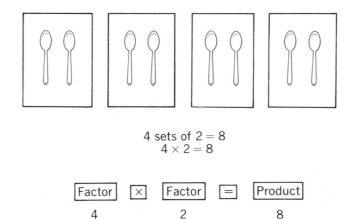

4 sets of 2 = 8
4 × 2 = 8

4. Develop the zero property of multiplication by using empty boxes. Each box can represent a set; thus these two boxes can represent

$$2 \text{ sets of } 0 = 0 \qquad 2 \times 0 = 0$$

Then place a third box with the other two. The children should write $3 \times 0 = 0$. Continue until the table is complete.

Number of sets	Elements in a set	Product
0	0	___
1	0	___
2	0	___
3	0	___
4	0	___
5	0	___
6	0	___
7	0	___
8	0	___
9	0	___

The children should generalize that any number multiplied by zero is zero.

5. Construct a multiplication table and use the zero property to fill in the first row and the first column.

6. Use sets as a model to develop the identity element of multiplication.

Model of sets	Multiples of 1	
▫	1 set of 1	$1 \times 1 = 1$
▫ ▫	2 sets of 1	$2 \times 1 = 2$
▫ ▫ ▫	3 sets of 1	$3 \times 1 = 3$
▫ ▫ ▫ ▫	4 sets of 1	$4 \times 1 = 4$
▫ ▫ ▫ ▫ ▫	5 sets of 1	$5 \times 1 = 5$
▫ ▫ ▫ ▫ ▫ ▫	6 sets of 1	$6 \times 1 = 6$
etc.	etc.	etc.

It is essential to use the commutative property of multiplication at this point. Using the commutative property of multiplication, the children should generalize that one times any number equals that number. Now fill in the second row and second column of the multiplication table.

7. Develop tables of multiples for each number by using sets as models.

Model of sets		Multiples of 2
	1 set of 2	$1 \times 2 = 2$
	2 sets of 2	$2 \times 2 = 4$
	3 sets of 2	$3 \times 2 = 6$
	4 sets of 2	$4 \times 2 = 8$
	5 sets of 2	$5 \times 2 = 10$
etc.	6 sets of 2 etc.	$6 \times 2 = 12$ etc.

Study the multiplication table to discover where each set of multiples will fit in.

8. Since children have difficulty in using charts of basic facts, the following procedure could be used. Construct two plastic strips of different colors so that the strips are slightly wider and longer than a row of the chart. Glue the two strips together at a 90-degree angle. At the overlapped end, cut out a rectangle the size of one of the rectangles on the chart. The student can use this device to find the product of two numbers on the basic fact chart (see below). This guide can also be used for addition.

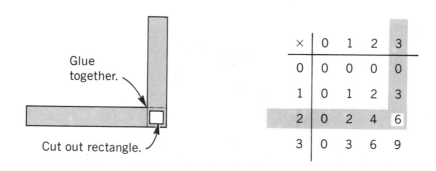

Glue together.

Cut out rectangle.

×	0	1	2	3
0	0	0	0	0
1	0	1	2	3
2	0	2	4	6
3	0	3	6	9

9. To make memorization of basic facts more interesting, Edmund the Eel could be used.

An eel is drawn on cardboard or construction paper. Irregularly shaped cards with basic facts written on them can be placed on the eel as the student memorizes them.

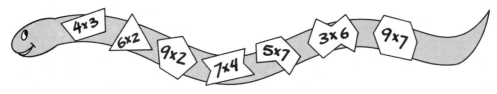

10. Fill in the blanks.

a) ____ × 2 = 6   e) 6 ÷ 2 = ____

b) ____ × 4 = 16   f) 16 ÷ 4 = ____

c) 5 × ____ = 15   g) 15 ÷ 5 = ____

d) 6 × ____ = 24   h) 24 ÷ 6 = ____

11. Use sets to extend the basic multiplication facts.

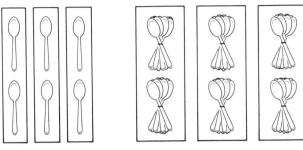

3 sets of 2   3 sets of 2 tens

$3 \times 2 = 6$ 3×2 tens $= 6$ tens
$3 \times 20 = 60$

12. a)

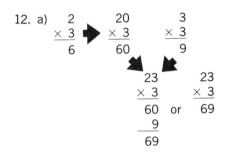

$$\begin{array}{r} 2 \\ \times\ 3 \\ \hline 6 \end{array} \quad \begin{array}{r} 20 \\ \times\ 3 \\ \hline 60 \end{array} \quad \begin{array}{r} 3 \\ \times\ 3 \\ \hline 9 \end{array}$$

$$\begin{array}{r} 23 \\ \times\ 3 \\ \hline 60 \\ 9 \\ \hline 69 \end{array} \quad \text{or} \quad \begin{array}{r} 23 \\ \times\ 3 \\ \hline 69 \end{array}$$

b) $42 = 40 + 2$
    $\underline{\times\ 2} = \underline{\times\quad 2}$

c)

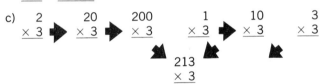

$$\begin{array}{r} 2 \\ \times\ 3 \end{array} \quad \begin{array}{r} 20 \\ \times\ 3 \end{array} \quad \begin{array}{r} 200 \\ \times\ 3 \end{array} \quad \begin{array}{r} 1 \\ \times\ 3 \end{array} \quad \begin{array}{r} 10 \\ \times\ 3 \end{array} \quad \begin{array}{r} 3 \\ \times\ 3 \end{array}$$

$$\begin{array}{r} 213 \\ \times\ 3 \end{array}$$

13. Use concrete materials for children to see how regrouping in multiplication works. They may need to use expanded notation before becoming familiar with the algorithm and being able to use the conventional short form. Base-ten blocks would be excellent to use here.

a) $\begin{array}{r} 23 \\ \times\ 4 \end{array}$ b) $\begin{array}{r} 36 \\ \times\ 2 \end{array}$ c) $\begin{array}{r} 48 \\ \times\ 3 \end{array}$ d) $\begin{array}{r} 426 \\ \times\ 5 \end{array}$

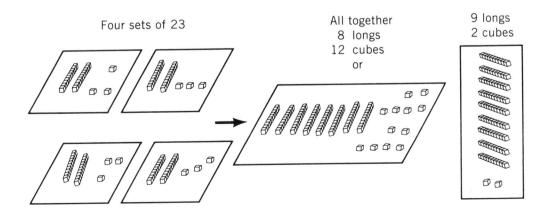

Four sets of 23

All together
8 longs
12 cubes
or

9 longs
2 cubes

14. Children need to learn how to multiply quickly using 10, 100, or 1000. Do not stress adding zeros, but emphasize place value.

a)
$$\begin{array}{cccc} 1 & 10 & 100 & 1000 \\ \times\,2 & \times\,2 & \times\,2 & \times\,2 \end{array}$$

b)
$$\begin{array}{cccc} 1 & 10 & 100 & 1000 \\ \times\,5 & \times\,5 & \times\,5 & \times\,5 \end{array}$$

c)
$$\begin{array}{cccc} 14 & 14 & 14 & 14 \\ \times\,1 & \times\,10 & \times\,100 & \times\,1000 \end{array}$$

15. Give each child 24 counters and several 5"-by-8" cards. Have the student model a variety of problems, such as "How many sets of 6 can be made from 24 counters?" Then have the student model four equal sets from 24 counters.

16. Use the cards with the words *factor* and *product* on them to develop the division sentence.

$$\boxed{\text{Factor}} \quad \boxed{\times} \quad \boxed{\text{Factor}} \quad \boxed{=} \quad \boxed{\text{Product}}$$

$$\boxed{\text{Product}} \quad \boxed{\div} \quad \boxed{\text{Factor}} \quad \boxed{=} \quad \boxed{\text{Factor}}$$

17. For each multiplication sentence write two related division sentences.

a) $3 \times 6 = 18$ c) $4 \times 9 = 36$
b) $7 \times 5 = 35$ d) $7 \times 8 = 56$

18. Use the arrays to help you complete each example.

a)
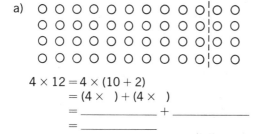

$$4 \times 12 = 4 \times (10 + 2)$$
$$= (4 \times \underline{}) + (4 \times \underline{})$$
$$= \underline{} + \underline{}$$
$$= \underline{}$$

b)

$$6 \times 13 = 6 \times (\underline{} + \underline{})$$
$$= (6 \times \underline{}) + (6 \times \underline{})$$
$$= \underline{} + \underline{}$$
$$= \underline{}$$

19. Place six items on the overhead projector and ask the children how many sets of 2 can be made from the six items.

Six spoons

Place small, colored, acetate squares on the overhead projector. As the acetates are placed, put two plastic spoons on each square.

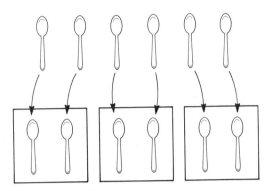

Six plastic spoons

Thus, there are three sets of 2 in 6. Children need many of these types of experiences using tangible objects.

20. Separate a set of plastic cups into two sets. If there are eight plastic cups, for instance, how many would go into each of two sets? Place two sheets of paper on the desk, one for each set. Now separate the eight plastic cups into the two sets. How many cups belong in each set?

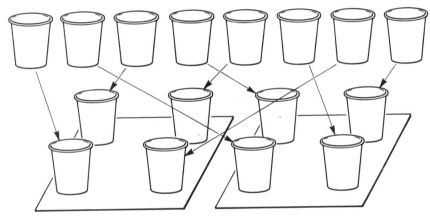

The children need many experiences on the concrete level manipulating materials for both measurement and partition division.

21. Division can be demonstrated by using Cuisenaire rods, Dienes Blocks, and Stern rods. Check the manuals for each of the materials.

22. Cassette tapes may also be used for memorization of basic facts of multiplication and division.

23. Write division sentences for each number-line model.

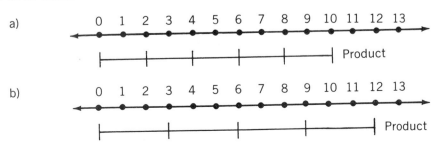

24. Find the quotients (missing factors).

   a) $12 \div 2 = $ _____   c) $4\overline{)36}$ e) $54 \div 9 = $ _____

   b) $21 \div 7 = $ _____   d) $6\overline{)24}$ f) $72 \div 8 = $ _____

25. Complete each example.

   a) $28 \div 2 = (20 + 8) \div 2$
   $= (20 \div 2) + (\_ \div 2)$
   $= 10 + \_$
   $= \_$

   c) $96 \div 3 = (90 + \_) \div 3$
   $= (\_ \div 3) + (\_ \div 3)$
   $= \_ + 2$
   $= \_$

   b) $842 \div 2 = (800 + \_ + 2) \div 2$
   $= (800 \div \_) + (40 \div \_) + (2 \div \_)$
   $= \_ + \_ + \_$
   $= \_$

   d) $105 \div 5 = (100 + 5) \div \_$
   $= (\_ \div 5) + (\_ \div 5)$
   $= 20 + \_$
   $= \_$

26. Find the quotients.

   a) $6\overline{)12}$ b) $5\overline{)30}$ c) $9\overline{)63}$ d) $8\overline{)64}$

27. The place-value box is an excellent device to use for beginning division because it can be used to model as many as three places in the dividend.

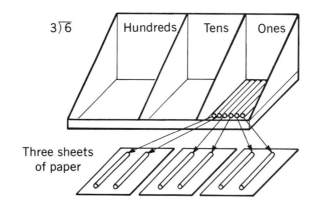

$3\overline{)6}$

Three sheets of paper

Six things separated into three sets. How many things go into each set?

28. The previous example can be expanded into 6 tens divided by 3.

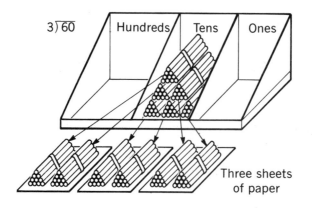

$3\overline{)60}$

Three sheets of paper

29. Division having a remainder must be presented using tangible objects.

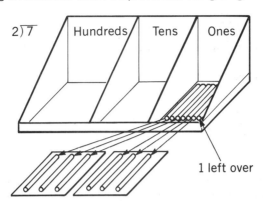

30. Invent a story using array cards, such as: "Last night, I had just finished making a set of array cards when I heard a strange sound and saw many colorful flashing lights. I quickly ran into the yard carrying my array cards. A strange machine was parked in the yard. Upon investigation, a hungry Wookie with square teeth grabbed my array cards. Here's all that's left. What can we do?"

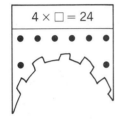

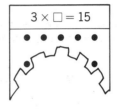

31. Find the quotients and remainders.

   a) $6\overline{)34}$ b) $2\overline{)11}$ c) $8\overline{)25}$ d) $5\overline{)34}$

32. Make bingo cards of products for each child in the class. Let one child draw multiplication flash cards at random and hold them up for the entire class to see. If a child has the product on his bingo card he may place a marker on it. The first child to get five in a row wins.

12	45	42	63	40
36	7	54	25	64
81	56	24	45	18
40	16	9	72	30
27	48	32	5	28

9	12	35	54	20
28	40	8	14	42
45	7	16	24	64
72	56	30	6	27
18	36	4	48	5

33. Make a playing board for a trip to the moon. Make small cardboard rocket ships to move on the board. Make three different colored cards.
   Red cards (worth 5 jumps) — hard multiplication facts, such as $\begin{array}{r} 9 \\ \times 7 \\ \hline \end{array}$

   Blue cards (worth 3 jumps) — middle difficulty multiplication facts, such as $\begin{array}{r} 6 \\ \times 5 \\ \hline \end{array}$

Yellow cards (worth 1 jump) — easy multiplication facts, such as $\begin{array}{r} 3 \\ \times 2 \\ \hline \end{array}$

Each child takes a turn drawing a red, blue, or yellow card of his choice. The other children check him and if he is correct, he can move his rocket 1, 3, or 5 places, depending on the card he has selected. The children can check each other for correct answers. The first one to arrive at the Moon wins.

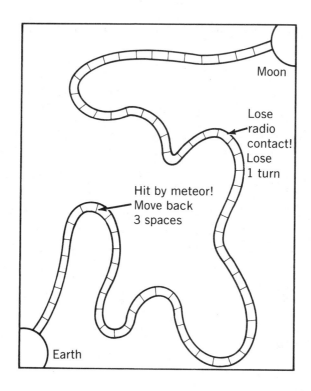

34. Fill in the blanks.

a) $1 \times 6 =$ ____   c) $1 \times 14 =$ ____
  $10 \times 6 =$ ____ $10 \times 14 =$ ____
  $100 \times 6 =$ ____ $100 \times 14 =$ ____

b) $1 \times 8 =$ ____   d) $1 \times 56 =$ ____
  $10 \times 8 =$ ____ $10 \times 56 =$ ____
  $100 \times 8 =$ ____ $100 \times 56 =$ ____

35. Find the missing factor.

a) $m \times 5 = 25$ c) $w \times 32 = 96$
b) $6 \times m = 54$ d) $7 \times z = 63$

36. Rewrite each division sentence as a related multiplication sentence; then find the product.

a) $n \div 7 = 5$ c) $d \div 9 = 8$
b) $c \div 9 = 7$ d) $m \div 7 = 6$

37. Cut octagons with diagonals about 10″ long out of cardboard. Draw the line segments as shown in the diagram. With a felt marking pen write the numerals as shown. Cover the entire cardboard octagon with clear self-adhesive plastic. Use a china marker to write a

factor inside the center circle. The children may write the products in the outer part of each segment. The octagon can be easily erased and used many times.

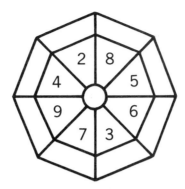

38. Loop the numeral naming the greatest multiple of ten that will make each sentence a true statement.

a) $3 \times n < 146$ 20   30   40   50   60
b) $5 \times n < 234$ 20   30   40   50   60
c) $4 \times n < 111$ 20   30   40   50   60
d) $6 \times n < 2354$ 100   200   300   400   500

39. Use the greatest multiple of 1, 10, 100, or 1000 to make each sentence a true statement.

a) ___ $\times 40 < 500$ b) ___ $\times 70 < 2100$
   ___ $\times 40 < 100$ ___ $\times 70 < 1000$
   ___ $\times 40 < 80$ ___ $\times 70 < 9000$
   ___ $\times 40 < 12{,}000$ ___ $\times 70 < 500$
   ___ $\times 40 < 2000$ ___ $\times 70 < 40{,}000$

40. Mark each true or false; then list a property for each.

a) $82 \times 39 = 39 \times 82$
b) $5 \times (6 \times 7) = (5 \times 6) \times 7$
c) $8 \times (7 \times 9) = (7 \times 9) \times 8$
d) $2354 \times 1 = 2354$
e) $0 \times 4782 = 0$
f) $(23 \times 14) \times 36 = 23 \times (14 \times 36)$
g) $(9 \times 37) \times 18 = 18 \times (9 \times 37)$

41.

$\times$ by 9		$\div$ by 7		$\times$ by 8	
7		49		11	
23		147		41	
41		231		7	
76		777		33	
38		217		9	
59		371		72	
18		294		56	
27		609		84	

42. Solve each.

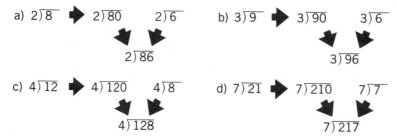

c) $4\overline{)12}$ ➡ $4\overline{)120}$ $4\overline{)8}$ d) $7\overline{)21}$ ➡ $7\overline{)210}$ $7\overline{)7}$

　　　　　　　$4\overline{)128}$　　　　　　　　　　　$7\overline{)217}$

43. True or false?

  a) $8 \div 4 = 4 \div 8$ c) $15{,}827 \div 19 = 19 \div 15{,}827$
  b) $24 \div 3 = 3 \div 24$ d) $(8 \div 4) \div 2 = 8 \div (4 \div 2)$

44. Using a number line, numbered by tens and/or hundreds, and a set of cards with two- and three-digit numbers, have the students place the numbers to the nearest ten, then to the nearest hundred.

45. In Grade 4 the children should practice with many division examples that have one-place divisors. Once they understand such examples well and have acquired reasonable skill in solving them, the children should be ready to move on to examples with two-place divisors. Encourage the children to check answers to division examples by using this idea:

$$\text{Dividend} = (\text{Quotient} \times \text{Divisor}) + \text{Remainder}$$

Complete these examples and check your answers.

a) $2\overline{)449}$
　$\underline{400}$ ⟵ _____ $\times 2$
　　$\underline{40}$ ⟵ _____ $\times 2$
　　　$\underline{8}$ ⟵ _____ $\times 2$

b) $30\overline{)935}$
　$\underline{900}$ ⟵ _____ $\times 30$
　　$\underline{30}$ ⟵ _____ $\times 30$

46. Find the quotient for each example. Check your answer by multiplication.

  a) $13\overline{)182}$ b) $11\overline{)913}$

  c) $40\overline{)165}$ d) $32\overline{)319}$

47. Again use short, simple, word problems to give students practice in translating problem situations into mathematical sentences. Write an equation for each problem. Then find the solution.

  a) 38 books on each shelf. 5 shelves. How many books?
  b) There are 10 pairs of socks on each section of the clothesline. 4 sections of clothesline. How many socks?
  c) 9 players on each team. 8 teams in the league. How many players in the league?
  d) 5 school days in each week. How many school days in 4 weeks?
  e) 8 wieners in each plastic pack. 12 packs. How many wieners?
  f) 24 hamburger buns. 8 in a package. How many packages?
  g) 16 scouts. 4 scouts per boat. How many boats will be needed?

48. Complete the table.

	+	−	×	÷
533 △ 13				
782 △ 34				
901 △ 53				
1645 △ 47				
899 △ 29				
837 △ 31				
1596 △ 42				
1118 △ 26				

Hand-Held Calculator Activities for the Intermediate Grades

1. The hand-held calculator should be used to check multiplication and division examples that the children have solved. Do not permit the students to use answer books.

2. Children can learn to use a constant for multiplication on the hand-held calculator. Procedures may vary with different calculators; some calculators require the constant to be entered first, and some calculators require the constant to be entered second. Using a constant in multiplication allows many multiplications by a given number without having to enter the constant each time. For instance, if the constant number is 3 and we want to multiply many numbers by 3, we would use the following procedure:

Any number	Operation	Constant	Equals	Display reads
2	×	3	=	6

Now the calculator has been set up to multiply any number by 3. If you strike the 7 key and the equals key, the display will read 21; if you strike the 9 key and the equals key, the display will read 27.

Example	Keys struck	Display shows
8 × 3 =	8 =	24
4 × 3 =	4 =	12
17 × 3 =	1 7 =	51
29 × 3 =	2 9 =	87

3. If we need to find the circumferences of many wheels, pi can be set up in the hand-held calculator as a constant. Then we need only strike the key(s) for the diameter and the equals key; the circumference will appear on the display screen.

Set up the hand-held calculator for pi:

Any number	Pi	Circumference
1	× 3.14 =	3.14

Now the hand-held calculator is set up to compute circumferences of circles. If the diameter of a circle is 7, just strike the 7 key and the equals key; 21.98, the circumference of a circle with a diameter of 7, will appear on the display screen.

Diameter	Keys struck	Display reads
8	8 =	25.12
10	1 0 =	31.4
23	2 3 =	72.44

4. The multiples of any given number can be generated using a constant. For instance, to generate the multiples of 4, set up the calculator with the constant 4. By entering the set of whole numbers one at a time and striking the equals key each time, the multiples of 4 will be displayed.

Example	Keys struck	Display will generate the multiples of 4
0×4	0 =	0
1×4	1 =	4
2×4	2 =	8
3×4	3 =	12
4×4	4 =	16
5×4	5 =	20
6×4	6 =	24
7×4	7 =	28
etc.		

Have the children practice by generating sets of multiples for any given number.

5. Have the children estimate answers to multiplication examples and then verify their answers using a hand-held calculator. Provide space on a worksheet for the children to write the estimated answer and the calculated answer. Example questions are:

a) How much money would you spend in a year if you spend a thousand dollars a day?
b) If you spend a dollar a minute, how much money would you spend in a year?
c) If you drop a penny in your piggy bank each hour, how much money would you have in your bank at the end of a leap year?
d) If you buy a new car every five years, how much money do you think you will spend on cars during your lifetime?
e) How many minutes are there in a regular year? In a leap year?
f) How many minutes old are you?
g) How many seconds old are you?

6. Children can find answers to problems that are too large for their hand-held calculators, by using generalizations. For instance, solve as many of the following examples on your calculator as you can. Study the patterns; then write the answers to the remaining examples.

$$1 \times 1 = \qquad\qquad 9 \times 2 =$$
$$11 \times 11 = \qquad\qquad 99 \times 2 =$$
$$111 \times 111 = \qquad\qquad 999 \times 2 =$$
$$1111 \times 1111 = \qquad\qquad 9999 \times 2 =$$
$$11111 \times 11111 = \qquad\qquad 99999 \times 2 =$$
$$111111 \times 111111 = \qquad\qquad 999999 \times 2 =$$
$$1111111 \times 1111111 = \qquad\qquad 9999999 \times 2 =$$
$$11111111 \times 11111111 = \qquad\qquad 99999999 \times 2 =$$
$$\text{etc.} \qquad\qquad\qquad \text{etc.}$$

Create similar examples for children to solve.

7. Look for patterns in a series of numbers, and then verify the pattern and extend it using the hand-held calculator. Study this exmple: 2, 6, 18, 54, 162, ___, ___, ___, ___, ___, etc. Children should discover that each number is three times the number that precedes it. This example can be set up in the hand-held calculator; enter a 2, then ×, then 3, and then continue to push the equals key. The sequence generated should be the same as indicated in this example; then it can be extended. Create other patterns for the children to study, and generate additional numbers in the sequence.

8. Solve problems such as the following: 480 children attend our school. If all the children attend an assembly, how many chairs will be needed in each of the 15 rows?

Microcomputer Activities for the Intermediate Grades

Multiplication is performed the same way in the computer as it is in arithmetic. The major difference is the symbolization. In arithmetic the × sign is used to indicate multiplication; on the computer, the * (asterisk) is used to symbolize multiplication. The same is true of division. In arithmetic we use the ÷ sign or the $\overline{)}$ sign to indicate division; on the computer, we use a / sign (slash) to symbolize division.

1. After children have a good understanding of mathematical operations and many basic facts have been memorized, they can use the computer in the immediate mode to solve arithmetic examples. Children need specific lessons on using the microcomputer to solve multiplication and division examples in the immediate mode. They should experiment with examples such as:

  a) 3 × 4 is entered into the microcomputer as ?3*4 (strike the ENTER or RETURN key).
  b) 53 × 71 is entered as ?53*71.
  c) 18 ÷ 2 is entered as ?18/2.
  d) 119 ÷ 17 is entered as ?119/17.

2. Programs are available to provide drill and practice for memorizing the basic multiplication and division facts. Help the children learn how to load software, so they can work independently on the microcomputer. Children can compete against themselves for greater accuracy or speed.

3. Intermediate school children can learn to write simple multiplication and division programs such as:

```
10 REM*MULTIPLICATION PROGRAM*
20 ?"WHAT IS ONE FACTOR":INPUT F
30 ?"WHAT IS THE OTHER FACTOR":INPUT G
40 ?"THE PRODUCT OF ";F;" TIMES ";G;" IS ";F*G
50 ?"TRY ANOTHER"
60 GOTO 20
```

```
10 REM*DIVISION PROGRAM*
20 ?"WHAT NUMBER DO YOU WANT TO DIVIDE":INPUT S
30 ?"WHAT DO YOU WANT TO DIVIDE THE NUMBER BY":INPUT F
40 ?S;" DIVIDED BY ";F;" IS ";S/F
50 ?"LET'S TRY ANOTHER"
60 GOTO 20
```

4. Teachers can easily write simple practice programs to meet the specific needs of any child or group of children. For example, this practice program is designed to provide basic multiplication fact drill. This program was written for a Pet microcomputer, but it can be easily changed to run on most microcomputers found in elementary school.

```
10   REM—MULTIPLICATION BASIC FACT DRILL—
20   ?"HI, WHAT IS YOUR NAME":INPUT N$
25   K=0
27   ?:?
30   ?"HELLO ";N$;" LET'S PRACTICE MULTIPLICATION FACTS"
40   X=INT(9*RND(1)+0):Y=INT(9*RND(1)+0)
50   ?X;" X ";Y;" = ":INPUT S
60   IF S< X*Y THEN?"TRY A LARGER NUMBER":GOTO 50
70   IF S> X*Y THEN?"TRY A SMALLER NUMBER":GOTO 50
80   IF S= X*Y THEN?"CORRECT, HERE IS ANOTHER"
90   K=K+1
100 IF K<25 THEN 40
110 IF K=25 THEN?"DO YOU WANT 25 MORE? (YES OR NO)"
120 INPUT Z$
130 IF Z$="YES"THEN GOTO 25
140 IF Z$="NO"THEN?"GOODBYE, ";N$;" SEE YOU AGAIN!"
```

5. The previous program can be changed to practice multiplying a two-place number by a one-place number, by changing line 40 to read:

```
40 X=INT(90*RND(1)+10):Y=INT(90*RND(1)+10)
```

6. The number of practice exercises can be easily changed, by changing the number 25 in lines 100 and 110 to the number of practice exercises you want the child to solve.

7. A microcomputer program for practicing basic division facts is harder to write, because only certain products can be used. One way to deal with this is to use a READ—DATA statement. This also avoids the random assignment of examples.

```
10   REM—DIVISION BASIC FACT PRACTICE—
20   ?"MY NAME IS MIKE, WHAT IS YOUR NAME":INPUT N$
30   ?"HI, ";N$;" LET'S PRACTICE SOME DIVISION BASIC FACTS"
40   K=0
50   FOR T=1 TO 1000:NEXT T
60   READY X,Y
70   DATA 16,4,35,7,48,8,24,6,72,8,49,7,15,3,21,7,
71   DATA 56,8,45,9,36,6,64,8,27,3,28,9,63,7,40,5,
72   DATA 54,9,12,2,24,3,32,8,18,6,25,5,42,7,56,7,
73   DATA 81,9,−1,0
80   IF X=−1 THEN GOTO 140
90   ?X;" DIVIDED BY ";Y;" = ":INPUT D
100 IF D<X/Y THEN?"YOUR ANSWER IS TOO SMALL.":GOTO 90
110 IF D>X/Y THEN?"YOUR ANSWER IS TOO LARGE.":GOTO 90
120 IF D=X/Y THEN?"YOU ARE CORRECT, TRY ANOTHER."
130 GOTO 60
140 ?"GOODBYE, ";N$;" SEE YOU AGAIN":END
```

Activities for the Upper Elementary Grades

All suggested activities and procedures for the lower grade levels are building blocks for developing an understanding of multiplication and division algorithms.

1. Provide the students with cards having incorrect computations of quotients. Challenge the students to locate and correct the errors.

$$\begin{array}{r} 81 \\ 5\overline{)4005} \end{array}$$

Give the following directions to the student: "Calamity Kate had committed careless computations. Each card has a computational error. See whether you can find the error and correct it for Calamity Kate."

2. Using 3"-by-5" (or 8 cm-by-13 cm) number and symbol cards, as shown, have the students write as many mathematical sentences as they can from the set of cards.

3. Begin with a magic square. Have the student multiply each number in the magic square by a given number. Is the result also a magic square?

4. Use a deck of cards with the face cards removed. Deal two cards to each player. Have the players multiply the numbers of the two cards together. A point is given for each correct answer.

5. For this activity a deck of 52 cards with the numbers between 1 and 25 is needed: three cards each of the numbers 1 to 10, two each of the numbers 11 to 17, and one each of the numbers 18 to 25. Five cards are turned face up. A sixth card is turned up on top of the deck. Players may add, subtract, multiply, or divide the numbers on the five cards in any order to attain the number on the sixth card.

6. Division can be used to compute the distance of lightning from an observer. Since it takes approximately five seconds after the lightning flash for the sound of thunder to travel one mile, the student can count the number of seconds between the flash and the sound, then divide by 5 to see how far away the lightning is.

7. Choose any three-place number (e.g., 234), repeat the three digits and use this number (234234) as the dividend. Use 91 as the divisor. The quotient will be the product of 11 and the three-place number (11 × 234 = 2574). There will never be any remainder. This is based upon number theory and the factors of 1,001.

8. The teacher writes the number 12345679 on the board and then asks a student, "What's your favorite number?" If the student responds "5," the teacher directs him or her to multiply the given number by 45 (9 × the favorite number). What's the product?

$$\begin{array}{r} 12345679 \\ \times\,45 \\ \hline 555555555 \end{array}$$

If the student had given 3 as a favorite number, the teacher would have asked him or her to multiply by 27 (3 × 9):

$$\begin{array}{r} 12345679 \\ \times\, 27 \\ \hline 333333333 \end{array}$$

Hand-Held Calculator Activities for the Upper Elementary Grades

1. Make the hand-held calculator display screen read 57, by using only the operation keys and digit keys 2 and 3. What is the least number of key punches necessary to reach 57?

2. Make the calculator display read 73, using only the operation keys and digit keys 2 and 4. What is the least number of key punches necessary to arrive at 73?

3. Make the calculator display screen read 93 with the least number of key punches, by using only the operation keys and the digit keys 7 and 2.

4. Use the hand-held calculator to solve each example. What can you discover about the products?

$$\begin{array}{r} 76923 \times\ \ 1 = \\ 76923 \times 10 = \\ 76923 \times\ \ 9 = \\ 76923 \times 12 = \\ 76923 \times\ \ 3 = \\ 76923 \times\ \ 4 = \end{array}$$

Now multiply 76923 by all other numbers between 0 and 13 (2, 7, 5, 11, 6, 8). What can you discover about these products?

$$\begin{array}{r} 76923 \times\ \ 2 = \\ 76923 \times\ \ 7 = \\ 76923 \times\ \ 5 = \\ 76923 \times 11 = \\ 76923 \times\ \ 6 = \\ 76923 \times\ \ 8 = \end{array}$$

5. Solve the following multiplication examples. Estimate the answers, and then check them on your hand-held calculator.

$$\begin{array}{r} 1 \times 8 + 1 = \\ 12 \times 8 + 2 = \\ 123 \times 8 + 3 = \\ 1234 \times 8 + 4 = \\ 12345 \times 8 + 5 = \\ 123456 \times 8 + 6 = \\ 1234567 \times 8 + 7 = \\ 12345678 \times 8 + 8 = \\ 123456789 \times 8 + 9 = \end{array}$$

6. Using only digits 1, 2, 3, 4, and 5, place numbers in the boxes of each example so that you will have the greatest possible product. Use each digit only once in each example. Use your hand-held calculator to check the answers.

$$
\begin{array}{r}
\square\,\square\,\square\,\square \\
\times \qquad \square \\
\hline
\end{array}
\qquad
\begin{array}{r}
\square\,\square\,\square \\
\times \quad \square\,\square \\
\hline
\end{array}
\qquad
\begin{array}{r}
\square\,\square\,\square \\
\times \qquad \square \\
\hline
\times \qquad\quad \square
\end{array}
$$

7. Use only digits 5, 6, 7, 8, and 9. Place numbers in the boxes of each example so that you will have the greatest possible product. Use each digit only once in each example. Use your hand-held calculator to check the answers.

$$
\begin{array}{r}
\square\,\square\,\square\,\square \\
\times \qquad \square \\
\hline
\end{array}
\qquad
\begin{array}{r}
\square\,\square\,\square \\
\times \quad \square\,\square \\
\hline
\end{array}
\qquad
\begin{array}{r}
\square\,\square\,\square \\
\times \qquad \square \\
\hline
\times \qquad\quad \square
\end{array}
$$

8. Use only digits 0, 1, 2, 3, and 4. Place numbers in the boxes of each example so that you will have the least possible product. Use each digit only once in each example. Use your hand-held calculator to check the answers.

$$
\begin{array}{r}
\square\,\square\,\square\,\square \\
\times \qquad \square \\
\hline
\end{array}
\qquad
\begin{array}{r}
\square\,\square\,\square \\
\times \quad \square\,\square \\
\hline
\end{array}
\qquad
\begin{array}{r}
\square\,\square \\
\times \quad \square \\
\hline
\times \quad \square \\
\hline
\times \quad \square
\end{array}
$$

9. It is easy to create examples similar to the preceding examples. Use different digits and different algorithms.

10. Have the children use the hand-held calculator to multiply numbers by 1, 10, 100, and 1000. Study the place-value relationship in each example. This will help children to understand why the partial products must be properly placed in multiplication. Multiplying by 10 causes the place value to change. Why? Do not say "we add a zero," because adding zero to a number does not change the value of the number.

$$
\begin{array}{r}
4563 \\
\times \quad 1 \\
\hline
4563
\end{array}
\qquad
\begin{array}{r}
4563 \\
\times \quad 10 \\
\hline
45630
\end{array}
\qquad
\begin{array}{r}
4563 \\
\times \quad 100 \\
\hline
456300
\end{array}
\qquad
\begin{array}{r}
4563 \\
\times \ 1000 \\
\hline
4563000
\end{array}
$$

11. Have the children explore the properties of multiplication, using the hand-held calculator. For instance, multiply 34 × 56 and then multiply 56 × 34. The commutative property of multiplication works for every multiplication example. Try the associative property or the distributive property of multiplication over addition.

Microcomputer Activities for the Upper Elementary Grades

1. The microcomputer can be used in the immediate mode the same way as the hand-held calculator. Have the children experiment on the microcomputer with multiplication and division examples in the immediate mode.

2. Students in the upper grade levels who have not yet memorized the basic multiplication or division facts should use software packages for practicing basic facts.

3. Children can find the products for long multiplication examples rather easily. Examples such as "what is the product of the first 12 counting numbers?" can be easily solved.

4. For solving difficult division examples (for example, 35864 divided by 56), have the children estimate trial quotients and then check their estimates on the computer.

5. Children can create simple BASIC microcomputer programs to solve long multi-place mathematics examples. For instance, a student created the following simple microcomputer program to complete his mathematics assignment.

```
10 REM*MY MULTIPLICATION SOLVER*
20 ?"WHAT IS THE VALUE OF ONE FACTOR"
30 INPUT X
40 ?"WHAT IS THE VALUE OF THE OTHER FACTOR"
50 INPUT Y
60 ?"THE PRODUCT OF ";X;" AND ";Y;" IS ";X*Y
70 GOTO 20
```

6. Teachers could write simple practice programs designed to reinforce specific multiplication or division concepts.

```
10   REM—TWO PLACE NUMBER BY A TWO PLACE NUMBER—
15   K=0
20   X=INT(90*RND(1)+10)
30   Y=INT(90*RND(1)+10)
35   CLS
40   ?"GOOD MORNING! WHAT IS YOUR NAME"
50   INPUT N$
55   CLS
60   ?"NICE TO SEE YOU TODAY ";N$
70   ?:?:?:?"LET'S PRACTICE MULTIPLICATION"
80   ?:?:?:?"YOU MAY USE A SHEET OF PAPER TO WRITE ON."
90   ?:?:?"IF YOU DO USE A SHEET OF PAPER GIVE"
100  ?"IT TO YOUR TEACHER AFTER YOUR PRACTICE."
110  ?:?:?
115  K=K+1
120  ?"SOLVE THIS EXAMPLE ";X;" X " ;Y
130  INPUT Z
140  IF Z=X*Y THEN 500
150  IF Z<>X*Y THEN ?"TRY AGAIN":GOTO 120
500  ?"GREAT! YOU ARE CORRECT"
505  IF K=10 THEN ?"THAT'S ALL ";N$:END
510  FOR T=1 TO 2000:NEXT T
520  ?"HERE IS ANOTHER EXAMPLE"
530  FOR T=1 TO 1000:NEXT T
540  GOTO 110
```

Suggested Readings

Ando, Masue, and Hitoshi, Ikeda. "Learning Multiplication Facts—More Than a Drill." *The Arithmetic Teacher*, vol. 18, no. 6, October 1971.

Bruni, James V., and Silverman, Helene J. "The Multiplication Facts: Once More with Understanding." *The Arithmetic Teacher*, vol. 23, no. 6, October 1976.

Connelly, Ralph, and Heddens, James W. "Remainders that Shouldn't Remain." *The Arithmetic Teacher*, vol. 18, no. 6, October 1971.

Dana, Marcia, and Lindquist, Mary Montgomery. "Thinking Up Your Own Practice Games." *The Arithmetic Teacher*, vol. 25, no. 5, February 1978.

Grossnickle, Foster E., and others. *Discovering Meanings in Elementary School Mathematics*. 7th ed. New York: Holt, Rinehart & Winston, 1983.

Higgins, Jon L., and Sachs, Larry A. *Mathematics Laboratories: 150 Activities for Elementary Schools*. Reston, Va.: National Council of Teachers of Mathematics, 1974.

Kennedy, Leonard M., and Michon, Ruth L. *Games for Individualizing Mathematics Learning*. Columbus, Ohio: Merrill, 1973.

Kurtz, Ray. "Fourth Grade Division: How Much Is Retained in Grade Five?" *The Arithmetic Teacher*, vol. 20, no. 1, January 1973.

National Council of Teachers of Mathematics. *Mathematics Learning in Early Childhood*. 37th Yearbook. Reston, Va.: NCTM, 1975.

Riedesel, C. Alan. *Teaching Elementary School Mathematics*. Englewood Cliffs, N.J.: Prentice-Hall, 1980.

Smith, C. Winston, Jr. "Tiger-Bite Cards and Blank Arrays." *The Arithmetic Teacher*, vol. 21, no. 8, December 1974.

Spitler, Gail. "Multiplying by Eleven—A Place-value Exploration." *The Arithmetic Teacher*, vol. 24, no. 1, February 1977.

Tucker, Benny F. "The Division Algorithm." *The Arithmetic Teacher*, vol. 20, no. 8, December 1973.

Vigilante, Nicholas J. "Access to Multiplication Facts." *The Arithmetic Teacher*, vol. 24, no. 1, September 1978.

8 Number Theory

Teaching Competencies

Upon completing this unit, you will be able to:

Write all possible two-factor product expressions for a given counting number

Draw all possible arrays that represent a given counting number

Classify counting numbers as prime or composite

Write the prime factorization of any given counting number

State the fundamental theorem of arithmetic

Calculate the greatest common factor for a given set of counting numbers

Calculate the least common multiple for a given set of counting numbers

State the rules for divisibility

Discussion

In this unit we will look closer at another aspect of the structural approach to teaching mathematics and the parts (factors) that comprise all numbers. Mathematics structures provide a solid foundation for building a stronger mathematics program. This will help students to develop mathematics and not just manipulate algorithms. Here we will consider some of the most efficient approaches to understanding numbers and their factors.

As a result of this close examination of number structure, it is hoped that each teacher will recognize the **fundamental theorem of arithmetic** as an idea that he has known for a long time. But of greater importance is the discovery of the way in which this theorem is basic to a thorough understanding of operations on whole and fractional numbers. The information in this unit is necessary background for every elementary classroom teacher.

Before getting into the subject of this unit, it is advisable for us to review some of the language used in discussing multiplication of whole numbers as that subject is presented in most elementary mathematics programs today. (See Unit 7). Let's begin by naming the parts of a mathematical sentence involving multiplication:

$$2 \times 3 = 6$$

In this sentence the 2 and the 3 are called **factors,** and the 6 is called the **product.** We also say that

2 is a **factor** of 6
3 is a **factor** of 6
6 is the **product** of the factors 2 and 3
6 is a **multiple** of 2
6 is a **multiple** of 3

When we say that 6 is a multiple of 2, we mean that we can multiply 2 by some whole-number factor to get 6 as a product. Each time we multiply 2 by a whole number, we get a multiple of 2. Thus the multiples of 2 are 0, 2, 4, 6, 8, 10 and so on. The multiples of 5 are 0, 5, 10, 15, 20, 25, and so on. In the primary grades we often have children practice counting by 2, by 3, and by 5. When they do

this, they are working with multiples of 2, multiples of 3, and multiples of 5.

As early as the primary grades the child learns that a number such as 12 can be named in many ways:

$11 + 1$	2×6
$15 - 3$	$24 \div 2$
3×4	$36 \div 3$

We will use the words **product expression** to talk about names, such as 3×4 and 2×6, that involve multiplication (or finding a product). In other words, 3×4 and 2×6 are product expressions for 12.

As we have seen in Unit 4, a product expression with two factors can be pictured by an array. For example, we can picture the product expression 3×4 with this array:

```
•  •  •  •
•  •  •  •
•  •  •  •
```

We call this a 3-by-4 array. The first number tells how many rows (3), and the second number tells how many columns (4).

We can use any of several different product expressions to represent the number 12. For example:

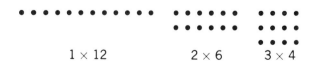

$1 \times 12 \qquad\qquad 2 \times 6 \qquad 3 \times 4$

Each of these product expressions for the number 12 has been expressed here as an array. Because of the commutative property, we need to use only these three product expressions for 12. Notice that these are rectangular arrays; this means that they have one or more rows and columns. Every number can be represented by a rectangular array having only one row.

In the case of the number 6, there are two product expressions containing two factors (plus two more that are omitted because of the commutative property):

We have formed rectangular arrays with 12 objects (1 × 12, 2 × 6, and 3 × 4) and with 6 objects (1 × 6 and 2 × 3). Now let's consider other numbers:

NUMBER	PRODUCT EXPRESSION	ARRAY
14	1 × 14	• • • • • • • • • • • • • •
	2 × 7	• • • • • • • • • • • • • •
20	1 × 20	• • • • • • • • • • • • • • • • • • • •
	2 × 10	• • • • • • • • • • • • • • • • • • • •
	4 × 5	• • • • • • • • • • • • • • • • • • • •

But what happens in the case of the number 13? With 13 objects or symbols we can form a rectangular array of only a single row (1 × 13) or a single column (13 × 1):

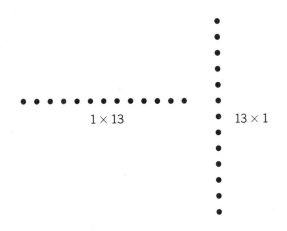

What other numbers can be represented by a rectangular array of only a single row or column?

Examining the following table, we find that 2, 3, 5, 7, and 11 also can be represented only by single rows or single columns.

NUMBER	PRODUCT EXPRESSION	ARRAY
2	1 × 2	• •
3	1 × 3	• • •
4	1 × 4	• • • •
	2 × 2	• • • •
5	1 × 5	• • • • •
6	1 × 6	• • • • • •
	2 × 3	• • • • • •
7	1 × 7	• • • • • • •
8	1 × 8	• • • • • • • •
	2 × 4	• • • • • • • •
9	1 × 9	• • • • • • • • •
	3 × 3	• • • • • • • • •
10	1 × 10	• • • • • • • • • •
	2 × 5	• • • • • • • • • •
11	1 × 11	• • • • • • • • • • •

What about a greater number—for example, 30?

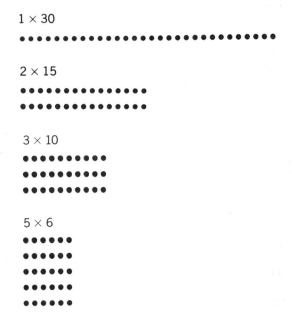

1 × 30

2 × 15

3 × 10

5 × 6

From this brief examination we can draw several conclusions:

1. A product expression for a number is another name for the number itself. For example, product expressions for 12 (1 × 12, 2 × 6, 3 × 4) are different ways of naming 12.
2. Every whole number greater than 1 can be named by at least two product expressions: 1 times the number itself and (by using the commutative property) the number itself times 1.
3. Many numbers can be named by more than two product expressions—for example, 4, 6, 8, 9, 10, 12, 14, 20, and 30.

From our review of the language of multiplication, we know that the numbers making up a product expression are called factors. We know that many of the numbers we've discussed have more than two factors. For example, we can name the set of all factors of 12: {1, 2, 3, 4, 6, 12}. But many numbers have only two factors: 1 and the number itself. The only factors of 11, for example, are 1 and 11, so the set of factors of 11 is {1, 11}.

Another way of examining numbers in the light of their factors comes to us from ancient Greece. Eratosthenes, a famous geographer of the third century B.C., first devised the method that has come to be called the **Sieve of Eratosthenes.** The following arrangement of numerals is one example of a pattern for a sieve.

	2	3	4	5	6	7	8	9	10
11	12	13	14	15	16	17	18	19	20
21	22	23	24	25	26	27	28	29	30
31	32	33	34	35	36	37	38	39	40
41	42	43	44	45	46	47	48	49	50
51	52	53	54	55	56	57	58	59	60
61	62	63	64	65	66	67	68	69	70
71	72	73	74	75	76	77	78	79	80
81	82	83	84	85	86	87	88	89	90
91	92	93	94	95	96	97	98	99	100

To begin our examination of the sieve, let us recall our discussion of rectangular arrays. The number 2 can be represented by a rectangular array of a single row or column only. The product expression for 2 is 1 × 2, but every multiple of 2 (other than 2 itself) can be represented by rectangular arrays with more than a single row or column.

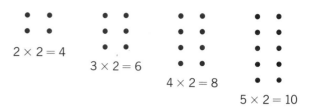

$2 \times 2 = 4$

$3 \times 2 = 6$

$4 \times 2 = 8$

$5 \times 2 = 10$

and so on

Now, referring to the table, or sieve, loop the numeral 2 and cross out all the other multiples of 2 (4, 6, 8, 10, . . ., 100).

Next, consider 3. You will recall that 3 can be represented by only a single row or column array; the only factors of 3 are 1 and 3. Multiples of 3 (other than 3 itself), however, can be represented by rectangular arrays with 3 columns. On the sieve, loop the 3 and then cross out all other multiples of 3 (6, 9, 12, 15, 18, . . ., 99).

The next consecutive numeral not looped or crossed out is 5. Loop the 5 and cross out all other multiples of 5 (10, 15, 20, 25, . . ., 100). You will notice that many of the multiples of 5 have already been crossed out, because some multiples of 5 are also multiples of 2 or 3.

The next numeral not crossed out is 7. Loop the 7 and cross out all other multiples of 7 (14, 21, 28, . . ., 98).

The next numeral not crossed out is 11. Loop the 11 and cross out all other multiples of 11 (22, 33, 44, . . ., 99). You will observe that all the multiples of 11 (other than 11 itself) have already been crossed out.

At this point, what generalization could you make about the multiples of 13? (All multiples of 13, other than 13 itself, have already been crossed out.)

You will notice that there are still numerals left on the chart that have not been crossed out. What generalization could you make about the arrays that illustrate these numbers? (In each case the array consists of either a single row or a single column. We cannot form rectangular arrays for these numbers.) For each of these numbers, what are the only factors? (For each number, the only factors are 1 and the number itself.) Make a list of the numerals on the chart that are not crossed out. (2, 3, 5, 7, 11, 13, 17, 19, 23, 29, 31, 37, 41, 43, 47, 53, 59, 61, 67, 71, 73, 79, 83, 89, and 97.) These whole numbers are greater than 1 and have only 1 and themselves as factors; they are called **prime numbers.** Whole numbers greater than 1 that have whole-number factors other than 1 and themselves are called **composite numbers.**

What do you notice that is common to all prime numbers except 2? (They are all odd. This is true because every even number has 2 as a factor.)

We have now examined the structure of certain numbers in two ways—by making arrays of physical objects or symbols and by marking off multiples of certain numbers on a chart. Comparing the results of these two approaches, what conclusions can we draw? You will remember that certain numbers cannot be represented by rectangular arrays. These are the prime numbers that we discovered on our chart. These prime numbers (the numbers still on the chart—the ones that were not crossed off the sieve) are numbers that can be represented in an array only by one row or one column of physical objects or symbols. What can we say about the factors that make up the product expressions of these numbers? (The only factors these numbers have are 1 and the numbers themselves.)

We have not included the number 1 in this discussion. The number 1 is unique. It is a factor of every number ($2 = 1 \times 2$, $3 = 1 \times 3$, $15 = 1 \times 15$, $189 = 1 \times 189$, and so on), because it is the identity element for multiplication. To say that 1 is a factor of a number, then, does not really tell us much about the number. By definition, **the number 1 is neither prime nor composite.** But remember that any number greater than 1 that has only 1 and the number itself as factors is a prime number. Any whole number greater than 1 must therefore be either prime or composite (nonprime). Using arrays and the sieve of Eratosthenes, we have sorted the set of whole numbers between 2 and 100 inclusive into prime and composite numbers.

A further remark on the work of Eratosthenes will explain the term "sieve." Working with numerals arranged on a parchment sheet, Eratosthenes physically punched out all the multiples of 2, except for 2 itself, leaving holes in the parchment. The multiples of 3, except for 3 itself, were cut from the sheet in the same way, then the multiples of 5 and so on. The end result was a sheet on which only the prime numbers remained. This parchment filled with holes where the composite numbers had dropped through closely resembled a sieve.

Interesting patterns can be discovered by placing varying amounts of numbers in a row. Let's look at the pattern that develops when the numbers are placed into a table with six columns. Where are the prime numbers located? Will a prime number ever appear in the column headed by 4 or 6? Justify your response.

1	2	3	4	5	6
7	8	9	10	11	12
13	14	15	16	17	18
19	20	21	22	23	24
25	26	27	28	29	30
31	32	33	34	35	36
37	38	39	40	41	42
43	44	45	46	47	48
49	50	51	52	53	54
55	56	57	58	59	60
61	62	63	64	65	66
67	68	69	70	71	72
73	74	75	76	77	78
79	80	81	82	83	84
85	86	87	88	89	90
91	92	93	94	95	96
97	98	99	100	101	102

We have found that every composite number can be renamed as a product expression other than 1 times the number. For instance, 24 can be renamed using any of the following product expressions:

2×12
3×8
4×6

This can also be shown in another way:

EXAMPLE A: EXAMPLE B: EXAMPLE C:

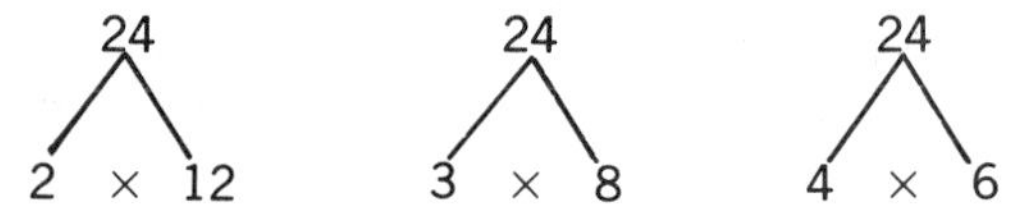

In Example A we know that 12 can be renamed as 2 × 6 or as 3 × 4, so Example A can be extended in two possible ways:

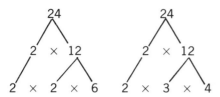

We can see in these two cases that 6 and 4 are both composite numbers, but each can be factored in only one way (excluding 1 as a factor):

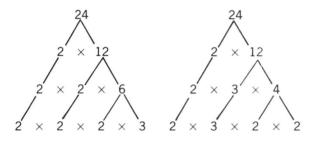

We see now that every number named in the last row is a prime number. Because of the shape of these particular diagrams, they are sometimes referred to as **factor trees.**

In Example B we know that 8 can be expressed only as 2 × 4. Hence the following factor tree:

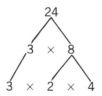

Examining the last row of this factor tree, we find the composite number 4, which can be named by the product expression 2 × 2:

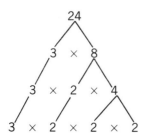

By examination we see that every number named in the last row is now a prime number.

In Example C, both 4 and 6 are composite numbers and can be shown by the product expressions 2 × 2 and 2 × 3, respectively. The following factor tree results.

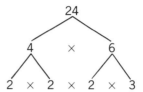

Since every number named in the last row is a prime number, the factor tree is complete.

Now examine the last row in each of the factor trees.

EXAMPLE A: 2 × 2 × 2 × 3
             2 × 3 × 2 × 2
EXAMPLE B: 3 × 2 × 2 × 2
EXAMPLE C: 2 × 2 × 2 × 3

You will notice that in each example the final result is a product expression for 24 in which each factor is a prime number. Furthermore, each product expression uses the same set of factors. Because of the commutative property of multiplication, the fact that they are arranged in a different order is not important.

Now examine another number, 18, and the appropriate factor trees:

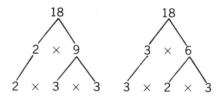

Notice that whether we use 2 × 9 or 3 × 6 as the first product expression, the last product expression in the factor tree is composed of the same set of factors. Again the fact that they are arranged in a different order is not significant.

Factor trees for the number 36 look like these:

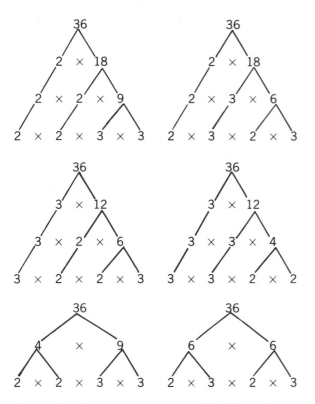

We see that the factor trees look a bit different from each other. Nevertheless, the same set of factors is to be found in the last product expression of all the trees. Can there ever be more than one set of factors in the last row of the factor trees for a particular number? (No.) This important conclusion is formally known as the **fundamental theorem of arithmetic.**

> The fundamental theorem of arithmetic states that except for the order of the factors, a composite number can be expressed as a product of prime numbers in only one way.

When a composite number is expressed as a product of prime numbers, we often refer to this as **prime factorization,** or complete factorization. The following are some examples of prime factorization.

$42 = 2 \times 21$
$ = 2 \times 3 \times 7$

$45 = 3 \times 15$
$ = 3 \times 3 \times 5$

$50 = 2 \times 25$
$ = 2 \times 5 \times 5$

$56 = 2 \times 28$
$ = 2 \times 2 \times 14$
$ = 2 \times 2 \times 2 \times 7$

$72 = 2 \times 36$
$ = 2 \times 2 \times 18$
$ = 2 \times 2 \times 2 \times 9$
$ = 2 \times 2 \times 2 \times 3 \times 3$

Notice that the product expression for prime factorization of a number is found when each factor in the final product expression is a prime number.

Now let's investigate some practical applications involving prime factors. Many times in mathematics we will need to factor numbers into primes. For example, we can use prime factorizations when we write fractions in simplest form and when we find least common denominators (see Units 10, 11, and 12). Thus we should know how to factor a number most efficiently.

To decide whether any given number is prime or factorable, a successive division test is applied. First we attempt to divide the given number by the least prime number, 2; then we use successively greater prime divisors. For example, let's test 92:

$$\begin{array}{r} 2\,\overline{)\,92} \\ 2\,\overline{)\,46} \\ 23 \end{array}$$

By starting with the divisor 2, it becomes evident that 92 can be factored, since we obtain a quotient and a zero remainder. 46 is also divisible by 2. Remember that in testing each quotient, we always begin with the least prime number, 2, as the divisor. The next quotient, 23, we find is not divisible by 2, 3, 5, 7, 11, 13, or 19. It is a prime number, so our factoring is complete. The prime factorization of 92 is thus shown to be $2 \times 2 \times 23$. By the inverse relationship of division and multiplication, we know that a divisor and a quotient can be expressed in a related multiplication form as two factors. In the example above, the divisor 2 and the quotient 46 are factors of 92 in the related multiplication equation, $2 \times 46 = 92$. Similarly, 2 and 23 are factors in the multiplication equation $2 \times 23 = 46$.

Now try a number with more factors, 468:

$$\begin{array}{r} 2\,\overline{)\,468} \\ 2\,\overline{)\,234} \\ 3\,\overline{)\,117} \\ 3\,\overline{)\,39} \\ 13 \end{array}$$

In this case the divisor 2 is effective in the first two steps. But the quotient 117 cannot be divided by 2. Our next step, then, is to see if 117 is divisible by the next prime number, 3. It is, so the division is performed and the new quotient obtained is 39. Obviously 39 is not divisible by 2, since it is an odd number. However, it is divisible by the next prime number, 3. Since the quotient 13 is prime, this is as far as our factoring can be carried. The prime factorization is a combination of *all* the divisors *and* the final quotient. (Divisors are of course factors.) The following expression shows the prime factorization of 468.

$$2 \times 2 \times 3 \times 3 \times 13$$

Since some greater numbers are prime, much time can be wasted attempting to find divisors (other than 1 and the numbers themselves) for greater numbers that are in fact prime. However, there is an aid that can save us some time. We should try only divisors that are *not* greater than the square root of the number being tested. (If you need to review the meaning of "square root," see Unit 16.)

Consider the number 97 and test it for factorization, beginning with the least prime number as divisor. The number 97 is obviously not divisible by 2, because 97 is not an even number. It is also not divisible by 3. Next we try the divisors 5 and 7, still unsuccessfully. There is no reason to try any greater primes as divisors. The square root of 97 is less than 10 (since $10 \times 10 = 100$), and 7 is the greatest prime divisor that isn't greater than this square root. Therefore, 97 is prime.

Students should understand the reasons we do not attempt to use divisors greater than the square root of the number involved.

Do *not* ask children to apply a rote rule. To illustrate the reasoning, let us consider what happens when a divisor is selected. For example

$$2\overline{)24} \atop 12$$

We see that factors appear in pairs. As soon as one number is used as a divisor, a second number appears as a quotient. In dividing 24 by 2, another factor, 12, appears automatically. For the moment let's consider all pairs of factors of 24: 1×24, 2×12, 3×8, and 4×6. Notice that in each case a greater factor is paired with a lesser factor:

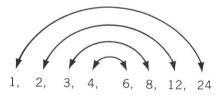

1,   2,   3,   4,   6,   8,   12,   24

Clearly, if no lesser number (other than those listed) is a factor of 24, then no greater number is a factor either. We see that 4 is the greatest factor we need to divide into 24 in order to list all the factors of 24 (if we have already divided by 1, 2, and 3). Hence, generalizing from the example of 24 to all whole numbers, we need to consider only the lesser numbers as divisors—that is, numbers that aren't greater than the square root of the number under consideration. Note that the square root of 24 lies between

the square root of 25 (written $\sqrt{25}$) and the square root of 16 ($\sqrt{16}$):

$$\sqrt{25} = 5; \qquad 5 \times 5 = 25$$
$$\sqrt{16} = 4; \qquad 4 \times 4 = 16$$

Since $25 > 24$, we do not need to test any divisors greater than 4 to obtain *all* the factors of 24.

Consider the number 100.

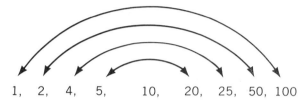

1,   2,   4,   5,   10,   20,   25,   50,   100

If we divide 100 only by factors of 100 up to and including the square root of 100 ($\sqrt{100} = 10$), we will obtain all the factors of 100. What is our procedure for finding the prime factorization of 100?

1. Begin by trying the least prime number, 2, as divisor:

$$2\overline{)100} \atop 50$$

2. We can divide by 2 again, since the quotient, 50, is an even number:

$$\begin{array}{r} 2\overline{)100} \\ 2\overline{)\;50} \\ \hline 25 \end{array}$$

3. This quotient is not divisible by 2 or by the next prime number, 3; but it is divisible by the next prime number, 5:

$$\begin{array}{r} 2\overline{)100} \\ 2\overline{)\;50} \\ 5\overline{)\;25} \\ \hline 5 \end{array}$$

4. Our prime factorization of 100 is now complete, since the quotient 5 is prime:

$$2 \times 2 \times 5 \times 5$$

With large numbers it is extremely helpful to use only prime-number divisors that are less than the square root of the dividend. For example, consider the number 469. Is this a prime number? If not, what is its prime factorization?

Our first step is to determine the greatest prime number that we need to try as a divisor. To determine this, we need to find only the square root, or the approximate square root, of 469. We know that $20 \times 20 = 400$. What are the prime numbers closest to 20? They are 19 and 23. Since $23 \times 23 = 529$ (and $529 > 469$), we know that 19 is the greatest prime number we need to try as a divisor.

Dividing 469 by primes (beginning, as always, with 2), we find that 2, 3, and 5 will not divide 469 evenly. The next prime number is 7, which does divide 469 evenly:

$$7 \overline{)469} \\ 67$$

Since 469 is not a multiple of 2, 3, or 5, neither can the number 67 be a multiple of 2, 3, or 5. By trying 7, 11, 13, 17, and 19 as divisors, we find that 67 is prime. Or, since $\sqrt{67}$ is approximately 8, we find that we have tested as far as is necessary with a divisor of 7. In either case, 67 is prime, and the prime factorization of 469 is 7×67.

Now let's test 73. We know that $\sqrt{73}$ lies somewhere between 8 and 9, since $8 \times 8 = 64$ and $9 \times 9 = 81$. The greatest prime divisor to test, then, is 7.

Is 73 divisible by 2? (No.)
Is 73 divisible by 3? (No.)
Is 73 divisible by 5? (No.)
Is 73 divisible by 7? (No.)

Any attempt to go further in division is unnecessary, since the next prime, 11, is greater than $\sqrt{73}$. The number 73, then, is prime.

To factor numbers completely and efficiently

1. We must understand prime factors.
2. We must have a systematic approach to factorization.
3. We must have some simple rules for determining whether or not a number is divisible by the most common prime numbers.

The sieve we have discussed can be used to point out simple rules of divisibility for the numbers 2, 3, and 5. By inspecting the multiples of 2, 3, and 5, children can discover the structural peculiarities of any number divisible by 2, 3, or 5. First, by examining the multiples of 2, children can see that the digit in the ones place is always 0, 2, 4, 6, or 8. Only whole numbers ending in one of these digits are divisible by 2. In other words, only even numbers are multiples of 2 (that is, divisible by 2).

Next, children should inspect the multiples of 3. A more complex development becomes apparent here. Any number divisible by 3 is a number whose digits add up to another number that is divisible by 3. For example, consider the following:

NUMBER	SUM OF DIGITS	FACTORS OF NUMBERS
12	$1 + 2 = 3$	3×4
15	$1 + 5 = 6$	3×5
18	$1 + 8 = 9$	3×6
21	$2 + 1 = 3$	3×7
24	$2 + 4 = 6$	3×8
27	$2 + 7 = 9$	3×9
96	$9 + 6 = 15$	3×32
168	$1 + 6 + 8 = 15$	3×56
4035	$4 + 0 + 3 + 5 = 12$	3×1345

In each case above, the sum of the digits is divisible by 3, and the original number is also divisible by 3. On the other hand, any number the sum of whose digits is not a multiple of 3 is not itself divisible by 3. This can be verified by examining such numbers as 11, 13, 14, 76, and 371.

Finally, children should inspect the multiples of 5. Every number that is divisible by 5 contains 0 or 5 in the ones place:

$$2 \times 5 = 10$$
$$3 \times 5 = 15$$
$$4 \times 5 = 20$$
$$5 \times 5 = 25$$
$$6 \times 5 = 30$$
$$7 \times 5 = 35$$
$$8 \times 5 = 40$$
$$9 \times 5 = 45$$
$$10 \times 5 = 50$$
and so on

On the other hand, any whole number that doesn't end with 0 or 5 is not divisible by 5. For example: 11, 17, and 134. These simple rules of divisibility can be very helpful, and children learn more about number structure by applying such tests than by going through the more cumbersome process of division by trial and error.

A very useful technique for children is to know, understand, and use the divisibility rules. A child should be able to look at a number and know very quickly if it is divisible by a given number. Children need a great deal of guidance and help in discovering and using divisibility rules. Many examples need to be carefully examined; then children should discuss how the examples are alike and how they are different.

Let us summarize divisibility and the divisibility rules. By divisibility we mean that a given number may be divided by a given divisor so that there is a zero remainder. Look at the examples below. We say

9 is divisible by 3 because we receive a zero remainder:

$$3\overline{)9}$$
$$\underline{-9}$$
$$0$$

In the example

$$3\overline{)7}$$
$$\underline{-6}$$
$$1$$

we say 7 is not divisible by 3 because when 7 is divided by 3 we have a nonzero remainder—in this case, 1.

Now let us summarize the divisibility rules. To obtain a prime factor of any number, a systematic approach should be used. Use the prime numbers in order from least to greatest. Consider these examples:

$$2\overline{)6}$$
$$\underline{-6}$$
$$0 \longleftarrow \text{zero remainder}$$

$$2\overline{)7}$$
$$\underline{-6} \qquad \text{This is not a}$$
$$1 \longleftarrow \text{zero remainder.}$$

Is 6 a composite number or a prime number? Use the prime numbers as factors in order from least to greatest. Is 6 divisible by 2? The answer is yes because when 6 is divided by 2 a zero remainder is obtained. Is 7 a prime number or a composite number? Divide 7 by the first prime number. We have 7 divided by 2. A remainder of 1 is obtained. Is 7 divisible by 3? Again a remainder of 1 is obtained. Since the square root of 7 is between 2 and 3 we have checked far enough. Use this procedure and check a sample of numbers so that children can justify the divisibility rules.

1. Any even number is divisible by 2. Two is a factor of any even number and a zero is obtained as a remainder.
2. A number is divisible by 3 if the sum of the digits is a multiple of 3. We know 144 is divisible by 3 because by adding the digits 1, 4, and 4, we obtain a sum of 9, and 9 is divisible by 3.
3. A number is divisible by 5 if there is either a 0 or 5 in the ones place.

Use this procedure to verify the following divisibility rules. These rules will be very valuable tools as we study rational numbers written in fraction or decimal form.

4. A number is divisible by 4 if the last two places, taken together as a number, are evenly divisible by 4. The number 328 is divisible by 4 because we know 28 is divisible by 4; therefore, 328 is divisible by 4.
5. A number is divisible by 6 if the number is divisible by both 2 and 3. The number 546 is even; therefore, it is divisible by 2. It is divisible by 3 because 5 + 4 + 6 = 15, and 15 is divisible by 3. Therefore 546 is divisible by 6 because it is divisible by both 2 and 3.
6. A number is divisible by 8 if the last three digits, taken together as a number, are divisible by 8; 9864 is divisible by 8 because we know 864 is divisible by 8.
7. A number is divisible by 9 if the sum of the digits is divisible by 9. The number 756 is divisible by 9 because 7 + 5 + 6 = 18 and we know 18 is divisible by 9.
8. A number is divisible by 10 if there is a zero in the ones place.

Now that every composite number has been shown to have a unique prime factorization, we can use this fact to help us find other information. For example, it is often very useful to know the **greatest common factor** (or greatest common divisor) of two numbers.

The ideas of GCF and LCM will be used extensively in the next three units to develop concepts about operations on fractional numbers. These are mentioned here because of their relation to prime factors. The practical applications shown in the next unit will be of interest to the teacher and of great importance throughout the study of fractional numbers.

Let's first examine the concept of greatest common factor. By this we mean that we want to find the greatest number that will divide evenly into two given numbers. Consider the two numbers 24 and 36. What is the greatest common factor of these two numbers? What are the factors of 24? (1, 2, 3, 4, 6, 8, 12, and 24) What are the factors of 36? (1, 2, 3, 4, 6, 9, 12, 18, and 36) The common factors of 24 and 36 are 1, 2, 3, 4, 6, and 12. Twelve is the greatest factor common to both 24 and 36.

We can also find the greatest common factor of 24 and 36 by using prime factorization. To do this we first write prime factorizations for 36 and 24:

$$36 = 2 \times 2 \times 3 \times 3$$
$$24 = 2 \times 2 \times 2 \times 3$$

By inspecting these factorizations, we can select each factor that is common to both numbers. Clearly, $2 \times 2 \times 3$ appears in both sets of factors. Since each number is "built" with these factors, each of the numbers is divisible by these factors. Thus the greatest common factor (GCF) of 36 and 24 is $2 \times 2 \times 3$, or 12. This tells us simply that the greatest factor by which both 36 and 24 can be divided is 12.

The previous development of prime factorization and factor trees should clarify why the method described leads to the determination of the GCF. You will recall that a number can be factored (with factor trees) into successive product expressions until the prime factorization is reached. When, for example, 36 is factored successively, it becomes apparent that any factor or combination of factors is actually a divisor of 36:

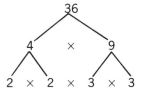

It can be seen that any factor or combination of factors expressed in the last line of the above factor tree is a divisor of 36. From this list of factors, (2, 2, 3, 3), we can take any two, three, or four factors and multiply them together to find another factor, one that is greater than any of the single factors listed. In this case we discover the following factors.

$$2 = 2$$
$$3 = 3$$
$$2 \times 2 = 4$$
$$2 \times 3 = 6$$
$$3 \times 3 = 9$$
$$2 \times 2 \times 3 = 12$$
$$2 \times 3 \times 3 = 18$$
$$2 \times 2 \times 3 \times 3 = 36$$

We have found, by drawing a factor tree to discover the prime factorization, that $24 = 2 \times 2 \times 2 \times 3$. From the list of factors (2, 2, 2, 3) we can take any two, three, or four factors and multiply them together to find other factors that are greater than the single factors listed. Thus we discover the following factors.

$$2 = 2$$
$$3 = 3$$
$$2 \times 2 = 4$$
$$2 \times 3 = 6$$
$$2 \times 2 \times 2 = 8$$
$$2 \times 2 \times 3 = 12$$
$$2 \times 2 \times 2 \times 3 = 24$$

By comparing the set of factors of 36 and the set of factors of 24, we can see that the greatest number that is a factor of both 36 and 24 is 12 (or $2 \times 2 \times 3$).

In addition to finding the greatest common factor of two numbers, we can also find the **least common multiple** of two numbers. What do we mean by least common multiple? First, we know that a **multiple** of any number is evenly divisible by that number. For instance, the multiples of 2 (0, 2, 4, 6, 8, 10 . . .) can all be divided evenly by 2. Second, when we say **common** multiple, we know that we are speaking of a number that is a multiple of each of at least two numbers. For example, 24 is a common multiple of 12 and 8, since it can be divided evenly by either 12 or 8. Third, when we speak of the **least** common multiple, we mean the smallest (least) nonzero number that is a multiple of all the numbers being considered.

Now let us find the least common multiple of 24 and 36. We can begin by listing multiples of each number until we find a common multiple.

The multiples of 24 are 0, 24, 48, 72, 96, 120, 144, 168, 192, and 216. The multiples of 36 are 0, 36, 72, 108, 144, 180, 216, 252, etc. Carefully examining the multiples of these two numbers, we find that some of the common multiples are 0, 72, 144, 216, ... The least common nonzero multiple of 24 and 36 is 72.

Now let's find the least common multiple for 24 and 36 by using prime factorization.

$$36 = 2 \times 2 \times 3 \times 3$$
$$24 = 2 \times 2 \times 2 \times 3$$

Since a multiple of a number must contain that number, it must also contain the prime factorization of that number. This stands to reason, since the prime factorization is the basic structure or composition of the number. Hence we can conclude that a multiple of a number must, at the very least, include the prime factorization of that number. Now we want to construct a multiple of both 36 and 24. This must contain the prime factorizations of both 36 and 24 in order to be a common multiple:

$$36 = 2 \times 2 \times 3 \times 3$$
$$24 = 2 \times 2 \times 2 \times 3$$

The LCM must contain $2 \times 2 \times 3 \times 3$ to accommodate 36. And it must contain $2 \times 2 \times 2 \times 3$ to accommodate 24. By comparing the two product expressions we see that, in addition to the factors in the product expression for 36 ($2 \times 2 \times 3 \times 3$), we need an additional 2 to make sure that the prime factorization of 24 is included. Clearly, then, the least common multiple of 24 and 36 must be $2 \times 2 \times 3 \times 3 \times 2$, or 72.

Notice that the least common multiple contains the prime factorizations of both 36 and 24 (2 × 2 × 3 × 3) × (2 × 2 × 2 × 3), but it is not simply the product of 36 and 24. If a factor appears in both numbers, then it must appear in the LCM only as often as it appears in the number (of the two numbers) in which it appears most often. For example, the factor 2 appears twice in 36 (2 × 2 × 3 × 3), and three times in 24 (2 × 2 × 2 × 3); therefore it must appear exactly three times in the LCM. Again, the factor 3 appears once in 24 (2 × 2 × 2 × 3) and twice in 36 (2 × 2 × 3 × 3); therefore it must appear exactly twice in the LCM. Clearly 72 (2 × 2 × 2 × 3 × 3) is the least number that contains three 2's and two 3's as factors.

We have examined number theory applicable to the elementary school mathematics program. Some children will become interested in number theory and will want to do additional study on their own. There are many other aspects of number theory that children might find interesting.

Terminology, Symbols, and Procedures

Composite number   A composite number is a whole number greater than 1 that has whole-number factors other than 1 and itself.

Divisible   A number is said to be divisible by another number if a zero is obtained as a remainder, when it is divided by that number.

Factorization (or factoring)   Factorization is the process of expressing a whole number as the product of whole numbers greater than 1.

Factors   Factors are two or more numbers that, under the operation of multiplication, result in a single, unique number (called the product). A first number is a factor of a second number if the first divides evenly into the second. (For example, 2 and 3 are factors of 6.)

Fundamental theorem of arithmetic   The fundamental theorem of arithmetic states that except for the order of the factors, a composite number can be expressed as a product of prime numbers in only one way.

Greatest common factor (GCF)   The greatest common factor (GCF) of two whole numbers is the greatest whole number that is a factor of each of the two numbers.

Least common multiple (LCM)   The least common multiple of two whole numbers is the smallest (least) nonzero number that is a multiple of both numbers.

Prime factorization   Prime factorization is the process of expressing a composite number as the product of prime numbers only (2 × 2 × 3 × 3 is the prime factorization of 36).

Prime number A prime number is a whole number greater than 1 that cannot be expressed as the product of two lesser whole numbers (each greater than 1). A prime number has only two factors, itself and 1. The number 1 is by definition neither prime nor composite. Prime numbers include 2, 3, 5, 7, 11, 13, 17, etc.

Product A product is the single, unique number that results from the operation of multiplication on two or more numbers (called factors).

Product expression A product expression for a number is an expression composed of two or more factors expressed as a multiplication operation. For example, 2 × 3 is a product expression for 6.

Rectangular array A rectangular array is an array that has one or more rows and one or more columns. These are arrays:

Practice Exercises

1. List the set of all factors for each number.

   a) 8   b) 17   c) 24   d) 100   e) 10

2. List all possible product expressions containing two factors for each number.

   a) 12   b) 27   c) 48   d) 100   e) 10

3. Draw all the possible arrays for each number.

   a) 9   b) 11   c) 10   d) 4

4. List the set of prime factors for each composite number.

   a) 8   b) 14   c) 36   d) 80   e) 41

5. Factor each composite number completely (into prime factors).

   a) 28   b) 78   c) 38   d) 92   e) 110

6. Use the principles of divisibility to determine whether each number is divisible by 2, 3, or 5.

   a) 99   b) 831   c) 615   d) 118,590   e) 458

7. Study the following numerals.

   a) 459   b) 675   c) 27

Devise a rule that will allow you to determine quickly if a given number is divisible by 9.

8. Twin primes are two prime numbers that have exactly one composite number between them. For example, 3 and 5 are considered to be twin primes. Name all the twin primes between 4 and 100.

9. Determine the greatest common factor for each set of numbers.

    a) {372, 390}
    b) {168, 714}
    c) {340, 390}
    d) {80, 84}

10. Determine the least common multiple for each set of numbers.

    a) {36, 60}
    b) {20, 42}
    c) {8, 14}
    d) {9, 15}

11. Study the following number sentences.

$$4 = 2 + 2$$
$$6 = 3 + 3$$
$$8 = 5 + 3$$
$$10 = 7 + 3 = 5 + 5$$
$$12 = 7 + 5$$

What kind of numbers do the numerals on the left-hand side of the equals sign represent? Are the addends on the right-hand side of the equals sign prime numbers? Can you formulate a statement that relates this information in the form of a general conjecture?

12. Study the following:

$2^2 = 4$, which has divisors 1, 2, 4
$3^2 = 9$, which has divisors 1, 3, 9
$5^2 = 25$, which has divisors 1, 5, 25
$7^2 = 49$, which has divisors 1, 7, 49
$11^2 = 121$, which has divisors 1, 11, 121

After studying this, see if you can formulate a general formula that summarizes it. Use your formula to determine the divisors of 169.

13. A number is called perfect if it is the sum of all the numbers (except itself) that divide it. For example, 6 is a perfect number because $6 = 1 + 2 + 3$, where 1, 2, and 3 are divisors of 6. Find another perfect number between 6 and 35.

Discussion Questions

1. Discuss the set of numbers having an odd number of factors. Make a generalization about these numbers.

2. Discuss methods of convincing children that zero is an even number.

3. Why do we use only prime numbers when we are checking divisibility?

4. Locate and study Goldbach's Conjecture; then present your findings to the class.

5. Discuss materials that can be used for the concrete development of number theory.

6. Discuss the dot pictures that can be drawn for square numbers and triangular numbers and the relationships between these dot pictures.

7. Discuss how a student could know whether a sum will be even or odd without actually adding the addends.

Activities for the Primary Grades

1. Have children stack ten cubes into two stacks, alternating between stacks. Then have them stack seven cubes. If the two stacks of cubes are the same height, the number is even. If the two stacks of cubes are uneven, then the number of cubes is odd.

Ten is even.   Seven is odd.

2. Use the same procedure as suggested previously. Have the children examine the sum of two even numbers, the sum of two odd numbers, and the sum of one even and one odd number.

3. Look for a pattern that will help you fill in the blanks.

   a) 2, 4, 6, 8, _____, _____, _____, _____
   b) 3, 6, 9, _____, 15, _____, _____, _____
   c) 4, 8, 12, _____, _____, 24, _____, _____
   d) 5, _____, 15, 20, _____, _____, _____, _____
   e) 10, 100, 1000, _____, _____, _____, _____

4. Write the first seven nonzero multiples of each number.

a) 9   b) 10   c) 11

5. Two whole numbers have been multiplied to yield a product of zero. What can you say about either of the original factors?

6. A puzzle game can be used to develop facility with factorizations of numbers. A home-made puzzle game may be made in the following way: 1) cut out a magazine picture, 2) dry mount it to a cardboard base, 3) cover it with clear self-adhesive plastic, 4) cut it into several jigsaw puzzle pieces and write numerals on the backs. Children can play this game

in the following way. A child takes a puzzle piece, say one with the numeral 18. If he can name all the factors of 18, he gets to use the puzzle piece in his attempt to construct the puzzle. If he is unable to state the factors of 18, he must try again with another piece.

7. A useful material for practice with factorizations of numbers is the roller board ("home-made TV"). The materials used to construct this are a cardboard box, shelf paper, dowels (at least 4″ longer than the box), and paint. The following method of construction can be used to make your roller board:

    a) Cut two slits in the cardboard box so that the paper may slide through without tearing.

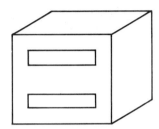

    b) With a sharp object, make two sets of two holes large enough for the dowels to fit into.

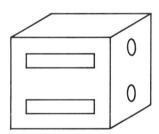

    c) Paint the box.
    d) After putting the dowels in, thread shelf paper through slits and tape the loose ends to the bottom dowel.

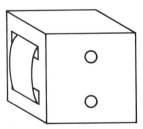
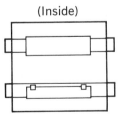

(Inside)

    e) Write on the "screen"; then turn the bottom dowel until the screen is clear. Continue until all desired information is on the roll; then cut the other end and tape it to the top dowel.

        This roller board or "homemade TV" can be helpful in illustrating many different mathematical concepts. For example, children may be asked to name many different pairs of factors for a number shown on the screen.

Hand-Held Calculator Activities for the Primary Grades

1. Have the children use hand-held calculators to add many even numbers. Ask the children to study their examples and generalize a rule. An even number added to another even number will yield an even sum.

2. Have the children use their calculators to add odd numbers. Ask the children to generalize a rule for adding two odd numbers. An odd number added to another odd number will yield an even sum.

3. Have the children use the hand-held calculators to add an even number to an odd number. Ask the children to generalize a rule for adding an odd number to an even number. An odd number added to an even number will yield an odd sum.

4. Request that the children use their hand-held calculators to multiply many numbers by zero and then generalize a rule for multiplying by zero. Use the same procedure, and multiply by 1.

5. Have the children use their calculators to add zero to many numbers. The children should generalize a rule for adding zero to a number.

Microcomputer Activities for the Primary Grades

All the calculator activities for the primary grades can also be used on a microcomputer in the immediate mode.

Activities for the Intermediate Grades

Knowledge of prime numbers and factorization provides another tool for the child to use in developing his mathematical skills, especially in his work with fractional numbers where he must find common denominators and rewrite fractions in simplest form.

The study of prime numbers and factorization can also introduce children to the exciting topic of number theory. Long an intriguing topic to mathematicians and nonmathematicians alike, the study of number lore can be a motivating topic for children to consider. For example, in Greek numerology two was considered a female number while three was considered male. Numbers have also had supernatural connotations. According to St. Augustine, God created the world in six days because six is a perfect number (six is the sum of all its divisors except itself).

FACTORS AND PRIME NUMBERS

1. Wooden cubes and a sheet of paper with the headings *Numeral, Dimensions of Rectangles,* and *Number of Rectangles* are used for this activity (see below). Beginning with one cube, the student records the numeral 1 under the column marked *Numeral,* records the dimensions of the rectangle (i.e., 1 × 1) formed by the cube, and records the number of rectangles formed (i.e., 1). Have the children record the numbers with only two rectangles, the numbers with more than two rectangles, and the numbers with less than two rectangles. Continue recording information until children have enough information to make a generalization.

Numeral	Dimensions of Rectangle	Number of Rectangles
1	1 × 1	1
2	1 × 2, 2 × 1	2
.	.	.
.	.	.
.	.	.
6	1 × 6, 6 × 1, 2 × 3, 3 × 2	4
.	.	.
.	.	.
.	.	.

2. Divide children into small groups (of four or five) and have them play "buzz" by taking turns counting; in place of prime numbers, however, they say "buzz." Taking turns, children might say: 1, buzz, buzz, 4, buzz, 6, buzz, 8, 9, 10, buzz, 12, buzz, 14, 15, 16, buzz, and so forth. "Buzz" is said in place of the prime numbers, 2, 3, 5, 7, 11, 13, 17 and so on. A variation of this game is to change the direction of play (clockwise to counterclockwise around the circle or vice versa) every time someone says "buzz."

3. Write each number as the product of two whole numbers in as many ways as you can.

   a) 28   b) 42   c) 63   d) 72   e) 124   f) 108

4. Complete the table.

Number	Whole-Number Factors	Prime Number?
9		
14		
19		
55		
73		

5. Children can play a game called Road Race. This game provides practice in identifying prime numbers and correct factorizations. Make a board showing a winding road consisting of a series of squares. Two players start off by flipping a coin and placing their tokens at the start position. The winner starts by drawing a card from the card deck illustrated. If he answers the question on the card correctly, he moves one space. If he misses the

question, he goes back one space (a flat tire or pit stop has been ordered). Some sample questions that could be pulled from the card deck are: "Name all the factors for 72," or, "Is 13 a prime number?"

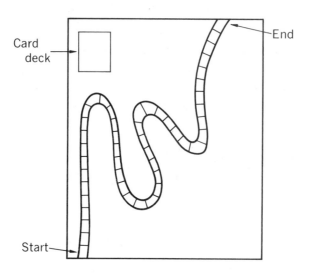

Hand-Held Calculator Activities for the Intermediate Grades

1. Use your hand-held calculator to find the prime factors for each of the following numbers. Use the prime numbers in order, beginning with two. The divisibility rules will also help you make good estimations. The teacher will want to use the hand-held calculator to generate examples for children to solve. Here are some sample beginning examples:

a) 3570   d)   510
b)   789   e) 27,761
c) 5083   f) 13, 860

2. Children can learn to use the add-on feature for exponents. For example, 3^5 means $3 \times 3 \times 3 \times 3 \times 3$, which equals 243. Using the hand-held calculator, we would enter ③ ☒ ⊟ ⊟ ⊟ ⊟; the display screen should read 243. Provide the children with many examples for practice. Discuss with the children how this procedure functions.

3. Numbers can be easily factored and the results expressed in exponent form. For example, $256 = 2^\square$. To find the exponent for this example the following procedure should be followed on the calculator: ② ⑤ ⑥ ⊟ ② ⊟ ⊟ ⊟ ⊟ ⊟ ⊟ ⊟ ⊟. 256 is divided by 2 continuously until the display screen shows 1. Since the equals key was pressed eight times, eight is the power of two necessary to equal 256. Discuss this procedure with the children. (The procedures suggested in examples 2 and 3 can be used as checks for each other.)

4. The hand-held calculator can be easily used to generate a set of multiples for any given number. For instance, what are the multiples of 7? The calculator can be set up for this example by pressing ⑦ ⊞ ⊟ ⊟ ⊟ . . . The first number to appear on the display screen is 7, which is the result of 1 × 7. Each time the equal key is pressed, the next multiple of 7 is displayed. The screen should show 7, 14, 21, 28, etc.

   Generate and list multiples for 63 and 42; then locate the least common multiple for the two numbers. You should locate the least common multiple as 126. Provide other practice for children to locate LCMs.

5. Use the procedure suggested in example one to locate the greatest common factor for a given pair of numbers. What is the greatest common factor for 1548 and 1505?

Microcomputer Activities for the Intermediate Grades

1. The hand-held calculator activities listed previously will apply to a microcomputer used in the immediate mode. Don't forget to begin each immediate-mode entry with either PRINT or a question mark.

2. Write a microcomputer program to generate a set of multiples for any given number.

```
5    CLS
10   PRINT " TELL ME A NUMBER AND"
20   PRINT"I WILL LIST 15 MULTIPLES FOR YOUR NUMBER"
30   PRINT:PRINT "FOR WHAT NUMBER DO YOU WISH MULTIPLES"
40   INPUT N
50   CLS
60   PRINT"FIFTEEN  MULTIPLES FOR ";N;" ARE LISTED."
70   A=0
90   X=A*N
100 A=A+1
110 PRINT X
120 IF X=15*N THEN END
130 GOTO 90
```

3. Change the preceding program to list the multiples in fields (columns).

4. Change the program to print the multiples horizontally rather than in a column.

5. Change the program example so it will list 25 multiples.

6. Change the preceding program so it will list 100 multiples.

7. Change the program again so that it will ask if you want to continue or stop. Change some statements, and add the following statements.

```
120 IF X=100*N THEN GOTO 150
150 PRINT"DO YOU WANT TO DO ANOTHER(YES,NO)"
160 INPUT Z$
170 IF Z$="YES"THEN 30
180 IF Z$="NO"THEN PRINT "GOODBYE"
```

Activities for the Upper Elementary Grades

FACTORS AND PRIME NUMBERS

1. What pairs of primes will result in each of the following products?

   a) 14   b) 35   c) 18   d) 22   e) 55
   f) 26   g) 86

2. Complete the factor trees so that you have only prime factors on the bottom row.

   a)   36
   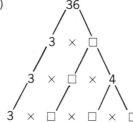

   b)   40
   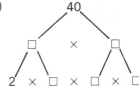

   c)   98

   d)   84
   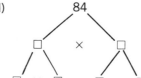

3. One game for finding prime factors is called Prime Spin. Cut out a large (24-inch diameter) cardboard circular region and mark it into sections as shown below. Mount a cardboard arrow in the middle with a brass fastener.

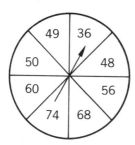

For more efficient use, the circle could be covered with clear self-adhesive plastic so that numerals could be written with a grease pencil and then erased. This would provide greater variety to the game.

   To play the game, separate the class into two teams. Have each team member alternately spin the wheel. A member of the rival team must then provide the prime factors of the number the arrow points to. If he is correct, then the team scores the number that has been spun. If the same number is spun twice, another spin should be performed so that new numbers will be factored. The team with the highest point total is declared the winner.

4. a) What number is a factor of every number?
    b) Every prime number has exactly _____ factors.
    c) Every prime number is odd except _____.
    d) What is the only prime number between 61 and 71? between 113 and 131? between 79 and 89? between 103 and 109?

5. List all the whole-number factors of each number.

    a) 8   c) 20   e) 18   g) 108   i) 98
    b) 19   d) 14   f) 28   h) 42   j) 120

6. a) List the set of even numbers between 3 and 55.
    b) List the set of prime numbers between 1 and 55.
    c) Can you write a name for any even number, 4 or greater, that is the sum of two of the primes in the list for part (a)?

    Example: Is 4 in the list? Is 2 in the list? Is $2 + 2 = 4$? Is this the sum of two of the primes in the list?

    How many more can you find?

7.
	1		13		5	8		18	4	
		3		9		11	15			7
2					17				16	
	14	6		12			10			

A game called Name That Prime can be used to help practice finding prime numbers. Numerals may be drawn on the chalkboard as shown above. The class is then separated into two teams. The teacher calls out a number—for example, 35. The first team that reports the correct prime factors (from the original set of numerals placed on the chalkboard) gets a point. If the number cannot be factored with the numerals on the board, the first team that states this gets a point. Again, the team with the most points is the winner.

PRIME FACTORIZATION

1. Use the Sieve of Eratosthenes to find the prime numbers up to 200.

2. Crossnumber puzzles may be used for practice in locating greatest common factors; the students fill in the squares of the table with the greatest common factor of the two numbers on the vertical and horizontal axes. An example of a crossnumber puzzle is:

	18	35	24	32
6	6	1	6	2
28		7		
54				
12				

3. Write the set of factors for each number in the given pair. Then write the set of common factors of the given numbers.

  a) 14 and 20   b) 36 and 24   c) 15 and 25   d) 40 and 16   e) 18 and 36

4. What is the GCF of each pair of numbers in Activity 1?

5. Write each number as the product of primes.

  a) 90   b) 144   c) 220   d) 420   e) 275

6. a) List the multiples of 16:   {   }
      List the multiples of 24:   {   }
      What is the LCM of 16 and 24?   _____

    b) List the multiples of 42:   {   }
      List the multiples of 4:   {   }
      What is the LCM of 4 and 42?   _____

    c) List the multiples of 12:   {   }
      List the multiples of 9:   {   }
      What is the LCM of 12 and 9?   _____

7. Find the LCM of each of these pairs:

  a) (6, 10)   b) (16, 18)   c) 15, 6)   d) (60, 36)   e) (64, 54)

8. A baseball game may be played to practice the concept of least common multiples. Two teams of pupils may be formed. One team is given a set of cards with two numerals on them (for example: 18, 36). This team is the defensive team. The team in the field selects a pitcher who then shows one of these cards to the offensive team. If the offensive team can find the LCM for the given numbers, they have a man on first base. If they answer incorrectly, they have one out. After three outs, the teams switch sides and play continues. The team that scores the most runs is the winner.

9. Which number (or numbers) less than 100 has the greatest number of factors?

10. What two numbers less than 100 have the greatest number of common multiples?

11. Make a table for the Sieve of Eratosthenes by placing only six numbers in a row. Make the table to at least 100. Study the patterns in the table and list any interesting discoveries.

Hand-Held Calculator Activities for the Upper Elementary Grades

1. All calculator activities for the intermediate grades can be adapted for the upper elementary grades.

2. Study this sequence of numbers: 2, 4, 6, . . . Use your hand-held calculator to generate the next 20 numbers in the sequence. The calculator should be set up by pressing ② ⊞ ②
⊟ ⊟ ⊟ ⊟, etc. How many numbers in this series are prime numbers?
    Study this sequence of numbers: 5, 11, 17, 23, . . . Use your hand-held calculator to generate the next 20 numbers in the sequence. Set up the calculator by pressing the following keys: ⑤ ⊞ ⑥ ⊟ ⊟ ⊟ ⊟ . . . How many numbers in the series are prime numbers?
    Experiment with other sequences. Can you find the sequence with the most prime numbers?

3. The number 37 is a strange number. Can you determine the product of 37 × 333 without using your calculator? Hint: Multiply 37 by the multiples of 3, beginning with 3. When you think you know the product of 37 and 333, write the answer. Check this on your calculator. Write the answer for 37 × 3333; then check on your calculator. Then try 37 × 33333 and 37 × 333333.

4. Use your hand-held calculator to experiment with these examples. Write the answers and look for patterns.

$$9 \times 6 =$$
$$99 \times 6 =$$
$$999 \times 6 =$$
$$9999 \times 6 =$$

Using the pattern you just discovered, write the answers for these examples; then check your guesses on your calculator.

$$9999999 \times 6 =$$
$$9999999 \times 9 =$$
$$9999999 \times 3 =$$

Microcomputer Activities for the Upper Elementary Grades

1. The hand-held calculator activities listed previously apply to the microcomputer when used in the immediate mode. Don't forget to begin each immediate-mode entry with PRINT or a question mark.

2. Use example 3 from the calculator activities; then use the microcomputer in the immediate mode, and experiment with the number 37 and many larger multiples of 3. At what point does your computer start using an "E" in the answer. Can you change the E answer into a base-ten number without an E? Write the product of this example without the E: 37 × 333333333333. Is your answer the same as the microcomputer's?

3. Use example 4 from the calculator examples. Use the microcomputer in the immediate mode to experiment with numbers that follow the same pattern but have many more decimal places. At what point does your microcomputer begin using the E notation?

4. Write a different program than the one provided at the intermediate grade level for printing multiples of a number. Your program should run on most microcomputers that use the BASIC language. The only change should be a command to clear the screen. One example might look like this:

```
10  CLS
20  PRINT"TELL ME A NUMBER"
30  PRINT"I WILL TELL YOU"
40  PRINT"15 MULTIPLES FOR YOUR NUMBER."
45  B=0
50  PRINT"WHAT IS YOUR NUMBER"
60  INPUT A
70  PRINT B
80  IF B<>15*A THEN 100
90  B=B+A
95  GOTO 70
100 END
```

Now change the program, giving the user a choice to continue or to quit the program. You might want to add these statements:

```
100 PRINT"DO YOU WANT TO TRY ANOTHER NUMBER(YES,NO)"
110 INPUT Z$
120 IF Z$="YES" THEN 45
130 IF Z$="NO" THEN PRINT"SEE YOU AGAIN"
```

Suggested Readings

Burton, Grace M., and Knifong, J. Dan. "Definitions for Prime Numbers." *The Arithmetic Teacher,* vol. 27, no. 6, February 1980.

Davidson, Jessica. *Using the Cuisenaire Rods.* New Rochelle, N.Y.: Cuisenaire Company of America, 1969.

Dubisch, Roy. "Generalizing a Property of Prime Numbers." *The Arithmetic Teacher,* vol. 21, no. 2, February 1974.

———. "The Sieve of Eratosthenes." *The Arithmetic Teacher,* vol. 18, no. 4, April 1974.

Hoffer, Alan R. "What You Always Wanted to Know About Six but Have Been Afraid to Ask." *The Arithmetic Teacher,* vol. 20, no. 3, March 1973.

Jeffrey, Neil J. "GCF and LCM on a Geoboard." *The Arithmetic Teacher,* vol. 24, no. 5, January 1977.

LeBlanc, John F.; Kerr, Donald R., Jr.; and Thompson, Maynard, eds. *Mathematics-Methods Program: Number Theory.* Reading, Mass.: Addison-Wesley, 1976.

Lichtenberg, Betty Plunkett. "Zero Is an Even Number." *The Arithmetic Teacher,* vol. 19, no. 7, November 1972.

Mar, Charlene Oliver. "Gus's Magic Number: A Key to the Divisibility Test for Primes." *The Arithmetic Teacher,* vol. 19, no. 3, March 1972.

Ore, Oystein. *Number Theory and Its History.* New York: McGraw-Hill, 1948.

Padberg, Friedhelm F. "Using Calculators to Discover Simple Theorems—An Example from Number Theory." *The Arithmetic Teacher,* vol. 27, no. 8, April 1981.

Sherzer, Laurence. "A Simplified Presentation for Finding the LCM and GCF." *The Arithmetic Teacher,* vol. 21, no. 5, May 1974.

Unenge, Jan. "A Crossnumber Game with Factors." *The Arithmetic Teacher,* vol. 22, no. 5, May 1975.

9 Rational Numbers Expressed as Fractions

Teaching Competencies

Upon completing this unit, you will be able to:

Use any of three models to develop understanding of nonnegative rational numbers expressed as fractions

Identify a given fraction by stating the numerator, denominator, and fraction bar

Distinguish whether a given fraction is a proper fraction, improper fraction, or mixed numeral

Write a fraction in its simplest form

Indicate whether one fraction is less than, equal to, or greater than a second fraction

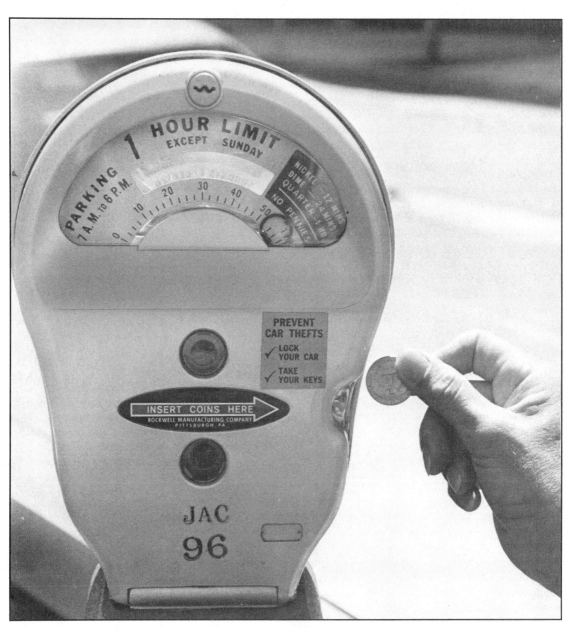

Discussion

In reviewing the early history of number development, we find that the growth of number ideas is directly related to the increasing complexity of civilization. Just as very limited tallying or matching became insufficient, so eventually whole numbers alone did not satisfy human needs. It became necessary to describe parts of whole things or groups of things. To meet this need, fractional numbers were created.

The word "fraction" is derived from the Latin "frangere," meaning "to break." Fractions have always described parts of a "broken" whole.

The first fractions were quite awkward, as one might suspect. The Egyptians, with few exceptions, employed unit fractions—fractions whose numerators were 1 and whose denominators varied (but were never zero). To express nonunit fractions, the Egyptians simply added the necessary unit fractions. For example, the fraction $\frac{5}{8}$ was expressed as $\frac{1}{2} + \frac{1}{8}$. The difficulties involved in such a system are obvious. The Egyptians were also hampered by cumbersome numerals (see Unit 4). The symbol for a fractional number was the hieroglyph $\bigcirc$, which was placed over a numeral that indicated the number of parts into which the whole was divided:

$$\underset{||||}{\bigcirc} = \frac{1}{4} \qquad \underset{\cap\cap|}{\bigcirc} = \frac{1}{21} \qquad \underset{9}{\bigcirc} = \frac{1}{100}$$

The Babylonian system was vastly superior to the Egyptian, which helps to account for Babylonian advances in astronomy and construction. Theirs was a sexagesimal system (that is, it was based, like their system of whole numbers, on groupings of sixty). The many possible factors and multiples of sixty (2, 3, 4, 5, 6, 10, 12, 15, 20, 30, 60, 120, 180, and so on) greatly facilitated work with fractions. The denominator was a factor or multiple of sixty, while the numerator, in contrast to the Egyptian system, was allowed to vary. The symbols used for fractional numbers, however, were extremely complicated.

The Roman fraction system was used largely for commerce. The Romans used denominators that were based on twelve and multiples of twelve, and names were given to twelfths and twenty-fourths of whole things, these parts of the whole becoming subunits. By using these subunits, they avoided the use of fractions in computation, much as we avoid it today by saying "one ounce" rather than "one-sixteenth of a pound."

The development of our familiar representation of fractional numbers comes from Hindu mathematicians, who began the convention of writing one numeral over another: $\frac{2}{3}$. The bar separating the numerator from the denominator was an Arabic device, not generally used in the Western world until the late Middle Ages.

Today, the trend is toward changing the emphasis on rational numbers expressed as fractions and decimals. Because of new emphasis on the metric system and the increasing emphasis on technology in our society (calculators and computers use decimals only), some elementary mathematics programs are teaching rational numbers expressed as decimals before teaching rational numbers expressed as fractions. When the teaching strategy is based on the concrete level and models, this sequence can be easily interchanged. However, when the teaching of fractions and decimals are dependent upon each other, is it much more difficult to change the teaching sequence. We believe that units 8 and 9 and units 10 and 11 can be easily interchanged with only a few minor alterations.

Today, considering the different systems of numbers, fractions are a subset of the set of rational numbers. Rational numbers may be expressed in two different forms—as fractions or decimals. This unit deals with rational numbers expressed as fractions.

> A rational number is any number that can be written in the form $\frac{a}{b}$, where a is any integer and b is any integer other than zero.

Fractional numbers are rational numbers written in fraction form; fractions are the symbols that we use for writing fractional numbers. Thus three-fourths is a rational number. When this number is written in fraction form, we call it a fractional number; the symbol $\frac{3}{4}$ is a fraction.

Children enter school with the concept that one-half means one of two pieces. We do not cut food items exactly in half; we cut them in two, and children always take the "larger" piece. When children say they will take the larger piece, they do not really demonstrate a true understanding of one-half.

Since whole numbers are a subset of rational numbers, students know a great deal about rational numbers before they begin formal study. Mothers divide candy bars or apples in half for children and introduce them to the concept of fractions at a very early age. The task then becomes to help the students develop a good understanding of what a rational number and fraction is.

There are basically three different models that can be used to develop students' understanding of fractions: regions, sets, and number lines. Fractions can also be considered as indicated division. Indicated division is abstract and should not be introduced at this time. For example, the fraction $\frac{3}{4}$ can mean 3 divided by 4. Either circular or rectangular regions are customarily used in teaching the concept of fractions.

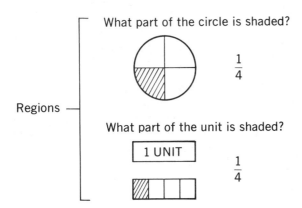

Regions

What part of the circle is shaded? $\frac{1}{4}$

What part of the unit is shaded?

1 UNIT $\frac{1}{4}$

What part of the set of dots is shaded?

Sets $\frac{1}{4}$

What part of the number line is marked?

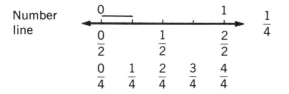

Number line $\frac{1}{4}$

Materials such as Cuisenaire rods, Stern rods, Dienes Blocks, and fraction bars are excellent in developing students' understanding of fractions. Cuisenaire rods may be used with a number line. Carefully examine the teacher's manuals for each set of materials; these manuals give specific directions for using these manipulative materials.

Let us carefully examine each of these models— regions, sets, and number lines—as we discuss fractions.

The concept of fractions should be presented by having children manipulate physical models showing a whole and fractions of that whole. Rectangular regions, such as the region pictured below, are often used as physical models. Usually we start with a **basic unit,** cut from cardboard and divided into congruent parts. Congruent parts are parts that have the same size and shape. For example, let this rectangular region be the basic unit, or unit region:

BASIC UNIT OR UNIT REGION

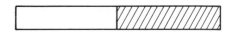

If we wish to identify the shaded part of the basic unit with a fractional number, that number is one-half, which can be written $\frac{1}{2}$. The 2 denotes the number of congruent pieces into which the basic unit is divided. The 1 denotes how many of these two congruent pieces we are concerned with. Children can recognize parts of regions and name the parts or they can color appropriate physical models. In these physical models children can, by counting, identify the part of each region that is shaded, name the appropriate fractional number, and write the corresponding fraction.

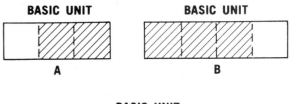

BASIC UNIT A **BASIC UNIT** B

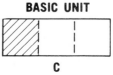

BASIC UNIT C

In A, two out of three equivalent parts are shaded; the corresponding fraction is $\frac{2}{3}$. In B, three out of four equivalent parts are shaded; this can be represented by the fraction $\frac{3}{4}$. In C, one part out of three equivalent parts is shaded; the appropriate fraction is $\frac{1}{3}$.

As an extension of this activity, children can be asked to shade, or color, given parts of regions.

For example, color one-sixth of the following circular region.

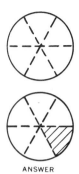

ANSWER

What fraction names the colored part of this circular region? $\left(\frac{1}{6}\right)$ Now color one-half of the region below.

It should be emphasized that this can be done in several ways; three are indicated here.

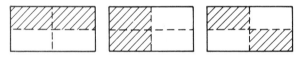

These examples stress the fact that fractions can be used to indicate parts of a whole. In each drawing two out of four congruent regions have been shaded. Thus we can write the fraction $\frac{2}{4}$. The 4 is the **denominator** of the fraction, which tells us how many equivalent parts the whole is separated into. The name *fourth* is assigned to each of the four pieces. The word *denominator* comes to us from the Latin word *nomen*, which means "to name." Thus the denominator functions as the "namer" of the number of congruent parts into which a unit has been separated. The denominator does not function as a number.

And the 2 is the **numerator,** which tells us how many of these pieces we are considering. In this example we have considered two of the pieces called fourths. The numerator of the fraction is the number that expresses how many of the pieces we are considering. In the fraction $\frac{2}{4}$, the 2 and the 4 are called the **terms** of the fraction.

FRACTION   2 ⟵— NUMERATOR
                  – ⟵— FRACTION BAR
                  4 ⟵— DENOMINATOR

TERMS OF
THE FRACTION

Now examine fractions using circular regions. The picture of the circle below is defined as a unit.

UNIT REGION

Children should cut circular regions out of paper, then subdivide the units into fractions, $\frac{1}{2}$, $\frac{1}{4}$, and $\frac{1}{8}$, by folding, then cutting. Since it is very difficult to fold a circular region into thirds, you may want to provide a pattern for thirds and any other fractional parts you want the children to make. Give each child an envelope in which to place the fractions of the circular regions.

Once the children have made these fraction kits, discuss how the fractional parts of the unit relate to the whole. Two equivalent pieces are called halves. If we consider one of the pieces then we would call that piece one-half, written in fraction form as $\frac{1}{2}$. The numerator 1 tells us how many pieces we are considering, and the 2 tells us the name of the pieces.

Consider a circular region separated into four equivalent pieces.

UNIT REGION

Since the unit is separated into four equivalent pieces we will name each piece a fourth. The one piece that is shaded would be represented by the fraction $\frac{1}{4}$ because we are considering one of the four pieces. If two are shaded we would write $\frac{2}{4}$

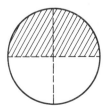

because two of the pieces we call fourths are shaded.

If three are shaded we would write $\frac{3}{4}$

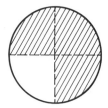

because three of the pieces we name fourths are being considered.

Once children have had many experiences using rectangular and circular regions to help them understand fractions, then introduce other shapes. For example $\frac{1}{2}$ of this region is shaded

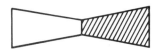

and $\frac{3}{4}$ of this region is shaded.

Emphasize that the shape of the region does not indicate the fraction.

Children should also have an opportunity to develop an understanding of fractional numbers by working with sets, the second model we will use. Children must actually manipulate set materials. Fractions can be used to name parts of sets of objects.

Consider the set of six objects pictured below.

By separating the set into two equivalent subsets and considering one of those subsets, one-half of the set is considered. A ring can be drawn round one-half of the set, or one-half of the objects can be colored, to indicate the fractional number $\frac{1}{2}$:

Many other fractional numbers can be represented in the same way:

In the first set pictured above, we can separate the twelve elements into four equivalent subsets by considering only columns of elements. Then by drawing a ring round one of the columns, we represent the fractional number $\frac{1}{4}$. In the second set we can separate the eight elements into four equivalent subsets by considering only rows of elements. Then if we enclose one of the rows with a ring, the number $\frac{1}{4}$ is again represented. Similarly, the third set illustrates $\frac{1}{3}$.

Suppose that now, however, we consider the elements of sets separately, not as rows or columns. Again taking the set of twelve elements pictured above, let's consider separately the elements of the column that was enclosed. We can do this by enclosing each of the elements of that column separately:

In this way we illustrate the number $\frac{3}{12}$, since there are twelve elements and we are separately considering three of them. Notice that in both cases exactly three elements out of the twelve are under consideration, but that in one case we are illustrating the number $\frac{1}{4}$ while in the other we are illustrating $\frac{3}{12}$. Evidently $\frac{1}{4}$ and $\frac{3}{12}$ are equivalent fractions:

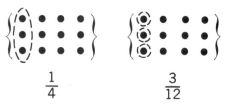

$$\frac{1}{4} \qquad \frac{3}{12}$$

In a similar fashion we can demonstrate that $\frac{1}{4} = \frac{2}{8}$ and that $\frac{1}{3} = \frac{3}{9}$.

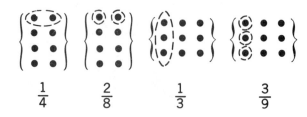

$$\frac{1}{4} \qquad \frac{2}{8} \qquad \frac{1}{3} \qquad \frac{3}{9}$$

Children should make a number of representations like these to help them identify two distinct concepts:

1. A fraction can represent part of a whole.
2. A fraction can represent part of a set.

And now let us reiterate that a fraction is a number written in the form $\frac{a}{b}$ (where $b \neq 0$) in which a and b are integers. Of course, fractions can also be written as decimals: .1 and $\frac{1}{10}$ are the same number, although only the second one is a fraction according to our definition.

A third model may be used to help us understand fractions: the number line. We can ask the question "How do fractions fit in with the numbers we have already studied on the number line?" So far we have matched equally spaced points on the number line with whole numbers (the numbers 0, 1, 2, 3, . . .):

But what about points that are located *between* the whole-number points? Are there no numbers to match with these points? We will find that many of these "in-between" points can be matched with fractional numbers.

When we considered the whole numbers under the operation of division, we found that division is not closed for this set. We discovered division examples in which the missing factor could not be expressed as a whole number. By way of illustration, consider $4 \div 5 = \square$. This example indicates the need for another set of numbers if we are to solve examples such as this. Another indication of the need for fractional numbers is observed as we attempt to express measurement more accurately. Using a ruler, one seldom finds a measurement of an exact number of inches. A method of expressing measurements that include parts of inches, feet, and yards is provided by the set of fractional numbers.

If we change entirely to the metric system of measurement there will be less need for fractions in measurement. The metric system is based on a decimal relationship. Measurements in the metric system will be recorded in tenths, hundredths, or thousandths (.1, .01, or .001).

Before developing fractional numbers on the number line, children should be familiar with the way we show basic operations with whole numbers on the number line. Draw a number line and indicate a reference point on it. For convenience, let's label that point "0," calling it zero. Now select another point, anywhere on the line to the right of zero, and

label that point "1." Use this segment from 0 to 1 as a standard unit, and mark off line segments equal in length to the standard unit. Each point should be matched with one of the whole numbers.

Now let's play a game and pretend that we are at the point named 0. If we make a jump of one unit to the right, where do we land? We land at the point named 1. If we make another jump of 1 unit to the right, where do we land this time? We land at the point named 2. Now, starting at 2, if we take a jump of one unit to the left, where do we land? We land back at 1. But suppose that we are now getting tired and, when we jump to the left, we do not make it all the way back to 0 but land at the point labeled "A."

How can we name this point where we have landed? Every point on the number line that we have seen so far has had a name. What do you think the name of this point should be? We have found that point A is equidistant from 0 and 1. The length of the line segment between 0 and A is the same as the length of the line segment between A and 1. The segment that we have defined as one unit for this particular number line has been divided by point A into two segments of equal length. How can we express this idea? We can express it by the notation $\frac{1}{2}$. Of the two equivalent segments between 0 and 1, we are one of the two segments away from 0. The notation $\frac{1}{2}$ expresses this fact. Another name for point A, therefore, is $\frac{1}{2}$.

Now suppose that we are at the point named by $\frac{1}{2}$ and jump to the point named by 1. How far are we then from the starting point, 0? How many one-half units separate us from 0? Clearly, we are two one-half units from the starting point. This is expressed by the fraction $\frac{2}{2}$. We divide the whole into two equivalent parts and consider them both:

If we now start at 1 and jump another one-half unit to the right, where do we land? Halfway between 1 and 2. How many one-half units are we away from 0? Three. We can express this fact by the fraction $\frac{3}{2}$, which can be interpreted to mean that, if we divide each unit length into two equivalent parts, we are considering three of the resulting half-unit segments:

We can continue in this way, naming each whole number and each point halfway between any pair of whole numbers. The resulting collection of points names the set of halves:

What is another name for 1? Two halves, $\frac{2}{2}$, is another name for 1, because $\frac{2}{2}$ and 1 name the same point on the number line. What is another name for 2? Four halves, $\frac{4}{2}$, is another name, because $\frac{4}{2}$ and 2 name the same point.

There are many names for any point on the number line. For the number 1 we have written the symbols 1 and $\frac{2}{2}$; for the number 2 we have written 2 and $\frac{4}{2}$. Is there another way in which we can write $\frac{3}{2}$, $\frac{5}{2}$, and other fractional numbers in which the numerator is greater than the denominator? Consider the point labeled $\frac{3}{2}$. This point is half a unit $\left(\frac{1}{2}\right)$ to the right of 1, so another way to indicate $\frac{3}{2}$ is $1 + \frac{1}{2}$, or $1\frac{1}{2}$. If the expression $1 + \frac{1}{2}$ is rewritten as $\frac{2}{2} + \frac{1}{2}$, which clearly equals $\frac{3}{2}$, it becomes obvious that $1 + \frac{1}{2}$ and $\frac{3}{2}$ are different names for the same number. Now consider the fraction $\frac{5}{2}$. By looking at the number line, we find that the point named by $\frac{5}{2}$ is half a unit $\left(\frac{1}{2}\right)$ to the right of 2. This point, therefore, can be indicated by $2 + \frac{1}{2}$, or $2\frac{1}{2}$. If $2 + \frac{1}{2}$ is rewritten as $\frac{4}{2} + \frac{1}{2}$, which is clearly equal to $\frac{5}{2}$, it becomes evident that the symbols $\frac{5}{2}$ and $2\frac{1}{2}$ $\left(\text{or } 2 + \frac{1}{2}\right)$ are merely different names for the same number. Numerals such as $1\frac{1}{2}$, $3\frac{1}{2}$, and $6\frac{1}{2}$ (for $\frac{3}{2}$, $\frac{7}{2}$, and $\frac{13}{2}$ respectively) are called **mixed numerals.** In this form we combine, or mix, a numeral naming a counting number and a fraction.

But remember, $1\frac{1}{2}$ can also be expressed as $\frac{3}{2}$:

$$1\frac{1}{2} = 1 + \frac{1}{2}$$
$$= \frac{2}{2} + \frac{1}{2}$$
$$= \frac{3}{2}$$

Circular regions should also be used to develop the concept of mixed numerals. Consider three of the pieces that we have named half of a circle.

We can write $\frac{3}{2}$ as a fraction for these regions. By rearranging the regions we can easily see that we have one and one-half circular regions.

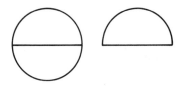

Children need many experiences manipulating regions that they have cut from paper and included in their fraction kits.

Also develop the concept of mixed numerals using rectangular regions:

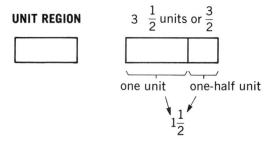

Children can rearrange the pieces to see why $\frac{3}{2}$ and $1\frac{1}{2}$ are the same.

Rectangular regions are more difficult than circular regions to divide, since it is harder to visualize unit regions of rectangles. You can easily see whether a circular region is complete or not, but it is difficult to visualize the size of a rectangular unit region.

A fraction, such as $\frac{3}{2}$, in which the numerator is greater than or equal to the denominator is called an **improper fraction.** Thus $\frac{3}{2}$, $\frac{7}{5}$, $\frac{6}{6}$, and $\frac{13}{8}$ are examples of improper fractions. A **proper fraction** is one in which the numerator is less than the denominator. Examples of proper fractions are $\frac{2}{3}$, $\frac{4}{5}$, $\frac{2}{9}$, and $\frac{24}{25}$.

The mixed form for writing fractional numbers gives us another way of naming the numbers represented on the number line:

Children should be given the opportunity to discover relations between the set of halves and other numbers on the number line. They may make the generalization that, in adding parts by moving to the right on the number line, the denominators remain the same and the numerators are added the way whole numbers are added. Children have had experience in counting by ones, fives, and tens. Now the opportunity is provided for them to count by halves: $\frac{1}{2}$, $\frac{2}{2}$, $\frac{3}{2}$, $\frac{4}{2}$, $\frac{5}{2}$, and so on (or $\frac{1}{2}$, 1, $1\frac{1}{2}$, 2, $2\frac{1}{2}$, and so on). The patterns in the set of halves should become clear.

Now let's develop the set of fourths, again using a number line. Each unit-long line segment is divided into four segments of equal length.

If the segment between 0 and 1 is divided into four equivalent parts, what can we name one of these parts? We can name it one-fourth. Thus, we can label the first point to the right of zero on the number line above as $\frac{1}{4}$, or one-fourth. Similarly, we can label the second point $\frac{2}{4}$, or two-fourths; the third point $\frac{3}{4}$, or three-fourths; and the fourth point $\frac{4}{4}$, or four-fourths:

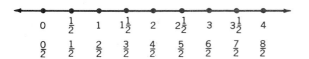

We can continue in this manner indefinitely, naming the set of fourths:

It is evident now that another name for 1 is $\frac{4}{4}$. Similarly, another name for 2 is $\frac{8}{4}$. We can also use other names to designate the points on the number line that represent fractional numbers greater than 1; we can use mixed numerals to designate these points. For example, the point labeled $\frac{5}{4}$ can be renamed with the mixed numeral $1\frac{1}{4}$. And the next point can be designated $1\frac{2}{4}$ instead of $\frac{6}{4}$.

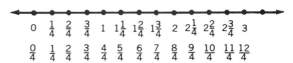

Now let's represent the set of halves and the set of fourths on the same number line. We should encourage children to discover as many relations as possible.

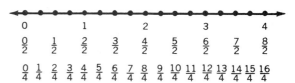

What are some other names for 1? $\left(\frac{2}{2} \text{ and } \frac{4}{4}\right)$ After children have examined the point named by 1, they should be able to make the generalization that when any counting number (1, 2, 3, or 4, and so on) appears as both numerator and denominator, the resulting fraction is another way to name 1. This means that there are infinitely many fraction names for 1.

$$\left\{\frac{1}{1}, \frac{2}{2}, \frac{3}{3}, \frac{4}{4}, \cdots\right\}$$

Similarly, children should discover many ways to write 2, 3, 4, 5, and other counting numbers as fractions. The children may then be ready to draw the following important conclusion: Since every whole number can be named by a fraction with a whole-number numerator and a counting-number denominator, *every whole number is also a fractional number*. This means that the set of whole numbers is a subset of the set of fractional numbers.

The point named by 1 can be indicated by either $\frac{1}{1}$ or $\frac{2}{2}$, because these are merely different names for the same point $\left(\frac{1}{1} = \frac{2}{2}\right)$. Children should then be shown that $\frac{1 \times 2}{1 \times 2} = \frac{2}{2}$, and also that $\frac{1 \times 3}{1 \times 3} = \frac{3}{3}$. The important thing for children to recognize here is that in each example the same factor is used in the numerator as in the denominator. Moreover, $\frac{1}{2}$ and $\frac{2}{4}$ name the same number $\left(\frac{1}{2} = \frac{2}{4}\right)$, and the relation $\frac{2 \times 1}{2 \times 2} = \frac{2}{4}$ is thus valid. We call fractions that name the same number **equivalent fractions.**

The concept of equivalent fractions can also be presented by using regions.

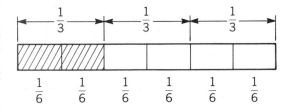

The basic unit pictured above is divided into thirds. It has also been divided into sixths. The shaded part of the unit region is $\frac{2}{6}$ of the entire unit region (two parts out of a total of six). But the shaded part is also $\frac{1}{3}$ of the entire unit region. When $\frac{2}{6}$ is renamed as $\frac{1}{3}$, we say that it is then in **simplest form.** A fraction is in simplest form if the numerator and the denominator have no common factor other than 1. For example, we have seen that $\frac{2}{6} = \frac{1}{3}$:

$$\frac{2}{6} = \frac{1 \times 2}{3 \times 2}$$
$$= \frac{1}{3} \times \frac{2}{2}$$
$$= \frac{1}{3} \times 1$$
$$= \frac{1}{3}$$

We use the term *simplest form* rather than the traditional phrase: *reduce to lowest terms. Reduce to lower terms* means "make smaller," but the fraction is really still the same size and amount. We are

actually writing a fraction in a form that is easier to comprehend. Students are not just mechanically following an algorithm; they are developing the meaning of the concept of renaming fractions. (We know that multiplying the numerator and the denominator by the same counting number, in this case 2, does not change the value of a fractional number, since this is the same as multiplying the fractional number by 1, the identity element for multiplication.) In the fraction $\frac{2}{6}$, the numerator and the denominator have the factor 2 in common; therefore $\frac{2}{6}$ is not in simplest form. The fraction $\frac{1}{3}$, however, is expressed in simplest form, for the numerator and the denominator have no common factor except 1.

Combining regions to form a chart is an excellent way to develop students' concept of equivalent fractions and the relationship among fractional numbers. Children can discover visually that any fraction has many names. For example, we know that $\frac{1}{2} = \frac{2}{4} = \frac{4}{8}$. A child can discover this truth by manipulating materials or by using a chart such as this one:

Units	1							
Halves	$\frac{1}{2}$				$\frac{1}{2}$			
Fourths	$\frac{1}{4}$		$\frac{1}{4}$		$\frac{1}{4}$		$\frac{1}{4}$	
Eighths	$\frac{1}{8}$	$\frac{1}{8}$	$\frac{1}{8}$	$\frac{1}{8}$	$\frac{1}{8}$	$\frac{1}{8}$	$\frac{1}{8}$	$\frac{1}{8}$

In this chart the unit interval on the number line is represented in four different ways. At the top it is represented by a single rectangular region, labeled 1 because it spans the entire interval. Below this the unit interval is represented by two rectangular regions; these are labeled $\frac{1}{2}$ because each region spans only one-half of the interval. Next the unit interval is represented by four rectangular regions, each labeled $\frac{1}{4}$ to indicate that it spans only one-fourth of the interval. And finally there are eight rectangular regions, each labeled $\frac{1}{8}$.

By shading some of the regions on the chart, children can see that fractional numbers can be renamed in various ways.

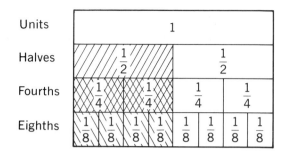

Units	1			
Halves	$\frac{1}{2}$		$\frac{1}{2}$	
Fourths	$\frac{1}{4}$	$\frac{1}{4}$	$\frac{1}{4}$	$\frac{1}{4}$
Eighths	$\frac{1}{8}$ $\frac{1}{8}$	$\frac{1}{8}$ $\frac{1}{8}$	$\frac{1}{8}$ $\frac{1}{8}$	$\frac{1}{8}$ $\frac{1}{8}$

For example, in the chart above, there are eight rectangular regions labeled $\frac{1}{8}$. Four of these have been shaded. This fact can be indicated by the fraction $\frac{4}{8}$, the denominator (8) indicating the total number of regions, and the numerator (4) indicating the number of these regions that are shaded. Considering the rectangular regions labeled $\frac{1}{4}$, we see that an equal area has been shaded. There are four regions labeled $\frac{1}{4}$, two of which have been shaded. This fact is indicated by the fraction $\frac{2}{4}$. Clearly, $\frac{4}{8}$ and $\frac{2}{4}$ are equivalent fractions. Now considering the rectangular regions labeled $\frac{1}{2}$, we see that an equal area has again been shaded. There are two regions labeled $\frac{1}{2}$, only one of which has been shaded. The fraction $\frac{1}{2}$ indicates this fact. Obviously $\frac{1}{2}$ is equivalent to $\frac{2}{4}$ and $\frac{4}{8}$ $\left(\frac{1}{2} = \frac{2}{4} = \frac{4}{8}\right)$. Other charts can be made that illustrate equivalent fractions.

Unit	1					
Thirds	$\frac{1}{3}$		$\frac{1}{3}$		$\frac{1}{3}$	
Sixths	$\frac{1}{6}$	$\frac{1}{6}$	$\frac{1}{6}$	$\frac{1}{6}$	$\frac{1}{6}$	$\frac{1}{6}$
Twelfths	$\frac{1}{12}$ $\frac{1}{12}$	$\frac{1}{12}$ $\frac{1}{12}$	$\frac{1}{12}$ $\frac{1}{12}$	$\frac{1}{12}$ $\frac{1}{12}$	$\frac{1}{12}$ $\frac{1}{12}$	$\frac{1}{12}$ $\frac{1}{12}$

In the chart above, for example, the equivalence of $\frac{1}{3}$, $\frac{2}{6}$, and $\frac{4}{12}$ is illustrated $\left(\frac{1}{3} = \frac{2}{6} = \frac{4}{12}\right)$.

Practice with these charts helps to clarify the meaning of equivalent fractions and to build a foundation for examining methods of finding equivalent fractions. Now let's construct a chart that includes all denominators from 2 to 10. Such a chart emphasizes the fact that increasing the value of the denominator, while leaving the numerator unchanged, reduces the value of the fraction.

1 Unit									
$\frac{1}{2}$									
$\frac{1}{3}$									
$\frac{1}{4}$									
$\frac{1}{5}$									
$\frac{1}{6}$									
$\frac{1}{7}$									
$\frac{1}{8}$									
$\frac{1}{9}$									
$\frac{1}{10}$									

On such a chart, equivalent fractions can be found, and comparisons can be made between fractions of different values. For example, it can be seen that $\frac{1}{2} = \frac{2}{4} = \frac{4}{8}$. In this way rows of equivalent fractions can be determined:

$$\frac{1}{2} = \frac{2}{4} = \frac{3}{6} = \frac{4}{8} = \frac{5}{10}$$
$$\frac{2}{3} = \frac{4}{6} = \frac{6}{9}$$

Furthermore, the relation between fractional numbers such as $\frac{1}{3}$ and $\frac{1}{7}$ can readily be seen:

$$\frac{1}{3} > \frac{1}{7} \text{ or } \frac{1}{7} < \frac{1}{3}$$

The number line can also be used to model fractions. For instance, the truth of the statement $\frac{1}{2} = \frac{2}{4}$ can be shown by using the number line. In the illustration below, the unit segment is divided into two segments of equal length.

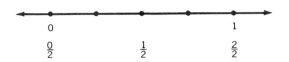

$$\begin{array}{ccc} 0 & & 1 \\ \frac{0}{2} & \frac{1}{2} & \frac{2}{2} \end{array}$$

Similarly, the segment between 0 and $\frac{1}{2}$ is separated into two equivalent parts, and the segment between $\frac{1}{2}$ and 1 is also divided into two equivalent parts. The unit segment has then been separated into four equivalent parts, and the point $\frac{1}{2}$ $\left(\text{or } \frac{2}{4}\right)$ is two of the $\frac{1}{2}$ units from 0. Notice that $\frac{1}{2}$ and $\frac{2}{4}$ each name the same point and that $\frac{1 \times 2}{2 \times 2} = \frac{2}{4}$. If the numerator and the denominator of a fraction are each multiplied by the same counting number, we are only finding another name for the same number. This is an application of the identity element for multiplication, which states that any number times 1 is the number itself ($a \times 1 = a$). Of course, we can substitute any equivalent name for 1, for example, $\frac{2}{2}$ or $\frac{3}{3}$. If $a = \frac{1}{2}$ in the mathematical sentence $a \times 1 = a$, then we can write $\frac{1}{2} \times 1 = \frac{1}{2}$. And since $\frac{2}{2}$ is another name for 1, we can also write $\frac{1}{2} \times \frac{2}{2} = \frac{1}{2}$ or $\frac{1 \times 2}{2 \times 2} = \frac{2}{4} = \frac{1}{2}$. Similarly, since $\frac{3}{3}$ is another name for 1, we can also write $\frac{1}{2} \times \frac{3}{3} = \frac{1}{2}$ or $\frac{1 \times 3}{2 \times 3} = \frac{3}{6} = \frac{1}{2}$. By using the identity element this way, we can find many different names for any point on the number line. Eventually pupils will observe that a fraction can be rewritten as an equivalent fraction if the numerator and the denominator of the fractional number are multiplied by the same counting number.

$$\frac{1}{4} = \frac{1 \times 2}{4 \times 2} = \frac{2}{8} \qquad\qquad \frac{1}{4} = \frac{1 \times 3}{4 \times 3} = \frac{3}{12}$$

$$\frac{1}{4} = \frac{1 \times 5}{4 \times 5} = \frac{5}{20}$$

We realize that children have not yet studied multiplication of fractions. However, we feel that the relationships between the fractions can be studied to justify that fractions can be renamed, using the identity element of multiplication.

Children should have an opportunity to discover as many names as possible for any point on the number line. They will want to expand their concept of fractions to include other fractions such as thirds, sixths, and eighths.

The number line is an excellent device for developing the order of fractions. Children should discover that the numerators of the set of halves follow the same pattern as the counting numbers, that the denominators are the same (2) in every case, and that any fraction named on the number line is greater than (>) each fraction to its left.

When two fractions are compared, one of three possible relations between them will hold (as we learned in the law of trichotomy in a previous unit). One fraction is either equal to (=), greater than (>), or less than (<) the other. Using the number line, children can begin to see relations between fractions that do not name the same number.

When several sets of related fractions appear on one number line, children can readily tell which one of any two fractional numbers is greater. They should acquire experience in writing statements such as 1 < 2. This statement is read, "One is less than two." The statement 2 > 1 is read, "Two is greater than one." Mathematicians read the symbol < as "less than" and the symbol > as "greater than." With young children the term "more than" may be clearer at first than "greater than"; children have experienced situations in which one child has more marbles or more pieces of candy than another. Teachers should introduce the correct terminology in its proper place, and children will come to understand this terminology by using it. In work with whole numbers, children learn that as they move to the right on the number line the numbers become greater, and as they move to the left the numbers become less. Fractional numbers, of course, follow the same pattern.

Teachers should provide many opportunities for children to show the relation between two fractional numbers by placing the proper sign between two fractions. Use placeholders between fractions as shown below and have children fill in the correct relation symbol.

$$\frac{1}{4} \bigcirc \frac{3}{4} \qquad \frac{1}{4} \enspace \text{\small$<$}\enspace \frac{3}{4}$$

$$\frac{1}{8} \bigcirc \frac{2}{4} \qquad \frac{1}{8} \enspace \text{\small$<$}\enspace \frac{2}{4}$$

$$\frac{3}{4} \bigcirc \frac{7}{8} \qquad \frac{3}{4} \enspace \text{\small$<$}\enspace \frac{7}{8}$$

$$\frac{3}{2} \bigcirc \frac{11}{8} \qquad \frac{3}{2} \enspace \text{\small$>$}\enspace \frac{11}{8}$$

Another way to look at a fraction is as a number obtained when an integer is divided by an integer other than 0. No rational number is named by $\frac{2}{0}$ (or $\frac{3}{0}$ or $\frac{4}{0}$ or so on), since $\frac{2}{0}$ indicates division by 0.

Every whole number is an element of the set of fractional numbers, since every whole number can be considered the result of dividing some whole number by a counting number. For example, every whole number is equal to itself (a whole number) divided by one (a counting number). Look at the following examples.

$$2 = 4 \div 2 \quad \text{or} \quad 2 = \frac{4}{2}$$

$$21 = 21 \div 1 \quad \text{or} \quad 21 = \frac{21}{1}$$

$$6 = 48 \div 8 \quad \text{or} \quad 6 = \frac{48}{8}$$

But not every fraction is an element of the set of whole numbers—for example $\frac{1}{3}$, $\frac{2}{13}$, and $\frac{5}{14}$. Zero, however, can be renamed by a fraction. Zero divided by any counting number is zero; so $\frac{0}{2} = 0$, $\frac{0}{3} = 0$, $\frac{0}{27} = 0$, and so on. (Again, 0 can never be the denominator of a fraction.)

All mixed numerals name fractions because all whole numbers can be written as fractions.

$$2\frac{1}{7} = 2 + \frac{1}{7}$$
$$= (1 + 1) + \frac{1}{7}$$
$$= \left(\frac{7}{7} + \frac{7}{7}\right) + \frac{1}{7}$$
$$= \frac{14}{7} + \frac{1}{7}$$
$$= \frac{15}{7}$$

Every fraction, like every whole number, can be named in many ways. For example, $\frac{2}{3}$ can be named as $\frac{4}{6}$, $\frac{6}{9}$, $\frac{8}{12}$, and so on. Similarly, $\frac{1}{4}$ can be named as $\frac{2}{8}$, $\frac{3}{12}$, $\frac{4}{16}$, and so on. In each case the fractional number remains the same, but different fractions are used to name the same point on the number line. Fractions that name the same fractional number are called equivalent fractions. (It might be helpful at this time to review the previous discussion of equivalent fractions.)

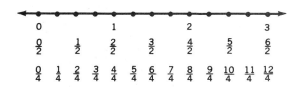

A number line showing equivalent fractions is a useful aid in preparing to develop the four basic operations with respect to fractional numbers.

Fractions can also be shown using regions. Have the children lay out one-half of a circular region and find how many fourths can be placed on top to completely cover half the region.

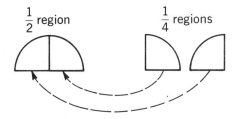

$\frac{1}{2}$ region $\frac{1}{4}$ regions

How many $\frac{1}{8}$ circular regions may be placed on top of the $\frac{1}{2}$ region? Continue this process until children realize:

$$\frac{1}{2} = \frac{2}{4} = \frac{4}{8} = \frac{5}{10} \text{ and so forth}$$

It is also very important that the children master the structure of the fraction form $\frac{a}{b}$:

1. The b is the **denominator,** named by the numeral below the fraction bar. The denominator indicates the number of parts into which a whole (region, set of objects, segment of a number line, or whatever) is divided.

2. The a is the **numerator,** named by the numeral above the fraction bar. The numerator indicates the number of parts being considered in a given whole.

Terminology, Symbols, and Procedures

Denominator   The denominator is the number below the fraction bar, indicating the number of equivalent pieces into which something is being divided. For example, the denominator of $\frac{5}{7}$ is 7.

Equivalent fractions   Equivalent fractions are fractions that name the same number. For example, $\frac{2}{3}$ and $\frac{4}{6}$ and $\frac{8}{12}$ are equivalent fractions $\left(\frac{2}{3} = \frac{4}{6} = \frac{8}{12}\right)$.

Fraction   A fraction is a numeral of the form $\frac{a}{b}$ (where $b \neq 0$); a and b may be integers.

Fraction bar   The line segment drawn horizontally between the numerator and denominator is the fraction bar.

Improper fraction   An improper fraction is a fraction in which the numerator is greater than or equal to the denominator, such as $\frac{7}{2}, \frac{3}{3}, \frac{6}{2}$.

Mixed numeral   A mixed numeral is a two-part numeral, such as $2\frac{3}{4}$, that consists of a whole number and a fraction. $2\frac{3}{4}$ is an abbreviated form of $2 + \frac{3}{4}$.

Numerator   The number above the fraction bar indicating how many "pieces" we are considering is the numerator. For example, the numerator in $\frac{5}{7}$ is 5.

Proper fraction   A proper fraction is a fraction in which the numerator is less than the denominator, such as $\frac{2}{3}, \frac{1}{2}, \frac{7}{8}$.

Simplest form   The form in which a fraction is written if the numerator and the denominator have no common factors other than 1 is called the simplest form. For example, $\frac{2}{3}, \frac{6}{7}, \frac{6}{25}$ are fractions written in simplest form.

Practice Exercises

1. Shade part of each region as suggested by the given fraction:

a)

$\dfrac{1}{4}$

b)

$\dfrac{2}{3}$

c)

$\dfrac{5}{6}$

d)

$\dfrac{3}{8}$

2. Shade part of each set as indicated by the given fraction.

$\dfrac{5}{7}$

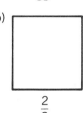

$\dfrac{3}{4}$

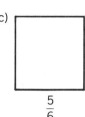

$\dfrac{3}{5}$

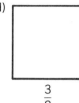

$\dfrac{7}{11}$

3. Shade part of each region as suggested by the given fraction:

$\dfrac{1}{3}$

$\dfrac{3}{4}$

$\dfrac{5}{8}$

$\dfrac{2}{3}$

$\dfrac{7}{8}$

4. Make a number line from 0 to 2; locate and label each of the following fractions.

$$0, 1, 2, \frac{1}{2}, \frac{1}{3}, \frac{1}{4}, \frac{2}{3}, \frac{3}{4}, \frac{2}{2}, \frac{4}{2}, \frac{2}{4}, \frac{1}{6}, \frac{2}{6}, \frac{4}{6}, \frac{3}{6}, \frac{5}{6}, \frac{4}{3}, 1\frac{1}{2}, 1\frac{1}{3}, \frac{5}{3}, 1\frac{2}{3}$$

5. Place the following fractions in order from least to greatest.

a) $\dfrac{1}{6}, \dfrac{1}{2}, \dfrac{1}{4}, \dfrac{1}{5}, \dfrac{1}{3}, \dfrac{1}{7}, \dfrac{1}{9}, \dfrac{1}{8}$

c) $\dfrac{3}{6}, \dfrac{1}{3}, \dfrac{4}{6}, \dfrac{1}{6}, \dfrac{5}{6}, \dfrac{3}{3}$

b) $\dfrac{3}{5}, \dfrac{1}{5}, \dfrac{2}{5}, \dfrac{5}{5}, \dfrac{4}{5}, \dfrac{6}{5}$

d) $\dfrac{5}{8}, \dfrac{1}{3}, \dfrac{3}{8}, \dfrac{2}{3}, \dfrac{3}{4}, \dfrac{1}{4}, \dfrac{1}{8}, \dfrac{4}{4}$

6. Place the correct relation symbol ($<, =, >$) between each pair of fractions to make a true statement.

a) $\dfrac{1}{10} \bigcirc \dfrac{2}{20}$

c) $\dfrac{3}{8} \bigcirc \dfrac{2}{3}$

e) $\dfrac{2}{3} \bigcirc \dfrac{5}{6}$

g) $\dfrac{5}{8} \bigcirc \dfrac{3}{4}$

b) $\dfrac{3}{4} \bigcirc \dfrac{3}{8}$

d) $\dfrac{1}{2} \bigcirc \dfrac{5}{12}$

f) $\dfrac{11}{8} \bigcirc \dfrac{5}{4}$

h) $\dfrac{3}{14} \bigcirc \dfrac{6}{28}$

7. Write each of the following as a fraction in simplest form.

a) $\dfrac{8}{12}$

e) $\dfrac{16}{24}$

b) $\dfrac{4}{16}$

f) $\dfrac{91}{161}$

c) $\dfrac{18}{32}$

g) $\dfrac{125}{5}$

d) $\dfrac{15}{18}$

h) $\dfrac{34}{51}$

8. Write each mixed numeral as a fraction.

a) $3\dfrac{3}{5}$

e) $4\dfrac{1}{2}$

b) $5\dfrac{3}{10}$

f) $16\dfrac{3}{8}$

c) $1\dfrac{7}{8}$

g) $5\dfrac{2}{5}$

d) $3\dfrac{1}{7}$

h) $7\dfrac{1}{7}$

9. Fill in the blanks in the following lists of equivalent fractions. Keep the denominators as small as you can (without using a fraction already in the list).

a) $\dfrac{1}{2}$, _____ , _____ , $\dfrac{4}{8}$, _____ , _____ , _____

b) $\dfrac{3}{8}$, $\dfrac{6}{16}$, _____ , _____ , _____ , _____ , _____

c) $\dfrac{5}{7}$, _____ , $\dfrac{15}{21}$, _____ , _____ , _____ , _____

10. Complete the following explanation of why the fraction $\dfrac{3}{5}$ is equivalent to $\dfrac{21}{35}$. If a rectangular region is divided into 5 regions of the same size, we can shade _____ (how many?) of these regions to represent $\dfrac{3}{5}$. If each of the 5 regions into which the original region is divided is itself divided into 7 equivalent regions, then the original rectangular region will have been divided into 5 × _____ equivalent regions. The portion that was shaded will then consist of _____ × 7 of these smaller regions. Thus the portion of the original rectangular region that is shaded can also be represented by the fraction $\dfrac{\_\_\_ \times 7}{5 \times \_\_\_}$. Since $\dfrac{21}{35}$ and $\dfrac{3}{5}$ both indicate what portion of the original region is shaded, we can conclude that $\dfrac{21}{35}$ and $\dfrac{3}{5}$ are _____ fractions.

11. Use reasoning similar to that in exercise 7 to argue that $\dfrac{4}{7}$ is equivalent to $\dfrac{400}{700}$.

12. Write each improper fraction as a mixed numeral.

a) $\frac{29}{5}$ c) $\frac{37}{7}$ e) $\frac{43}{12}$ g) $\frac{49}{6}$ i) $\frac{25}{13}$

b) $\frac{17}{4}$ d) $\frac{24}{9}$ f) $\frac{31}{4}$ h) $\frac{19}{5}$ j) $\frac{44}{9}$

13. Mark each statement true or false.

a) The number $1\frac{2}{7}$ can be named with a proper fraction.

b) It is incorrect to call $2\frac{2}{3}$ a fractional number, because it is' the sum of a whole number and a fractional number.

c) Every improper fraction names a number greater than or equal to 1.

d) Every mixed numeral can be rewritten as an improper fraction.

e) The number $\frac{10}{5}$ is a fraction but not a whole number.

f) Every proper fraction names a number greater than 0.

g) Every proper fraction names a number less than 1.

h) An infinite number of fraction names are possible for the number 1.

Discussion Questions

1. Discuss situations that the teacher can create in the primary classroom to involve children with fractions from the real world.

2. Examine the fraction program in several elementary school textbooks, and discuss with your peers the similarities and differences between the programs.

3. In preparation for a discussion on which subject be taught first (rational numbers expressed as *decimals* or rational numbers expressed as *fractions*), separate a page into two columns. List the advantages and disadvantages of teaching decimals first in one column and the advantages and disadvantages of teaching fractions first in the second column.

4. Fractions should be introduced on the concrete level and then carried through the semiconcrete, semiabstract, and abstract levels. Discuss materials that can be used at each level of student development.

5. Discuss how pure discovery and guided discovery can be used in introducing fractions to children.

6. Research the following materials used to introduce fractions. Present your findings to the class.

   a) Cuisenaire rods
   b) Dienes Blocks
   c) Stern rods
   d) attribute blocks
   e) squared paper

7. Prepare a list of readiness activities that can be used in the primary grades as a foundation for the formal introduction of fractions.

8. Use transparent colored plastic to prepare a fraction kit that can be used on the overhead projector. Demonstrate the use of the kit to your class. You might want to make both circular and rectangular regions.

9. Make a set of number-line overlays for the overhead projector, illustrating fractions marked on the number line. Demonstrate the use of the number-line transparencies to your class.

10. Discuss how problem solving should be incorporated into the study of fractions.

Activities for the Primary Grades

The contemporary approach to elementary school mathematics provides a consistent pattern of experiences designed to extend the child's understanding of concepts with each successive step. This sequential approach includes an introduction to fractional numbers at the primary level. A basic understanding of the meaning of fractions beginning in the primary grades not only meets the mathematical needs of the child; it also gives him a proper perspective of number structure. The child who is introduced to concepts of fractional numbers at the primary level sees their relation to whole numbers at an advantageous time. When he reaches the point of operations with fractional numbers, they are not something completely new and different.

It is important to remember that concrete and semiconcrete experiences and demonstrations should be used frequently to provide the background of understanding necessary for working with the more abstract concepts later.

Since so many children have wanted the "biggest half of the candy bar," there is a need to provide many situations that will help children understand the precise meaning of the denominator and the numerator in a fraction. This understanding must precede any computation with fractional numbers. Manipulation of real objects, demonstrations on the felt board with regions separated into fractional parts, and simple exercises involving folding and cutting paper not only increase understanding of fractional parts but introduce computational skills as well. Use Cuisenaire rods, Dienes Blocks, Stern rods, and fraction bars in presenting the concept of fractions.

Use transparent colored plastic, and cut out circular regions about 6 millimeters in diameter. Use a different color for each set of fractions, and make 5 circular regions of each color. Cut one set of 5 circular regions into halves, and cut the remaining sets into thirds, fourths, fifths, sixths, sevenths, eighths, ninths, and tenths. Keep each set in a small envelope marked to indicate the type of pieces inside. The pieces can be easily manipulated on the overhead projector by both teacher and students, and students can easily see the relationships among the pieces.

At the primary grade levels it is particularly important to establish visual perception of the concept of fractional parts. Use of the number line will help in establishing the idea of $\frac{1}{2}$, $\frac{1}{4}$, and so on, and the fact that a fractional number has many names.

0				1
$\frac{0}{2}$		$\frac{1}{2}$		$\frac{2}{2}$
$\frac{0}{4}$	$\frac{1}{4}$	$\frac{2}{4}$	$\frac{3}{4}$	$\frac{4}{4}$

$\frac{0}{8}$ $\frac{1}{8}$ $\frac{2}{8}$ $\frac{3}{8}$ $\frac{4}{8}$ $\frac{5}{8}$ $\frac{6}{8}$ $\frac{7}{8}$ $\frac{8}{8}$

Use the chalkboard or pictures of articles to give children opportunities to talk about fractions. For example:

Jimmy and Johnny were playing together at Johnny's house. Johnny's sister came home with a candy bar for Johnny. She didn't know that Jimmy was going to be there too. She cut the candy bar into two pieces so that Jimmy and Johnny could each have one-half. Have a child come to the chalkboard and point out the candy bar that is cut into halves (or to the proper picture, if pictures are used).

Use this same kind of activity but have children make up stories about the pictures. This activity can be extended to include one-fourth, one-third, and so on.

The following models can be made by the teacher to demonstrate the relationships among fractions and equivalent fractions.

A fraction board can be made from plywood. Construct a frame from a piece of plywood on which narrow strips of wood are nailed or glued. Construct rectangles of plywood so that the rectangles will fit between the wooden strips. Cut each rectangle into different fractional parts.

1 Unit				
$\frac{1}{2}$			$\frac{1}{2}$	
$\frac{1}{3}$		$\frac{1}{3}$		$\frac{1}{3}$
$\frac{1}{4}$	$\frac{1}{4}$		$\frac{1}{4}$	$\frac{1}{4}$
$\frac{1}{5}$	$\frac{1}{5}$	$\frac{1}{5}$	$\frac{1}{5}$	$\frac{1}{5}$

The same type of fraction model may be made on plywood using heavy cardboard and staples.

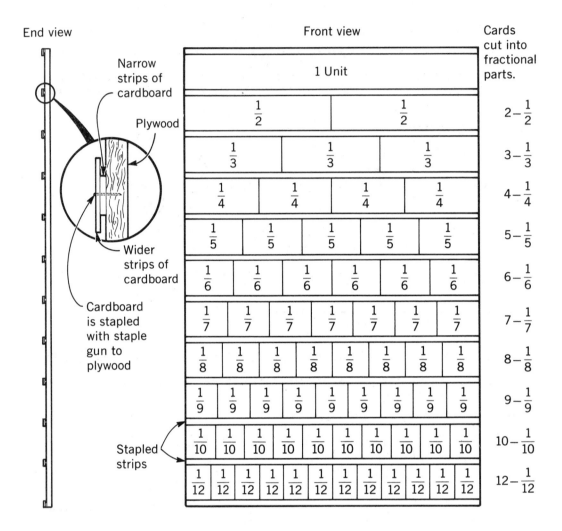

Attach a long string (the length of the fraction board) to a thumb tack. The children can see which fractions are related, by placing the thumb tack on the top edge of the fraction board and drawing the string taut. For instance, place the thumb tack in the top of the fraction board directly above the division between the two one-half pieces. Tighten the string down the center of the board so the children can see that two one-fourths, three one-sixths, four one-eighths, five one-tenths, and six one-twelfths are the same in length as one-half. Thus one-half is equivalent to two-fourths, three-sixths, four-eighths, five-tenths, and six-twelfths. A similar procedure can be used with the other fractional parts.

To construct a fraction kit, trace sixteen large circles on construction paper (or use paper plates if available). Cut them as follows: three regions intact (units), two regions in two parts (halves), two regions in three parts (thirds), two regions in four parts (fourths), two regions in five parts (fifths), two regions in six parts (sixths), two regions in eight parts (eighths), and one region in twelve parts (twelfths). The teacher may want to make a fraction kit out of colored transparencies to use on an overhead projector.

CONCEPT OF FRACTIONAL PARTS

1. Open a manila file folder and write the fraction $\frac{1}{2}$ on one side; on the other write the fraction $\frac{1}{4}$. Cut out a number of geometric shapes and color either $\frac{1}{4}$ or $\frac{1}{2}$ of each. Make five or ten folders so that many children can sort the shapes by placing them on the proper side of the folder. When the child is finished, he should raise his hand so that you can check his folder.

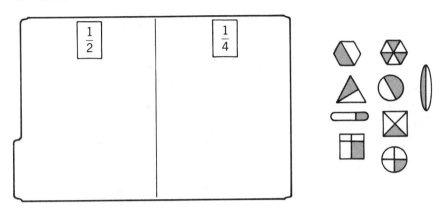

2. Tape another piece of cardboard to some of the folders and put the fraction $\frac{1}{3}$ on this section. Make figures with $\frac{1}{3}$ of them colored to add to the set.

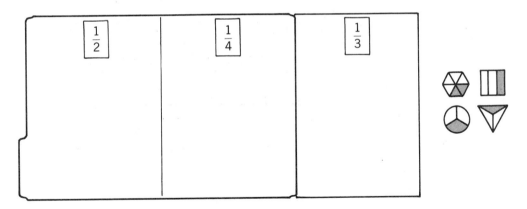

3. Mark each figure that has $\frac{1}{2}$ of the region shaded.

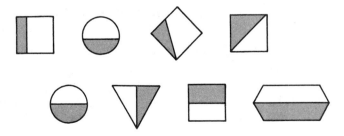

4. Mark each figure that has $\frac{1}{4}$ of the region shaded.

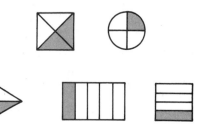

5. Shade $\frac{1}{3}$ of each figure.

6. Make a set of cardboard dominoes. Draw a figure on both ends of each domino and shade either $\frac{1}{2}$, $\frac{1}{3}$, or $\frac{1}{4}$ of the figure. Play regular dominoes by matching shapes that have the same fractional part shaded.

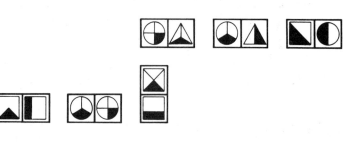

7. Use the felt board or chalkboard for simple diagrams. Ask a child to draw a ring around one-half, one-third, or one-fourth of the objects pictured.

CONCEPT OF FRACTIONS

1. Each child is given two congruent circles of different colors cut from construction paper. Instruct the children to fold one circle in half and cut with a scissors along the fold. Fit both halves over the other circle. Have the children trade halves with another student to see if two halves still make a whole.

2. Give each child two squares of construction paper of different colors. Instruct the children to fold one square in half and cut along the fold (do not demonstrate this). Fit both

halves over the other square. Trade halves with another student. Often, some students will cut a square along the diagonal, which provides excellent material for discussion.

Student A

Student B

Results when
Student A and Student B
exchange halves

3. Give a student eight checkers: five red and three black. Have the student write the fractions for the part of the set that is red and the part of the set that is black. A teacher may use discs cut from colored transparencies and placed on the overhead projector. Have the children orally tell the fraction for a given part of the set.

4. Draw a ring around the correct fraction.

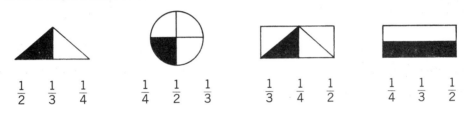

$\frac{1}{2}$ $\frac{1}{3}$ $\frac{1}{4}$ $\qquad$ $\frac{1}{4}$ $\frac{1}{2}$ $\frac{1}{3}$ $\qquad$ $\frac{1}{3}$ $\frac{1}{4}$ $\frac{1}{2}$ $\qquad$ $\frac{1}{4}$ $\frac{1}{3}$ $\frac{1}{2}$

5. Color $\frac{1}{4}$ of each picture.

   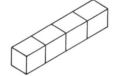 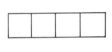

6. Draw a ring around the correct fraction.

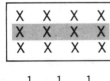 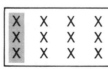 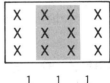

$\frac{1}{4}$ $\frac{1}{3}$ $\frac{1}{2}$ $\qquad$ $\frac{1}{4}$ $\frac{1}{3}$ $\frac{1}{2}$ $\qquad$ $\frac{1}{4}$ $\frac{1}{3}$ $\frac{1}{2}$

7. Color $\frac{1}{2}$ of each set.

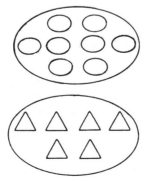 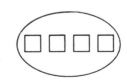

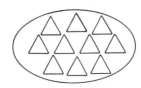

8. Color $\frac{1}{4}$ of each set.

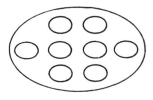 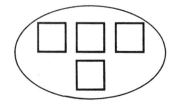 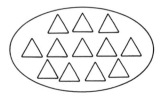

9. a) Color $\frac{1}{3}$ of each picture.   b) Color $\frac{2}{3}$ of each picture.

 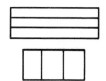   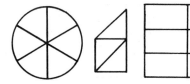

c) Color $\frac{3}{4}$ of each picture.   d) Color $\frac{1}{3}$ of each set.

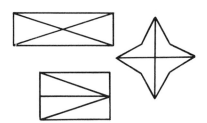   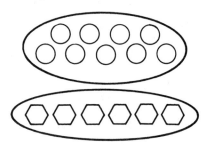

10. Draw a ring around $\frac{1}{3}$ of the objects in each set.

11. Draw a ring around $\frac{2}{3}$ of the objects in each set.

12. Draw a ring around $\frac{1}{4}$ of the objects in each set.

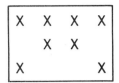

13. Draw a ring around $\frac{3}{4}$ of the objects in each set.

14. Loop the correct fraction for each bar.   One unit

$\frac{1}{4}$ $\frac{2}{4}$ $\frac{3}{4}$ $\frac{4}{4}$

$\frac{1}{4}$ $\frac{2}{4}$ $\frac{3}{4}$ $\frac{4}{4}$

$\frac{1}{4}$ $\frac{2}{4}$ $\frac{3}{4}$ $\frac{4}{4}$

$\frac{1}{4}$ $\frac{2}{4}$ $\frac{3}{4}$ $\frac{4}{4}$

$\frac{1}{3}$ $\frac{2}{3}$ $\frac{3}{3}$

$\frac{1}{3}$ $\frac{2}{3}$ $\frac{3}{3}$

$\frac{1}{3}$ $\frac{2}{3}$ $\frac{3}{3}$

15. Write the correct fraction for each.

Shaded $\frac{}{2}$

Not shaded $\frac{}{2}$

Shaded $\frac{}{4}$

Not shaded $\frac{}{4}$

Shaded $\frac{}{4}$

Not shaded $\frac{}{4}$

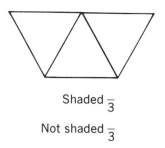

Shaded $\dfrac{}{3}$

Not shaded $\dfrac{}{3}$

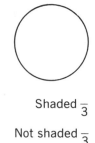

Shaded $\dfrac{}{3}$

Not shaded $\dfrac{}{3}$

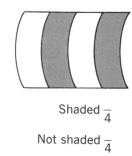

Shaded $\dfrac{}{4}$

Not shaded $\dfrac{}{4}$

Hand-Held Calculator Activities for the Primary Grades

The display screen of a hand-held calculator cannot display fractions. All rational numbers are expressed as decimals on a calculator. Fractions can be converted to decimals, by thinking of a fraction as division, but this concept was not developed in Unit 8 so we will save that discussion until Unit 10. Since the hand-held calculator does not function with rational numbers expressed as fractions, no activities are included in this section.

Microcomputer Activities for the Primary Grades

The previous comments about hand-held calculators also apply to microcomputers used in the immediate mode. Programs are available and can be developed for use with fractions on a microcomputer. Computers that have excellent graphics can be used to draw regions on the video screen, and the children can be asked to identify the fraction that names a certain region. Programming graphics for children, however, is beyond the scope of this textbook. Teachers might want to evaluate available software for the primary grades and fractions, but we do not recommend microcomputer programs to be used with fractions.

Activities for the Intermediate Grades

Activities suggested for the primary grades can also be used in the intermediate grades.

1. Give the student two yellow buttons, eight blue buttons, and five cards. Ask the student to tell what fraction of the buttons is yellow. $\left(\dfrac{2}{10}\right)$ What fraction is blue? $\left(\dfrac{8}{10}\right)$ Have the student place two buttons on each card with the two yellow ones together. Now ask what fraction of the cards with buttons is yellow. $\left(\dfrac{1}{5}\right)$ Blue? $\left(\dfrac{4}{5}\right)$ Variations of this activity can be done by changing the number of buttons and cards.

2. Give each child a copy of the following chart; the children can cut out strips, or rows, to solve the questions that follow.

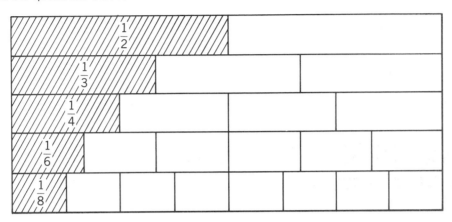

a) Which is greater?

$\frac{1}{2}$ or $\frac{1}{4}$ $\frac{1}{2}$ or $\frac{1}{6}$ $\frac{1}{8}$ or $\frac{1}{4}$ $\frac{1}{6}$ or $\frac{1}{3}$ $\frac{1}{2}$ or $\frac{2}{3}$ $\frac{2}{3}$ or $\frac{5}{6}$ $\frac{3}{8}$ or $\frac{1}{4}$ $\frac{5}{8}$ or $\frac{3}{4}$

b) Which is less?

$\frac{1}{3}$ or $\frac{1}{2}$ $\frac{1}{4}$ or $\frac{1}{6}$ $\frac{1}{8}$ or $\frac{1}{6}$ $\frac{3}{4}$ or $\frac{5}{6}$ $\frac{3}{4}$ or $\frac{2}{3}$ $\frac{1}{2}$ or $\frac{3}{4}$ $\frac{3}{8}$ or $\frac{1}{4}$

c) Which are equivalent?

$\frac{1}{2}$ and $\frac{2}{4}$ $\frac{2}{3}$ and $\frac{3}{4}$ $\frac{3}{8}$ and $\frac{2}{4}$ $\frac{1}{4}$ and $\frac{1}{6}$ $\frac{4}{6}$ and $\frac{2}{3}$ $\frac{6}{8}$ and $\frac{3}{4}$

3. Write the correct fraction for the shaded part of each figure.

4.   a) Color $\frac{1}{3}$ c) Color $\frac{2}{6}$ e) Color $\frac{2}{4}$ g) Color $\frac{3}{8}$

  b) Color $\frac{2}{3}$ d) Color $\frac{4}{6}$ f) Color $\frac{3}{4}$ h) Color $\frac{6}{8}$

5. Write the correct fraction for the part that you did not color in each of the preceding figures.

a) _____   c) _____   e) _____   g) _____
b) _____   d) _____   f) _____   h) _____

Use the chart from activity 2 as an aid for activities 6 and 7.

6. Write the correct symbol ($<$, $>$, or $=$) in each $\bigcirc$.

a) $\frac{1}{3}$ $\bigcirc$ $\frac{1}{4}$ c) $\frac{2}{4}$ $\bigcirc$ $\frac{1}{2}$ e) $\frac{3}{8}$ $\bigcirc$ $\frac{4}{8}$

b) $\frac{1}{6}$ $\bigcirc$ $\frac{1}{4}$ d) $\frac{2}{4}$ $\bigcirc$ $\frac{1}{8}$ f) $\frac{1}{6}$ $\bigcirc$ $\frac{2}{6}$

7. Write four fractions that are names for, or equal, 1.

8. Examine these figures. Write a fraction for the shaded part of each figure. Then write a fraction for the unshaded part of each figure.

a) 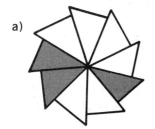   b) 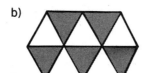   c)

9. Write the correct fraction below each point labeled with a letter.

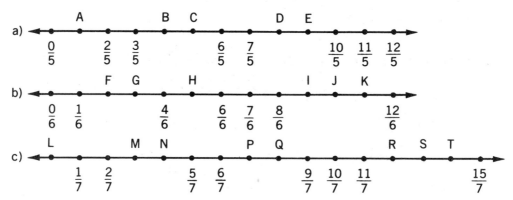

10. Use the number lines in Activity 9 to help you answer these questions.

a) What whole number is named by $\frac{5}{5}$, $\frac{6}{6}$, and $\frac{7}{7}$?

b) What whole number is named by $\frac{10}{5}$, $\frac{12}{6}$, and $\frac{14}{7}$?

11. For this activity, cardboard cutouts of circles, squares, rectangles, triangles, and diamond shapes (rhombuses) are cut into halves, thirds, and fourths. Construct a die with the fractions $\frac{1}{2}$, $\frac{1}{3}$, and $\frac{1}{4}$. Roll the die. The one with the largest fraction rolls first. Roll the die in turn and select a corresponding region to match the die. With the cardboard cutout

regions, try to form (1) one whole figure. The first person to get 1 whole figure can be declared winner, or the score can be kept and the game played for a certain time period with the high scorer declared the winner. This game can be varied by trying to get one of each of the shapes listed.

Hand-Held Calculator Activities for the Intermediate Grades

Since the hand-held calculator does not display fractions on the screen, no calculator activities are included here. The hand-held calculator can be used to change fractions to decimal form, if fractions are interpreted as division. The numerator divided by the denominator will produce a decimal on the display screen. (This concept will be discussed in Unit 10.)

Microcomputer Activities for the Intermediate Grades

The preceding comments about the hand-held calculator also apply to the microcomputer used in the immediate mode. The microcomputer can be programmed to print fractions on the screen, written in division form using the slash (/) key. Three-fourths is written 3/4. Tutorial and practice programs for fractions can be written for the computer.

1. A short test in fractions can be programmed for a microcomputer. This progam can be altered to include the type of questions you would like to ask about fractions. The program is appropriate for a Radio Shack TRS-80 computer, but it can be adapted for other computers by changing a few statements. The "clear the screen" (CLS) command varies with different computers. Remember: If you are using an Atari computer, the string variable must be dimensioned. The program will run on a Commodore machine (Commodore 64, Pet or Vic-20), if the clear-the-screen command is changed. This program can also be made to run on the Apple computer, by changing CLS to HOME.

```
10   REM FRACTION TEST
20   CLS
30   ?"WHAT IS YOUR NAME"
40   INPUT N$
50   ?:?:?:?"HELLO, ";N$;", TODAY WE WILL TAKE A FRACTION TEST."
60   ?:?:?:?"ARE YOU READY, HERE WE GO!"
70   FOR T=1 TO 4000:NEXT T
80   CLS
90   ?"STUDY THIS FRACTION  3/4."
100 ?:?:?:?"WHAT NUMBER IS IN THE NUMERATOR"
110 INPUT A
120 IF A=3 THEN?"CORRECT"
130 IF A<>3 THEN?"WRONG, TRY AGAIN!":GOTO 90
140 FOR T=1 TO 2000:NEXT T
150 CLS
160 ?"IN THE FRACTION 3/4, WHAT NUMBER IS IN THE DENOMINATOR"
170 INPUT B
180 IF B=4 THEN?"CORRECT"
190 IF B<>4 THEN?"WRONG, TRY AGAIN!":GOTO 160
```

```
200 FOR T=1 TO 2000:NEXT T
210 CLS
220 ?"WHAT IS THE LINE BETWEEN THE NUMERATOR AND THE DENOMINATOR
CALLED"
230 INPUT Z$
240 IF Z$="FRACTION BAR"THEN?"CORRECT"
250 IF Z$<>"FRACTION BAR"THEN?"WRONG, TRY AGAIN!":GOTO 220
260 FOR T=1 TO 2000:NEXT T
270 ?"NICE JOB, ";N$;", GOODBYE"
```

More questions could be placed in the program, following the same format. The teacher can easily construct a test for students on any given subject. In this program, we only made provisions for one correct or incorrect answer to each question; no provision has been made to help the student or to give more options for each response. This program may be enhanced by adding more comments to the user, a counter to keep track of the number of questions asked, or a counter to keep track of the number of correct and incorrect answers. The program could also be made more friendly, by adding more interaction.

2. The following microcomputer program is appropriate for the Atari computer. The graphics must be changed for other computers.

```
10   REM—IDENTIFYING FRACTIONS—
20   ?:?:?:?"MY NAME IS ATARI, WHAT IS YOUR NAME"
30   DIM N$(25)
40   INPUT N$
50   ?:?:?"HOWDIE, ";N$;", TODAY WE WILL WRITE FRACTIONS FOR SETS."
60   GR.8
70   PL.160,20
80   DR.320,20:DR.320,40:DR.160,40:DR.160,20
90   PL.200,20:DR.200,40:PL.240,40:DR.240,40
95   PL.280,20:DR.280,40
100  PL.160,60:DR.280,60:DR.280,80:DR.160,80:DR.160,60
110  PL.200,60:DR.200,80:PL.240,60:DR.240,80
120  ?"HOW MANY SQUARES ARE DRAWN ON THE TOP ROW
130  INPUT A
140  IF A=4 THEN?"YOU ARE RIGHT":FOR T=1 TO 2000:NEXT T
150  IF A<>4 THEN?"WRONG, TRY AGAIN!":FOR T=1 TO 2000:NEXT T:G.120
160  ?:?:?:?"HOW MANY SQUARES IN THE SECOND ROW"
170  INPUT B
180  IF B=3 THEN?"YOU ARE CORRECT":FOR T=1 TO 2000:NEXT T
190  IF B<>3THEN?"WRONG, TRY AGAIN!":FOR T=1 TO 2000:NEXT T:G.160
200  ?:?:?:?"HOW MANY SQUARES ALL TOGETHER"
210  INPUT C
220  IF C=7 THEN?"GREAT, YOU ARE CORRECT":FOR T=1 TO 2000:NEXT T
230  IF C<>7 THEN?"WRONG, TRY AGAIN!":FOR T=1 TO 2000:NEXT T:G.200
240  ?:?:?:?"WHAT FRACTION OF THE SQUARES ARE IN THE TOP ROW"
250  DIM Z$(4)
260  INPUT Z$
270  IF Z$="4/7"THEN?"YOU UNDERSTAND":FOR T=1 TO 2000:NEXT T
280  IF Z$<>"4/7"THEN?"WRONG, TRY AGAIN!":FOR T=1 TO 2000:NEXT T:G.240
290  ?:?:?:?"WHAT FRACTION OF THE SQUARES ARE IN THE SECOND ROW"
300  DIM W$(4)
310  INPUT W$
320  IF W$="3/7"THEN?"CORRECT AGAIN":FOR T=1 TO 2000:NEXT T
330  IF W$<>"3/7"THEN?"WRONG, TRY AGAIN!":FOR T=1 TO 2000:NEXT T:G.290
340  GR.0
350  ?"NICE JOB TODAY, ";N$;", SEE YOU TOMORROW."
```

Statements 60 through 330 can be repeated, using new values to develop different numbers of squares and fractions. A program of this type can be expanded to contain as many examples as you wish. The program can also be made more friendly by adding more interaction with the user or made more elegant by adding counters, color, and sound. The possibilities are limited only by the teacher's computer knowledge.

Activities for the Upper Elementary Grades

1. Examine a ruler or measuring cup and discuss how each is divided.

2. Give the students paper plates, graph paper, or construction paper; then ask them to shade various fractional regions of the materials.

3. Using several rectangular regions with the same dimensions, have the student find as many ways as possible to illustrate a given fraction $\left(\text{for instance, } \frac{1}{4}\right)$.

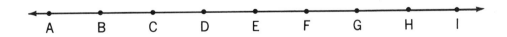

4. On graph paper, have the students model $\frac{1}{2} = \frac{2}{4}$, $\frac{2}{3} = \frac{4}{6}$, $\frac{1}{4} = \frac{2}{8}$, and $\frac{2}{5} = \frac{4}{10}$. This requires the students to think at a sophisticated level.

  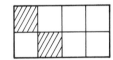

$$\frac{2}{4} \quad = \quad \frac{1}{2}$$

5. Demonstration activity: Draw a number line on the chalkboard. Label the points.

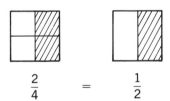

A   B   C   D   E   F   G   H   I

   a) Which point is one-half the distance between points A and I?

   b) Which point is one-fourth the distance between points E and I?

   c) Which point is three-fourths the distance between points A and I?

   d) Which point is six-eighths the distance between points A and I?

e) Which point is four-eighths the distance between points A and I?

f) The distance from C to D can be named by what fraction?

g) The distance from E to G can be named by what fraction?

This activity can be used with sketches of number lines that include points labeled with various sets of fractions. Other questions can be included to reinforce the concept. Children should be given the opportunity to pose questions of their own to other members of the group.

6.

Set	Number of the Set	Parts Shaded	Fraction Shaded	Parts Not Shaded	Fraction Not Shaded
a) ⭘⬤⭘⬤⭘					
b) ▲▽▲▽▲					
c) ⭘⬤⭘⬤⭘⭘					
d) ⬤⭘⬤⭘⬤⭘⬤⭘⭘					
e) ⬣⬡⬡⬡					
f) ⭘⬤⭘⭘⬤⭘					
g) ⬤⬤⭘⬤⬤⭘⬤⬤⭘					

7. Hand each child a dittoed page of number lines. Give the children the name of the first and last points on each number line. Have the children name all the points marked on each line.

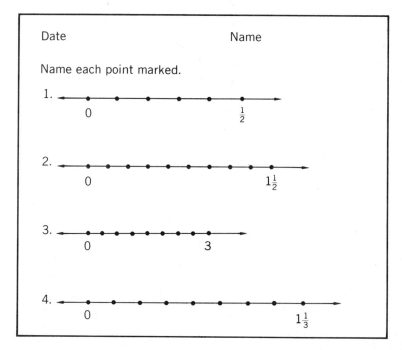

Date   Name

Name each point marked.

1.

0        $\frac{1}{2}$

2.

0        $1\frac{1}{2}$

3.

0   3

4.

0        $1\frac{1}{3}$

8. Construct a deck of about 60 cards. Write a fraction on each card. You may start by using fractions with the denominators of 2, 3, 4, 6, and 8. Five cards are dealt to each player and are placed face up in front of the player in the order in which they are dealt.

Example: $\dfrac{5}{8}$ $\dfrac{1}{4}$ $\dfrac{5}{6}$ $\dfrac{1}{8}$ $\dfrac{3}{4}$

Each player draws a card or takes a discard from the pile in order. The first person to have five fractions in order from smallest to largest is the winner. For instance, the player's first

draw is $\dfrac{2}{3}$, so he or she discards $\dfrac{1}{8}$.

$\dfrac{5}{8}$ $\dfrac{1}{4}$ $\dfrac{5}{6}$ $\dfrac{2}{3}$ $\dfrac{3}{4}$

The fraction $\dfrac{5}{8}$ must be replaced by some fraction less than $\dfrac{1}{4}$, and $\dfrac{5}{6}$ must be replaced by some fraction more than $\dfrac{1}{4}$ and less than $\dfrac{2}{3}$ for the player to win.

9. See if you can locate a pattern; then complete the sequence.

  a) 3, $2\dfrac{1}{2}$, 2, ____, ____, ____, ____

  b) 1, $\dfrac{1}{2}$, 2, ____, ____, ____, ____

  c) 8, 4, 2, 1, ____, ____, ____, ____

  d) 18, 10, 6, 4, ____, ____, ____

10. Arrange the elements of the following sets of fractional numbers in order from least to greatest.

  $A = \left\{\dfrac{1}{2}, \dfrac{6}{6}, \dfrac{6}{3}, \dfrac{3}{4}\right\}$ $B = \left\{\dfrac{9}{10}, \dfrac{2}{5}, \dfrac{2}{10}, \dfrac{3}{6}\right\}$ $C = \left\{\dfrac{2}{3}, \dfrac{3}{2}, \dfrac{4}{3}, \dfrac{3}{4}\right\}$

11. Draw a number line or diagram if you need it to help you fill in the blanks.

  a) $\dfrac{1}{2}$ is 4 times as great as ____.   d) $\dfrac{1}{5}$ is 2 times as great as ____.

  b) $\dfrac{1}{4}$ is ____ times as great as $\dfrac{1}{8}$.   e) $\dfrac{1}{2}$ is 5 times as great as ____.

  c) $\dfrac{1}{8}$ is ____ times as great as $\dfrac{1}{16}$.   f) $\dfrac{1}{3}$ is 3 times as great as ____.

12. The following activity can be used to reinforce the students' understanding of equivalent fractions. Construct a deck of 42 cards with the following sets of fractions: halves, thirds, fourths, fifths, sixths, eighths, and tenths. One card should also be constructed for each of the whole numbers 1, 2, 3, and 4. The cards are then: $\dfrac{1}{2}, \dfrac{2}{2}; \dfrac{1}{3}, \dfrac{2}{3}, \dfrac{3}{3}; \dfrac{1}{4}, \dfrac{2}{4}, \dfrac{3}{4}, \dfrac{4}{4}; \dfrac{1}{5}, \dfrac{2}{5},$

$\dfrac{3}{5}, \dfrac{4}{5}, \dfrac{5}{5}; \dfrac{1}{6}, \dfrac{2}{6}, \dfrac{3}{6}, \dfrac{4}{6}, \dfrac{5}{6}, \dfrac{6}{6}; \dfrac{1}{8}, \dfrac{2}{8}, \dfrac{3}{8}, \dfrac{4}{8}, \dfrac{5}{8}, \dfrac{6}{8}, \dfrac{7}{8}, \dfrac{8}{8}; \dfrac{1}{10}, \dfrac{2}{10}, \dfrac{3}{10}, \dfrac{4}{10}, \dfrac{5}{10}, \dfrac{6}{10}, \dfrac{7}{10}, \dfrac{8}{10}, \dfrac{9}{10}, \dfrac{10}{10}; 1, 2, 3, 4.$

Each player is dealt seven cards. The deck is placed in the middle of the playing area, and a card off the deck is turned face up. Players take turns in playing their cards. A card with the same denominator or a card with an equivalent fraction is discarded on top of the card that is face up, on the discard pile. If a player has a card with a whole number, he or she can play the card and change the denominator to be played next. If a player does not have a card that can be played, he or she must draw from the deck and lose a turn. The game ends when one player gets rid of all of his or her cards.

13. Using graph paper, draw diagrams of rectangular or square regions to model each fraction.

a) $\dfrac{1}{4}$ b) $\dfrac{2}{3}$ c) $\dfrac{5}{6}$ d) $\dfrac{7}{8}$ e) $\dfrac{3}{5}$ f) $\dfrac{5}{2}$

14. Cut out 70 2″ by 3″ cardboard cards and label each with one of the ten different names for one of the fractions $\dfrac{1}{2}, \dfrac{1}{4}, \dfrac{3}{4}, \dfrac{1}{8}, \dfrac{3}{8}, \dfrac{5}{8},$ and $\dfrac{7}{8}.$ Continue until all seven fractions have ten cards, each with one name. Place all cards face down on a table between two players to play Concentration. The player with the most pairs wins.

15. Write a set of ten fractions for the number 1.

16. Use the many names for one and generate a set of equivalent fractions for each.

Names for 1	$\dfrac{2}{2}$	$\dfrac{3}{3}$	$\dfrac{4}{4}$	$\dfrac{5}{5}$	$\dfrac{6}{6}$	$\dfrac{7}{7}$	$\dfrac{8}{8}$	$\dfrac{9}{9}$
Fractions for $\dfrac{1}{2}$								
Fractions for $\dfrac{2}{3}$								
Fractions for $\dfrac{3}{4}$								

17. Have each child make two sets of multiple strips (as shown) for each number 1 through 10. Cut the strips apart. Consider the fraction $\dfrac{2}{3}$. If you place the *two* strip over the *three* strip, you have a set of equivalent fractions that names the fractional number $\dfrac{2}{3}$. A set of equivalent fractions can be shown for fractions with denominators less than ten by putting the two strips together.

1	2	3	4	5	6	7	8	9	10
2	4	6	8	10	12	14	16	18	20
3	6	9	12	15	18	21	24	27	30
4	8	12	16	20	24	28	32	36	40
5	10	15	20	25	30	35	40	45	50
6	12	18	24	30	36	42	48	54	60
7	14	21	28	35	42	49	56	63	70
8	16	24	32	40	48	56	64	72	80
9	18	27	36	45	54	63	72	81	90
10	20	30	40	50	60	70	80	90	100

18. Which pairs of fractions are equivalent?

a) $\frac{9}{25}, \frac{4}{10}$ b) $\frac{8}{10}, \frac{40}{50}$ c) $\frac{17}{25}, \frac{9}{12}$ d) $\frac{13}{16}, \frac{9}{10}$ e) $\frac{11}{22}, \frac{72}{144}$ f) $\frac{2}{6}, \frac{20}{60}$

19. Place the correct relation symbol ($<$, $=$ or $>$) in each circle.

a) $\frac{2}{3} \bigcirc \frac{5}{6}$ c) $\frac{3}{8} \bigcirc \frac{3}{4}$ e) $\frac{4}{5} \bigcirc \frac{4}{7}$ g) $\frac{2}{5} \bigcirc \frac{4}{10}$

b) $\frac{3}{4} \bigcirc \frac{6}{8}$ d) $\frac{8}{15} \bigcirc \frac{8}{14}$ f) $\frac{0}{3} \bigcirc \frac{0}{6}$ h) $\frac{2}{3} \bigcirc \frac{3}{4}$

20. Prepare a set of cards and a call sheet with the fractions $\frac{1}{2}, \frac{1}{3}, \frac{2}{3}, \frac{1}{4}, \frac{3}{4}, \frac{1}{5}, \frac{2}{5}, \frac{3}{5}, \frac{4}{5}, \frac{1}{6}, \frac{5}{6}, \frac{1}{8}, \frac{3}{8}, \frac{5}{8}, \frac{7}{8}, \frac{1}{9}, \frac{2}{9}, \frac{4}{9}, \frac{5}{9}, \frac{7}{9}, \frac{8}{9}$. Prepare bingo cards with equivalent fractions of $\frac{2}{4}, \frac{3}{6}, \frac{4}{8}, \ldots$; $\frac{2}{6}, \frac{3}{9}, \frac{4}{12}, \ldots$, and etc. Play proceeds according to usual bingo rules.

21. Complete the following table.

Fraction	Prime Factors	Fraction in Simplest Form
$\frac{10}{12}$	$\frac{2 \times 5}{2 \times 6}$	$\frac{5}{6}$
$\frac{27}{36}$		
$\frac{78}{117}$		
$\frac{85}{51}$		

22. Complete the following chart. Use the example as a guide.

Fraction	Factors of the Numerator	Factors of the Denominator	GCF	Simplest Form
$\frac{6}{8}$	2, 3, 6, 1	2, 4, 8, 1	2	$\frac{3}{4}$
$\frac{8}{12}$				
$\frac{5}{15}$				
$\frac{14}{10}$				
$\frac{4}{3}$				
$\frac{16}{9}$				

Hand-Held Calculator Activities for the Upper Elementary Grades

No hand-held calculator activities are presented here, because of the limitations of the calculator.

Microcomputer Activities for the Upper Elementary Grades

The microcomputer programs for the intermediate grade levels can also be used at the upper grade levels.

The following sample program can be easily enlarged; follow the format of statements 30 through 82. Many sets can be made from whatever symbols are available on your classroom computer. This program is written for the Vic-20 and can be used on a Pet or a Commodore 64. With minor changes the program will function equally well on a Radio Shack TRS-80, or an Atari computer. Remember: If you use an Atari, all the string variables must be dimensioned.

```
5    REM—SETS & FRACTIONS
7    ?"♡"
10   ?:?:?:?"WILL YOU TELL ME YOUR NAME"
12   INPUT N$
15   ?:?:?:?"I WILL SHOW YOU A SET, ";N$;", THEN YOU TELL ME A FRACTION FOR
     PART OF THE SET."
16   FOR T=1 TO 4000:NEXT T
20   ?"♡"
30   ?"HERE IS A SET OF ♡ AND ♤."
40   ?:?:?:?"        [♤ ♡ ♤ ♡ ♤ ♡ ♤ ♡ ♤]"
50   ?:?:?"WHAT FRACTION OF THE SET IS ♡"
60   INPUT A$
70   IF A$="4/9"THEN?"GREAT, YOU ARE CORRECT!":FOR T=1 TO 2000:NEXT T
80   IF A$<>"4/9"THEN?"WRONG, TRY AGAIN!":FOR T=1 TO 2000:NEXT T:GOTO 40
82   ?"♡"
85   ?:?:?:?"        [♧ ♡ ♤ ♡ ♧ ♡ ♤ ♡ ♤]"
90   ?:?:?:?"WHAT FRACTIONAL PART OF THE SET IS ♧"
100  INPUT B$
110  IF B$="2/9"THEN?"THAT'S CORRECT>":FOR T=1 TO 2000:NEXT T
120  IF B$<>"2/9"THEN?"WRONG, TRY AGAIN!":FOR T=1 TO 2000:NEXT T:GOTO 85
125  ?"♡"
130  ?"LOOK AT THIS SET":FOR T=1 TO 2000:NEXT T
140  ?:?:?:?" [♢ ♧ ♧ ♢ ♧]
150  ?"WHAT FRACTIONAL PART OF THE SET IS ♧"
160  INPUT C$
170  IF C$="3/5"THEN?"CORRECT!":FOR T=1 TO 2000:NEXT T:?"♡"
180  IF C$<>"3/5"THEN?"WRONG, TRY AGAIN!":FOR T=1 TO 2000:NEXT T:GOTO 140
185  ?" [♢ ♧ ♧ ♢ ♧]
190  ?"WHAT FRACTIONAL PART OF THE SET IS ♢"
200  INPUT D$
210  IF D$="2/5"THEN?"CORRECT":FOR T=1 TO 2000:NEXT T
220  IF D$<>"2/5"THEN?"WRONG, TRY AGAIN!":FOR T=1 TO 2000:NEXT T:GOTO 185
230  ?"HOPE YOU HAD FUN, ";N$;", SEE YOU LATER."
```

Suggested Readings

Brown, Christopher N. "Fractions on Grid Paper." *The Arithmetic Teacher*, vol. 26, no. 5, January 1979.

Dana, Marcia, and Lindquist, Mary Montgomery. "From Halves to Hundredths." *The Arithmetic Teacher*, vol. 26, no. 3, December 1979.

Dienes, Zoltan P. *Fractions: An Operation Approach*. New York: Herder & Herder, 1967.

Dumas, Enoch. *Math Activities for Child Development*. Boston: Allyn & Bacon, 1971.

Duquette, Raymond J. "Some Thoughts on Piaget's Findings and the Teaching of Fractions." *The Arithmetic Teacher*, vol. 19, no. 4, April 1972.

National Council of Teachers of Mathematics. *Games and Puzzles for Elementary and Middle School Mathematics*. Reston, Va.: NCTM, 1975.

National Council of Teachers of Mathematics. *Mathematics Learning in Early Childhood*. 37th Yearbook. Reston, Va.: NCTM, 1975.

National Education Association. *Manipulative Activities and Games in the Mathematics Classroom*. Washington, D.C.: NEA, 1979.

Post, Thomas. "Fractions: Results and Implications from National Assessment." *The Arithmetic Teacher*, vol. 28, no. 9, May 1981.

Sowder, Larry. "Models for Fractional Numbers—A Quiz for Teachers." *The Arithmetic Teacher*, vol. 18, no. 1, September 1971.

Usiskin, Zalman P. "The Future of Fractions." *The Arithmetic Teacher*, vol. 26, no. 5, January 1979.

10 Operations on Fractions

Teaching Competencies

Upon completing this unit, you will be able to:

Use models (regions, sets, and number lines) to develop an understanding of addition, subtraction, multiplication, and division of fractions

Describe an instructional sequence for addition, subtraction, multiplication, and division of fractions

Use standard algorithms for addition, subtraction, multiplication, and division of fractions

Use basic numerical properties in calculating with fractions

Use the least common denominator and greatest common fraction as tools for solving examples with fractions

Discussion

In Unit 9, models of regions, sets, and number lines were used as basic techniques to help students develop an understanding of rational numbers written in fraction form. After the children have developed an understanding of rational numbers, they are ready to learn the operations of addition, subtraction, multiplication, and division, as applied to fractions. A strong understanding of whole numbers and operations with whole numbers form the base for developing operations with fractions. Many concepts and structures of whole numbers can be directly applied to the fundamental operations on fractional numbers.

The binary operations of addition and multiplication and the inverse operations of subtraction and division can be extended to fractions so that basic numerical properties are preserved. Addition and multiplication remain commutative and associative; multiplication is still distributive over addition; and 0 and 1 continue to be the identity elements for addition and multiplication, respectively. Once children grasp the idea that the operations and structure already studied extend naturally to fractions, they have learned a great deal about the system of fractional numbers.

Approaches using regions, sets, and number lines, as well as Dienes Blocks, Cuisenaire rods, Stern rods, and other manipulative materials can help to develop students' understanding of operations on fractions. Locate and study manuals designed to help teachers instruct children using the above materials. Let's begin our study by examining the addition of fractional numbers.

The following figures illustrate the use of rectangular regions in modeling addition of fractional numbers. The fraction board (as illustrated in Unit 8) is an excellent device for children to use.

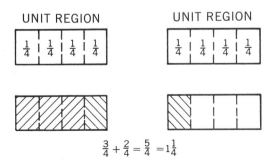

$$\tfrac{3}{4} + \tfrac{2}{4} = \tfrac{5}{4} = 1\tfrac{1}{4}$$

The two unit regions are both divided into fourths. Each smaller region therefore represents $\tfrac{1}{4}$. Suppose we want to add $\tfrac{3}{4}$ and $\tfrac{2}{4}$. To represent $\tfrac{3}{4}$ in the diagram we shade three of the smaller regions, and to represent $\tfrac{2}{4}$ we shade two more regions. This gives us a total of five regions that are shaded, each representing $\tfrac{1}{4}$. We can indicate four of these regions as $\tfrac{4}{4}$, which equals 1. And since the fifth region remaining represents $\tfrac{1}{4}$, we can represent the sum of the five shaded regions by the numeral $\tfrac{5}{4}$, that is, $\tfrac{4}{4} + \tfrac{1}{4}$ or $1\tfrac{1}{4}$.

Circular regions can also be used as models to illustrate addition of fractions. Consider the same example using circular regions as models. Using fraction kits, each child should model the example.

UNIT REGION   UNIT REGION

$\tfrac{3}{4}$ shaded $\tfrac{2}{4}$ shaded

The two circular regions above have been separated into fourths. Each small region then represents $\tfrac{1}{4}$ of the region. If we wish to add $\tfrac{3}{4}$ and $\tfrac{2}{4}$ we shade $\tfrac{3}{4}$ of one circular unit region and $\tfrac{2}{4}$ of a second circular region, then combine the shaded regions:

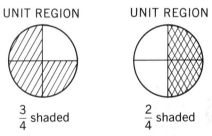

$$\tfrac{3}{4} + \tfrac{2}{4}$$
$$\left(\tfrac{3}{4} + \tfrac{1}{4}\right) + \tfrac{1}{4}$$
$$\left(\tfrac{4}{4}\right) + \tfrac{1}{4}$$
$$1 + \tfrac{1}{4} = 1\tfrac{1}{4}$$

Note that by moving one of the fourths to the first region, one complete unit can be made and $\tfrac{1}{4}$ of a unit is left. So the result of adding $\frac{3}{4}$ and $\frac{2}{4}$ must be $1\frac{1}{4}$.

This same example can also be illustrated with sets:

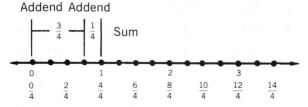

$$\frac{3}{4} + \frac{2}{4} = \frac{5}{4} = 1\frac{1}{4}$$

Each set of four elements represents a unit, 1, and each individual element represents $\frac{1}{4}$. To represent $\frac{3}{4}$ we draw a dotted line around three elements, and to represent $\frac{2}{4}$ we draw a dotted line around two more elements. This gives us a total of five elements that have been enclosed, and indicates a value of $\frac{5}{4}$ or $1\frac{1}{4}$. We can represent this by drawing a dotted line around all five elements, as shown previously.

We have used rectangular regions, circular regions, and sets to model addition of fractions; we can also use the number line. Remember that children have already modeled addition on the number line using whole numbers. We can use the number line to develop children's understanding of addition of fractions. Consider $\frac{3}{4} + \frac{1}{4} = \square$, for example.

Addend Addend

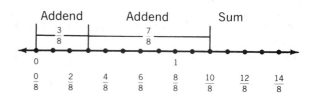

Children should have no difficulty finding the point on the number line that names $\frac{3}{4}$ and (since this is addition) jumping one-fourth of a unit to the right. To start at $\frac{3}{4}$ and jump one-fourth $\left(\frac{1}{4}\right)$ of a unit to the right puts us at the point labeled $\frac{4}{4}$. We know, of course, that $\frac{4}{4}$ is another name for 1, and therefore

$$\frac{3}{4} + \frac{1}{4} = \frac{4}{4} = 1$$

Some children may wonder about the example $\frac{1}{4} + \frac{3}{4} = \square$. They would start at $\frac{1}{4}$ and jump three-fourths $\left(\frac{3}{4}\right)$ of a unit to the right.

Addend   Addend

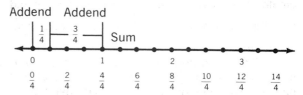

These children will write

$$\frac{1}{4} + \frac{3}{4} = \frac{4}{4} = 1$$

From these two examples some children might conclude that since $\frac{3}{4} + \frac{1}{4} = 1$ and $\frac{1}{4} + \frac{3}{4} = 1$, then $\frac{3}{4} + \frac{1}{4} = \frac{1}{4} + \frac{3}{4}$. This tends to confirm the commutative property for addition of fractional numbers. Here is an excellent chance for children to apply the basic structure that they have learned.

Consider this example: $\frac{3}{8} + \frac{7}{8} = \square$.

Locate $\frac{3}{8}$ on the number line; then jump, or count, $\frac{7}{8}$ unit (seven-eighths of a unit) to the right. This puts us at $\frac{10}{8}$. But $\frac{10}{8}$ has another name. We have passed the point named by 1 and moved another $\frac{2}{8}$ unit (two-eighths of a unit) to the right. Another name for $\frac{10}{8}$, then, is $1\frac{2}{8}$. But since $\frac{2}{8}$ can be renamed in simplest form as $\frac{1}{4}$, another name for $\frac{10}{8}$ is $1\frac{1}{4}$.

$$\frac{3}{8} + \frac{7}{8} = \frac{10}{8}$$
$$= \frac{8}{8} + \frac{2}{8}$$
$$= 1 + \frac{2}{8}$$
$$= 1 + \frac{1}{4}$$
$$= 1\frac{1}{4}$$

After many examples, children should be able to generalize: to add fractional numbers with like denominators, we add the numerators as we would add any pair of whole numbers and keep the same denominator. We may want, as in the preceding example, to express the sum as a mixed numeral and to write it in simplest form $\left(\frac{2}{8} = \frac{1}{4}\right)$ for greater convenience.

Children can discover how to add using mixed numerals while they are learning to add fractional numbers with like denominators. Consider the example $\frac{4}{3} + \frac{5}{3} = \square$.

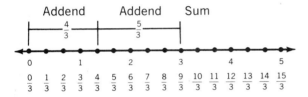

Locate $\frac{4}{3}$ on the number line; from this point jump $\frac{5}{3}$ units to the right. This puts us at the point named by $\frac{9}{3}$; so $\frac{4}{3} + \frac{5}{3} = \frac{9}{3}$. But this can also be expressed with mixed numerals: $1\frac{1}{3} + 1\frac{2}{3} = 3$, since $\frac{4}{3} = 1\frac{1}{3}$ and $\frac{5}{3} = 1\frac{2}{3}$ and $\frac{9}{3} = 3$. If we were given the example $1\frac{1}{3} + 1\frac{2}{3} = \square$, therefore, we could approach it by first translating it into fraction form, then solving it, and finally translating it back into mixed-numeral form. There is, however, a more direct method for solving examples written in mixed-numeral form. We know that $1\frac{1}{3}$ can be expressed as $1 + \frac{1}{3}$ and that $1\frac{2}{3}$ can be expressed as $1 + \frac{2}{3}$. Thus $1\frac{1}{3} + 1\frac{2}{3} = \square$ can be rewritten as $\left(1 + \frac{1}{3}\right) + \left(1 + \frac{2}{3}\right) = \square$. We can then solve the example as follows:

$$1\frac{1}{3} + 1\frac{2}{3} = \left(1 + \frac{1}{3}\right) + \left(1 + \frac{2}{3}\right) \quad \text{Renaming}$$

$$= (1 + 1) + \left(\frac{1}{3} + \frac{2}{3}\right) \quad \begin{array}{l}\text{Commutative and}\\\text{associative}\\\text{properties}\end{array}$$

$$= 2 + \frac{3}{3}$$

$$= 2 + 1$$

$$= 3$$

This written form illustrates how we want children to think of this example. Do not require children to write each of these steps. So we can add using mixed numerals by adding their whole-number parts separately $(1 + 1 = 2)$, then adding their fractional parts separately $\left(\frac{1}{3} + \frac{2}{3} = \frac{3}{3}\right)$, and, if necessary, rewriting the sum $\left(2 + \frac{3}{3} = 3\right)$.

Regions can also be used as models to help children understand how to add using mixed numerals. You can see that three one-thirds equals one unit. $\frac{4}{3}$ is $\frac{1}{3}$ more than a unit and $\frac{5}{3}$ is $\frac{2}{3}$ more than 1 unit. When put together there are 2 and $\frac{3}{3}$ or 3 units.

1 unit			1 unit			1 unit		
$\frac{1}{3}$	$\frac{1}{3}$	$\frac{1}{3}$	$\frac{1}{3}$	$\frac{1}{3}$	$\frac{1}{3}$	$\frac{1}{3}$	$\frac{1}{3}$	$\frac{1}{3}$

$$\frac{4}{3} \qquad + \qquad \frac{5}{3} \qquad = \frac{9}{3} = 3$$

Now you should experiment using circular regions as a model or using models of Cuisenaire rods, Dienes Blocks, or any other manipulative material. Children should be encouraged to experiment with different models.

Children have little difficulty adding fractions with like denominators. Addition of fractions with unlike denominators is much more difficult. Gradually move into unlike denominators by beginning with examples of unlike but related denominators. Examples of these would include $\frac{1}{3} + \frac{1}{6}$. In this case, one of the denominators is the common denominator. After children become proficient with unlike but related denominators, move on to unlike but *unrelated* denominators, such as $\frac{1}{3} + \frac{1}{4}$. Note that in this case neither denominator is the common denominator. Next, examples such as $\frac{1}{4} + \frac{1}{6}$ may be studied.

How can we add fractions when the denominators of the addends are unlike? Consider the example $\frac{1}{3} + \frac{5}{6} = \square$. Let's use a number-line model.

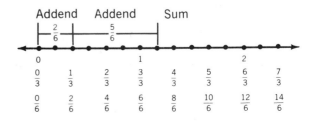

Locate $\frac{1}{3}$ on the number line. We can see that $\frac{1}{3}$ has another name, $\frac{2}{6}$. After locating $\frac{1}{3}$ (or $\frac{2}{6}$) we can add $\frac{5}{6}$ by moving $\frac{5}{6}$ unit to the right, which brings us to the point named by $\frac{7}{6}$. The fact that $\frac{1}{3}$ can be rewritten as $\frac{2}{6}$, which has the same denominator as $\frac{5}{6}$, should suggest another way of obtaining the sum $\frac{7}{6}$:

$$\frac{1}{3} + \frac{5}{6} = \frac{2}{6} + \frac{5}{6}$$
$$= \frac{7}{6} \left(\text{or } 1\frac{1}{6} \right)$$

1 unit		
$\frac{1}{3}$	$\frac{1}{3}$	$\frac{1}{3}$

$\frac{1}{6}$	$\frac{1}{6}$	$\frac{1}{6}$	$\frac{1}{6}$	$\frac{1}{6}$	$\frac{1}{6}$

The example $\frac{1}{3} + \frac{5}{6} = \square$ may also be modeled using rectangular regions. Separate the region into thirds and sixths, since those are the denominators of the two fractions to be added. The student can easily see that $\frac{2}{6}$ is another name for $\frac{1}{3}$. When one third is put with $\frac{5}{6}$ we see that we have $\frac{1}{6}$ more than one; thus we have $\frac{7}{6}$. This will be an easy step for children if many models have been used to develop a basic understanding of what rational numbers expressed as fractions really are. Understanding the generation of sets of fractions and renaming fractions is necessary also.

1 unit					
$\frac{1}{3}$	$\frac{1}{6}$	$\frac{1}{6}$	$\frac{1}{6}$	$\frac{1}{6}$	$\frac{1}{6}$

$$\frac{1}{3} \quad + \quad \frac{5}{6} \quad = \frac{7}{6} = 1\frac{1}{6}$$

We cannot stress too much the importance of developing understanding through models. If more emphasis is placed on developing an understanding of fractions, less time will be needed to develop an understanding of *operations* with fractions.

Experiment using circular regions as well.

In general, if two fractional addends have unlike denominators, we can rename one (or both) of the addends so that the denominators are the same and then find the sum in the usual manner. In very simple examples it is usually easy to see how to use this procedure. In less simple examples we must use a more complicated procedure, which will be discussed presently.

After studying equivalent fractions, children should not have difficulty with addition of fractions having unlike denominators. They can apply knowledge they already have. The only new idea they should discover is that in addition of fractions, the fractions naming the numbers must have like denominators.

Consider $\frac{1}{3} + \frac{1}{6} = \square$.

$$\frac{1}{3} + \frac{1}{6} = \frac{2}{6} + \frac{1}{6} \left(\text{since } \frac{1 \times 2}{3 \times 2} = \frac{2}{6} \right)$$
$$= \frac{3}{6}$$

We would prefer to express our answer, $\frac{3}{6}$, in simplest form, usually the most convenient way to name fractions. Reviewing simplest form briefly, we know from number-line models that $\frac{3}{6} = \frac{1}{2}$. At this point of development you may wish to review simplifying fractions and renaming fractions using the identity element of multiplication. We can multiply the numerator and the denominator by the same factor without changing the value of the fractional number. (Remember that the factor cannot be 0.) The inverse of this is also true. The numerator and denominator can be divided by the same nonzero number without changing the value of the fractional number; thus

$$\frac{3}{6} = \frac{3 \div 3}{6 \div 3} = \frac{1}{2}$$

Now let us consider addition of unlike and unrelated fractions. How can we add $\frac{1}{4}$ and $\frac{1}{3}$? Begin with models to help children understand why a common denominator is necessary and how a common denominator can be found. If circular regions are used as models, we can place $\frac{1}{4}$ of a circle with $\frac{1}{3}$ of a circle, but the children probably do not know what the name of the new region is.

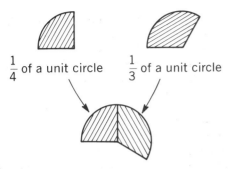

$\frac{1}{4}$ of a unit circle $\quad$ $\frac{1}{3}$ of a unit circle

What part of a circular region is this?

By placing other parts of circular regions on top of these two regions, children should discover that twelfths would fit. After much experimentation, children should develop a systematic technique to solve examples of this type.

Before fractional numbers like $\frac{1}{4}$ and $\frac{1}{3}$ can be added (or subtracted), a common denominator must be found. Since a common denominator must be divisible by each of the two original denominators, it must be a multiple of each of the denominators. In the case of $\frac{1}{4} + \frac{1}{3} = \square$, the common denominators are 12, 24, 36, 48, or any multiple of 12. Any one of these common denominators could be used in adding the two fractional numbers; however, it is usually convenient to use the **least common denominator (LCD),** 12 in this case.

Finding the least common denominator is actually a process of finding the **least common multiple (LCM)** of the denominators. When the least common multiple is used as a common denominator, it is usually easier for us to express our answer in lowest terms so that we work with smaller numbers.

Consider the example suggested above, $\frac{1}{4} + \frac{1}{3}$.

The easiest and most direct method of determining the least common multiple (LCM) is by factoring the denominators completely—that is, by factoring them into prime factors:

$$\frac{1}{4} = \frac{1}{2 \times 2}$$
$$\frac{1}{3} = \frac{1}{3}$$

The least common multiple (LCM) can be constructed from the prime factorizations of the denominators. First, the LCM must have 2×2 as a factor in order to be a multiple of 4:

$$\text{LCM} = 2 \times 2 \times ?$$

The 2×2 ensures that the LCM is divisible by 4, and the question mark indicates that there may be other factors. Next, we know that the LCM must contain the factor 3 to be divisible by 3:

$$\text{LCM} = 2 \times 2 \times 3$$

Now it is apparent that the number we have constructed is divisible by both 4 and 3. Consequently, $2 \times 2 \times 3$, or 12, is the least common multiple and hence the least common denominator.

The least common multiple is always built by factoring the denominators completely and then finding the least number that is a multiple of both denominators. Let's consider another example:

$$\frac{1}{6} + \frac{1}{8} + \frac{1}{3} = \square$$

Factor the denominators completely:

$$\frac{1}{6} = \frac{1}{2 \times 3} \qquad \frac{1}{8} = \frac{1}{2 \times 2 \times 2} \qquad \frac{1}{3} = \frac{1}{3}$$

Now build the least common multiple of 6, 8, and 3. The LCM must contain 2×3 to be divisible by 6:

$$\text{LCM} = 2 \times 3 \times ?$$

It must also contain $2 \times 2 \times 2$ to be divisible by 8. That is, the LCM must contain 2 as a factor three times. But since we have already recorded 2 as a factor once (LCM = $2 \times 3 \times ?$), it is necessary to record it only twice more for the LCM to accommodate 8:

$$\text{LCM} = 2 \times 3 \times 2 \times 2 \times ?$$

Finally, the LCM must contain the factor 3 so that it can be divided by 3. But 3 has already been indicated as a factor (LCM = $2 \times 3 \times 2 \times 2 \times ?$), so it doesn't have to be recorded again. Thus we have identified the LCM as

$$2 \times 3 \times 2 \times 2 = 24$$

The basic structure that we have studied shows that multiplying a number by the identity element for multiplication (1) does not change the value of the number ($a \times 1 = a$). We have also learned how to name 1 by using fractions such as $\frac{2}{2}, \frac{3}{3}, \frac{4}{4}, \frac{5}{5}$, and $\frac{6}{6}$.

Therefore any fraction can be multiplied by an equivalent value of 1 (any fraction whose numerator and denominator are identical other than 0) without changing the value of the fraction. With this in mind, let's return to our original example and find the sum.

$$\frac{1}{6} + \frac{1}{8} + \frac{1}{3} = \square$$

$$\frac{1}{6} = \frac{\square}{24} \longrightarrow \frac{1 \times \square}{6 \times \square} = \frac{\square}{24} \longrightarrow \frac{1 \times 4}{6 \times 4} = \frac{4}{24}$$

$$\frac{1}{8} = \frac{\square}{24} \longrightarrow \frac{1 \times \square}{8 \times \square} = \frac{\square}{24} \longrightarrow \frac{1 \times 3}{8 \times 3} = \frac{3}{24}$$

$$\frac{1}{3} = \frac{\square}{24} \longrightarrow \frac{1 \times \square}{3 \times \square} = \frac{\square}{24} \longrightarrow \frac{1 \times 8}{3 \times 8} = \frac{8}{24}$$

We have now found equivalent fractions for each fraction in the original example. Since these new fractions have a common denominator, we can easily find the sum by adding their numerators.

$$\frac{4}{24} + \frac{3}{24} + \frac{8}{24} = \frac{15}{24}$$

$$\frac{15}{24} = \frac{15 \div 3}{24 \div 3} = \frac{5}{8}$$

Now let's consider another example: $\frac{3}{8} + \frac{5}{6} = \square$. First we must find the least common denominator for $\frac{3}{8}$ and $\frac{5}{6}$, that is, the least common multiple (LCM) of 8 and 6:

$$\frac{3}{8} = \frac{3}{2 \times 2 \times 2}$$

$$\frac{5}{6} = \frac{5}{2 \times 3}$$

LCM $= 2 \times 2 \times 2 \times$?	(The LCM is divisible by 8.)
LCM $= 2 \times 2 \times 2 \times 3$	(The LCM is also divisible
LCM $= 24$	by 6.)

Then we must rename $\frac{3}{8}$ and $\frac{5}{6}$ as fractions having the common denominator 24.

$$\frac{3}{8} = \frac{\square}{24}$$

$$\frac{3}{8} \times 1 = \frac{\square}{24} \qquad \text{What equivalent fraction can we use for 1?}$$

$$\frac{3}{8} \times \frac{3}{3} = \frac{9}{24} \qquad \text{We can use } \frac{3}{3}, \text{ to make the denominator 24.}$$

$$\frac{5}{6} = \frac{\square}{24}$$

$$\frac{5}{6} \times 1 = \frac{\square}{24} \qquad \text{What equivalent fraction can we use for 1 this time? We can}$$

$$\frac{5}{6} \times \frac{4}{4} = \frac{20}{24} \qquad \text{use } \frac{4}{4}. \text{ The denominator is then 24.}$$

Now we can add:

$$\frac{3}{8} + \frac{5}{6} = \frac{9}{24} + \frac{20}{24}$$

$$= \frac{29}{24}$$

$$= \left(\frac{24}{24} + \frac{5}{24} \right)$$

$$= 1 + \frac{5}{24} \text{ or } 1\frac{5}{24}$$

The concept of finding common denominators must be extended to mixed numerals. Begin with examples like $1\frac{1}{2} + \frac{1}{3}$; then move to examples with two mixed numerals, such as $1\frac{1}{2} + 4\frac{1}{3}$. Then move to examples that will require renaming, such as $3\frac{4}{5} + 2\frac{3}{4}$.

Subtraction of fractions can be introduced shortly after beginning addition of fractions. Regions, sets, and number lines may be used as models for subtraction, as well as addition. The children should manipulate the pieces in their fraction kits, or pieces from the fraction board, before attempting to use the more abstract number line.

Let's model the example $\frac{3}{4} - \frac{1}{4} = \square$ using regions. The unit has been separated into fourths and we begin with three one-fourths. One-fourth may be taken away from the $\frac{3}{4}$, leaving $\frac{2}{4}$. Another name for $\frac{2}{4}$ is $\frac{1}{2}$.

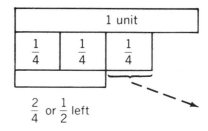

$\frac{2}{4}$ or $\frac{1}{2}$ left

Through use of the number line (using whole numbers), children should know that subtraction is the inverse operation of addition and that we can use the number line to model subtraction.

Consider this example:

$$\frac{3}{4} - \frac{1}{4} = \square$$

We could also use the idea that subtraction is the inverse of addition and rewrite the subtraction example $\frac{3}{4} - \frac{1}{4} = \square$ as $\frac{1}{4} + \square = \frac{3}{4}$. The addition example can then be solved on the number line as follows:

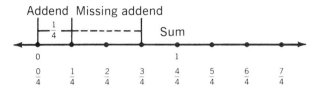

Therefore $\square = \frac{2}{4} = \frac{1}{2}$; so $\frac{3}{4} - \frac{1}{4} = \frac{1}{2}$.

Notice that $\frac{2}{4}$ is renamed as $\frac{1}{2}$. This is possible because $\frac{2}{4}$ and $\frac{1}{2}$ are equivalent fractions. We rename $\frac{2}{4}$ as $\frac{1}{2}$ in order to express the answer in simplest form.

After working through a great many examples such as this, children should be able to make some generalizations about subtraction of fractions:

1. In order to subtract fractional numbers, we must represent them by fractions having like denominators.
2. The numerators are then subtracted in the same way that whole numbers are subtracted.
3. The denominator of the difference is the same as the common denominator found in step 1.
4. The answer is usually written in simplest form for convenience.

Now consider another example, $\frac{5}{8} - \frac{3}{8} = \square$.

Again using the idea that subtraction is the inverse of addition, we can think of $\frac{5}{8}$ as the sum and $\frac{3}{8}$ as the addend. What is the missing addend? The example could be rewritten $\frac{3}{8} + \square = \frac{5}{8}$. The example can then be modeled on the number line as follows:

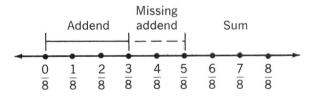

We find that the missing addend is $\frac{2}{8}$. Another name for this point is $\frac{1}{4}$. (Notice that $\frac{2}{8}$, in simplest form, is $\frac{1}{4}$, or $\frac{2 \div 2}{8 \div 2} = \frac{1}{4}$.) Therefore $\frac{5}{8} - \frac{3}{8} = \frac{2}{8} = \frac{1}{4}$. The region model can be used to find the missing addend also.

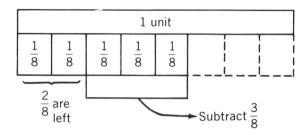

If we begin with $\frac{5}{8}$ and take away $\frac{3}{8}$, we find $\frac{2}{8}$ are left; $\frac{2}{8}$ can be renamed as $\frac{1}{4}$.

Use circular regions and see if you can solve $\frac{5}{8} - \frac{3}{8}$. Try using sets and see if you can model $\frac{5}{8} - \frac{3}{8}$.

Can we find a way to subtract $\frac{7}{8}$ from $\frac{19}{8}$?

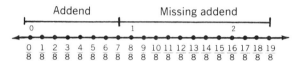

Mark the addend $\frac{7}{8}$ and then locate the sum $\frac{19}{8}$. The missing addend is $\frac{12}{8}$, but another name for $\frac{12}{8}$ is $\frac{3}{2}$, that is, $\frac{12 \div 4}{8 \div 4} = \frac{3}{2}$ of $1\frac{1}{2}$. Can you also use regions to model this example?

$$\frac{19}{8} - \frac{7}{8} = \frac{12}{8}$$
$$= \frac{3}{2} \text{ or } 1\frac{1}{2}$$

Children should apply their basic knowledge of addition to the subtraction of fractions to discover how a problem such as the following can be solved: $\frac{7}{8} - \frac{3}{4} = \square$. They should recall that fractions must have like denominators before computation (addition or subtraction) can be performed. One of the fractions must therefore be renamed. We can rename $\frac{3}{4}$ as $\frac{6}{8}$. The example can now be solved.

$$\frac{7}{8} - \frac{3}{4} = \frac{7}{8} - \frac{6}{8}$$
$$= \frac{1}{8}$$

The example, of course, can also be solved using the number line as a model:

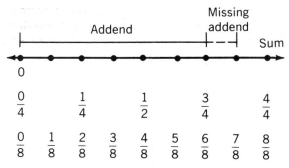

Again, the answer is clearly $\frac{1}{8}$.

Now let's consider a slightly more complex example:

$$\frac{11}{12} - \frac{5}{8} = \square$$

By applying their knowledge of least common multiples, children should be able to factor both denominators and find the LCM:

$$\frac{11}{12} = \frac{11}{2 \times 2 \times 3}$$

$$\frac{5}{8} = \frac{5}{2 \times 2 \times 2}$$

Then they should build the LCM by using the factors of 12 and 8. The least common denominator is thus shown to be $2 \times 2 \times 3 \times 2$, or 24. Finally they should rename $\frac{11}{12}$ and $\frac{5}{8}$ and perform the indicated subtraction:

$$\frac{11}{12} = \frac{11 \times 2}{12 \times 2} = \frac{22}{24}$$

$$\frac{5}{8} = \frac{5 \times 3}{8 \times 3} = \frac{15}{24}$$

$$\frac{22}{24} - \frac{15}{24} = \frac{7}{24}$$

Each of these subtraction examples can also be solved by using regions or sets. Let's demonstrate the region and set approaches to solving the example $\frac{7}{8} - \frac{7}{16} = \square$.

Consider the following unit region, which has been divided into 16 parts (subregions) to illustrate eighths and sixteenths.

UNIT REGION

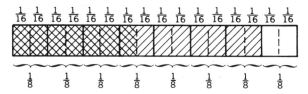

We can represent $\frac{7}{8}$ by shading seven of the eight regions that illustrate eighths. And we can represent $\frac{7}{16}$ by shading seven of the sixteen regions that illustrate sixteenths. In order to represent $\frac{7}{8} - \frac{7}{16}$, however, the shaded region indicating $\frac{7}{16}$ must be entirely contained within the shaded region indicating $\frac{7}{8}$ (because we are subtracting $\frac{7}{16}$ from $\frac{7}{8}$), so the region indicating $\frac{7}{8}$ and $\frac{7}{16}$ must be shaded differently:

UNIT REGION

In the unit region above, the difference between $\frac{7}{8}$ and $\frac{7}{16}$ is indicated by that part of the region shaded only once. This region contains seven smaller regions illustrating sixteenths; therefore it represents $\frac{7}{16}$. So $\frac{7}{8} - \frac{7}{16} = \frac{7}{16}$.

Now let's approach this example using sets. Consider the set of 16 elements pictured below.

If this set represents one unit, then each individual element represents $\frac{1}{16}$ unit, and each column of elements represents $\frac{1}{8}$. Now, if we enclose seven of the eight columns with a ring, the 14 enclosed elements illustrate the fractional number $\frac{7}{8}$. And if we draw another ring round 7 of these elements (already enclosed), we illustrate $\frac{7}{16}$ (since there are 16 elements in the entire set and 7 of them are enclosed by this second ring). The difference between $\frac{7}{8}$ and $\frac{7}{16}$, is indicated by all those elements enclosed by the first ring but not by the second. In the following figure, these elements are shaded.

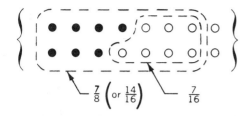

$$\frac{7}{8} \left(\text{or } \frac{14}{16} \right) \qquad \frac{7}{16}$$

Since there are 7 elements shaded (out of a total of 16 elements in the set) and since each of the elements represents $\frac{1}{16}$, the difference between $\frac{7}{8}$ and $\frac{7}{16}$ is clearly $\frac{7}{16}$, or $\frac{7}{8} - \frac{7}{16} = \frac{7}{16}$.

Often we need to work with mixed numerals as well as ordinary fractions. For example, solve $5\frac{7}{8} - 4\frac{5}{8} = \square$. It is not difficult to extend our understanding of subtraction to include mixed numerals. Our approach here is very similar to that used for addition with mixed numerals:

$$
\begin{aligned}
5\frac{7}{8} &= & 5 + \frac{7}{8} \\
- 4\frac{5}{8} &= & - \left(4 + \frac{5}{8} \right) \\
\hline
& & 1 + \frac{2}{8} \\
&= & 1 + \frac{1}{4} \\
&= & 1\frac{1}{4}
\end{aligned}
$$

Note that with the two + signs, one in front of the $\frac{7}{8}$ and one in front of the $\frac{5}{8}$, children are likely to subtract the whole numbers and add the fractions. Call their attention to the parentheses and explain that both the whole numbers and the fractions must be subtracted.

We write the mixed numerals as the sum of whole numbers and fractional numbers. Then we subtract whole numbers to obtain the whole-number difference, and fractional numbers to obtain the fractional-number difference. Notice that we write the fractional-number difference in simplest form.

In subtraction with mixed numerals, it is important to develop an understanding of renaming. For instance, consider the following subtraction example:

$$
\begin{aligned}
& 3\frac{1}{4} \\
- & 2\frac{3}{4}
\end{aligned}
$$

Even though the fractions already have a common denominator, we cannot subtract the numerators. Therefore we must find another way of expressing $3\frac{1}{4}$ so that we can subtract.

$$
\begin{aligned}
3\frac{1}{4} &= 3 + \frac{1}{4} \\
&= (2 + 1) + \frac{1}{4} \\
&= \left(2 + \frac{4}{4} \right) + \frac{1}{4} \\
&= 2 + \left(\frac{4}{4} + \frac{1}{4} \right) \\
&= 2 + \frac{5}{4} \\
&= 2\frac{5}{4}
\end{aligned}
$$

By renaming 3 as $2 + 1$ and expressing 1 as $\frac{4}{4}$, we can rewrite $3\frac{1}{4}$ as $2\frac{5}{4}$ and proceed.

$$
\begin{aligned}
3\frac{1}{4} &= & 2\frac{5}{4} \\
- 2\frac{3}{4} &= & - 2\frac{3}{4} \\
\hline
& & \frac{2}{4} = \frac{1}{2}
\end{aligned}
$$

Another example of this kind is $8\frac{1}{6} - 3\frac{5}{6} = \square$.

$$
\begin{aligned}
8\frac{1}{6} &= & 8 + \frac{1}{6} &= 7 + \left(\frac{6}{6} + \frac{1}{6} \right) = & 7 + \frac{7}{6} \\
- 3\frac{5}{6} &= & - \left(3 + \frac{5}{6} \right) = & - \left(3 + \frac{5}{6} \right) = & - \left(3 + \frac{5}{6} \right) \\
\hline
& & & & 4 + \frac{2}{6} \\
& & & = & 4 + \frac{1}{3} \\
& & & = & 4\frac{1}{3}
\end{aligned}
$$

Now let's examine another example:

$$
\begin{aligned}
& 7\frac{3}{8} \\
- & 2\frac{3}{4}
\end{aligned}
$$

First we must obtain a common denominator. Since $\frac{3}{4} = \frac{6}{8}$, we can rename $2\frac{3}{4}$ as $2\frac{6}{8}$:

$$
\begin{aligned}
7\frac{3}{8} &= & 7\frac{3}{8} \\
- 2\frac{3}{4} &= & - 2\frac{6}{8}
\end{aligned}
$$

Now we must find another way to name $7\frac{3}{8}$, since we cannot subtract the numerators (6 from 3):

$$7\frac{3}{8} = 7 + \frac{3}{8}$$
$$= \left(6 + 1\right) + \frac{3}{8}$$
$$= \left(6 + \frac{8}{8}\right) + \frac{3}{8}$$
$$= 6 + \left(\frac{8}{8} + \frac{3}{8}\right)$$
$$= 6 + \frac{11}{8}$$
$$= 6\frac{11}{8}$$

Now we can solve the example:

$$6\frac{11}{8} - 2\frac{6}{8} = 4\frac{5}{8}$$

In general, the difference between two fractions named by mixed numerals can be determined in the following way.

1. Find a common denominator for the fractional-number parts, if necessary.
2. Rewrite the first mixed numeral, if necessary, so that the numerators of the fractional-number parts can be subtracted.
3. Find the difference between the whole-number parts of the two numbers.
4. Find the difference between the fractional-number parts of the two numbers.
5. Express the difference in simplest form.

The number line, physical models, and sets have been utilized to develop the operations of addition and subtraction with respect to fractional numbers. We must emphasize that we are not teaching new ideas. Rather we are helping children to discover how to apply the operations and basic structure they have already learned about whole-number operations to a new situation: operations with fractions.

Study the following models and note that the number line and regions support the commutative property of addition as it applies to fractions.

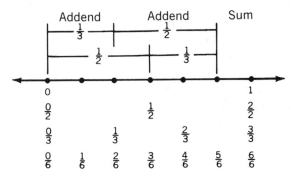

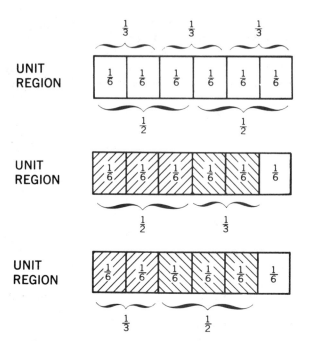

After examining many examples we can generalize that $\frac{a}{b} + \frac{c}{d} = \frac{c}{d} + \frac{a}{b}$. We have carefully demonstrated that fractional numbers are commutative with respect to the fundamental operation of addition. But what about the operation of subtraction? Let's consider the example $\frac{1}{2} - \frac{1}{3} = \Box$.

$$\frac{1}{2} - \frac{1}{3} = \frac{3}{6} - \frac{2}{6}$$
$$= \frac{1}{6}$$

The difference is clearly $\frac{1}{6}$. But the solution to $\frac{1}{3} - \frac{1}{2} = \Box$ is very definitely not $\frac{1}{6}$.

$$\frac{1}{3} - \frac{1}{2} = \frac{2}{6} - \frac{3}{6}$$
$$= ?$$

Consequently, $\frac{1}{2} - \frac{1}{3} \neq \frac{1}{3} - \frac{1}{2}$. We must conclude from this counterexample that fractions are not commutative with respect to subtraction.

In our study of the whole numbers we explored the concept of **associativity** as well as commutativity. We discovered that whole numbers are associative with respect to the operation of addition—that is, we can combine (or associate) addends in any way we choose without altering the value of the sum. For example, $(1 + 2) + 4 = 1 + (2 + 4)$. The whole numbers are not, however, associative with respect to subtraction. For example, $(9 - 5) - 2 \neq 9 - (5 - 2)$.

Now let's find out whether or not fractions are associative with respect to addition and subtraction. If we are given any three fractions, we know that their sum can be expressed as the sum of three numerators over a common denominator. For example, $\left(\frac{5}{2} + \frac{3}{2}\right) + \frac{1}{2}$ can be expressed as $\frac{(5+3)+1}{2}$:

$$\left(\frac{5}{2} + \frac{3}{2}\right) + \frac{1}{2} = \left(\frac{5+3}{2}\right) + \frac{1}{2}$$
$$= \frac{(5+3)}{2} + \frac{1}{2}$$
$$= \frac{(5+3)+1}{2}$$

But we know that $\frac{(5+3)+1}{2}$ is another name for $\frac{5+(3+1)}{2}$, since $(5+3)+1 = 5+(3+1)$, and that $\frac{5+(3+1)}{2}$ is equal to $\frac{5}{2} + \left(\frac{3}{2} + \frac{1}{2}\right)$:

$$\frac{5+(3+1)}{2} = \frac{5}{2} + \frac{(3+1)}{2}$$
$$= \frac{5}{2} + \left(\frac{3+1}{2}\right)$$
$$= \frac{5}{2} + \left(\frac{3}{2} + \frac{1}{2}\right)$$

Clearly, $\left(\frac{5}{2} + \frac{3}{2}\right) + \frac{1}{2} = \frac{5}{2} + \left(\frac{3}{2} + \frac{1}{2}\right)$. Fractional numbers, then, are associative with respect to addition, since this relation can be demonstrated for any three fractional addends in any order.

The associative property of the fractional numbers under addition can be illustrated by using a number line. Let's consider the preceding example.

The set of fractions can be shown to be associative under addition by means of regions, too. Let's examine the example above using regions.

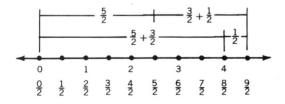

UNIT REGIONS (5)

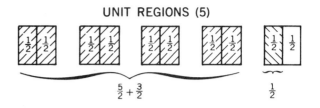

UNIT REGIONS (5)

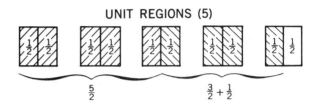

After looking at more examples, we can generalize the associative property for addition of fractions as:

$$\left(\frac{a}{b} + \frac{c}{d}\right) + \frac{e}{f} = \frac{a}{b} + \left(\frac{c}{d} + \frac{e}{f}\right)$$

We have now shown in several ways that fractions are associative with respect to the fundamental operation of addition. But what about subtraction? Let's consider the example $\frac{6}{7} - \frac{3}{7} - \frac{2}{7} = \square$. This example can be interpreted in either of two ways, depending upon how we associate the fractional numbers.

$$\left(\frac{6}{7} - \frac{3}{7}\right) - \frac{2}{7} = \frac{3}{7} - \frac{2}{7} = \frac{1}{7}$$

or

$$\frac{6}{7} - \left(\frac{3}{7} - \frac{2}{7}\right) = \frac{6}{7} - \frac{1}{7} = \frac{5}{7}$$

Most certainly the way in which we group (or associate) the numerals in order to perform the necessary operations does make a difference. If we work the example one way, associating the $\frac{6}{7}$ and the $\frac{3}{7}$ first, we get $\frac{1}{7}$ for an answer. But if we work the example the other way, associating the $\frac{3}{7}$ and the $\frac{2}{7}$ first, we get an answer of $\frac{5}{7}$. Obviously, $\left(\frac{6}{7} - \frac{3}{7}\right) - \frac{2}{7} \neq \frac{6}{7} - \left(\frac{3}{7} - \frac{2}{7}\right)$. This counterexample proves that fractions are not associative under subtraction.

What about 0, the **identity element for addition?** In working with the whole numbers, we discovered that the sum of any whole number and 0 is always that whole number. But what about 0 when we are working with fractions? Since 0 can be expressed as a fraction simply by using 0 for the numerator and any counting number for the denominator, and since fractions are added by adding their numerators (provided they have been named with common denominators), it is clear that fractions are not changed by the addition of 0. For example, consider $\frac{13}{5} + 0$.

$$\frac{13}{5} + 0 = \frac{13}{5} + \frac{0}{5}$$
$$= \frac{13 + 0}{5}$$
$$= \frac{13}{5}$$

So it is evident that 0 is the identity element for addition when we are working with the set of fractions, as well as when we are working with the set of whole numbers.

In this unit we have examined the fundamental operations of addition and subtraction with respect to fractions. We have also looked at the basic properties of fractions with respect to these two operations. Now let's consider multiplication of fractions. Begin with examples in which a fraction is multiplied by a whole number. Children should work with a variety of models.

Multiplication of whole numbers, with which children are familiar, always results in a product that is either equal to or greater than either factor. When children begin to apply the operation of multiplication to fractional numbers, they will, for the first time, find that a product can be less than both factors.

Look at the number line below and the example $3 \times \frac{1}{4} = \square$.

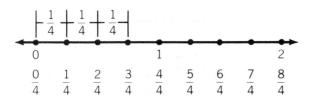

If we start at the point named 0 and make three jumps to the right, each jump $\frac{1}{4}$ of a unit in length, where do we land? We land at the point named $\frac{3}{4}$. By using the number line in this way, we can show the product of $3 \times \frac{1}{4}$ to be $\frac{3}{4}$.

$$3 \times \frac{1}{4} = \frac{3}{4}$$

This example can also be written

$$\frac{3}{1} \times \frac{1}{4} = \frac{3}{4}$$

Now let's look at another example:

$$6 \times \frac{2}{3} = \square$$

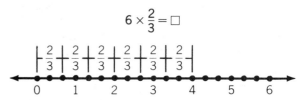

On the number line we can model $6 \times \frac{2}{3}$ with six line segments, each $\frac{2}{3}$ of a unit in length, placed end to end. In doing so we find that the resulting line segment is 4 units long. Thus the product of 6 and $\frac{2}{3}$ is shown to be 4:

$$6 \times \frac{2}{3} = \frac{2}{3} + \frac{2}{3} + \frac{2}{3} + \frac{2}{3} + \frac{2}{3} + \frac{2}{3}$$
$$= \frac{12}{3}$$
$$= \frac{12 \div 3}{3 \div 3}$$
$$= \frac{4}{1} \text{ or } 4$$

On the same number line we can also show $\frac{2}{3} \times 6$. This is pictured as $\frac{2}{3}$ of a line segment 6 units long. If the segment from 0 to 6 is divided into three parts, each 2 units long, $\frac{2}{3} \times 6$ is represented by two of these parts:

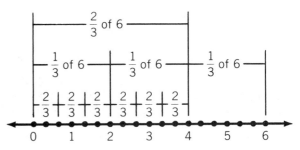

In this way the **commutative property of multiplication** is clearly illustrated:

$$6 \times \frac{2}{3} = \frac{2}{3} \times 6$$

The number line can be used as a teaching aid, without undue difficulty, to illustrate examples in which one factor is a whole number. The number line is not the best model, however, to explain situations in which neither factor can be written as a whole number—for example, $\frac{2}{3} \times \frac{4}{5} = \square$ and $\frac{7}{21} \times \frac{2}{9} = \square$. To illustrate examples like these we can use regions.

To explore the way in which regions are used to illustrate multiplication of fractional numbers, let's look at the example $6 \times \frac{2}{3} = \square$ again.

UNIT REGION

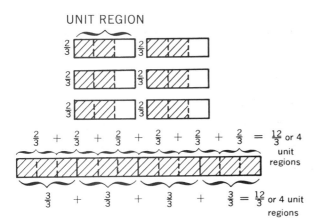

$$\frac{2}{3} + \frac{2}{3} + \frac{2}{3} + \frac{2}{3} + \frac{2}{3} + \frac{2}{3} = \frac{12}{3} \text{ or } 4 \text{ unit regions}$$

$$\frac{3}{3} + \frac{3}{3} + \frac{3}{3} + \frac{3}{3} = \frac{12}{3} \text{ or } 4 \text{ unit regions}$$

This illustration indicates the way in which multiplication can be modeled as repeated, or successive, addition:

$$6 \times \frac{2}{3} = \frac{2}{3} + \frac{2}{3} + \frac{2}{3} + \frac{2}{3} + \frac{2}{3} + \frac{2}{3}$$
$$= \frac{12}{3} \text{ or } 4$$

We can count the number of shaded parts (one-thirds) and see that there are 12 one-thirds, $\frac{12}{3}$. Another name for $\frac{12}{3}$ we know is 4:

$$\frac{12}{3} = \frac{3}{3} + \frac{3}{3} + \frac{3}{3} + \frac{3}{3}$$
$$= 1 + 1 + 1 + 1$$
$$= 4$$

Another valuable device to teach multiplication of fractions is a **unit square** (a square with each side one unit long). The unit square may be subdivided into smaller squares. Let us examine the several models drawn below.

UNIT SQUARES

This unit square is divided into 100 smaller squares.

This unit square is divided into 144 smaller squares.

By placing a colored rubber band around a unit card, you can illustrate $\frac{1}{2}$ of the card, $\frac{1}{4}$ of the card, or whatever fraction you choose. Using rubber bands and the unit card, let's consider this example:

$$\frac{1}{2} \times \frac{1}{3} = N$$

First we construct a unit square.

UNIT SQUARE

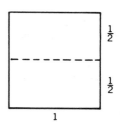

Next we divide the unit square horizontally into halves:

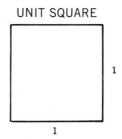

Then we divide the unit square vertically into thirds:

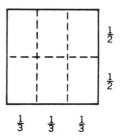

Examining the unit square, we see that it has been partitioned into 6 congruent regions. To show the result of $\frac{1}{2} \times \frac{1}{3}$, we shade any $\frac{1}{3}$ of the unit square (shading one way) and then either the lower (or upper) $\frac{1}{2}$ of the unit square (shading another way).

By observation we can see that there is one part of the unit square that has been shaded twice. The double-shaded region indicates the product of $\frac{1}{2}$ and $\frac{1}{3}$:

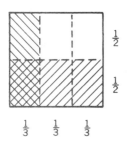

Comparing the double-shaded region with the total square, we see that 1 of the 6 parts (smaller regions) has been shaded twice. This leads us to the conclusion that $\frac{1}{2} \times \frac{1}{3} = \frac{1}{6}$. The same diagram, or one similar to the following, can be used to illustrate $\frac{1}{3} \times \frac{1}{2} = \frac{1}{6}$.

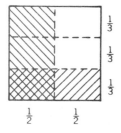

This is another illustration of the commutative property of multiplication.

Now let's see how we can use the same reasoning to find the product of two fractions whose values are both greater than 1:

$$\frac{3}{2} \times \frac{4}{3} = n$$

First we construct a unit square, dividing the square horizontally into halves and vertically into thirds. We divide the square into halves and thirds because they are the fractional parts being considered (indicated by the denominators) in this particular example.

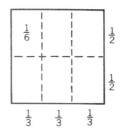

Notice that the square is now divided into 6 congruent parts. Since we have established our unit square, we can extend it horizontally and vertically to form a region that is $\frac{3}{2}$ by $\frac{4}{3}$ in size. We do this

because $\frac{3}{2}$ and $\frac{4}{3}$ are the two factors being considered.

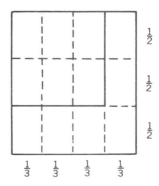

Again, notice that each small region is actually $\frac{1}{6}$ of a unit square. In this case we have more small regions than are necessary to make up 1 unit square. In fact, there are 12 small regions, or $\frac{12}{6}$ of a unit square. Since $\frac{12}{6}$ is another name for 2, we can see that there are actually enough small regions to complete two unit squares. Consequently, $\frac{3}{2} \times \frac{4}{3} = \frac{12}{6} = 2$.

After children have solved many examples of this kind and have developed an understanding of multiplication of fractions, the familiar algorithm for multiplying fractions should be introduced. Children should be led to see that in multiplying two fractions, the numerators of the two factors can be multiplied to obtain the numerator of the product and the denominators of the two factors can be multiplied to obtain the denominator of the product. The last two examples can be solved using this algorithm:

$$\frac{1}{2} \times \frac{1}{3} = \frac{1 \times 1}{2 \times 3} = \frac{1}{6}$$
$$\frac{3}{2} \times \frac{4}{3} = \frac{3 \times 4}{2 \times 3} = \frac{12}{6} \text{ (or 2)}$$

In each case we get the same answer that we obtained by using regions. Notice that after we have determined the numerator and denominator of the product, we may wish to rewrite the product in another form (as an equivalent fraction or as a whole number, for example). In the second example above, the product $\frac{12}{6}$ can be rewritten as 2. Since whole numbers and fractional numbers named by mixed numerals can be expressed in fraction form, we can find the product of any two fractional numbers by means of the algorithm.

$$6 \times \frac{2}{3} = \frac{6}{1} \times \frac{2}{3}$$

$$= \frac{6 \times 2}{1 \times 3}$$

$$= \frac{12}{3} \text{ (or 4)}$$

$$2\frac{1}{2} \times \frac{1}{3} = \frac{5}{2} \times \frac{1}{3}$$

$$= \frac{5 \times 1}{2 \times 3}$$

$$= \frac{5}{6}$$

$$3 \times \frac{1}{4} = \frac{3}{1} \times \frac{1}{4}$$

$$= \frac{3 \times 1}{1 \times 4}$$

$$= \frac{3}{4}$$

$$2 \times 5 = \frac{2}{1} \times \frac{5}{1}$$

$$= \frac{2 \times 5}{1 \times 1}$$

$$= \frac{10}{1} \text{ (or 10)}$$

We can now generalize that to multiply any two fractions (whole numbers are understood as having the denominator 1), the following steps should be performed.

1. Multiply the numerators of the factors to obtain the numerator of the product.
2. Multiply the denominators of the factors to obtain the denominator of the product.
3. If desired, rename the product (as an equivalent fraction or whole-number numeral, for example).

If $\frac{a}{b}$ and $\frac{c}{d}$ are any two fractions such that $b \neq 0$ and $d \neq 0$, then

$$\frac{a}{b} \times \frac{c}{d} = \frac{a \times c}{b \times d}$$

After completing a multiplication example, it is necessary to simplify the product. For instance

$$\frac{2}{3} \times \frac{3}{4} = \frac{2 \times 3}{3 \times 4} = \frac{6}{12} = \frac{1 \times 6}{2 \times 6} = \frac{1}{2}$$

It is much easier if the example is simplified before multiplying. Consider the example $\frac{2}{3} \times \frac{3}{4}$ again.

$$\frac{2}{3} \times \frac{3}{4} = \frac{2 \times 3}{3 \times 2 \times 2} \qquad \text{factor}$$

$$= \frac{3 \times 2 \times 1}{3 \times 2 \times 2} \qquad \text{rewrite}$$

$$= \frac{3}{3} \times \frac{2}{2} \times \frac{1}{2} \qquad \text{rewrite}$$

$$= 1 \times 1 \times \frac{1}{2} \qquad \text{rename}$$

$$= \frac{1}{2}$$

Factor the numerator and denominator completely. Look for values of one. Thus you have simplified the example prior to multiplication.

$$\frac{5}{6} \times \frac{3}{10} = \frac{1 \times 5 \times 3}{2 \times 3 \times 5 \times 2}$$

$$= \frac{1 \times 3 \times 5 \times 1}{2 \times 3 \times 5 \times 2}$$

$$= \frac{1}{2} \times 1 \times 1 \times \frac{1}{2}$$

$$= \frac{1}{4}$$

Before going on to division of fractions, let's look at the example $\frac{1}{2} \times \square = 1$.

$$\frac{1}{2} \times \square = 1$$

$$\left(\frac{2}{1} \times \frac{1}{2}\right) \times \square = \frac{2}{1} \times 1$$

$$= \frac{2}{1} \times \frac{1}{1}$$

$$\left(\frac{2 \times 1}{1 \times 2}\right) \times \square = \frac{2 \times 1}{1 \times 1}$$

$$\frac{2}{2} \times \square = \frac{2}{1}$$

$$1 \times \square = \frac{2}{1}$$

$$\square = \frac{2}{1} \text{ (or 2)}$$

$$\therefore \frac{1}{2} \times \frac{2}{1} = 1$$

If we work through some more examples like this one, we begin to see a pattern:

$$\frac{1}{5} \times \square = 1 \rightarrow \square = \frac{5}{1} \qquad \therefore \frac{1}{5} \times \frac{5}{1} = 1$$

$$\frac{4}{7} \times \square = 1 \rightarrow \square = \frac{7}{4} \qquad \therefore \frac{4}{7} \times \frac{7}{4} = 1$$

$$\frac{5}{3} \times \square = 1 \rightarrow \square = \frac{3}{5} \qquad \therefore \frac{5}{3} \times \frac{3}{5} = 1$$

$$\square \times \frac{11}{4} = 1 \rightarrow \square = \frac{4}{11} \qquad \therefore \frac{4}{11} \times \frac{11}{4} = 1$$

In each of the examples we discover a pair of fractional numbers whose product is equal to 1. (You will recall that the number 1 is the identity element for multiplication of whole numbers. We shall see a little later in this unit that 1 is also the identity element for multiplication of fractions.) Two fractions whose product is 1 are called **multiplicative inverses** or **reciprocals** of each other. For instance, the last three examples show that the reciprocal (or multiplicative inverse) of $\frac{4}{7}$ is $\frac{7}{4}$, that the reciprocal of $\frac{3}{5}$ is $\frac{5}{3}$, and that the reciprocal of $\frac{4}{11}$ is $\frac{11}{4}$. We also observe that for the fractions in each example, the numerator of the first fraction equals the denominator of the second, and the denominator of the first equals the numerator of the second. Is it possible to use this idea to find reciprocals? Let's see. If we interchange the numerator and denominator in the fraction $\frac{2}{3}$, we obtain $\frac{3}{2}$. Is $\frac{3}{2}$ the reciprocal of $\frac{2}{3}$, that is, is $\frac{3}{2} \times \frac{2}{3}$ equal to 1? Yes, since $\frac{3 \times 2}{2 \times 3} = \frac{6}{6} = 1$. Is it always true that if $\frac{a}{b}$ is a fraction, then its reciprocal is $\frac{b}{a}$? We can ask this question in a slightly different way. Is it true, for every fraction $\frac{a}{b}$, that $\frac{a}{b} \times \frac{b}{a} = 1$? The answer is yes, provided neither a nor b is equal to zero. (Why must we exclude these cases?)

> If $\frac{a}{b}$ is any fraction such that $a \neq 0$ and $b \neq 0$, then
> $$\frac{a}{b} \times \frac{b}{a} = 1.$$

Thus we have the following procedure for finding the reciprocal (or multiplicative inverse) of a nonzero fractional number:

1. Express the given number in fraction form.
2. Interchange the numerator and denominator of the fraction in step 1. The result is the reciprocal (or multiplicative inverse) of that fraction.

What is the reciprocal of $2\frac{3}{8}$? Use the procedure suggested. First, write the mixed numeral in fractional form:

$$2\frac{3}{8} = 2 + \frac{3}{8} = \frac{16}{8} + \frac{3}{8} = \frac{19}{8}$$

Second, interchange the numerator and denominator of the fraction $\frac{19}{8}$. This gives the fraction $\frac{8}{19}$. Clearly $\frac{8}{19}$ is the reciprocal of $2\frac{3}{8}$, since $2\frac{3}{8} \times \frac{8}{19} = \frac{19}{8} \times \frac{8}{19} = \frac{152}{152} = 1$.

Now let's examine the binary inverse operation of multiplication (division) with respect to fractions. This is often a difficult topic for children to master and for teachers to develop. Actually, division of fractions is not really relevant to everyday life. (Try

to create a story problem involving the division of two fractions.)

Recall that the operation of division on whole numbers was defined as the process of finding a missing factor (Unit 7). Let's apply this definition of division to the set of fractions. Consider the example $\frac{1}{4} \div \frac{1}{2} = \square$. Applying the definition, we can rewrite this example as the multiplication sentence $\frac{1}{2} \times \square = \frac{1}{4}$. Written in this form, the example asks us to find a number that will yield $\frac{1}{4}$ when multiplied by $\frac{1}{2}$. The example can also be expressed as follows:

$$\frac{1 \times \bigcirc}{2 \times \triangle} = \frac{1}{4}$$

Since we know that $1 \times 1 = 1$, the numerator of the missing factor is clearly 1. And since we know that $2 \times 2 = 4$, the denominator is seen to be 2. Therefore the answer is $\frac{1}{2}$:

$$\frac{1 \times 1}{2 \times 2} = \frac{1}{4}, \frac{1}{2} \times \frac{1}{2} = \frac{1}{4}, \text{ or } \frac{1}{4} \div \frac{1}{2} = \frac{1}{2}.$$

Consider the example $\frac{3}{4} \times \square = \frac{6}{16}$. It can be expressed in this form:

$$\frac{3 \times \bigcirc}{4 \times \triangle} = \frac{6}{16}$$

The answer here is $\frac{2}{4}$ ($\bigcirc = 2$ and $\triangle = 4$), which can be renamed as $\frac{1}{2}$.

$$\frac{3}{4} \times \frac{2}{4} = \frac{6}{16} \text{ or } \frac{3}{4} \times \frac{1}{2} = \frac{3}{8}$$

This procedure has been successful so far, but some examples could become very difficult if no alternative procedure were available. Consider the example $\frac{3}{7} \times \square = \frac{5}{9}$, which can be rewritten as

$$\frac{3 \times \bigcirc}{7 \times \triangle} = \frac{5}{9}$$

Three times what number equals 5, and seven times what number equals 9? This method gives us a very cumbersome answer, $\dfrac{1\frac{2}{3}}{1\frac{2}{7}}$. How can children comprehend the meaning of such a fraction? How can they possibly translate it into something with more meaning for them? We clearly need another method for division of fractions.

The meaning of the inverse operation of division, as related to rational numbers expressed as fractions, can be thought of in another way. The children are familiar with the symbol $\overline{)}$, which they interpret as division; they are also familiar with division of whole numbers. With these two ideas as prerequisite learning, children are ready for division of rational numbers expressed as fractions. Parallel the discussion of the division of whole numbers with the division of fractions. First, review a whole number example such as, "What does $2\overline{)6}$ mean?" This example can mean that we have six things and we want to know how many sets of two can be made.

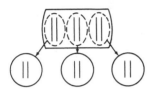

Three sets of two can be made from six things.

If we have six eighths, how many sets of two eighths can we make from six eighths?

$$2 \text{ eighths}\overline{)\begin{array}{l} 3 \\ 6 \text{ eighths} \\ \underline{6 \text{ eighths}} \end{array}}$$

$$\frac{6}{8}$$

$$\frac{2}{8}\overline{)\begin{array}{l} 3 \\ \frac{6}{8} \end{array}}$$

One set of $\frac{2}{8}$

On the concrete level, by using $\frac{1}{8}$ sectors of a circle, we can show that there can be three sets of $\frac{2}{8}$ each made from a set of $\frac{6}{8}$. Thus $\frac{6}{8} \div \frac{2}{8} = 3$.

Let's compare another division example using fractions with an example using whole numbers.

$$3\overline{)\begin{array}{l} 3 \\ 9 \end{array}}$$

$$\frac{9}{10}$$

$$\frac{3}{10}\overline{)\begin{array}{l} 3 \\ \frac{9}{10} \\ \underline{\frac{9}{10}} \end{array}}$$

One set of $\frac{3}{10}$ One set of $\frac{3}{10}$ One set of $\frac{3}{10}$

Thus we can see that there are 3 sets of $\frac{3}{10}$ in $\frac{9}{10}$.

Sometimes an example does not divide evenly, such as $2\overline{)\begin{array}{l} 4\frac{1}{2} \\ 9 \\ \underline{-8} \\ 1 \end{array}}$.

Now relate this example to $\frac{2}{10}\overline{)\begin{array}{l} \frac{9}{10} \end{array}}$.

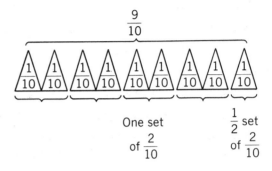

One set of $\frac{2}{10}$ $\frac{1}{2}$ set of $\frac{2}{10}$

Thus

$$\frac{2}{10}\overline{)\begin{array}{l} 4\frac{1}{2} \\ \frac{9}{10} \\ \underline{-\frac{8}{10}} \\ \frac{1}{10} \end{array}}$$

The $\frac{1}{10}$ is $\frac{1}{2}$ of a set of $\frac{2}{10}$.

In developing an alternative method for division of fractions, it is imperative that we understand the meaning of division by 1. Consider this example: $\frac{5}{3} \div 1 = \square$. This can be rewritten in the following form: $\frac{5}{3} = \square \times 1$. The missing factor here is clearly $\frac{5}{3}$, since the product of any number and 1 is that number. And the quotient for $\frac{5}{3} \div 1 = \square$ is therefore $\frac{5}{3}$.

$$\frac{5}{3} \div 1 = \frac{5}{3}$$

After working a number of similar examples, we can generalize: any fraction divided by 1 is the number itself. That is, division by 1 leaves any fraction unchanged. Now we are prepared to develop another method for dividing fractions.

Let's reconsider the example

$$\frac{5}{9} \div \frac{3}{7} = \square$$

We know that $\frac{5}{9} \div \frac{3}{7}$ can be written as $\dfrac{\frac{5}{9}}{\frac{3}{7}}$. And since the identity element for multiplication (1) is a valid concept in the set of fractions, just as it is in the set of whole numbers (this fact will be definitely established later in the unit), we can multiply $\dfrac{\frac{5}{9}}{\frac{3}{7}}$ by 1 and by doing so translate the example into a new form:

$$\frac{5}{9} \div \frac{3}{7} = \frac{\frac{5}{9}}{\frac{3}{7}}$$

$$= \frac{\frac{5}{9}}{\frac{3}{7}} \times 1$$

$$= \frac{\frac{5}{9}}{\frac{3}{7}} \times \frac{\frac{7}{3}}{\frac{7}{3}}$$

Since we know that the reciprocal of the denominator $\frac{3}{7}$ is $\frac{7}{3}$, and that if we multiply any number by its reciprocal the result is 1, we choose here to multiply the fractional number $\dfrac{\frac{5}{9}}{\frac{3}{7}}$ by $\dfrac{\frac{7}{3}}{\frac{7}{3}}$ (another name for 1)

$$= \frac{\frac{5}{9} \times \frac{7}{3}}{\frac{3}{7} \times \frac{7}{3}}$$

$$= \frac{\frac{5}{9} \times \frac{7}{3}}{1}$$ (the product of reciprocals is 1)

$$= \frac{5}{9} \times \frac{7}{3}$$ (division by 1)

In this manner the example $\frac{5}{9} \div \frac{3}{7} = \square$ has been rewritten as $\frac{5}{9} \times \frac{7}{3} = \square$. The division example has been translated into a multiplication example (which we know how to solve) by changing the division sign into a multiplication sign and by replacing the fraction after the operation sign $\left(\frac{3}{7}\right)$ with its reciprocal $\left(\frac{7}{3}\right)$.

Thus we can determine the quotient for $\frac{5}{9} \div \frac{3}{7} = \square$.

$$\frac{5}{9} \div \frac{3}{7} = \frac{5}{9} \times \frac{7}{3}$$

$$= \frac{5 \times 7}{9 \times 3}$$

$$= \frac{35}{27}$$

We could do this by the other method, but with greater difficulty.

Intermediate steps could have been omitted in the determination of the answer, because they are unnecessary. For whenever one fraction is to be divided by another we can bypass these steps by inverting the second fraction and multiplying (instead of dividing).

> If $\dfrac{a}{b}$ and $\dfrac{c}{d}$ are any two fractions such that $b \neq 0$, $c \neq 0$, $d \neq 0$, then
> $$\frac{a}{b} \div \frac{c}{d} = \frac{a}{b} \times \frac{d}{c}$$

The basic properties of fractions apply, of course, to all fractions, including numbers expressed as mixed numerals. A mixed numeral, we know, names a whole number and a fraction together. For example, the number named by the mixed numeral $2\frac{1}{2}$ is the sum of the whole number 2 and the fraction $\frac{1}{2}$.

Now let us consider the multiplication example $3 \times 2\frac{1}{2} = \square$. We can solve this example by expressing the factors in fraction form and multiplying as we would any two fractions:

$$3 \times 2\frac{1}{2} = \frac{3}{1} \times \frac{5}{2}$$ renaming

$$= \frac{3 \times 5}{1 \times 2}$$ procedure for multiplying with fractions

$$= \frac{15}{2}$$ multiplication

$$= \frac{14}{2} + \frac{1}{2}$$ renaming

$$= 7 + \frac{1}{2} \text{ or } 7\frac{1}{2}$$ renaming

But there is another way of solving this example if we remember that a mixed numeral names the sum of a whole number and a fraction. That is, $2\frac{1}{2}$ can be written as $2 + \frac{1}{2}$:

$$3 \times 2\frac{1}{2} = 3 \times \left(2 + \frac{1}{2}\right)$$ renaming

$$= (3 \times 2) + \left(3 \times \frac{1}{2}\right)$$ distributive property of multiplication over addition

$$= 6 + \frac{3}{2}$$ multiplication

$$= 6 + \left(\frac{2}{2} + \frac{1}{2}\right)$$ renaming

$$= 6 + \left(1 + \frac{1}{2}\right)$$ renaming

$$= (6 + 1) + \frac{1}{2} \qquad \text{associative property}$$

$$= 7 + \frac{1}{2} \qquad \text{addition}$$

$$= 7\frac{1}{2} \qquad \text{renaming}$$

Therefore $3 \times 2\frac{1}{2} = 7\frac{1}{2}$.

Now let's try another example, $6\frac{3}{8} \times 7 = \square$. We can solve this by renaming the first number as the sum of a whole number and a fraction. (We have given the justification for each step, for your information. Do *not* ask children to write their reasons for each step.)

$$6\frac{3}{8} \times 7 = \left(6 + \frac{3}{8}\right) \times 7 \qquad \text{renaming}$$

$$= (6 \times 7) + \left(\frac{3}{8} \times 7\right) \qquad \text{distributive property}$$

$$= 42 + \frac{21}{8} \qquad \text{multiplication}$$

$$= 42 + \left(\frac{16}{8} + \frac{5}{8}\right) \qquad \text{renaming}$$

Applying the same reasoning described in the preceding examples, solve $4\frac{1}{2} \times 3\frac{1}{4} = \square$ and $5\frac{2}{3} \times 7\frac{5}{6} = \square$.

Teaching multiplication of numbers named by mixed numerals is simply an extension of what has been taught previously. Multiplication with mixed numerals should provide an opportunity for children to apply basic structure and discover how to solve new examples.

It is important to note that children should not be taught to omit intermediate steps right away. It is not easy for children to understand division of fractions; only after they have developed such an understanding can they use shortcuts and know what they are doing. In no case should they be taught shortcuts until they have demonstrated a thorough understanding of division of fractions, and never should shortcuts be presented without an adequate explanation of their use and purpose.

We have carefully examined some basic structures (properties) related to multiplication with fractions. If we follow the procedure that we used with properties of whole numbers, we would find that:

1. Fractions are commutative with respect to multiplication but *not* commutative with respect to division.
2. Fractions are associative with respect to multiplication but *not* associative with respect to division.
3. The number 1 is the identity element for multiplication with fractions.
4. Multiplication is distributive over addition and subtraction for the set of fractions.
5. Division is *not* distributive over addition or subtraction for the set of fractions.

Terminology, Symbols, and Procedures

Addition of fractions having like denominators Add the numerators in the same way that all whole numbers are added. The denominator remains the same. For example, $\frac{3}{8} + \frac{2}{8} = \frac{5}{8}$. In general, $\frac{a}{b} + \frac{c}{b} = \frac{a + c}{b}$.

Addition of fractions having unlike denominators Rewrite the fractions as fractions having a common denominator (the least common denominator is the easiest to work with). Then add as usual. For example:

$$\frac{3}{4} + \frac{5}{8} = \frac{6}{8} + \frac{5}{8} = \frac{11}{8} \left(\text{or } 1\frac{3}{8}\right)$$

Addition of fractions named by mixed numerals having like denominators Add the whole-number parts; then add the fraction parts. The fraction in the answer should be expressed in simplest form. For example:

$$1\frac{3}{7}$$
$$+\ 3\frac{5}{7}$$
$$4\frac{8}{7},\ \text{or}\ 5\frac{1}{7}$$

Associative property of multiplication Multiplication of fractions is an associative operation; for any fractions $\frac{a}{b}$, $\frac{c}{d}$, and $\frac{e}{f}$ (where $b \neq 0$, $d \neq 0$, and $f \neq 0$):

$$\left(\frac{a}{b} \times \frac{c}{d}\right) \times \frac{e}{f} = \frac{a}{b} \times \left(\frac{c}{d} \times \frac{e}{f}\right)$$

Division of fractional numbers is not associative:

$$\left(\frac{a}{b} \div \frac{c}{d}\right) \div \frac{e}{f} \neq \frac{a}{b} \div \left(\frac{c}{d} \div \frac{e}{f}\right)$$

Commutative property of multiplication Multiplication of fractions is commutative; for any fractions $\frac{a}{b}$ and $\frac{c}{d}$ (where $b \neq 0$ and $d \neq 0$):

$$\frac{a}{b} \times \frac{c}{d} = \frac{c}{d} \times \frac{a}{b}$$

Division of fractional numbers is not commutative:

$$\frac{a}{b} \div \frac{c}{d} \neq \frac{c}{d} \div \frac{a}{b}$$

Determining the least common denominator The least common denominator of two fractions is determined by finding the least common multiple (LCM) of their denominators. The LCM of two denominators is found by factoring them completely (prime factorization) and taking the smallest whole number that contains all the factors of each denominator. For example:

$$\frac{3}{4} = \frac{3}{2 \times 2}$$
$$\frac{5}{8} = \frac{5}{2 \times 2 \times 2}$$

LCM $= 2 \times 2 \times ?$ (The LCM is divisible by 4.)
LCM $= 2 \times 2 \times 2$ (The LCM is also divisible by 8.)
LCM $= 8$
$\therefore \frac{3}{4} = \frac{6}{8}$ and $\frac{5}{8} = \frac{5}{8}$

Distributive properties In the set of fractional numbers, multiplication is distributive over addition and over subtraction:

$$\frac{a}{b} \times \left(\frac{c}{d} + \frac{e}{f}\right) = \left(\frac{a}{b} \times \frac{c}{d}\right) + \left(\frac{a}{b} \times \frac{e}{f}\right) \text{ and } \left(\frac{c}{d} + \frac{e}{f}\right) \times \frac{a}{b} = \left(\frac{c}{d} \times \frac{a}{b}\right) + \left(\frac{e}{f} \times \frac{a}{b}\right)$$

$$\frac{a}{b} \times \left(\frac{c}{d} - \frac{e}{f}\right) = \left(\frac{a}{b} \times \frac{c}{d}\right) - \left(\frac{a}{b} \times \frac{e}{f}\right) \text{ and } \left(\frac{c}{d} - \frac{e}{f}\right) \times \frac{a}{b} = \left(\frac{c}{d} \times \frac{a}{b}\right) - \left(\frac{e}{f} \times \frac{a}{b}\right)$$

Division is distributive over addition and subtraction on the right, but not on the left:

$$\left(\frac{c}{d}+\frac{e}{f}\right)\div\frac{a}{b}=\left(\frac{c}{d}\div\frac{a}{b}\right)+\left(\frac{e}{f}\div\frac{a}{b}\right) \text{ but } \frac{a}{b}\div\left(\frac{c}{d}+\frac{e}{f}\right)\neq\left(\frac{a}{b}\div\frac{c}{d}\right)+\left(\frac{a}{b}\div\frac{e}{f}\right)$$

$$\left(\frac{c}{d}-\frac{e}{f}\right)\div\frac{a}{b}=\left(\frac{c}{d}\div\frac{a}{b}\right)-\left(\frac{e}{f}\div\frac{a}{b}\right) \text{ but } \frac{a}{b}\div\left(\frac{c}{d}-\frac{e}{f}\right)\neq\left(\frac{a}{b}\div\frac{c}{d}\right)-\left(\frac{a}{b}\div\frac{e}{f}\right)$$

Identity element for multiplication   The number 1 is the identity element for multiplication.
For any fractional number $\frac{a}{b}$ (where $b\neq0$):

$$\frac{a}{b}\times1=\frac{a}{b} \text{ and } 1\times\frac{a}{b}=\frac{a}{b}$$

Procedure for dividing two numbers expressed in fraction form   To divide one number expressed in fraction form by another number expressed in fraction form, multiply the first number by the reciprocal of the second number.
For example:

$$\frac{1}{7}\div\frac{1}{3}=\frac{1}{7}\times\frac{3}{1}=\frac{3}{7}$$

Procedure for multiplying two numbers expressed in fraction form   To multiply two numbers expressed in fraction form, multiply the numerators of the two numbers to obtain the numerator of the product, and multiply the denominators of the two numbers to obtain the denominator of the product. For example:

$$\frac{2}{3}\times\frac{1}{5}=\frac{2\times1}{3\times5}=\frac{2}{15}$$

Reciprocal, or multiplicative inverse   The reciprocal or multiplicative inverse of any nonzero number is the number whose product with the given number is 1. If a nonzero fraction is expressed in fraction form, interchange the numerator and denominator to find the reciprocal. For example, if we interchange the numerator and denominator of $\frac{3}{4}$, we get $\frac{4}{3}$; the reciprocal of $\frac{3}{4}$ is indeed $\frac{4}{3}$, since $\frac{3}{4}\times\frac{4}{3}=\frac{3\times4}{4\times3}=\frac{12}{12}=1$.

Subtraction of fractions having like denominators   Subtract the numerators in the same way that whole numbers are subtracted. The denominator remains the same. For example, $\frac{5}{9}-\frac{1}{9}=\frac{4}{9}$. In general, $\frac{a}{b}-\frac{c}{b}=\frac{a-c}{b}$.

Subtraction of fractions having unlike denominators   Rewrite the fractions as fractions having a common denominator (the least common denominator is the easiest to work with). Then subtract as explained above. For example:

$$\frac{3}{4}-\frac{5}{8}=\frac{6}{8}-\frac{5}{8}$$
$$=\frac{1}{8}$$

Subtraction of fractions named by mixed numerals having like denominators Subtract the whole-number parts; then subtract the fraction parts. For example:

$$\begin{array}{r} 6\frac{4}{5} \\ -\,2\frac{1}{5} \\ \hline 4\frac{3}{5} \end{array}$$

In cases where the two numerators cannot be subtracted, it is necessary to rewrite the first of the two mixed numerals before subtracting. For example:

$$\begin{array}{rcrcr} 8\frac{2}{5} & = & 7+\left(\frac{5}{5}+\frac{2}{5}\right) & = & 7\frac{7}{5} \\ -\,5\frac{4}{5} & = & -\left(5+\frac{4}{5}\right) & = & -\,5\frac{4}{5} \\ \hline & & & & 2\frac{3}{5} \end{array}$$

Practice Exercises

1. Write an addition sentence for each model.

a) 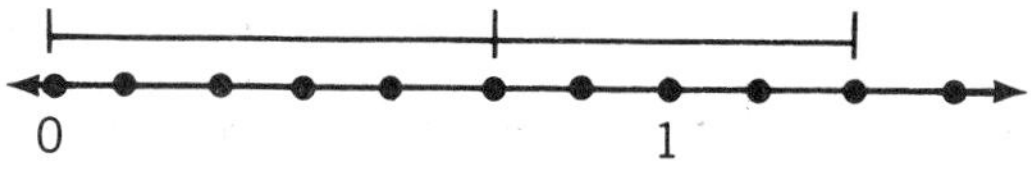

b) 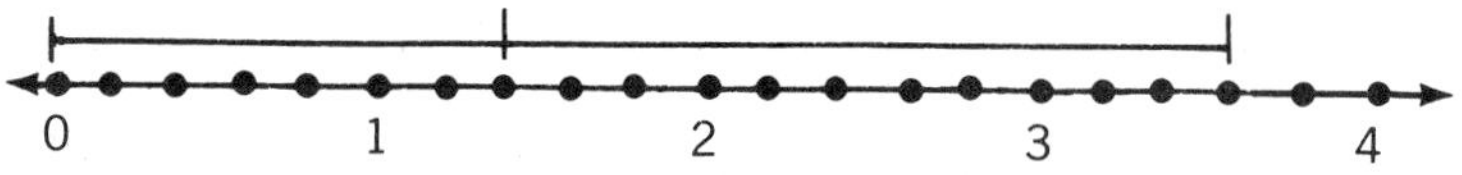

c) 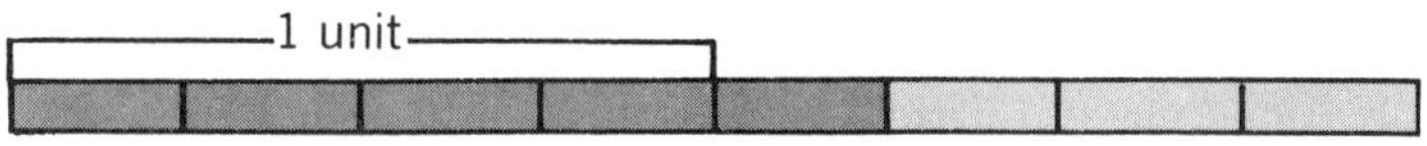

2. Complete the table; write answers in simplest form.

		Addend												
	+	$\frac{5}{12}$	$\frac{1}{12}$	$\frac{7}{12}$	$\frac{11}{12}$	$\frac{1}{4}$	$\frac{17}{12}$	$\frac{2}{3}$	$\frac{5}{6}$	$\frac{2}{5}$	$\frac{1}{2}$	$\frac{1}{3}$	$\frac{3}{4}$	$\frac{1}{7}$
Addend	$\frac{3}{12}$													
Addend	$\frac{3}{4}$													

3. Solve each example and model it with number lines and regions.

a) $\frac{3}{16}+\frac{7}{16}=\square$ b) $\frac{6}{7}+\frac{5}{7}=\square$ c) $\frac{7}{8}+\frac{3}{8}=\square$ d) $\frac{2}{9}+\frac{7}{9}=\square$

4. Consider each set of numbers as denominators. Find the LCM for each set of denominators.

  a) 4, 6   b) 15, 12   c) 8, 12   d) 3, 5, 9   e) 6, 15, 10

5. Write a subtraction sentence for each model.

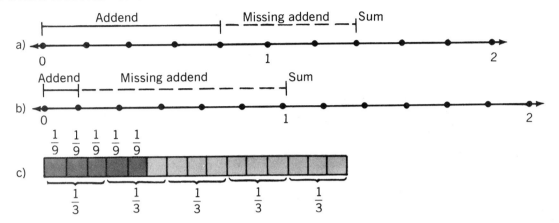

6. Complete the table. Write all answers in simplest form.

								Sums					
$-$	$\frac{7}{12}$	$\frac{5}{12}$	$\frac{11}{12}$	$\frac{3}{4}$	$\frac{13}{16}$	$\frac{23}{24}$	$\frac{31}{36}$			$\frac{1}{2}$	$\frac{5}{6}$	$\frac{7}{8}$	$\frac{9}{10}$
Addend $\frac{5}{12}$							$\frac{23}{60}$						
Addend $\frac{3}{4}$									$\frac{3}{28}$				

7. Solve each example and model each one on the number line and with regions.

  a) $\frac{4}{5} - \frac{3}{10} = \square$ b) $\frac{7}{8} - \frac{3}{4} = \square$ c) $\frac{5}{6} - \frac{1}{3} = \square$ d) $\frac{2}{3} - \frac{1}{4} = \square$

8. Model each multiplication example on the number line.

  a) $3 \times \frac{1}{4} = \square$ d) $6 \times \frac{1}{2} = \square$

  b) $4 \times \frac{2}{5} = \square$ e) $8 \times \frac{5}{6} = \square$

  c) $5 \times \frac{2}{3} = \square$ f) $5 \times \frac{3}{4} = \square$

9. Model each multiplication example by using regions.

  a) $\frac{1}{2} \times \frac{3}{4} = \square$ d) $\frac{5}{6} \times \frac{1}{8} = \square$

  b) $\frac{2}{3} \times \frac{1}{4} = \square$ e) $\frac{3}{8} \times \frac{4}{5} = \square$

  c) $\frac{2}{5} \times \frac{1}{6} = \square$ f) $\frac{2}{3} \times \frac{4}{5} = \square$

10. Solve each division example by using a drawing.

a) $2\overline{)\dfrac{8}{9}}\dfrac{8}{9}$
b) $\dfrac{1}{4}\overline{)\dfrac{3}{4}}$
c) $\dfrac{5}{11}\overline{)\dfrac{10}{11}}$
d) $\dfrac{1}{4}\overline{)\dfrac{3}{8}}$
e) $\dfrac{2}{3}\overline{)\dfrac{5}{6}}$
*f) $\dfrac{4}{5}\overline{)\dfrac{4}{3}}$

11. Name the reciprocal of each number.

a) $\dfrac{3}{5}$ c) $\dfrac{5}{6}$ e) $\dfrac{9}{5}$ g) 17   i) $6\dfrac{7}{8}$

b) $\dfrac{1}{4}$ d) $\dfrac{7}{8}$ f) $2\dfrac{1}{4}$ h) $3\dfrac{4}{9}$

12. Solve the examples by rewriting each one in the form $\dfrac{\frac{a}{b}}{\frac{c}{d}}$. Then multiply the numerator

and denominator by the reciprocal of $\dfrac{c}{d}$.

a) $\dfrac{2}{9} \div \dfrac{8}{9} = \square$
d) $\dfrac{3}{8} \div \dfrac{1}{4} = \square$
g) $\dfrac{2}{3} \div \dfrac{1}{4} = \square$
j) $\dfrac{5}{9} \div \dfrac{3}{5} = \square$

b) $\dfrac{3}{4} \div \dfrac{1}{4} = \square$
e) $\dfrac{5}{6} \div \dfrac{2}{3} = \square$
h) $\dfrac{3}{7} \div \dfrac{2}{3} = \square$
k) $\dfrac{1}{3} \div \dfrac{7}{8} = \square$

c) $\dfrac{10}{11} \div \dfrac{5}{11} = \square$
f) $\dfrac{4}{3} \div \dfrac{4}{5} = \square$
i) $\dfrac{4}{5} \div \dfrac{6}{7} = \square$
l) $\dfrac{5}{6} \div \dfrac{3}{4} = \square$

13. Suppose $\dfrac{x}{z}$ and $\dfrac{y}{z}$ are two fractional numbers. Complete the following by supplying the correct relation symbol (=, <, or >).

a) If $x < y$, then $\dfrac{x}{z} \bigcirc \dfrac{y}{z}$.
b) If $x = y$, then $\dfrac{x}{z} \bigcirc \dfrac{y}{z}$.
c) If $x > y$, then $\dfrac{x}{z} \bigcirc \dfrac{y}{z}$.

14. If $a, b, c,$ and d are any counting numbers and $a \times d < b \times c$, then $\dfrac{a}{b} < \dfrac{c}{d}$. This fact enables us to compare two fractional numbers by comparing products of counting numbers. Use this test to decide which is the lesser of each pair of fractional numbers.

a) $\dfrac{13}{27}, \dfrac{27}{55}$ b) $\dfrac{71}{81}, \dfrac{18}{21}$ c) $\dfrac{6}{17}, \dfrac{23}{67}$

15. Solve each example.

a) $\left(\dfrac{3}{4} \times \dfrac{5}{6}\right) \div \dfrac{2}{3} = \square$
b) $\left(\dfrac{7}{8} \div \dfrac{4}{5}\right) \times \dfrac{1}{2} = \square$
c) $\dfrac{2}{5} \times \left(\dfrac{2}{3} \div \dfrac{3}{4}\right) = \square$
d) $\dfrac{5}{7} \div \left(\dfrac{4}{9} \times \dfrac{2}{5}\right) = \square$

16. Internally simplify each example before multiplying.

a) $\dfrac{7}{9} \times \dfrac{3}{8} = \square$
c) $\dfrac{6}{7} \div \dfrac{4}{5} = \square$
e) $\dfrac{5}{6} \div \dfrac{20}{21} = \square$
g) $2\dfrac{5}{6} \div 3\dfrac{1}{4} = \square$

b) $\dfrac{4}{5} \times \dfrac{15}{28} = \square$
d) $\dfrac{8}{9} \div \dfrac{4}{18} = \square$
f) $\dfrac{3}{11} \times 2\dfrac{4}{9} = \square$
h) $1\dfrac{3}{8} \times 4\dfrac{2}{3} = \square$

17. If a room measures $12\dfrac{1}{2}$ feet by $11\dfrac{3}{4}$ feet, how many square yards of carpeting will be needed?

Discussion Questions

1. Discuss the importance of learning the operations with fractions as we move toward metric measure, hand-held calculators, and microcomputers.

2. What are the best means for developing children's understanding of the operations using fractions?

3. Discuss the relationship between regrouping with whole numbers and regrouping using fractions. How are they alike? How are they different?

4. What are the advantages and disadvantages of allowing children to develop and use their own fraction kits? Should the kits be made with circular or rectangular regions (or both)?

5. Make a list of cases where the identity element of multiplication is used with fractions. How important is the identity element of multiplication in operations with fractions?

6. Discuss the important concepts that children must comprehend before the teacher should introduce division with fractions.

7. Research the Stretchers and Shrinkers Program, as developed by the University of Illinois Committee on School Mathematics, and present your findings to your class.

8. Discuss teaching materials and aids that can be used to teach children operations with fractions.

9. Discuss the difficulties that are encountered when children attempt to use hand-held calculators and microcomputers for operations on fractions.

10. Discuss microcomputer programs that can be developed for use with fractions.

Activities for the Primary Grades

Children need many examples of addition, subtraction, multiplication, and division of fractions before they can proceed to perform these operations themselves. Such examples should be on the concrete, semiconcrete, and semiabstract levels first, in that order. Real objects should be used to show parts of sets and regions. The number line is also an excellent model to help children understand addition of fractions.

By the fourth grade, some children need many experiences with diagrams, shading of fractional parts, intersection of shaded parts, and so forth; others need relatively few. It is important to remember that as long as children need to refer to diagrams to understand a concept they should be permitted to do so. It is also important to allow children who already understand a concept to go ahead and apply what they have learned; holding them back or barraging them with pictures can be just as harmful as pushing them into abstractions before they are ready.

Children should not be presented with shortcuts to operations with fractions before they completely understand how the operations work; this can confuse them and rob them of the joy of discovering for themselves why the operations function as they do. If they completely understand the basic concepts involved, they can develop true proficiency in working with fractions.

In the primary grades we use activities to prepare children to work with fractions; they should not, of course, be expected to perform operations with fractions themselves. The children should manipulate concrete objects to show the relations involved in discovering that equivalent fractions exist, how they relate to one another, and comparisons between them. Provide models, such as Cuisenaire rods and Dienes Blocks, to prepare children to add, subtract, multiply and divide fractions.

1. Discuss with the children the idea of one-half of a class. After several discussions they should begin to realize that one-half and one-half make up the entire class. This is particularly apparent when you choose teams for games.

2. Discuss how many of certain pieces of something make up the whole—that is, that it takes three one-thirds (for instance) to make one whole item.

3. Give children sets of objects and ask them to show one-fourth of the set.

4. Give children egg cartons and counters and ask them to show one-half dozen.

Hand-Held Calculator Activities for the Primary Grades

For the same reasons that we mentioned in the previous unit, no hand-held calculator activities are suggested for this unit.

Microcomputer Activities for the Primary Grades

Bright primary children might be asked to run some microcomputer software packages that require students to identify fractional parts of regions or sets.

Activities for the Intermediate Grades

The intuitive level of understanding fractions has been used in the primary grades. At the intermediate grade level, an intuitive understanding of operations with fractions must first be developed with Dienes Blocks, Cuisenaire rods, paper folding, and graph paper. Then activities can be used to develop understanding of the operations.

ADDITION AND SUBTRACTION OF FRACTIONS

1. Using the fraction kit described in the previous unit, ask the child to model:

$$\frac{1}{3}+\frac{1}{3}, \quad \left(\frac{1}{3}+\frac{1}{3}\right)+\frac{1}{3}, \quad \frac{1}{2}+\frac{1}{4}, \quad \frac{3}{6}+\frac{1}{2}, \text{ and so forth}$$

2. Give a child two egg cartons, each half full of counters. Ask the child what part of each egg carton is full. Have the child put the "eggs" all in one carton. Now ask the child what part of the egg carton is full. The teacher should write the mathematical sentence $\frac{1}{2}+\frac{1}{2}=1$.

3. Using a ruler marked in eighths of an inch, have the child add $\frac{1}{8}$ and $\frac{5}{8}$.

4. Children who have had experiences using measuring cups will be ready to use such measuring cups as models for addition of rational numbers expressed as fractions.

$$\frac{1}{4}+\frac{1}{4}=\frac{2}{4}=\frac{1}{2}$$

$$\begin{array}{r} 1 \text{ fourth} \\ + \ 1 \text{ fourth} \\ \hline 2 \text{ fourths} = \frac{2}{4} = \frac{1}{2} \end{array}$$

$$\frac{1}{2}$$

5. Divide a paper plate into sixths. Color $\frac{2}{6}$ blue and $\frac{3}{6}$ green. Show that:

$$\frac{2}{6}+\frac{3}{6}=\frac{5}{6}, \quad \frac{6}{6}-\frac{5}{6}=\frac{1}{6}, \quad \frac{5}{6}-\frac{2}{6}=\frac{3}{6}=\frac{1}{2}, \quad \frac{5}{6}-\frac{3}{6}=\frac{2}{6}=\frac{1}{3}.$$

6. Using the fraction kit described in the previous unit, have the children model:

$$\frac{5}{8}-\frac{2}{8}, \quad \frac{1}{2}-\frac{1}{4}, \quad \frac{5}{6}-\frac{1}{2}, \text{ and so forth}$$

7. Have the children study and discuss simple addition examples.

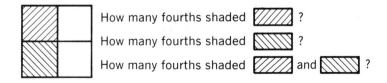

How many fourths shaded [///] ?
How many fourths shaded [\\\] ?
How many fourths shaded [///] and [\\\] ?

Relate how $\frac{1}{4}+\frac{1}{4}=\frac{2}{4}$ records the idea as discussed above.

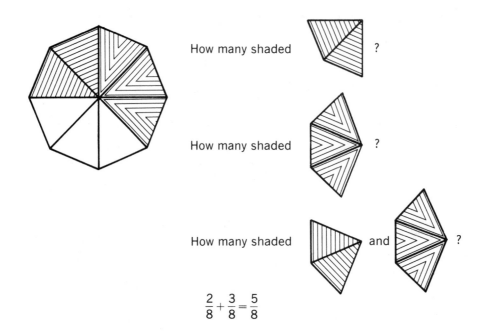

How many shaded 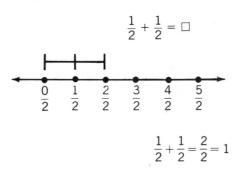 ?

How many shaded ?

How many shaded and ?

$$\frac{2}{8} + \frac{3}{8} = \frac{5}{8}$$

8. Children who have used the number line as a model for addition of whole numbers will find little difficulty in relating it to fractions.

$$\frac{1}{2} + \frac{1}{2} = \square$$

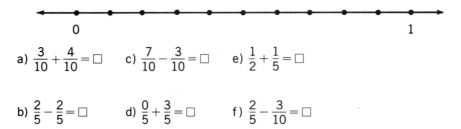

$$\frac{0}{2} \quad \frac{1}{2} \quad \frac{2}{2} \quad \frac{3}{2} \quad \frac{4}{2} \quad \frac{5}{2}$$

$$\frac{1}{2} + \frac{1}{2} = \frac{2}{2} = 1$$

9. Use the number line below to help you find the sums. Label the points on the number line to show halves, fifths, and tenths.

0   1

a) $\frac{3}{10} + \frac{4}{10} = \square$ c) $\frac{7}{10} - \frac{3}{10} = \square$ e) $\frac{1}{2} + \frac{1}{5} = \square$

b) $\frac{2}{5} - \frac{2}{5} = \square$ d) $\frac{0}{5} + \frac{3}{5} = \square$ f) $\frac{2}{5} - \frac{3}{10} = \square$

10. Make number-line diagrams to help solve the following examples.

a) $\frac{1}{4} + \frac{1}{4} = \square$ c) $\frac{2}{4} + \frac{1}{4} = \square$ e) $\frac{3}{4} - \frac{1}{4} = \square$ g) $\frac{4}{6} + \frac{1}{6} = \square$

b) $\frac{1}{6} - \frac{1}{6} = \square$ d) $\frac{2}{6} + \frac{1}{6} = \square$ f) $\frac{3}{6} + \frac{1}{6} = \square$ h) $\frac{5}{6} - \frac{1}{6} = \square$

11. Draw diagrams to help you complete each equation.

a) $\frac{1}{4}+\frac{1}{2}=\square$ d) $\frac{5}{8}+\frac{1}{4}=\square$ g) $\frac{1}{2}+\frac{1}{3}=\square$

b) $\frac{3}{8}+\frac{2}{8}=\square$ e) $\frac{1}{2}+\frac{0}{4}=\square$ h) $\frac{5}{8}+\square=\frac{3}{4}$

c) $\frac{1}{2}+\square=\frac{4}{6}$ f) $\frac{2}{4}+\square=\frac{3}{4}$ i) $\frac{1}{6}+\square=\frac{1}{3}$

12. Find the missing addends. Draw a number-line diagram for each example.

a) $\underline{\hspace{2cm}}+\frac{2}{4}=\frac{3}{4}$ c) $\frac{2}{5}+\underline{\hspace{2cm}}=\frac{5}{5}$

b) $\frac{3}{4}-\frac{2}{4}=\underline{\hspace{2cm}}$ d) $\frac{5}{5}-\frac{2}{5}=\underline{\hspace{2cm}}$

13. Find the differences.

a) $9\frac{6}{7}$ b) $5\frac{4}{9}$ c) $6\frac{13}{15}$ d) $10\frac{8}{11}$ e) $3\frac{17}{20}$

   $-3\frac{2}{7}$ $-1\frac{1}{9}$ $-4\frac{11}{15}$ $-5\frac{2}{11}$ $-2\frac{3}{20}$

14. Write the fraction that represents the shaded area. The unit region is the large rectangular region.

A $\underline{\hspace{2cm}}$ B $\underline{\hspace{2cm}}$ C $\underline{\hspace{2cm}}$ D $\underline{\hspace{2cm}}$

A + B + C + D = $\underline{\hspace{2cm}}$

a) Write an addition sentence expressing the sum of A and B.
b) Write a subtraction sentence using A and B.
c) Write an addition sentence using C and D.
d) Write a subtraction sentence using C and D.

15. Allow children to test fractions for commutativity and associativity. Let them discuss their results and justify their reasoning. For example:

Is $\frac{1}{4}+\frac{2}{4}=\frac{2}{4}+\frac{1}{4}$?   Is $\left(\frac{1}{5}+\frac{2}{5}\right)+\frac{2}{5}=\frac{1}{5}+\left(\frac{2}{5}+\frac{2}{5}\right)$?

16. Emphasis on the inverse relation is evident in the use of equations with missing addends. For example:

$$\frac{3}{5} - \frac{1}{5} = \square \quad \text{or} \quad \frac{1}{5} + \square = \frac{3}{5}$$

WRITING MATHEMATICAL SENTENCES

Children in the intermediate grades should be able to translate some simple problem situations that involve fractions into mathematical sentences.

1. Write a mathematical sentence for each problem; then solve the problems.

a) It took Lewis $2\frac{1}{2}$ hours to mow Mrs. Huffie's lawn. It took him $1\frac{3}{4}$ hours to mow Mrs. Martin's lawn. How much more time did he spend on Mrs. Huffie's lawn?

b) Linda's library books weighed $2\frac{1}{4}$ pounds and Diane's weighed $3\frac{1}{4}$ pounds. Henry carried both stacks of books for the girls. How many pounds of books did he carry?

c) Fred fed $2\frac{1}{4}$ bags of peanuts to the elephants and $3\frac{3}{4}$ bags to the monkeys. He kept 1 bag for himself. How many bags of peanuts did Fred buy?

d) Mitch picked 3 rows of corn on Monday and 8 rows on Tuesday. There were 18 rows of corn in the garden. What fractional part of the corn did he have left to pick?

2. Make a set of 50 cards about 2″ by 3″. Write one fraction on each card. Some fractions may be repeated. Shuffle the cards and deal five to each player. The object is to put together a set of fraction cards that add up to one. Two or more cards may be used. During a child's turn he draws a card and lays down as many sets of cards that add up to one as he can. The pupil who has the most sets wins.

3. Use a file folder to make a game board as shown. Use two different colors of cardboard and make about 25 cards of each color, each just a little smaller than the squares drawn on the board. On the cards, write addition and subtraction examples whose answers are the same as the fractions written on the board. Two individuals may play the game. Randomly place the cards face down. One player uses one color set and the other player uses the other. Each player takes turns drawing one of his own cards, solving it, and placing it on the board on its proper answer. The players check each other. Once a card is placed on the board and judged correct it cannot be moved to view the fraction beneath the card. If the other player has a card with the same answer, his card is placed on top of the first player's card. Each player tries to get three of his cards in a row. The first to do so wins the game.

Write
sums
on
board

$\frac{5}{8}$	$\frac{2}{3}$	$\frac{3}{8}$
$\frac{1}{3}$	$\frac{1}{6}$	$\frac{1}{2}$
$\frac{7}{8}$	$\frac{3}{4}$	$\frac{5}{6}$

4. Use sponge rubber or wooden cubes to make a set of dice with fractions written on the faces.

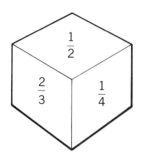 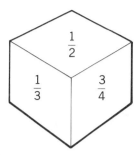

Have the children roll the dice and use the fractions on the top side as addends to find the sum.

5. Use the dice from the previous activity. After rolling them, subtract the lesser value from the greater.

MULTIPLICATION OF FRACTIONS

In the intermediate grades the major emphasis is on preparing students to multiply fractions and on multiplication examples in which one of the factors is a whole number. The children need to understand that when we find $\frac{1}{5}$ of a set, we are partitioning or separating the set into five equivalent subsets. If we separate a set of twenty objects into five equivalent subsets, each subset will contain four objects. We therefore say that $\frac{1}{5}$ of 20 = 4 or $\frac{1}{5}$ × 20 = 4.

1. Have children use their fraction kits to solve the following examples.

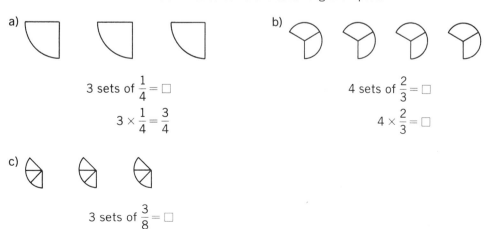

a)

3 sets of $\frac{1}{4} = \square$

$3 \times \frac{1}{4} = \frac{3}{4}$

b)

4 sets of $\frac{2}{3} = \square$

$4 \times \frac{2}{3} = \square$

c)

3 sets of $\frac{3}{8} = \square$

$3 \times \frac{3}{8} = \square$

2. Give each student a set of 12 counters. Have them model $\frac{1}{4}$ of the set of 12 counters.

3. Which part of each region is shaded? (This can be done as a group activity first.)

a) 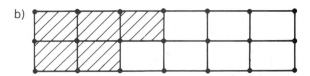   b)

c) 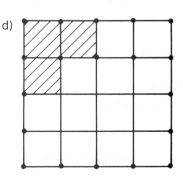   d)

4. What part of each region is double-shaded?

a)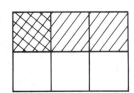

_____ is double-shaded.

$\frac{1}{3}$ of $\frac{1}{2}$ is _____.

b)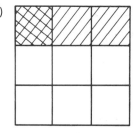

_____ is double-shaded.

$\frac{1}{3}$ of $\frac{1}{3}$ is _____.

c)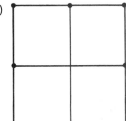

Color $\frac{1}{2}$ of the region blue.

Color $\frac{1}{2}$ of the blue region red.

$\frac{1}{2}$ of $\frac{1}{2}$ is _____.

What part of the region has been colored twice? _____

5. Complete the sentence under each diagram.

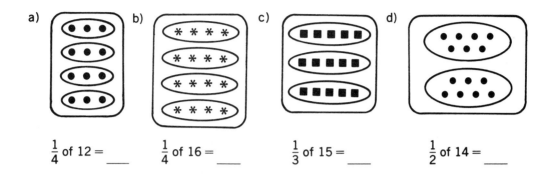

a) $\frac{1}{4}$ of 12 = ____

b) $\frac{1}{4}$ of 16 = ____

c) $\frac{1}{3}$ of 15 = ____

d) $\frac{1}{2}$ of 14 = ____

6. The number-line model will help you understand multiplication of rational numbers expressed as fractions.

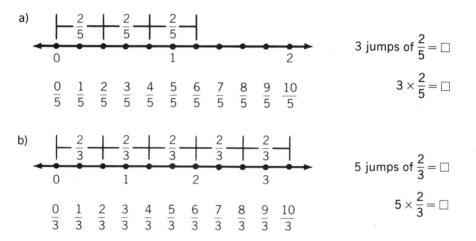

a) 3 jumps of $\frac{2}{5}$ = □

$3 \times \frac{2}{5}$ = □

b) 5 jumps of $\frac{2}{3}$ = □

$5 \times \frac{2}{3}$ = □

7. Further readiness activities can be presented by giving the children practice with repeated addition of fractional numbers.

a) $\frac{2}{3} + \frac{2}{3} + \frac{2}{3} = \square$

$\therefore 3 \times \frac{2}{3} = \square$

b) $\frac{3}{8} + \frac{3}{8} + \frac{3}{8} = \square$

$\therefore 3 \times \frac{3}{8} = \square$

c) $\frac{2}{7} + \frac{2}{7} + \frac{2}{7} = \square$

$\therefore 3 \times \frac{2}{7} = \square$

d) $\frac{4}{5} + \frac{4}{5} + \frac{4}{5} + \frac{4}{5} = \square$

$\therefore 4 \times \frac{4}{5} = \square$

e) $\frac{1}{9} + \frac{1}{9} + \frac{1}{9} + \frac{1}{9} = \square$

$\therefore 4 \times \frac{1}{9} = \square$

f) $\frac{7}{6} + \frac{7}{6} + \frac{7}{6} = \square$

$\therefore 3 \times \frac{7}{6} = \square$

8. Complete the following.

a) $\frac{1}{2}$ of 6 = 3 or $\frac{1}{2} \times 6 =$ ____

b) $\frac{1}{2}$ of 8 = ____ or $\frac{1}{2} \times 8 =$ ____

c) $\frac{1}{5}$ of 10 = ____ of $\frac{1}{5} \times 10 =$ ____

d) $\frac{1}{3}$ of 12 = 4 or $\frac{1}{3} \times 12 =$ ____

e) $\frac{1}{4}$ of 12 = ____ or $\frac{1}{4} \times 12 =$ ____

f) $\frac{1}{3}$ of 9 = ____ or $\frac{1}{3} \times 9 =$ ____

9.   On a sheet of cardboard draw a figure as shown. Make each diagonal about six to eight inches long; laminate the card. Use a china marker to write examples on the figure. The children may write the products in the outside ring.

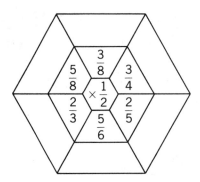

Hand-Held Calculator Activities for the Intermediate Grades

For the same reasons that we mentioned in the previous unit, no hand-held calculator activities are suggested for this unit.

Microcomputer Activities for the Intermediate Grades

Microcomputer software packages are available using graphics to help children learn beginning operations with fractions.

1.   Drill packages with addition and subtraction of fractional numbers can be easily constructed by the classroom teacher. Here is a sample program for a Commodore Vic-20 or Pet 2001 computer.

```
10 REM—ADDITION OF FRACTIONS—
20 ?"♡"
30 ?:?:?:?"          I AM YOUR PET."
40 ?:?:?"        WHO ARE YOU"
50 INPUT N$
60 ?"♡"
70 ?:?:?:?"          HELLO, ";N$
80 ?:?"          TODAY IS"
90 ?:?"    *_*_*_*_*_*_*_*"
100 ?:?"      ADDITION"
110 ?"            OF"
120 ?"        FRACTIONS"
130 ?"            DAY"
140 ?:?    *_*_*_*_*_*_*_*"
150 FOR T=1 TO 4000:NEXT T:?"♡"
160 ?"        THIS IS A RECTANGLE."
170 ?"        _____"
180 ?"        _____"
```

```
190 ?"              "
200 ?"              "
210 FOR T=1 TO 3000:NEXT T
220 ?:?"            WHAT PART OF THE RECTANGLE IS SHADED"
230 INPUT A$
240 IF A$="3/5"THEN?"CORRECT!"
250 IF A$<>"3/5"THEN?"WRONG, TRY AGAIN!":GOTO 160
260 FOR T=1 TO 3000:NEXT T
270 ?"▢"
280 ?:?:?"WHAT PART OF THE RECTANGLE IS SHADED"
290 ?"    _____"
300 ?"                    "
310 ?"                    "
320 INPUT B$
330 IF B$="1/5"THEN?"CORRECT"
340 IF B$<>"1/5"THEN?"WRONG, TRY AGAIN!":GOTO 270
350 FOR T=1 TO 3000:NEXT T
360 ?"▢"
370 ?:?:?:?"NOW ADD THE SHADED PARTS OF THE TWO RECTANGLES."
380 ?" _____"
390 ?"              "
400 ?"              "
410 FOR T=1 TO 5000:NEXT T
420 ?:?:?:?:?"WHAT PART OF THE RECTANGLE IS SHADED NOW."
430 INPUT C$
440 IF C$="4/5"THEN?"CORRECT!"
450 FOR T=1 TO 5000:NEXT T
460 IF C$<>"4/4"THEN?"WRONG, TRY AGAIN!":GOTO 370
470 ?:?:?"YOU HAVE NOW ADDED 3/5 WITH 1/5 TO GET 4/5."
480 FOR T=1 TO 5000:NEXT T
490 ?"▢"
500 ?"NOTE"
510 ?:?:?"WHEN 3/5 IS ADDED WITH 1/5 THE SUM IS 4/5."
520 FOR T=1 TO 5000:NEXT T
530 ?:?:?"3 + 1 = 4"
540 ?:?:?:?"THE 5 IS NOT ADDED WITH THE OTHER 5."
550 FOR T=1 TO 5000:NEXT T
560 ?:?:?:?"ADD THE TOP NUMBERS."
570 ?:?:?:?"DO NOT ADD THE BOTTOM NUMBERS!"
580 ?:?:?:?"WHY DO WE ADD THE TOP NUMBERS AND NOT ADD THE BOTTOM
       NUMBERS?"
590 ?:?:?:?"DISCUSS THIS QUESTION WITH THE MEMBERS OF YOUR CLASS."
```

2. The preceding program can easily be adapted for the Atari computer:

   a) Change line statements 20, 60, 270, 360, and 490 to GR.0.
   b) Use GR.8 screen.
   c) Use the window for the printed material.
   d) Use PLOT and DRAWTO statements for the graphics.
   e) Dimension all string variables.

3. This program can also be adapted for a Radio Shack TRS-80 computer, as follows:

   a) Change lines 20, 60, 270, 360, and 490 to CLS.
   b) Draw the graphics by using

   ```
   FOROVER = 10 TO 20
   SET(OVER, 10)
   NEXTOVER
   ```

```
FORDOWN=10 TO 13
SET(20,DOWN)
NEXTDOWN
FOROVER=20 TO 10 STEP−1
SET(OVER,13)
NEXTOVER
FORDOWN=13 TO 10 STEP−1
SET(10,DOWN)
NEXTDOWN
FORDOWN=10 TO 13
SET(12,DOWN)
NEXTDOWN
FORDOWN=10 TO 13
SET(14,DOWN)
NEXTDOWN
FORDOWN= 10 TO 13
SET(16,DOWN)
NEXTDOWN
FORDOWN=10 TO 13
SET(18,DOWN)
NEXTDOWN
```

c) Use random numbers and the SET statement to shade regions of the rectangle.

Activities for the Upper Elementary Grades

ADDITION AND SUBTRACTION OF FRACTIONS

Any of the preceding activities may be adapted for the upper elementary grades. Remember that the introduction to fractions should begin on a concrete level.

SUMS AND DIFFERENCES

1. Using the fraction kit described in the activities for Unit 10, have the student model:

a) $\frac{5}{8} + \frac{2}{8}$ b) $\frac{5}{6} - \frac{2}{6}$ c) $\frac{7}{10} + \frac{1}{5}$ d) $\frac{1}{2} - \frac{1}{4}$

2. Use the geoboard (see pp. 404–405) and establish that the entire area is called one (1). What is the value of each small square? $\left(\frac{1}{36}\right)$ (Answers will vary with the size of the geoboard.)

What is the value of six small squares?

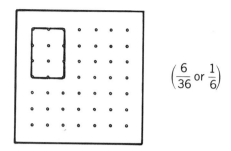

$\left(\dfrac{6}{36} \text{ or } \dfrac{1}{6}\right)$

Have students use geoboards or dot paper to represent fractions:

$$\frac{1}{3} \qquad \frac{2}{6} \qquad \frac{1}{2} \qquad \frac{3}{6}$$

On the same geoboard have the student model $\dfrac{1}{2} + \dfrac{1}{8}$. The task is to count the squares to arrive at a sum.

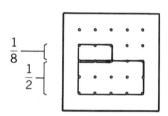

3. From construction paper of different colors construct a rectangle so that two unit squares fit over it. Next construct two triangles by cutting another unit square along the diagonal. This will give you Triangle A. Take the other half of the unit square and cut it in half. This will give you Triangle B. Questions such as the following can be asked: What part of the square is Triangle A? What part of Triangle A is Triangle B?

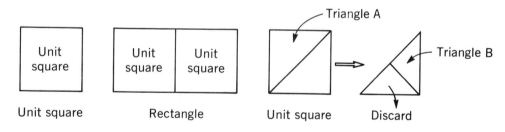

4. Using a number line, have the student diagram examples such as:

a) $\dfrac{5}{8} + \dfrac{7}{8}$ \qquad b) $\dfrac{7}{4} - \dfrac{5}{4}$ \qquad c) $\dfrac{4}{5} + \dfrac{3}{10}$ \qquad d) $\dfrac{5}{6} - \dfrac{2}{3}$

5. Complete the tables.

+	$\frac{1}{3}$	$\frac{5}{6}$	$7\frac{1}{8}$
$\frac{1}{2}$			
$2\frac{1}{3}$			
$2\frac{1}{4}$			

−	$\frac{1}{2}$	$\frac{2}{3}$	$\frac{7}{12}$
$\frac{5}{6}$			
$\frac{25}{12}$			
$7\frac{2}{3}$			

6. Have the student fill in the missing numbers.

Addend	Addend	Sum
	$\frac{1}{2}$	$\frac{7}{8}$
$\frac{1}{3}$	$\frac{4}{6}$	
$\frac{3}{10}$		$\frac{4}{5}$

7. Use what you have learned about whole numbers and fractions to complete each sentence.

a) If $\frac{1}{2}+\frac{1}{2}=1$, then $1\frac{1}{2}+\frac{1}{2}=$ ____.

b) If $\frac{1}{4}+\frac{3}{4}=1$, then $2\frac{1}{4}+\frac{3}{4}=$ ____.

c) If $\frac{1}{4}+\frac{1}{4}=\frac{1}{2}$, then $3\frac{1}{4}+1\frac{1}{4}=$ ____.

d) If $\frac{1}{3}+\frac{2}{3}=1$, then $2\frac{1}{3}+\frac{2}{3}=$ ____.

e) If $\frac{1}{2}+\frac{1}{4}=\frac{3}{4}$, then $2\frac{1}{2}+\frac{1}{4}=$ ____.

f) If $\frac{1}{2}+\frac{1}{3}=\frac{5}{6}$, then $4\frac{1}{2}+2\frac{1}{3}=$ ____.

8. Place the correct sign of operation in each $\triangle$.

a) $\frac{9}{12}\,\triangle\,\frac{3}{6}=1\frac{1}{4}$

b) $\frac{4}{5}\,\triangle\,\frac{3}{10}=\frac{1}{2}$

c) $\frac{6}{16}\,\triangle\,\frac{3}{8}=\frac{3}{4}$

d) $\frac{3}{4}\,\triangle\,\frac{11}{12}=1\frac{2}{3}$

9. Mark each statement true or false.

a) $\frac{1}{4}+\frac{2}{3}=\frac{2}{3}+\frac{1}{4}$

b) $1-\frac{3}{8}=\frac{3}{8}-1$

c) $\frac{3}{4}-\frac{4}{4}=\frac{4}{4}-\frac{3}{4}$

d) $\frac{1}{8}+0=0-\frac{1}{8}$

e) $\frac{1}{3}+0=0+\frac{1}{3}$

f) $\frac{1}{6}+1=\frac{7}{7}+\frac{2}{12}$

10. Find the prime factors of the numerator and denominator of each fraction.

a) $\frac{6}{10}$ b) $\frac{9}{12}$ c) $\frac{4}{8}$ d) $\frac{12}{15}$ e) $\frac{15}{25}$

In each fraction above, did you find a common prime factor for the numerator and denominator? Are any of the fractions in simplest form? Rename each fraction in simplest form.

11. Are the following fractions in simplest form? If not, rewrite them in simplest form.

a) $\frac{7}{30}$ b) $\frac{10}{12}$ c) $\frac{4}{6}$ d) $\frac{15}{16}$ e) $\frac{7}{8}$ f) $\frac{24}{27}$

12. Find the GCF of the numerator and denominator of each fraction.

a) $\frac{6}{9}$ b) $\frac{8}{12}$ c) $\frac{16}{12}$ d) $\frac{25}{15}$ e) $\frac{8}{8}$ f) $\frac{64}{80}$

13. Construct several cardboard flash cards. On each card place several fractions with unlike denominators. Show the card to the student. The student should state the least common denominator. Pencil and paper may be used if necessary.

14. Find the least common multiple of the denominators. Express the fractions using the LCD as the common denominator; then add or subtract as indicated. Examples should be written in both vertical and horizontal form.

Example: $\frac{1}{2} + \frac{1}{4}$ LCD = 4 $\frac{1}{2} + \frac{1}{4} = \frac{2}{4} + \frac{1}{4} = \frac{3}{4}$

a) $\frac{2}{5} + \frac{4}{3} =$ _____

b) $\frac{3}{8} + \frac{3}{16} =$ _____

c) $\frac{1}{2} - \frac{1}{4} =$ _____

d) $\frac{5}{6} - \frac{1}{2} =$ _____

e) $\frac{8}{10} + \frac{15}{20} =$ _____

f) $\frac{5}{12} + \frac{6}{15} =$ _____

MIXED NUMERALS

1. Rewrite the following mixed numerals as improper fractions. Use either Example A or Example B as a guide.

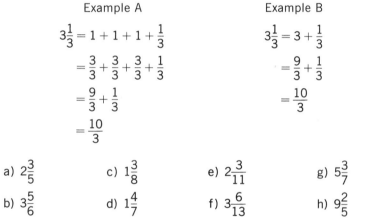

Example A

$$3\frac{1}{3} = 1 + 1 + 1 + \frac{1}{3}$$
$$= \frac{3}{3} + \frac{3}{3} + \frac{3}{3} + \frac{1}{3}$$
$$= \frac{9}{3} + \frac{1}{3}$$
$$= \frac{10}{3}$$

Example B

$$3\frac{1}{3} = 3 + \frac{1}{3}$$
$$= \frac{9}{3} + \frac{1}{3}$$
$$= \frac{10}{3}$$

a) $2\frac{3}{5}$

b) $3\frac{5}{6}$

c) $1\frac{3}{8}$

d) $1\frac{4}{7}$

e) $2\frac{3}{11}$

f) $3\frac{6}{13}$

g) $5\frac{3}{7}$

h) $9\frac{2}{5}$

2. Use examples like the following to reinforce children's understanding of addition and subtraction. (Some children will have difficulty with the + sign in the middle of a subtraction example. They will add the fractions and subtract the whole numbers.)

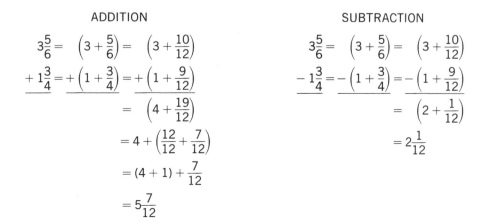

ADDITION

$$3\frac{5}{6} = \left(3 + \frac{5}{6}\right) = \left(3 + \frac{10}{12}\right)$$
$$+ 1\frac{3}{4} = +\left(1 + \frac{3}{4}\right) = +\left(1 + \frac{9}{12}\right)$$
$$= \left(4 + \frac{19}{12}\right)$$
$$= 4 + \left(\frac{12}{12} + \frac{7}{12}\right)$$
$$= (4 + 1) + \frac{7}{12}$$
$$= 5\frac{7}{12}$$

SUBTRACTION

$$3\frac{5}{6} = \left(3 + \frac{5}{6}\right) = \left(3 + \frac{10}{12}\right)$$
$$- 1\frac{3}{4} = -\left(1 + \frac{3}{4}\right) = -\left(1 + \frac{9}{12}\right)$$
$$= \left(2 + \frac{1}{12}\right)$$
$$= 2\frac{1}{12}$$

3. Find the sum or difference.

a) $6\frac{2}{3} + 2\frac{1}{4} = \square$ b) $12\frac{1}{2} - 8 = \square$

c) $2\frac{7}{16} - 1\frac{3}{8} = \square$ d) $7\frac{5}{6} + 4\frac{3}{3} = \square$

e) $5\frac{1}{2} + 3\frac{1}{4} = \square$ f) $9\frac{1}{6} - 5\frac{3}{4} = \square$

4.

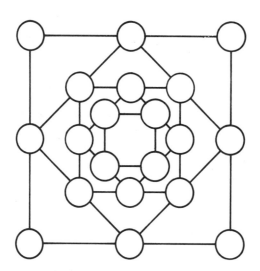

On a sheet of white cardboard, draw a figure as shown above. Cover the drawing with clear self-adhesive plastic so that you can use a china marker to write on it. Write a fraction in each circular region in the four corners of the square. Find the difference between the larger fraction and the smaller one and write the difference in the circular region between the fractions subtracted. Continue this process, moving toward the center of the figure. Can you find four fractional numbers to put in the first four circular regions so that you end with zeros in the innermost circular regions?

5. For this activity, construct two decks of cards from cardboard of different colors. On each card, write an addition or subtraction example with one of the following answers: $\frac{1}{2}, \frac{3}{4}, \frac{7}{10}, \frac{5}{8}, \frac{4}{5}, \frac{5}{6}, \frac{3}{5}, \frac{3}{8}$, or $\frac{1}{4}$. On a file folder, place a grid on the inside of one page (see p. 349). Place the fractions listed above in squares of the grid. Place the folder between two players. One player uses a deck all of one color and the other player uses the deck of the other color. The players take turns drawing a card and solving the example. The other player checks the example after the player places his or her card on the answer board. Players may place cards on top of cards played by the other player. After cards are placed on the board, the players may not look at the answers underneath. The first player to get three in a row or column wins the game.

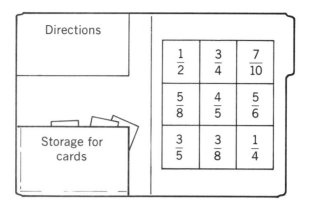

WRITING MATHEMATICAL SENTENCES

Present a variety of word problems that involve addition and subtraction of fractions. Have the students write and solve an appropriate mathematical sentence for each problem. Word problems of this kind provide valuable experience in analyzing problems, and they provide practice in performing operations on fractions. Perimeter problems offer a chance to review various ideas of geometry while giving practice in computation.

MULTIPLICATION OF FRACTIONS

Activities in the upper grades should review and then extend concepts developed in intermediate grades. The overhead projector can greatly facilitate guided discovery at this level. Begin on the concrete level, manipulating models.

1. Draw equal-sized squares on a series of transparencies for the overhead projector. On each transparency shade a different sector of the square. Place two transparencies on top of each other to model different multiplication examples. Make two transparencies for each model.

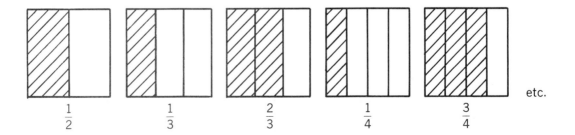

2. Use the diagrams to help you find the products. Also use the overhead transparencies discussed previously.

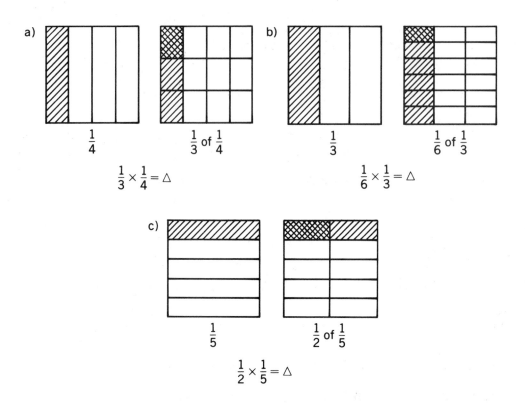

a) $\frac{1}{4}$ $\frac{1}{3}$ of $\frac{1}{4}$

$$\frac{1}{3} \times \frac{1}{4} = \triangle$$

b) $\frac{1}{3}$ $\frac{1}{6}$ of $\frac{1}{3}$

$$\frac{1}{6} \times \frac{1}{3} = \triangle$$

c) $\frac{1}{5}$ $\frac{1}{2}$ of $\frac{1}{5}$

$$\frac{1}{2} \times \frac{1}{5} = \triangle$$

3. Using the fraction kit and sheets of paper to represent sets, have the student model three sets of $\frac{2}{5}$. Have the student manipulate the regions and write the multiplication sentence.

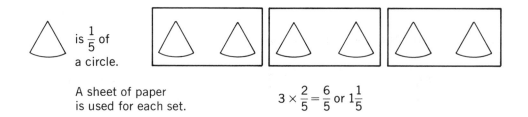

is $\frac{1}{5}$ of a circle.

A sheet of paper is used for each set.

$$3 \times \frac{2}{5} = \frac{6}{5} \text{ or } 1\frac{1}{5}$$

4. Have the children shade parts of regions to solve examples such as the following.

a) $\frac{1}{2} \times \frac{1}{7} = \square$ b) $\frac{2}{3} \times \frac{1}{2} = \square$ c) $\frac{4}{5} \times \frac{1}{3} = \square$ d) $\frac{3}{4} \times \frac{1}{5} = \square$

5. The number line should also be used for modeling examples such as $3 \times \frac{2}{5} = \frac{6}{5}$.

6. Solve each of the following sentences.

a) $\frac{7}{8} \times \frac{2}{3} = n$ c) $\frac{3}{7} \times \frac{2}{3} = n$ e) $\frac{4}{5} \times \frac{3}{7} = n$ g) $\frac{3}{4} \times \frac{4}{5} = n$

b) $\frac{5}{6} \times \frac{1}{3} = n$ d) $\frac{1}{4} \times \frac{5}{8} = n$ f) $\frac{2}{5} \times \frac{3}{5} = n$ h) $\frac{3}{7} \times \frac{4}{9} = n$

7. Factor the numerator and denominator of each fraction before multiplying. Then use what you know about other names for 1 and the multiplication property of 1 to express the product in simplest form.

$$\text{Example:} \quad \frac{7}{10} \times \frac{2}{3} = \frac{7 \times 2}{2 \times 5 \times 3}$$
$$= \frac{2 \times 7}{2 \times 5 \times 3}$$
$$= \frac{2}{2} \times \frac{7}{5 \times 3}$$
$$= 1 \times \frac{7}{15}$$
$$= \frac{7}{15}$$

a) $\frac{5}{6} \times \frac{2}{3}$

b) $\frac{21}{35} \times \frac{42}{64}$

c) $\frac{3}{8} \times \frac{3}{4}$

d) $\frac{6}{10} \times \frac{9}{15} \times \frac{11}{30}$

e) $\frac{3}{10} \times \frac{5}{25}$

f) $\frac{9}{49} \times \frac{7}{56}$

8. Rewrite each mixed numeral as an improper fraction. Then multiply to find n.

a) $1\frac{7}{8} \times 2\frac{1}{5} = n$

b) $3\frac{1}{7} \times 2\frac{1}{5} = n$

c) $1\frac{2}{7} \times 8\frac{1}{4} = n$

d) $5\frac{1}{3} \times 5\frac{1}{3} = n$

e) $4\frac{1}{6} \times 5\frac{1}{2} = n$

f) $8\frac{1}{3} \times 2\frac{2}{5} = n$

9. Which product is not another name for 1?

a) $1\frac{1}{2} \times \frac{2}{3}$

b) $\frac{7}{8} \times \frac{8}{7}$

c) $\frac{1}{10} \times 1$

d) $1\frac{5}{6} \times \frac{6}{11}$

e) $\frac{16}{4} \times \frac{1}{4}$

10. Write the reciprocal of each fractional number.

a) $\frac{5}{8}$

b) $\frac{1}{2}$

c) $\frac{9}{8}$

d) $\frac{4}{9}$

e) $\frac{12}{10}$

f) $9\frac{1}{2}$

g) 0

11. Complete each table.

a)

n	$\frac{2}{3} \times n$
0	
1	
2	$\frac{4}{3}$
3	
4	

b)

n	$\frac{1}{5} \times n$
$\frac{1}{2}$	
$\frac{2}{3}$	
$\frac{3}{4}$	
$\frac{4}{5}$	
$\frac{5}{6}$	

c)

n	$2 \times n$
$1\frac{1}{2}$	
2	
$2\frac{1}{2}$	
3	
$3\frac{1}{2}$	

DIVISION OF FRACTIONS

Trying to demonstrate division of fractions *concretely* presents difficulties in interpretation. However, it is not impossible. At this point children are accustomed to seeing an example in division written in three ways:

$$8 \div 4 = n \qquad 4\overline{)8} \qquad n \times 4 = 8$$

It is not difficult for them to understand that if we begin with a set of 8 objects, we can divide this set into 2 sets of 4 objects or 4 sets of 2 objects. With this reasoning as a reference point, division of fractions can be demonstrated in a way that makes sense.

Example: $\dfrac{8}{9} \div \dfrac{4}{9} = n \qquad \dfrac{4}{9}\overline{)\dfrac{8}{9}} \qquad n \times \dfrac{4}{9} = \dfrac{8}{9}$

Let's examine the concept in terms of regions. Consider the example $2 \div \dfrac{1}{3} = n$. We are asking how many one-thirds there are in 2.

$$\frac{1}{3}\overline{)\,2} = \frac{1}{3}\overline{)\,\dfrac{6}{3}}\;{\scriptstyle 6}$$

Clearly there are 6 one-thirds in 2. Now, suppose that we have one unit region divided into fourths. How many three-fourths are contained in one unit region?

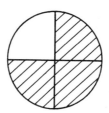

The shaded area is three-fourths of the unit region, but there is one-fourth of the unit region left over.

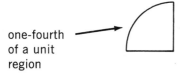

one-fourth of a unit region

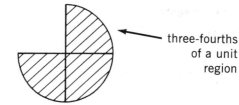

three-fourths of a unit region

The one-fourth left over is one-third of the three-fourths unit region. So there are $1\frac{1}{3}$ three-fourths in one unit region.

$$1 \div \frac{3}{4} = 1\frac{1}{3}$$

The number line is an excellent device to use for developing an understanding of the division of fractions.

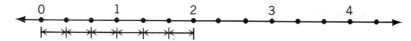

How many one-thirds are there in 2? You can readily see that there are 6 one-thirds in 2.

Thus 2 divided by $\frac{1}{3}$ is 6. Draw a number line and show how many three-fourths are in 1.

Throughout their study of division of whole numbers, the children have been made aware of the inverse relationship between multiplication and division. This relationship should again be stressed to help the children understand division of fractions. It is also important for the children to understand that every expression of the form $a \div b$ can be written in the form $\frac{a}{b}$, and vice versa. A factor multiplied by a factor equals a product, or a product divided by a factor equals a missing factor.

1. Complete the following.

   a) Since $\frac{2}{3} \times 6 = 4$, we know that $4 \div \frac{2}{3} = $ _____ and $4 \div 6 = \frac{2}{3}$.

   b) Since $\frac{3}{5} \times 5 = 3$, we know that $3 \div \frac{3}{5} = 5$ and $3 \div 5 = $ _____.

   c) Since $\frac{4}{7} \times 7 = 4$, we know that $4 \div \frac{4}{7} = $ _____ and $4 \div 7 = $ _____.

   d) Since $\frac{8}{5} \times 5 = 8$, we know that $8 \div \frac{8}{5} = $ _____ and $8 \div 5 = $ _____.

   e) Since $\frac{13}{16} \times 16 = 13$, we know that $13 \div \frac{13}{16} = $ _____ and $13 \div 16 = $ _____.

2. Complete each of the following.

   a) $1 \div \frac{1}{3} = $ _____

   b) $1 \div \frac{7}{6} = $ _____

   c) $1 \div \frac{2}{3} = $ _____

   d) $1 \div \frac{10}{3} = $ _____

   e) $1 \div \frac{3}{4} = $ _____

   f) $1 \div \frac{4}{9} = $ _____

   g) $1 \div \frac{5}{6} = $ _____

   h) $1 \div \frac{13}{8} = $ _____

Several different approaches to division of fractions are possible. One excellent method that stresses structure and properties of operations is the method just explained. The sensitive teacher will be aware of the difficulties that individual children are experiencing and whenever possible will vary the approach to meet individual needs. Children should eventually discover the usual algorithm for division of fractions, but it is essential that the algorithm be used only after the children understand why it works.

3. Solve each sentence for n.

   a) $\frac{6}{7} \div \frac{7}{6} = n$

   b) $\frac{1}{9} \div \frac{7}{15} = n$

   c) $\frac{3}{5} \div \frac{8}{7} = n$

   d) $\frac{4}{9} \div \frac{7}{12} = n$

   e) $\frac{5}{4} \div \frac{9}{10} = n$

   f) $\frac{35}{64} \div \frac{7}{8} = n$

   g) $\frac{13}{6} \div \frac{1}{4} = n$

   h) $\frac{6}{5} \div \frac{14}{15} = n$

4. Solve each sentence.

   a) $2\frac{1}{6} \div \frac{1}{3} = n$

   b) $2\frac{5}{7} \div \frac{1}{14} = n$

   c) $1\frac{3}{8} \div \frac{6}{24} = n$

   d) $5 \div 4\frac{1}{2} = n$

5. Rewrite each of the following as a multiplication sentence and solve.

   a) $\frac{4}{5} \div \frac{5}{9} = \square$

   b) $\frac{2}{2} \div \frac{7}{8} = \square$

   c) $\frac{3}{2} \div \frac{5}{3} = \square$

   d) $8\frac{3}{4} = \square$

6. Write $<$, $>$, or $=$ in each circle.

   a) $5\frac{1}{2} - 4\frac{11}{12} \bigcirc 2\frac{3}{4} \div 11$

   b) $7\frac{1}{3} \div 2\frac{1}{5} \bigcirc 5 - 1\frac{2}{3}$

c) $\frac{5}{6} \div \frac{5}{12}$ ◯ $17\frac{8}{10} \div \frac{9}{10}$ d) $\frac{5}{2} \times \frac{2}{5}$ ◯ $\frac{2}{3} \times \frac{2}{3}$

e) $1\frac{1}{2} \div \frac{3}{3}$ ◯ $\frac{5}{3} \times \frac{3}{4}$ f) $10 \div \frac{4}{9}$ ◯ $5 \div \frac{2}{9}$

g) $\frac{8}{3} \times \frac{1}{4}$ ◯ $\frac{8}{3} \div \frac{1}{4}$ h) $5 \div 3\frac{1}{2}$ ◯ $\frac{1}{5} \times \frac{7}{2}$

7. Write only the answers to the following examples. Do all computation mentally.

a) $5 \times 15 = $ ____   b) $2 \times 3\frac{1}{2} = $ ____

c) $7 \times 13 = $ ____   d) $3 \times 2\frac{2}{3} = $ ____

e) $6 \times 16 = $ ____   f) $4\frac{1}{4} \times 4 = $ ____

g) $4 \times 18 = $ ____   h) $5\frac{3}{4} \times 2 = $ ____

8. Complete the following chart. The first example has been done for you.

Example	Unknown factor is between:	Unknown factor is between:	Unknown factor is closer to:
$24 \div 3\frac{5}{6}$	$24 \div 3$ and $24 \div 4$	8 and 6	6
$16 \div 2\frac{2}{3}$			
$18 \div 3\frac{1}{3}$			
$9 \div 2\frac{3}{4}$			

9. Write a mathematical sentence for each problem. Then solve the sentence.

a) Richard went to a movie that was $1\frac{1}{2}$ hours long. He watched only $\frac{2}{3}$ of the movie. How long did he stay?

b) Mr. Mosley traveled for $4\frac{1}{4}$ hours at a speed of 40 miles an hour. How far did he go?

c) A rectangle is $2\frac{3}{8}$ inches long and $1\frac{1}{4}$ inches wide. What is its area in square inches?

d) A rectangle has an area of 60 square inches. It is $3\frac{3}{4}$ inches wide. How long is it?

e) In a class of 30 students, $\frac{1}{6}$ of the boys have brown hair. The boys make up $\frac{3}{5}$ of the class. How many boys are there with brown hair?

10. Complete the table by finding fraction pairs.

Sum	Fraction Pair	Product
1	$\frac{1}{2}, \frac{1}{2}$	$\frac{1}{4}$
$\frac{14}{48}$		$\frac{1}{48}$
$\frac{17}{12}$		$\frac{1}{2}$
$1\frac{7}{30}$		$\frac{2}{6}$
$\frac{11}{8}$		$\frac{7}{16}$
$1\frac{7}{15}$		$\frac{8}{15}$
$1\frac{5}{24}$		$\frac{7}{24}$
$\frac{61}{56}$		$\frac{15}{56}$

11. Prepare 48 cards with a fraction example on each card (multiplication, division, addition, and subtraction). Deal all the cards. Each player places his or her cards face down. Taking the top card of the deck, the player solves the example on that card. The player whose example yields the highest answer wins all of the cards played. At the end of the period, the person with the most cards is declared the winner.

12. Use three small wooden or sponge cubes. Write a fraction on each face of two of them. On the third put operation signs. Let the children take turns rolling the dice and solving the examples.

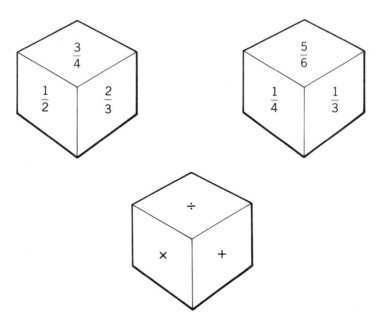

Hand-Held Calculator Activities for the Upper Elementary Grades

Hand-held calculator activities are not appropriate for operations with fractions, since calculators do not have the capabilities of displaying fractions on the screen.

Microcomputer Activities for the Upper Elementary Grades

The following program will function with fractions on the Apple computer. Teachers should first run the program and then edit it to meet the needs of the children in each classroom.

```
10 HOME
20 PRINT "IN THIS PROGRAM YOU WILL BE GIVEN THREE"
30 PRINT "NUMBERS LIKE THOSE SHOWN BELOW."
40 PRINT : PRINT
50 PRINT "1/3","3/4","3/12"
60 PRINT : PRINT
70 PRINT "YOU'LL HAVE TO SELECT THE OPERATION "
80 PRINT "THAT WAS USED ON THE TWO NUMBERS ON THE"
90 PRINT "LEFT TO GET THE ANSWER ON THE RIGHT"
100 PRINT "CAUTION: FRACTIONS WILL NOT ALWAYS BE"
110 PRINT "IN THEIR SIMPLEST FORM."
140 PRINT
150 PRINT "READY (TYPE YES OR NO) ";: INPUT A$
160 IF A$ <> "YES" THEN GOTO 400
170 HOME
180 LET X = INT ( RND (1) * 10) + 1
190 LET Y = INT ( RND (1) * 10) + 1
200 LET Q = INT ( RND (1) * 10) + 1
210 LET R = INT ( RND (1) * 10) + 1
215 IF (X * R) − (Y * Q)<0 THEN GOTO 180
220 PRINT X;"/";Y,Q;"/";R,
230 LET S = INT ( RND (1) * 4) + 1
240 ON S GOTO 250,260,270,280
250 PRINT (X * R) + (Y * Q);"/";(Y * R): GOTO 290
260 PRINT (X * R) − (Y * Q);"/";(Y * R): GOTO 290
270 PRINT (X * Q);"/";(Y * R): GOTO 290
280 PRINT (X * R);"/";(Y * Q): GOTO 290
290 PRINT : PRINT "TYPE THE NUMBER OF THE OPERATION THAT WAS USED"
300 PRINT : PRINT "_____1. ADDITION
310 PRINT : PRINT "_____2. SUBTRACTION
320 PRINT : PRINT "_____3. MULTIPLICATION
330 PRINT : PRINT "_____4. DIVISION
340 PRINT : INPUT A
350 IF A = S THEN PRINT "FANTASTIC!!!": FOR X = 1 TO 1000: NEXT X: GOTO 150
360 IF A <> S THEN PRINT "SORRY, TRY AGAIN": FOR X = 1 TO 1000: NEXT X:
    GOTO 340
```

```
400 PRINT : PRINT "WOULD YOU LIKE TO TRY AGAIN";
410 INPUT A$
420 IF A$ = "YES" THEN GOTO 10
430 END
```

Suggested Readings

Bright, George W. "Ideas." *The Arithmetic Teacher*, vol. 24, no. 1, January 1977.

Coxford, Arthur, and Ellerbruch, Lawrence W. "Fractional Numbers," in *Mathematics Learning in Early Childhood*, Thirty-Seventh Yearbook. Reston, Va.: National Council of Teachers of Mathematics, 1975.

Dienes, Zoltan P. *Fractions: An Operational Approach*. New York: Herder & Herder, 1967.

Ellerbruch, Lawrence W., and Payne, Joseph N. "A Teaching Sequence from Initial Fraction Concepts Through the Addition of Unlike Fractions," in *Developing Computational Skills, 1978 Yearbook*. Reston, Va.: National Council of Teachers of Mathematics, 1978.

Heddens, James W., and Hynes, Michael. "Division of Fractional Numbers." *The Arithmetic Teacher*, vol. 16, no. 2, February 1969.

Kolesnik, Theodore. "Illustrating the Multiplication and Division of Common Fractions." *The Arithmetic Teacher*, vol. 10, no. 5, May 1963.

Madell, Robert L. "Children Can Understand Mathematics." *The Arithmetic Teacher*, vol. 29, no. 5, January 1982.

Moulton, J. Paul. "A Working Model for Rational Numbers." *The Arithmetic Teacher*, vol. 22, no. 4, April 1975.

Ockenga, Earl, and Duea, Joan. "Ideas." *The Arithmetic Teacher*, vol. 25, no. 4, January 1978.

Platts, Mary E., ed. *Plus*. Stevensville, Mich.: Educational Services, 1964.

Ruaid, Ronald W. "A Low-Stress Algorithm for Fractions." *Mathematics Teacher*, vol. 71, no. 4, April 1978.

Silvia, Evelyn M. "A Look at Division of Fractions." *The Arithmetic Teacher*, vol. 30, no. 5, January 1983.

Smith, Seaton E., Jr., and Backman, Carl A. *Teacher-Made Aids for Elementary School Mathematics*. Reston, Va.: National Council of Teachers of Mathematics, 1974.

Sowder, Larry. "Models for Fractional Numbers—A Quiz for Teachers." *The Arithmetic Teacher*, vol. 18, no. 1, January 1971.

Virginia Council of Teachers of Mathematics. *Practical Ways to Teach the Basic Skills*. Reston, Va.: National Council of Teachers of Mathematics, 1979.

Wassmandorf, M. "Reducing Fractions Can Be Easy, Maybe Even Fun." *The Arithmetic Teacher*, vol. 21, no. 2, February 1974.

11 Rational Numbers Expressed as Decimals

Teaching Competencies

Upon completing this unit, you will be able to:

Use models (including Dienes Blocks, regions, money, and the number line) to develop understanding of decimals and their operations

Change and write any given rational number in fraction form, decimal form, or expanded notation

Perform basic operations and inverse operations on numbers expressed in decimal form

Express numbers in scientific notation

Use ratio and proportion to describe problem situations and to solve percentage problems

Rewrite any terminating or repeating decimal in fraction form

Discussion

In the two previous units, we discussed rational numbers expressed as fractions; in this unit, we will carefully examine rational numbers expressed as **decimals.** Decimals are convenient and efficient to use for computational purposes. They permit the place-value notation used for whole numbers to be extended to rational numbers. For these reasons and others, decimals are widely used in science, industry, and commerce in applications involving the metric system, calculators, and computers.

The beginning step in teaching children rational numbers expressed as decimals is to develop an understanding of what a decimal actually represents. Several models can be used with children. Let's begin to develop an understanding of decimals by using Dienes Blocks.

At this stage of development, children should have had many experiences with Dienes Blocks in learning the concept of place value. You might want to review whole-number place-value concepts at this point. With whole numbers, children understand the value of the Dienes Blocks as follows:

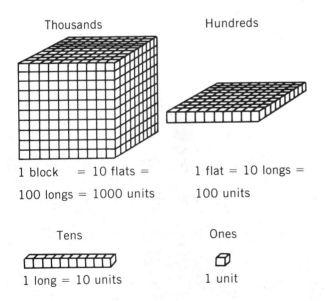

Thousands   Hundreds

1 block = 10 flats =   1 flat = 10 longs =
100 longs = 1000 units   100 units

Tens   Ones

1 long = 10 units   1 unit

Now let's redefine the blocks. These blocks are always defined in terms of the block placed in the ones place. When a cube is defined, a long, a flat, and a block then become defined. Begin by using a block defined as one.

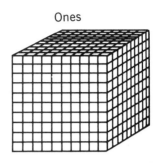

Ones

Then discuss with the children the relationships among the blocks, as tenths, hundredths, and thousandths are defined. If a block equals one, a flat is defined as one tenth of a block, a long is one tenth of a flat, and a cube is one tenth of a long.

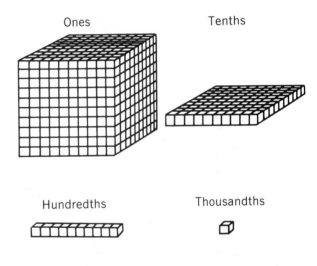

Ones   Tenths

Hundredths   Thousandths

Children need to manipulate the blocks, see the new relationship, extend the place-value chart, and discuss the extension of the place-value system. This is really not a new concept for the children; it only extends a concept developed in earlier grades. (If decimals are introduced before fractions, then using Dienes Blocks and the concept of place value is an excellent procedure for introducing rational numbers.)

Another material that should be used with children is squared-paper models. Squared-paper models are more dependent upon fractions than are Dienes Blocks. Let's examine the models and their usefulness for introducing students to decimals.

Since students have worked with fractions, they should understand the concept of tenths and hundredths. Squared paper is a good way to illustrate .1 and .01, or $\frac{1}{10}$ and $\frac{1}{100}$.

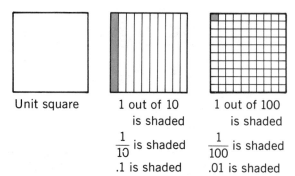

Unit square   1 out of 10   1 out of 100
is shaded   is shaded

$\frac{1}{10}$ is shaded $\frac{1}{100}$ is shaded

.1 is shaded   .01 is shaded

Circular regions can be used in a similar manner:

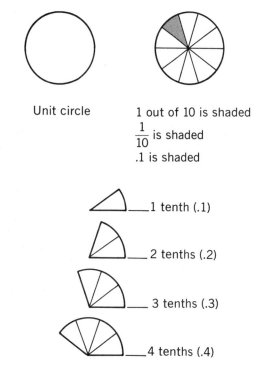

Unit circle   1 out of 10 is shaded

$\frac{1}{10}$ is shaded

.1 is shaded

_____1 tenth (.1)

_____2 tenths (.2)

_____3 tenths (.3)

_____4 tenths (.4)

Students have modeled many fractions on the number line. After having done halves, thirds, fourths, fifths, sixths, and eighths, modeling tenths on a number line will be easy.

0										1		
$\frac{0}{10}$	$\frac{1}{10}$	$\frac{2}{10}$	$\frac{3}{10}$	$\frac{4}{10}$	$\frac{5}{10}$	$\frac{6}{10}$	$\frac{7}{10}$	$\frac{8}{10}$	$\frac{9}{10}$	$\frac{10}{10}$	$\frac{11}{10}$	...
0	.1	.2	.3	.4	.5	.6	.7	.8	.9	1.0	1.1	

The concept of place value is fundamental to an understanding of decimals. In order that students may be able to discover the meaning of decimals for themselves, it is necessary for them to review place value. Consider the values of the places shown in the following chart.

THOUSANDS	HUNDREDS	TENS	ONES
1	1	1	1

The value of the tens place is how many times the value of the ones place? The 1 in the tens place has ten times the value of the 1 in the ones place. The value of the hundreds place is how many times the value of the tens place? The 1 in the hundreds place has 10 times the value of the 1 in the tens place. Now let's reverse our procedure and compare the tens place with the hundreds place.

The 1 in the tens place has $\frac{1}{10}$ the value of the 1 in the hundreds place. What is the relation between the ones place and the tens place? The 1 in the ones place has $\frac{1}{10}$ the value of the 1 in the tens place. Do you think there is another place to the right of the ones place? If there is, what relation exists between this new place and the ones place?

If the pattern that we have discovered is consistent, this new place should have $\frac{1}{10}$ the value of the ones place. Since $\frac{1}{10}$ of 1 is $\frac{1}{10}$, we can name this new place the **tenths** place. What about the next place to the right of the tenths place? What relation exists between this new place and the tenths place? The value of this place should be $\frac{1}{10}$ the value of the tenths place. Since $\frac{1}{10}$ of $\frac{1}{10}$ is $\frac{1}{100}$, we can name this place the **hundredths** place. Using the pattern developed, we can continue this procedure to find the values of as many places as we wish.

All the places to the right of the ones place represent fractional parts of 1, so we need a way to indicate this fact. We do this with a **decimal point**. The decimal point is our reference point to indicate the separation of whole-number values from fractional-number parts in a decimal (base-ten) numeral. The decimal point is marked between the ones place and the tenths place.

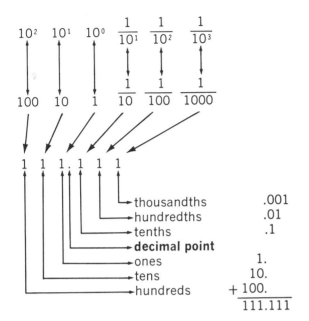

Can you now continue this place-value scheme to both the left and the right? Can you name the first ten places to the right of the decimal point? Using the pattern developed, you should be able to name each of these places and, in so doing, see clearly the structure and meaning of the **decimal system.**

Money can also be used to develop an understanding of tenths and hundredths. Place a one-dollar bill in the ones place; then a dime is one tenth of a dollar, and a penny is one hundredth of a dollar. A dime is written as .10 and a penny is written as .01. Discuss money with the children, and relate the writing of money values to the place-value system.

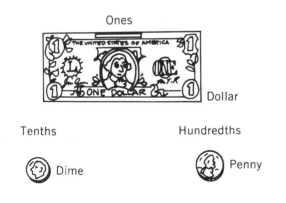

Numeral Expanders can also be used to help children understand decimal notation, as follows:

Place the *Numeral Expander* that has the zeros printed on it in front of you. Make sure that the small section of the *Numeral Expander* is on the left and that the longer sections are on the right. This is the

opposite of the way that the *Numeral Expander* is placed for whole numbers. Using the special marking pencil, mark a large dot so everyone in the classroom can see it, in the lower left-hand corner of the small section. This dot is the reference point. We call this dot the *decimal point.*

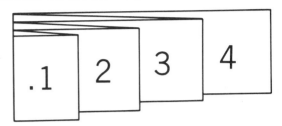

Note: Numeral expanders can be purchased along with a manual directly from James Heddens, Elementary-Secondary Education, Kent State University, Kent, Ohio 44242.

On each of the next three panels with zeros printed on it, mark a large dot in the lower left-hand corner. Also write a large numeral on each of the four panels.

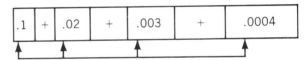

When the *Numeral Expander* is ready for use with decimals, it will look like this model. Note that four decimal points have been written on the *Expander*—one on the tenths panel, one on the hundredths panel, one on the thousandths panel, and one on the ten-thousandths panel.

Now let's examine a procedure that might be used to teach understanding of decimals. Write a numeral for a three- or four-place whole number on the chalkboard. Label the place-value name above each numeral. Using a heuristic approach, review the relation between each value of the places. For example:

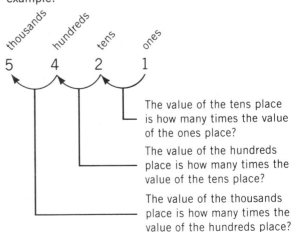

The children's response to each of these questions should be that each place value on the left is 10 times the place value on its right.

Now, using the same procedure, compare the value of each place to the value of the place to its immediate right.

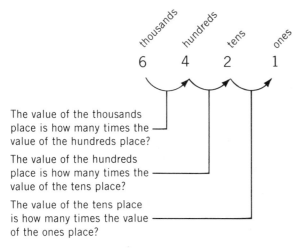

The value of the thousands place is how many times the value of the hundreds place?

The value of the hundreds place is how many times the value of the tens place?

The value of the tens place is how many times the value of the ones place?

The answers to each of these three questions should be that the place value on the right is one tenth of the place value on its immediate left.

These questions merely review the place-value understanding that children have already developed. Now ask the children to pretend that there is a place to the *right* of the ones place. What relationship might exist between the ones and this *new* place? Permit the children to discuss their ideas about this new place.

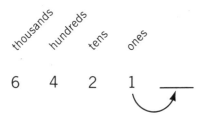

The students should respond that the value of the new place should be one tenth that of the ones place (assuming that the same pattern continues). From their understanding of fractions, the children know that

$$\frac{1}{10} \times 1 = \frac{1}{10}$$

Therefore, we agree to call this new place the **tenths place.** This procedure should be continued to the right for three or four places. The children can discover the name for each place by using fractions.

Now use the prepared *Numeral Expander* with the decimal points marked. Hold the *Numeral Expander* as illustrated, so that the tenths and hundredths places face the students.

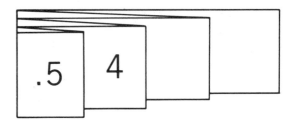

Next, fold back the thousandths and ten-thousandths places so they do not show. Now the tenths and hundredths places can be expanded by unfolding these two places.

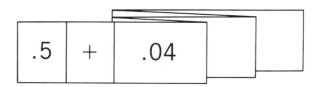

Have the students write the number in standard notation when the expanded notation is shown and in expanded notation when the standard notation is shown.

Children are shown	Children write
.4 + .07	.4 + .07 = .47
.2 + .09	.2 + .09 = .29
.36	.36 = .3 + .06
.23	.23 = .2 + .03

When the children have a good understanding of tenths and hundredths, they are then ready to consider additional places.

Use similar procedures to develop standard notation for tenths, hundredths, thousandths, and ten-thousandths. The *Numeral Expander* will help children understand the standard and expanded notation for these four places. When children have a good understanding of these four decimal places, and of expanded and standard notation, then they can easily develop additional places to the right.

To use the *Numeral Expander* for addition and subtraction of decimals, adapt the procedures that we explained for addition and subtraction of whole numbers.

In our discussion of structure of place-value numeration systems, we saw that every whole number can be renamed in several ways. For example, 427 can be written in expanded notation:

$$427 = 400 + 20 + 7$$

We can also write it using exponential notation:

$$427 = (4 \times 10^2) + (2 \times 10^1) + (7 \times 10^0)$$

Can all decimal numerals be written in similar alternative forms? Yes, this is possible. Consider, for example, the numeral 23.56; we can rewrite it in expanded notation as follows:

$$23.56 = 20 + 3 + .5 + .06$$

We can continue and write the numeral in several other forms:

$$
\begin{aligned}
23.56 &= 20 + 3 + .5 + .06 \\
&= 20 + 3 + \frac{5}{10} + \frac{6}{100} \\
&= (2 \times 10) + (3 \times 1) + \left(5 \times \frac{1}{10}\right) + \left(6 \times \frac{1}{100}\right) \\
&= (2 \times 10^1) + (3 \times 10^0) + \left(5 \times \frac{1}{10^1}\right) + \\
&\quad \left(6 \times \frac{1}{10^2}\right)
\end{aligned}
$$

Children in the intermediate grades should be able to rewrite decimal numerals in these alternative forms to demonstrate an understanding of place value in decimal numerals. Some children in Grade 6 may be ready to use negative exponents to write decimals in yet another form. If the children understand the meaning of negative integers (see Unit 12), you might use the patterns in the following chart to help the children discover the meaning of 10^{-1}, 10^{-2}, and so on.

Decimal	Exponential Notation
1000	10^3
100	10^2
10	10^1
1	10^0
.1	$10^?$
.01	$10^?$
.001	$10^?$

Children should be familiar with the way exponential notation is used in the first four rows of the chart. What exponents could we use to complete the right-hand column of powers of 10? We observe that as we go down the right-hand column, the exponents decrease by 1 each time. If this pattern continues, what exponent should we use to replace the first question mark? Yes, $^-1$ (the integer which is 1 less than 0). What integer should replace the second question mark? Clearly the answer is $^-2$, since $^-2$ is the integer which is 1 less than $^-1$. What integer should replace the third question mark? Yes, $^-3$. In this way the children can discover the following kind of facts about negative exponents:

$$
\begin{aligned}
10^{-1} &= \quad .1 = \frac{1}{10} \quad \text{or} \quad \frac{1}{10^1} \\
10^{-2} &= \quad .01 = \frac{1}{100} \quad \text{or} \quad \frac{1}{10^2} \\
10^{-3} &= .001 = \frac{1}{1000} \quad \text{or} \quad \frac{1}{10^3}
\end{aligned}
$$

From these and similar facts the children should be able to make the generalization that for any whole number n,

$$10^{-n} = \frac{1}{10^n}$$

Expanded notation and powers of 10 that involve negative exponents can be used to reinforce ideas about place value:

$$
\begin{aligned}
34.1 &= 30 + 4 + .1 \\
&= (3 \times 10) + (4 \times 1) + \left(1 \times \frac{1}{10}\right) \\
&= (3 \times 10^1) + (4 \times 10^0) + (1 \times 10^{-1})
\end{aligned}
$$

$$
\begin{aligned}
234.12 &= 200 + 30 + 4 + .1 + .02 \\
&= (2 \times 100) + (3 \times 10) + (4 \times 1) + \\
&\quad \left(1 \times \frac{1}{10}\right) + \left(2 \times \frac{1}{100}\right) \\
&= (2 \times 10^2) + (3 \times 10^1) + (4 \times 10^0) + \\
&\quad (1 \times 10^{-1}) + (2 \times 10^{-2})
\end{aligned}
$$

$$
\begin{aligned}
764.123 &= 700 + 60 + 4 + .1 + .02 + .003 \\
&= (7 \times 100) + (6 \times 10) + (4 \times 1) + \\
&\quad \left(1 \times \frac{1}{10}\right) + \left(2 \times \frac{1}{100}\right) + \left(3 \times \frac{1}{1000}\right) \\
&= (7 \times 10^2) + (6 \times 10^1) + (4 \times 10^0) + \\
&\quad (1 \times 10^{-1}) + (2 \times 10^{-2}) + (3 \times 10^{-3})
\end{aligned}
$$

Note: Do *not* ask children to write these steps. These are here only to help you understand the concepts. Teachers should be able to understand and write these steps.

This use of expanded notation should further clarify the meaning of decimals in our number system (a **base-ten** or **decimal system**).

Since the children have studied fractions, place value, and addition of whole numbers, adding decimals should not be too difficult. Let's look at an addition example involving decimals by comparing it to regions of a circle. Using tenths of a circle, let's examine the example .2 + .3 = □. The students understand basic addition and know that:

2 tenths + 3 tenths = 5 tenths

We can write:

.2 + .3 = .5   or   2 tenths   or   .2
                    + 3 tenths   + .3
                      5 tenths   .5

Now let's look at the same example modeled on the number line, illustrated just like any other addition example.

Always begin at 0. Mark off an addend of 2 tenths, then mark off an addend of 3 tenths, and you arrive at the point we call the sum, which in this case is 5 tenths. Therefore .2 + .3 = .5.

In addition of whole numbers, ones are aligned in the ones column, tens in the tens column, and so on. The same idea applies to addition of decimals. Tenths are added to tenths and are aligned in the tenths column; hundredths are added to hundredths and are aligned in the hundredths column, and so on. If the children understand place value, they should discover that in the addition of decimals, the decimal points are always aligned. The meaning of place value should be reviewed and stressed as often as necessary in introducing children to rational numbers in decimal form.

Consider another addition example:

$$\frac{3}{10} + \frac{4}{10} = \frac{7}{10}$$

After our study of fractions, this example should not be difficult. We know from our examination of decimals that we can rewrite these fractions.

$$\frac{3}{10} = \quad .3$$
$$+\frac{4}{10} = + .4$$
$$\frac{7}{10} = \quad .7$$

Thus another way to add $\frac{3}{10}$ and $\frac{4}{10}$ is to rewrite these fractions as decimals.

.3 (three-tenths)
+ .4 (four-tenths)
.7 (seven-tenths)

Take another example:

$$\frac{23}{100} + \frac{14}{100} = \frac{37}{100}$$

Another way of stating this example is shown below.

.23
+ .14
.37

A longer example illustrates the procedure more clearly.

$$.234 = \frac{234}{1000} = \frac{2340}{10,000} \longrightarrow .2340$$

$$.1742 = \frac{1742}{10,000} = \frac{1742}{10,000} \longrightarrow .1742$$

$$+.11 = +\frac{11}{100} = +\frac{1100}{10,000} \longrightarrow +.1100$$

$$\frac{5182}{10,000} \longrightarrow .5182$$

(Again, do not ask children to write these steps.) By working through a number of similar examples, children should soon realize why decimal points are aligned in addition and subtraction. Alignment of decimal points is comparable to finding a common denominator, as we see in the example above. A shorter analysis of the example is shown below. Notice the use of zeros in illustrating place value.

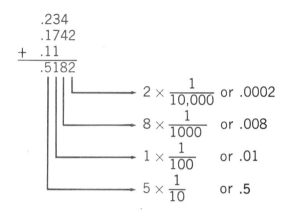

$$.234$$
$$.1742$$
$$+ \; .11$$
$$\overline{.5182}$$

$2 \times \dfrac{1}{10,000}$ or .0002

$8 \times \dfrac{1}{1000}$ or .008

$1 \times \dfrac{1}{100}$ or .01

$5 \times \dfrac{1}{10}$ or .5

Notice that in the hundredths column we obtain a sum of .11, or $\dfrac{11}{100}$. We record the .01 $\left(\dfrac{1}{100}\right)$ in the hundredths column and add the 0.1 $\left(\dfrac{1}{10}\right)$ to the tenths column; we add this .1 to the .4 and indicate the sum, .5, in the tenths column.

Consider this example: $.8 + .6 = \square$. We can solve this example as follows.

$$.8$$
$$+ \, .6$$

We know that $\dfrac{8}{10} + \dfrac{6}{10} = \dfrac{14}{10} = 1\dfrac{4}{10}$ or $1 + \dfrac{4}{10}$.

Therefore

$$.8$$
$$+ \, .6$$
$$\overline{1.4} \longleftarrow (1 + .4)$$

Again, notice the alignment of the decimal points.

After working many such examples involving decimals, children should discover that the decimal points are always aligned in addition and that numerals must be expressed with their proper place value just as in addition of whole numbers. If children know their basic addition facts and can relate fractions and decimals, they should have very little difficulty with addition of decimals. The basic structure of whole numbers and fractional numbers is merely applied in a new way.

From a knowledge of addition, children should be able to discover some basic generalizations concerning subtraction of decimals. They should begin subtraction of decimals using models, such as circular regions. Let's consider an example: $.5 - .3 = \square$.

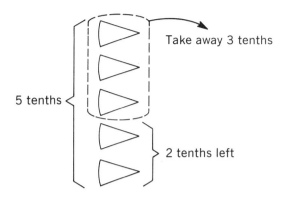

Take away 3 tenths

5 tenths

2 tenths left

We write:

5 tenths	or	.5
$-$ 3 tenths		$-$ .3
2 tenths = .2		.2

When using the number line as a model, we always begin at 0. In the example $.5 - .3 = \square$, the .3 is an addend and .5 is the sum. From 0 we mark off the addend .3 and then mark the sum .5. What is the missing addend?

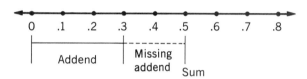

Thus we can see that $.5 - .3 = .2$.

Children should discover that the decimal points are always aligned in subtraction and that the numbers must be expressed with their proper place value, just as in addition of decimals. This is illustrated in these examples:

$$\dfrac{7}{10} - \dfrac{3}{10} = \dfrac{4}{10} \qquad \begin{array}{r} .7 \\ - \, .3 \\ \hline .4 \end{array}$$

$$\dfrac{29}{100} - \dfrac{12}{100} = \dfrac{17}{100} \qquad \begin{array}{r} .29 \\ - \, .12 \\ \hline .17 \end{array}$$

Another example illustrates conversion of fractions with unlike denominators:

$$.73 = \dfrac{73}{100} = \dfrac{73}{100} \qquad .73$$

$$- \, .4 = - \dfrac{4}{10} = - \dfrac{40}{100} \qquad - \, .40$$

$$\dfrac{33}{100} \qquad .33$$

Again, alignment of decimal points is associated with finding a common denominator. By aligning tenths under tenths, we are subtracting numbers named with like denominators.

$$.73 - .4 = (.7 + .03) - .4$$
$$= (.7 - .4) + .03$$
$$= .3 + .03$$
$$= .33$$

$$.73 - .4 = \left(\frac{7}{10} + \frac{3}{100}\right) - \frac{4}{10}$$
$$= \left(\frac{7}{10} - \frac{4}{10}\right) + \frac{3}{100}$$
$$= \frac{3}{10} + \frac{3}{100}$$
$$= \frac{30}{100} + \frac{3}{100}$$
$$= \frac{33}{100} = .33$$

After working a number of examples and developing the generalizations, children should be provided with practice exercises until the process is clearly understood. Students need a great deal of practice and drill of subtraction involving ragged decimals and decimals with more places, as in these examples:

27.4	42.78	74.2	80
− 3.5	− 17.2	− 38.176	− 29.63

Such exercises provide the teacher with an opportunity to evaluate the students' knowledge of basic subtraction facts and of place value.

Now let's consider multiplication of decimals. Begin with models on the concrete level. Consider the example $3 \times .2 = \square$. What does it mean? It means you have three sets with 2 tenths in each set. If ▷ is a tenth of a circle then you have 2 of them in each of 3 sets.

  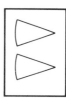

By observation we can conclude that 3 sets of 2 tenths will equal 6 tenths. We write:

$$3 \times .2 = .6 \quad \text{or} \quad \begin{array}{r} 2 \text{ tenths} \\ \times 3 \\ \hline 6 \text{ tenths} = .6 \end{array} \quad \text{or} \quad \begin{array}{r} .2 \\ \times 3 \\ \hline .6 \end{array}$$

The same example can also be modeled on a number line:

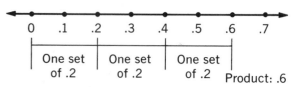

Thus, $3 \times .2 = .6$.

Another approach to teaching multiplication with decimals is to have children use what they have learned about multiplication with fractions. Suppose we are given a multiplication example where both factors are written as decimals. Rewrite the decimals as fractions. Multiply as usual; the result will be the product expressed in fraction form. Rewrite this fraction as a decimal; this gives the answer for the original example (expressed in decimal form).

Let's look at an example that is solved by this procedure. Suppose we wish to solve the example $2.7 \times .3 = \square$.

1. Use place-value and basic properties to help rewrite the decimals as fractions.

DECIMALS

$$2.7 \times .3 \quad = 2\frac{7}{10} \times \frac{3}{10}$$
$$= \left(2 + \frac{7}{10}\right) \times \frac{3}{10}$$
$$= \left(\frac{20}{10} + \frac{7}{10}\right) \times \frac{3}{10}$$
$$= \frac{27}{10} \times \frac{3}{10}$$

FRACTIONS

2. Use the fraction form; multiply as usual (numerator times numerator, denominator times denominator).

$$\frac{27}{10} \times \frac{3}{10} = \frac{27 \times 3}{10 \times 10}$$
$$= \frac{81}{100}$$

3. Rewrite the fraction obtained in Step 2 as a decimal to get the final answer.

$$\frac{81}{100} = .81$$
$$\therefore 2.7 \times .3 = .81$$

Now let us use the same procedure to solve $14.5 \times 2.17 = \square$.

1. Write the example in fraction form.

$$14.5 \times 2.17 = 14\frac{5}{10} \times 2\frac{17}{100}$$

$$= \left(\frac{140}{10} + \frac{5}{10}\right) \times \left(\frac{200}{100} + \frac{17}{100}\right)$$

$$= \frac{145}{10} \times \frac{217}{100}$$

2. Multiply.

$$\frac{145}{10} \times \frac{217}{100} = \frac{145 \times 217}{10 \times 100}$$

$$= \frac{31465}{1000}$$

3. Rewrite the answer in decimal form.

$$\frac{31465}{1000} = 31.465$$

$$\therefore 14.5 \times 2.17 = 31.465$$

Children who understand and practice this procedure are not likely to encounter the old difficulty of not knowing "where to put the decimal point." Eventually the children can make the transition to the usual short algorithm:

$$\begin{array}{c} 16.2 \\ \times .357 \\ \hline 1134 \\ 8100 \\ 48600 \\ \hline 5.7834 \end{array} \qquad \frac{162}{10} \times \frac{357}{1000} = \frac{57834}{10,000}$$

tenths × thousandths = ten-thousandths

Tenths times thousandths gives ten-thousandths. So the final digit in the answer should occupy the ten-thousandths place. After practice with many examples of this sort, the children will probably discover that the location of the decimal point can be determined by counting to see how many digits are to the right of the decimal points in the factors.

It is hoped that this method will provide children with insight into the meaning of multiplication of decimals. When pupils come to understand multiplication of decimals thoroughly and discover that the location of the decimal point can be determined by counting the number of places in the factors, they can use this shortcut.

Now let's examine division of decimals. Division of decimals can also be begun with models. Let us examine: $2\overline{)}.6$. What does it mean? It could mean 6 tenths are to be separated into two sets. This is 1 tenth of a circular region: ▷ .

Six tenths

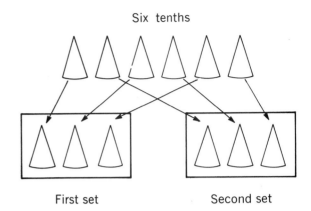

First set   Second set

Thus when 6 tenths are separated into two sets there are 3 tenths in each set:

$$2\overline{)}.6 \atop .3$$

The number line can also be used to demonstrate this. Mark off the product (.6) and then separate this line segment into two equivalent segments.

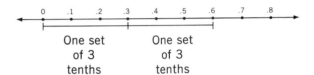

One set   One set
of 3   of 3
tenths   tenths

There are two sets of .3 in .6:

$$2\overline{)}.6 \atop .3$$

Now consider .6 divided by .2.

$$.2\overline{)}.6$$

This can mean that we have a product of .6 and want to make sets of .2. How many sets of .2 can we make from a set of .6?

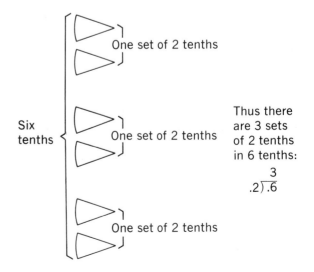

One set of 2 tenths

Six tenths

One set of 2 tenths

One set of 2 tenths

Thus there are 3 sets of 2 tenths in 6 tenths:

$$.2\overline{)}.6 \atop 3$$

The number line can also be used. Mark off a product of .6 and then mark off sets of 2 tenths.

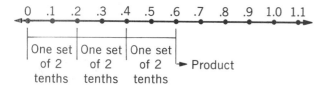

There are three sets of .2 in .6:

$$.2\overline{)\,.6}^{\,3}$$

Now consider an example such as $\dfrac{.8}{.4} = \Box$. We know that we can multiply the numerator and the denominator by the same number to get an equivalent fraction. In this case let's multiply them both by 10. That is, let's multiply the fractional number by $\dfrac{10}{10}$.

$$\frac{.8}{.4} \times \frac{10}{10} = \frac{8}{4} = 2$$

What about an example like $\dfrac{.84}{.21} = \Box$? We can multiply $\dfrac{.84}{.21}$ by $\dfrac{100}{100}$, which is another name for 1.

$$\frac{.84}{.21} \times \frac{100}{100} = \frac{84}{21} = 4$$

Now let's relate this to the long-division form:

$$.21\overline{)\,.84}$$

In this case both the product and the known factor should be multiplied by 100 to obtain a whole-number divisor:

$$21\overline{)\,84}^{\,4}$$

In this way we rationalize the traditional shortcut process of "moving" the decimal point in long division to obtain a whole-number divisor.

Relate this procedure to the use of common denominators for division of rational numbers expressed in fraction form. (See Unit 9.)

Now we are ready to take a closer look at the relation between decimals and fractions in the form $\dfrac{a}{b}$. We have said that any fractional number $\dfrac{a}{b}$ can be thought of as a quotient obtained from the division of a whole number by a counting number. This can also be stated another way: a fractional number is any number (y) that satisfies an equation of the form $b \times y = a$, where a is a whole number and b is a counting number. For such an equation, the solution can be expressed either by $y = a \div b$ or by $y = \dfrac{a}{b}$. Thus the fraction $\dfrac{a}{b}$ means the same thing as $a \div b$. That is, $\dfrac{6}{2}$ is the same as $6 \div 2$ and $\dfrac{.6}{.2}$ is the same as $.6 \div .2$.

We have seen that any fraction whose numerator is a whole number and whose denominator is a power of 10 (1, 10, 100, 1000, and so on) can be easily expressed as a decimal. What about other fractions? Consider the fraction $\dfrac{1}{4}$.

$$\begin{aligned}
\frac{1}{4} &= \frac{1}{4} \times \frac{25}{25} \\
&= \frac{1 \times 25}{4 \times 25} \\
&= \frac{25}{100} \\
&= .25
\end{aligned}$$

We could also find the decimal for $\dfrac{1}{4}$ by recalling that $\dfrac{1}{4}$ means 1 divided by 4 ($1 \div 4$).

$$
\begin{array}{r}
.25 \\
4\overline{)\,1.00} \\
-\,80 \\
\hline
20 \\
-\,20 \\
\hline
0
\end{array}
$$

In view of this, let's ask, what is the decimal name for $\dfrac{5}{8}$?

$$
\begin{aligned}
\frac{5}{8} &= \frac{5}{8} \times \frac{125}{125} \\
&= \frac{5 \times 125}{8 \times 125} \\
&= \frac{625}{1000} \\
&= .625
\end{aligned}
$$

We chose $\dfrac{125}{125}$, another name for 1, because 125 is the least number that when multiplied by 8 will give a product in the denominator that is a power of ten: $8 \times 125 = 1000$.

But since $\frac{5}{8}$ means 5 divided by 8, let's examine the division form:

$$
\begin{array}{r}
.625 \\
8\overline{)5.000} \\
-\underline{4\,800} \\
200 \\
-\underline{160} \\
40 \\
-\underline{40} \\
0
\end{array}
$$

The decimal for $\frac{5}{8}$, then, is .625 (six hundred twenty-five thousandths).

What are the decimal names for the following common fractions?

a) $\frac{3}{8}$ b) $\frac{4}{5}$ c) $\frac{3}{4}$

a) $\frac{3}{8} = \frac{3}{8} \times \frac{125}{125} = \frac{375}{1000} = .375$

or

$$
\begin{array}{r}
.375 \\
8\overline{)3.000} \\
-\underline{2\,4} \\
60 \\
-\underline{56} \\
40 \\
-\underline{40} \\
0
\end{array}
$$

b) $\frac{4}{5} = \frac{4}{5} \times \frac{2}{2} = \frac{8}{10} = .8$

or

$$
\begin{array}{r}
.8 \\
5\overline{)4.0} \\
-\underline{4\,0} \\
0
\end{array}
$$

c) $\frac{3}{4} = \frac{3}{4} \times \frac{25}{25} = \frac{75}{100} = .75$

or

$$
\begin{array}{r}
.75 \\
4\overline{)3.00} \\
-\underline{2\,8} \\
20 \\
-\underline{20} \\
0
\end{array}
$$

Note that in many cases the division method is far simpler to use, as in this example: $\frac{21}{32}$.

$$
\begin{array}{r}
.65625 \\
32\overline{)21.00000} \\
-\underline{19\,2} \\
1\,80 \\
-\underline{1\,60} \\
200 \\
-\underline{192} \\
80 \\
-\underline{64} \\
160 \\
-\underline{160} \\
0
\end{array}
$$

It can be readily discovered that certain fractions, when renamed by a decimal, do not terminate but yield a quotient that repeats endlessly. An example is $\frac{1}{3}$.

$$
\begin{array}{r}
.333 \ldots \\
3\overline{)1.0000}
\end{array}
$$

We put three dots after the third digit in the quotient to show that it continues in the same way—an endless succession of threes. We can never get a remainder of zero, regardless of how many places we calculate in the quotient.

Observe the result in performing the indicated division in $\frac{3}{7}$, or $3 \div 7$. We obtain the quotient .428571428571 . . . . Again, we can never obtain a zero remainder, regardless of how many places we calculate in the quotient. Notice that in this quotient a particular sequence of numerals occurs repeatedly: 428571. A fractional number whose quotient repeats a particular sequence of digits is called a **repeating** or **periodic decimal.** A periodic decimal is often indicated by a bar over the digits that repeat. For example: $.\overline{428571}$ . . . . All fractions whose decimal forms do not terminate are periodic (though we will not prove this here). Thus we see that fractional numbers named in decimal form give either **repeating decimals** (in which one or more digits repeat endlessly) or **terminating decimals** (in which the quotient terminates, that is, eventually has a zero remainder).

We can easily determine whether the decimal for a fraction terminates or repeats by inspecting the prime factorization of its denominator.

Fraction	Prime factorization of denominator	Decimal
$\dfrac{1}{4}$	2×2	.250 or .25
$\dfrac{1}{2}$	2	.50 or .5
$\dfrac{1}{10}$	2×5	.10 or .1
$\dfrac{1}{20}$	$2 \times 2 \times 5$	.050 or .05
$\dfrac{1}{50}$	$2 \times 5 \times 5$	.020 or .02

Notice that each prime factorization listed above contains only factors that are also factors of 10, the base of our number system. Fractions whose denominators, when factored into primes, contain only 2's and 5' as factors form terminating decimals. But let's examine some fractions whose denominators contain factors other than 2's and 5's.

Fraction	Prime factorization of denominator	Decimal
$\dfrac{1}{3}$	3	.333 . . .
$\dfrac{1}{6}$	2×3	.1666 . . .
$\dfrac{1}{12}$	$2 \times 2 \times 3$	.08333 . . .

These fractions contain, in the prime factorization of their denominators, factors other than 2 or 5. Fractions of this kind form repeating decimals. Note that we usually round off repeating decimals such as .333 . . . . We usually refer to this as .33, but this is only an approximation.

Decimal fractions can be indicated on the number line in the same manner as whole numbers or common fractions.

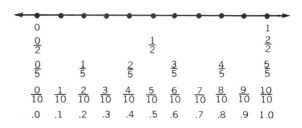

Note that points on the number line are now named in decimal form. We can see that

$$\frac{1}{5} = \frac{2}{10} = .2$$

$$\frac{1}{2} = \frac{5}{10} = .5$$

$$1 = \frac{2}{2} = \frac{5}{5} = \frac{10}{10} = 1.0$$

and so on.

Other number lines can be drawn that show other decimal names. For example

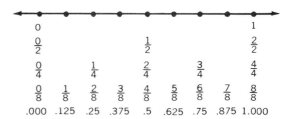

The number line is an extremely useful device for demonstrating order relationships between different decimals; for example, to show that .5 > .375 and .125 < .625. It is also useful for showing the decimal equivalents of common fractions, as on the preceding number line. How would we locate the point named by a repeating decimal? This is not difficult if we have a method for converting a repeating decimal into an ordinary fraction.

Let's examine how this is done by writing the periodic decimal 0.$\overline{63}$ . . . as a fraction. If we let n equal the repeating decimal .636363 . . . , we can find the value of $100 \times n$ by multiplying .63$\overline{63}$ . . . by 100.

$$n = .6363\overline{63} \ . \ . \ .$$
$$100 \times n = 63.6363\overline{63} \ . \ . \ .$$

Now we subtract the first of these two equations from the second.

$$
\begin{array}{r}
100 \times n = 63.6363\overline{63} \ . \ . \ . \\
- \quad (n = \quad .636363 \ . \ . \ .) \\
\hline
99 \times n = 63
\end{array}
$$

We find that if $99 \times n = 63$, then $n = \frac{63}{99}$. Translating into simplest form, we find that $n = \frac{7}{11}$. We can now write .636363 . . . as the fraction $\frac{7}{11}$.

Now try converting $.33\overline{3}$ . . . and $.037\overline{037}$ . . . into fraction form. First multiply $.33\overline{3}$ by 10 and $.\overline{037}$ by 1000. (Notice that in the first example the single digit 3 is repeated, so we multiply the decimal by 10^1, or 10. But in the second example the three digits .037 are repeated, so we multiply the decimal by 10^3, or 1000.) After proceeding as before to solve these two examples (getting $\frac{1}{3}$ and $\frac{1}{27}$ for answers), we can draw some generalizations for changing periodic decimals into fraction form.

1. Let an unknown (such as n) represent the repeating decimal.
2. Multiply the equation in Step 1 by some power of 10 so that the decimal point is shifted to the right as many places as there are digits that repeat.
3. Subtract the equation in Step 1 from the equation in Step 2.
4. Solve the new equation obtained in Step 3; write the solution as a fraction.

Now apply these generalizations to the periodic decimal $.015\overline{015}$ . . .

Step 1. Let $n = .015\overline{015}$ . . .

Step 2. Multiply the equation in Step 1 by 1000 so that the decimal point is moved three places to the right (since there are three digits, 015, in the repeating period).
$1000 \times n = 015.015\overline{015}$ . . .

Step 3. Subtract the equation in Step 1 from the equation in Step 2.

$$
\begin{array}{r}
1000 \times n = 015.015\overline{015} \ldots \\
- \quad (n = \quad .015\overline{015} \ldots) \\
\hline
999 \times n = \quad 15
\end{array}
$$

Step 4. Solve the equation obtained in Step 3.

$$n = \frac{15}{999} = \frac{5}{333}$$

We have discovered that in our number system we can name numbers in many ways. One of the ways we found to rename numbers is by using expanded notation. For example, 123 can be written as $100 + 20 + 3$. We can also express 123 in terms of powers of ten:

$$(1 \times 10 \times 10) + (2 \times 10) + 3$$

Consider another way to name 123. If we are multiplying two tens together, we can use exponential notation, as we did in discussing place value (see Unit 5). Thus we can write 10^2 for 10×10 (the small 2 is called an exponent). Using exponential notation, 123 is written

$$123 = (1 \times 10^2) + (2 \times 10^1) + (3 \times 10^0)$$

There are many other ways of naming 123. For example

$$
\begin{array}{ll}
12.3 \times 10 & \text{or } 12.3 \times 10^1 \\
1.23 \times 100 & \text{or } 1.23 \times 10^2 \\
.123 \times 1000 & \text{or } .123 \times 10^3
\end{array}
$$

If 123 is expressed as 1.23×10^2, it is said to be expressed in **scientific notation.** The table below shows some numbers expressed in scientific notation.

Number	Scientific Notation
24	2.4×10^1
324	3.24×10^2
1324	1.324×10^3
12,000	1.2×10^4
140,000	1.4×10^5
1,750,000	1.75×10^6

Examine the numbers expressed in scientific notation. What generalization can we make about writing numerals in this way? In scientific notation a number is expressed as some number equal to or greater than 1 and less than 10, multiplied by ten to a certain power. For example, 24 is expressed as 2.4 (a number greater than 1 and less than 10) multiplied by 10^1, or 2.4×10^1. Similarly, the number 140,000 is expressed as 1.4 (again, a number greater than 1 and less than 10) multiplied by 10^5, or 1.4×10^5. Since 10^5 equals 100,000, we have

$$
\begin{aligned}
1.4 \times 10^5 &= 1.4 \times 100,000 \\
&= 140,000
\end{aligned}
$$

Scientific notation, as the name suggests, is an efficient way for people in technical fields to express and work with very large numbers. The following table lists some astronomical distances expressed in scientific notation.

Planet	Distance from the Sun in Miles
Mercury	3.6×10^7
Venus	6.71×10^7
Earth	9.29×10^7
Mars	1.42×10^8
Jupiter	4.83×10^8
Saturn	8.86×10^8
Uranus	1.78×10^9
Neptune	2.79×10^9
Pluto	3.67×10^9

Just as very large numbers can be expressed conveniently in scientific notation, so can very small numbers. We have examined fractional parts expressed in decimal form and, earlier, the use of negative exponents to name fractional parts. Now let's examine the use of scientific notation to express very small numbers. First, we have seen that $\frac{1}{10}$ can be expressed as .1 or 10^{-1}. (Remember that 10^{-1} means $\frac{1}{10^1}$ or $\frac{1}{10}$ since any number raised to the first power is equal to the number itself.) Then, $\frac{1}{100} = .01 = 10^{-2}$. Again, 10^{-2} means $\frac{1}{10^2}$ or $\frac{1}{100}$. If we continued in this way, we could make a chart.

Fraction	Decimal	Scientific Notation
$\frac{1}{10}$	.1	1×10^{-1}
$\frac{1}{100}$	.01	1×10^{-2}
$\frac{1}{1000}$	.001	1×10^{-3}
$\frac{1}{10,000}$	.0001	1×10^{-4}
$\frac{1}{100,000}$	.00001	1×10^{-5}
$\frac{1}{1,000,000}$	.000001	1×10^{-6}
$\frac{1}{10,000,000}$	.0000001	1×10^{-7}
$\vdots$	$\vdots$	$\vdots$

The pattern is evident. Now, let's simply apply our knowledge of scientific notation to this sequence. In scientific notation we express a number as the product expression of a number between 1 and 10, and 10 raised to some power. For example, 300,000 is expressed as 3×10^5. How could we express $\frac{3}{100,000}$? This rather awkward fraction could be rewritten as

$$3 \times 10^{-5}$$

The relation of this numeral to the fraction form is

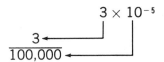

Now suppose you wished to express the time required for an electronic computer to perform one addition operation. It has been calculated that the IBM 3031 computer requires 115 nanoseconds per processing step. This would be written as .000000115 or, in fraction form, $\frac{115}{1,000,000,000}$ (115 billionths). Scientific notation would be much simpler: 1.15×10^{-8}.

Many elementary school mathematics programs introduce and teach the concept of **ratio** in conjunction with rational numbers expressed as fractions. We have chosen to introduce ratios at this point in the mathematics program, as a means of reviewing fraction ideas and as a vehicle for teaching percents. The concept of ratio is another aspect of rational numbers that is useful in solving a variety of examples. Look at a problem such as this:

Balloons are sold at the rate of 2 balloons for 5¢. How many balloons can you buy for 10¢?

The problem can be interpreted this way: "Two balloons for five cents" suggests a fixed rate (a comparison between two numbers), which we can call a ratio. If this ratio is constant, we should be able to find out how many balloons we could buy for ten cents or twenty cents, or how much it would cost to buy four balloons, or six balloons.

One way we can express the ratio of balloons to cents is 2:5 (2 balloons for 5 cents). A somewhat more convenient notation is the familiar fraction form:

$$\frac{2}{5} \begin{array}{l} \longleftarrow \text{(two balloons)} \\ \longleftarrow \text{(five cents)} \end{array}$$

Young students need to manipulate real objects so that they can easily see and then understand this relationship.

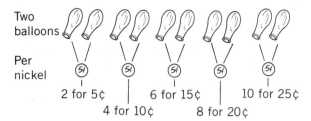

Two balloons
Per nickel

2 for 5¢ | 6 for 15¢ | 10 for 25¢
4 for 10¢ | 8 for 20¢

Now suppose we want to find the number of balloons we can buy for ten cents. If "two balloons for five cents" can be expressed as a ratio, $\frac{2}{5}$ (read "two to five"), then there is some number of balloons that we can buy for ten cents. Suppose we let n stand for the number of balloons we can buy for ten cents. Then we can write

$$\frac{n}{10} \begin{array}{l} \longleftarrow (n \text{ balloons}) \\ \longleftarrow (\text{ten cents}) \end{array}$$

Thus we see that you can buy two balloons for five cents, four balloons for ten cents, and so on. We can write $\frac{2}{5}, \frac{4}{10}, \frac{6}{15}, \frac{8}{20}, \frac{10}{25}$ .... These are **equivalent ratios** because each ratio expresses the same relationship; 2 to 5 is the same relationship as 4 to 10.

An equation of two equivalent ratios, such as $\frac{2}{5} = \frac{n}{10}$, is called a **proportion**. When the problem is stated in this way, we can see that if $\frac{n}{10}$ is equal to $\frac{2}{5}$, then the numerator and denominator of $\frac{2}{5}$ must be multiplied by the same number to obtain $\frac{n}{10}$. Since the denominator, 5, must be multiplied by 2 to get 10, so must the numerator, 2, be multiplied by 2. The value of n, then, is clearly 2×2, or 4. We can buy four balloons for ten cents.

$$\frac{2}{5} = \frac{4}{10}$$

Helping students look for patterns is an excellent technique for locating missing numbers in a proportion. Let us examine ratios in several different ways.

Relationship between denominators and between numerators

$$\frac{2}{5} \frac{\square}{10} \qquad \frac{\square}{10} \frac{2}{5}$$

Since one denominator is twice as large as the other, the corresponding numerator must be twice as large.

$$\frac{2}{5} \overset{\times 2}{=} \frac{4}{10} \qquad \frac{4}{10} \overset{\times 2}{=} \frac{2}{5}$$

Relationship between numerator and denominator

$$\frac{4}{8} = \frac{\square}{2} \qquad \frac{4}{8} = \frac{1}{\square}$$

Since the numerator is one half of the denominator in one ratio, it must be half in the other.

Since the denominator is twice as large as the numerator in one ratio, it must be twice as large in the other.

$$\times \frac{1}{2} \; \frac{4}{8} = \frac{1}{2} \; \times \frac{1}{2} \qquad \times 2 \; \frac{4}{8} = \frac{1}{2} \; \times 2$$

As we mentioned, when two equivalent ratios are expressed as an equality, they form a proportion. A proportion is a mathematical sentence.

$$\frac{2}{5} = \frac{4}{10}$$

This proportion is read, "Two is to five as four is to ten." Since a ratio always expresses a relation between two quantities, this proportion means, "Two balloons for five cents indicates the same price as four balloons for ten cents."

If one uses notation of the form $a{:}b$ to express the ratios, then the proportion $\frac{2}{5} = \frac{4}{10}$ would be written $2{:}5 = 4{:}10$. Some textbook authors prefer to use the symbol :: in place of the equals sign (=) when ratios are expressed in the form $a{:}b$. The proportion would then be written $2{:}5{::}4{:}10$.

We can, by this method, find the cost of any number of balloons or the number of balloons we can buy for any given amount of money.

$$\frac{2}{5} = \frac{4}{10} \longleftarrow \begin{bmatrix} 2 \text{ balloons for 5¢} \\ 4 \text{ balloons for 10¢} \end{bmatrix}$$
$$\therefore \frac{2}{5} = \frac{40}{100} \longleftarrow 40 \text{ balloons for 100¢}$$

Establish a pattern with the children by first setting up a table to find the cost of 2, 4, 6, 8 . . . balloons.

Number of Balloons	Cost
2	5¢
4	10¢
6	15¢
8	20¢
10	25¢
12	30¢
14	35¢
.	.
.	.
.	.

Children can see that the ratio is always $\frac{2}{5}$, and that different proportions can be set up:

$$\frac{2}{5} = \frac{4}{10} \quad \frac{2}{5} = \frac{8}{20} \quad \frac{2}{5} = \frac{14}{35} \quad \text{and so on}$$

A ratio is an expressed relation between two numbers: two tickets for \$3 $\left(\frac{2}{3.0}\right)$, or 3 cans of juice for 99¢ $\left(\frac{3}{99}\right)$. A proportion is a statement of equality for two ratios:

$$\frac{2}{5} = \frac{4}{10} \quad \frac{3}{7} = \frac{21}{49} \quad \frac{1}{3} = \frac{4}{12}$$

Here is an interesting property often used in solving proportions: If two equivalent ratios are written in fraction form, then the two products formed by multiplying the numerator of one fraction by the denominator of the other are equal. In symbols we can say:

$$\text{if } \frac{a}{b} = \frac{c}{d}, \text{ then } a \times d = c \times b$$

To see why this is always true, multiply both sides of $\frac{a}{b} = \frac{c}{d}$ by the product of the denominators:

$$\frac{a}{b} \times (b \times d) = \frac{c}{d} \times (b \times d)$$

$$\frac{a \times (b \times d)}{b} = \frac{c \times (b \times d)}{d}$$

$$\frac{(a \times d) \times b}{b} = \frac{(c \times b) \times d}{d}$$

$$(a \times d) \times \frac{b}{b} = (c \times b) \times \frac{d}{d}$$

But $\frac{b}{b} = 1$ and $\frac{d}{d} = 1$, so the last equation simplifies to

$$(a \times d) \times 1 = (c \times b) \times 1$$

or

$$a \times d = c \times b$$

The products $a \times d$ and $c \times b$ are often called **cross products,** because they are formed according to this scheme:

$$\frac{a}{b} \diagdown \diagup \frac{c}{d}$$

Let's solve some proportions by using both patterns and the cross-product method. Consider this example: "Suppose 3 waitresses can service 17 tables. How many waitresses are needed to service 51 tables?" This problem can be expressed by the proportion

$$\frac{3}{17} = \frac{w}{51}$$

Looking for patterns, we might recognize that $17 \times 3 = 51$.

If the denominator of the second ratio is three times the denominator of the first ratio, then the numerator of the second ratio must be three times the numerator of the first ratio.

$$\frac{3}{17} \times 1 = \frac{w}{51}$$

$$\frac{3}{17} \times \frac{3}{3} = \frac{w}{51}$$

$$\frac{3}{17} \times \frac{3}{3} = \frac{9}{51}$$

Using the cross-product method, we find that

$$3 \times 51 = w \times 17$$
$$\text{or } w \times 17 = 153$$
$$\therefore w = 153 \div 17 = 9$$

So 9 waitresses are needed to service 51 tables.

Comparing the two techniques for solving ratio examples, we find using patterns easier if one term of a proportion is a multiple of another term of the proportion.

Consider another example: "Arnold kept a record of number of hits for times at bat. He found that he had 32 hits for 40 times at bat. At this rate, how many hits will he have for 45 times at bat?" The example can be expressed by means of the following proportion:

$$\frac{32}{40} = \frac{h}{45}$$

Using the cross-product method gives

$$32 \times 45 = h \times 40$$
$$\text{or} \quad h \times 40 = 1440$$
$$h = 1440 \div 40 = 36$$

So Arnold can expect 36 hits out of 45 times at bat.

In studying baseball facts, the following information was gathered:

Player	Hits	Times at Bat	Ratio
Mary Ann	6	24	$\frac{6}{24}$
Cecelia	4	10	$\frac{4}{10}$
Tom	3	30	$\frac{3}{30}$
Dan	5	25	$\frac{5}{25}$
Jim	2	8	$\frac{2}{8}$

Which player has the best batting average? We know that a batting average is calculated from the number of hits compared with the number of times at bat. It is very difficult to compare the ratios for the players above to know who the best batter is because each ratio is based on a different number of times at bat. To compare the batting averages we need to rewrite the ratios so that they all have the same second term or denominator. For convenience, let's select 100 as a common denominator.

Player	Ratio	Rewritten Ratio
Mary Ann	$\frac{6}{24}$	$\frac{25}{100}$
Cecelia	$\frac{4}{10}$	$\frac{40}{100}$
Tom	$\frac{3}{30}$	$\frac{10}{100}$
Dan	$\frac{5}{25}$	$\frac{20}{100}$
Jim	$\frac{2}{8}$	$\frac{25}{100}$

Now that the ratios have been written with a common denominator, 100, we can compare them and can easily see that Cecelia has the best batting average and Tom has the poorest. Ratios that have a common denominator of 100 can be called percentages. The symbol for percent is %. The word **percent** comes from the Latin "per centum," meaning "for a hun-

dred." By percent we mean "per hundred," or "parts of a hundred." Thus 1 percent means one per hundred, or one out of every hundred $\left(\frac{1}{100}\right)$; 25 percent means twenty-five per hundred, or twenty-five out of every hundred $\left(\frac{25}{100}\right)$; 50 percent means fifty per hundred, or fifty out of every hundred $\left(\frac{50}{100}\right)$.

The best model for developing children's understanding of percentage is a hundreds board. Use a heavy cardboard square and divide it into 100 smaller squares:

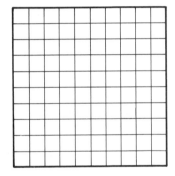

Children may want to draw on squared paper by marking off ten-by-ten squares. By definition the entire card represents 100%—or all of the squares.

In the square on the left, one small square is shaded. We can see that $\frac{1}{100}$ of the square is shaded. Changing the fraction to a decimal we see that .01 of the square is shaded. Each small square on the card is 1%. In the center square, 10 small squares are shaded; $\frac{10}{100}$ of the large square is shaded. The fraction $\frac{10}{100}$ is another name for $\frac{1}{10}$ so we can say .1, .10, or 10% of the center square is shaded. A rubber band could be stretched around the large square to illustrate 10%. The square on the right has a rubber band up two rows from the bottom. This card shows 20% below the rubber band and 80% above the rubber band.

Students need to work with other shapes and objects to understand the concept that all of something is 100%.

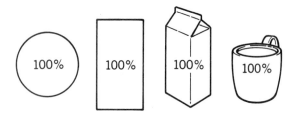

What percentage of each region below is shaded?

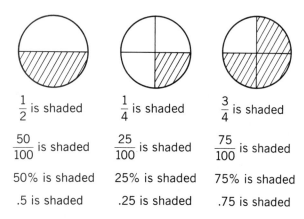

$\frac{1}{2}$ is shaded	$\frac{1}{4}$ is shaded	$\frac{3}{4}$ is shaded
$\frac{50}{100}$ is shaded	$\frac{25}{100}$ is shaded	$\frac{75}{100}$ is shaded
50% is shaded	25% is shaded	75% is shaded
.5 is shaded	.25 is shaded	.75 is shaded

We have seen that .01, $\frac{1}{100}$, and 1% are three names for the same number (one one-hundredth). Similarly the number seventeen one-hundredths can be represented as a decimal, as a fraction, or as a percent: .17, $\frac{17}{100}$, or 17%. Each of these numerals can be thought of as expressing a ratio (17 per 100).

Several different ways may be used to express each comparison—a fraction, a ratio, a decimal, or a percent. For example, we say that $\frac{1}{2}$, $\frac{50}{100}$, .50, and 50% are equivalent. The following table shows some equivalent names for percents.

Fractions	Ratios	Decimals	Percents
$\frac{1}{2}$	$\frac{50}{100}$	.50	50%
$\frac{1}{4}$	$\frac{25}{100}$	.25	25%
$\frac{1}{3}$	$\frac{33\frac{1}{3}}{100}$	$.33\frac{1}{3}$	$33\frac{1}{3}\%$
$\frac{1}{8}$	$\frac{12\frac{1}{2}}{100}$	$.12\frac{1}{2}$	$12\frac{1}{2}\%$
$\frac{3}{4}$	$\frac{75}{100}$	.75	75%

When one form for percent is known, how do we find the other form? One of the basic structures of mathematics that we must use is the identity element of multiplication. Consider a pack of gum that contains five sticks. If a child is chewing two sticks of gum, what part or percent of the gum does he have? Since he is chewing two sticks out of a pack of five we would say that he is chewing $\frac{2}{5}$ of the gum. How can we find the ratio for $\frac{2}{5}$ that has a denominator of 100? We know that $\frac{2}{5} \times 1 = \frac{2}{5}$ and that 1 has many names, such as $\frac{2}{2}, \frac{3}{3}, \frac{4}{4}, \ldots$ etc. What value for 1 should be selected so that the denominator becomes 100? Because $5 \times 20 = 100$ we should select the value for 1 of $\frac{20}{20}$. Now, since

$$\frac{2}{5} \times 1 = \frac{2}{5}$$

and

$$1 = \frac{20}{20}$$

we write

$$\frac{2}{5} \times \frac{20}{20} = \frac{40}{100}$$

So the fraction $\frac{2}{5}$ can be written as an equivalent ratio of $\frac{40}{100}$. From our study of decimals we know that $\frac{40}{100}$ can be written as .40 and that .40 can be written as 40%.

Some fractions have denominators that are not factors of 100. How are these fractions changed to ratios, decimals, and percents? Either of two techniques learned earlier in this unit may be applied in this situation. You know that the fraction bar can also mean "divide," so a fraction can be changed to a decimal by dividing the numerator by the denominator. And we also know that when an element is missing in a proportion it may be found by using the cross-products method.

Consider the fraction $\frac{5}{6}$. We see that 6 is not a factor of 100. Using the first method, we divide the numerator by the denominator:

$$\frac{5}{6} = 6\overline{)5.00} \qquad .83\frac{2}{6} = .83\frac{1}{3} = 83\frac{1}{3}\%$$

Thus we say $\frac{5}{6}$ equals $.83\frac{1}{3}$ equals $83\frac{1}{3}$ percent.

Now let us consider the cross-products method.

$$\frac{5}{6} = \frac{n}{100}$$

$$5 \times 100 = n \times 6$$

$$500 = n \times 6$$

$$500 \times \frac{1}{6} = n \times 6 \times \frac{1}{6}$$

$$\overset{250}{\cancel{500}} \times \frac{1}{\underset{3}{\cancel{6}}} = n$$

$$250 \div 3 = n$$

$$83\frac{1}{3} = n$$

So
$$\frac{5}{6} = \frac{83\frac{1}{3}}{100} = .83\frac{1}{3} = 83\frac{1}{3}\%$$

Ratio and proportion play a major role in the study of percentage. In the traditional mathematics program, three rather mechanical approaches to percentage problems were taught. Today only one (but a more meaningful) approach is presented. By defining percent as parts of a hundred we eliminate the traditional mechanical formula requiring children to move decimal points back and forth and to drop and add percent signs. The examples below use the ratio approach to percent.

1. 20% of 10 = ___
2. ___% of 10 = 2
3. 20% of ___ = 2

Example 1. In some programs, 20% is expressed as $\frac{20}{100}$, or 20 per 100. Therefore 20% of some number (in this case, 10) can be expressed by equivalent ratios: 20 per 100 is equivalent to some number n per 10.

$$\frac{20}{100} = \frac{n}{10}$$

or

$$\frac{n}{10} = \frac{20}{100}$$

The numerator and denominator of $\frac{n}{10}$ must both be multiplied by the same number to get $\frac{20}{100}$. Since the denominator, 10, must be multiplied by 10 to get 100, the numerator, n, must also be multiplied by 10 to get 20.

$$n \times 10 = 20$$

$$n = 2$$

Thus n is equal to 2:

$$\frac{2}{10} = \frac{20}{100}$$

and 20% of 10 = 2.

Example 2. Examples of this kind can be solved by recognizing that the percent is not known but can be expressed as some part, n, of 100. We see that 2 out of 10 is equivalent to some part, n, of 100.

$$\frac{n}{100} = \frac{2}{10}$$

or

$$\frac{2}{10} = \frac{n}{100}$$

The value of n is clearly 20 and $\frac{20}{100}$ can be expressed as 20%.

20% of 10 = 2

Example 3. This example should be written as

$$\frac{20}{100} = \frac{2}{n}$$

or

$$\frac{2}{n} = \frac{20}{100}$$

We can determine the value of n by examining the proportion in terms of equivalent fractions. The value of n is thus shown to be 10.

Simple examples involving percent, such as those above, are more easily understood in the elementary grades when interpreted by means of proportions (equivalent ratios). Moreover, since ratio is a rather complex topic, it is not elaborated at this point but introduced to children in terms of a familiar topic, equivalent fractions.

Ratio is one method taught to children to solve percentage problems. Let us examine another method. After children have used models such as squared paper so that they understand the meaning of percentage, then the formula method may be introduced. In the formula method, students must learn to identify the **rate, base,** and **percentage.** Consider this example:

20% of 40 = 8
The rate is 20%.
The base is 40.
The percentage is 8.

The formula the student must learn is $r \times b = p$ which means *rate times base equals percentage.*

Consider the following problem. Sam correctly solved 60% of the 30 mathematics examples on the last test. How many examples did Sam solve correctly? In this problem, 60% is the rate, 30 is the base, and the percentage needs to be found. Substitute the values in the percentage formula and solve the example. Remember that 60% must be expressed as .60 to keep track of the decimal point when calculating.

$$r \times b = p$$
$$.60 \times 30 = \square$$
$$18.00 = \square$$

Sam solved 18 examples correctly. Let us change the example to illustrate another case of percentage. On a mathematics test Sam solved 18 out of 30 examples correctly. What percentage of the mathematics examples did Sam solve correctly? Thirty is the base, 18 is the percentage, and we are to find the rate.

Now the values can be substituted in the percentage formula, and it can be solved for the rate:

$$r \times b = p$$
$$\square \times 30 = 18$$

When given a product and a factor, the student should understand how to solve the example:

$$\square \times 30 = 18$$
$$\square = \frac{18}{30} = \frac{3 \times 6}{5 \times 6} = \frac{3}{5} \times \frac{6}{6}$$
$$\frac{3}{5} \times 1 = .60$$
$$.60 \text{ is } 60\%$$

Thus Sam solved 60% of the mathematics examples correctly.

If Sam solved 60% of the examples correctly and he solved 18 correctly, how many examples are on the mathematics test? The rate is 60%, which can be written as .60. The percentage is 18. Substituting these values in the percentage formula $r \times b = p$ we get:

$$r \times b = p$$
$$.60 \times \square = 18$$

The product is 18, and .60 is a factor.

$$\square = \frac{18}{.60}$$
$$\square = 30$$

There are 30 examples on Sam's mathematics test.

Terminology, Symbols, and Procedures

Decimal A fractional number may be expressed in several ways. We have found that fractions such as $\frac{2}{10}$, $\frac{3}{100}$, $2\frac{24}{1000}$, and so on, whose denominators are powers of 10, can be rewritten (using a decimal point) in a form called decimal form.

$$\frac{2}{10} = .2 \qquad \frac{3}{100} = .03 \qquad 2\frac{24}{1000} = 2.024$$

Fractions whose denominators are not powers of 10 such as $\frac{3}{4}$, $\frac{5}{8}$, and $\frac{4}{7}$, can be changed to decimal form. These examples could be treated like division ($3 \div 4$, $5 \div 8$, and $4 \div 7$). This technique is used to change a fraction to a decimal.

Decimal point The decimal point is a mark (.) that is used (in the base-ten system) in recording numbers to separate the whole-number parts of numbers from the fractional-number parts. For example, consider the mark (.) in 29.05.

$$29 \longleftarrow \overset{\displaystyle 29.05}{\underset{\displaystyle \frac{5}{100}}{\vrule height 1em \qquad \vrule height 1em}} \longrightarrow$$

Where there is no whole-number part, for example $\frac{32}{100}$, we write .32 (or 0.32).

Exponential notation Exponential notation permits us to represent powers of numbers by means of superscripts (or raised numerals). In exponential notation, a number is represented in terms of another number taken as a factor a specified number of times. The first number is called the *base*, and the superscript is called the *exponent*.The absolute value of the exponent indicates how many times the base is used as a factor. In the example 10^5, the base is 10 and the exponent is 5.

$$10^5 = (10 \times 10 \times 10 \times 10 \times 10)$$

Percent Percent means a certain number of hundredths. For example, 25 percent, written 25%, means twenty-five hundredths, 25 out of 100, $\frac{25}{100}$, or 25 parts of a hundred.

Periodic or repeating decimal A periodic or repeating decimal is a decimal in which some digit or series of digits repeats endlessly. In $.0575\overline{57}$ . . . , for example, the three dots indicate that an endless number of digits follows, and the bar over the last 57 indicates that this pair of digits is repeated endlessly. Every fraction can be expressed as either a terminating decimal or a periodic decimal.

Proportion A proportion is a mathematical sentence stating that two ratios are equal. For example

$$\frac{2}{5} = \frac{4}{10} \qquad \frac{n}{3} = \frac{16}{12}$$

Ratio A ratio is a comparison between two numbers. The ratio of two to five, for example, is written as 2:5 or $\frac{2}{5}$.

Scientific notation A number that is expressed as some number equal to or greater than 1 and less than 10, multiplied by a power of 10, is said to be expressed in scientific notation. For example, 82,000,000 is expressed in scientific notation as 8.2×10^7.

Terminating decimal A terminating decimal is a decimal that can be written with a finite number of digits—for example, .315 or .7590452.

Practice Exercises

1. Write 346.128 in expanded form.

2. Translate each decimal into a fraction.

   a) 2.1896   c) .12$\overline{12}$ e) .88 . . .   g) .35$\overline{8}$
   b) .003201   d) .46$\overline{46}$ f) .25   h) .072$\overline{072}$

3. Translate each fraction into a decimal.

   a) $\frac{4}{7}$ b) $1\frac{12}{13}$ c) $\frac{8}{11}$ d) $\frac{11}{12}$ e) $\frac{5}{15}$ f) $\frac{2}{3}$

4. Is it possible that there is a fraction with a whole-number numerator and a counting-number denominator that, when changed to a decimal, is neither terminating nor repeating? How can you be sure of your answer?

5. Complete the indicated operation in each example.

   a) $2.34 + 17.1 + .0234 + .123$ c) 7.43×2.1

   b) $43.7 - 12.684$ d) $6.2\overline{)8.928}$

6. Solve each problem by using ratios.

   a) Tomato juice is on sale at 3 cans for 39 cents. How much must you pay for a dozen cans?

   b) Mr. DeMarco's class is going to the art museum. If 5 children can ride in each car, how many cars are needed to carry all 35 children in the class?

   c) If 100 centimeters measure the same length as 1 meter, how many centimeters are needed to measure the same length as 3 meters?

   d) If 1 kilometer is approximately .6 miles, how many kilometers will measure the same length as one mile?

7. Solve each problem by using ratios and proportions.

   a) A chair that normally sells for $150.00 has been marked down to sell for $100.00. What is the percent of discount?

   b) The price for regular gasoline has increased at a particular station from 61.9 cents per gallon to 98.9 cents per gallon. What percent of increase has there been at that station?

   c) In a fourth-grade class, 10 percent of the children received perfect scores in an arithmetic test. If 33 children received perfect scores, how many children took the test?

   d) At Maywood School, 56 percent of the children walk to school every day. How many children walk to school if there are 500 pupils in the school?

   e) At Greenfield School, 391 children attended the school play. If this is 17 percent of the number of children in the school, what is the total number of children who attend Greenfield School?

8. Use the percentage formula and solve each problem in Exercise 7. Study how the solutions differ.

9. Express each of the following with an ordinary base-ten numeral.

   a) 9.38×10^5 c) 4.66×10^9 e) 8.31×10^{-2} g) 2.2×10^{-3}

   b) 2.37×10^4 d) 5.3×10^6 f) 3.641×10^{-6} h) 4.681×10^{-5}

10. Express each number in scientific notation.

    a) 7300   c) 8,900,000,000   e) 16,432

    b) 24,000,000   d) 123   f) 437.56

11. Change each of these fractions, $\frac{1}{3}$, $\frac{5}{7}$, and $\frac{6}{13}$, to decimals. How often does the sequence repeat? Formulate a general principle that will allow you to predict the maximum number of decimal places that can occur before a digit is repeated. (Hint: be sure to consider the denominator of each of the examples.)

12. How could you use a 10×10 square cut from graph paper to show that $\frac{1}{2}$ and $\frac{1}{2}\%$ are different concepts?

13. Translate each fraction to a percent.

    a) $\frac{7}{8}$ b) $\frac{9}{11}$ c) $\frac{13}{25}$ d) $\frac{7}{13}$ e) $\frac{3}{4}$ f) $\frac{8}{9}$

Discussion Questions

1. Examine a number of elementary school mathematics textbooks; compare and contrast the techniques for introducing decimals to children.

2. Discuss the use of decimals in society today. Which is most useful: decimals or fractions?

3. Discuss the advantages of teaching decimals before fractions and teaching fractions before decimals.

4. Compare the common characteristics of a specific operation on decimals with that operation on whole numbers.

5. Discuss problem-solving techniques that can be applied to decimals.

6. What homemade or commercial teaching aids can be used in developing an understanding of decimals?

7. List the advantages of using decimals instead of fractions with a calculator or a computer.

8. Discuss the prerequisite knowledge necessary for studying decimals.

9. Discuss useful evaluation techniques for assessing the understanding of decimals on the concrete level.

10. Explain how to make provision for individual differences teaching decimals to children.

11. Discuss how the overhead projector can be used for teaching decimals to children.

12. Discuss why, when dividing 1 by 6, some calculators display 0.1666666 and others display .16666667. What is the *real* value and how do we write it?

Activities for the Primary Grades

With continuing emphasis on place value and understanding of our number system, there is no reason why children should approach decimals with the idea that they are something completely isolated from concepts that have already been discovered and used. What the children should discover is the relation of decimals to the total structure of our number system. When they begin to recognize that operations with decimals can be more convenient in many situations than operations with fractions, they realize the importance of decimal notation. Moreover, increased emphasis on the metric system of measurement calls for a clear understanding of decimals.

The concepts developed with whole numbers can easily be extended to decimals. Children will soon realize that the basic facts they have memorized also apply to decimals, thus there are no new basic facts to memorize. Two add three is five regardless of the place value that it occupies. The place-value generalization must only be extended to the left of the decimal point.

Children should discover for themselves that the fraction-decimal-percent relation is merely a matter of renaming. This approach eliminates a great deal of the confusion and misunderstanding that was previously considered a necessary evil in elementary school mathematics.

Children already have an understanding of fractions, and the number line provides an excellent visual presentation of the relation between fraction and decimal forms. The place-value grid, or chart, and squared paper are other aids to present this relationship.

One way of preparing children to understand decimals is to use real money; dollars and cents are expressed in decimals. You can "buy" some item such as shoes or books from the children at the beginning of the class period with real money, then they can buy them back at the end of the class period.

1. Construct a deck of cards with the numerals .10 through .99. Shuffle the deck and deal the cards face down. Players turn one card over at a time. The player with the highest numeral on the cards gets to take the cards from the other players. The player who has the most cards at the end of the period is declared the winner.

2. Point out to the children ratios they have seen or see every day, such as one bean pod to five beans, one flower to six petals, one car to four wheels, two wheels to one bicycle, two feet to one child, and so forth. Materials on a flannel board and semiconcrete materials can be used for illustration.

Hand-Held Calculator Activities for the Primary Grades

1. When children play with a hand-held calculator, they will press keys just to experiment. In this process, they will eventually divide a smaller number by a larger number. Many hand-held calculators will display the results of $1 \div 6$ as 0.1666666, so children are bound to ask questions about decimals.

2. Using the newspaper, have the children prepare shopping lists and compute the totals of their grocery bills.

3. Use the hand-held calculator for computing change to be given to a customer.

4. Play store; have the cashier use the calculator.

Microcomputer Activities for the Primary Grades

All calculator activities suggested for primary grade children can also be used on the microcomputer in the immediate mode.

1. The microcomputer activities suggested for operations on whole numbers can be applied to decimals by changing the whole-number values to decimal numbers. Primary grade children should work only with money in decimal values.

2. Use the microcomputer as a read-out on a cash register. Children can play store and calculate totals for their transactions.

Activities for the Intermediate Grades

NOTATION AND PLACE VALUE

1. Use a ten-by-ten square cut from squared paper to illustrate .5, .05, .60, .68.

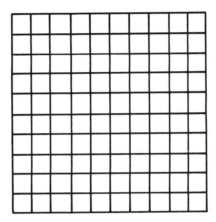

2. A game using teacher-made cardboard dominoes can be helpful in learning to recognize equivalent fractions and decimals. A set of twenty-eight dominoes is required. Each domino should show numerals for positive rational numbers as fractions or as decimals or both. For example:

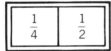  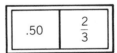

Some of the cards should be doubles, as

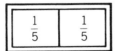   or

Place dominoes face down on the table and shuffle. Each player selects five; the others are left on the table in a pile. The player with the largest double begins by placing it on the table. The player to his left may play a domino if he has one with a numeral equal to the sum of the two on the double or one with a numeral naming a fraction or decimal equivalent to the original domino. If he cannot play, he must draw from the pile until he can. The next player may play either on the other side of the double, if he has the sum, or on the last domino played, if he has a fraction or decimal equal to the open end or to the sum of the two fractions or decimals. The game is ended when one player has no more dominoes. To score this game, each player gets one point per play.

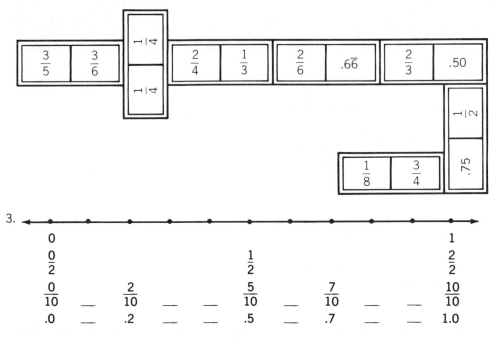

3.

	0			1
0		1		2
2		2		2

| 0 | 2 | | 5 | 7 | | 10 |
| 10 | 10 | | 10 | 10 | | 10 |

| .0 | .2 | | .5 | .7 | | 1.0 |

Label the remaining points on the number line.

4. Write the correct numeral in each blank space.

    a) .58 means _____ tenths _____ hundredths.
    b) .06 means _____ tenths _____ hundredths.
    c) .309 means _____ tenths _____ hundredths _____ thousandths.
    d) .572 means _____ tenths _____ hundredths _____ thousandths.

5. Prepare two sets of numeral cards with 0, 1, 2, . . . 9 and a card with a decimal point on it for each set of numerals. Have one member from each team come to the table or chalk rack and place the cards in order when the caller dictates a number (e.g., 1325.76). Additional sets of cards can eliminate the competition element. If there is enough space, the game can be made more active: each student can be given a numeral or decimal point, then the students, in teams, arrange themselves to form the numeral.

6. Complete the sequences.

    a) .14, .16, .18, ____, ____
    b) .43, .49, .55, ____, ____
    c) .56, .50, .44, ____, ____
    d) .80, .40, .20, .10, ____, ____

7. Mark 40 cards with decimals. For example:

    | .06 | | .8 | | .25 |

One person mixes the cards and deals one at a time, face down, until each player has three cards. When the dealer says "Grab," each player then picks up his cards and arranges them in the correct order. The first person to declare "Between" and display the correct sequence wins a point. A person who says "Between" first but illustrates an incorrect sequence loses two points.

The first person to get twelve points is the winner.

8. Which of the following statements are true?

a) $.84 > .76$ c) $.23 < \dfrac{23}{100}$ e) $.07 = \dfrac{7}{10}$

b) $\dfrac{40}{100} = .04$ d) $\dfrac{4}{100} \neq .4$ f) $.72 > .8$

9. Write the correct relation symbol ($<$, $>$, or $=$) in each $\bigcirc$.

a) $.8 \bigcirc 1$ d) $1.1 \bigcirc 1$ g) $1 \bigcirc 0.999$

b) $.2 \bigcirc 1$ e) $1 \bigcirc .001$ h) $1.01 \bigcirc 1$

c) $.02 \bigcirc .8999$ f) $1 \bigcirc \dfrac{1}{10}$ i) $.0901 \bigcirc 1$

10. Tell whether the first number is to the left or right of the second number on the number line.

a) .48 is to the _____ of .61
b) 3.98 is to the _____ of 2.876
c) .094 is to the _____ of 4.0
d) 4.0 is to the _____ of 2.989
e) 4.301 is to the _____ of 4.3001
f) .11 is to the _____ of .9

11. Rename each of the following as a decimal.

a) $\dfrac{3}{10}$ b) $\dfrac{85}{100}$ c) $\dfrac{14}{100}$ d) $\dfrac{89}{10}$ e) $\dfrac{5}{100}$ f) $3\dfrac{4}{10}$

12. Rename each of the following as a proper fraction or a mixed numeral.

a) 0.13   d) 8.9   g) .09
b) 1.06   e) 4.87   h) .101
c) 4.15   f) 6.05   i) 6.70

13. A game can be developed for practice in renaming fractions as decimals and vice versa. Make a set of forty cards. Mark twenty with fractions and the other twenty with the equivalent decimal numerals. The cards are shuffled and then placed face down on a table (like a Concentration board). The first player turns up any two cards; if they are equivalent names (one fraction and one decimal) for the same number, he keeps the pair of cards and takes another turn. If the cards do not name equivalent decimals and fractions, he places the cards back on the table face down and the next player takes his turn. When all the cards have been paired the game is over. The player with the most pairs (one fraction and one decimal) is the winner.

14. Complete each pair of equations.

a) $\dfrac{6}{10} + \dfrac{9}{10} = \triangle$ b) $1\dfrac{4}{10} + \dfrac{3}{10} = \triangle$ c) $3 + \dfrac{9}{10} = \triangle$ d) $\dfrac{11}{10} + \dfrac{3}{10} = \triangle$

$.6 + .9 = \square$ $1.4 + .3 = \square$ $3 + .9 = \square$ $1.1 + .3 = \square$

15. Fill in the blanks to complete each example.

a)   .37 = ___ tenths ___ hundredths
  + .82 + 8 tenths 2 hundredths

b)   2.6 = ___ ones   ___ tenths
  + 4.7 + 4 ones   7 tenths
             ___ ones   13 tenths
            7 ones   ___ tenths

c)   .06 = ___ tenths ___ hundredths
  + .24 + 2 tenths ___ hundredths
           ___ tenths 10 hundredths
          3 tenths ___ hundredths

d)   4.3 = ___ ones   ___ tenths
  + .9 + _____ 9 tenths
           4 ones   ___ tenths
          ___ ones   2 tenths

16. The following activity can be used for adding and subtracting decimals. Mark off a square area with masking tape. Divide the area into several sections and mark each section with different decimals. Have the student throw two bean bags into the square. The student should then add or subtract the numbers that his or her bean bags landed on.

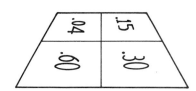

17. Add.

a)   2.34   b)   .206   c)   9.44   d)   4.003   e)   6.009   f)   4.987
  + 1.05   + .472   + .35   + 2.099   + .432   + .498

18. Subtract.

a)   31.9   c)   28.7   e)   81.6   g)   19.7
  − 10.6   − 11.3   − 20.6   − 10.8

b)   42.8   d)   8.21   f)   6.34   h)   77.31
  − 2.65   − .17   − 1.75   − 9.41

19. Find the following sums and differences. Show your work in vertical form. Be sure the digits are lined up according to place-value positions.

a) 7.38 + 5.1   c) 32.1 + 9.46   e) 4.0 + .905   g) 663.4 + 8
b) 73.2 − 8.06   d) 3.72 − .5   f) 130 − 2.4   h) 18 − .42

20. A magic square for decimals might be a useful vehicle for practice with addition and subtraction. Remember that in a magic square, the sum of each row horizontally, vertically, and diagonally should be the same (in the following one, the sum of each row is 7.5).

3.25	1.5	2.75
2.0	2.5	3.0
2.25	3.5	1.75

21. Use a dollar sign and a decimal point to express each of the following amounts of money.

   a) 6 dimes 4 pennies
   b) $3\frac{1}{2}$ dollars
   c) 1 quarter 3 dimes 2 pennies
   d) 8 dimes 2 nickels 7 pennies
   e) 2 dimes 4 pennies
   f) 3 quarters 1 nickel
   g) 23 pennies
   h) 1 half-dollar 1 quarter

22. How much change would you get if you bought a quart of oil for $1.05 and then filled your gas tank with fifteen gallons of gasoline at 98.9 cents a gallon and paid for all of this with a $20 bill?

23. Many children in Grades 4 and 5 have some knowledge of the metric system. A variety of problems can be presented that will reinforce basic concepts of measurement and help children understand some of the uses and advantages of decimal notation. For example, have the children draw polygons on pieces of paper. Ask them to measure the sides of the polygons to the nearest millimeter and to the nearest $\frac{1}{8}$ inch. Which measurements are easier to make? Have the children calculate the perimeters of the polygons they drew in millimeters and in inches (using the measurements they have obtained). Which measurements are easier to add?

24. Draw sets to show that the following ratios are equivalent.

8 to 10	3 to 9	4 to 12	3 to 1
4 to 5	9 to 27	8 to 24	12 to 4

25. Children may be given directions to construct two sets, one containing four red counters and the other containing five black counters. The ratio of red to black counters is thus $\frac{4}{5}$. They should then be asked to place four more red counters and five black counters on the table. Now the ratio of red to black counters is $\frac{8}{10}$. It should be noted that these two ratios are equivalent because for every four red counters there are five black counters.

26. Express the following as ratios in fraction form.

   a) 1 inch to 1 foot
   b) 1 quart to 1 gallon
   c) 2 runs in 3 innings
   d) 2 cookies for 5 cents
   e) 1 millimeter to 1 decimeter
   f) 6 milligrams to 1 kilograms

27. Write an equivalent ratio for each given ratio.

a) $\frac{8}{12} =$ ____   c) $\frac{14}{21} =$ ____   e) $\frac{32}{24} =$ ____   g) $\frac{15}{10} =$ ____   i) $\frac{3}{8} =$ ____

b) $\frac{4}{6} =$ ____   d) $\frac{12}{18} =$ ____   f) $\frac{2}{3} =$ ____   h) $\frac{27}{18} =$ ____

28. Study the following table.

Father's Age	Son's Age	$\frac{\text{Son's Age}}{\text{Father's Age}}$
24	0	0
26	2	$\frac{1}{13}$
28	4	$\frac{1}{7}$
32	8	$\frac{1}{4}$
36	12	$\frac{1}{3}$
48	24	$\frac{1}{2}$

What can you say about the ratio of the son's age to the father's as each gets older?

29. Have children write simple verbal problems involving ratios. This is an excellent way to find out whether they understand the basic ideas. Give them opportunities to discuss the problems and explain their thinking.

Hand-Held Calculator Activities for the Intermediate Grades

1. Have the children divide fractions and study the patterns of the decimals. For example:

One divided by eleven
Two divided by eleven
Three divided by eleven
Four divided by eleven
Five divided by eleven
Six divided by eleven
Seven divided by eleven
Eight divided by eleven
Nine divided by eleven
etc.

2. When 9 is divided by 17, the calculator display screen will read 0.5294117. How can the example be entered into the calculator so it will have eight decimal places?

3. Provide many experiences for children to change rational numbers written in fraction form to decimal form, by interpreting fractions as division.

4. Select any two-digit number; multiply that number by 10 two consecutive times. Now divide the number on the display screen by 10 four consecutive times. Discuss what happens to the number on the display screen after each multiplication or division.

5. Have the children change decimal names for numbers into decimals and then add the numbers. Check the exercise against a given sum. Study the following example.

Thirty-one and forty-two thousandths   = _____._____

Sixty and four tenths   = _____._____

Twenty-six and seven hundredths   = _____._____

Total   _____._____

Check   1 1 7 . 5 1 2

6. Count on your hand-held calculator, using decimal values. For instance, begin with the number 7.8 and add .1 ten consecutive times. Observe what happens as each number is added; then discuss the results with the class.

7. Check the addition and subtraction of decimal numbers, using a calculator.

8. Solve each example given in the first column of the following table. Write the answer in the second column. Write the digit in the appropriate place in the last column, and add the numbers in the last column. If the sum is the same as the sum written below the example, the child knows her work is correct. If the sums are not the same, she must check her work to find the mistake. Study this example:

Example	Answer	Place	Number
4.35 + 7.8 =		Tenths	
9.84 − 6.37 =		Hundredths	
10.7 − 3.58 =		Ones	
			Total
			Check 7.07

Microcomputer Activities for the Intermediate Grades

Most calculator activities suggested for the intermediate grades can also be used on the microcomputer.

1. The microcomputer programs suggested for operations on whole numbers can also be applied to decimals by changing the whole numbers to decimals.

2. Microcomputer software is available for drill and practice of operations on decimals. Examine catalogs from computer software companies.

3. Using the immediate mode, we can provide the computer with an example and it will print the answer. For example, if we type 4.7 − 2.93 and press RETURN (some computers have an ENTER key), the computer immediately displays 1.77 on the screen. How can we get the computer to print the example along with the answer? Try this example. Type into the computer

PRINT " 6.21 × 4.3 =";6.21*4.3

We have used the × for multiplication when we ask the computer to print multiplication on the screen. When we are communicating with the computer, we use an asterisk (∗) to indicate multiplication. You might want to use the ∗ symbol in both cases.

Create other decimal examples, using different operations. Remember that you want the computer to print out the example as well as calculate and print the answer. The computer will print whatever is typed inside the quotation marks. The semicolon causes the next part of the statement to be printed alongside the previous part. The computer will print the results of the mathematics occurring outside the quotation marks.

Activities for the Upper Elementary Grades

1. A place-value pocket chart may be easily constructed by using a piece of tag board 24″ by $5\frac{1}{2}$″. Fold $1\frac{1}{2}$″ and staple or sew as marked.

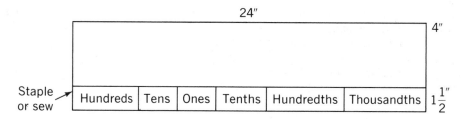

The teacher can use this place-value pocket chart by calling a number, such as 258.025. Using cards labeled with numerals 2, 5, 8, 0 and 2, the pupil tries to place the proper card in its correct pocket.

2. Tell what place value each digit(s) with the line segment under it represents.

   a) 71.57　　f) 8.798
   b) 4.666　　g) 2.09
   c) 122.32　　h) 8.23
   d) 4.666　　i) 4.96
   e) 15.7　　j) 243.6

3. Write the decimal numeral for each of the following.

   a) 89 and 4 tenths　　　　d) 584 and 24 hundredths
   b) 9 and 798 thousandths　　e) 42 and 59 hundredths
   c) 6 and 6 thousandths　　　f) 33 and 547 thousandths

4. Mark the decimal in each column that represents the greatest fractional number.

A	B	C	D
3.6	.065	1.003	35.505
3.4	.65	1.133	35.550
4.4	.0605	1.303	35.555
2.9	.0655	1.330	35.500

5. Write five decimals that name numbers that fit the description.

   a) greater than .11 and less than .2   c) greater than .01 and less than 0.1
   b) greater than .09 and less than 0.1   d) greater than 0.9 and less than 1.0

6. Complete each sequence.

   a) 1.78, 2.88, 3.98, ____, ____   c) 3.5, 3.4, 3.3, ____, ____
   b) 8.5, 9.0, 9.5, ____, ____   d) 3.076, 3.086, 3.096, ____, ____

7. A game providing practice with order relations of decimals can easily be developed by using three different colored dice. Each die represents place value of a decimal numeral. For example, a red die could stand for tenths, blue for hundredths, and green for thousandths. One pupil rolls the die and records the numeral represented. Another repeats the process. The pupil with the greatest valued decimal numeral is the winner.

8. A modification of Rummy can be a helpful game that provides valuable practice in renaming fractions as decimals and vice versa. A pack of cards, each marked with a fraction or decimal, is needed. For each number, there must be three cards, each with the number shown in different forms—for example: $\frac{1}{2}$, .50, .500. There should be approximately 20 of these sets.

   Two to four players may play the game, which proceeds as follows. Each player is dealt five cards. Place the remainder of the deck face down with the top card turned up. The player to the left of the dealer begins. He may take either the turned-up card or the top card of the face-down deck. If he has three cards showing equivalent fractions or decimals, he lays them down on the table. When he is finished, he discards one card face up. Play continues. When one player has no cards, the game ends and the one with most sets of three wins.

9. Rename as decimals.

   a) $\frac{33}{200}$ b) $\frac{19}{20}$ c) $\frac{27}{500}$ d) $\frac{4}{5}$ e) $\frac{16}{50}$ f) $\frac{17}{25}$ g) $3\frac{5}{6}$

10. Rewrite each decimal as a fraction.

   a) 0.7   b) 1.67   c) 0.064   d) 0.06   e) 5.5   f) 2.25

11. Find the sums.

   a)   5.67   b)   87.4   c)   68.08   d)   481.32   e)   .11
      + 2.24   + 39.56   + 9.92   + 25.60   .80
                                                                      7.00

12. Find the differences.

   a)   6.34   b)   24.302   c)   .0700   d)   72.302   e)   75.2
      − 2.18   − 16.756   − .0245   − 26.298   −   .13

13. Complete the table. What pattern do you find?

Factors	Number of Decimal Places	Product	Number of Decimal Places
.36 and .2			
3.56 and .08			
.345 and .8			
.1245 and .18			

14. Use 10×10 squares cut from graph paper to model the sum of

$$\begin{array}{r} .89 \\ + .47 \\ \hline \end{array}$$

It is advisable to stress the comparison between fraction and decimal notation frequently as children begin to extend their working knowledge in the operations of arithmetic. This is not to imply that every example must be translated from one form into the other, which would defeat the purpose. When a child understands the relation and can select the notation that is most efficient in a given situation, then the purpose has been accomplished.

This is particularly true in the operations of multiplication and division involving decimals. The memorized rules of "counting the decimal places" and "moving the decimal point" should be replaced by sound mathematical reasoning that can be justified.

15. Study and complete the following examples.

a) $.1 \times 6 \;\; = \dfrac{\square}{10} \times 6$

b) $.25 \times .3 = \dfrac{25}{\square} \times \dfrac{3}{\triangle}$

c) $\begin{array}{r} .36 \\ \times \;\; 4 \\ \hline \end{array}$

 3 tenths 6 hundredths
$\times$ _____4 ones_____
 12 tenths 24 hundredths
 14 tenths __ hundredths
__ ones __ tenths __ hundredths

d) $\begin{array}{r} .26 \\ \times \;\; .4 \\ \hline \end{array}$

 2 tenths 6 hundredths
$\times$ 4 tenths _____
 8 hundredths 24 thousandths
 __ hundredths __ thousandths
__ tenths __ hundredths __ thousandths

e)

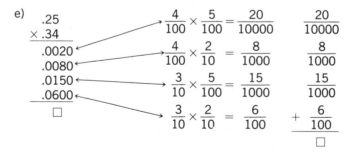

$$\begin{array}{r} .25 \\ \times .34 \\ \hline .0020 \\ .0080 \\ .0150 \\ .0600 \\ \hline \square \end{array}$$

$\dfrac{4}{100} \times \dfrac{5}{100} = \dfrac{20}{10000} \qquad \dfrac{20}{10000}$

$\dfrac{4}{100} \times \dfrac{2}{10} = \dfrac{8}{1000} \qquad \dfrac{8}{1000}$

$\dfrac{3}{10} \times \dfrac{5}{100} = \dfrac{15}{1000} \qquad \dfrac{15}{1000}$

$\dfrac{3}{10} \times \dfrac{2}{10} = \dfrac{6}{100} \qquad + \dfrac{6}{100}$

$\qquad\qquad\qquad\qquad\qquad \square$

f) $\begin{array}{r} .34 \\ \times .08 \\ \hline \end{array}$

16. Find the products.

a) 0.8×0.05 b) 8.96×4.3 c) 37.6×3.75 d) $\dfrac{7}{10} \times \dfrac{36}{100}$

17. Multiply each of the following by $\frac{10}{10}$, $\frac{100}{100}$, or $\frac{1000}{1000}$ to make the denominator a whole number.

   a) $\frac{6.72}{3.2}$ b) $\frac{8.51}{.23}$ c) $\frac{1.59}{.4}$ d) $\frac{69.3}{.31}$ e) $\frac{45}{1.5}$

18. Rewrite each example in fraction form and find the quotient.

   a) $7 \div 4$ b) $.44 \div .4$ c) $172.8 \div 0.12$ d) $38.6 \div 6.8$

19. Find the quotients.

   a) $.8\overline{)2.4}$ c) $.11\overline{)1.21}$ e) $4\overline{).875}$

   b) $.05\overline{)15.00}$ d) $.02\overline{).134}$ f) $68.77\overline{)14,304.16}$

20. Bingo cards should be constructed with a variety of numbers expressed as percentages, decimals, and fractions in the nine squares. A list of fractions and their equivalent decimals and percentages should be devised.

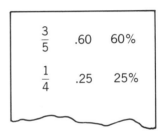

.60	15%	$\frac{1}{4}$
37.5%	FREE	.05
$\frac{2}{3}$	.8	75%

$\frac{3}{5}$	.60	60%
$\frac{1}{4}$	.25	25%

The caller chooses one of the numbers, and students may cover any equivalent number on their cards. The first person to get three in a row or column is the winner. The card may be extended to five rows and five columns.

21. Write a message, then construct a grid on the inside of a file folder with a space for each letter of the message. Make a set of cards with a fraction on one side of each card and a letter on the other side. Have the student take one card at a time and change the fraction written on the card to its decimal equivalent. Find the decimal equivalent on the board. Turn the card over and place the card on the board so that the letter is showing. If the child has placed each card correctly, he or she will receive a message.

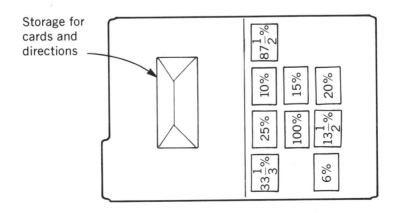

Storage for cards and directions

22. A shoebox can be used to facilitate practice with equivalent fractions, decimals, and percents. Take the lid off the shoebox and cut out eight rectangular slits.

$\frac{1}{2}$ 65%   .06   75% $\frac{1}{3}$ 20%   .45 $\frac{2}{3}$

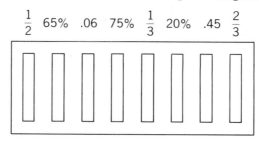

Write a fraction, decimal, or percent above each slit; then partition the shoebox into eight sections and replace the lid. Make cards representing the value in at least three ways.

For example, for the slit marked $\frac{1}{2}$, the following cards should be made.

Make approximately 50 to 60 cards. The student's task is to place the appropriate card in a slit named by an equivalent decimal, fraction, or percent. After students are finished, they may open the box and check the bottom of the shoebox where the correct representations are listed.

23. Write the correct relation symbol (<, >, or =) in each loop.

a) $\frac{2.54}{100} \bigcirc \frac{2.54}{10}$

b) $16 \div 0.4 \bigcirc .4 \div 16$

c) $62.4 \times \frac{10}{24} \bigcirc 62.4 \div 2.4$

d) $\frac{5}{6} \div \frac{5}{12} \bigcirc \frac{178}{10} \div \frac{89}{10}$

e) $.6 \bigcirc 6\%$

f) $1 \bigcirc 100\%$

g) $50\% \bigcirc \frac{1}{2}$

h) $2 \bigcirc 200\%$

i) $25.5 \div 5.1 \bigcirc 255 \div 51$

j) $\frac{174}{1000} \bigcirc \frac{17.4}{1000}$

k) $7 \div .75 \bigcirc .75 \div 7$

l) $7 \bigcirc 7\%$

m) $.04 \bigcirc 4\%$

n) $\frac{1}{2} \bigcirc \frac{1}{2}\%$

24. Use your knowledge of scientific notation to complete each of the following:

a) $780 = 7.8 \times$ _____

b) $4800 = 4.8 \times$ _____

c) $6790 = 6.79 \times$ _____

d) $23,800 =$ _____ $\times 10^4$

e) _____ $= 4.98 \times 10^4$

f) $495,000 =$ _____ $\times 10^5$

25. Collect a variety of inexpensive materials and place them in a shoebox or container. For example:

15 nails	9 circular regions
24 paper clips	12 triangular regions
18 straws	6 cup hooks

Prepare a question sheet that may be laminated, for students to write on, or else provide a separate answer sheet. Ask such questions as:

What is the ratio of the straws to the paper clips? (8:24 or 1:3)

What is the ratio of the straws to the cup hooks? (8:6 or 4:3)

26. Find the number represented by the letter in each of the proportions.

a) $\frac{2}{1} = \frac{24}{n}$ b) $\frac{5}{m} = \frac{9}{27}$ c) $\frac{13}{a} = \frac{17}{17}$ d) $\frac{16}{18} = \frac{24}{y}$

27. Write a mathematical sentence for each problem. Then solve the sentence and answer the question.

a) If a space capsule travels at a speed of 28,800 kilometers per hour, how many kilometers does it travel in one minute? How many kilometers per second?

b) A car can travel 33 kilometers on one liter of gasoline. How far will it go on 5 liters of gasoline?

c) David's father drives 104 kilometers in one hour. At this speed, how many hours will it take him to drive 520 kilometers?

d) George can run 75 meters in 12 seconds. How long will it take him to run 175 meters if he doesn't change his pace?

Hand-Held Calculator Activities for the Upper Elementary Grades

All activities suggested for the intermediate grades can be easily adapted for the upper elementary grades.

1. Have children use the hand-held calculator to check their completed worksheets of decimal operations.

2. Assume that a sheet of paper measures 0.001 inches thick. How thick will the paper be, if it is folded in half? in fourths? in eighths? How many sheets of paper will it take to make a stack 1 inch thick? Many similar questions could be posed.

3. Use the repeated add function discussed in Unit 6 and a constant of .1. What is the answer after the equals key is pressed 20 times? 25 times? 50 times?

4. Provide children with decimal multiplication examples that have been solved numerically without decimal points. Have the children provide the decimal points and check their answers, using a hand-held calculator.

5. Have children use the calculator to multiply a given number by .1 and then .01, .001, etc. Compare the answers. Discuss with the children the effect of multiplying by tenths, hundredths, and thousandths. Also try multiplying decimals by 1, 10, 100, and 1000; discuss the effect with the class.

6. Have children use the calculator to divide a given number by .1, .01, .001, etc. Compare the answers. Discuss with the class the effects of dividing by tenths, hundredths, and thousandths. Also try dividing a *decimal* number by 1, .1, .01, .001, etc. Discuss the effects with the class.

7. Provide children with decimal division examples solved numerically without decimal points. Have the children supply the necessary decimal points in the answers and check their results on a hand-held calculator.

8. Teach children how to change a number to a percent using the percent key. For instance, place the number 250 on the screen, then press the % key. Now what appears on the screen?

9. The percent add-on key is very useful in the business world. The use of the percent add-on key is not commonly understood. The best way to explain this function is by carefully examining a problem. If a suit that regularly sells for $175 is on sale at 20% off, what will a customer have to pay for the suit (including a 5% sales tax)? Solve the problem by pressing the following keys:

$$\boxed{1}\,\boxed{7}\,\boxed{5}\,\boxed{-}\,\boxed{2}\,\boxed{0}\,\boxed{\%}\,\boxed{=}\,\boxed{+}\,\boxed{5}\,\boxed{\%}\,\boxed{=}$$

Study this example and discuss with the class how the add-on percent key functions. Create additional examples for the children to solve before you ask them to generalize.

10. Use the athletic data from the newspaper and calculate batting averages, percent of wins, and percent of losses. Use football data to calculate the percent of passes completed, etc.

11. Walk 100 meters three times; calculate the average length of one pace. Predetermine how many decimal places you will consider. How many steps must you take to walk 1,000,000 meters?

12. How many aluminum pop cans will be needed to make a stack 1,000,000 meters high?

13. Guess-My-Number Game: Set up the hand-held calculator by selecting a number between 1 and 100; key it into the calculator, followed by $\boxed{\div}\,\boxed{=}$. This makes the selected number a constant divisor. Hand the calculator to another student and ask him to guess the number that was entered. Enter another number and hit the $\boxed{=}$ key. A decimal will appear on the display screen. Students should be able to discover the hidden number by analyzing the number on the display screen.

Microcomputer Activities for the Upper Elementary Grades

Many of the hand-held calculator activities suggested for the upper elementary grades can also be used with the microcomputer in the immediate mode.

1. Check software catalogs for programs that provide the drill and practice needed for the upper elementary grades. Many software programs also keep records for the teacher. In these cases, the teacher can easily check the computer to find out how many examples each child has practiced, the number of correct and incorrect answers, the percent of accuracy, and the amount of time consumed.

2. Children in the upper elementary grades should be able to write simple computer programs to accomplish a specific purpose. Ask the children to write a computer program to calculate sales tax. For this example, we will assume that the state sales tax is 4.5%. This

sample program should run on most microcomputers. The "clear the screen" statement will vary, depending on which computer you are using. We have used CLS with the TRS-80 microcomputer.

```
10 REM—SALES TAX PROGRAM—
15 CLS
20 ?"ENTER THE TOTAL FOR A SALE AND I WILL CALCULATE THE TAX."
30 ?:?"I WILL ALSO PRINT THE TOTAL AMOUNT WITH TAX."
40 FOR T=1 TO 5000:NEXT T
50 CLS
60 ?"WHAT IS THE AMOUNT OF THE SALE."
70 INPUT A
80 S=.045*A
90 ?"SALES TAX IS $";S
100 ?:?"SALES PLUS TAX IS $";A+S
110 END
```

3. Write a computer program to compute commissions for a salesperson, based on:

   a) A straight 20-percent commission
   b) A 15-percent commission on the first $2000 and 20 percent on all sales above $2000
   c) An eight-percent commission on the first $1000 in sales, 10 percent on sales between $1000 and $2000, 12 percent on sales between $2000 and $3000, and 14 percent on all sales above $3000.

Suggested Readings

Ashlock, Robert B. "Introducing Decimal Fractions with the Meterstick." *The Arithmetic Teacher*, vol. 23, no. 3, March 1976.

Bright, George W. "Ideas." *The Arithmetic Teacher*, vol. 24, no. 3, March 1977.

Firl, Donald H. "Fractions, Decimals, and Their Future." *The Arithmetic Teacher*, vol. 24, no. 3, March 1977.

Hatfield, Larry L. "Teaching Mathematics with Microcomputers: Junior High School." *The Arithmetic Teacher*, vol. 30, no. 6, February 1983.

Heck, William. "Teaching Mathematics with Microcomputers: Primary Grades." *The Arithmetic Teacher*, vol. 30, no. 6, February 1983.

Higgins, Jon L., and Sachs, Larry A. *Mathematics Laboratories: 150 Activities and Games for Elementary Schools*. Reston, Va.: National Council of Teachers of Mathematics, 1974.

Immerzel, George, and Wiederanders, Don. "Ideas." *The Arithmetic Teacher*, vol. 21, no. 2, February 1974.

Molinaski, Marie. "Fracto." *The Arithmetic Teacher*, vol. 21, no. 4, April 1974.

National Council of Teachers of Mathematics. *Games and Puzzles for Elementary and Middle School Mathematics*. Reston, Va.: NCTM, 1975.

Ockenga, Earl. "Calculator Ideas for the Junior High Classroom." *The Arithmetic Teacher*, vol. 23, no. 7, November 1976.

Virginia Council of Teachers of Mathematics. *Practical Ways to Teach the Basic Mathematics Skills*. Reston, Va.: National Council of Teachers of Mathematics, 1979.

Wahl, M. Stoessel. "A Percentage Visualizer." *Manipulative Activities and Games in the Mathematics Classroom*. Reston, Va.: National Education Association, 1979.

Winter, Mary Jean. "Teaching Mathematics with Microcomputers: Middle Grades." *The Arithmetic Teacher*, vol. 30, no. 6, February 1983.

12 The Real Number System

Teaching Competencies

Upon completing this unit, you will be able to:

Define the terms *integer, rational number,* and *real number*

Match integers and rational numbers with points on the number line

Use the number line to illustrate addition and subtraction of integers

Use additive inverses to solve subtraction examples involving integers

Perform the fundamental operations on integers and rational numbers

State the relations between the system of real numbers and its subsystems

Discussion

In previous units we have examined various aspects of our number system. We began with concrete items; then we moved to the study of number. After that we looked at some of the various sets of numbers that make up our mathematical system—counting numbers, whole numbers, and fractional numbers.

The study of the real-number system is rather a crucial point in a student's mathematical development. It brings together all of the number systems studied in the elementary school. Let's look at the number systems that make up the real-number system. The elementary school mathematics program is based upon a very logical organization that begins with the numbers we call the counting numbers. You should recall that counting numbers begin with 1 and continue with 2, 3, 4, and so forth, in that pattern. We symbolize the counting numbers [1, 2, 3, . . .].

The next logical set of numbers we consider is the set of whole numbers, the counting numbers with the inclusion of zero (0). The whole numbers are symbolized [0, 1, 2, 3, 4, 5, . . .]. Note that one new element has been included in this system of numbers. A diagram can illustrate the relation between counting numbers and whole numbers.

Counting numbers
[1, 2, 3, 4, 5, 6, . . .]

Whole numbers [0]

Note that whole numbers include all counting numbers.

Another set of numbers we will examine in this unit is the set of integers. Counting numbers and whole numbers are included in the set of integers. We now show the counting numbers as positive numbers [$^+$1, $^+$2, $^+$3, $^+$4, $^+$5, . . .]. Zero is included as an integer. By extending the number line to the left, we see that there is a logical need for negative numbers. So three sets of numbers make up the integers: counting numbers, negative numbers, and 0. (Negative numbers will be explained in more detail later.) We can show the relationship among the numbers with a diagram.

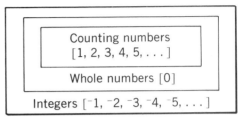

The system of numbers is now extended to include rational numbers. Rational numbers may be written in two different forms—fractions and decimals. Rational numbers were in Units 9, 10, and 11. Since counting numbers, whole numbers, and integers are rational numbers, we can extend the diagram of the number system as follows:

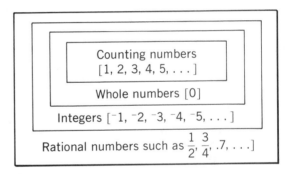

In this unit we will also examine irrational numbers. It will be shown that irrational numbers are not related to counting numbers, whole numbers, integers, or rational numbers, so they are set off to one side.

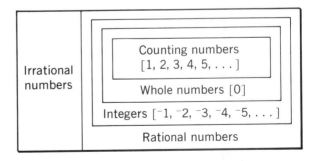

All of the systems of numbers make up the real number system, which will be discussed in this unit. The final diagram is shown on the following page.

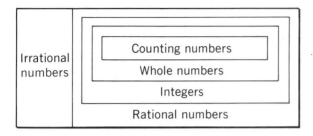

Real Number System

These number systems—counting numbers, whole numbers, and rational numbers—have all been related to the number line; we found that any number can be matched with a unique point on the number line. If we examine the number line closely, we can see that there are many points on it that we have not yet named. In this unit we will investigate some of these unnamed points of the number line.

As we worked with whole numbers, we found that the sum of any two whole numbers is a whole number, but sometimes the difference between two whole numbers is not a whole number. Consider, for example, $4 + \square = 3$, or $3 - 4 = \square$. There is no whole number that satisfies this equation. Thus we need another kind of number to solve examples such as this.

The need for a number system that includes numbers less than zero was answered by the invention of negative numbers. To explore this concept, let's take a look at a familiar number line that we all use in our everyday lives—a thermometer.

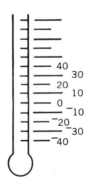

We see that 0 is the reference point on this thermometer and that numerals are marked at regular (equal) intervals to indicate temperature. We are all familiar with readings such as 25°, 32°, and 59°. But what about midwinter readings, or readings on a deep-freeze thermometer—10 below 0, 15 below 0, and so on? Temperatures below zero, when recorded in the newspaper, are written as ⁻10° and ⁻15°.

Essentially, a thermometer is a number line with equivalent divisions on both sides of the zero

point. The numerals on one side of the zero are exactly like the numerals on the following number line, which is used in the primary grades.

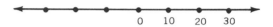

Can we, on our number line, mark and label points to show the part of the number line that corresponds to the below-zero readings of a thermometer?

Obviously, we must distinguish between the numerals written to the left of the zero and those written to the right. One way of doing this is to place a sign (⁻) in front of any numeral written to the left of 0 to indicate that it represents a number *less than zero:*

A number represented by a numeral with this sign is called a **negative number,** and the sign (⁻) is called a **negative sign.** The numerals written to the right of the zero represent what are called **positive numbers,** and a positive number is sometimes written with a **positive sign** (⁺) placed in front of it (for example, ⁺10 or ⁺20). Numerals written without signs are understood to represent positive numbers. The number zero is neither positive nor negative. Numbers that are named by numerals with signs to indicate that the numbers named are positive (⁺) or negative (⁻) are called **directed numbers.** Notice that the positive and negative signs are raised to prevent confusion with the signs for addition and subtraction. The raised ⁺ (positive) and ⁻ (negative) signs should not be mistakenly thought of by pupils as operation signs. The raised ⁺ and ⁻ signs are part of the names of the numbers. When first introducing positive and negative numbers to children, it is best to place the ⁺ sign with every positive number under discussion. Later, children will recognize that positive numbers can sometimes be written with the ⁺ understood.

Some individuals read ⁻2 as "minus two" and ⁺2 as "plus two." When the terms *minus* and *plus* are associated with positive and negative numbers, children confuse the concept of integers with the concepts of addition and subtraction. This is why in Unit 6 we suggested reading the + sign as *add;* now with integers we will read the + sign as *positive.* The − sign with integers will be read as *negative.* The difficulties that children experience in developing an understanding of integers are usually caused by confusion between these uses of the + and − signs.

Examine the following number-line diagram.

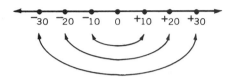

Notice that the points labeled $^+20$ and $^-20$ are the same distance from 0, but that one is to the right of 0, while the other is to the left of 0. We call such pairs of numbers **opposites.** In general, if two points are the same distance from the 0 point, but on opposite sides of the 0 point, the numbers that correspond to these points are called opposites. Thus $^+10$ and $^-10$ are opposites, as are $^+5$ and $^-5$, $^+3$ and $^-3$, and so on. So that every number will have an opposite, it is customary to say that *zero is its own opposite*.

A number is an **integer** if it is a whole number or the opposite of a whole number. We can indicate the integers as follows:

$$\{\ldots, ^-4, ^-3, ^-2, ^-1, 0, ^+1, ^+2, ^+3, ^+4, \ldots\}$$

The integers that are greater than zero form the set of **positive integers:**

$$\{^+1, ^+2, ^+3, ^+4, ^+5, \ldots\}$$

The integers that are less than zero form the set of **negative integers:**

$$\{^-1, ^-2, ^-3, ^-4, ^-5, \ldots\}$$

The number 0 is an integer, but it is usually considered to be neither positive nor negative.

We have seen that we can represent the integers on the number line. On the number line below, locate the point named by $^+5$. As we have just seen, the 5 indicates how many unit lengths from zero, and the $^+$ indicates the direction.

Considering the line segment that begins at 0 on the number line, the arrow indicates the direction (the **sign** of the number), and the length indicates the number of unit lengths from zero (the value of the number regardless of its sign). This line segment stands for the value $^+5$.

Consider the value $^-2$. The negative sign indicates direction, and the 2 indicates magnitude.

Magnitude or **absolute value** refers to the length of the line segment in unit lengths.

This line segment stands for $^-2$ because it is two units long and has a negative direction. Remember that, starting at zero, we move left from zero to indicate negative numbers, and right from zero to indicate positive numbers.

Using the number line, children learned number relations in whole numbers and in fractional numbers. They found that beginning with zero, numbers increase in value to the right on the number line. This is, of course, still valid when the negative integers are located on the number line.

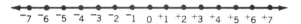

Since children have already learned relations such as $4 > 2, 5 < 7, 3 > 0$, and so on, it is not difficult to extend this concept to include negative integers. Any number on the number line is greater than any number to its left, as we have seen. So, on the number line above, we see that $^-1 > ^-2, ^-3 > ^-7, 0 > ^-1, ^+2 > ^-3, ^+1 > ^-10$, and so on. This extension of children's knowledge of relations on the number line is consistent and logical. The evident truth of statements such as $^+1 > ^-7$, seen on the number line, will help children understand the meaning of negative integers. A number is still greater than any number named to its left on the number line. However, 0 is not a "beginning" point now but a point of reference between positive and negative numbers. The set of integers extends endlessly to the left and to the right of zero.

To further clarify the meaning of $^-8 < ^+1$, for example, the familiar analogy of being in debt, or "in the hole," could be mentioned. If Mr. Smith owes $8, and Mr. Brown has $1, who has more money? Mr. Brown, since Mr. Smith is $8 in debt, or has $^-8$ dollars, while Mr. Brown has $^+1$ dollar.

The positive integers have the properties of the whole numbers with which the child is familiar, but should always be labeled with the $^+$ sign when the set of integers is being considered. By the time they are in high school, pupils will be familiar enough with integers to consider positive integers without labeling them $^+$ when they are named.

Now let's look at some examples of addition of integers modeled on the number line. In each of the following examples, find the indicated sum.

a) $^-3 + ^-2 = \square$

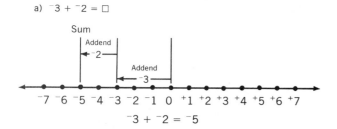

$^-3 + ^-2 = ^-5$

b) $^+3 + ^-5 = \square$

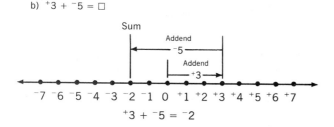

$^+3 + ^-5 = ^-2$

c) $^-7 + ^+2 = \square$

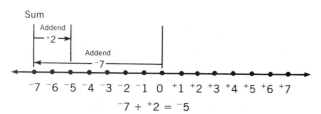

$^-7 + ^+2 = ^-5$

In each example, all the arrows are drawn according to the magnitude and direction indicated in the equation. Generalizing from these examples, we see that if we wish to represent sums of positive and negative numbers as moves on the number line, we can observe the following procedure.

1. Start at zero on the number line and draw an arrow so that its length in unit lengths equals the first addend to be added (regardless of its sign) and the direction in which the arrow is drawn corresponds to the sign of the number (left for $^-$ and right for $+$).

2. Starting from the end of the first arrow (and just above it), draw an arrow so that its length in unit lengths equals the second addend to be added (regardless of its sign) and the direction in which the arrow is drawn corresponds to the sign of the number.

3. The point on the number line where the second addend ends names the sum. The sum is also called the **resultant** in this case. The resultant is always the sum of an addition example and it is read from the end of the arrow that names the second addend. It is named by a point on the number line.

You will readily see that if we add two integers which are opposites, we get 0 for the sum. For example, $^+4 + ^-4 = 0$:

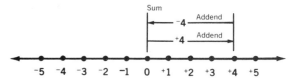

The arrow for the first addend ($^+4$) takes us to $^+4$, and the arrow for the second addend ($^-4$) brings us back to 0. If we read the point at the end of the second arrow, we find the sum to be 0. Nevertheless, it should be clear from the diagram that $^+4 + ^-4 = 0$. Similarly, the sum of any two opposites is zero:

Addend		Addend		Sum
$^+7$	$+$	$^-7$	$=$	0
$^-9$	$+$	$^+9$	$=$	0
$^+12$	$+$	$^-12$	$=$	0
		and so on		

The fact that any two opposites have a sum of zero is often referred to as the **addition property of opposites.**

Besides the addition property of opposites, what other properties exist for addition of integers? Using number-line models, it is easy to see that addition of integers has all the basic properties that we found for whole numbers and fractional numbers:

1. Addition of integers is **commutative.**
2. Addition of integers is **associative.**
3. Zero (0) is the **identity** element for addition of integers.

At this point we will leave it to the student to draw number-line models to convince himself that these properties do indeed hold.

From number-line diagrams, it is easy to see that the sum of two positive integers must be positive: $^+3 + ^+5 = ^+8$, $^+6 + ^+7 = ^+13$, and so on. It is equally clear that the sum of two negative integers must be negative: $^-2 + ^-3 = ^-5$, $^-7 + ^-1 = ^-8$, and so on. What about the sum of a positive integer and a negative integer?

Consider this example: $^+8 + ^-4 = \square$. The property of opposite numbers tells us that $^+4 + ^-4 = 0$. We can use the concept of opposites and the number line to find a solution:

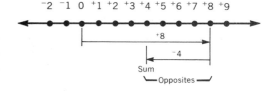

Let's look at another example: $^+3 + {}^-9 = \square$.

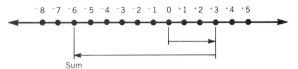

Sum

Another example: $^+10 + {}^-7 = \square$.

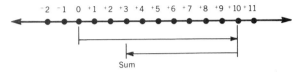

Sum

And another: $^-17 + {}^+19 = \square$.

Sum

Locate where the opposites are apparent in each example.

Notice that integers, like other numbers, can be renamed in many different ways. For example, we can rename 12 as $11 + 1$, $10 + 2$, $9 + 3$, and so on. We can, in the same manner, rename $^-12$ in different ways: $^-11 + {}^-1$, $^-10 + {}^-2$, $^-9 + {}^-3$, and so on.

Now let's look at the inverse operation of subtraction in relation to the set of integers. Subtraction, we know, is the inverse operation of addition.

Addend		Addend		Sum
6	+	8	=	14
∴ 14	−	6	=	8
or 14	−	8	=	6
Sum		Addend		Addend

Let's examine the way in which the inverse operation of subtraction is performed using the number line. Consider $^+4 - {}^+2 = \square$. We can rewrite as the addition example $^+2 + \square = {}^+4$. First draw an arrow that is two units long and points to the right (the positive direction) to represent the first addend. The arrow for the second addend, which is the missing addend, must go from the tip of the first arrow to the point for $^+4$ (the sum). Draw this arrow; use a dotted line to indicate that it represents the missing addend.

Missing
addend

Addend ┤- - - - -┤ Sum

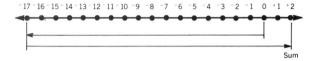

What integer does the dotted arrow represent? Since it is two units long and points in the positive direction, it represents $^+2$. The sum of the addition example, and hence of the subtraction example, is therefore $^+2$. Thus

Sum		Addend		Addend
$^+4$	−	$^+2$	=	$^+2$

Consider this example: $^-5 - {}^+3 = \square$. This example can be rewritten as an addition example: $^+3 + \square = {}^-5$. This example can be modeled on the number line by beginning at the reference point, zero, and laying off the addend 3 in a positive direction. Next locate the point $^-5$, which is the sum. We know that the missing addend must begin at the end of the first addend and end at the sum. The number-line model can be drawn in the following way:

Sum   Missing addend   Addend

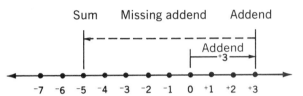

Addend
$^+3$

The diagram shows that $\square = {}^-8$. Therefore

$$^-5 - {}^+3 = {}^-8.$$

Look at the following subtraction examples, which have been rewritten in terms of addition and solved.

SUBTRACTION	ADDITION	SOLUTION
$^+4 - {}^+2 = \square$	$^+2 + \square = {}^+4$	$\square = {}^+2$
$^+4 - {}^+1 = \square$	$^+1 + \square = {}^+4$	$\square = {}^+3$
$^+4 - 0 = \square$	$0 + \square = {}^+4$	$\square = {}^+4$
$^+4 - {}^-1 = \square$	$^-1 + \square = {}^+4$	$\square = {}^+5$
$^+4 - {}^-2 = \square$	$^-2 + \square = {}^+4$	$\square = {}^+6$

These five examples have been rewritten to illustrate the generalization that subtracting a number gives the same result as adding its opposite. You will note by looking at the number line that the opposite of zero is zero itself.

$^+4 - {}^+2 = \square$	$^+4 + {}^-2 = \square$	$\square = {}^+2$
$^+4 - {}^+1 = \square$	$^+4 + {}^-1 = \square$	$\square = {}^+3$
$^+4 - 0 = \square$	$^+4 + 0 = \square$	$\square = {}^+4$
$^+4 - {}^-1 = \square$	$^+4 + {}^+1 = \square$	$\square = {}^+5$
$^+4 - {}^-2 = \square$	$^+4 + {}^+2 = \square$	$\square = {}^+6$

The concept of subtracting integers closely parallels subtraction of whole numbers. The number line has been used as a model to help develop an understanding. Inverse sentences have been used to help children comprehend the existing relationships. After the children have had many experiences with subtraction as related to integers, they should begin to look for patterns to help them generalize. Teachers should not rush the children by pushing them into generalizing prematurely.

Can we make a generalization about solving subtraction examples? Yes. When we are to subtract one number from another, we can obtain the difference by adding the opposite of that number. For example:

$$^+3 - {}^+2 = \square \longrightarrow {}^+3 - {}^+2 = {}^+1$$
$$^+3 + {}^-2 = \square \longrightarrow {}^+3 + {}^-2 = {}^+1$$
$$\therefore {}^+3 - {}^+2 = {}^+3 + {}^-2$$

We mentioned earlier that addition of integers has all of the properties of addition of whole numbers and fractional numbers. What properties does subtraction have? When we studied subtraction of whole numbers we found that it was neither commutative nor associative. The same is true for subtraction of integers. For example $^+2 - {}^+4 = {}^-2$, but $^+4 - {}^+2 = {}^+2$; therefore $^+2 - {}^+4 \neq {}^+4 - {}^+2$, which is enough to show that subtraction is not commutative. Can you devise a counterexample to show that subtraction is not associative? So far we have found two properties that subtraction of integers does *not* have. (Subtraction of whole numbers did not have them either.) An important property that subtraction of integers *does* have is that for any integers a and b, $a - b$ is also an integer. In the system of whole numbers, there is no way to subtract a greater number from a lesser one, but in the system of integers, there is.

Let us turn our attention now to multiplication of integers. Multiplication of two nonnegative integers is just like multiplication of whole numbers. For instance

Factor		Factor		Product
$^+3$	$\times$	$^+2$	$=$	$^+6$
0	$\times$	$^+5$	$=$	0
$^+6$	$\times$	$^+7$	$=$	$^+42$
$^+1$	$\times$	$^+8$	$=$	$^+8$

and so on

Multiplication examples such as 2×4 can be interpreted to mean "two sets of four." We can model the example on the number line:

If we interpret $^+2 \times {}^+4$ as two jumps of $^+4$ in a positive direction, we arrive at $^+8$. Following the same logic, we can interpret $^+2 \times {}^-4$ as two jumps of $^-4$ in the negative direction. Thus we see that $^+2 \times {}^-4 = {}^-8$.

Thus we see that $^+2 \times {}^-4 = {}^-8$.

Using the commutative property of multiplication, we can change $^+2 \times {}^-4 = {}^-8$ to $^-4 \times {}^+2 = {}^-8$.

Patterns are helpful for children to justify the results of multiplication of integers. Now let's look at the operation of multiplication using negative numbers and looking for patterns. Consider the following examples:

Factor		Factor		Product
$^+5$	$\times$	$^+3$	$=$	$^+15$
$^+5$	$\times$	$^+2$	$=$	$^+10$
$^+5$	$\times$	$^+1$	$=$	$^+5$
$^+5$	$\times$	0	$=$	0
$^+5$	$\times$	$^-1$	$=$	$\square$
$^+5$	$\times$	$^-2$	$=$	$\square$
$^+5$	$\times$	$^-3$	$=$	$\square$

Examining the pattern found here, we discover that the product becomes five less every time the second factor becomes one less. If this pattern is extended to include the last three examples in the series above, we get negative products:

$$^+5 \times {}^-1 = {}^-5$$
$$^+5 \times {}^-2 = {}^-10$$
$$^+5 \times {}^-3 = {}^-15$$

Notice that $^+5 \times {}^-3 = {}^-15$ while $^+5 \times {}^+3 = {}^+15$. Changing the sign of the second factor from positive to negative merely results in changing the sign of the product also from positive to negative. The same is true of the other two examples: $^+5 \times {}^-2 = {}^-10$ while $^+5 \times {}^+2 = {}^+10$, and $^+5 \times {}^-1 = {}^-5$ while $^+5 \times {}^+1 = {}^+5$.

A similar approach can be used to discover how to define multiplication when the first factor is negative and the second factor is positive. Look for the pattern in these examples:

Factor		Factor		Product
$^+3$	$\times$	$^+5$	$=$	$^+15$
$^+2$	$\times$	$^+5$	$=$	$^+10$
$^+1$	$\times$	$^+5$	$=$	$^+5$
0	$\times$	$^+5$	$=$	0
$^-1$	$\times$	$^+5$	$=$	$\square$
$^-2$	$\times$	$^+5$	$=$	$\square$
$^-3$	$\times$	$^+5$	$=$	$\square$

Examining the pattern, we see that the second factor is the same in all the examples. The first factor is decreasing by one and the product is decreasing by five. If this pattern continues, the last three examples will give negative products:

$$^-1 \times {}^+5 = {}^-5$$
$$^-2 \times {}^+5 = {}^-10$$
$$^-3 \times {}^+5 = {}^-15$$

Again, changing the sign of the first factor from positive to negative also results merely in changing the sign of the product from positive to negative. We can generalize from these examples by saying that the product of a positive integer and a negative integer is the same as the product of two positive integers, except that the sign of the product is negative.

Now consider the following examples.

Factor Factor Product

$$^-4 \times {}^+3 = {}^-12$$
$$^-4 \times {}^+2 = {}^-8$$
$$^-4 \times {}^+1 = {}^-4$$
$$^-4 \times 0 = 0$$
$$^-4 \times {}^-1 = \square$$
$$^-4 \times {}^-2 = \square$$
$$^-4 \times {}^-3 = \square$$

We can discover a pattern here: every time the second factor beomes one less, the product becomes four greater. Extending this pattern to include the last three examples in the series, we get positive products:

$$^-4 \times {}^-1 = {}^+4$$
$$^-4 \times {}^-2 = {}^+8$$
$$^-4 \times {}^-3 = {}^+12$$

Notice that $^-4 \times {}^-3 = {}^+12 = {}^+4 \times {}^+3$. Changing the signs of both factors from positive to negative doesn't affect the value of the product at all. Similarly for the other two examples, $^-4 \times {}^-2 = {}^+8 = {}^+4 \times {}^+2$ and $^-4 \times {}^-1 = {}^+4 \times {}^+1$. We can generalize from these examples by saying that the product of two negative numbers is the same as the product of two positive numbers.

This examination of the multiplication of negative numbers has revealed that the product of a negative number and a positive number is negative, and that the product of two negative numbers is positive. And, of course, the product of two positive numbers is positive. Therefore we can observe the following steps in the multiplication of signed numbers.

1. Determine the value of the product, regardless of its sign, by multiplying the two factors as though they were both positive.
2. Determine the sign of the product. If the factors have identical signs (both positive or both negative), the sign of the product is positive. If the factors have different signs (one positive and the other negative), the sign of the product is negative.

By following these steps we see that $^+5 \times {}^-3 = {}^-15$, $^+3 \times {}^+5 = {}^+15$, $^-4 \times {}^-3 = {}^+12$, and $^+4 \times {}^+3 = {}^+12$, the same answers we obtained when we solved the examples before.

Statements such as $^+3 \times {}^+5 = {}^+15$ and $^+3 \times {}^-5 = {}^-15$ can be illustrated on the number line if we use the idea of repeated addition.

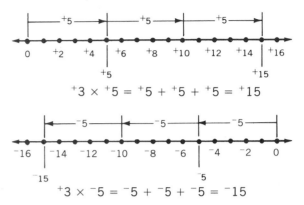

$$^+3 \times {}^+5 = {}^+5 + {}^+5 + {}^+5 = {}^+15$$

$$^+3 \times {}^-5 = {}^-5 + {}^-5 + {}^-5 = {}^-15$$

Multiplication examples in which the first factor is negative can be solved with number-line models, but the models are not so "natural" or so easily interpreted as in the examples above. Probably the best approach is to use patterns such as those we have been discussing.

Multiplication of integers, like multiplication of whole numbers, is a binary operation. Multiplication of integers has the same basic properties that we found for multiplication of whole numbers: it is commutative, associative, and distributive over addition. The number $^+1$ is the identity element for multiplication of integers.

Now let's examine the operation of division with respect to integers. Consider the following multiplication examples and the division examples that have been derived from them.

Factor	Factor	Product		Product	Factor	Factor
$^+3$	$\times$ $^+4$	$=$ $^+12$		$^+12$	$^+4$	$=$ $^+3$
$^-3$	$\times$ $^+4$	$=$ $^-12$		$^-12$	$^-3$	$=$ $^+4$
				$^-12$	$^+4$	$=$ $^-3$
$^-3$	$\times$ $^-4$	$=$ $^+12$		$^+12$	$^-4$	$=$ $^-3$

We know that the multiplication examples are correct, because we have just examined multiplication with integers. And we know that the division examples are correct, because we discovered in Unit 7 that the operation of division can be interpreted as the inverse operation of multiplication. Examining the division examples and generalizing from them, we see that we can observe the following steps when dividing one number by another.

1. Determine the value of the quotient, regardless of its sign, by performing the indicated division as though both the divisor and the dividend were positive.

2. Determine the sign of the quotient. If the divisor and dividend have the same signs (both positive or both negative), the sign of the quotient is positive. If the divisor and dividend have different signs (one positive and the other negative), the sign of the quotient is negative.

Division with negative numbers can also be modeled on the number line. However, this is considerably more complex than the development of multiplication and would not prove useful to an elementary-level pupil.

The system of integers was formed as an extension of the system of whole numbers. For each whole number greater than zero, we included the opposite negative number. By including numbers less than zero with our system we were able to label an infinite set of points to the left of zero on the number line.

Now let us consider the system of fractional numbers and form a larger system by including the opposites of all the fractional numbers. When we do this, we obtain a system of numbers that includes not only $\frac{1}{2}, \frac{3}{7}, \frac{4}{5}, \frac{9}{8}$ (and so on), but also numbers such as $^-\left(\frac{1}{2}\right), ^-\left(\frac{3}{7}\right), ^-\left(\frac{4}{5}\right), ^-\left(\frac{9}{8}\right)$ (and so on). This larger set of numbers, consisting of all the fractional numbers and their opposites, is called the system of **rational numbers.** The set of rational numbers can also be thought of as the set of all quotients $\frac{a}{b}$, where a is an integer and b is a nonzero integer. (Notice the similarity between this last statement and the definition of a fractional number as the quotient $\frac{a}{b}$ of a whole number and a counting number.)

The system of numbers called rational numbers may be written in two different forms — as fractions or decimals.

Let's look at a number line on which some of the points have been labeled with rational numbers expressed as fractions.

We know that the point halfway between 0 and $^+1$ is $^+\left(\frac{1}{2}\right)$. Then, from our knowledge of opposites, the point halfway between 0 and $^-1$ is $^-\left(\frac{1}{2}\right)$. The point named $^+1$ could be renamed as $^+\left(\frac{1}{1}\right)$, or $^+\left(\frac{2}{2}\right)$, and so on. Then, in the same way, we could rename $^-1$ as $^-\left(\frac{1}{1}\right)$, or $^-\left(\frac{2}{2}\right)$, and so on. So, it should be clear that every rational number has an opposite.

$^+\left(\frac{1}{2}\right) + ^-\left(\frac{1}{2}\right) = 0, \; ^+\left(\frac{2}{3}\right) + ^-\left(\frac{2}{3}\right) = 0$, and so on

Operations with signed rational numbers follow the same patterns that we discovered in the set of integers.

$$^+2 + ^+3 = ^+5 \qquad ^+\left(\frac{1}{2}\right) + ^+\left(\frac{1}{3}\right) = ^+\left(\frac{5}{6}\right)$$

$$^-3 \times ^-2 = ^+6 \qquad ^-\left(\frac{1}{2}\right) \times ^-\left(\frac{1}{4}\right) = ^+\left(\frac{1}{8}\right)$$

$$^+8 \div ^-2 = ^-4 \qquad ^+\left(\frac{1}{2}\right) \div ^-2 = ^-\left(\frac{1}{4}\right)$$

$$^+2 - ^+5 = ^-3 \qquad ^+\left(\frac{1}{8}\right) - ^+\left(\frac{3}{8}\right) = ^-\left(\frac{1}{4}\right)$$

Of course, rational numbers can be named in many ways. For example

$$^+\left(\frac{1}{4}\right) = ^+\left(\frac{2}{8}\right) = ^+\left(\frac{3}{12}\right) = ^+\left(\frac{4}{16}\right) \text{ (and so on)}$$

Also

$$^+\left(\frac{1}{4}\right) = \frac{^+1}{^+4} = \frac{^-1}{^-4} = \frac{^-2}{^-8} \text{ (and so on)}$$

Similarly

$$^-\left(\frac{2}{3}\right) = \frac{^-2}{^+3} = \frac{^+2}{^-3} = \frac{^+10}{^-15} \text{ (and so on)}$$

Obviously a full discussion of all the fundamental operations as they apply to rational numbers would be long and time-consuming, and we shall not give one. It will probably come as no surprise that in the system of rational numbers these operations enjoy all of the properties that they had in the systems studied earlier. You will perhaps find it helpful to convince yourself of this fact by testing each property with several examples.

We have now extended our number line in the negative direction, thus increasing the number of points we are familiar with. If we take any two points on the number line that represent rational numbers, there is at least one other point between them that represents another rational number. This third number is necessarily greater than one of the first two numbers and less than the other; that is, the third number is necessarily intermediate in value between the first two. Consider, for example, the points labeled 0 and 4. Between them we find points labeled 1, 2, and 3, to name just a few. Consider the points labeled 0 and 1. Between them we find points labeled $\frac{1}{4}, \frac{1}{2}$, and $\frac{5}{8}$, again naming just a few. We can also perform this process without benefit of the number line. For example, between the rational numbers $\frac{1}{4}$ and $\frac{3}{4}$ we find such other rational numbers as $\frac{1}{2}$ and

$\frac{5}{8}$. The fact that we can always perform this process is due to the density property of rational numbers.

The **property of density for rational numbers** means that between any two rational numbers there exists a third rational number of intermediate value. Not all sets of numbers possess this property. The set of whole numbers, for example, does not possess it. By way of illustration, consider the whole numbers 11 and 12; between them there is no third whole number. The set of rational numbers, however, does possess the property of density. Given any two rational numbers, we can always find a third rational number between them. Another way of illustrating this property is to add the two given numbers and divide the sum by 2. For example, given $\frac{1}{5}$ and $\frac{2}{5}$, we know that $\frac{3}{10}$ is between them:

$$\frac{1}{5} + \frac{2}{5} = \frac{3}{5} \quad \text{ADDING THE TWO NUMBERS}$$
$$\frac{3}{5} \div 2 = \frac{3}{10} \quad \text{DIVIDING THE SUM BY 2}$$

Of course, there are also many other rational numbers between $\frac{1}{5}$ and $\frac{2}{5}$.

In an earlier unit we discussed repeating decimals, indicating at that time that repeating decimals are rational numbers. In addition to terminating decimals and repeating decimals, both of which we have already discussed, there are also decimals that neither terminate nor repeat. Numbers named by such decimals are called **irrational numbers.** Consider, for example, .12112111211112111112 . . . This is an irrational number because it is a nontermi-

nating, nonrepeating decimal. It is nonrepeating because each successive 2 has one more 1 immediately preceding it than the preceding 2. Another irrational number is the square root of two ($\sqrt{2}$). By the square root of two we mean the number that when multiplied by itself equals 2. The Greek mathematician Pythagoras proved, some 2400 years ago, that $\sqrt{2}$ is not a rational number.

There are also negative irrational numbers; for example the opposite of $\sqrt{2}$, which we write as $^-\sqrt{2}$, is an irrational number.

The union of the set of rational numbers and the set of irrational numbers gives us an all-inclusive set called the set of **real numbers.** One of our goals has been to show how number systems are enlarged step by step and how each move to a larger system allows us to label more points on the number line. With the set of real numbers we are able to match a unique number with any point on the number line. In fact the real numbers can be placed in one-to-one correspondence with the points on the number line.

We have now considered all the different kinds of points on the number line. The easiest method for developing the relations between the different sets of numbers that we have considered is to draw a diagram showing the set of real numbers (the most comprehensive of the sets we have considered) broken down successively into the different kinds of numbers that make up the set.

The teaching of the structure of the real-number system is begun in first grade with the concept of number developed from sets and leading into the counting numbers. Children are gradually introduced to different kinds of numbers and have usually studied the complete system of real numbers by the time they complete the eighth grade.

Technology, Symbols, and Procedures

Addition property of opposites   Any two opposites when added have a sum of zero, the addition property of opposites.

$$^+3 + {}^-3 = 0$$
$$^+a + {}^-a = 0$$

Counting numbers   The set of counting numbers is the set $\{1, 2, 3, \ldots\}$. The set of counting numbers is sometimes referred to as the set of natural numbers.

Directed numbers   Directed numbers are numbers that are expressed by a numeral and a positive ($^+$) or negative ($^-$) sign. Examples of directed numbers are $^+4$, $^-15$, $^-.714$, $^+\left(\frac{3}{5}\right)$, and $^-\sqrt{2}$.

Integers   The set of integers is the set consisting of the counting numbers and their opposites and zero.

Irrational numbers   The set of irrational numbers is the set of all real numbers that aren't rational. For example, the square root of 2 (that is, $\sqrt{2}$, the number which when multiplied by itself yields 2) is an irrational number.

Magnitude or **absolute value**   The magnitude or absolute value of a number is its value without a positive or negative sign. On a number line, it is the unit length of the line segment regardless of direction.

Opposites   Opposites are pairs of numbers corresponding to points on the number line that are equidistant from the zero point, but in different directions from zero. For example, $^+3$ and $^-3$ are opposites. The sum of any pair of opposites is equal to zero. For example, $^+3 + {}^-3 = 0$.

Rational numbers   The set of rational numbers is the set of all numbers that can be expressed as the quotient of two integers. Both fractional numbers and the integers themselves are rational numbers. (Don't forget that a number cannot be expressed with zero in the denominator.)

Real numbers   The set of real numbers is the set of all numbers that can be represented by points on the number line. The set of real numbers includes all rational numbers (positive numbers, negative numbers, and zero) and all irrational numbers ($\sqrt{2}$, $\sqrt{3}$, π, and so on).

Whole numbers   The set of whole numbers is the set containing zero and the counting numbers; thus the set of whole numbers is the set $\{0, 1, 2, 3, \ldots\}$.

Practice Exercises

1. Complete the following tables. Study the tables and look for patterns.

a)

Addend

+	$^-5$	$^-4$	$^-3$	$^-2$	$^-1$	0	$^+1$	$^+2$	$^+3$	$^+4$	$^+5$
$^+5$											
$^+4$											
$^+3$											
$^+2$											
$^+1$											
0											
$^-1$											
$^-2$											
$^-3$											
$^-4$											
$^-5$											

Addend

b)

Factor

×	⁻5	⁻4	⁻3	⁻2	⁻1	0	⁺1	⁺2	⁺3	⁺4	⁺5
⁺5											
⁺4											
⁺3											
⁺2											
⁺1											
0											
⁻1											
⁻2											
⁻3											
⁻4											
⁻5											

F a c t o r

2. Name six different number systems and list several subsets of each.

3. Name the opposite of each number.

a) $^+2$ e) $\dfrac{^-2}{3}$ i) $^+73$

b) $^-3$ f) $^+217$ j) $^-49$

c) 0 g) $^-43$ k) $\dfrac{^+7}{8}$

d) $\dfrac{^+1}{4}$ h) $^-47$ l) $\dfrac{^-14}{23}$

4. Draw a number-line model for each example and name the sum.

a) $^+3 + {}^-2 = \square$ e) $^+6 + {}^+2 = \square$
b) $^-5 + {}^+2 = \square$ f) $^-8 + {}^+5 = \square$
c) $^-4 + {}^-5 = \square$ g) $^-2 + {}^-4 = \square$
d) $^+7 + {}^-3 = \square$ h) $^+1 + {}^-6 = \square$

5. Solve each addition example.

a) $^-43 + {}^+17 = \square$ d) $^-83 + {}^+69 = \square$ g) $^-68 + {}^+73 = \square$
b) $^-57 + {}^-78 = \square$ e) $^+47 + {}^+34 = \square$ h) $^-37 + {}^-53 = \square$
c) $^+61 + {}^-56 = \square$ f) $^-92 + {}^-89 = \square$ i) $^+48 + {}^-84 = \square$

6. Draw a number-line model for each example and name the missing addend.

a) $^+7 - {}^-8 = \square$ d) $^-9 - {}^+3 = \square$
b) $^-4 - {}^-3 = \square$ e) $^-1 - {}^-8 = \square$
c) $^+6 - {}^+2 = \square$ f) $^+4 - {}^-7 = \square$

7. Solve each subtraction example.

a) $^-24 - {}^-42 = \square$ d) $^-73 - {}^+91 = \square$
b) $^-51 - {}^+68 = \square$ e) $^+86 - {}^-27 = \square$
c) $^+23 - {}^-19 = \square$ f) $^+39 - {}^+93 = \square$

8. Use the rules for multiplying integers and solve each example.

a) $^+7 \times {}^-9 = \square$ e) $^+32 \times {}^-23 = \square$ i) $^-85 \times {}^-19 = \square$
b) $^-8 \times {}^+6 = \square$ f) $^-47 \times {}^-18 = \square$ j) $^-39 \times {}^+17 = \square$
c) $^-9 \times {}^-6 = \square$ g) $^-68 \times {}^+42 = \square$ k) $^+74 \times {}^-51 = \square$
d) $^-43 \times {}^-17 = \square$ h) $^+53 \times {}^+65 = \square$ l) $^-67 \times {}^+37 = \square$

9. Solve each division example.

a) $^-48 \div {}^+6 = \square$ e) $^-69 \div {}^-3 = \square$ i) $^+98 \div {}^-14 = \square$
b) $^+72 \div {}^+9 = \square$ f) $^-144 \div {}^+6 = \square$ j) $^-204 \div {}^-34 = \square$
c) $^-63 \div {}^-7 = \square$ g) $^-72 \div {}^-4 = \square$ k) $^-208 \div {}^+26 = \square$
d) $^-42 \div {}^-7 = \square$ h) $^+84 \div {}^-12 = \square$ l) $^+378 \div {}^-42 = \square$

10. Solve these examples selected from the system of real numbers.

a) $\dfrac{^+3}{4} \times \dfrac{^-7}{8} = \square$ e) $\dfrac{^-3}{5} + \dfrac{^-5}{9} = \square$ i) $\dfrac{^-5}{8} \times \dfrac{^-4}{15} = \square$

b) $\dfrac{^-5}{6} \div \dfrac{^-2}{3} = \square$ f) $^+7.8 - {}^-.21 = \square$ j) $^-1.84 \div {}^+2.3 = \square$

c) $^+.8 \times {}^-.06 = \square$ g) $\dfrac{^+7}{8} - \dfrac{^+2}{3} = \square$ k) $^+2.03 - {}^+1.45 = \square$

d) $^-.96 \div {}^+1.2 = \square$ h) $^-3.41 + {}^+2.9 = \square$ l) $\dfrac{^+9}{13} + \dfrac{^-2}{7} = \square$

11. Suppose that we use letters to designate the following sets of numbers we have studied.

A = set of all counting numbers
B = set of all whole numbers
C = set of all integers
D = set of all fractional numbers
E = set of all rational numbers
F = set of all irrational numbers
G = set of all real numbers

a) Which of these sets contains all of the other sets in the list?
b) Which of the sets listed does *not* contain Set A?
c) Which of the sets contain Set E?
d) Which of the sets are contained in Set E?

e) Which of the sets have $^-\left(\dfrac{2}{3}\right)$ as an element?

f) In which set is division by zero possible?

Discussion Questions

1. Some mathematics educators suggest that, following the structures of mathematics, integers should be taught before rational numbers. Have each member of the class take a stand either supporting or rejecting this statement; debate the question in class.

2. Discuss the similarities and differences between the set of whole numbers and the set of integers.

3. Discuss why 1 is not a prime number.

4. Describe the relationship of the set of integers to the operation of subtraction.

5. Discuss the points on the number line in relation to the set of rational numbers, irrational numbers, and integers.

6. Using a reference book, locate the height of the tallest mountain in the world (Mt. Everest) and the depth of the deepest ocean (Pacific Ocean—Mariana Trench). Which of these varies most from sea level? Relate the discussion to integers.

7. Examine elementary school mathematics textbooks. How and when are integers introduced? Have a class discussion on the merits of teaching integers in the elementary classroom.

8. Locate a copy of Dr. Marijane Werner's book, *Teaching the Set of Integers to Elementary School Children*; discuss the suggested teaching techniques.

9. Examine standardized achievement tests for children. Itemize the number of examples related to each set of numbers defined in this unit. Discuss the appropriateness of the distribution of examples.

10. Research the literature, and provide evidence to support teaching integers to elementary school children.

Activities for the Primary Grades

If children's experiences with mathematical concepts are developed through an organized systems approach, then many topics, including integers, may be introduced much earlier than in traditional programs. When a child looks at a thermometer and observes that the temperature has dropped below zero, he begins to see the need for negative numbers. If integers are used to describe concrete situations in mathematical terms, they may be introduced easily in the primary and intermediate grades. Some elementary mathematics programs are allowing children to have experiences with integers beginning in first grade. The concepts of integers are expanded at each grade level. In order to lay a good foundation, it is important to draw on situations in which children can see a real need or use for integers. Problems dealing with the thermometer, the altitude in respect to sea level, and simple statistics of gain and loss can be easily discussed with the aid of integers.

1. Children may draw "maps" such as the following on long sheets of paper. Questions about the "maps" may either be printed on cards (for independent study) or asked orally by the teacher (see the following page).

Questions such as the following may be asked.

    a) How many blocks will I travel going from Jane's house to the theater?

    b) If I go 3 blocks east starting from Jane's house, where will I land?

    c) How many blocks will I travel going from Jane's house to the pet shop?

    d) If I want to go to the zoo from Jane's house, how many blocks will I go? Which direction?

    e) If I start at Jane's house and go 3 blocks west and then 5 blocks east, where will I be? How many blocks from Jane's house will I be? Which direction from Jane's house will I be?

To stress the idea of an origin, Jane's house should always be used as the starting point.

2. Make copies of a number line like the one shown so that each child has one on his desk to use.

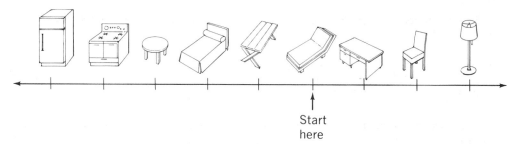

Start
here

You may use the overhead projector and have children locate items of furniture shown on the number line. For example, write on the overhead transparency "Move 3 ⟶." Let a child explain that he would be at the floor lamp if he moved 3 ⟶ to the right. After many oral experiences as described above, the child could work on a work sheet. For example: Mark the object designating your location with an X.

Move	Land on			
⟵ 2	refrigerator	bed	stool	chair
⟶ 2	chair	chaise	stove	desk
⟵ 4	stool	bed	chair	stove
⟵ 1	floor lamp	desk	cot	chaise
⟶ 3	floor lamp	desk	chair	stool

3. Number lines may be drawn with numerals of a different color on each side of "our house."

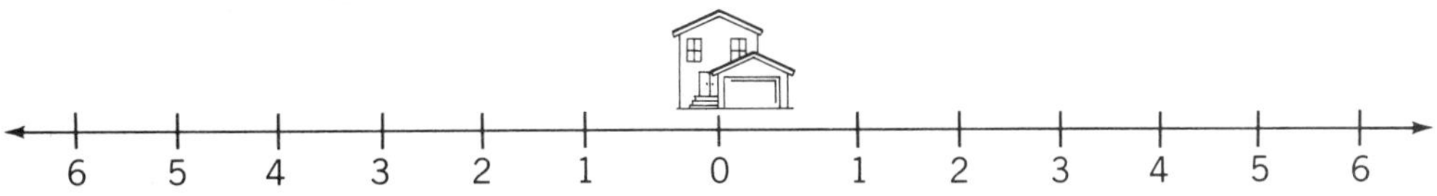
Our house
6 5 4 3 2 1 0 1 2 3 4 5 6
Red numerals
Black numerals

Discuss with the children how many blocks you would be from home if you walked $\overrightarrow{4}$. Where are you? Four blocks in the black. If you walk $\overleftarrow{2}$ where are you? In the red 2. If you walk $\overrightarrow{3}$ and then $\overleftarrow{4}$ where are you?

4. Make an integer number line on the floor with masking tape for the children to walk on.

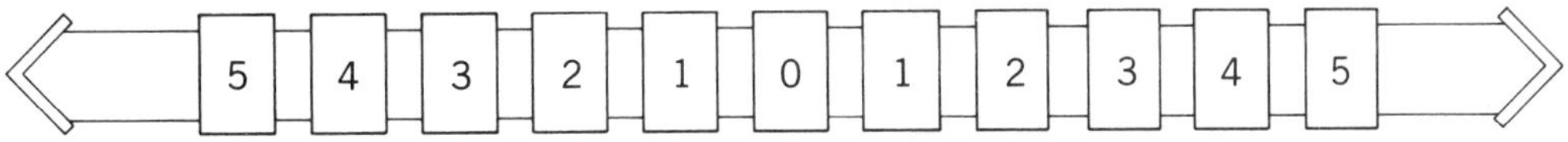
5 4 3 2 1 0 1 2 3 4 5

Each side of the number line may be made from different colors of tape. Provide many opportunities for the children to walk on this number line.

Hand-Held Calculator Activities for the Primary Grades

1. Have the children place a number on the calculator display screen. Subtract 1 from the number on the display screen. Continue to subtract 1; the display screen will soon show numbers with a subtraction sign in front of them. Discuss with the children why this happens and relate the discussion to the number line. Model the number line on the overhead projector. Extend it to the left of zero.

2. Set up the calculator for a constant. Subtract one (−1) and continue to just push the equals key. First press any number key followed by a subtraction sign and the number 1; then continuously press the equals key. For instance, try entering this sequence of key punches: $\boxed{7}$ $\boxed{-}$ $\boxed{1}$ $\boxed{=}$ $\boxed{=}$ $\boxed{=}$ $\boxed{=}$ . . . . What happens when the equals key is pushed eight times? nine times? What appears on the display screen each time the equals key is pushed after the eighth time?

3. Turn on the calculator, and display zero on the screen. For this activity, set up the calculator by entering $\boxed{-}$ $\boxed{1}$ $\boxed{=}$ $\boxed{=}$ $\boxed{=}$ $\boxed{=}$ $\boxed{=}$ $\boxed{=}$. Record each number in a column as it appears on the display screen. Then clear the screen. Again, begin with zero on the display screen and enter $\boxed{+}$ $\boxed{1}$ $\boxed{=}$ $\boxed{=}$ $\boxed{=}$ $\boxed{=}$ $\boxed{=}$ $\boxed{=}$. In a second column parallel to the first column, write the numbers as they appear on the display screen. Your record should look like this:

0	0
−1	+1
−2	+2
−3	+3
−4	+4
−5	+5
−6	+6

Discuss the two outputs with the chidren. How are these outputs alike? How are they different? What can the children discover about integers?

Microcomputer Activities for the Primary Grades

1. The preceding activities suggested for the hand-held calculator can also be used on the microcomputer in the immediate mode.

2. Write a computer program to count by ones.

```
10 REM—THIS PROGRAM WILL COUNT BY ONE—
20 CLS
30 ?"LET'S COUNT BY ONES!"
40 X = X + 1
50 PRINT X
55 FOR T=1 TO 300:NEXT T
60 GOTO 40
```

Children should be able to answer the following questions.

   a) How long will the microcomputer continue to count by ones?
   b) How do you stop the microcomputer from counting?
   c) What would happen if line 50 is changed to the following:

   50 PRINT X; (or PRINT X" ";)

   d) What would happen if line 50 is changed to the following:

   50 PRINT X,

3. Write a program to count using negative numbers.

```
10 CLS
20 X=X−1
30 PRINT X
35 FOR T=1 TO 300:NEXT T
40 GOTO 20
```

4. Allow the children to experiment and create imaginative counting programs.

Activities for the Intermediate Grades

When children see a need for integers in real situations, understanding comes naturally and very rapidly. If the set of integers is developed before that of rational numbers, a completely different type of elementary mathematics program exists. Some elementary school mathematics programs have developed a rather extensive approach to the system of integers for the intermediate grades. Rational numbers, which are then taught following the integers, stressing both positive and negative value, can be taught almost simultaneously.

1. Story problems can be useful in activities. The children can also make up interesting stories. Some of the stories may be dramatized, and the children should be encouraged to be imaginative with the situations they invent.

Example: John started at the top of a flight of stairs and walked down 8 stairs, then down 7 more stairs, and then back up 15 stairs. What stair was he on then? (The top of the flight of stairs, where he started.)

You may want to number the middle step zero and then number the steps both ways from the zero step.

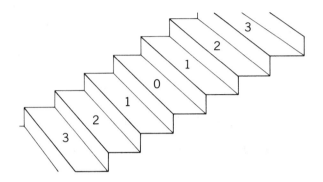

2. Children enjoy number-line games. The following activity helps to develop ideas of distance and directions, important aspects of the understanding of integers. The children should be divided into two teams—the Reds and the Blues, for example. Each member of the Reds is paired with an opponent from the Blues. Each pair of opponents should have a playing board. The board may be a copy of the race track shown below. The children on each team each have a marker that corresponds to the color of their team. Each marker represents a red or blue racing car. You should prepare a deck of cards with instructions for moves written on them. Each instruction card should give a distance to travel and a direction of travel. For example, a card with $^+4$ written on it might mean "travel 4 miles toward the finish line." A card with $^-2$ written on it would then mean "travel 2 miles toward the repair shop." The Reds alternate with the Blues in making the moves called by the teacher as cards are drawn from the pile. The game ends when the first cars reach the finish line. If one team's cars enter the repair shop first, then that team is declared out of the race and the other team wins.

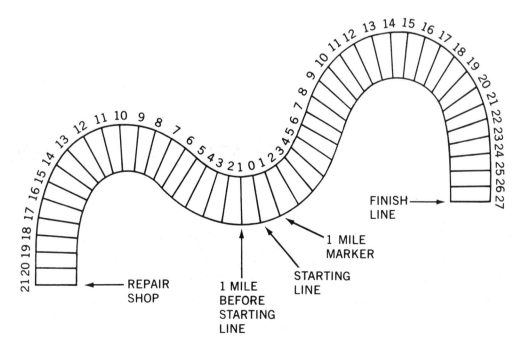

3. Children should realize that a number line may have any position—vertical or diagonal as well as horizontal. A thermometer is an example of a vertical number line. Use a large demonstration thermometer, if one is available; otherwise, sketch one on the chalkboard. Ask questions such as the following:

    a) If the thermometer reads 72 degrees and the temperature drops 15 degrees, what is the reading on the thermometer then?

    b) If the thermometer reads 54 degrees after it has dropped 7 degrees, what was the original reading?

    c) If the thermometer reads 12 degrees below zero and rises 20 degrees, what is the temperature then?

    d) If the thermometer reads 3 degrees below zero and drops 8 degrees, what is the temperature reading then?

Hand-Held Calculator Activities for the Intermediate Grades

All hand-held calculator activities suggested for the primary grades can also be adapted for the intermediate grades.

1. Use Exercise 3 from the calculator activities for the primary grades, and then conduct a discussion of opposites.

2. Discuss how to display a negative number on the screen of a hand-held calculator. The subtraction sign can be used with a numerical value.

3. Use the and-on principle to add a constant of ⁻2. Set up the calculator by pressing the following keys: ⊞ ⊟ ② ▤ ▤ ▤ . . . . Now the calculator will add a negative two each time the equals key is pressed.

4. Discuss the relation between subtraction and negative numbers.

5. Set up the hand-held calculator as illustrated: ⊟ ② ⊠ ▤ ▤ ▤ ▤ ▤ . . . . Why are the numbers alternately negative and positive? Have the children experiment with many examples, using negative numbers and multiplication. Discuss with the class the numerical value and the sign value.

6. Introduce the children to the ⌷+/−⌷ key. Study your calculator manual for the many uses of this key.

Microcomputer Activities for the Intermediate Grades

The microcomputer activities listed for the primary grades can also be used for the intermediate grades.

1. Run the following program to illustrate a limited counting program. This program will run on most microcomputers, when the clear-the-screen statement is adjusted.

```
10 CLS
20 FOR X = 1 TO 25
30 PRINT X
40 NEXT X
```

What will hapen if . . . ?

   a) Line 30 is changed to

      30 PRINT X,

   b) line 30 is changed to

      30 PRINT X;

   c) line 20 is changed to

      20 FOR X = 1 TO 25 STEP 2

   d) line 20 is changed to

      20 FOR X = 25 TO 1 STEP −2

2. Write a computer program to list all even numbers between 1 and 25. Can the program in Exercise 2 be modified to print even numbers?

3. Permit the children to experiment and write many different counting programs. If you have a printer, print out these programs. Otherwise, have the children copy their programs on paper. Make a bulletin board of computer programs to accomplish the same goal, but use a different set of statements.

4. Can the program in Exercise 2 be programmed on one line only? Try this program:

10 CLS:FOR 1 TO 25:?X:NEXT X

What does the colon tell the computer?

Activities for the Upper Elementary Grades

1. Maps may be used as number lines to develop a feeling for magnitude and direction. Children may use different techniques for recording directions. Some suggestions are:

                L2 or R2 for left 2 or right 2,
                N3 or S3 for north 3 or south 3,
                E4 or W4 for east 4 or west 4,
                U5 or D5 for up 5 or down 5,

2. You may make copies of number lines without numerals; the chidren can then label the points representing positive and negative integers. Use the number line to help you decide which relation symbol (< or >) you should write in each circle.

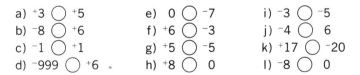

a) ⁺3 ◯ ⁺5   e) 0 ◯ ⁻7   i) ⁻3 ◯ ⁻5

b) ⁻8 ◯ ⁺6   f) ⁺6 ◯ ⁻3   j) ⁻4 ◯ 6

c) ⁻1 ◯ ⁺1   g) ⁺5 ◯ ⁻5   k) ⁺17 ◯ ⁻20

d) ⁻999 ◯ ⁺6   h) ⁺8 ◯ 0   l) ⁻8 ◯ 0

3. For each child, make a large integer number line (10 cm by 50 cm) from cardboard, allowing about 2 cm between the numbers. Cover the number line with clear self-adhesive plastic or else laminate it and provide china marking pencils so the children can model examples on it.

4. Bend two different colors of pipe cleaners into crescent-shaped curves to represent positive and negative integers. For instance, one white pipe cleaner would be $^+1$ and one red pipe cleaner would be $^-1$. Matching the two half circles together (one red and one white) would form a 0. To represent the sum of $^+4 + {}^-5 = {}^-1$, use pipe cleaners as diagramed below.

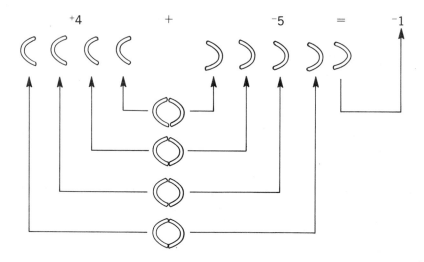

5. Model each addition of integers example on the number line.

   a) Begin with examples of like signs of direction.

   $^+3 + {}^+7 = \square, \qquad {}^-4 + {}^-5 = \square$

   b) Follow like signs of direction examples with examples of unlike signs of direction.

   $^-3 + {}^+4 = \square, \qquad {}^+6 + {}^-9 = \square, \qquad {}^+5 + {}^-3 = \square$

6. After many addition-of-integer examples have been solved, have the children study them and look for patterns. Through guided discovery they should develop some generalizations about addition of integers.

7. Rewrite each subtraction example as an addition sentence.

   a) $^+7 - {}^+3 = \square$ c) $^+6 - {}^-3 = \square$ e) $^+11 - \square = {}^-15$
   b) $^-8 - {}^+5 = \square$ d) $^-9 - \square = {}^+4$ f) $^-19 - \square = {}^-23$

8. Rewrite each subtraction example as an addition sentence; then model it on the number line.

   a) $^+9 - {}^+7 = \square$ c) $^-5 - {}^-3 = \square$ e) $^-12 - \square = {}^-15$
   b) $^-8 - {}^+5 = \square$ d) $^-6 - {}^+9 = \square$ f) $^+17 - \square = {}^-2$

9. After many subtraction-of-integer examples have been solved, encourage the children to study them for patterns. Through guided discovery, help the children develop some generalizations that will help them subtract within the set of integers.

10. Provide an opportunity for the children to develop addition and multiplication tables as displayed in Exercise 1.

11. List the sets of integers that are

   a) less than $^-5$ and greater than $^-10$ c) less than $^+4$ and greater than $^-1$
   b) greater than $^-2$ and less than $^+4$ d) greater than $^-10$ and less than $^+1$

12. Describe these sets of integers in words.

   a) $\{^-5, ^-4, ^-3, ^-2\}$ b) $\{11, 12, 13, 14\}$ c) $\{1, 0\}$

13. Arrange in order from least to greatest.

   $^-26$ $^+4$ $^+9$ $^+12$ $^-2$ $^-11$

14. Choose the greater integer from each pair of opposites.

   a) $^+6, ^-6$ b) $^-212, ^+212$ c) $0, 0$ d) $^-8, ^+8$

15. Write the opposite of each integer.

   a) $^-112$ b) $^+270$ c) 0 d) $^+256$

16. Choose the greatest integer in each set.

   $A = \{^+23, ^-41, ^-30, ^+29, ^+20\}$ $B = \{^-3, 0, ^-7, ^-2, ^-6\}$

17. Which of the following are true statements?

   a) $^+17 > ^-88$ c) $^-1 > 0$ e) $^+2 < ^+5$ g) $^-14 < ^+14$
   b) $^-17 > ^-88$ d) $0 > ^-6$ f) $^-2 < ^-5$ h) $^-89 < ^-87$

18. Write the correct operation sign (+ or −) in each △.

   a) $^-5 \triangle ^-9 = ^+4$ c) $^+26 \triangle ^+11 = ^+15$ e) $^-1 \triangle ^+8 = ^+7$
   b) $^+10 \triangle ^-10 = 0$ d) $^-9 \triangle ^+5 = ^-4$ f) $^+18 \triangle ^-3 = ^+21$

19. Complete the chart.

Integers	+7, □	□ , ⁻6	⁻9, ⁻7	+18, ⁻18	⁻3, +6	+9, ⁻9	□ , ⁻4
Result	⁻5	+9	⁻16	0			⁻9
Operation	addition	subtraction			addition	subtraction	subtraction

20. Solve each equation. If you wish, draw a number line and use it for help.

   a) $^+2 + ^-5 = n$ d) $^+2 + ^+4 = n$ g) $^-3 + ^-2 = n$
   b) $^-7 + ^+3 = n$ e) $^+8 + ^-6 = n$ h) $^-6 + ^-4 = n$
   c) $^-4 + ^+9 = n$ f) $0 + ^-5 = n$ i) $^+4 + 0 = n$

21. Football situations offer excellent opportunities for children to work with integers. A gain of yardage is considered as a positive number and a loss of yardage is considered a negative one.

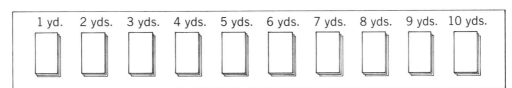

   The children can make game boards as scale models of real football fields and prepare cards with examples on them. Separate stacks of cards can be made for the various amounts of yardage possible, so that children can collect yardage cards. More difficult examples should be worth more yards than the easy examples, and the example cards should be labeled with the amount of yardage they are worth.

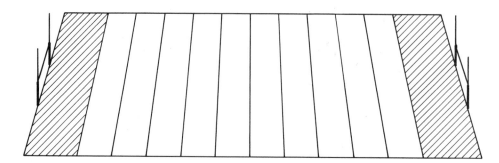

A child must make ten yards in four downs (attempts) or he loses the ball. If he misses his example, he loses the yardage on the example card. The child who gets the ball over the goal line receives six points. Other rules can be made for specific classroom situations.

22. Make a set of cubes with integers written on the faces. As children roll the dice, use the top two numbers as an example to solve.

The dice could also be used for addition of integers in a game to be played on an open manila folder. In this game, students put playing pieces on a tee (Tee 1 first) and for each correct example they get to move the piece one space forward. The first one to arrive at the green wins. If students want to continue the game, they move to Tee 2, and so forth.

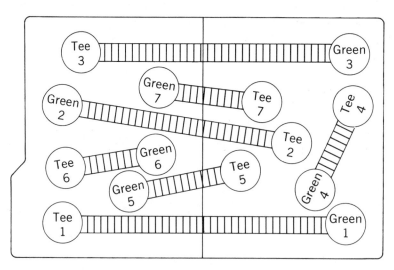

23. After all the operations and inverse operations have been learned, three dice may be used. The third die should provide the operation for each turn.

24. Make a number-line diagram to illustrate each of these equations.

a) $^+3 + {}^-4 = {}^+1$ c) $^-6 + {}^-2 = {}^-8$ e) $^+4 + {}^-4 = 0$
b) $^-6 - {}^+8 = {}^-14$ d) $^+3 + {}^+7 = {}^+10$ f) $^-8 - {}^-1 = {}^-7$

25. Solve each equation.

   a) $^+2 + n = 0$
   b) $^+9 + n = 0$
   c) $n + {}^+15 = 0$

   d) $^-3 + n = 0$
   e) $n + {}^-6 = 0$
   f) $n + {}^+7 = 0$

   g) $^-4 + n = 0$
   h) $n + {}^-10 = 0$
   i) $n + 0 = 0$

26. Rewrite each subtraction equation as an addition equation. Then find the solution.

   a) $^+9 - {}^+4 = n$
   b) $^-3 - {}^-2 = n$
   c) $^+9 - {}^-4 = n$

   d) $^+6 - {}^-3 = n$
   e) $^+10 - {}^+2 = n$
   f) $^-8 - {}^+1 = n$

   g) $^-2 - {}^+3 = n$
   h) $^+10 - {}^+10 = n$
   i) $^-6 - {}^-9 = n$

27. A profit and loss game may be played after addition and subtraction have been presented. Prepare sets of cards with "P" or "L" on them. Cards of two different colors may also be used (for example, red cards for loss and white cards for profit). Some example cards are shown below.

Profit cards   Loss cards   White cards   Red cards

Now make a set of operation cards such as the following:

| $^+5 + {}^-3$ | $^-2 + {}^+4$ | $^+5 - {}^-3$ | $^-1 - {}^+4$ |

In the example at left, $^+5$ means to take five "P" cards; $^-3$ means to take three "L" cards. The operation sign $+$ means to take the cards as indicated. The player would take five "P" cards ($^+5$) and three "L" cards ($^-3$).

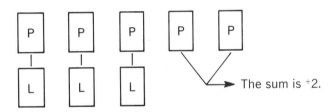

The sum is $^+2$.

Now let's examine the third card from the left; $^+5$ means the player takes five "P" cards. Here we have the operation sign $-$, which means the player takes the opposite of the next number indicated. Therefore $^-3$ means to take 3 "P" cards.

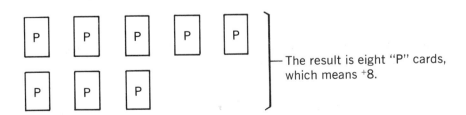

The result is eight "P" cards, which means $^+8$.

28. Find the products.

   a) $^+2 \times {}^-3 = \square$
   b) $^+3 \times {}^-4 = \square$
   c) $^+8 \times {}^-3 = \square$

   d) $^+3 \times {}^-5 = \square$
   e) $^+6 \times {}^+2 = \square$
   f) $^+7 \times {}^-8 = \square$

   g) $^+3 \times {}^-1 = \square$
   h) $^+10 \times {}^-3 = \square$
   i) $^+4 \times {}0 = \square$

29. Find the following products. Do you see a pattern?

    a) $^+3 \times ^-1 = \square$ c) $^+12 \times ^-1 = \square$ e) $^+16 \times ^-1 = \square$
    b) $^+50 \times ^-1 = \square$ d) $^+132 \times ^-1 = \square$ f) $^+654 \times ^-1 = \square$

30. Complete the tables.

(a)

×	0	$^+2$	$^+4$	$^+6$	$^+8$
0			0		
$^-2$					
$^-4$			$^-24$		
$^-6$					
$^-8$					

(b)

×	$^+1$	$^-1$	$^+2$	$^-2$	$^+3$
$^+1$					
$^-1$					
$^+2$			$^+4$		
$^-2$					$^-6$
$^+3$					

31. Complete the second column of each table.

(a)

n	$^-2 \times n$
$^+2$	
$^+1$	$^-2$
0	
$^-1$	
$^-2$	
$^-3$	
$^-4$	

(b)

n	$n \times ^+3$
$^+10$	
$^+5$	
0	
$^-5$	
$^-10$	$^-30$
$^-15$	
$^-20$	

(c)

n	$^-5 \times n$
$^+4$	$^-20$
$^+2$	
$^+0$	
$^-2$	
$^-4$	
$^-6$	
$^-8$	

32. Find the missing factors.

    a) $^-2 \times n = ^+8$ c) $^-3 \times n = ^-12$ e) $^+1 \times n = ^-9$
    b) $^+4 \times n = ^-20$ d) $^+4 \times n = ^+20$ f) $^+7 \times n = ^-14$

33. For this activity several 3-by-3 grids should be used; you may want to laminate the grids and have the children use grease pencils for writing on them. Place four numbers in four squares of the grid (see below). Have the students add across and down the rows and place their sums in the empty squares. This activity can also be used for subtraction, multiplication, and division of integers.

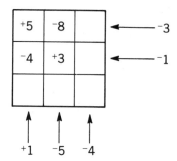

34. On the floor, form a large square (two feet on a side) by using masking tape. Divide the square into eight equivalent squares. Place a different integer in each square. Construct a large die and place an operation sign on each of the 6 sides of the die: addition, subtraction, multiplication, or division. Give the student two counters. The student tosses the die to determine the operation to be used. The student then takes the counters and tosses them onto the square. He or she must add, subtract, multiply, or divide the given numbers according to the results of the die toss.

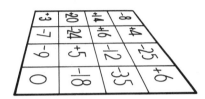

Hand-Held Calculator Activities for the Upper Elementary Grades

All hand-held calculator activities for the intermediate grades can be adapted for the upper elementary grades.

1. Remind the children that the negative sign takes one place on the display screen; this means that only seven-place negative numbers can be displayed on the screen.

2. Some hand-held calculators have a $\boxed{+/-}$ "change sign" key. This key changes the sign of the number on the display screen. Have the children experiment with this key. For example:

   a) $\boxed{-}$ $\boxed{8}$ $\boxed{5}$ $\boxed{\div}$ $\boxed{5}$ $\boxed{+/-}$ $\boxed{=}$
   b) $\boxed{9}$ $\boxed{1}$ $\boxed{\div}$ $\boxed{3}$ $\boxed{+/-}$ $\boxed{=}$
   c) $\boxed{-}$ $\boxed{4}$ $\boxed{8}$ $\boxed{\div}$ $\boxed{2}$ $\boxed{+/-}$ $\boxed{=}$ $\boxed{=}$ $\boxed{=}$ $\boxed{=}$ $\boxed{=}$ $\boxed{=}$ . . .

Microcomputer Activities for the Upper Elementary Grades

1. Write a countdown program for a rocket blast-off.

```
10 PRINT"COUNTDOWN"
20 FOR X = 10 TO 0 STEP −1
30 PRINT X
40 FOR T = 1 TO 1000
50 NEXT T
60 NEXT X
70 PRINT"BLASTOFF!!"
```

2. Have the children write a computer program to generate a given number of even numbers and then sum them.

```
10 PRINT"SUM OF EVEN NUMBERS UP TO "
20 INPUT N
30 B = 0
40 FOR X = 2 TO N STEP 2
45 PRINT X
50 B = B + X
60 NEXT X
70 PRINT "THE SUM IS ";B
80 PRINT:GOTO 10
```

Answer these questions.

    a) What is the sum of all even numbers up to 100?
    b) What is the sum of the even numbers up to 1000?

3. Write a program to sum the odd numbers up to a given point.

4. Write a program to sum the numbers occurring between two given numbers.

```
10 PRINT"WHAT IS THE SUM OF THE NUMBERS"
15 PRINT " BETWEEN TWO GIVEN NUMBERS?"
20 PRINT:PRINT"WHAT IS THE BEGINNING NUMBER"
30 INPUT M
40 PRINT:PRINT"WHAT IS THE ENDING NUMBER"
50 INPUT N
55 IF M>N THEN GOTO 20
60 FOR X = M TO N
70 PRINT X
80 B = B + X
90 NEXT X
100 PRINT "THE SUM IS ";B
110 PRINT: GOTO 10
```

Suggested Readings

Bennett, A. B., and Musser, G. L. "A Concrete Approach to Integer Addition and Subtraction." *The Arithmetic Teacher*, vol. 23, no. 5, May 1976.

Biggs, Edith E., and MacLean, James R. *Freedom to Learn: An Active Learning Approach to Mathematics.* Don Mills, Ontario: Addison-Wesley (Canada), 1969.

Henderson, George L., and Glunn, Lowell D. *Let's Play Games in Mathematics.* Skokie, Ill.: National Textbook, 1971.

Kennedy, Leonard M., and Michon, Ruth L. *Games for Individualizing Mathematics Learning*. Columbus, Ohio: Merrill, 1973.

Kohn, Judith B. "A Physical Model for Operations with Integers." *The Mathematics Teacher*, vol. 71, no. 9, December 1978.

LeBlanc, John F.; Kerr, Donald R., Jr.; and Thompson, Maynard, eds. *Mathematics Methods Program: Rational Numbers with Integers and Reals*. Reading, Mass.: Addison-Wesley, 1976.

National Council of Teachers of Mathematics. *Games and Puzzles for Elementary and Middle School Mathematics*. Reston, Va.: NCTM, 1975.

National Council of Teachers of Mathematics. *Teacher-Made Aids for Elementary School Mathematics*. Reston, Va.: NCTM, 1974.

Werner, Marijane. *Teaching the Set of Integers to Elementary School Children*. Dubuque, Iowa: Kendall Hunt, 1973.

13 Measurement

Teaching Competencies

Upon completing this unit, you will be able to:

Describe the metric and the English systems of measurement

Describe the relationship among different measuring units

Add, subtract, multiply, and divide, using denominate numbers

Describe an approach for teaching time to children

Enumerate steps in the acquisition of money concepts.

Relate some of the historical development of measurement.

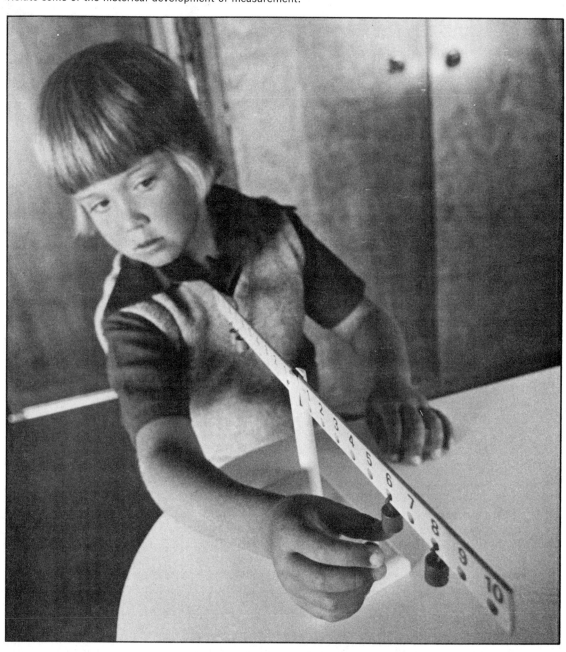

Discussion

One of the first mathematical needs of any society is a system of standard measurement. Even primitive man had to have some rudimentary way to mark the passage of time or to describe the distance from one place to another—for example, the distance from the tribe's camp to a herd of animals that could provide food and clothing.

The Egyptian and Babylonian civilizations developed the first known systems of measurement in the Western world. The Egyptians were primarily concerned with agriculture and so developed an elaborate system of land measurement for laying out crops and for marking the annual loss and subsequent restoration of land resulting from the great floods of the Nile. They also developed a system for measuring volume—for example, the amount of grain in a container—but this system of volume measurement was extremely complex and awkward.

The Babylonians developed the science of measurement much more than the Egyptians. We have seen that their number system was a great improvement over that of the Egyptians, and this in turn made measurement much more accurate. As an example, the Babylonians calculated the length of the sidereal year to be 365 days, 6 hours, and 11 minutes—a figure that is within three minutes of the modern calculation. (The sidereal year is computed from the apparent movement of the stars, which gives a more accurate measurement of time than the earth's movement round the sun. Even today, astronomical observations help to standardize the measure of time to a high degree of accuracy.)

Both the Egyptians and the Babylonians used units of measure that for the most part were based on the dimensions of the human body. For example, the length of the forearm was used in measurement by the Babylonians and other early peoples. This length was called a "cubit." The ancient Greeks and Romans also used units of measure derived from the human body. Some of the units they used for measuring length are the length of a foot, the width of a finger, and the width of the palm of a hand. The development of systems of measure led the peoples of the ancient world to create the science of geometry, which reached its highest point with the Greeks. As we mentioned in an earlier unit, the English word "geometry" comes from Greek "geo" (meaning "earth") and "metron" (meaning "measure"), and thus "geometry" means "earth measure." This clearly indicates that the practical activity of measurement was the origin of the abstract discipline of geometry.

For centuries after the Greeks, units of measure continued to be derived from the human body. In the early Middle Ages, the following units of length were commonly used:

fathom—the distance between a man's hands with arms outstretched
cubit —the distance from the elbow to the tip of the middle finger
hand —the width of the hand
digit —the width of the index finger
foot —the distance from the heel of the foot to the tip of the great toe
yard —the length of the arm from shoulder to tip of the middle finger (later revised to equal 3 feet)

The limitations of these units of measure should become evident with a little thought. The distance from the elbow to the tip of the middle finger varies from person to person. The width of the hand is greater for a large person than for a small person. Not all people have feet of the same length. In short, these units of measure were inconsistent in that they varied from person to person. Measurement would not be precise and invariable until people devised a system of **standard measurement**—units of measure that would be the same for everyone.

During the late medieval period, attempts were made to establish some standard units of measure. The length of a standard yard was originally determined in the following way. The length of three barleycorns was to be an inch; twelve inches were to be a foot; three feet were to be a yard. Later, Henry I of England (1068-1135) decreed that the distance from his nose to the thumb of his outstretched arm would be one yard. Edward I of England (1239-1307) established the first fixed standard—an iron rod whose length was defined as one yard.

Over the last three centuries, with the perfection of machine tools and accurate instruments, measurement has become an extremely precise science. In the nineteenth century, England, France, and the United States established bureaus of standards to maintain fixed units of standard measure. Not only the units of linear measurement but also those of weight and time have been standardized by defining standard units. Each country has its standard yardsticks and meter sticks, usually made of platinum and maintained under constant conditions to prevent day-to-day variations.

Today there are two main systems of measurement in use, the **English system** and the **metric system.** The English system, with which most of us are familiar, is the system commonly used by the layman in the United States and in some countries of the British Commonwealth. The United Kingdom began conversion to the metric system in 1965, Australia followed in 1970, and Canada in 1971. The metric system predominates in most countries of the world and in scientific work in all nations.

The English system of measurement is in many cases difficult to work with because of the odd relations between the various units. This confusion is due to the long historical development of the system, which has its roots in the units of measure that were in use before the development of standardized measure.

Even standardized measurement presents difficulties; for instance, a dry quart is larger than a liquid quart and a British quart is smaller than either quart. An ounce that measures liquid is not the same as an ounce that is used to measure dry material; also, the avoirdupois ounce (which we normally use) is lighter than the troy ounce or the apothecary's ounce.

The following table shows the principal units of the English system that are recognized in the United States.

LENGTH

12 inches = 1 foot
3 feet = 1 yard
$5\frac{1}{2}$ yards = 1 rod
40 rods = 1 furlong
8 furlongs = 1 mile

AREA

144 square inches = 1 square foot
9 square feet = 1 square yard
4840 square yards = 1 acre
640 acres = 1 square mile

VOLUME

3 teaspoons = 1 tablespoon
16 tablespoons = 1 cup
2 cups = 1 pint
2 pints = 1 quart
4 quarts = 1 gallon
2 gallons = 1 peck
4 pecks = 1 bushel

WEIGHT

$437\frac{1}{2}$ grains = 1 ounce
16 ounces = 1 pound
100 pounds = 1 hundredweight
20 hundredweights = 1 ton

As we examine the table, we can find no clear and logical pattern of relations between the various units. This accounts for the awkwardness of the English system. The growth of science and industry in the eighteenth century, however, required an efficient and convenient way to measure length, weight, and volume. The **metric system** of measurement was created to satisfy this need.

The metric system did not evolve out of the capricious customs of the ancient and medieval world, but was first suggested by various French scientists in the eighteenth century. A number of countries, including France, eventually came to adopt this system. In 1875 the International Bureau of Weights and Measures was established in an attempt to create a uniform and efficient system of measurement. The system that was adopted by the bureau is the metric system. All the countries of the world, except some countries of the British Commonwealth, have adopted the metric system and made it the official system of measurement. Moreover, most scientists throughout the world, including those of the United States and the British Commonwealth, do their work with metric units. Consequently, as American society becomes more scientifically and technically oriented, it becomes necessary for us to understand the metric system. For this reason the metric system is now being introduced into mathematics programs in the elementary schools.

The metric system has evolved over the decades and been modified into what it is today. The system, called *le système international d'unités,* is known today as SI. SI provides seven basic units.

Measurement	Standard unit	Symbol
length	meter	m
time	second	s
mass	kilogram	kg
electric current	ampere	A
amount of substance	mole	mol
temperature	Kelvin	K
luminous intensity	candela	cd

In elementary school we teach only length, time, mass, and temperature. The temperature we teach, however, is Celsius or Fahrenheit, not the Kelvin scale.

The basic unit of linear measurement (length) in the metric system is the **meter.** Originally the standard meter was based on a calculation of one ten-millionth of the distance between the North Pole and the equator, through Paris. Today, having more precise instruments of measurement, we know that this measurement is slightly inaccurate.

The meter has been redefined as the distance between two microscopic lines engraved on a particular platinum-iridium bar maintained under specified conditions at the International Bureau of Weights and Measures at Sevres, France. Later the meter was alternatively defined as the length of 1,553,164.13 wavelengths of red cadmium light waves under specified conditions. On October 14, 1960 the General Conference on Weight and Measures defined the meter as 1,650,763.73 wavelengths of the orange-red line of krypton 86. These modern definitions serve to determine the length of the meter to a phenomenally high degree of accuracy.

The other units of length in the metric system are related to the meter by powers of ten, as shown in the following table.

Em	1 exameter	= 1 000 000 000 000 000 000.	meters
Pm	1 petameter	= 1 000 000 000 000 000.	meters
Tm	1 terameter	= 1 000 000 000 000.	meters
Gm	1 gigameter	= 1 000 000 000.	meters
Mm	1 megameter	= 1 000 000.	meters
km	1 kilometer	= 1 000.	meters
hm	1 hectometer	= 100.	meters
dam	1 dekameter	= 10.	meters
m	1 meter	= 1.	meter
dm	1 decimeter	= .1	meter
cm	1 centimeter	= .01	meter
mm	1 millimeter =	.001	meter
um	1 micrometer	= .000 001	meter
nm	1 nanometer	= .000 000 001	meter
pm	1 picometer	= .000 000 000 001	meter
fm	1 femtometer =	.000 000 000 000 001	meter
am	1 attometer	= .000 000 000 000 000 001	meter

The names of the units of length based on the meter are composed of two parts, the base "-meter" and a prefix that indicates the relation of the unit to the meter. For example, "kilo-" is a prefix meaning "one thousand," so the term "kilometer" designates a unit of length equal to one thousand meters. Most foreign automobile speedometers measure speed in kilometers per hour, just as ours measure miles per hour. Similarly, "centi-" is a prefix meaning "one-hundredth," so the term "centimeter" designates a unit of length equal to one-hundredth of a meter. Notice the clear and logical pattern of relations between the various units; this makes for ease and efficiency in scientific work.

We do not teach children all the prefixes. In elementary school, we teach only kilo-, deci-, centi-, and milli-. The existing prefixes are listed here just to familiarize the teacher with the complete system of naming measures. You should *not* memorize the entire table. We do not memorize all the measures in the English system of measurement.

On December 23, 1975, Gerald Ford, then president, signed the Metric Conversion Act of 1975. The bill called for a voluntary conversion to the metric system and established a U.S. Metric Board to handle the coordination of the conversion. Immediately after the passage of the act there was a great deal of enthusiasm for changing to metric, but the momentum seems to be waning. The effects of evolution in measurement can be observed in the motor industry. The Ford Motor Company used measurements to sixty-fourths of an inch in constructing the Model T and to one-hundredth of an inch in constructing the Model A. The Pinto was constructed using the metric system. In 1975 the Chevette was mostly based upon metric measure. And many items in grocery stores are being labeled both in the metric and English systems. So the United States is gradually making the change to metric.

From the seven basic units of the metric system (SI) all other measurements are developed. The table below shows the most commonly used measurements.

Quantity	Common units	Symbol
length	kilometer	km
	meter	m
	centimeter	cm
	millimeter	mm
area	square kilometer	km^2
	square meter	m^2
	square centimeter	cm^2
	square millimeter	mm^2
volume	cubic meter	m^3
	cubic decimeter	dm^3
	cubic centimeter	cm^3
mass	kilogram	kg
	gram	g
temperature	degree Celsius	°C

Now let us examine some of these different metric measurements. Units of area measurement in the metric system are based on the convenient relation of powers of ten. Area measurement is square measurement. For example, one square meter is the amount of area covered by a square one meter on a side:

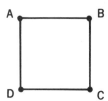

$$\overrightarrow{AB} = \overrightarrow{BC} = \overrightarrow{CD} = \overrightarrow{DA} = 1 \text{ meter}$$
Area of square ABCD = 1 square meter

So we can arrange a table to show square metric units.

sq km	1 square kilometer	=	$(1000.)^2$	square meters
sq m	1 square meter	=	1.	square meter
sq dm	1 square decimeter	=	$(.1)^2$	square meter
sq cm	1 square centimeter	=	$(.01)^2$	square meter
sq mm	1 square millimeter	=	$(.001)^2$	square meter

The metric system uses the kilogram and gram instead of the English units of pounds, ounces, and so forth. Originally, the gram was defined as the weight of one cubic centimeter of pure water under specified conditions (a cubic centimeter being the volume contained by a cube one centimeter on a side). Today, using more precise instruments, we have redefined the gram as one-thousandth of the weight of a particular platinum-iridium cylinder maintained under specified conditions. This is an absolute measurement; therefore, it has the same value in outer space or on other planets or moons that it does on earth. The kilogram (1,000 grams) is now used as the basic unit of weight in the metric system. The other units of weight are related to the kilogram by powers of ten as shown in the following table. (From this point on we will only show the most commonly used units. The student can expand the tables as necessary.)

kg	1 kilogram	=	1.	kilogram
g	1 gram	=	.001	kilogram

The names of the units of weight other than the gram are composed of two parts, the base "-gram"

and a prefix that indicates the relation of the unit to the gram. For example, "mega-" is a prefix meaning "one million," so the term "megagram" names a unit equal to one million grams. Similarly, the prefix "micro-" means "one-millionth," so the term "microgram" designates a unit of weight equal to one-millionth of a gram. Again, a clear and logical pattern exists in the relations between the various units.

The basic unit of volume in the metric system is the **liter,** which is defined as the volume of one kilogram of pure water under specified conditions. The standard liter was originally intended to equal .001 cubic meter, or 1 cubic decimeter; but because of the inaccuracy in fixing the units of weight, this equality is only approximate. As is shown in the table below, the other units of volume in the metric system are related to the liter by powers of ten. (Again we will not complete the entire table; the student can complete additional parts of the table as necessary.)

l	1 liter	=	1.	liter
cl	1 centiliter	=	.01	liter
ml	1 milliliter	=	.001	liter

The names of the other units of volume have two parts, the base "-liter" and a prefix indicating the relation of the unit to the liter. For example, "deka-" is a prefix meaning "ten," so the term "dekaliter" names a unit of volume equal to ten liters. Similarly, the prefix "deci-" means "tenth," so the term "deciliter" names a unit of volume equal to one-tenth of a liter. Notice once more the clear and logical pattern of relations between the various units.

The relations between the metric units of length, weight, and volume are summarized in the following table. The basic unit for each kind of measure is shaded.

Prefix		Linear Measure	Weight	Volume or Capacity
10^3	× base	kilometer	kilogram	kiloliter
10^2	× base	hectometer	hectogram	hectoliter
10^1	× base	dekameter	dekegram	dekaliter
10^0	× base	meter	gram	liter
10^{-1}	× base	decimeter	decigram	deciliter
10^{-2}	× base	centimeter	centigram	centiliter
10^{-3}	× base	millimeter	milligram	milliliter

Because the units of the metric system are related in a simple and logical way by powers of ten, it is very easy to change from one unit to another. We need only to multiply or divide by the appropriate power of ten. Consider, for example, two farmhouses that are 1300 meters apart. Suppose we want to express this distance in kilometers. We know that 1000 meters is equal to 1 kilometer, that each meter is equal to $\frac{1}{1000}$ of a kilometer. Therefore we can multiply 1300 by $\frac{1}{1000}$ (or .001) and obtain 1.3, which is the distance between the two farmhouses in kilometers.

$$1300 \text{ meters} = 1.3 \text{ kilometers}$$

Clearly it is quite easy to change units in the metric system.

In the English system, however, it is much more cumbersome to change units. Suppose, for example, that the two farmhouses are 1.3 miles apart and that we wish to express this distance in feet. There are 5280 feet in one mile. So we must multiply 1.3 by 5280 to find the distance in feet between the two farmhouses.

$$1 \text{ mile} = 5280 \text{ feet}$$
$$1.3 \text{ miles} = 1.3 \times 5280$$
$$= 6864 \text{ feet}$$

$$
\begin{array}{r}
5280 \\
\times \quad 1.3 \\
\hline
1584.0 \longleftarrow (.3 \times 5280) \\
5280 \quad \longleftarrow (1 \times 5280) \\
\hline
6864.0
\end{array}
$$

Then 1.3 miles is equal to 6864 feet and the two farmhouses are 6864 feet apart.

At this point we can begin to appreciate the efficiency of the metric system. To convert 1.3 miles into 6864 feet, we had to perform a three-step mathematical operation. Even if we had memorized the fact that there are 5280 feet in one mile, we would still have had to multiply 1.3 by 5280. But to convert 1300 meters into 1.3 kilometers, we had only to multiply 1300 by $\frac{1}{1000}$ (or .001).

If a measurement is expressed in metric units, a computation can be performed to express the same measurement in English units. Similarly, if a measurement is expressed in English units, a computation can be performed to convert the measurement into metric units. The most common relations between metric and English units are listed below.

While these relations are for the most part only approximate, they are adequate for ordinary practical purposes. The symbol $\approx$ is read "approximately equal to."

Conversion of measures from one system to another is not taught as part of the elementary school mathematics program. Students only need an understanding of the relative sizes of the measures. Usually, if a measure is given in metric units, the calculating will also be done in metric measure. Do *not* ask children to convert from one system of measurement to another.

LINEAR MEASURE

1 meter ≈ 39.37 inches	1 centimeter ≈ .3937 inch
1 meter ≈ 3.28 feet	1 centimeter ≈ .0328 foot
1 meter ≈ 1.09 yards	1 centimeter ≈ .0109 yard

1 kilometer ≈ .62 mile
1 inch ≈ 2.54 centimeters ≈ .0254 meter
1 foot ≈ 30.48 centimeters ≈ .3048 meter
1 yard ≈ 91.44 centimeters ≈ .9144 meter
1 mile ≈ 1609 meters ≈ 1.609 kilometers

WEIGHT

1 gram ≈ .035 ounce ≈ .0022 pound
1 kilogram ≈ 2.2 pounds
1 pound ≈ 453.6 grams ≈ .4536 kilogram
1 ounce ≈ 28.35 grams ≈ .02835 kilogram

VOLUME

1 liter ≈ 61.025 cubic inches
1 liter ≈ .264 gallon
1 liter ≈ 1.057 quarts
1 gallon ≈ 231 cubic inches ≈ 3.785 liters
1 quart ≈ 57.75 cubic inches ≈ .946 liter

The distance from Minneapolis to Chicago is approximately 350 miles. How many kilometers is this?

$$1 \text{ mile} = 1.609 \text{ kilometers}$$

$$
\begin{array}{r}
1.609 \\
\times \quad 350 \\
\hline
80.450 \\
482.7 \quad \\
\hline
563.150
\end{array}
$$

The distance is approximately 563 kilometers.

Throughout this unit we have been talking about measurement, but we have not explained what we mean by the term. What is measurement? **Measurement** is the determination of the size of a thing, or a comparison between some aspect of a thing and a standard unit of measurement. When we determine the height of a building, we are using measurement. When we determine the time it takes to run a race, we are using measurement. When we count the number of pupils in a classroom, we are using measurement. In each of these situations our measurement is expressed by a combination of two things:

(1) the **measure,** which shows us "how many," and
(2) a **standard unit,** which shows us the unit of measurement with which the quantity to be measured is compared.

For instance, consider these examples:

The building is 350 feet high.
The racetrack is 100 meters long.
The race took 17 seconds.

In the first example, the unit of measurement is feet and the measure is 350; in the second, the unit is meters and the measure is 100; in the third, the unit is seconds and the measure is 17.

Let's develop the idea of measurement with respect to linear measurement. Linear measurement, as the name suggests, is concerned with measurement of length. Children in the primary grades can begin to develop some concept of linear measurement by using any suitable object as a measuring device. A child could measure his desk using a pencil, an eraser, a book, or a card, for example. One child might measure his desk as "7 pencils long," and another child measure his as "14 erasers long." Through a discussion and comparison of such measurements, children will soon realize the need for standard units of measurement. Each class might develop its own standard unit of measurement; one class might use a Popsicle stick, for example. They will soon discover that if two different children use the same measuring instrument carefully, they will arrive at the same measurement of a given object. Each pupil might find that his desk is 6 Popsicle sticks long.

After manipulating familiar objects, children are ready for the more abstract level of comparing line segments, choosing one line segment as a standard unit. Children should be asked to compare the lengths of two line segments:

They can do this by tracing $\overset{\bullet\!-\!\bullet}{AB}$ on another sheet of paper and then placing this tracing on top of $\overset{\bullet\!-\!\bullet}{YZ}$. Clearly $\overset{\bullet\!-\!\bullet}{AB}$ is shorter than $\overset{\bullet\!-\!\bullet}{YZ}$, or $m(\overset{\bullet\!-\!\bullet}{AB}) < m(\overset{\bullet\!-\!\bullet}{YZ})$. The letter m in front of $(\overset{\bullet\!-\!\bullet}{AB})$ means "the measure of." We can therefore read the sentence $m(\overset{\bullet\!-\!\bullet}{AB}) <$

$m(\overset{\bullet\!-\!\bullet}{YZ})$ as "the measure of line segment AB is less than the measure of line segment YZ." In the same manner the two line segments below can be compared in length.

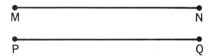

This time the two line segments are of equal length, $m(\overset{\bullet\!-\!\bullet}{MN}) = m(\overset{\bullet\!-\!\bullet}{PQ})$. Children should be encouraged to make a number of such comparisons so that they can gain an understanding of relative (or comparative) lengths.

Now let's introduce a standard unit of length. Let the distance between points S and T, the length of $\overset{\bullet\!-\!\bullet}{ST}$, be called a "unit length."

Children can compare the length of the following line segment, $\overset{\bullet\!-\!\bullet}{GH}$, with this standard unit.

They should trace $\overset{\bullet\!-\!\bullet}{ST}$ on another sheet of paper and label the tracing $\overset{\bullet\!-\!\bullet}{S'T'}$. Then they should place $\overset{\bullet\!-\!\bullet}{S'T'}$ on the top of $\overset{\bullet\!-\!\bullet}{GH}$ so that points G and S' coincide. The point on $\overset{\bullet\!-\!\bullet}{GH}$ that coincides with point T' can be labeled A.

Children should then place $\overset{\bullet\!-\!\bullet}{S'T'}$ on top of $\overset{\bullet\!-\!\bullet}{GH}$ so that points A and S' coincide and so that point T' coincides with a point to the right of point A (that is, between points A and H). The point that coincides with T' can be labeled E.

Then, by placing $\overset{\bullet\!-\!\bullet}{S'T'}$ on top of $\overset{\bullet\!-\!\bullet}{GH}$ so that points E and S' coincide, it will be discovered that points H and T' also coincide. Children can thus see that the length of $\overset{\frown}{GH}$ is three times the length of $\overset{\frown}{S'T'}$. Since we have defined the length of $\overset{\frown}{ST}$ to be a unit length, we can say that the length of $\overset{\frown}{GH}$ is 3 unit lengths. (3 shows the measure; "unit lengths" shows the unit of measure.)

The process described above for measuring the length of $\overset{\frown}{GH}$ is a bit awkward. It would be much easier if we had a line segment like the following:

K   L   M   N   P

in which the lengths of $\overset{\frown}{KL}$, $\overset{\frown}{LM}$, $\overset{\frown}{MN}$, and $\overset{\frown}{NP}$ are each equal to one unit length. Children should trace $\overset{\frown}{KP}$ on another sheet of paper and label the points coinciding with K, L, M, N, and P as K′, L′, M′, N′, and P′ respectively. They should then place $\overset{\frown}{K'P'}$ on top of $\overset{\frown}{GH}$ so that points G and K′ coincide. Clearly, that part of the tracing labeled $\overset{\frown}{K'N'}$ coincides with $\overset{\frown}{GH}$. Since the length of $\overset{\frown}{K'N'}$ is 3 unit lengths, the length of $\overset{\frown}{GH}$ must also be 3 unit lengths.

This measurement can be seen more clearly if $\overset{\frown}{KP}$ and its tracing are relabeled as follows:

0   1   2   3   4

The distance in unit lengths between the point labeled 0 and any other labeled point on the line segment is equal to the number naming the second point. For example, the distance between the points labeled 0 and 2 is 2 unit lengths, the distance between the points labeled 0 and 4 is 4 unit lengths, and so on. If we place the relabeled $\overset{\frown}{K'P'}$ on top of $\overset{\frown}{GH}$ so that point G and the point labeled 0 coincide, point H coincides with the point labeled 3. The distance between the points labeled 0 and 3 is 3 unit lengths. Therefore, the length of $\overset{\frown}{GH}$ is also 3 unit lengths.

We have now developed a standard unit for measuring distance—the unit length. The distance between any two points and the dimensions of any object can be measured by comparing the appropriate distances with this standard unit of measure. Such measurements have meaning because the unit length is a fixed unit of measure—it has the same length today as it did yesterday and will have the same length tomorrow—and because a quantitative relation exists between any distance and the unit length. For example, the height of a particular building is equal to 2300 unit lengths.

We use a number of different units for measuring distance. We have already discussed the most important of these—the inch, the foot, the meter, and so on. Understanding of these units can be developed in much the same way that understanding of the unit length was developed. For example, children can construct a line segment AB such that the distance between the end points is one inch:

A   B

Then they can construct a line segment like the one below, which is composed of three smaller segments each one inch long.

T   U   V   W

Each of these smaller segments is congruent to $\overset{\frown}{AB}$. If $\overset{\frown}{TW}$ is matched with the whole numbers 0 through 3, as in the illustration below, then we can use it to measure distance in inches, just as we used a similar line segment three unit lengths long to measure distances in unit lengths.

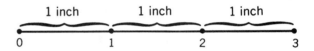

0   1   2   3

Let's create a line segment, XY, that is 1 centimeter long, another standard unit of measurement. If we use the $\overset{\frown}{XY}$ line segment four consecutive times, we say that the line segment is 4 centimeters long.

By developing the idea of measure in this way, we can enable children to understand much more clearly what they are doing when they use a ruler marked off in inches or centimeters to measure something. The various kinds of linear measurement should become clear to them. Other units of length can now be developed in terms of this understanding. For example, having gained an understanding of what inches are, children will be much better prepared to comprehend the meaning of feet, yards, miles, and so on. Their understanding of the metric units of linear measurement (centimeter, meter, millimeter, kilometer) can be developed in much the same manner.

When a distance is measured with a ruler, we say that we are making a **direct measurement.** A direct measurement is any measurement that is obtained by placing a measuring instrument directly on the object whose dimensions are to be measured. When we move a yardstick or a meter stick along the floor to find the length and width of a room, we are making a direct measurement. When we compare the dimensions of two windows by applying a tape measure to each of them, we are again making a direct measurement. An indirect measurement, on the other hand, is any measurement that is not a direct measurement. For example, if we wish to determine the distance across a river, we must employ scientific instruments or a mathematical technique; we cannot simply place a yardstick, meter stick, or tape measure on the surface of the water.

Children in the first grade should be introduced to inches, feet, centimeters, and meters as standard units of linear measure. Rulers in this grade should have only the points marking inches or centimeters. Units smaller than an inch (for example, half inches and quarter inches) will probably only confuse young children at this level. If the number line has been used to develop basic number concepts, children should easily be able to apply these concepts to linear measurement. The yard and meter should also be introduced as standard units of measure in the first or second grade.

The teacher should provide many opportunities for children to measure objects in the classroom. In measuring a line segment, the edge of the ruler is placed along the line segment as illustrated in the following drawing.

The end of the ruler marked 0 is placed at one of the end points of the line segment. The mark on the ruler that is closest to the other end point indicates the length of the line segment being measured. In the above drawing the other end point is closest to the mark labeled 2. This means that the length of the line segment is two inches.

The measurement we have just made is necessarily only an **approximation.** It is impossible to measure distance exactly. Any ruler or tape measure cannot be other than an imperfect instrument. The marks on a ruler or tape measure are physical marks (that is, they have length and width), and a geomet-

ric point cannot be exactly represented by a mark that has dimensions. Moreover, the human eye is incapable of perceiving the precise points at which an object to be measured begins and ends.

In addition to these barriers to exact measurement, there is another difficulty. Examine the following drawing.

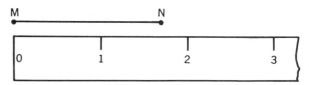

The length of $\overline{MN}$ is greater than 1 inch, but it is less than 2 inches. There is no whole number of inches that represents exactly the length of $\overline{MN}$. The best estimate we can make is that the length of $\overline{MN}$ is approximately 2 inches—that is, it is closer to 2 inches than to any other whole number of inches. This is hardly an exact measurement, but most of the measurements that children make are obviously approximate in this same manner.

As children progress through elementary school and are introduced to fractional numbers on the number line, they should also be introduced to smaller units of linear measure. The half inch can be introduced in the second grade, the quarter inch in the third grade, and the eighth inch and sixteenth inch whenever the children have developed a sufficient understanding of the number line and the rational numbers.

In the metric system, measures of centimeter and meter can be presented in the first grade. Then millimeters can be introduced in the second grade. The units should be used independently; other metric units should not be presented until children have had some experience with decimals.

Now let's return to the measurement of $\overline{MN}$. When we measured this line segment before, we found that its length was approximately 2 inches. Once children have become familiar with half inches, however, $\overline{MN}$ can be measured again, this time with a ruler that is marked to indicate half inches.

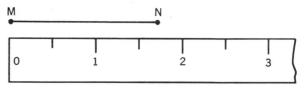

In the ruler pictured above, the long lines labeled with numerals indicate inches, while the unlabeled short lines indicate half inches. For example, the distance between the zero mark and the line labeled 2 is 2 inches, and the distance between the end of the ruler and the unlabeled short line just to the left of the line labeled 2 is $1\frac{1}{2}$ inches. Clearly the length of $\overset{\bullet\,\bullet}{MN}$ cannot be expressed exactly in terms of whole inches and half inches. However, it is closer to $1\frac{1}{2}$ inches than to 2 inches. Therefore we can say that the length of MN is approximately $1\frac{1}{2}$ inches.

But this poses a problem. Our first measurement indicates that the length of $\overset{\bullet\,\bullet}{MN}$ is approximately 2 inches, while our second measurement indicates that this same length is approximately $1\frac{1}{2}$ inches. How can we reconcile these two measurements? The key to answering this question is the difference in the **precision** of the measurements. The first measurement was made in terms of whole inches, the second in terms of half inches. The second measurement is more precise than the first, though both are approximately correct. To the nearest inch, the length of $\overset{\bullet\,\bullet}{MN}$ is 2 inches. To the nearest half inch, the length of $\overset{\bullet\,\bullet}{MN}$ is $1\frac{1}{2}$ inches.

Now let's measure the length of $\overset{\bullet\,\bullet}{MN}$ to the nearest quarter inch.

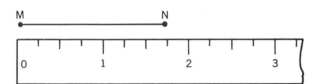

This time we must use a ruler, like the one pictured above, with each one-inch interval divided into four equivalent parts. Each small interval is therefore one-quarter of an inch long. Examining the above drawing, we see that the length of $\overset{\bullet\,\bullet}{MN}$ is less than $1\frac{3}{4}$ inches but greater than $1\frac{1}{2}$ (or $1\frac{2}{4}$) inches and that it is closer to $1\frac{3}{4}$ than it is to $1\frac{1}{2}$. Thus the length of $\overset{\bullet\,\bullet}{MN}$ is approximately $1\frac{3}{4}$ inches. This is more precise than either of the other two measurements.

Let's now measure the length of $\overset{\bullet\,\bullet}{MN}$ to the nearest eighth inch.

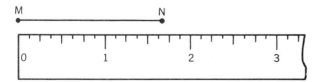

Clearly, of all the lengths indicated in the drawings above, $1\frac{3}{4}$ $\left(\text{or } 1\frac{6}{8}\right)$ inches best approximates the length of $\overset{\bullet\,\bullet}{MN}$. To the nearest eighth inch, $\overset{\bullet\,\bullet}{MN}$ is $1\frac{6}{8}$ inches long. The smaller the unit of measure used, the more precise the measurement is.

At this point it should be said that the first step in measurement is to select the units to be used. A measurement is always made in terms of units. It is therefore impossible for children to measure something until they have decided whether they are going to use inches or meters or days or dollars or something else. It is important that the units be appropriate. It would be ridiculous to use inches for finding the distance between New York and Chicago. It would be equally ridiculous to weigh a small bag of candy on the scales at a truck-weighing station. The first step, therefore, is to select a unit of measurement appropriate for the situation at hand.

Many children have a tendency to be careless in naming units. In solving a word problem, they may want to give the answer as a measure (a number) without naming the units. For example, consider the following problem.

If John weighs 89 pounds and Peter weighs 82 pounds, how much do John and Peter weigh together?

When asked the answer to this problem, children may reply, "171." But this is wrong. Do they mean "171 yards," "171 days," "171 apples," or what? The reply "171" is insufficient because a measurement is always made in terms of some unit. A measurement therefore must always be expressed as a measure and a unit of measure. The numerical answer to the word problem above is then "171 pounds" ("171" shows the measure; "pounds" shows the unit of measurement). This point must be emphasized. Remember in Unit 4 it was stated that a word problem should be answered with a complete sentence. Therefore the complete answer to the story problem above would be "Together John and Peter weigh 171 pounds."

Quantities expressed with a numeral and a unit of measure are called **denominate numbers.** Some people criticize work with denominate numbers on the grounds that we cannot perform operations on measurements, but only on numbers. In a sense, this argument is correct. Yet if we look at the real world, we see many practical situations in which we must deal with measurements and hence with denominate numbers. Denominate numbers are not numbers in the mathematical sense, they are measurements of physical attributes of objects, and we use operations on numbers to help us compare and operate with these measurements.

Children should be given the opportunity to work many problems involving units of measure. These may or may not be in the form of word problems, like the one on the previous page. Consider the following addition example.

$$1 \text{ foot } 5 \text{ inches}$$
$$+ 1 \text{ foot } 2 \text{ inches}$$

This example is not expressed in terms of a single unit. Rather the measurements have been made in two units—feet and inches. This is quite acceptable. We can solve this example by adding the numbers expressed in the feet column and then adding the numbers expressed in the inches column separately.

$$1 \text{ foot } 5 \text{ inches}$$
$$\underline{+ 1 \text{ foot } 2 \text{ inches}}$$
$$2 \text{ feet } 7 \text{ inches}$$

The sum is clearly 2 feet 7 inches. Here is another example in metric measure.

$$3 \text{ meters } 34 \text{ centimeters}$$
$$\underline{+ 2 \text{ meters } 27 \text{ centimeters}}$$
$$5 \text{ meters } 61 \text{ centimeters}$$

Note how easy it is to rewrite the example all in one unit and then add the numbers. We can change 3 meters 34 centimeters to 334 centimeters and change 2 meters 27 centimeters to 227 centimeters. Now the example becomes

$$334 \text{ centimeters}$$
$$\underline{227 \text{ centimeters}}$$
$$561 \text{ centimeters}$$

Note that the addition of metric measure can conveniently be changed to an addition example familiar to most children. Adding denominate numbers is much easier in metric than in English measure.

Now let's consider another example.

$$4 \text{ pounds } 10 \text{ ounces}$$
$$\underline{+ 3 \text{ pounds } 9 \text{ ounces}}$$

The answer here is 7 pounds 19 ounces. But 19 ounces is equal to 1 pound 3 ounces. The answer can therefore be expressed as 8 pounds 3 ounces.

$$
\begin{aligned}
7 \text{ pounds } 19 \text{ ounces} &= 7 \text{ pounds} + 19 \text{ ounces} \\
&= 7 \text{ pounds} + (1 \text{ pound} + \\
&\quad 3 \text{ ounces}) \\
&= (7 \text{ pounds} + 1 \text{ pound}) + \\
&\quad 3 \text{ ounces} \\
&= 8 \text{ pounds} + 3 \text{ ounces} \\
&= 8 \text{ pounds } 3 \text{ ounces}
\end{aligned}
$$

Note that the concept of regrouping place value can be applied to regrouping here: 19 ounces becomes 1 pound 3 ounces. In general, as a matter of convenience, when a measurement is expressed in two or more units, each unit is written with as great a number as possible. The answer to the preceding example can be written in a number of different ways:

$$8 \text{ pounds } 3 \text{ ounces}$$
$$7 \text{ pounds } 19 \text{ ounces}$$
$$6 \text{ pounds } 35 \text{ ounces}$$
$$\text{and so on}$$

It is more convenient, however, to write the answer as 8 pounds 3 ounces. By writing the answer with a lesser number of pounds, the expression for ounces would necessarily be more cumbersome.

Below are three more examples in which the answers have been expressed in the most convenient form.

(a)
$$4 \text{ yards } 2 \text{ feet } 5 \text{ inches}$$
$$\underline{\times 5}$$
$$20 \text{ yards } 10 \text{ feet } 25 \text{ inches}$$

$$
\begin{aligned}
20 \text{ yards } &10 \text{ feet } 25 \text{ inches} \\
&= 20 \text{ yards} + 10 \text{ feet} + 25 \text{ inches} \\
&= 20 \text{ yards} + 10 \text{ feet} + (2 \text{ feet} + 1 \text{ inch}) \\
&= 20 \text{ yards} + (10 \text{ feet} + 2 \text{ feet}) + 1 \text{ inch} \\
&= 20 \text{ yards} + 12 \text{ feet} + 1 \text{ inch} \\
&= (20 \text{ yards} + 4 \text{ yards}) + 1 \text{ inch} \\
&= 24 \text{ yards} + 1 \text{ inch} \\
&= 24 \text{ yards } 1 \text{ inch}
\end{aligned}
$$

If one wanted the largest unit of measurement to be a rod, then this example could be rewritten as 4 rods + 2 yards + 1 inch or 4 rods 2 yards 1 inch.

(b) $8 \times 77¢ = \square$

$8 \times 77¢ = \$6.16$

$$\$ .77$$
$$\underline{\times 8}$$
$$\$6.16$$

(c)
$$7 \text{ grams } 4 \text{ decigrams}$$
$$\underline{\times 6}$$
$$42 \text{ grams } 24 \text{ decigrams}$$
$$= 44 \text{ grams } 4 \text{ decigrams}$$

or, more conveniently, since 7 grams 4 decigrams = 7.4 grams

$$7.4$$
$$\underline{\times 6}$$
$$44.4 \text{ grams}$$
$$(\text{or } 444 \text{ decigrams})$$

Notice that in the last example 7 grams 4 decigrams is rewritten as 7.4 grams before the indicated multiplication is performed. This is not necessary, but computation is easier in that form. Such simplification is possible because the metric system is based on powers of ten. The expression "4 decigrams" can be rewritten as ".4 gram"; the sum of 7 grams and .4 gram can be expressed as 7.4 grams.

We have said that a measurement is always expressed by a numeral together with a unit of measurement. For example, if a line segment has a length of 4 centimeters, the "4 centimeters" is composed of two parts—"4," showing the measure, and "centimeters," showing the unit of measurement. Consider the following example, in which 4 inches and 7 inches represent the lengths of two line segments.

$$
\begin{array}{r}
4 \text{ inches} \\
+ \ 7 \text{ inches} \\
\hline
11 \text{ inches}
\end{array}
$$

It is incorrect to say that we are adding two lengths. We are not adding 4 inches and 7 inches, for we are not adding the "inches" of the expressed sum. Rather we are adding the measures of the two lengths—4 and 7.

Children should be introduced to the concept of measuring money early—beginning in kindergarten and continuing until perhaps the end of the fourth grade. First have the children sort attribute blocks according to different characteristics; then have them separate a collection of coins into piles of coins that are alike. Successfully separating the coins into different piles indicates that the child can identify those that are alike and those that are different. Have the children examine each of the different coins and discuss the likenesses and the differences.

The next stage will require the children to recognize the relative value of the coins. How many pennies does it take to have the same value as a nickel? (Do not say to young children, "How many pennies are there in a nickel?" We are interested in

Nickel	Dime	Quarter	
5 pennies	10 pennies	25 pennies	3 nickels
			1 dime
	2 nickels	5 nickels	
			3 nickels
	5 pennies	2 dimes	10 pennies
	1 nickel	1 nickel	
			2 nickels
		1 dime	15 pennies
		15 pennies	
			1 dime
			2 nickels
		1 dime	5 pennies
		1 nickel	
		10 pennies	
		(and so on)	

the relative value of the coins—there are no pennies in a nickel, strictly speaking.)

Next, children need to recognize the various combinations of coins that are equivalent in value. Ask the children how many different combinations of coins are equivalent in value to 25 cents. The concept of making change should be presented next. Use real objects with price tags on them and have children pretend to buy and sell them. The prices should be realistic so that the children begin to develop a concept of value. Money notation with the use of ¢ and $ can then be introduced. Word problems that involve money should be presented at this point.

Another aspect of measurement that children should be familiar with is time. Children generally have some knowledge of time when they enter school. Time has regulated their lives since birth so they have developed an intuitive understanding of it; for example, they have seldom missed their favorite television shows.

Readiness activities necessary for an understanding of how time is measured and how to read a clock should begin in kindergarten. By the end of third grade all children should be able to read a clock to the nearest minute.

Development of time concepts begins in kindergarten and continues each year thereafter. Begin to develop an understanding of *day* and *week* through discussion with the children. In the first and second grades, *month* and *year* can be developed, and A.M., P.M., and the calendar can be introduced.

For our purposes, one year is defined as the amount of time required for the earth to make one complete revolution around the sun. A month is the amount of time required for the moon to make one revolution around the earth. A day is the period of time required for the earth to make one revolution on its axis. There is no relationship among these three different phenomena; they are independent events.

This information is presented as background material for the teacher to use when appropriate. Do not hold primary children responsible for knowing this information.

After children have some understanding of numbers, the teacher can begin to use a clock to give times to do certain activities. It is better to use even hours (such as two o'clock or three o'clock).

Do not rush children into reading clocks, because it is a very abstract and difficult task. Do not teach "quarter after," "half past," or "quarter to." A child knows a quarter as twenty-five cents; suddenly his teacher wants him to know it as fifteen minutes. So as not to confuse him, reserve "quarter" for money. Also, since he has not been introduced to rational numbers, he cannot comprehend one half or half past an hour.

A child is not ready to learn to read a clock until he or she can

1. understand a number-line segment from 0 to 60,
2. visualize number lines, and
3. count by fives from 0 to 60.

Cut twelve 2"-by-5" rectangle shapes from colored cardboard or acetate. With a paper punch, punch holes in the lower corners of each rectangle. Use brass fasteners to hook the twelve cards together. Write one numeral on the right-hand end of each card. Thus you have a flexible number-line segment from 1 to 12.

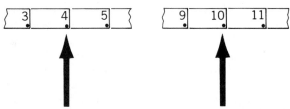

← From the same color of cardboard, cut an arrow-shaped hand for the clock.

Introduce the children to the number-line segment in a horizontal position by laying it on the floor, in the chalk trough, or on a flannel board. Place the hand so that it points to a numeral and have the children read it.

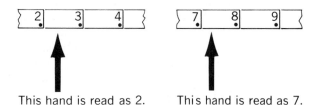

Now place the hand so that it is pointing somewhere between two numerals.

This hand is read as 2.   This hand is read as 7.

The children need to realize that the number is read as the least value until the hand reaches the next number.

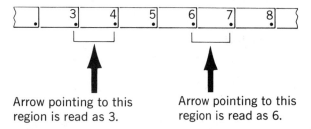

Arrow pointing to this region is read as 3.

Arrow pointing to this region is read as 6.

After the children are successful in reading the arrow pointing to the horizontal number-line segment, connect the two ends together with a brass fastener to make a circular shape and place it on the floor or on a flannel board.

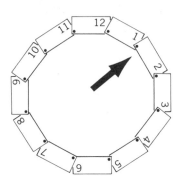

Place the arrow in the center and have the children practice reading what numeral the hand is pointing toward.

Extend the number-line segment to 60 and practice counting from 1 to 60. Introduce counting by 5 beginning with 5 and counting to 60. Cut twelve more 2"-by-5" cards from a different color of cardboard. Punch holes in their lower corners and fasten them with brass fasteners. Print the numerals 5, 10, 15 . . . 60 on the cards and place five equally spaced marks on each card.

Cut a longer arrow out of the same color of cardboard as this number-line segment.

Give the children practice in reading the number the arrow is pointing toward.

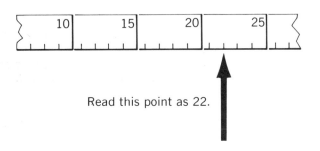

Read this point as 22.

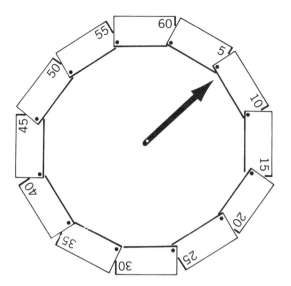

Continue having the children practice reading the arrow as it points toward marks between the numerals written on the number-line segment. After the children are successful in reading the number-line segment horizontally, change the arrangement to a circular one.

Place the long arrow in the middle of the clock and have the children practice reading what number the hand is pointing toward.

Now place the number-line segment with numerals from 1 to 12 on top of the segment that has numerals from 5 to 60. Place the two arrows or hands together and discuss how they are different. The hands are not "big" and "little"; one is called the "short hand" and the other is called the "long hand." Read the short hand first with the top number-line segment and then read the long hand using the number-line segment that is underneath. If the children have difficulty, permit them to check by looking at the number-line segment underneath.

This clock is read as 5:10.

Now the children have developed all the necessary skills they need to read a clock. Continually provide opportunities for them to tell time.

After they have become efficient in reading the clock, the idea of "to the hour" may be introduced. It is much more difficult for children to understand this, so wait until they are proficient in reading "after the hour" before introducing "to the hour."

In this unit we have concentrated on linear measurement. However, all the most common types of measurement—length, area, volume, weight, time, and money—should be developed in the elementary grades. For the most effective teaching, these concepts should be developed with real materials. Ideas can then be discovered and understood rather than superficially learned and mechanically applied. Time must be provided for children to explore and discover the basic concepts of measurement and the relations that exist between the various units of measurement.

Terminology, Symbols, and Procedures

Denominate number A quantity expressed by an ordinary numeral in combination with a unit of measurement is a denominate number. For example, if one measures one's height with a yardstick, the measurement might be expressed by one of the following denominate numbers: 67 inches, 5 feet 7 inches, or 1 yard 2 feet 7 inches.

Direct measurement A measurement obtained by placing a standard unit next to an object to be measured is a direct measurement; for example, a metric ruler is laid next to a textbook and the length is measured in centimeters.

Indirect measurement   A measurement in which the measuring instrument cannot be placed directly next to or on an object to be measured is an indirect measurement; for instance, finding the distance to the moon or the distance across a river.

Measurement   A measurement is a comparison with a known unit. It often involves a determination of the size of something or a comparison of some aspect of an object with a unit accepted as a standard. A measurement is always expressed in two parts:

1. A unit of measure (standard or nonstandard) with which the quantity to be measured is compared.
2. The measure, a number comparing the quantity to be measured with an accepted unit of measurement.

For example, if a river is 100 feet wide, "100" shows the measure and "feet" shows the unit of measure. If a book is 7 paper clips long, "7" shows the measure and "paper clips" shows the unit of measure.

Standard measure   A measure generally accepted by everyone is a standard measure. Examples of standard measures are the kilogram, second, nickel, day, inch, meter, square centimeter, and so forth.

Practice Exercises

1. Measure each of the following line segments to the nearest

   inch,   sixteenth inch,
   half inch,   decimeter,
   quarter inch,   centimeter, and
   eighth inch,   millimeter,

   a) A _____ B

   b) M _____ N

   c) X _____ Y

   d) C _____ D

2. Place the symbol <, =, or > in the circle to make each statement true.

   a) 5 centimeters ◯ 52 millimeters   h) 7 decimeters ◯ 1 meter

   b) 1 meter ◯ 99 centimeters   i) 1 bushel ◯ 2 pecks

   c) 1 yard ◯ 36 feet   j) 8 pints ◯ 1 gallon

   d) 4 liters ◯ 401 milliliters   k) 9 pounds ◯ 140 ounces

   e) 1 mile ◯ 5280 feet   l) 2 feet ◯ 0.5 yards

   f) 4 kilograms ◯ 453.6 grams   m) 3 meters ◯ 300 centimeters

   g) 23 centimeters ◯ 2.3 millimeters

3. Write each measure in meters. Use the reference chart in this unit to help you.

   a) 72 decimeters   d) .0672 hectometers   g) 92 centimeters
   b) 41 dekameters   e) .8 decimeters   h) 1241 millimeters
   c) 5000 centimeters   f) .04 hectometers   i) 824 hectometers

4. Write the equivalent of 720 milliliters in each unit as indicated. Use the reference chart in the unit to help you.

   a) liters   c) deciliters   e) hectoliters
   b) centiliters   d) dekaliters   f) kiloliters

5. Answer each statement true or false.

   a) Most countries of the world use the English system of measurement.
   b) The metric system is a base-ten system.
   c) The metric system is compatible with our place-value system.
   d) The metric system is much older than the English system.
   e) All linear measurement is approximate.
   f) The smaller the unit of measure, the more precise the measure.

6. Express each measurement in the units indicated. Use the reference chart in the unit to help you.

   a) 5.4 meters   = ___ centimeters   e) 72 liters   = ___ microliters
   b) 81 kilometers = ___ meters   f) 524 milliliters = ___ deciliters
   c) 1 megaliter   = ___ microliters   g) 2473 micrograms = ___ grams
   d) 5497 grams   = ___ kilograms   h) 7 meters   = ___ decimeters

7. Solve each example using denominate numbers. Rewrite the metric examples to make them easier to solve. For example, in h) 3 cm 8 mm = 38 mm; thus the example should be written as: 38 mm
                                                                                             $\times$ 3
                                                                                           _____

   a)   3 ft. 4 in.   d) 2 rd. 9 ft.   g)   7 yds. 3 in.   i) $5\overline{)12\text{ gal. 3 pt.}}$
           7 ft. 9 in. $\times$ 6 $-$ 2 yds. 8 in.
        $+$ 6 ft. 5 in.   _____
        _____

   b)   8 hrs. 43 min.   e)   17 ft. 7 in. h) 3 cm 8 mm   j)   4 m 54 cm
       $+$ 1 hr. 39 min. $-$ 6 ft. 9 in. $\times$ 3   6 m 63 cm
       _____   _____ _____   9 m 37 cm
                                                                   $+$ 1 m 52 cm
   c) $4\overline{)6\text{ m 8 cm}}$ f)   5 m 23 cm   _____
                                      $-$ 1 m 67 cm
                                      _____

8. Express each measurement in the units indicated.

   a) 17 feet   = ___ yards   f) 7 miles   = ___ feet
   b) $1\frac{3}{4}$ yards   = ___ inches   g) 1815 sq. yards = ___ acres
   c) 20 pints   = ___ gallons   h) 43 cups   = ___ pints
   d) $1\frac{3}{8}$ pounds   = ___ ounces   i) 49 sq. yards   = ___ sq. feet
   e) 3 cups   = ___ tablespoons j) 3 gallons   = ___ cups

9. List all of the possible combinations of coins that will make 50 cents if only dimes, nickels, and quarters are used.

10. Use a metric ruler calibrated in millimeters to calculate the thickness of a penny. (Hint: you might want to use more than one penny.)

11. List all possible combinations of coins that will make one dollar if only dimes, nickels, and quarters are used.

12. Use a metric ruler calibrated in millimeters to calculate the thickness of a dime.

Discussion Questions

1. Discuss situations in which standard units of measure are not used.

2. Examine how several elementary school mathematics textbooks teach children how to tell time. Discuss the similarities and differences between methods used by other elementary textbooks and the method used in this text to introduce the concept of time.

3. Discuss and compare operations using English measurement with the metric system.

4. Discuss the advantages and disadvantages of the United States' conversion to the metric system.

5. Research and discuss the development of a metric interest center (mathematics metric lab) within the classroom.

6. Discuss appropriate measuring instruments for each grade level.

7. Discuss the similarities and differences between addition of whole numbers and addition of denominate numbers.

8. Compare and contrast addition of measures in English units and addition of measures in metric units.

9. Discuss situations where fractions are most useful and situations where decimals are most useful for measurement.

10. Compare methods of measurement used on earth with measurements made in space.

Activities for the Primary Grades

To young children the concept of measurement is most meaningful when it is expressed in terms of concepts like "longer," "shorter," "taller," "later," and "farther." In the spring they realize the days are longer and they are allowed to play outside later. In winter the days are shorter, and it seems that they must go to bed earlier. They know that some children are taller than others, that some stores are farther away than others, that some people are older than others. All of these familiar situations create a perfect setting for developing the concepts of measurement.

When faced with a simple situation that demands measurement of length, a child should understand the need for measuring and be able to decide on the proper units to use and perform the measurement with a degree of accuracy appropriate to his age and maturity.

Measurement presents unique situations for the classroom teacher. It is an excellent opportunity to use a laboratory approach to teaching. Children learn measurement best by measuring. Provide many materials (some can be made by the PTA) for children to use in experimenting and discovering. In learning and teaching metric measurement, children, teachers, and parents are in a unique position, for children can learn the metric system in school and then go home and teach their parents some mathematics they probably do not know.

BASIC CONCEPTS OF MEASUREMENT

1. Stimulating interest in measuring objects or people in the student's real world is a logical starting point in Grade 1. Many activities result from appropriate questions asked by the teacher:

Who is the tallest?
Who can reach the widest?
Who is heaviest?
Who can jump the highest?
Which is longer, the chalk tray or the windowsill?
Which is later in the day—breakfast or bedtime?
Which holds more—a milk glass or a coffee cup?

2. To measure the chalk tray, for example, have a long stick available to use as a unit. Have children measure the length of the tray in "stick units." It is advisable to have two children work together. This kind of measuring activity can be performed by several pairs of children and their results compared. The sticks used should not have markings of any sort.

Have sticks of various lengths available. Ask children to measure the width of the room in stick-length units. Repeat the activity using sticks of greater length and sticks of shorter length. Have children compare and discuss their results, then decide which stick length is the most practical to use for this project.

Give children ample time to follow through on this activity. Have groups of three or four children work together measuring various objects or distances in the classroom. Let them compare their results and present their findings to the class for discussion.

Select an object in the room for children to measure, one that does not allow the stick length to fit an even number of times. Have children estimate the amount of a unit (or stick length) left over and lead them into the idea of rounding to the nearest whole unit. (If the object measured is approximately one-half of a unit, children may call it this.)

3. Select groups to work together measuring objects that you have already measured. Have each group record their results and then check with you to see if their measurements are reasonably correct. Many children may lack the dexterity and coordination needed to obtain precise results, and this should be taken into account.

4. Have one child stretch his arms horizontally; tell him to hold still while you measure the distance from the tip of the middle finger of his right hand to the tip of the middle finger of his left hand. Record the distance. Then measure the same child's height. Record the height. Repeat the activity with enough children to indicate whether or not, for each child, these two measurements tend to be almost identical.

5. Distribute several unmarked foot rulers (wooden, plastic, or stiff cardboard straight-edges, all one foot long). Ask the children to compare these rulers and find out if they are the same length. Have them compare the foot ruler with the yardstick. Encourage them to think about various uses for each. For example, "Which one would you use to measure the bookcase?" "Which one would you use to measure the length of a sheet of paper?"

6. Use heavy cardboard and have children make rulers one decimeter long. Create a "Bureau of Standards" that is in charge of deciding what length each unit will be on the cardboard rulers (1 meter, 1 centimeter, and so on); the students model their rulers after those of the "Bureau of Standards." Each child can mark his own ruler into centimeters. Discuss the concept of the U.S. Bureau of Standards.

7. Place strips of masking tape of various lengths in different parts of the room. Use lengths between 1 foot and 8 feet, preferably. Have children use their foot rulers to measure these lengths, and have them record and compare their results.

After this activity, have one child use his foot ruler to measure a 10-inch strip. Rounded to the nearest foot, this would be recorded as 1 foot. Ask another child to measure a 3-inch strip with his foot ruler. Rounded to the nearest foot, this would be recorded as zero feet. At this point the children should be asked to think about this idea of zero feet. Is it really zero or not? Hopefully, this will generate the idea of using smaller units.

8. Distribute one-inch-cube blocks to the children and let them use these blocks to discover how many of them will fit on their foot ruler. (Remember, we have been using sticks for foot rulers, with no calibrations up to this point.) They will discover that 12 of these one-inch units will fill their foot ruler; consequently we can say that one foot unit of measure is equivalent to 12 one-inch units of measure. The children should now be able to use standard rulers with inch or half-inch markings. Discuss the convenience of using this kind of ruler and let them practice measuring objects.

9. Draw several triangles or quadrilaterals, at least 1 foot on each side, on 24-by-36-inch newsprint or tagboard. Have children measure the lengths of the line segments forming the sides of the figures. Use both a foot ruler and a meter stick.

10. Have the children line up one at a time, tallest to shortest. Discuss who is the tallest and who is the shortest. Another day have them line up shortest to tallest and discuss the relationship.

11. Have children name objects that are longer than their reading books. Then have them name objects that are shorter than the tops of their desks.

12. Ask the children: who lives farthest from school? Have children who walk to school count their steps as they walk. Children must be able to count at least to several hundred to do this activity.

TIME

1. Present a variety of activities related to the number line from 0 to 12. You can present many addition and subtraction activities that will develop readiness for telling time.

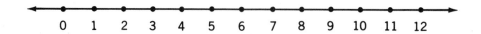

After these activities, review counting by five and present many experiences counting by fives from 0 to 60. Supplement these activities with work on the number line from 0 to 60. Label only those points that correspond to multiples of 5.

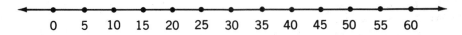

Relate the two number-line diagrams. Be sure that children do not become confused by the use of different unit lengths in the two number-line diagrams.

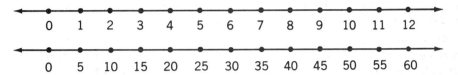

2. Now make the number lines into "number circles" by cutting off the excess portions at the ends of the diagrams and forming a circle (so that the 12 falls on top of the zero). To do this you can use number lines made of cardboard segments that are hinged at the places where the numerals go. First work with the "number circle" that shows numerals from 1 to 12 (remember the 12 has covered the 0). Introduce the hour hand and have children tell which numeral it points to as you move it from one position to another. In a similar manner, make a "number circle" from a number-line model that is marked in intervals of 5 from 0 to 60. Introduce the minute hand and let the children practice reading the numeral to which the minute hand is pointing.

3. Discuss with the children the difference between A.M. and P.M. Throughout the year, discuss the calendar, the day of the week and month.

4. Place a large clock in the room and set the hands of the clock for a certain activity—for instance, a snack. The clock is not running. When the hands of the clock on the wall (the clock you use to tell time) are the same as the hands on the activity clock, it will be time for the snack. Have the children observe that the long hand must go around the clock once for the short hand to move to the next number.

LIQUID MEASURE AND WEIGHT

1. Allow children to explore various measures for liquids by comparing the capacities of different containers with those of gallon, quart, pint, and liter containers. You may use sand instead of water for this activity.

2. Allow the children to compare the weight of various objects in the classroom to a one-pound weight or a one-ounce weight. Use this activity only to compare weights, not to determine the actual weight of an object.

3. Construct a pan balance so that the children can place items in the pans and determine if the items have the same or different weights. Drill three holes through a narrow stick (as shown in the following diagram). One hole should be in the center of the stick; the other two placed at an equivalent distance from the two ends. Hang the balance from a table or tall piece of furniture by a string attached to the center hole. The pans can be made of plastic containers and hung by string as shown.

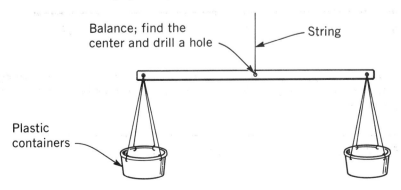

MONEY

In teaching children about money, it is recommended that real money be used, since if play money is used the children must jump to one more level of abstraction to associate each unit of play money with the corresponding unit of real money. To avoid loss of money, try "buying" something from the child (like a shoe) for a fixed amount (say 75 cents). Place a large box in the room and have each child put one shoe in it, then give the child 75 cents. At the end of the period when the child returns the 75 cents, he or she gets the shoe back.

1. Have children sort money into different denominations. Then discuss with them why they sorted the coins as they did. Study each coin and list its characteristics.

2. Place a coin under a sheet of paper on a table. Describe the coin to a group of children sitting around the table; when they think they know what the coin is, they should raise their hands. Note how many cues are needed for different children to recognize the coin being described. After everyone is sure what the coin is, turn the sheet of paper over to see if the children are correct.

Hand-Held Calculator Activities for the Primary Grades

1. Use the hand-held calculator to make a chart for the ticket seller at the movie theater. Tickets sell for $2.50 for adults and $1.25 for children. Make one chart for adults and another chart for children.

Adults' tickets	
Number of tickets	Cost
1	$2.50
2	
3	
4	
5	
6	
7	
8	
9	
10	

Children's tickets	
Number of tickets	Cost
1	$1.25
2	
3	
4	
5	
6	
7	
8	
9	
10	

2. Use your hand-held calculator to fill each space in the following table.

Cost of Item	Money Given	Change
$1.79	$2.00	
3.49	5.00	
2.19	3.00	
1.28		.22
3.31		1.69

3. Provide the children with newspaper ads and have them prepare a shopping list from the ads. Find the total amount of the bill.

4. Use catalogs and calculate the costs of orders.

Microcomputer Activities for the Primary Grades

1. Use the microcomputer in the immediate mode to perform the activities suggested for the hand-held calculator.

2. Primary grade children can type in and run this program. To do so, the children must have some reading skills and recognize numbers.

```
10 PRINT "HOW MUCH IS THE ITEM"
20 INPUT C
30 PRINT "HOW MANY DID YOU BUY"
40 INPUT N
50 Z=N*C
60 S=S+Z
70 PRINT:PRINT"COST FOR ";N;" ITEMS AT ";C;", IS ";Z
80 PRINT:PRINT"YOU HAVE SPENT ";S
90 PRINT:PRINT"DO YOU WANT TO BUY MORE(YES,NO)"
100 INPUT X$
110 IF X$="YES"THEN 10
120 IF X$="NO"THEN PRINT"GOODBYE"
```

Activities for the Intermediate Grades

LINEAR MEASURE

The activities from the primary grades should be continued into the intermediate grades. Provide many opportunities for the children to measure various items. Use English rulers marked only in inches and metric rulers marked only in centimeters. Children seem to find that too many markings on a ruler are confusing. As children become competent at measuring, add the $\frac{1}{2}$ inch line and the millimeter markings. Children need a great deal of experience estimating measurements and then measuring to check their estimates.

1. Use string to measure objects or things that are not in a straight line. Have the children take measurements of their waists, wrists, necks, heads, arms, and so forth.

2. Have the children use straightedges to draw line segments of a given length (say 5 centimeters). Then have them use a ruler to check how close their measurements really were.

3. Children can now begin adding and subtracting denominate numbers. Give the children two cards of different sizes. They should measure each card and tell how much longer or how much wider one card is than another.

DEVELOPING LINEAR UNITS

1. Through various experiences, children will discover the need for a measuring instrument that is longer than a foot. Again, appropriately initiated discussion questions can provide a point of departure.

> How long do you think the room is?
> How long is the fence along the soccer (or baseball) field?
> How long is the bulletin board?
> Could you measure the length of any of these with the measuring units we have been using? (inch and foot units)
> Does anyone know another way we could measure these things?

If children suggest that the measurement could be made in yards or meters, encourage further response to check for understanding. Then present the uncalibrated yardstick, the foot ruler, and the one-inch cubes for observation and comparison. Also introduce the uncalibrated meter stick and the decimeter.

2. Have one child measure the length of the bulletin board with the yardstick. Have another measure the length of the same bulletin board with the foot ruler. Use several activities of this kind involving comparisons to establish the idea of selecting an appropriate unit of measure. Use this same activity with metric measures.

It is important to provide experiences such as these that will constantly reinforce awareness of the relation between the one-inch, one-foot, and one-yard units. If this understanding is developed at the primary level, then linear measurement will present no problem as the child progresses to the more abstract kinds of measurement at the intermediate and junior-high levels.

3. While the concept of a mile is difficult for a small child to comprehend, there are many ways of creating an intuitive understanding. Almost every child rides in an automobile and realizes that distance traveled is measured in miles on the odometer. Many groups take walks that measure one mile or more in length. In some areas a familiar place or a certain building, such as the library, may be a distance of one mile from the school. Any practical experiences that can be interpreted by the child can be valuable in helping him to understand the meaning of mile. It will be much more difficult to teach the concept of a kilometer, because Americans do not use it as much as the mile.

4. Have the children play a question-and-answer game. One question might be:

> What unit of measure would I use to measure the length of my desk?

The child who responds with an appropriate unit is then asked to think of another question to present.

As a variation of this activity, have one child select a unit of measure—the one-inch cube, the foot ruler, or the yardstick—and ask, "What three lengths could I measure with this?"

5. In a school hallway, use small strips of masking tape to mark a line the length of a kilometer. Have the children walk the distance. They will probably be surprised at how many times they will need to walk down the same hall. A kilometer might also be marked off outside. Have the children walk the kilometer during recess.

LIQUID MEASURE

1. The activities for the primary grades can be reviewed and extended. Introduce the smaller measures of cup, tablespoon, and teaspoon. Remember that if you use sand, you must discuss the difference between heaping and level spoonsful, since liquids form level spoonsful.

LIQUID MEASURE AND WEIGHT

1. Allow the children to discover the relationships between standard units of liquid measure (gallon, quart, and pint). Provide the children with standard size containers, and let them pour sand from the smaller containers into the larger containers. Be sure to have the children keep records of their findings.

2. In the intermediate grades, children should be able to determine the approximate weight of an object by using a balance scale and various combinations of pound, ounce, gram, and kilogram weights.

3. Obtain a large metal ball bearing and a large piece of styrofoam (such as the kind used as packing in a box). Have the children place the ball bearing in one hand and the styrofoam in the other hand and guess which is heavier. Use a pan balance to show which object really is the heavier.

4. Have the children guess the weight of a variety of objects; then place them on a scale and weigh them to see how close the estimates really are. Children need many experiences like this with both metric and English measurements. Do not convert from one system to the other; either work entirely in the metric system or entirely in the English system.

TIME

1. As soon as the children are successfully reading the two clocks described in the activities for the primary grades, review the relationship between the two number lines, this time using the two clocks. Introduce the hour hand and the minute hand on the clock face.

2. Follow the procedure described earlier in this chapter to teach the children to read a clock.

3. Using paper plates, have each child make a clock by writing the numbers on the face, cutting out the hands, and fastening them to the plate with a brass fastener.

4. Multiple use overhead transparencies are very valuable in working with children. Make two transparencies, one with clock faces and one with the hands of the clock. The centers of the clocks and the hands should be positioned at the vertices of a square, as in the following example:

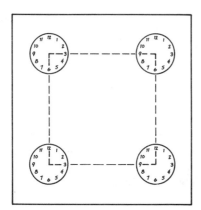 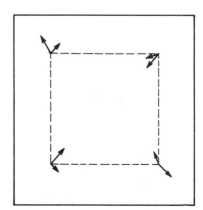

Dotted lines should not be on the transparency; these are only lines to help you make the transparency. Note that the transparency with the hands can be rotated so that it can be placed on the clock faces four different ways. If you rotate the transparency with the clock hands 90 degrees, you will have four more clock faces for children to read. This will provide four clocks to read in each position, and with four positions you have 16 clocks to read.

Now you can flip the transparency over and place it on the clocks again. Rotate the transparency; you will have another 16 clocks for the children to read. This will provide a total of 32 clock faces for the children.

5. Review the clock face. At this level (assuming that the children can read the clock to minute intervals), the concepts of "quarter past," "half past," and "quarter to" can be presented. Relate the concepts to fractional numbers.

Hand-Held Calculator Activities for the Intermediate Grades

The calculator activities for the primary grades can also be adapted for the intermediate grades.

1. Use the hand-held calculator to find the price of one item when you know the price for several items. For example: if three items sell for $1.79, what is the price per item? Some children will have difficulty rounding the number into a value that they can understand. Using the hand-held calculator, 1.79 divided by 3 is 0.5966666. What does this number mean in terms of money?

2. Extend the preceding concept into unit price. If 4 ounces sell for $1.35, what is the price per ounce? Using the calculator, divide 1.35 by 4; the display screen will show 0.3375. Discuss with the children what this means.

3. The grocery store has three brands of soup.

Brand A has 539 grams for $.69
Brand B has 305 grams for $.32
Brand C has 553 grams for $1.29

Which brand is the best buy? Use the unit price to make a valid comparison:

Brand A .69/539 = 0.0012801
Brand B .32/305 = 0.0010491
Brand C 1.29/553 = 0.0023327

Brand B seems to be the best buy, since you pay 0.0010491 cents (less than a penny) per ounce for the soup.

Microcomputer Activities for the Intermediate Grades

1. Use the microcomputer program suggested for the primary grades.

2. Use the calculator activities on the microcomputer in the immediate mode.

3. Write a microcomputer program for calculator exercise 1 on page 450.

```
10 PRINT "HOW MANY ITEMS IN A GROUP"
20 INPUT I
30 PRINT"HOW MUCH DOES THE GROUP OF ITEMS COST"
40 INPUT C
50 X = C/I
60 PRINT "THEN ONE ITEM COSTS ";X
```

The children will need help interpreting the answers. Teach the children what 0.6274355 means in terms of money. Use newspaper ads to get data to feed into this computer program.

Activities for the Upper Elementary Grades

MEASUREMENT AND COMPARISON

1. Use strings to compare the lengths of the line segments and other curves represented here. Write "longer" or "shorter" in the spaces provided.

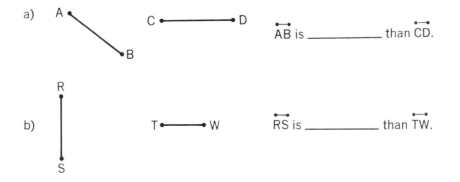

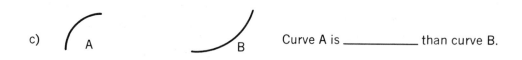

c) A ⌒ B   Curve A is _____ than curve B.

d) Z ∿ N   Curve Z is _____ than curve N.

2. Use your compass to help you compare the line segments below. Which is longer?

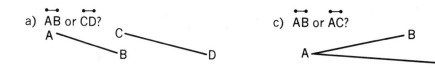

a) $\overleftrightarrow{AB}$ or $\overleftrightarrow{CD}$?

c) $\overleftrightarrow{AB}$ or $\overleftrightarrow{AC}$?

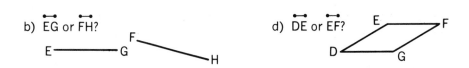

b) $\overleftrightarrow{EG}$ or $\overleftrightarrow{FH}$?

d) $\overleftrightarrow{DE}$ or $\overleftrightarrow{EF}$?

3. Complete each sentence.

a) Our family drinks 3 quarts of milk each day.
   The unit of measure is _____.
   The measure is _____.
   The amount of milk is _____.

b) My desk is 9 chalk pieces long.
   Its length is _____.
   Its measure is _____.
   The unit of measure is _____.

4. Find the measures of these segments to the nearest unit. Use the units shown.

a) A —————————————— B
   $m(\overleftrightarrow{AB}) >$ _____ but $m(\overleftrightarrow{AB}) <$ _____
   $m(\overleftrightarrow{AB}) =$ _____ (to the nearest unit)

   _____
   unit

b) C —————————————— D
   $m(\overleftrightarrow{CD}) >$ _____ but $m(\overleftrightarrow{CD}) <$ _____
   $m(\overleftrightarrow{CD}) =$ _____ (to the nearest unit)

   _____
   unit

c) R —————————————— S
   $m(\overleftrightarrow{RS}) >$ _____ but $m(\overleftrightarrow{RS}) <$ _____
   $m(\overleftrightarrow{RS}) =$ _____ (to the nearest unit)

   _____
   unit

5. Use your compass to find the measures of the line segments. Use $\overset{\bullet\rightarrow}{AB}$ as the unit segment. Since the unit is one inch, give your answers to the nearest inch.

A _____ B
inch

a) C _____ D

   $m(\overset{\bullet\rightarrow}{CD}) =$ _____ inches

b) E _____ F

   $m(\overset{\bullet\rightarrow}{EF}) =$ _____ inches

c) G _____ H

   $m(\overset{\bullet\rightarrow}{GH}) =$ _____ inches

d) L _____ M

   $m(\overset{\bullet\rightarrow}{LM}) =$ _____ inches

6. Answer the questions in each column.

	Which is longer?	How much longer?
a) 23 inches or 1 foot		
b) 18 inches or 2 feet		
c) 4 feet or 1 yard		
d) 1 foot 8 inches or 19 inches		
e) 1 yard 4 inches or 42 inches		
f) 1 yard 2 feet or 7 feet		
g) 1 mile or 3495 feet		

7. Answer each question below. The symbol $\overset{m}{=}$ means "has the same measure as." The first example has been worked for you.

a)   24 in. $\overset{m}{=}$ _2_ ft.

b)   27 in. $\overset{m}{=}$ ____ ft. ____ in.

c)   32 in. $\overset{m}{=}$ ____ ft. ____ in.

d)   18 in. $\overset{m}{=}$ ____ ft. ____ in.

e)   78 in. $\overset{m}{=}$ ____ ft. ____ in.

f) 108 in. $\overset{m}{=}$ ____ ft. ____ in.

g)   6 ft. $\overset{m}{=}$ ____ yd.

h)   9 ft. $\overset{m}{=}$ ____ yd.

i)   7 ft. $\overset{m}{=}$ ____ yd. ____ ft.

j)   5 ft. $\overset{m}{=}$ ____ yd. ____ ft.

k) 10 ft. $\overset{m}{=}$ ____ yd. ____ ft.

l) 30 ft. $\overset{m}{=}$ ____ yd. ____ ft.

THE METRIC SYSTEM

Activities dealing with the metric system should stress the relationship of various metric units of linear measure to decimal notation, as well as the relationships between English and metric units.

Remember: compare measures but do *not* convert from one measuring system to another.

1. Distribute several meter sticks so that each group of four or five children has one. Then pass a yardstick around the class. Have children compare the length of the meter stick with that of the yardstick.

Have one group of children measure the length of the classroom in yards and another group measure it in meters. Have other groups of children find the width of the room in yards and in meters.

Children might also be asked to measure and cut various simple shapes from construction paper according to lengths expressed in centimeters. This would provide an opportunity to compare the centimeter with the inch. Have the children measure lengths of some objects in inches and in centimeters. Ask them to compare an inch with a centimeter. Which is longer? How many times longer is it? Measure the height of several children in centimeters and in inches.

2. In the following exercises use $\overset{\bullet\;\;\bullet}{RS}$ as a unit. Since your unit is the centimeter, express your answers to the nearest centimeter.

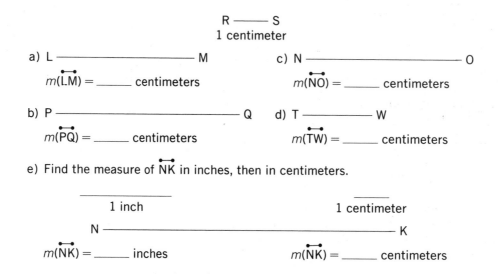

R ——— S
1 centimeter

a) L ————————— M

$m(\overset{\bullet\;\bullet}{LM}) =$ _____ centimeters

c) N ————————— O

$m(\overset{\bullet\;\bullet}{NO}) =$ _____ centimeters

b) P ——————————— Q

$m(\overset{\bullet\;\bullet}{PQ}) =$ _____ centimeters

d) T ——————— W

$m(\overset{\bullet\;\bullet}{TW}) =$ _____ centimeters

e) Find the measure of $\overset{\bullet\;\bullet}{NK}$ in inches, then in centimeters.

_____   _____

1 inch   1 centimeter

N ————————————————— K

$m(\overset{\bullet\;\bullet}{NK}) =$ _____ inches $m(\overset{\bullet\;\bullet}{NK}) =$ _____ centimeters

3. Make a set of ten cards and on each one paste a picture of an object to be measured. Have the children measure the objects in at least two ways so they can be compared. If you laminate the cards, they can easily be erased. For example:

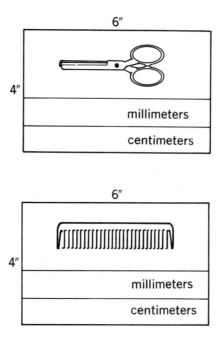

4. Play metric bingo. You will need to make a set of cards with metric measures on them for the caller to use. You will also need a set of bingo cards with metric measures on them. Play the game like regular bingo. Here are some sample cards:

2 milliliters

1 centimeter

100 centimeters

Metric bingo

2 l	.8 l	.1 m	7 m	10 ml
6 km	2 g	10 m	35 cm	.1 cm
100 cm	5 dm	1 kg	.1 km	68 cm
.01 km	.7 cm	5 m	1 cm	55 g
2 kg	2 ml	40 l	.5 dm	10 m

Metric bingo

1 cm	10 ml	.7 cm	2 ml	2 kg
.5 dm	.1 l	2 g	7 m	.1 m
68 cm	5 m	1 kg	.1 km	55 g
100 mm	.8 l	.1 m	35 cm	6 km
40 l	.01 km	5 dm	.1 cm	100 cm

Metric bingo

1 kg	6 km	1 m	2 kg	5 dm
.1 cm	.5 dm	10 ml	10 mm	35 cm
.1 km	.7 cm	100 cm	78 cm	.1 m
2 g	10 l	1 cm	2 ml	5 m
55 g	7 m	.8 l	.01 km	40 l

5. Play a game of Concentration with a set of cards each of which has a metric measure on it. Use 24 cards that are about 6 centimeters by 9 centimeters and mark them with pairs of equivalent measures, as in the examples shown.

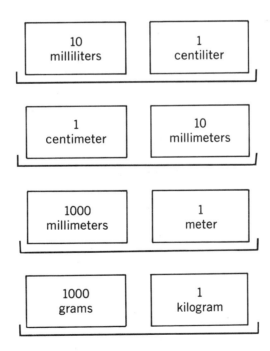

Place all cards face down. Players take turns turning over pairs of cards. If the cards have equivalent measures, the player keeps the set of cards. If the cards are not equivalent, they are replaced. The game continues until all the cards are picked up. The player with the most cards is the winner. As the children learn the game, you can increase the number of cards to 50.

6. Have the children construct metric measurement instruments out of heavy cardboard. Make a ruler marked in millimeters that is 10 centimeters long. Then construct a cube that is 10 centimeters on a side. A pattern is shown. Tape each of the seams.

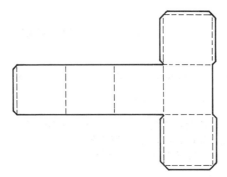

This cube is 1000 cubic centimeters. It will hold 1 liter. Its mass is 1 kilogram when it is full of water.

Hand-Held Calculator Activities for the Upper Elementary Grades

The hand-held calculator activities suggested for the primary and intermediate grades can be adapted for the upper elementary grades.

1. The heart pumps an average of 80 milliliters of blood per second. Use your hand-held calculator to compute the amount of blood pumped

a) per hour
b) per day
c) per week
d) in the month of January
e) in the month of February
f) in the month of April
g) in a year

2. Use the calculator to change 12 feet into yards.

3. Now use the constant key and set up the calculator to solve many examples of changing feet to yards. Enter the following into the calculator: 1 2 ÷ 3 =. Now you can enter any number of feet and press the equals key; the display screen will show the number of yards. Try using 2 4 =; 8 should appear on the display screen. This is the number of yards that equals 24 feet. Try many more examples.

4. Set up the calculator constant so it will change yards to feet.

5. Set up the constant so it will change grams to kilograms.

6. Experiment with the constant key to change units. Remember: do not convert measures between the English and metric systems. Only convert measures within one measuring system.

Microcomputer Activities for the Upper Elementary Grades

Microcomputer activities suggested for the intermediate grades can be adapted to the upper elementary grades.

1. Write a computer program that can be used for unit price comparisons.

```
10 PRINT "WHAT IS THE PRICE OF ITEM A"
20 INPUT P
30 PRINT "BE SURE TO USE THE SAME UNIT OF WEIGHT"
40 PRINT "OUNCES, POUNDS, GRAMS, KILOGRAMS"
50 PRINT:PRINT"WHAT IS THE WEIGHT OF ITEM A"
60 INPUT W
70 U = P/W
80 PRINT "UNIT PRICE FOR ITEM A IS ";U
90 PRINT "DO YOU WANT TO DO ANOTHER(YES,NO)"
100 INPUT Z$
110 IF Z$ ="YES" THEN 10
120 IF Z$ = "NO" THEN END
```

2. Write a program to change yards to feet.

```
10 PRINT "HOW MANY YARDS DO YOU HAVE"
20 INPUT Y
30 F = Y*3
40 PRINT Y ;"YARDS IS THE SAME AS ";F;" FEET"
```

3. Now write a program to change feet to yards.

4. Write a program to change kilograms to grams.

5. Write a program to change grams to kilograms.

6. Change the preceding program so that the user has a choice: of solving another example or stopping the program.

Suggested Readings

Biggs, Edith E., and MacLean, James R. *Freedom to Learn: An Active Learning Approach to Mathematics.* Don Mills, Ontario: Addison-Wesley (Canada), 1969.

Bitter, Gary G.; Mikesell, Jerald L.; and Maurdeff, Kathryn. *Activity Handbook for Teaching the Metric System.* Boston: Allyn & Bacon, 1976.

Bruni, James V., and Silverman, Helene. "Developing the Meaning of Linear Measurement." *The Arithmetic Teacher,* vol. 21, no. 7, November 1974.

Carpenter, Thomas P. "The Performance of First-Grade Students on a Non-Standard Set of Measurement Tasks." In *Technical Report No. 211.* Madison, Wisc.: Wiconsin Research and Development Center for Cognitive Learning, 1971.

Donovan, Frank. *Prepare Now for a Metric Future.* New York: Weybright & Talley, 1970.

Hiebert, James. "Units of Measure: Results and Implications from National Assessment." *The Arithmetic Teacher,* vol. 29, no. 6, February 1981.

Higgins, Jon L., ed. *A Metric Handbook for Teachers.* Reston, Va.: National Council of Teachers of Mathematics (no date).

Leutzinger, Larry P., and Nelson, Glenn. "Meaningful Measurements." *The Arithmetic Teacher,* vol. 28, no. 7, March 1980.

Metric Commission. *Introduction to the Metric System.* Manitoba, Canada: Manitoba Department of Education, 1973.

Nelson, Doyal, ed. *Measurement in School Mathematics: 1976 Yearbook.* Reston, Va.: National Council of Teachers of Mathematics, 1976.

National Council of Teachers of Mathematics. *A Metric Handbook.* Reston, Va.: NCTM, 1974.

O'Daffer, Phares G., and Clemens, Stanley R. *Metric Measurement for Teachers: An Activity Approach.* Menlo Park, Calif.: Addison-Wesley, 1976.

Ostergard, S.; Silva, E.; and Wheeler, B. *The Metric World—A Survival Guide.* St. Paul, Minn.: West Publishing Company, 1975.

Thiessen, Diane. "Measurement Activities Using the Metric System." *The Arithmetic Teacher,* vol. 27, no. 2, October 1979.

Whitman, Nancy C., and Braun, Frederick G. *The Metric System: A Laboratory Approach for Teachers.* New York: John Wiley & Sons, 1978.

Zalewski, Donald. "Some Dos and Don'ts for Teaching the Metric System." *The Arithmetic Teacher,* vol. 26, no. 4, December 1978.

14 Geometry

Teaching Competencies

Upon completing this unit, you will be able to:

Understand some basic geometry terms as demonstrated by using them correctly

Use correct mathematical notation for figures such as lines, line segments, rays, and angles

Classify angles according to their measures

Use the measures of two angles to tell whether the angles are complimentary or supplementary

Use a straightedge and compass to bisect a given angle

Discussion

Today's elementary mathematics programs introduce geometry concepts in the elementary grades that were traditionally reserved for secondary school. Children live in a geometric world. Many of their toys are geometric—blocks, balls, boxes, etc. Because of this geometric environment, it seems logical that geometry be emphasized at every grade level, but many teachers skip geometry in their teaching programs. There are two probable reasons for this: teachers in general do not have sound geometry backgrounds and they also feel that basic operations are more important. Today we must reevaluate the significance of geometry in the elementary mathematics program.

Geometry is defined as the study of **space** and **shapes in space.** It has been found that children develop concepts of geometry by observing geometric shapes in the world around them; they learn by observation and intuitive processes rather than by complex or formal analysis.

Children have had many experiences with geometry before they enter school. The blocks that children play with are basically cubes, prisms (such as long blocks), and cylinders. Children learn a great deal about blocks from their own play and observation but they don't usually have ample opportunities to verbalize their discoveries. For instance, when building something, children could select the appropriate block for their immediate needs and yet not be able to verbalize their observations.

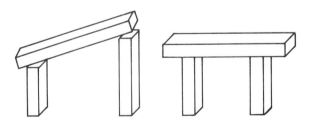

In the drawing on the left, the top block is unstable; in the drawing on the right, it is stable. Children perceive this and can choose the configuration of blocks on the right. Intuitively children compare blocks and develop the ability to visualize the geometric shapes. They need a great deal of experience manipulating the different objects, however.

To help children develop spatial perception, let them examine three blocks such as a cube, a prism, and a pyramid. Provide directions for them to follow in using the blocks—for example:

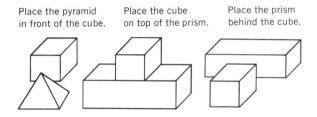

Place the pyramid in front of the cube. Place the cube on top of the prism. Place the prism behind the cube.

Using blocks or pictures of items, illustrate words of position or spatial arrangement for the class. A suggested list might include the following:

under/over	above/below
first/last	underneath/on top of
high/low	in front of/behind
far/near	beside/by/next to
bottom/middle/top	between/around
right/left	inside/outside

Provide children with many formal and informal experiences in sorting, classifying, and playing with attribute blocks. Check the literature for teacher's manuals giving precise instructions for using these materials.

Certain fundamental concepts of geometry must be presented before more formal work can be started—concepts such as point, space, curve, line, line segment, ray, and angle. Some of these geometric concepts are undefined terms; we can attach meaning to them only by assuming particular properties about them. Basic statements, assumed to be true, that express these assumptions are called *axioms* or *postulates*.

The term **point** is an example of an undefined term in geometry. A geometric point can be thought of as an immovable or fixed **location** in geometric space. Similarly, geometric space, which is also undefined, can be thought of as the **set of all points.** Geometric space and geometric points, like numbers, are abstractions.

A geometric point is a precise, fixed location in geometric space. We cannot see a geometric point because, unlike a pencil or chalk mark, a geometric point has no physical length, width, or thickness—only position.

When we say that space is the set of all points (location), we mean that we can think of the physical universe as being filled with these points. When we "pinpoint" the location of an object, we are specifying its position as precisely as we know how. We can think of a geometric point as providing the most precise way possible of specifying a position. Perhaps it is helpful to imagine a dot that shrinks to the smallest imaginable size. This "smallest imaginable dot" corresponds fairly well with our intuitive idea of a geometric point.

Geometric points and geometric space are ideas with no physical existence. In constructing figures, however, we represent geometric ideas by physical representations—dots and lines drawn on paper or chalkboard. Just as a number is an idea, physically represented by a numeral, so is a geometric point an idea, physically represented by a dot. The dot we draw is a convenient approximation. No matter how small we make our dot, it still covers countless geometric points; but a dot is the most satisfactory way we have of representing a geometric point. Points represented by dots are labeled with capital letters, as in the following example.

• A   (read "point A")

What is a plane? To understand the concept of geometric **plane,** think of a flat tabletop. Imagine the surface of the flat tabletop extending horizontally in all directions limitlessly.

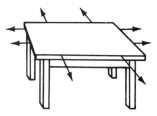

The flat surface of the table extended horizontally in all directions without end suggests a geometric plane. Like all other geometric figures, a plane is a set of points. A plane is a subset of space. A flat surface, such as a tabletop, occupies an infinite number of geometric points. If the table is removed, can you still imagine the set of points that the flat surface of the table represented? Now imagine this set of points extended horizontally in all directions indefinitely. This exercise should help you develop an understanding of geometric plane. In the diagram below, the arrows indicate that the plane p extends endlessly.

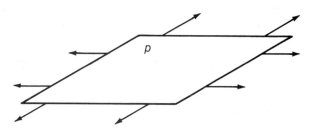

The primary-school child is best introduced to the concept of plane through physical representations of parts of planes. The simplest representations for him to understand are the surface of his desk, a wall, a chalkboard, the sheet of paper on which he is drawing, a book cover, the floor of a basketball court, and so on. It should be emphasized that these are physical representations of parts of planes. If he imagines the set of points occupied by his desk top, or by the floor of the basketball court, going on forever, he is imagining a geometric plane. This geometric plane is a subset of space; it is a particular set of points. These points are fixed locations. The set of points occupied by a chalkboard remains even if the chalkboard is removed.

A sheet of cardboard can also be used to represent a part of a plane. Have two pupils each hold a sharpened pencil with the point up. Attempts to balance the cardboard (representing a plane) on the two pencil points (representing two points) will not be successful. But if another pupil holds a third pencil near the other two (not in line with them), the cardboard will rest steadily on the three pencils.

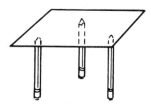

This fact can be reinforced by asking why a three-legged stool never wobbles, even if each of the three legs has a different length. Both of these situations emphasize an important geometric fact: *Any three points not in a straight line determine a plane.*

If three points are not in a straight line, how many planes can be passed through them? Only one. For example, any other sheet of cardboard resting on the three pencil points would lie in the same plane as the first.

The shortest or most direct path between two given points in Euclidean space is called a line segment. A **line segment** is a set of points (and a subset of geometric space) that represents the shortest distance between two given points. A line segment has a first (or initial) point and a last (or terminal) point. These are called the **end points.** A line segment has a definite length.

A •————————————————————• B

The symbol for the line segment from point A to point B (with the end points included) is $\overset{\bullet\,\bullet}{AB}$. This is also written $\overline{AB}$, read "line segment AB." In working with small children, it might be better to use the "•—•" symbol at first. Since they learn that a line segment has a first and a last point (as marked in the drawing above), the symbol showing dots at each end is easier to associate with the drawing representing a line segment. A tightly stretched string is a good physical representation of a line segment. Others include the intersection of two walls, the edges of a chalkboard, the edges of a book, and so on.

The concept of line is also undefined in geometry. A line is a set of points and therefore a subset of space. If we draw a representation of a line segment on paper with pencil and straightedge and imagine that this representation is extended endlessly in both directions, the result can be thought of as a geometric line. To help children understand the concept of a line, ask them to imagine line segments extending from their pencil points

1. to the doorknob (have the end points named in each case);
2. to the top of the school flagpole;
3. to the top of the Washington Monument, the Empire State Building, or some other prominent (and pointed) landmark they know; and
4. to a star

Having stretched their imaginations to envision the two end points of an imaginary line segment, the children should now be ready for the broader concept of line.

A line has no end points, but continues endlessly in each of two opposite directions. To represent a line, we draw a line segment and place arrowheads at each end to show that the line has no end points but extends endlessly in both directions.

We can name a line by a small letter, as above, or by labeling two points on the line. In the drawing above we can refer to the figure as "line ℓ." We can refer to the figure in the drawing below as "line RS."

Line RS is also indicated by the symbol $\overset{\leftrightarrow}{RS}$. When we name two points on a line, we have also named a line segment—in this case, line segment RS, or $\overset{\bullet\!\bullet}{RS}$. Every line segment is a subset of a line. It would be helpful to explain to children that "segment" means "part." Line segment RS is a subset, or part, of line RS.

Suppose we name several points on a line:

Since we can name a line with any two points on the line, what names can we give the line above?

$\overset{\leftrightarrow}{CE}$	$\overset{\leftrightarrow}{ED}$		$\overset{\leftrightarrow}{GD}$	$\overset{\leftrightarrow}{DE}$
$\overset{\leftrightarrow}{CF}$	$\overset{\leftrightarrow}{EG}$		$\overset{\leftrightarrow}{GF}$	$\overset{\leftrightarrow}{DC}$
$\overset{\leftrightarrow}{CD}$	$\overset{\leftrightarrow}{FD}$	as well as	$\overset{\leftrightarrow}{GE}$	$\overset{\leftrightarrow}{FE}$
$\overset{\leftrightarrow}{CG}$	$\overset{\leftrightarrow}{FG}$		$\overset{\leftrightarrow}{GC}$	$\overset{\leftrightarrow}{FC}$
$\overset{\leftrightarrow}{EF}$	$\overset{\leftrightarrow}{DG}$		$\overset{\leftrightarrow}{DF}$	$\overset{\leftrightarrow}{EC}$

Note that when we have named a line with two points, for example $\overset{\leftrightarrow}{CE}$ above, the same line is named by $\overset{\leftrightarrow}{EC}$. This is true for any line or line segment.

We have established the fact that a line segment is a set of points, and therefore a subset of space. A line segment is also defined as the shortest path between two points in a plane.

There are other paths, however, between points A and B. Some of these are illustrated in the following diagram.

Paths between two points, as between points A and B above, are examples of curves. In the above diagram the curves that are represented are called simple curves because they don't pass through the same point twice. A **simple curve** is defined as a curve that passes through no point more than once. A line segment is a special kind of simple curve.

A **closed curve** is a curve that returns to its starting point. A closed curve has no end points. A **simple closed curve,** then, is a curve that returns to its starting point without crossing itself at any point. Is a triangle a simple closed curve? Yes. Some examples of simple closed curves are represented below.

Students should practice drawing simple closed curves, including simple closed curves that pass through one, two, three, or more given points.

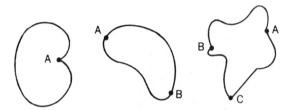

The possibilities are limitless.

Careful notice should be taken of the fact that a curve that crosses itself does not form a simple closed curve. None of the following is a simple closed curve.

Any curve that does form a simple closed curve, however, divides the plane in which it lies into three sets of points:

1. The set of points composing the simple closed curve itself.
2. The set of points composing the interior of the simple closed curve.
3. The set of points composing the exterior of the simple closed curve.

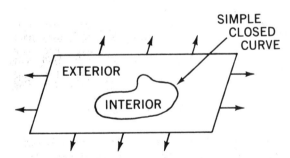

The set of points formed by the union of a simple closed curve and its interior is called a **simple closed region.**

A **ray** is another kind of subset of a line. It consists of a point on the line and all points on the line extending in one direction from the point.

The point from which the ray extends is part of the ray and is called the **end point,** or the **initial point,** of the ray.

On the line above, we have marked point A. This point is the end point (or initial point) of two rays, one beginning at point A and extending endlessly to the right, the other beginning at point A and extending endlessly to the left. Obviously there are an infinite number of rays contained in a line, since any point on the line can be selected as an end point and there are an infinite number of points on the line.

By naming a point on either side of point A, we can now name the two rays (sometimes referred to as **opposite** rays) that extend from this point:

We can name a ray with two letters, representing two points, as $\overrightarrow{AB}$. This name represents the ray that starts at point A and extends endlessly to the right (through point B). The bar with one arrowhead on it ($\bullet\!\!\rightarrow$) indicates that a ray is being named, and the fact that there is no arrowhead above the A indicates that point A is the end point of the ray. Similarly, $\overrightarrow{AC}$ represents the ray that starts at point A and extends endlessly to the left (through point C). It is interesting to note that the two rays have one point in common (point A).

$$\overrightarrow{AB} \cap \overrightarrow{AC} = \{A\}$$

Notice also that the two rays are the line named $\overleftrightarrow{AB}$, $\overleftrightarrow{AC}$, or $\overleftrightarrow{CB}$. A simple physical representation of a ray is a flashlight or searchlight beam. A child can easily imagine a beam of light beginning at the flashlight and continuing endlessly in space in one direction.

With these concepts in mind, children's intuitive perception can be developed. With pencil and straightedge they can practice drawing "lines" on paper and, as symbols are introduced, add these to their drawings. Remember that when a student uses a straightedge to draw a line segment (or any other geometric figure) he is only picturing the abstract geometric figure. It is no more correct to say that what he has drawn is a line segment than it is to say that a sketch of a person is a human being. (It is not necessary that lines always be drawn horizontally; any direction is satisfactory. Freedom of interpretation, not slavish imitation, is to be encouraged.)

Next, children should practice drawing lines through a given point. They should quickly realize that there is no limit to the number of lines that they can draw through any one point.

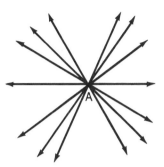

At this stage children are ready for another major concept—a line through two points. Have them mark two points on a sheet of paper and label them. Then have them draw lines through the two points. They soon realize, after several trials, that only one line can be drawn through two points. Because they are marking dots with a pencil to represent points, children may try to draw two lines through two points. Remind them that their pencil-drawn dots should be as small as possible (they will still cover many geometric points) so that only one line will pass through two points.

In these exercises the line a child draws through two points should extend beyond the points. He can then be introduced to the concept of line segment by drawing a figure that does not extend beyond two points. When he has drawn a figure that terminates in this way, it is evident that the segment has a definite length (between the end points). The child can emphasize this fact by drawing more line segments between any two marked points. Practice in drawing geometric figures should be given through exercises such as the following.

1. Draw a line, mark and name four points on the line, and use these points to name the line in several different ways.

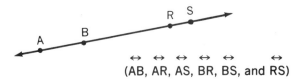

(↔AB, ↔AR, ↔AS, ↔BR, ↔BS, and ↔RS)

2. Given point A, draw lines through point A.

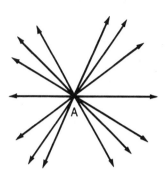

3. Given two points, A and B, draw a line through them.

4. Draw a line segment, name seven points on the line segment, and then use these points to name different line segments.

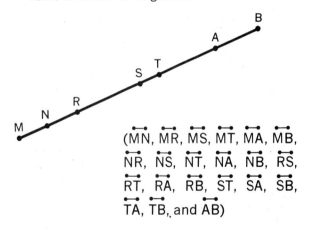

(MN, MR, MS, MT, MA, MB, NR, NS, NT, NA, NB, RS, RT, RA, RB, ST, SA, SB, TA, TB, and AB)

5. Given point R, draw a ray with point R as the end point and name the ray by naming any other point on the ray.

Do $\overrightarrow{RT}$ and $\overrightarrow{TR}$ both name this ray we have drawn? No, they don't. $\overrightarrow{RT}$ names this ray, but $\overrightarrow{TR}$ names a ray (not drawn here) whose end point is T. The first letter always indicates the end point of a ray.

If the drawings (and what they represent) are understood, the pupils will have no difficulty with later drawings and concepts. All figures are built with the basic building blocks that we have studied so far in this unit:

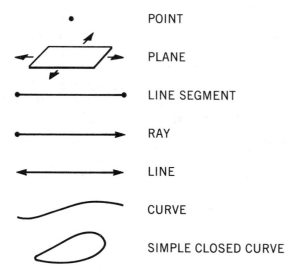

POINT

PLANE

LINE SEGMENT

RAY

LINE

CURVE

SIMPLE CLOSED CURVE

The concepts of space and point are undefined. Space is understood to be the set of all points. And conversely, points are understood to be immovable locations in space. A line segment is defined as a set of points in space (that is, as a subset of space) that is the shortest path between two points. A geometric line is undefined. It extends endlessly in two opposite directions. A ray is defined as part of a line consisting of a point on the line and all the points on the line extending endlessly in one direction from the initial point.

We are now ready to introduce the angle. An **angle** is defined in most mathematics programs as the union of two rays that have a common end point and do not lie on the same line. The common end point of the two rays is called the **vertex** of the angle. And each of the two rays is called a **side** of the angle. In order to name an angle, we must name three points on the angle—the vertex and a point on each of the sides:

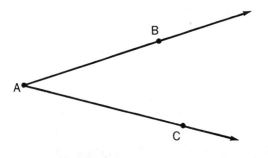

In the above diagram the angle is named by the three points A, B, and C. In symbols we can name

the angle as ∠BAC or ∠CAB. The symbol ∠ is the symbol for angle; it indicates an angle named by the three points listed after the symbol. Notice that the vertex A is the second point named in the expression ∠BAC. When we name any angle this way, the vertex is always between two other points.

One standard unit of angle measure is called a **degree.** The number of degrees measures the opening between the sides of an angle:

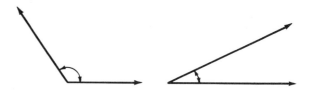

The instrument most commonly used to find the measures of angles is called a protractor.

The primary-school pupil, perceiving geometric shapes and relations intuitively, will not be concerned with the measurement of angles.

By fifth grade, however, the student can use a simple protractor to draw angles of a given measure or to determine angle measure. To determine the measure of an angle, the protractor is placed with its horizontal center point on the vertex of the angle (B) and its base parallel to one of the sides ($\overleftrightarrow{BC}$):

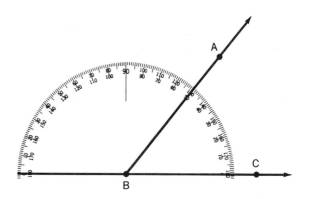

In the diagram, the measure of ∠ABC (50°) is read directly on the inside semicircular scale. The symbol $m\angle ABC$ represents the measure of ∠ABC. Thus $m\angle ABC = 50°$.

On the intuitive level, children in the primary grades should practice drawing angles of all sizes. In order to learn that an angle is the union of two rays with a common end point and not lying on the same line, they should practice by naming a point

•
A

and then drawing any two rays from that point, for example

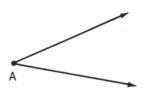

Again, encourage the children to draw in any direction. Teachers tend to draw angles on chalkboards with a horizontal base. Teachers should give themselves the same freedom to draw angles in many positions on the chalkboard.

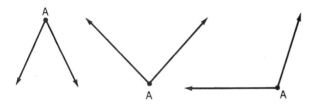

The only discipline to be observed is that drawings such as the following are incorrect (by our definition of angle) and should be discouraged.

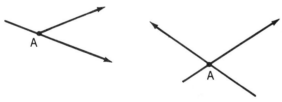

Suppose we have two angles such as the following and wish to compare them to see whether they have the same "size."

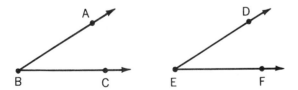

On another sheet of paper, trace ∠ABC and call it ∠A′B′C′ (read "angle A prime, B prime, C prime"). We can compare ∠ABC with ∠DEF by placing the tracing, ∠A′B′C′, on top of ∠DEF. If we place the tracing, ∠A′B′C′, on ∠DEF so that $\overrightarrow{B'C'}$ falls on $\overrightarrow{EF}$, we can decide whether ∠ABC has the same measure as ∠DEF. If, after we have placed point B′ over point E and $\overrightarrow{B'C'}$ over $\overrightarrow{EF}$, we find that $\overrightarrow{B'A'}$ coincides with $\overrightarrow{ED}$, then we know that the two angles have the same measure. If ∠ABC and ∠DEF have the same measure, we say that they are **congruent** or that ∠ABC *is*

congruent to ∠DEF. The symbol "≅" is used to indicate congruence, so we can write

∠ABC ≅ ∠DEF   or $m∠ABC = m∠DEF$

This is read, "Angle ABC is congruent to angle DEF."

If B′A′ does not fall on ED, then ∠ABC is not congruent to ∠DEF. This relation can be written

∠ABC ≇ ∠DEF   or $m∠ABC ≠ m∠DEF$

We read this, "Angle ABC is not congruent to angle DEF."

Angles are classified according to their properties. So we should examine some of the properties of angles. Consider $\overleftrightarrow{AB}$ below and point D not on $\overleftrightarrow{AB}$. Point C on $\overleftrightarrow{AB}$ is marked directly under point D.

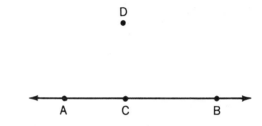

Now draw ray CD.

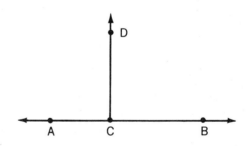

Ray CD determines two angles, ∠ACD and ∠BCD. If these two angles are congruent, then they are called **right angles,** and $\overrightarrow{CD}$ is said to be **perpendicular** to $\overleftrightarrow{AB}$ (in mathematical symbols, $\overrightarrow{CD} ⊥ \overleftrightarrow{AB}$). A right angle has a measure of 90°.

Consider $\overleftrightarrow{XY}$, point Z on $\overleftrightarrow{XY}$, and point O not on $\overleftrightarrow{XY}$. Ray ZO is drawn.

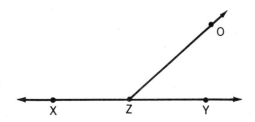

Trace ∠YZO on another sheet of paper, and label the tracing ∠Y′Z′O′. Then compare the tracing, ∠Y′Z′O′, with ∠BCD (the right angle in the previous example). Place the tracing so that point Z′ falls on point C and Z′Y′ falls on CB. Clearly, ∠Y′Z′O′ ≇ ∠BCD; therefore ∠YZO ≇ ∠BCD. Since ∠YZO is less than a right angle, we call ∠YZO an acute angle. An **acute angle** can be defined as an angle that is less than a right angle, or an angle whose measure is less than 90°. Using symbols, we can compare the measures of ∠BCD and ∠YZO in the following way: $m(∠YZO) < m(∠DCB)$. This is read, "The measure in degrees of angle YZO is less than the measure in degrees of angle DCB," or simply, "Angle YZO is less than angle BCD."

Now let's examine another situation in which we have line MN and point E on MN. Another point, G, not on MN is marked, and EG is drawn.

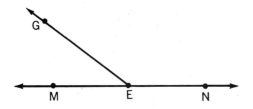

Trace ∠NEG on another sheet of paper, and label the tracing ∠N′E′G′. Compare ∠N′E′G′ with ∠BCD (the right angle in the earlier example) by placing point E′ on point C and E′N′ on CB. Clearly, ∠N′E′G′ ≇ ∠BCD, and therefore ∠NEG ≇ ∠BCD. Since ∠NEG has a measure greater than a right angle but less than 180°, we call ∠NEG an **obtuse angle.** Using symbols, we can compare the measures of ∠NEG and ∠BCD as follows: $m(∠NEG) > m(∠BCD)$. This is read, "The measure in degrees of angle NEG is greater than the measure in degrees of angle BCD," or simply, "Angle NEG is greater than angle BCD." An **obtuse angle** can be defined as an angle whose measure is greater than 90° but less than 180°.

We can point out physical representations of right angles in the classroom. The corner of the room, for example, suggests several right angles.

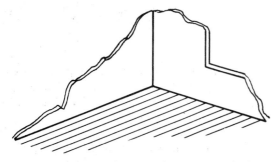

The corners of a window or of a chalkboard are also convenient representations of right angles. An ex-

cellent representation of a right angle is a sheet of paper, such as a page of this book, which has four right angles. Children will probably see the right angle best as the "square corner" of some object. Children should be able to draw representations of right angles, but these will be only approximate, since measurement of angles is not done in the early grades. Children can use the corner of a book (or any other object with a rigid "square corner") to draw representations of right angles.

Angles children draw that are not "square corner" angles but whose measures are less than a right angle are acute angles.

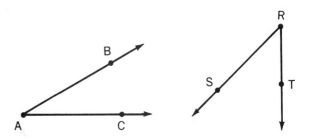

As we have seen, acute angles are angles having a measure of less than 90° (that is, angles whose measures are less than a right angle). Angles that are greater than a right angle but less than a straight angle are obtuse angles.

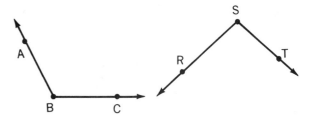

We have seen that obtuse angles are angles having a measure greater than 90° but less than 180°. What statements can we make about ∠DOC and ∠COB below?

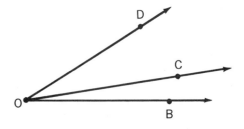

We see that ∠DOC and ∠COB have a common vertex, point O. The two angles also have a common ray, OC, between them. Two angles with a common vertex and a common ray (or side) between them are called **adjacent angles.** In the diagram above, ∠DOC is adjacent to ∠COB.

If the sum of the measures of two angles is equal to the measure of a right angle (90°), the two angles are said to be complementary; they are called **complementary angles.**

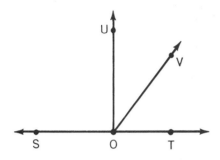

In the diagram above, if $\overrightarrow{OU}$ is perpendicular to $\overleftrightarrow{ST}$ ($\overrightarrow{OU} \perp \overleftrightarrow{ST}$) — that is, if ∠SOU and ∠UOT are right angles — then ∠UOV and ∠VOT are complementary angles, since the sum of the measures of ∠UOV and ∠VOT is equal to the measure of the right angle UOT:

$$m(\angle UOV) + m(\angle VOT) = m(\angle UOT)$$

Two angles do not have to be adjacent (as ∠UOV and ∠VOT are) to be complementary angles. In the diagram below, ∠JEK and ∠LEM are complementary, because the sum of their measures is 90°.

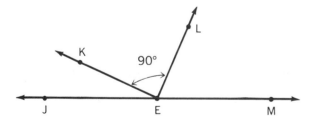

If the sum of the measures of two angles is equal to 180°, the two angles are said to be supplementary; they are called **supplementary angles.**

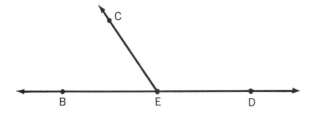

In the above diagram, ∠BEC and ∠CED are supple-

mentary, because the sum of their measures is equal to 180°:

$$m(\angle BEC) + m(\angle CED) = 180°$$

In this case ∠BEC and ∠CED are also adjacent angles. But two angles that are not adjacent can also be supplementary. In the following diagram ∠NUP and ∠QUR are supplementary, because the sum of their measures is 180°.

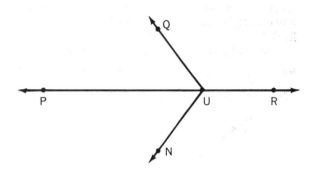

In some instances adjacent angles are congruent. For example, consider the following diagram.

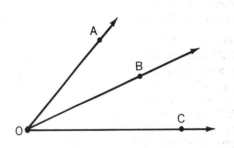

Clearly, ∠AOB and ∠BOC are adjacent angles. Trace ∠AOB and label the tracing ∠A'O'B'. Place the tracing so that O' falls on point O and ray O'B' falls on ray OC. We see that ∠AOB is congruent to ∠BOC. Since ∠AOB ≅ ∠BOC, ray OB is said to bisect ∠AOC. To **bisect** means to divide in half. Since ∠AOB ≅ ∠BOC, the measures of these two angles are equal. Therefore $\overrightarrow{OB}$ bisects ∠AOC.

As well as knowing the vocabulary related to lines and angles, children should learn the procedure for constructing lines and angles. The basic tools for geometric drawings are the straightedge, the compass, and a sharp pencil. (A straightedge is simply a ruler without numerals or other marks on it.) The challenge in constructing geometric models lies in trying to draw accurate models without the use of a ruler (to measure lengths) or protractor (to measure angles).

Let's begin with a simple exercise. Use a straightedge to construct a line segment, $\overline{AB}$.

Using the straightedge, draw another line segment. Label any point C on the line segment.

Now adjust your compass so that the metal point is at point A on $\overleftrightarrow{AB}$ and the pencil point of the compass falls on B. The arc struck by the compass should pass exactly through point B. Move the compass point to point C and strike an arc so that it intersects the line segment containing point C. Label this point of intersection point D.

We can now say that $\overleftrightarrow{CD} \cong \overleftrightarrow{AB}$.

Now let's construct an angle, ∠JEF, congruent to a given angle, ∠ABC.

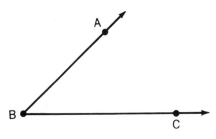

First, draw a ray and label it $\overrightarrow{EF}$.

With the metal point on point B, set the compass at any convenient radius and strike an arc through the sides of ∠ABC. Label the points of intersection of this arc and the sides of the angle as G and H.

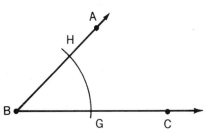

Using this same radius, set the metal compass point on E and strike an arc that intersects ray EF.

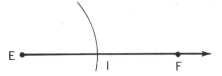

Label the point of intersection of the arc with $\overrightarrow{EF}$ as point I. With the compass, measure the distance from point G to point H. Using this measurement, strike an arc from point I that intersects the first arc we drew on this diagram. Label this intersection point J, and draw ray EJ with a straightedge and pencil.

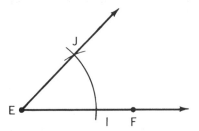

We can now say that ∠JEF ≅ ∠ABC. For practice in construction, use this procedure to draw several other angles congruent to given angles.

Now let's consider angle RST below, and construct the bisector of ∠RST.

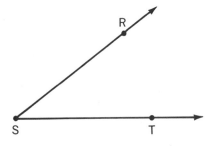

Placing the metal point of the compass at point S, strike an arc so that it intersects rays SR and ST. Label the two points of intersection U and V.

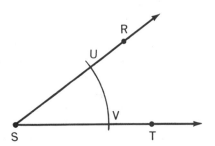

Placing the metal point of the compass at point U, strike an arc between $\overleftrightarrow{ST}$ and $\overleftrightarrow{SR}$. Then, using the same setting on the compass, strike an arc from point V that intersects the arc struck from point U. Label the intersection point M. Connect points S and M, using a straightedge and pencil. The ray SM is the bisector of ∠RST.

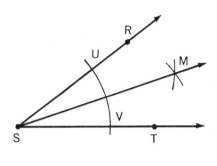

∠RSM ≅ ∠TSM

An excellent device for presenting basic geometric concepts to children is the geoboard. A geoboard is usually a square piece of material in which an array of nails or pegs has been placed. Very often a geoboard is made by using a square piece of plywood in which an array of nails has been driven part way into the wood. The nails should protrude about 1 centimeter.

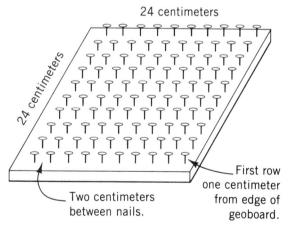

24 centimeters

24 centimeters

Two centimeters between nails.

First row one centimeter from edge of geoboard.

To make the nails a uniform height, use a pliers to hold the nails and drive the nails in until they hit the top of the pliers. Since the first row of nails is positioned 1 centimeter from the edge and the nails are 2 centimeters apart, several geoboards can be placed side by side for a large board.

By placing rubber bands around the nails driven into the geoboard, the student may represent line segments, squares, rectangles, triangles, and angles. Ask students to perform various tasks and

answer questions using the geoboard. Examples of more open-ended questions are:

1. Show a line segment on your geoboard. Using the nails, see who can make the longest line segment and who can make the shortest line segment. In a class discussion, have different children show why they think their line segment is the longest or shortest.
2. After the children have had time to experiment with making angles on the geoboard, ask them to make an angle with the fewest number of degrees. Have different children show why their angle contains fewest degrees. Will you accept an angle of 0°?
3. Make an angle with the greatest number of degrees. Will you accept an angle that a child says contains 390°?
4. Make an acute angle that contains the greatest number of degrees.
5. Make an obtuse angle that will contain the greatest number of degrees. Does a 360° angle fit the request?
6. After making open and closed curves, make a closed curve that has the greatest interior.

Make a closed curve that has the smallest interior.

Tangrams are excellent for children to work with in developing concepts of spatial relations. A set of tangrams has seven pieces that fit together as shown:

The seven pieces can be put together in hundreds of different ways. Often it is useful to give the students an outline of a figure and ask them to put the seven pieces inside the outline. Tangrams can help teach children about whole-part relationships, spatial relationships, congruence, similarity, perimeter, and area.

Mira Math is another excellent device to use in introducing geometry. A Mira is a red plastic device that has a reflective quality as well as a transparent quality. This device is especially helpful in studying transformational geometry. Reflections, rotations, slides, and flips can easily be demonstrated with a Mira. The device can be used for constructions as well as for the study of symmetry, congruence, line segments, angles, geometric shapes, and other geometric concepts, like parallel and perpendicular lines.

Consult the Mira Math teacher's manual for detailed instructions for teaching geometry with this unique device.

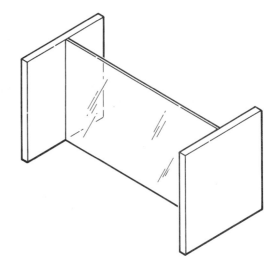

Terminology, Symbols, and Procedures

Acute angle   An acute angle is any angle that is less than a right angle. An acute angle has a measure of less than 90°.

Adjacent angles   Any two angles with a common vertex and a common ray (side) between them are called adjacent angles.

Angle   An angle is the union of two rays that have a common end point. If $\overrightarrow{AB}$ and $\overrightarrow{AC}$ are rays, then their union is an angle, which can be denoted by ∠BAC or ∠CAB.

Closed curve   A closed curve is a curve that returns to its starting point.

Complementary angles   Two angles are complementary angles if the sum of their measures is equal to the measure of a right angle (90°).

Congruent   Two angles whose measures are equal are said to be congruent. They are called congruent angles.

Geometry   Geometry is the study of space and shapes in space.

Line   The term *line* is an undefined term in geometry. Intuitively, a line is the figure one obtains by extending a line segment through each of its end points so that the figure extends endlessly in each of two opposite directions. If A and B are any two points on a line, then the line can be denoted by $\overleftrightarrow{AB}$ or $\overleftrightarrow{BA}$.

Line segment A segment can be thought of as a set of points that forms the shortest path between two points. The segment from point A to point B can be denoted by $\overset{\bullet-\bullet}{AB}$ or $\overset{\bullet-\bullet}{BA}$. Points A and B are called the end points of the line segment.

Obtuse angle An obtuse angle is any angle that has a measure between 90° and 180°.

Perpendicular Two lines that intersect at 90° or at right angles are said to be perpendicular.

Plane A plane is an undefined concept in geometry. It can be thought of as the set of points suggested by a flat surface extending endlessly in the directions established by any portion of the surface.

Point A point in geometry is undefined. A geometric point is considered to be a particular location in geometric space. A point does not have length, width, or depth. A point can be pictured by a small dot. We name points with capital letters.

Ray A subset of a line formed by a given point on the line and all points on the line extending in one direction from the given point is called a ray. The given point is called the end point of the ray. If C is the end point of a ray that passes through a second point D, then the ray can be denoted by $\overset{\bullet\longrightarrow}{CD}$.

Right angle If a given line is intersected by another line so that the two angles formed on one side of the given line are congruent, then the two angles are said to be right angles. The measure of a right angle is 90°.

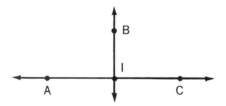

For example, if $m(\angle AIB) = m(\angle BIC)$, then $\angle AIB$ and $\angle BIC$ are both right angles.

Sides of an angle The two rays that form an angle are called the sides of the angle.

Simple closed curve A simple closed curve is a closed curve that does not cross itself at any point. Any simple closed curve divides a plane into three sets of points:

1. The set of points composing the simple closed curve.
2. The set of points composing the interior of the closed curve.
3. The set of points composing the exterior of the closed curve.

Simple closed region The union of a simple closed curve and its interior is called a simple closed region.

Space   Space is considered to be the set of all points (locations).

Supplementary angles   Two angles are supplementary angles if the sum of their measures is equal to the measure of a straight angle (180°).

Vertex   The vertex of an angle is the common end point of the rays that form the angle.

Practice Exercises

Obtain or make a geoboard (see page 471) and perform the following exercises.

1. Use rubber bands with a geoboard to make some line segments.

2. Make some open curves and some curves that are not open.

3. Make the following types of angles on the geoboard:
   a) an acute angle
   b) a right angle
   c) an obtuse angle
   d) a pair of adjacent angles
   e) supplementary angles

4. Show two perpendicular line segments.

5. a) Draw a model of a point. Name it A. How many lines can be drawn through point A?
   b) Draw a model for another point about 5 centimeters from point A. Name the second point B. Draw line segment AB. How many line segments can be drawn between points A and B?

6. a) Make a tracing of angle PEN. Name your angle P'E'N'. Use a compass and straight-edge and bisect angle P'E'N'. Since both angles have the same measure, we say that the two angles are _____.

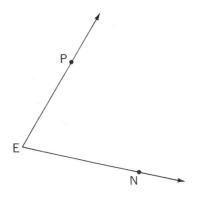

   b) Since angle PEN has a measure less than 90°, we would say that ∠PEN is an _____
      _____ angle.

7. Write the number of degrees in the complementary angle of each angle named below.

a) $m(\angle MAC) = 25°$ d) $m(\angle LOT) = 73°$
b) $m(\angle DEC) = 45°$ e) $m(\angle HAT) = 3°$
c) $m(\angle CAT) = 80°$ f) $m(\angle CAP) = 86°$

8. Write the number of degrees in the supplemental angle of each angle named below.

a) $m(\angle NOT) = 40°$ d) $m(\angle LOW) = 170°$
b) $m(\angle TOP) = 90°$ e) $m(\angle INA) = 45°$
c) $m(\angle BUT) = 150°$ f) $m(\angle SAC) = 109°$

9. Make a drawing that represents an acute angle, labeling it $\angle XYZ$. Construct an angle congruent to $\angle XYZ$, and label it $\angle X'Y'Z'$.

10. Identify the geometric concept suggested by each drawing below. If the figure can be represented by a symbol, write the symbol.

a)

b)

c)

d)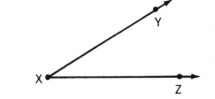

e)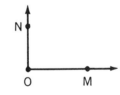

f)

g)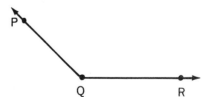

h)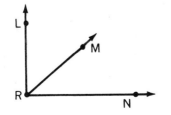

i)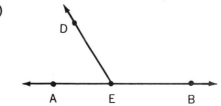

11. Tell whether each statement is true or false.

a) Line segments, rays, and angles are sets of points.
b) A line is an infinite set of points.
c) A line segment is a finite set of points.
d) The union of two adjacent angles is an angle.
e) Two perpendicular lines form four right angles.
f) If you make diagrams to represent two lines, $\overleftrightarrow{AB}$ and $\overleftrightarrow{CD}$, and the pencil lines do not cross in the diagram, then the two lines cannot intersect.
g) If two angles are supplementary angles, then they are also adjacent angles.

12. Name all the line segments marked in this picture.

Discussion Questions

1. Research the literature and learn about Mira Math. Make a presentation to your class. Compare and contrast Mira Math with traditional techniques for teaching geometry.

2. Discuss the merits of creating a geometric interest center in the classroom.

3. Examine elementary mathematics textbooks to find out what percent of each program is devoted to geometry. Is the geometric segment of these mathematics programs adequate or should it be increased or decreased?

4. Discuss how the overhead projector can be used to teach geometry to children.

5. Since the child's world is three-dimensional (blocks, balls, etc.), should a geometry program begin with solid geometry and then move to plane geometry?

6. Research the literature and then discuss the merits of using geoboards to teach geometry.

7. Compare and contrast Euclidean geometry with transformational geometry.

8. Why is the study of geometry essential for elementary school children?

Activities for the Primary Grades

Most of today's teachers were introduced to geometry at the secondary level in a traditional geometry course that utilized formal proof. It is difficult for us to realize that many basic ideas of geometry have a place in the elementary school curriculum. However, children can usually comprehend simple geometric concepts at this level.

The concepts of this unit have been presented to you as abstractions, but it is clear that young children cannot work easily with the abstract notions of point, line, line segment, and so on. Any consideration of these concepts at the primary level should be based on the child's intuitive understanding of the concepts and not on textbook descriptions or formal characterizations by means of axioms or postulates. An intuitive approach to geometry permits you to use a wealth of activities that can be exciting and mathematically sound. In presenting geometric concepts, it is important to consider the maturity, coordination, and attention span of children.

BASIC GEOMETRIC CONCEPTS

1. Provide the children with large sheets of construction paper, flattened straws, and paste. Have them arrange the straws in various geometrical patterns and paste them on the construction paper. Colored string or yard can be dipped in paste and arranged on construction paper in the same way.

2. Copy and distribute "Join the Dots" puzzles. These puzzles involve joining dots in consecutive order (by number) to obtain a picture. These puzzles are very useful in developing visual awareness of shapes.

3. Use large sheets of squared paper and let children trace over the lines on the paper to invent pictures made up of line segments.

4. Use any other easy-to-obtain, inexpensive materials you can think of that will give children experiences in forming simple figures: use toothpicks, drinking straws, pipe cleaners, and so on.

5. Some first graders have sufficient motor development to be able to work with a geoboard. Show the children how different shapes and lines can be modeled on the geoboard. Provide time for the children to experiment with the boards.

6. Children will enjoy working with tangrams and simple designs. First allow the children to become acquainted with the materials through free play. Provide the children with some simple designs, and ask them to place the tangrams inside the outline provided. Teachers can relate this activity to putting materials back into their storage boxes. In this type of activity, space relations (as defined by Piaget) are important for young children.

7. Some children will have the motor development to start drawing line segments with the aid of a straightedge. They may enjoy drawing angles of different types.

8. Have two children sit so that they cannot observe each other. Provide both children with identical sets of blocks. As one child builds with the blocks, he or she is to describe what is being built and give instructions to the other child to imitate; for example, "Place a cube in front of you, place a triangle on top of the cube, place the ball to the left of the cube. . . ." After all the blocks have been used, compare the two displays of blocks to see if they are alike.

9. Teachers should provide many opportunities for children to use vocabulary that has to do with location or position. Place a box on a table and have the children follow directions such as, "Place a sheet of paper under the box, place the doll behind the box, place a comb in the box, place a pencil to the side of the box . . ." and so forth.

Hand-Held Calculator Activities for the Primary Grades

Since this is a non-metric geometry unit, no activities are suggested for the hand-held calculator.

Microcomputer Activities for the Primary Grades

1. Big Track is a tank with a built-in computer. The tank can be programmed to complete simple tasks. It can be purchased in most toy stores. Obtain Big Track and allow the children to observe how it moves. Have the children sit on the floor in the shape of a circle. Place Big Track in front of the teacher, and have a discussion about it. Program Big Track so it will move to the center of the circle, turn toward a previously selected student, and then move toward her, stopping in front of her. Have that student program Big Track so it will use the same procedure, moving toward and stopping in front of another child. Continue the process until the children become proficient.

2. Big Track should be available in a work space during work time. Young children can become very effective programmers of Big Track. It provides an opportunity for children to experiment on the concrete level.

3. The BASIC language is not as effective as LOGO for activities in the primary grades. Use LOGO for drawing basic geometric shapes. Children's functioning has now moved from the concrete to the semiconcrete level. Children can learn to give commands such as FOR-WARD, BACK, RIGHT, and LEFT to direct a turtle around a microcomputer screen. Children must develop their language skills as they develop their programming skills. Should the basic word list for language arts programs be revised in view of the new computer world for children?

4. Have children dramatize what they want the LOGO turtle to do. Soon children will associate their own movements with the movements of the turtle.

5. Seat the children on the floor in the shape of a square. Provide each child with different models of squares, and discuss the figures with the children. After the children have developed a clear mental image of a square, have them try to draw a square on the video screen. Use the children's suggestions as a trial-and-error period. The final program should look something like this:

SQUARE
FORWARD 50
LEFT 90
FORWARD 50
LEFT 90
FORWARD 50
LEFT 90
FORWARD 50

6. Seat the children on the floor in the shape of a triangle. Provide the children with models of triangles so they can manipulate them. Discuss the necessary characteristics of a triangle. Ask a child to walk, using the shape of a triangle. Request that the children

experiment by drawing a triangle on the video screen. The completed program should look something like this:

TRIANGLE
FORWARD 50
RIGHT 120
FORWARD 50
RIGHT 120
FORWARD 50

Activities for the Intermediate Grades

BASIC GEOMETRIC CONCEPTS

1. Begin with a question to promote discussion. For example:
   "I'm thinking of a certain point on the chalkboard. How could I show you the point?" The usual response will be, "Make a dot with the chalk." If this is the reaction, show children a sheet of paper with a tiny pinhole. Then make a large dot on the chalkboard. This may stimulate some of the faster-thinking pupils to make a mental comparison. Direct their thinking toward the idea of a geometric point by encouraging this comparison of physical representations.

2. Draw two dots on the chalkboard. Ask which dot is larger. Then ask which dot is the better representation of a geometric point, and why.

3. Children enjoy drawing some of the many possible paths between two points and creating stories about the path from one point to the other. For example:

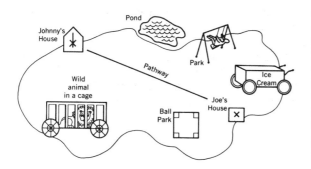

Johnny started to walk to his friend Joe's house. He walked by the pond and saw Arthur fishing. He stopped in the park to play on the swings for a while. Then he passed the ice cream man, but he didn't have any money with him so he couldn't buy anything. He went on to Joe's house, but Joe wasn't home, so Johnny decided to go back home the shortest way possible. Which path did Johnny take?

This is obviously a simplified situation. Children have the imagination to create much more involved and complex stories.

4. How many different objects can you think of that could be models of line segments? A pencil could be one model. What others can you think of?
   Which of the objects that you named are the best models of line segments? Is a pencil a better model than a tree? Why? Can you make a mark with your pencil that is a better picture of a line segment than the mark you make with your crayon?

5. Draw two dots on the chalkboard and connect them.

●━━━━━━━━━━━━━━━━━━━━━●

Ask whether the line could be longer or shorter and still connect the points. Lead the children to think about a "part of a line" in comparison with a "line." Draw a dot with a line through the point represented by the dot. Ask whether any other lines could be drawn through this point. Have children give you directions until the idea is established that there are infinitely many lines that can be drawn through the point.

At this grade level it may be easier for children to think of a line segment as a "part of a line" and end points as a "starting point" and an "ending point." Children should be allowed to use the vocabulary that is easiest for them in describing concepts. Also, they should be provided with a strip of cardboard to use as a straightedge. Since coordination varies considerably in children of this age, some children will have difficulty drawing line segments neatly.

Have children use cardboard straightedges to draw line segment AB.

  A •   • B

6. With the use of a straightedge and a pencil that is well sharpened, have the children draw angles. Some activities that can be used in drawing angles are:
   a) How many different kinds of right angles can you draw? Children will respond that ⌐ is a different kind of right angle than ∟. They need to place many right angles on top of each other to realize that there is only one type of right angle.
   b) How many different acute angles can you draw? Children should begin to realize that there is an infinite number.
   c) How many different obtuse angles can you draw?

7. Use a geoboard and make an angle with the greatest number of degrees possible. Compare different models and discuss which fits the criteria. Make an angle with the fewest possible degrees using the geoboard.

8. Use the geoboard and show open and closed curves. Examine each model made by the children and discuss why is it an open or closed curve.

9. Provide the children with many drawings of curves and ask them to classify all of the drawings either as open or closed.

10. Make many different curves on a geoboard and have the children tell whether they are simple closed curves or not.

11. Have the children reproduce on paper specific patterns displayed on a geoboard. Can children observe and reproduce a specific design? Children who cannot reproduce the pattern should be allowed to trace over the rubber bands on the geoboard.

12. The following can be used successfully as a group activity. Give directions orally. Draw a picture of line segment AB, with A and B as end points.

            •   •
            A   B

Draw a longer line segment, but keep A as one end point.

            ●━━━━━━━━━━━━━━●
            A   B

Place an arrow at the end of the line segment that goes through point B. What does the arrow mean?

13. This is a picture of line segment AB. Draw ray AB.

14. This is a picture of line segment CD. Draw ray DC.

15. a) Mark two points on your paper. Name the points E and F. Draw line segment EF.
b) Mark two points on your paper. Name the points G and H. Draw line GH.
c) Mark one point on your paper and name it N. Draw a ray having N as the end point.

16. Mark a point on your paper and name it S. Draw a ray having S as the end point. Draw another ray having S as the end point. Describe your drawing.

17. How would you describe this picture? Does the figure have an inside and an outside? Label the inside and the outside.

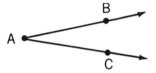

18. Draw pictures of four different angles on your paper. How many points will you need to mark to name each angle?

19. How would you describe this picture?

How many things can you find in your classroom that are models of this figure?

20. Study the following diagram carefully.

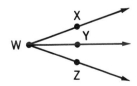

How many angles are pictured in this diagram?

Hand-Held Calculator Activities for the Intermediate Grades

Since this is a non-metric geometry unit, no activities are suggested for the hand-held calculator.

Microcomputer Activities for the Intermediate Grades

1. All microcomputer activities suggested for the primary grades can be easily adapted for the intermediate grades.

2. Obtain a software package for the LOGO language that is compatible with your microcomputer. Introduce the command TO. TO BOX should cause the computer to draw a square. Now draw two squares. Try this program:

To pinwheel
REPEAT 4(BOX)
End

We will use an asterisk (*) preceding the name of every entry. Try this program:

*PENS
REPEAT 2(*SQUARE)

Now try these programs:

REPEAT 3(*SQUARE)   REPEAT 4(*SQUARE)

3. Children in the intermediate grades who have learned to program in BASIC can easily learn to draw geometric figures on the screen. The first step is to learn to draw a line on the screen. Graphics capabilities vary a great deal among the popular microcomputers in the schools. Let's first examine the procedure for drawing a line on the TRS-80 microcomputer. A horizontal line might be drawn using these three statements:

```
10 FOR OVER = 10 TO 130
20 SET(OVER, 30)
30 NEXT OVER
```

After allowing the children to practice drawing horizontal lines, have them experiment by drawing vertical lines. How would you draw a diagonal line? Experiment!

4. Using a TRS-80, how do you create a program to draw a rectangle clockwise? (After the children master this task, ask them to program the computer to draw a rectangle counterclockwise.)

```
10   CLS
20   FOR OVER = 15 TO 112
30   SET(OVER, 10)
40   NEXT OVER
50   FOR DOWN = 10 TO 38
60   SET(112,DOWN)
70   NEXT DOWN
80   FOR OVER = 112 TO 15 STEP −1
```

```
90   SET(OVER, 38)
100  NEXT OVER
110  FOR DOWN = 38 TO 10 STEP −1
120  SET(15,DOWN)
130  NEXT DOWN
```

5. Students using Atari microcomputers must first change to a graphics screen and then learn to use the PLOT command to move the cursor and the DRAWTO command to draw lines. Diagonal lines on the Atari Graphics screen 3 are difficult to use for drawing triangles that look like triangles.

Activities for the Upper Elementary Grades

BASIC GEOMETRIC CONCEPTS

The beginning activities for Grade 4 will depend on how much background children have had in geometry. It is also advisable to review activities like those for Grades 2 and 3 to determine how much students know about geometry and to give the students practice.

1. Draw a large dot on the chalkboard. Then ask the following questions for class discussion.

   a) Is this a point? If I erase the chalk mark, does the point move?
   b) How many points are covered by a dot you make with a pencil?
   c) Does a big dot represent a larger point than a small dot?
   d) Did you ever see a real point?

2. Draw a representation of a line and of a line segment on the chalkboard. Then use the following questions for class discussion.

   a) What is a line?
   b) What is a line segment?
   c) How many end points does a line have?
   d) How many end points does a line segment have?
   e) Can you find three objects in the room that are examples of line segments?

3. Name all the different line segments you can find in this figure. One is $\overline{AC}$.

4. Name all the line segments you see represented in this figure.

5. Draw two line segments each having point A as one end point. Draw three line segments each having point A as one end point. How many different line segments can you draw each having A as an end point?

6. Show another way to name each line segment.

$$\overline{AB} \quad \overline{AC} \quad \overline{CB} \quad \overline{CD} \quad \overline{AE} \quad \overline{CA} \quad \overline{EF} \quad \overline{DC} \quad \overline{FB}$$

7. Draw a dot on your paper and label it point A.

 a) Use your straightedge to draw one line through point A.
 b) Draw a different line through point A.
 c) Draw three more lines through point A.
 d) Using the letters B, C, D, E, and F, label one point other than point A on each of these lines.
 e) Can you draw still more lines through point A?

8. Use your straightedge and pencil to help you answer the following questions.

 a) How many line segments can you draw having end points A and B?
 b) How many line segments can you draw that are extensions of $\overline{AB}$?
 c) How many lines contain both A and B?
 d) Is a line segment all of a line?
 e) Is a line segment part of a line?
 f) Is a line part of a line segment?

9. Find twenty different names for the line represented below.

10. Draw a picture of a line on your paper. Let A be a point on this line.
 a) Choose a point on the line different from A and label it B.
 b) Choose another point on the line in the opposite direction from A and label it C.
 c) Name two rays that are part of this line and have A as an end point.
 d) Are there any more rays on this line that have A as an end point?

11. Mark a point on your paper and label it A.

 a) Draw one ray having end point A.
 b) Draw another ray having end point A.
 c) Draw four more rays having end point A.
 d) How many rays are there having A as an end point?

12. Name all the angles you can find in the figure below.

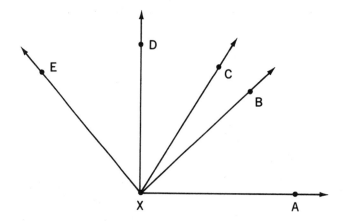

Do five different rays with a common end point always form this same number of angles? Explain.

13. Without using your protractor, tell whether the angles shown are acute angles or obtuse angles.

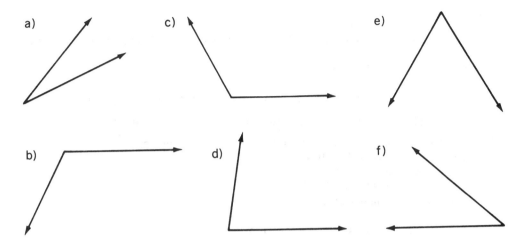

a) c) e)

b) d) f)

14. Use your protractor and draw angles with the following measures.

a) 35° b) 160° c) 90° d) 33° e) 179°

15. Use your compass to draw a circle. Then mark 5 points on the circle. How many line segments can you draw using pairs of these 5 points as end points?

16. a) Draw a line on a sheet of paper; mark a point on the line and label it A. Now mark a point not on the line and label it B. Draw ray AB. Use your compass and straightedge to bisect each of the two adjacent angles.

b) Measure the angle formed by the rays which are the bisectors. What is the measure of the angle? If you had marked point B in a different position, what would be the measure of the angle formed by the two bisectors?

Hand-Held Calculator Activities for the Upper Elementary Grades

Since this unit is a non-metric geometry unit, no activities are suggested for the hand-held calculator.

Microcomputer Activities for the Upper Elementary Grades

1. All microcomputer activities suggested for the primary and intermediate grades can be easily adapted for the upper elementary grades.

2. PILOT is a language that has an exciting approach to programming and graphics. It permits teachers to create their own educational software, related specifically to their

instructional style. Teachers of the intermediate and upper elementary grades are encouraged to study the PILOT language for use with teaching children.

3. Use the microcomputer activities suggested for the intermediate grades to experiment drawing horizontal and vertical lines on the video screen. Have the children use the TRS-80 to draw lines on the diagonal.

4. Have the children experiment drawing triangles on the TRS-80 video screen.

5. Using the Atari Graphics screen 8, it should be easy for children to write a program to draw a triangle on the screen.

6. Children can learn to program the Apple computer so it will display simple geometric shapes on the screen.

Suggested Readings

Aman, George. "Discovery on a Geoboard." *The Arithmetic Teacher,* vol. 17. no. 4, April 1974.

Brydegaard, Marguerite, and Inskeep, James E., Jr. *Readings in Geometry from the Arithmetic Teacher.* Reston, Va.: National Council of Teachers of Mathematics, 1970.

Jenkins, Lee, and McLean, Peggy. *It's a Tangram World.* San Leandro, Calif.: Educational Consultants, 1972.

Kerr, D. R., Jr. "The Study of Space Experiences: A Framework for Geometry for Elementary Teachers." *The Arithmetic Teacher,* vol. 23, no. 3, February 1976.

Lesh, Richard, ed. *Recent Research Concerning the Development of Spatial and Geometric Concepts.* Columbus, Ohio: ERIC Science, Mathematics and Environmental Education Clearinghouse, May 1978.

O'Daffer, Phares, "Geometry: What Shape for a Comprehensive, Balanced Curriculum?" In *Selected Issues in Mathematics Education.* 1981 Yearbook of the National Society for the Study of Education. Berkeley, Calif.: McCutchan, 1981.

Payne, Joseph N., ed. *Mathematics Learning in Early Childhood: Thirty-Seventh Yearbook.* National Council of Teachers of Mathematics. Reston, Va.: NCTM, 1975.

Piaget, Jean, and Inhelder, Barbel. *The Child's Conception of Geometry.* New York: Harper Torchbooks (Harper & Row), 1964.

Seymour, Dale. *Tangramath.* Palo Alto, Calif.: Creative Publications, 1971.

Wells, Peter. "Creating Mathematics with a Geoboard." *The Arithmetic Teacher,* vol. 17, no. 4, April 1970.

15 More Geometry

Teaching Competencies

Upon completing this unit, you will be able to:

Identify simple closed curves in the plane

Classify polygons according to the number of sides they contain

Classify triangles according to the measures of their angles and according to the measures of their sides

Calculate perimeters and areas of squares, rectangles, parallelograms, and triangles

Calculate the circumference and area of a circle, given its radius or diameter

Apply the Pythagorean theorem to find the length of any side of a right triangle, given the measures of the other two sides

State the basic concepts of transformational geometry

Recognize and classify space figures such as prisms, pyramids, cylinders, cones, and spheres

Use mathematical notation to name the parts of any given prism or pyramid

Calculate the volume and lateral area of a prism, given the necessary information about the base and height of the prism

Discussion

In Unit 13 we discussed measurement, and in Unit 14 we considered basic geometry. In this unit we will expand upon geometric concepts and then relate measurement to geometry. We are now ready to use the fundamental concepts developed in Unit 14 to examine a variety of geometric figures and relations based upon information we have already studied.

Simple closed curves composed of three or more line segments (referred to as sides) are called **polygons.** ("Poly-" comes from the Greek word "polys," meaning "many"; and "-gon" comes from the Greek word "gonia," meaning "angle.") The figures represented below are polygons.

Polygons are simple closed curves formed by the union of three or more line segments that lie in the same plane and touch only at their endpoints. Remember that a line segment is a particular kind of curve.

Polygons have special names according to the number of sides they have. A three-sided polygon, for example, is called a **triangle.** The following table names the more familiar kinds of polygons. We present this table to illustrate techniques used for naming polygons. Do *not* require children to memorize all these names, only those names that are appropriate for your children.

The prefixes listed in this table are the same prefixes that are used to name all plane and solid geometric figures. From this point on only several geometric shapes will be named, and it will be left to the student to use the given prefixes and to generate the additional geometric names needed.

Each student should have his or her own geoboard with a supply of rubber bands. As each of the different geometric shapes are discussed, the student should be given ample opportunity to experiment and make them on the geoboard. Few children *or* college students have enough experience creating polygons themselves. After students have each constructed a certain polygon, compare them and see how many different ways the polygon can be made on a geoboard.

Number of Sides	Prefix	Name of Polygon	Name of Region
3	tri-	triangle	triangular region
4	quad-	quadri-lateral	quadrilateral region
5	penta-	pentagon	pentagonal region
6	hexa-	hexagon	hexagonal region
7	hepta-	heptagon	heptagonal region
8	octa-	octagon	octagonal region
9	nona-	nonagon	nonagonal region
10	deca-	decagon	decagonal region
11	undeca-	undecagon	undecagonal region
12	dodeca-	dodecagon	dodecagonal region
.	.	.	.
.	.	.	.
.	.	.	.
many	poly-	polygon	polygonal region

A **pentagon** is a polygon with five sides. It is five line segments lying in a plane and forming a simple closed curve.

Pentagon ABCDE

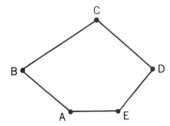

If each of the five line segments has the same length and each of the angles formed has the same measure, the figure formed is called a regular pentagon. Children are probably familiar with the Pentagon Building across the Potomac from Washington, D.C.

A **hexagon** is a polygon with six sides. It is six line segments lying in a plane and forming a simple closed curve.

Hexagon ABCDEF

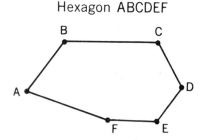

If the sides of a hexagon are all congruent (that is, of equal length) and the angles formed are all equal in measure, the figure is said to be a regular hexagon. The heads of bolts are often hexagonal.

An **octagon** is a polygon with eight sides. It is eight line segments lying in a plane and forming a simple closed curve.

Octagon ABCDEFGH

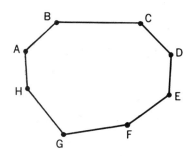

An octagon with all sides equal in length and all angles equal in measure is a regular octagon.

If all the sides of a polygon are congruent (that is, have the same length) and all its angles are of equal measure, it is a **regular** polygon. Since segments with the same length are congruent, and angles with the same measure are congruent, we can say that a regular polygon is a polygon with congruent sides and congruent angles. If the sides of a polygon are not all congruent or if the angles are not all equal in measure, it is an **irregular** polygon. Some examples of regular and irregular polygons are shown below.

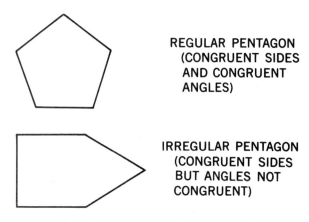

REGULAR PENTAGON (CONGRUENT SIDES AND CONGRUENT ANGLES)

IRREGULAR PENTAGON (CONGRUENT SIDES BUT ANGLES NOT CONGRUENT)

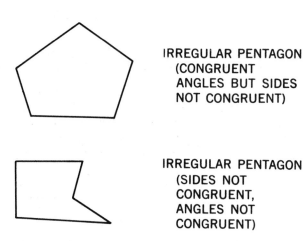

IRREGULAR PENTAGON (CONGRUENT ANGLES BUT SIDES NOT CONGRUENT)

IRREGULAR PENTAGON (SIDES NOT CONGRUENT, ANGLES NOT CONGRUENT)

REGULAR HEXAGON

IRREGULAR HEXAGON

REGULAR OCTAGON

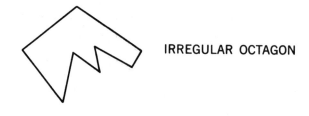

IRREGULAR OCTAGON

We will now consider two kinds of polygons: triangles and quadrilaterals. Mark any three points that are not on the same line, and connect the three points with line segments. The figure formed is a triangle. Let's look at triangles in detail.

We have said that an angle is two rays that have a common end point but do not lie on the same line.

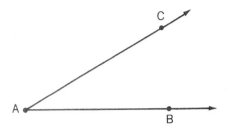

In the diagram above, the two rays, $\overrightarrow{AB}$ and $\overrightarrow{AC}$, determine the angle CAB (or angle BAC). This can be written as ∠CAB (or ∠BAC). Now suppose that B is selected as the end point of another ray that passes through (or contains) point C. Then extend $\overrightarrow{BA}$ with B as an end point.

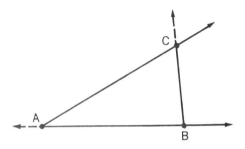

Clearly we have formed another angle. What can we name this angle whose vertex is point B? We can name it ∠CBA or ∠ABC.

A **closed plane region** is a set of points in one plane that is bounded by a closed curve (not necessarily a simple closed curve). The boundary of the closed plane region formed in the diagram above is a triangle. The triangles discussed in this unit are all plane triangles (that is, each triangle is considered to lie entirely within a plane).

Color the following triangle, △ABC (read "triangle ABC").

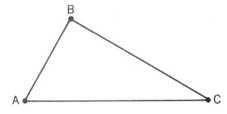

When you colored △ABC, you should have colored only the line segments—$\overline{AB}$, $\overline{BC}$, and $\overline{CA}$—since it is the union of line segments that forms a triangle. If you were to color the triangular region bounded by $\overline{AB}$, $\overline{BC}$, and $\overline{AC}$, you would color both the line segments (the sides) and the interior of △ABC. When we use the term "triangle," we mean only the set of

points that compose the closed curve. When we use the term "triangular region," we mean the union of the closed curve and the interior.

A triangle, then, can be seen as the boundary of a particular kind of closed plane region. A triangle partitions, or separates, a plane into three sets of points:

1. The set of points that make up the line segments forming the sides of the triangle.
2. The set of points that make up the interior of the triangle.
3. The set of points that make up the exterior of the triangle.

Since the sides of a triangle are line segments and a triangle is formed by three line segments, a triangle is a particular kind of simple closed curve. (A simple closed curve, remember, is a curve that returns to its initial point and does not cross itself.)

The vertices of a triangle determine three lines in the same plane, none of which is parallel to another. (**Parallel lines** are lines in the same plane. Clearly, two lines that intersect are not parallel.)

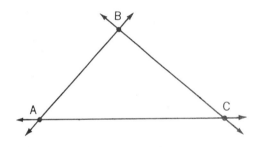

In the above diagram, how many points of intersection do you see? (Three: points A, B, and C.) The three points of intersection determine three line segments: $\overline{AB}$, $\overline{AC}$, and $\overline{CB}$.

Now let's take a closer look at the triangle we've been studying. In the drawing above, the three points of intersection are A, B, and C. What are the names of the three lines whose intersection determines these points? ($\overleftrightarrow{AB}$, $\overleftrightarrow{AC}$, and $\overleftrightarrow{BC}$.) What do we call the set of points that extends endlessly from the initial point A through point B? (Ray AB.) Is there another ray we can name that has A as its initial point? (Yes: $\overrightarrow{AC}$.) What do we call the set of points named by the union of these two rays? (Angle BAC.) From the information given, can you name two rays that have B as a common end point? (Yes: $\overrightarrow{BC}$ and $\overrightarrow{BA}$.) What angle does the union of these two rays name? (∠ABC.) Is there another angle we can name? (Yes: ∠BCA.)

Now let's examine the triangle below.

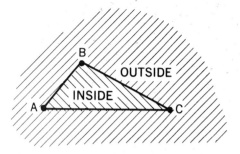

What do we call the part of the line that has A and B as end points? (Line segment AB.) Do you see other line segments? (Yes: $\overset{\bullet\!-\!\bullet}{BC}$ and $\overset{\bullet\!-\!\bullet}{AC}$.) What are some generalizations that we can make about triangles?

1. A triangle is a simple closed curve.
2. A triangle is made up of three line segments.

   For example, $\triangle ABC = \overset{\bullet\!-\!\bullet}{AB}, \overset{\bullet\!-\!\bullet}{AC}, \overset{\bullet\!-\!\bullet}{BC}$.
3. A triangle is made up of only those points that are elements of one or more of the three line segments that make up the triangle. In the drawing above, only those points forming $\overset{\bullet\!-\!\bullet}{AB}$, $\overset{\bullet\!-\!\bullet}{AC}$, and $\overset{\bullet\!-\!\bullet}{BC}$ are elements of $\triangle ABC$.
4. A triangle has an inside (or interior) and an outside (or exterior). The points forming the inside and outside, however, are not elements of the triangle itself.

Consider triangle ABC; if we take B as the common end point of two rays ($\overset{\longrightarrow}{BC}$ and $\overset{\longrightarrow}{AB}$) formed by extending line segments BC and BA indefinitely, we form $\angle ABC$. Notice that the inside of the triangle suggests three angles. Because we have defined an angle as the union of two rays with a common end point and because a triangle is made up of three line segments, we can say that any two line segments of a triangle "suggest," or "represent," an angle. The three angles suggested by $\triangle ABC$ are $\angle ABC$, $\angle ACB$, and $\angle BAC$. These are called the angles of $\triangle ABC$.

Since every triangle is made up of three line segments (called sides), we can name certain kinds of triangles according to the relations between the sides.

Equilateral Triangle: A triangle in which the sides are equal in length is called an equilateral triangle. Line segments that are equal in length are said to be **congruent.** So we can also say that an equilateral triangle is a triangle with three congruent sides.

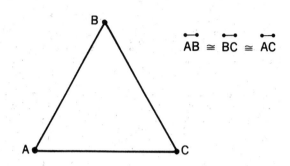

This is read, "Line segment AB is congruent to line segment BC, and line segment BC is congruent to line segment AC."

Isosceles Triangle: A triangle in which at least two sides are congruent (equal in length) is called an isosceles triangle.

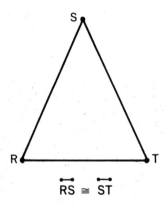

Are all equilateral triangles also isosceles triangles? Yes, because an equilateral triangle has at least two congruent sides.

Scalene Triangle: If no two sides of a triangle are congruent (equal in length), we call the triangle a scalene triangle.

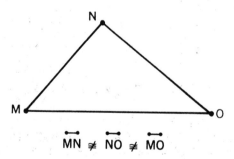

When we describe a triangle as being equilateral, isosceles, or scalene, we are describing it according to the relations that exist among its sides. Now let's see if we can name triangles according to the relations that exist among the angles suggested by the line segments bounding the triangles.

Right Triangle: This is a familiar triangle. You will notice that it has a "square corner," referred to as a 90° angle, or right angle. If one angle of a triangle is a right angle, the triangle is called a right triangle.

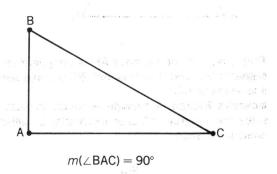

$$m(\angle BAC) = 90°$$

Unfortunately, right triangles are usually drawn on a horizontal base with the right angle on the left. Right triangles should be drawn in many positions. Use an overhead projector with a right triangle drawn on a transparency. After the triangle has been identified, move it to many different positions by rotating or flipping it; explain that it is still a right triangle.

Equiangular Triangle: An equiangular triangle is a triangle whose three angles are congruent.

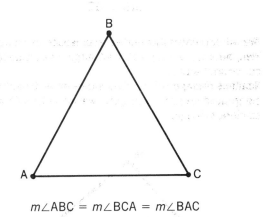

$$m\angle ABC = m\angle BCA = m\angle BAC$$

If we examine any equiangular triangle, we find that not only are its angles all equal in measure but its sides are all congruent. Consequently, any equiangular triangle is also an equilateral triangle.

Acute Triangle: We have learned that an angle with a measure of less than 90° is called an acute angle. If all three of the angles of a triangle are acute, the triangle is called an acute triangle.

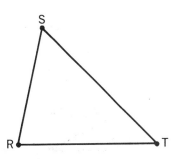

$$m\angle RST < 90°, \; m\angle STR < 90°, \; m\angle TRS < 90°$$

Obtuse Triangle: We have also learned that if an angle has a measure of more than 90° but less than 180°, it is called an obtuse angle. A triangle that has one obtuse angle is called an obtuse triangle.

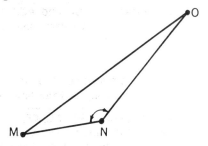

$$m\angle MNO > 90°, \; m\angle NOM < 90°, \; m\angle OMN < 90°$$

To demonstrate why we don't define an obtuse triangle as a triangle having more than one obtuse angle, have the children draw several large triangles on a sheet of paper and then find the measures of the angles of the triangles. After the children have found the measures of the angles for each triangle, ask them to take each triangle separately and add its angle measures. The results here will depend on the accuracy with which the children use their protractors. But generally they will find that the sum of the measures of the angles of a triangle is 180°. Because of inaccuracy in their measurements they may be off a few degrees, but they will be close enough to make the proper generalization. We should be able to generalize that, in any plane triangle ABC, the sum of the measures of the angles is 180°. In mathematical symbols, we can write

$$m\angle A + m\angle B + m\angle C = 180°$$

Now return to the question: Can a triangle have more than one obtuse angle? Remember that an obtuse angle has a measure of more than 90° but less than 180°. In a triangle the sum of the measures of the three angles is 180°. If the measure of one angle is more than 90°, then the sum of the measures of the other two angles must be less than 90°. Consequently the answer to the question is: No, a triangle cannot have more than one obtuse angle.

Children can also discover in another way that the sum of the measures of the angles represented by any triangle is 180°. Have children draw triangles of many different shapes on paper. If they cut these triangles out and tear off the corners

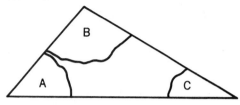

they will discover that the three angles of any one triangle, when placed together as shown here, form a straight line (sometimes thought of as a straight "angle" or an "angle" of 180°).

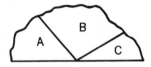

After several trials, children will discover that this is true for any triangle, no matter what its shape or what the measures of the separate angles are.

In Unit 14 we have seen that any three points determine a plane. Since any triangle has three vertices (the point at which two sides of a triangle intersect is called a vertex of the triangle) and since these vertices can be thought of as determining a plane, we can say that any triangle determines a plane. A triangle partitions the plane that it determines into three sets of points:

1. The set of points making up the interior of the triangle.
2. The set of points making up the line segments that form the sides of the triangle.
3. The set of points making up the exterior of the triangle.

These three sets of points put together constitute the plane itself.

Now let's look at the methods of constructing triangles with a straightedge and a compass. A scalene triangle can be constructed simply by using the straightedge to connect any three points not in a straight line, provided that no two of the line segments formed are congruent.

An isosceles triangle can be constructed in the following manner. Draw a line; then take any two points on this line and label them A and B.

Choose any convenient radius on the compass greater than one-half $\overset{\bullet\bullet}{AB}$. Place the point of the com-

pass at point A, and strike an arc on one side of line AB. Using the same compass measure, place the point of the compass at point B and strike an arc that intersects the first arc. Label the intersection of the two arcs point O. Then draw line segments AO and OB.

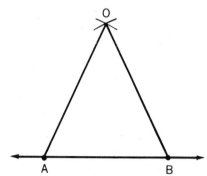

Since $\overset{\bullet\bullet}{AO} \cong \overset{\bullet\bullet}{OB}$, triangle AOB is an isosceles triangle.

Remember that each student should be constructing each of the triangles on a geoboard, as suggested earlier. Another nice device to introduce the children to is the Mira. Mira Math should be used for the children to draw each of the geometric figures suggested in this unit.

An equilateral triangle can be constructed in the following way. Draw a line. Take any two points on this line and label them D and E. Place the point of the compass at point D and measure $\overset{\bullet\bullet}{DE}$ with the compass. Using this compass measure, strike an arc on one side of line DE. Using the same compass measure, place the point of the compass at E and strike an arc that intersects the first arc. Label the point of intersection O, and draw line segments OD and OE.

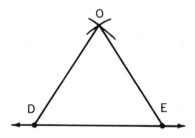

Triangle DOE is clearly an equilateral triangle, since $\overset{\bullet\bullet}{DO} \cong \overset{\bullet\bullet}{OE} \cong \overset{\bullet\bullet}{ED}$.

The ancient Egyptian culture developed an extensive practical use for geometry. The Egyptians used geometry in surveying lands after the annual spring floods of the Nile River. The floods washed away landmarks, and some method of reestablishing boundaries was necessary. Some historians state that one surveying tool used by the Egyptians was a rope with thirteen equally spaced knots. If the first and thirteenth knots are joined and a stake is placed at the fourth, the eighth, and the thirteenth knot, a right triangle is constructed:

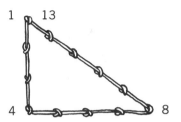

We do know that triangles of this kind were studied by the Greek geometer Pythagoras in the sixth century B.C. His statement on the relation between the sides of right triangles is known as the **Pythagorean theorem.** Consider triangle ABC below, in which $\angle$ACB has the measure of a right angle. In the diagram of this right triangle, we can mark the right angle by making a small square, as shown:

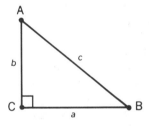

Since we label the vertices of a triangle with capital letters, we will use small letters to name the sides. By custom, the side opposite a given angle is named with the same letter as the angle, but with a small letter. For example, in the diagram above, the side opposite point A is labeled a. The longest side of a right triangle (the side opposite the right angle) is called the hypotenuse. The other two sides are called legs. The Pythagorean theorem states that the square of the measure of one leg of a right triangle plus the square of the measure of the other leg is equal to the square of the measure of the hypotenuse. (Or, alternatively, the square of the measure of the hypotenuse of a right triangle is equal to the sum of the squares of the measures of the other two sides.) Using the drawing above, we can state the theorem of Pythagoras mathematically:

$$a^2 + b^2 = c^2$$
$$\text{or} \quad m(AB)^2 = m(AC)^2 + m(BC)^2$$

Suppose we assign the following unit lengths to the sides of triangle ACB.

$a = 4$ units
$b = 3$ units
$c = 5$ units

Substituting these values in the mathematical statement of the theorem and performing the indicated computation, we can illustrate the Pythagorean theorem:

$$a^2 + b^2 = c^2$$
$$(4 \times 4) + (3 \times 3) = (5 \times 5)$$
$$16 + 9 = 25$$
$$25 = 25$$

There are more than three hundred proofs of the Pythagorean theorem. We will not attempt to give a general proof of this theorem, but we will verify and discuss in detail an example that illustrates the theorem.

Consider right triangle ABC.

Using $\overset{\bullet\!\!\bullet}{AC}$ as one side, construct the square ACMN.

Using $\overset{\bullet\!\!\bullet}{CB}$ as one side, construct the square CBOP.

Using $\overset{\bullet\!\!\bullet}{AB}$ as one side, construct the square ABRS.

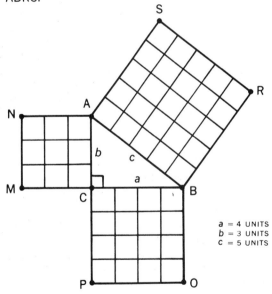

a = 4 UNITS
b = 3 UNITS
c = 5 UNITS

The three square regions we have just constructed are divided into smaller square regions of equal size, as shown in the diagram. The number of small square regions along a particular side of the triangle indicates the length of that side. For example, there are five small square regions along the hypotenuse AB because this side has a length of 5 units. The number of small square regions in a particular square region represents the square (a^2 or b^2) of the length of the side that the particular square region is next to. For example, the hypotenuse AB (named c) has a length of 5 units, so the square (c^2) of the hypotenuse is 25; and the square region ABRS is divided into 25 smaller square regions. It can be observed visually that the number of small squares in square CBOP (16) plus the number of small squares in square ACMN (9) is equal to the number of small squares in square ABRS (25).

$$a^2 + b^2 = c^2$$
$$4^2 + 3^2 = 5^2$$
$$16 + 9 = 25$$
$$25 = 25$$

The regions can be cut out and pasted together to demonstrate even to very young children the physical meaning of the Pythagorean theorem. This kind of verification can be used for any right triangle the lengths of whose sides can be represented by whole numbers.

Now let's examine the following right triangles in light of the Pythagorean theorem.

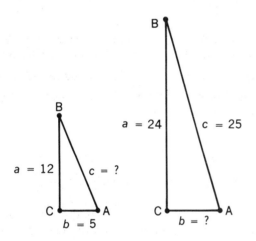

If you know the lengths of the legs of a right triangle, can you find the length of the hypotenuse? Yes, by applying the Pythagorean theorem. And if you know the lengths of the hypotenuse and one of the legs of a right triangle, can you find the length of the other leg? Yes, in the same way.

$a = 12$
$c = 13$
$b = 5$

$$a^2 + b^2 = c^2$$
$$12^2 + 5^2 = c^2$$
$$144 + 25 = c^2$$
$$169 = c^2$$
$$c = 13$$

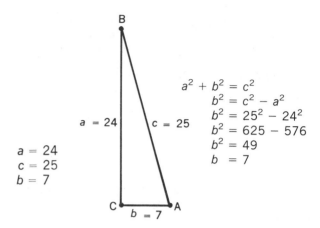

$a = 24$
$c = 25$
$b = 7$

$$a^2 + b^2 = c^2$$
$$b^2 = c^2 - a^2$$
$$b^2 = 25^2 - 24^2$$
$$b^2 = 625 - 576$$
$$b^2 = 49$$
$$b = 7$$

The term "congruent" was defined earlier with respect to angles. Now let's see how we can apply the concept of triangles. **Congruent triangles** are defined as triangles that have the same size and shape. That is, their corresponding sides are congruent and their corresponding angles are congruent. We define **similar triangles** as triangles that have the same shape but not necessarily the same size. Only the corresponding angles are congruent; the corresponding sides can have different lengths.

Compare the three triangles pictured below.

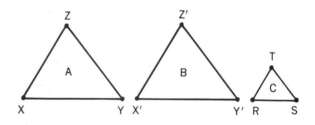

In the triangles pictured, the corresponding sides are as follows:

$\overline{XZ}$ corresponds to $\overline{X'Z'}$ corresponds to $\overline{RT}$
$\overline{YZ}$ corresponds to $\overline{Y'Z'}$ corresponds to $\overline{ST}$
$\overline{XY}$ corresponds to $\overline{X'Y'}$ corresponds to $\overline{RS}$

Triangle A is congruent to triangle B because the corresponding sides of triangles A and B are congruent and the corresponding angles are congruent. Triangle C is similar to triangles A and B because it has the same shape but not the same size. The angles of triangle C are congruent to the corresponding angles of triangle B (and triangle A), but the corresponding sides are not congruent (that is, they do not have the same length). We can express these relations in the following manner.

Triangle A is congruent to triangle B.

$$\triangle A \cong \triangle B$$

Therefore

$m(\overset{\leftrightarrow}{XZ}) = m(\overset{\leftrightarrow}{X'Z'})$ $m\angle X = m\angle X'$

$m(\overset{\leftrightarrow}{XY}) = m(\overset{\leftrightarrow}{X'Y'})$ $m\angle Y = m\angle Y'$

$m(\overset{\leftrightarrow}{YZ}) = m(\overset{\leftrightarrow}{Y'Z'})$ $m\angle Z = m\angle Z'$

Triangle C is similar to triangle B.

$\triangle C \sim \triangle B$ (The symbol $\sim$ means "is similar to.")

Therefore

$$m\angle X' = m\angle R$$
$$m\angle Y' = m\angle S$$
$$m\angle Z' = m\angle T$$

Let's compare the similar triangles ABC and DEF pictured in the following diagram.

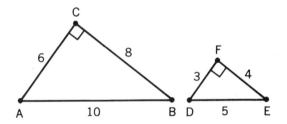

The line segment DF corresponds to $\overset{\leftrightarrow}{AC}$. The lengths of these two sides can be compared by a ratio, $\dfrac{m(\overset{\leftrightarrow}{DF})}{m(\overset{\leftrightarrow}{AC})}$ $= \dfrac{3}{6} = \dfrac{1}{2}$. That is, the length of side $\overset{\leftrightarrow}{DF}$ is to the length of side $\overset{\leftrightarrow}{AC}$ as 3 is to 6 (or as 1 is to 2). The ratio of the lengths is $\dfrac{1}{2}$. Compare the length of side $\overset{\leftrightarrow}{EF}$ with that of side $\overset{\leftrightarrow}{BC}$. This ratio is $\dfrac{m(\overset{\leftrightarrow}{EF})}{m(\overset{\leftrightarrow}{BC})} = \dfrac{4}{8} = \dfrac{1}{2}$. Similarly, comparing the lengths of $\overset{\leftrightarrow}{DE}$ and $\overset{\leftrightarrow}{AB}$, we find that $\dfrac{m(\overset{\leftrightarrow}{DE})}{m(\overset{\leftrightarrow}{AB})}$ $= \dfrac{5}{10} = \dfrac{1}{2}$. If two triangles are similar to each other, the lengths of their corresponding sides will have the same ratio. Applying this idea to triangles DEF and ABC, we see that the ratios of the lengths of corresponding sides is in each case $\dfrac{1}{2}$.

$$\frac{m(\overset{\leftrightarrow}{DF})}{m(\overset{\leftrightarrow}{AC})} = \frac{m(\overset{\leftrightarrow}{EF})}{m(\overset{\leftrightarrow}{BC})} = \frac{m(\overset{\leftrightarrow}{DE})}{m(\overset{\leftrightarrow}{AB})} = \frac{1}{2}$$

This is an application of the concepts of ratio and proportion, which were discussed in Unit 10.

On a geoboard make two triangles that are similar. How can you show that the two triangles are similar? What is the largest triangle that can be made on your geoboard? What is the smallest triangle that can be made on your geoboard?

If we are given two similar triangles and are told the lengths of three sides of one of the triangles and the length of one side of the other triangle, we can easily find the lengths of the other two sides of the second triangle. For example, suppose we are given the following two similar triangles.

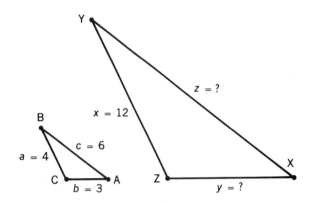

If we know that a and x are corresponding sides, then we know that the ratio of corresponding sides must be $\dfrac{1}{3}$ (since $\dfrac{a}{x} = \dfrac{4}{12} = \dfrac{1}{3}$, and since the corresponding sides of similar triangles all have the same ratio). Therefore $y = 9$ and $z = 18$.

$\dfrac{1}{3} = \dfrac{3}{y}$ $y = 9$ $\left(\text{since } \dfrac{1 \times 3}{3 \times 3} = \dfrac{3}{9}\right)$

$\dfrac{1}{3} = \dfrac{6}{z}$ $z = 18$ $\left(\text{since } \dfrac{1 \times 6}{3 \times 6} = \dfrac{6}{18}\right)$

Before we discuss quadrilaterals, let's take a quick look at parallel lines. We have already defined parallel lines as two lines in the same plane that never intersect. Similarly, we can call two line segments parallel if they are subsets of parallel lines.

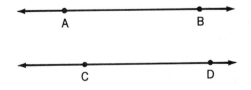

In the above diagram, $\overset{\leftrightarrow}{AB}$ is parallel to $\overset{\leftrightarrow}{CD}$ so the two lines never intersect. This is written $\overset{\leftrightarrow}{AB} \parallel \overset{\leftrightarrow}{CD}$, which is read, "Line AB is parallel to line CD." Now we can also write $\overset{\bullet\bullet}{AB} \parallel \overset{\bullet\bullet}{CD}$, which is read, "Line segment AB is parallel to line segment CD."

With this in mind, we can now discuss the important class of geometric figures called **quadrilaterals**. A quadrilateral was defined earlier as a simple closed curve composed of four line segments, none of which lie on the same line. A quadrilateral should not be confused with a quadrilateral region, which is defined as a quadrilateral and its interior.

We classified triangles according to angle measure and according to relative length of sides. Quadrilaterals are also classified according to the relations between their sides and angles. We can name several different kinds of quadrilaterals according to these relations.

Square: A square is a quadrilateral having four congruent sides and four angles of equal measure. All the angles of a square are right angles—that is, each angle has a measure of 90°. Opposite sides of a square are always parallel.

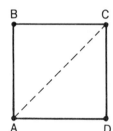

$$\overleftrightarrow{AB} \cong \overleftrightarrow{BC} \cong \overleftrightarrow{CD} \cong \overleftrightarrow{DA}$$
$$\overleftrightarrow{AB} \parallel \overleftrightarrow{CD}, \overleftrightarrow{BC} \parallel \overleftrightarrow{AD}$$

$$m\angle DAB = m\angle ABC$$
$$= m\angle BCD$$
$$= m\angle CDA$$
$$= 90°$$

A line segment joining any two opposite vertices of square ABCD divides the square into two right triangles. Any line segment that joins two opposite vertices is called a **diagonal.** In square ABCD we have marked diagonal $\overleftrightarrow{AC}$, forming right triangles ABC and ADC.

Rectangle: A rectangle is a quadrilateral in which sides opposite each other are both congruent (equal in length) and parallel, and each angle has a measure of 90°.

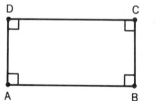

$$\overleftrightarrow{AD} \cong \overleftrightarrow{BC}, \overleftrightarrow{DC} \cong \overleftrightarrow{AB}$$
$$\overleftrightarrow{AD} \parallel \overleftrightarrow{BC}, \overleftrightarrow{DC} \parallel \overleftrightarrow{AB}$$

$$m\angle ABC = m\angle BCD$$
$$= m\angle CDA$$
$$= m\angle DAB$$
$$= 90°$$

Notice that all squares are also rectangles, though not all rectangles are squares.

Parallelogram: A parallelogram is a quadrilateral in which the opposite sides are congruent and parallel. Notice that the parallelogram differs from the rectangle in that the angles of a parallelogram are not necessarily 90° angles. A parallelogram whose angles are 90° angles is also a rectangle. Thus all rectangles are parallelograms, but not all parallelograms are rectangles.

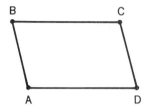

$$\overleftrightarrow{AB} \cong \overleftrightarrow{DC}, \quad \overleftrightarrow{AD} \cong \overleftrightarrow{BC}$$
$$\overleftrightarrow{AB} \parallel \overleftrightarrow{DC}, \quad \overleftrightarrow{AD} \parallel \overleftrightarrow{BC}$$

Rhombus: A rhombus is a quadrilateral in which all four sides are congruent and the opposite sides are parallel. Notice that the rhombus differs from the square in that the angles of a rhombus are not necessarily 90° angles. A rhombus whose angles are 90° angles is also a square. Thus all squares are rhombuses, but not all rhombuses are squares. A rhombus is a special kind of parallelogram—a parallelogram in which all four sides are congruent.

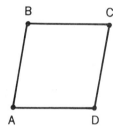

$$\overleftrightarrow{AB} \cong \overleftrightarrow{BC} \cong \overleftrightarrow{CD} \cong \overleftrightarrow{DA}$$

$$\overleftrightarrow{AB} \parallel \overleftrightarrow{DC}$$

$$\overleftrightarrow{AD} \parallel \overleftrightarrow{BC}$$

Trapezoid: A trapezoid is a quadrilateral in which one and only one pair of sides is parallel.

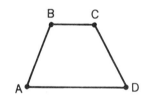
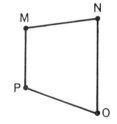

In trapezoid ABCD, $\overleftrightarrow{AD} \parallel \overleftrightarrow{BC}$.
In trapezoid MNOP, $\overleftrightarrow{PM} \parallel \overleftrightarrow{ON}$.

The relations between the various kinds of quadrilaterals can be shown clearly and quickly by means of a diagram. Suppose we take the set of all quadrilaterals as the universal set and then name the subsets of this universe.

U = the set of all quadrilaterals
A = the set of all parallelograms
B = the set of all rectangles
C = the set of all rhombuses
D = the set of all squares
E = the set of all trapezoids
F = the set of all other quadrilaterals

Then we can draw the following diagram.

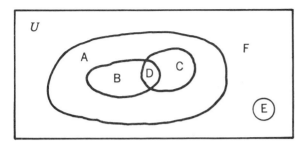

From this diagram we can make a number of observations:

1. All rectangles, rhombuses, and squares are also parallelograms.
2. All squares are both rhombuses of a special type and rectangles of a special type.
3. There are no squares that cannot also be called both rhombuses and rectangles; however, there are rectangles and rhombuses that are not squares.
4. There are rhombuses that are not rectangles.
5. There are rectangles that are not rhombuses.
6. There are no trapezoids that can be called parallelograms, rectangles, rhombuses, or squares.
7. The set of all other quadrilaterals includes all those quadrilaterals formed by four line segments of various lengths.

Another important simple closed curve is the circle. A **circle** is all points in one plane that are an equal distance from a given point, called the center. All the points of a circle, then, are an equal distance from the center. A line segment from the center to any point on the circle is called a **radius.** (The plural of "radius" is "radii.") A line segment extending from any point on the circle to another point on the circle, and passing through the center of the circle is called a **diameter.** A diameter can therefore be thought of as two radii lying on the same line.

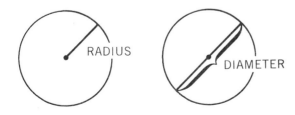

The distance round a circle is called the **circumference** of the circle. Any two points of a circle divide the circle into two parts. Either of these two parts is called an **arc.**

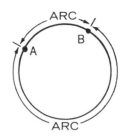

Remember that a circle, like any other geometric figure, is an abstract concept, and the model drawn on paper is merely a representation of a circle. There are three sets of points formed by a circle—the points forming the interior, the points forming the exterior, and the simple closed curve that forms the circle itself.

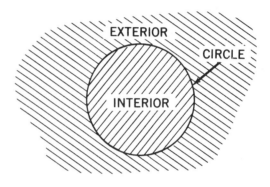

A circular region is the simple closed region formed by a circle and its interior—that is, by the points forming a circle and the points forming its interior.

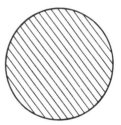

A circle is constructed with a compass. Set the compass at any desired radius and rotate the top of the compass with the fingers of one hand so that the circle is constructed in one continuous movement.

The relation of the radius and the diameter of a circle to the circumference can bring on some awkward moments. At what age do children need to develop an understanding of the meaning of **pi** (π)? Very often pi has been introduced to children as a numerical value that is used mechanically to find the circumference and area of a circle without their understanding anything of its derivation or meaning.

Programs today, however, are introducing the concept of pi fairly early, through experiences that provide children with the opportunity to discover what pi is and what it means. A simple approach to this topic is described below.

Provide a large circular object, such as a cardboard plate or pie pan, and a ruler. Use the ruler to measure the diameter of the circular object. We can then measure the approximate circumference (the distance round the rim or edge) of the circular object by rolling the circular object through one complete turn and measuring the linear distance traveled. To do this, mark a dot at some point on the circumference and place this dot on the table at point A. Then roll the circular object until the dot is again on the table, this time at point B. The distance between A and B on the table approximates the circumference of the circular object.

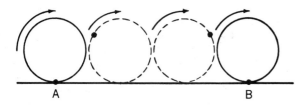

Another method would be to use a piece of string to measure around the object. A cloth tape measure would be very helpful in getting accurate measurements. We can compare the diameter with this measured circumference by means of the following ratio: $\frac{circumference}{diameter}$. This ratio, expressed as a decimal, should be approximately 3.1. By comparing the circumferences of many circular objects with their diameters, children should draw the conclusion that π, the ratio of the circumference to the diameter, is approximately 3.1, regardless of the size of the circular object. Students sometimes wonder what the exact value of π is. Mathematicians have been able to prove that π is an irrational number. This means that any fraction or decimal that we may write for π is only an approximation for the actual value of π. Commonly used approximations for π are 3.14, 3.1416, and $\frac{22}{7}$.

Children can use the hand-held calculator for dividing the circumference by the diameter. If these examples were entered into a large computer, the value of pi could be calculated more precisely.

Another aspect of geometry that we should investigate is the concept of area. **Area** gives us a measure of a plane region. Area, like any measure, is always expressed by a number value and an appropriate unit of measure. An area might be expressed,

for example, as 6 square inches (or 6 sq. in.). The unit of measure in this example is square inches; and the number value is 6, which indicates how many square inches.

We could just as well have used square centimeters and expressed the measure in metric units. If we have 12 square centimeters, it means that there are 12 squares that measure 1 centimeter each.

Let's consider the units of measure for area. The object to be measured is compared with a standard unit measure. A measurement of 6 feet tells us that an object has the same length as 6 one-foot rulers. The standard units for measuring area are square inches, square feet, square yards, square miles, square meters, square centimeters, and so forth. A square inch, by definition, is that area represented by a square region 1 inch on each side. Similarly, a square centimeter is that area represented by a square region 1 centimeter on each side.

In finding the area of a region we ask, How many square units are there in the given region? As an example, consider a rectangular region that is 4 units wide and 6 units long. How can we find the area of this region?

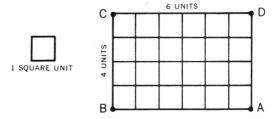

Use the geoboard and construct geometric shapes. Because the geoboard is in squares, the children can count the number of squares within a figure. The children can compare their calculated area with the counted area. The two answers should be approximately the same.

A simple method for determining the area of a rectangular region is to use a ratio. There are 6 square units in one row. This fact can be stated by means of a ratio: $\frac{6}{1}$, or "six square units per row." So, if there are 6 units per row, how many square units are there in 4 rows? This can be expressed as a proportion, using two equivalent ratios.

$$\frac{6}{1} = \frac{\square}{4}$$

The missing numerator is clearly 24.

$$\frac{6 \times 4}{1 \times 4} = \frac{\square}{4}$$
$$\square = 24$$

The denominator of the first ratio is multiplied by 4, so the numerator must also be multiplied by 4. So we see that there are 24 square units in the rectangular region. This fact can be verified by counting the number of square units in the region. If the unit is centimeters, then the area is 24 square centimeters; if the unit is inches, then the area is 24 square inches.

In order to obtain 24 square units we did not multiply 4 units by 6 units. Instead we multiply the number of square units in one row by the number of rows. Thus 6 square units is multiplied by 4: 4×6 square units = 24 square units.

Now let's consider another region:

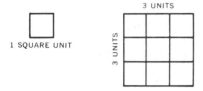

If there are 3 square units in one row, how many square units are there in 3 rows?

$$\frac{3}{1} = \frac{\square}{3}$$
$$\frac{3 \times 3}{1 \times 3} = \frac{\square}{3}$$
$$\square = 9$$

The answer is clearly 9 square units. This fact can be verified by counting the number of square units in the region. Thus 3×3 square units = 9 square units. Consider another region:

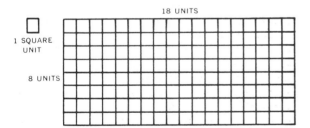

If there are 18 square units in one row, how many square units are there in 8 rows?

$$\frac{18}{1} = \frac{\square}{8}$$
$$\frac{18 \times 8}{1 \times 8} = \frac{\square}{8}$$
$$\square = 144$$

There are 144 square units in 8 rows. Again, the answer can be verified by counting the number of square units in the region.

After children have found the areas of several rectangular regions, they should be able to generalize their findings. The number of units in the

length times the number of units in the width gives the number of square units in the area. This fact can be expressed by a formula:

$$A = \ell \times w$$

In this formula A stands for area, ℓ stands for length, and w stands for width.

Now let's use the concepts of area and ratio to determine the area bounded by a parallelogram.

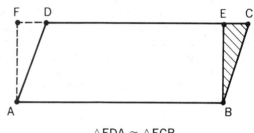

$$\triangle FDA \cong \triangle ECB$$
$$\therefore \text{Area } \triangle FDA = \text{Area } \triangle ECB$$

Cut off the triangular region BEC and place it on the other end of the parallelogram as shown above. The area within the parallelogram ABCD is exactly the same as the area within the rectangle ABEF that is formed. Thus we can determine the area within parallelogram ABCD by determining the area of the rectangular region ABEF.

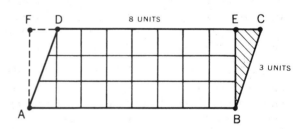

In the rectangular region ABEF, if there are 8 square units in one row, how many units are there in 3 rows?

$$\frac{8}{1} = \frac{\square}{3} \qquad A = \ell \times w$$
$$\frac{8 \times 3}{1 \times 3} = \frac{\square}{3} \qquad A = 8 \times 3$$
$$\square = 24 \qquad A = 24 \text{ square units}$$

The area within the parallelogram is therefore 24 square units.

We can generalize from this last example. If $\overset{\bullet\rightarrow}{AB}$ is called the base of the parallelogram (labeled b), and if $\overset{\bullet\bullet}{BE}$ is called the height of the parallelogram (labeled h), then the number of square units in the area (A) within the parallelogram is indicated by the product of the number of units in the base and the number of units in the height. We can express this fact by means of a formula:

$$A = b \times h$$

Now let's apply these concepts to finding the area of a triangular region.

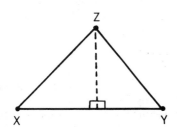

Make a tracing of triangle XYZ, and label it X'Y'Z'. Place △X'Y'Z' next to △XYZ, as in the following:

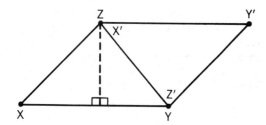

The area of one of the triangular regions is clearly one-half the area within the parallelogram. The formula for the area within the parallelogram is $A = b \times h$. Then the formula for finding the area of a triangle (one-half of a parallelogram) is

$$A = \frac{1}{2}bh$$

(Notice that this formula has been written without the multiplication sign, ×. This is acceptable. The multiplication sign between two factors in a formula can always be omitted provided the meaning of the expression or sentence remains clear.)

Consider the following triangular region RST, and find its area.

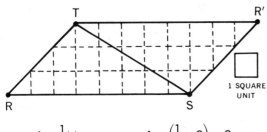

$$A = \frac{1}{2}bh \qquad A = \left(\frac{1}{2} \times 8\right) \times 3$$

$$A = \frac{1}{2} \times 8 \times 3 \qquad \begin{aligned} A &= 4 \times 3 \\ A &= 12 \end{aligned}$$

1 SQUARE UNIT

The area of the triangular region is 12 square units. These basic principles can also be applied to finding the areas of other triangular regions.

The process of finding the area of a circular region is much more difficult than finding the area of a polygonal region.

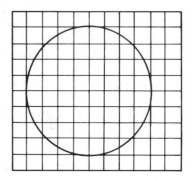

One method, which will give only an estimate, is to place the circular region on a square grid and count the number of square units covered by the circular region. The smaller the square unit, the more accurately the area of the circular region can be estimated.

A second method is to think of the circular region as being made up of many small congruent triangles, approximated by drawing a large number of radii to form many small regions that are approximately triangular. Notice that the radii must be drawn so that the resulting arcs of the circle are all equal in length if the small triangular regions are to be congruent.

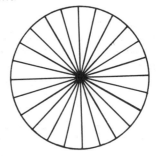

Let's consider this second method of determining the area of a circular region. Examine one of the small regions that has been formed:

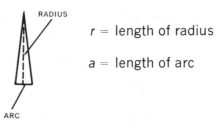

r = length of radius

a = length of arc

We can use the formula $A = \frac{1}{2}ra$ to find the approximate area of this region. The shape of the region is very nearly triangular, with the arc as a base and the radius as a height. The area within a triangle, remember, is equal to one-half the product of the base and the height. Then, multiplying the area of this region by the total number of regions, we obtain an approximation of the area of the circular region. If we consider each small region a triangle (this is approximately the case), we can state that the area of the circular region (A) is equal to the area within the first triangle $\left(\frac{1}{2}ra_1\right)$ plus the area within the second triangle $\left(\frac{1}{2}ra_2\right)$ plus the area within the third triangle $\left(\frac{1}{2}ra_3\right)$ plus the area within the fourth triangle $\left(\frac{1}{2}ra_4\right)$, and so on:

$$A = \frac{1}{2}ra_1 + \frac{1}{2}ra_2 + \frac{1}{2}ra_3 + \ldots + \frac{1}{2}ra_n$$

The term $\frac{1}{2}ra_n$ represents the area within the last triangle.

The sum of the lengths of the bases of the triangles is approximately equal to $a_1 + a_2 + a_3 + a_4 + \ldots + a_n$, which is the same length as that of the circumference of the circle. So the area within the circle can be expressed by the following equation:

$$A = \frac{1}{2}r(a_1 + a_2 + a_3 + a_4 + \ldots + a_n)$$
$$= \frac{1}{2}r(\text{circumference})$$

But we know that the circumference of a circle is used to calculate the value of π (pi). The value of π has been defined as the ratio of the circumference to the diameter:

$$\pi = \frac{\text{circumference}}{\text{diameter}}$$

Hence the circumference of a circle is equal to π times its diameter, or 2π times its radius.

$$\begin{aligned}
\text{circumference} &= \pi \times \text{diameter} \\
&= \pi \times (2 \times \text{radius}) \\
&= 2\pi \times \text{radius} \\
&= 2\pi r
\end{aligned}$$

Thus we can calculate the area within a circle to be equal to π times the square of its radius.

$$\begin{aligned}
A &= \frac{1}{2}r(\text{circumference}) \\
&= \frac{1}{2}r(2\pi r) \\
&= \left(\frac{1}{2} \times 2\right) \times (\pi \times r \times r) \\
&= \pi r^2
\end{aligned}$$

Now let's use this formula to find the area of a circular region with a radius of 10 units.

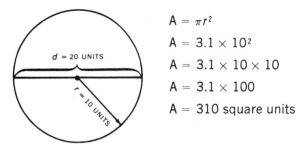

$$\begin{aligned}
A &= \pi r^2 \\
A &= 3.1 \times 10^2 \\
A &= 3.1 \times 10 \times 10 \\
A &= 3.1 \times 100 \\
A &= 310 \text{ square units}
\end{aligned}$$

The area of a circular region with a radius of 10 units is approximately 310 square units. Now determine the circumference of the same circular region.

$$\begin{aligned}
C &= \pi \times d \\
C &= 3.1 \times 20 \\
C &= 62 \text{ linear units}
\end{aligned}$$

The circumference is approximately 62 linear units.

The sum of the measures of the line segments that form a polygon is called the **perimeter** of the polygon. The perimeter of a polygon, such as the following scalene triangle, can be determined by adding the lengths of the sides.

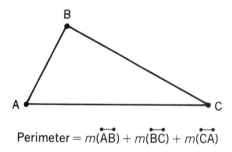

$$\text{Perimeter} = m(\overset{\bullet\!\!-\!\!\bullet}{AB}) + m(\overset{\bullet\!\!-\!\!\bullet}{BC}) + m(\overset{\bullet\!\!-\!\!\bullet}{CA})$$

The length of each side can be approximated by direct measurement with a ruler. The measure of a side can be expressed in symbols—for example, $m(\overset{\bullet\!\!-\!\!\bullet}{AB})$, is read "the measure of line segment AB."

$$P = m(\overset{\bullet\!\!-\!\!\bullet}{AB}) + m(\overset{\bullet\!\!-\!\!\bullet}{BC}) + m(\overset{\bullet\!\!-\!\!\bullet}{CA})$$

The perimeter (P) of an equilateral triangle is equal to three times the measure of one side, since the three sides are all congruent (equal in measure).

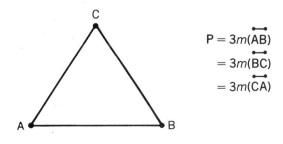

$$\begin{aligned}
P &= 3m(\overset{\bullet\!\!-\!\!\bullet}{AB}) \\
&= 3m(\overset{\bullet\!\!-\!\!\bullet}{BC}) \\
&= 3m(\overset{\bullet\!\!-\!\!\bullet}{CA})
\end{aligned}$$

We can express this fact in symbols by writing $P = 3s$, where s stands for any of the three sides.

The perimeter of a square is equal to four times the measure of one side, since all four sides are congruent.

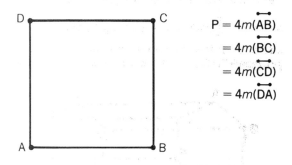

$$P = 4m(\overleftrightarrow{AB})$$
$$= 4m(\overleftrightarrow{BC})$$
$$= 4m(\overleftrightarrow{CD})$$
$$= 4m(\overleftrightarrow{DA})$$

This fact can also be expressed in symbols as $P = 4s$, where s stands for any of the four sides.

The perimeter of a rectangle is equal to twice the measure of one of the sides representing the length plus twice the measure of one of the sides representing the width. Let ℓ equal the measure of the length and w equal the measure of the width.

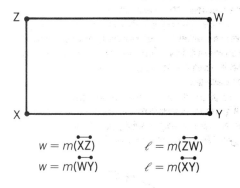

$$w = m(\overleftrightarrow{XZ}) \qquad \ell = m(\overleftrightarrow{ZW})$$
$$w = m(\overleftrightarrow{WY}) \qquad \ell = m(\overleftrightarrow{XY})$$

The perimeter can be determined according to the following formula.

$$P = 2\ell + 2w$$

In the elementary school, geometry is presented in an intuitive manner. Elementary geometry relies heavily on a visual approach. In high school the student has the opportunity to study geometry as a deductive mathematical system in which results are obtained through careful step-by-step logical reasoning, starting from basic assumptions called axioms or postulates. In the elementary school we take a much more informal approach to geometry. We want the students to become acquainted with some of the terminology of geometry and we want them to perceive various kinds of relationships and properties between geometric figures.

An excellent way to help students develop in these areas is to introduce some of the basic ideas of symmetry and geometric transformations. These ideas are helpful in exploring the properties of geometric figures.

Most of us are familiar with figures that are **symmetric about a line.** In each of the figures shown below, the given figure is symmetric about the dotted line. The dotted line is called a line of symmetry for the figure.

Have the children place a mirror on the line of symmetry of a figure and examine the figure. Then place a Mira in many different places; how do you know when you have placed the Mira on a line of symmetry?

If you were to trace any one of these figures, cut the figure out and fold along the dotted line, you would find that the parts on either side of the dotted line match perfectly. The part of the figure on one side of the dotted line is the "mirror image" of the part on the other side.

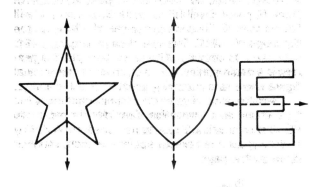

Symmetry with respect to a line can be described in mathematical terms. A figure is **symmetric with respect to a line** ℓ if for each point P of the figure (P not on the line ℓ) has a matching point P′ on the other side of ℓ such that the line ℓ bisects $\overleftrightarrow{PP'}$ and is perpendicular to $\overleftrightarrow{PP'}$.

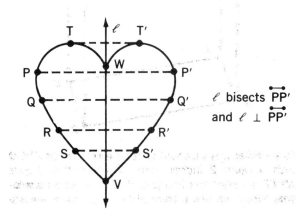

ℓ bisects $\overleftrightarrow{PP'}$ and $\ell \perp \overleftrightarrow{PP'}$

The point P' is called the **image** of P in line ℓ (or the image of P under **reflection** in line ℓ). Similarly, the image of Q is Q', the image of R is R', and so on. We could also think of P as the image of P', of Q as the image of Q', and so on. The point V at the tip of the heart shaped figure can be thought of as its own image; so can the point W labeled at the top of the figure. The word **flip** is often used in discussing the image of a figure in a line. Look at the following diagram.

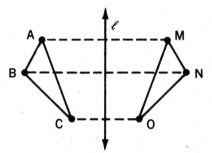

If we flip triangle ABC over line ℓ, point A will fall on point M, point B will fall on point N, and point C will fall on point O. Thus we can speak of △MNO as the **flip image** of △ABC. The operation of flipping △ABC over line ℓ to obtain △MNO is an example of a **geometric transformation.** For each point of the original figure there is a matching point in the flip image.

Another kind of geometric transformation is the type known as a **translation.** Consider the rectangle ABCD shown below. Suppose we transform ABCD by matching each vertex with a point two inches further down on the page.

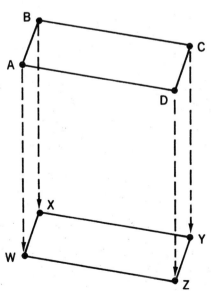

In a similar way we could match every point on ABCD with a point 2 inches lower. The resulting figure WXYZ is called the image of ABCD under a **translation.** When we use a translation on a figure, we are

finding the figure that we would obtain if it were possible to give the rectangle a straight shove in a certain direction and through a certain distance.

We can use an arrow to indicate both the direction and distance of a translation. For example, we can indicate a translation of $1\frac{1}{2}$ inches to the right by an arrow $1\frac{1}{2}$ inches and pointing to the right. If we use such a translation on polygon ABCDEF we get polygon RSTUVW as the **image** under the translation.

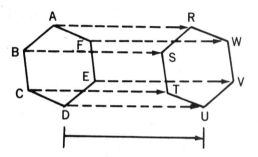

Each point of the image polygon is $1\frac{1}{2}$ inches to the right of its corresponding point in the given polygon. The arrow below the diagrams of the two polygons indicates how far and in what direction ABCDEF moves under the translation.

Since young students often have vocabulary problems when long words are used, many authors recommend that translations be called **slides.** The word is short and suggests the intuitive meaning of the concept.

Another transformation we can use on a geometric figure is a **rotation** or **turn.** If we apply a quarter turn to the triangle ABC, as shown in the diagram, we get AB'C' as the image figure.

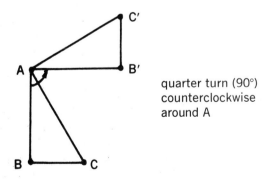

quarter turn (90°)
counterclockwise
around A

The point about which the given figure is turned is called the **center** of the turn. The curved arrow indicates that the turn is in a counter-clockwise direction.

Here are some more diagrams that show a given figure and its image under a turn transformation. Since all points of the original figure remain at the same distance from the center of rotation after rotation, the image figure has the same size and shape as the original.

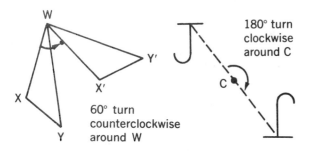

60° turn counterclockwise around W

180° turn clockwise around C

Flips, slides, and turns are connected with the very important geometric concept of **congruence.** If one figure is the image of another with respect to one of these motions, then the figures are congruent. Also, if two figures are congruent, then you can get from one figure to the other by a flip, a slide, or a turn, or a combination of these motions.

Flips, slides, and turns move figures from one position to another, but they do not change them in any other way. Figures stay the same size and shape, which is exactly what congruence means. For this reason flips, slides, and turns are called **rigid motions.**

Basic ideas of geometric transformations can be presented to children to help them understand a variety of ideas in geometry. This approach provides many opportunities for children to manipulate cutouts and tracings of geometric figures. A formal development of ideas of geometric transformations should not be the goal.

In our discussion of geometry so far, we have considered only figures lying entirely in one plane. Now we will examine spatial figures, or space figures. **Space figures** are geometric figures that do not lie entirely in one plane. Children are more familiar with representations of space figures than they are with representations of plane figures. Just as sheets of paper and chalkboards represent planes, so do shoeboxes, rooms, skyscrapers, silos, and basketballs represent various kinds of space figures.

The best introductory approach to the topic of space figures is to lead children to become more aware of familiar physical shapes around them and to associate these physical shapes with the geometric shapes that they suggest. For example, it is quite likely that children are in a classroom with a floor, a ceiling, and four walls and that one pair of opposite walls is longer than the other pair. A room like this represents a particular kind of geometric space figure.

Early in our study of plane figures we defined a simple closed curve. Let's begin our study of space figures by defining a simple closed surface. A simple closed curve, we found, consists of the points on a plane that divide the plane into three sets of points —the points forming the simple closed curve itself, the points forming the interior of the curve, and the points forming the exterior of the curve.

Analogously, a **simple closed surface** consists of the points in space that divide space into three sets of points—the points forming the simple closed surface itself, the points forming the interior of the space figure, and the points forming the exterior of the space figure.

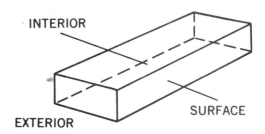

INTERIOR

EXTERIOR

SURFACE

In discussing plane regions we defined the union of a simple closed curve and its interior as a plane region. In spatial geometry we define the union of a simple closed surface and its interior as a **space region.**

If we examine the walls of a room, we see that the intersection of two walls can be thought of as representing a line segment. If we think of the two walls as representing or determining planes (remember that planes extend endlessly, without bounds), the intersection of these two planes is clearly a line. We can generalize by saying that *the intersection of two planes is always a line.*

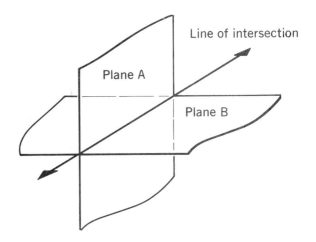

Line of intersection

Plane A

Plane B

But planes do not always intersect. If we examine the opposite walls of most rooms, we see that they do not meet and could not meet if the walls were extended indefinitely. And if we consider the planes that the two walls can be thought of as representing, we see that the planes do not intersect. Two planes that have no intersection, regardless of how far they are extended, are called **parallel planes.**

We are now prepared to consider a very important kind of simple closed surface, the prism. A **prism** can be defined as a simple closed surface formed by two congruent polygonal regions in parallel planes and three or more quadrilateral regions joining the two congruent polygonal regions so as to enclose the space between them completely. The following diagram illustrates one kind of prism.

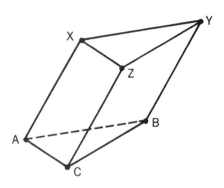

The triangular regions ABC and XYZ are the two congruent polygonal regions in parallel planes. And AXZC, CZYB, and BYXA are the quadrilateral regions joining triangular regions ABC and XYZ and enclosing completely the space between them. The two congruent polygonal regions are called the **bases** of the prism. In the prism pictured here, the triangular regions ABC and XYZ are the bases. The quadrilateral regions of a prism that join the two bases are called **lateral faces** or **sides.** In this prism the quadrilateral regions AXZC, CZYB, and BYXA are the faces. All of the polygonal regions that form the prism (the lateral faces and the two bases) are called the faces. The line segment formed by the intersection of two sides (faces) is called an **edge.** Each point where three edges intersect (or three faces) is called a **vertex.** (The plural of "vertex" is "vertices.") The prism pictured above has five **faces** (ABC, AXZC, CZYB, BYXA, and XYZ), nine edges (AB, BC, CA, XY, YZ, ZX, AX, BY, and CZ), and six vertices (points A, B, C, X, Y, and Z).

Many different kinds of space figures can be classified as prisms, and each is named according to the polygonal regions forming the bases. The following table shows some of the principal kinds of prisms.

NAME OF PRISM	POLYGONAL REGIONS FORMING THE BASES	NUMBER OF FACES	NUMBER OF EDGES	NUMBER OF VERTICES
TRIANGULAR PRISM	TRIANGULAR REGIONS	5	9	6
QUADRILATERAL PRISM	QUADRILATERAL REGIONS	6	12	8
HEXAGONAL PRISM	HEXAGONAL REGIONS	8	18	12

Many prisms are shaped so that is we could imagine setting them horizontally on one of their bases, their sides and the edges joining the two bases would be perpendicular to the bases. (Since all the lateral edges of a prism are parallel, we only need to know that one of the lateral edges is perpendicular to the bases.)

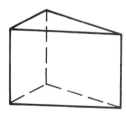

Such prisms are called **right prisms.** The prisms pictured in the preceding table are right prisms. Other prisms are shaped so that if placed horizontally on one of their bases, their sides and the edges joining the bases are not all perpendicular to the bases.

These prisms are not right prisms. The prisms we will examine in this unit will all be right prisms.

A quadrilateral prism with rectangular bases is called a **rectangular prism.** The following diagram pictures a rectangular prism.

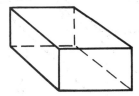

Like any other quadrilateral prism, it has six sides, twelve edges, and eight vertices. A rectangular prism that is also a right prism is referred to as a **right rectangular prism.**

Now let's look at a particular kind of right rectangular prism. The sides of this prism are all congruent square regions, and all the edges of the prism are congruent.

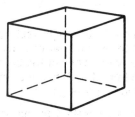

This particular space figure is called a cube. A **cube** is a quadrilateral prism in which the six faces are all congruent square regions.

A very important concept in spatial geometry is that of volume. **Volume** is a measure of the space occupied by a space region. Volume is named by a numeral and an appropriate unit name—for example, three cubic feet or four cubic centimeters. Notice that the unit name in this example is cubic feet. We always use **cubic units** in measuring volume—cubic inches, cubic feet, cubic centimeters, and so on. Cubic units may be English units or metric units. What does "cubic feet" mean? Consider a cube whose edges are each one foot long. (Remember the edges of a cube are all congruent, or equal in length.) The measure of the space enclosed by such a cube is defined as one cubic foot. We can define cubic inches or any other unit of volume in a similar way. What does "cubic centimeters" mean? A cube whose edges are each one centimeter in length is called a cubic centimeter.

Now let's examine the following right rectangular prism. (A right rectangular prism, remember, is a rectangular prism that is also a right prism. A right rectangular prism has a shape like a shoebox.) Remember, the units can be either English or metric.

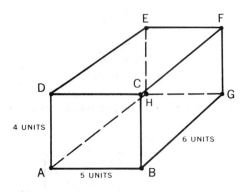

Let's see how we can find the volume within this rectangular prism. To do this we must determine how many cubic units can be fitted into the prism. How many cubic units can be placed end to end along the edge $\overset{\bullet\rightarrow}{AB}$?

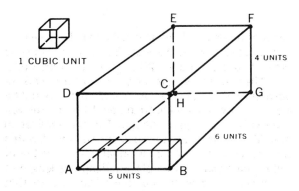

1 CUBIC UNIT

Clearly, 5 cubic units. How many cubic units can we place end to end along edge $\overset{\bullet\rightarrow}{BG}$?

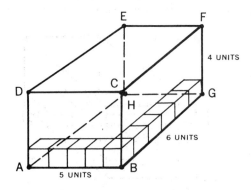

The answer is 6. How many cubic units can be placed on the lower base, rectangle ABGH? If there are 5 cubic units in one row, how many are there in 6 rows?

$$\frac{5}{1} = \frac{\square}{6}$$

$$\frac{5 \times 6}{1 \times 6} = \frac{\square}{6}$$

$$\square = 30$$

Thirty cubic units can be placed on the lower base.

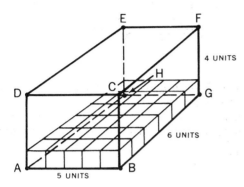

Since the prism is 4 units high, it can hold 4 layers of these cubic units. If there are 30 cubic units in one layer, 4 layers contain 120 (or 4 × 30) cubic units.

After solving a number of similar problems involving right rectangular prisms, children should be able to make a generalization about finding the volume within such spatial figures. Their generalization should be written as a formula. The volume, V, within a right rectangular prism is equal to the number of cubic units that can be placed along the length of the prism, ℓ, times the number of cubic units that can be placed along the width, w, times the number of cubic units that can be placed along the height, h:

$$V = \ell \times w \times h$$
$$\text{or} \quad V = \ell wh$$

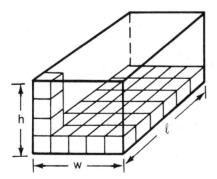

Using this formula, find the volume of a right rectangular prism 6 units wide, 15 units long, and 7 units high.

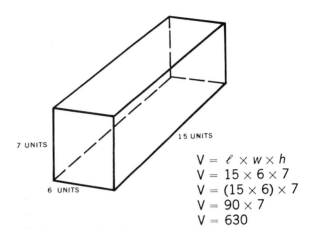

$$V = \ell \times w \times h$$
$$V = 15 \times 6 \times 7$$
$$V = (15 \times 6) \times 7$$
$$V = 90 \times 7$$
$$V = 630$$

The volume of this prism is 630 cubic units.

The following formula is another way of expressing the volume within a right rectangular prism.

$$V = B \times h$$
$$\text{or} \quad V = Bh$$

The volume, V, of a right rectangular prism is equal to the number of cubic units that can be placed on one of the bases, B, times the number of cubic units that can be placed along the height, h.

This formula is equivalent to the first formula, $V = \ell wh$, since the number of cubic units that can be placed on one of the bases of the prism (B) is determined by the product of the number of cubic units that can be placed along the length of the prism (ℓ) and the number of cubic units that can be placed along the width (w). In the formula $V = \ell wh$, we simply replace ℓw with its equivalent, B, to obtain

$$V = \ell \times w \times h$$
$$V = \quad B \quad \times h$$

An advantage of the formula $V = Bh$ is that it is valid for any right prism. It is not restricted to right rectangular prisms as is the other formula. For example, consider the following right triangular prism.

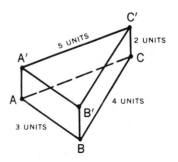

We know that the area of one of the bases (triangular region ABC or triangular region A'B'C') is 6 square units. (Triangles ABC and A'B'C' are right triangles, so the area of the triangular region ABC or A'B'C' is one-half the product of its legs: $\frac{1}{2} \times 3 \times 4$, or 6.) Therefore we can fit six cubic units on one of the bases of the prism. But there are two layers of these cubic units because the height of the prism is 2 units. Consequently 6×2, or 12, cubic units can be placed in the prism. So the volume of the right triangular prism is 12 cubic units. The same result can be obtained by using our second formula:

$$V = Bh$$
$$= \left(\frac{1}{2} \times 3 \times 4\right) \times 2$$
$$= 6 \times 2$$
$$= 12 \text{ cubic units}$$

In a similar manner we can determine the volume within any right prism.

A **pyramid** is a simple closed surface formed by a simple closed region, a point not in the plane of the region, and triangular regions joining the simple closed region and the point outside the region, completely enclosing the space between them.

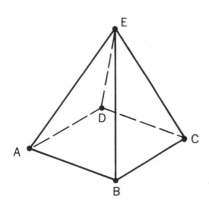

In the pyramid shown here, ABCD is the simple closed region, E is the point not in the plane of ABCD, and the triangular regions joining ABCD and point E are ABE, BCE, CDE, and DAE. The simple closed region ABCD is called the **base** of the pyramid, and the triangular regions ABE, BCE, CDE, and DAE are called **lateral faces.** The base and the lateral faces are also called the **faces** of the pyramid. The line segment formed by the intersection of two sides (faces) is called an edge, and the point formed by the intersection of three or more edges (or by the intersection of three or more sides) is called a vertex. In the diagram of the pyramid, the plane regions ABCD,

ABE, BCE, CDE, and DAE are the faces; $\overset{\bullet\!-\!\bullet}{AB}$, $\overset{\bullet\!-\!\bullet}{BC}$, $\overset{\bullet\!-\!\bullet}{CD}$, $\overset{\bullet\!-\!\bullet}{DA}$, $\overset{\bullet\!-\!\bullet}{AE}$, $\overset{\bullet\!-\!\bullet}{BE}$, $\overset{\bullet\!-\!\bullet}{CE}$, and $\overset{\bullet\!-\!\bullet}{DE}$ are the edges; and points A, B, C, D, and E are the vertices.

NAME OF PYRAMID	POLYGONAL REGION FORMING BASE	NUMBER OF FACES	NUMBER OF EDGES	NUMBER OF VERTICES
TRIANGULAR PYRAMID	TRIANGULAR REGION	4	6	4
QUADRILATERAL PYRAMID	QUADRILATERAL REGION	5	8	5
HEXAGONAL PYRAMID	HEXAGONAL REGION	7	12	7

Pyramids are classified according to the polygonal region forming the base. A quadrilateral pyramid whose base is formed by a rectangular region is called a rectangular pyramid.

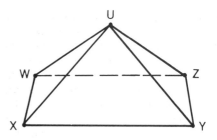

In the above diagram, if the quadrilateral region WXYZ (the base) is rectangular, then the space figure represented is a rectangular pyramid. A rectangular pyramid, like any quadrilateral pyramid, has 5 faces, 8 edges, and 5 vertices.

Another simple closed surface that children have often seen is the cylinder. A **cylinder** is a simple closed surface formed by two congruent simple closed regions (not polygonal regions) in parallel planes, and one or more surfaces (at least one of which is curved) formed by the union of those line segments that join corresponding points of the curves that bound the two congruent regions. The following drawings illustrate various kinds of cylinders.

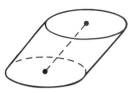

The simple closed regions at the ends of a cylinder are called the **bases** of the cylinder. The surface or surfaces that join the two bases are called the **lateral faces.** The bases and lateral faces of a cylinder are illustrated in the following drawing.

A cylinder whose bases are circular regions is called a **circular cylinder.**

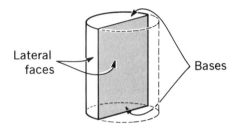

Lateral faces

Bases

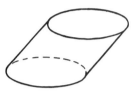

Some of the shapes that the bases of a cylinder can have are indicated in the diagram below.

A cylinder that is both a circular cylinder and a right cylinder is called a right circular cylinder.

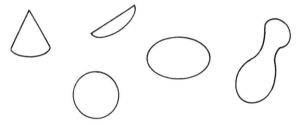

If the bases are polygonal regions, the simple closed surface is a prism rather than a cylinder. (Remember that a polygon is a simple closed curve formed by the union of line segments and that a polygonal region is formed by the union of a polygon and its interior.) If a simple closed surface is a prism, the edges of its two bases are all line segments; but if a simple closed surface is a cylinder, the sides of its bases are not all line segments. This is the essential difference between a prism and a cylinder.

In a right circular cylinder, the line segment joining the centers of the bases is perpendicular to both bases and parallel to the sides of the cylinder.

A cone is another space figure that is familiar to all children. What child does not know what an ice-cream cone is? A **cone** is a simple closed surface having a base, a vertex, and one or more lateral faces joining the base and the vertex. The base is a simple closed nonpolygonal plane region. The vertex is a point not in the plane of the base. The lateral face, or faces, consist of all those line segments joining the vertex and the simple closed curve bounding the base. The drawings below illustrate various kinds of cones.

If the line segment joining the centers of the bases of a cylinder is perpendicular to the bases, then the cylinder is a **right cylinder.**

If the line segment joining the centers of the bases is not perpendicular to the bases, the cylinder is not a right cylinder.

The simple closed region opposite the vertex is called the base of the cone. And the surface or surfaces that join the base with the vertex are called the lateral faces. The base, vertex, and lateral faces of a cone are illustrated in the following drawing.

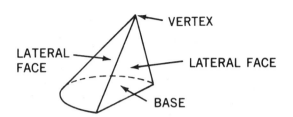

Some of the shapes that the base of a cone can have are indicated in the drawings below.

If a polygonal region forms the base, the simple closed surface is a **pyramid** rather than a cone. (Remember, again, that a polygon is a simple closed curve formed by the union of line segments and that a polygonal region is formed by the union of a polygon and its interior.) If a simple closed surface is a pyramid, the edges of the base are all line segments; but if a simple closed surface is a cone, the edges of the base are not all line segments. This is the essential difference between a pyramid and a cone.

A cone whose base is a circular region is referred to as a **circular cone.**

If the line segment joining the center of the base with the vertex of the cone is perpendicular to the base, then the circular cone is called a **right circular cone.**

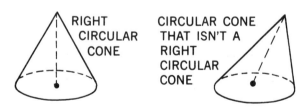

Another simple closed surface that should be familiar to all children is the sphere. Young children have all played with balls or other toys that have suggested spheres and are therefore familiar with physical representations, or models, of spheres. A **sphere** is a simple closed surface and is the set of all points in space that are the same distance from a given point, called the center. A sphere divides space into three sets of points—the points forming the sphere

itself, the points forming the interior of the sphere, and the points forming the exterior of the sphere.

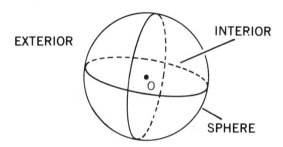

Any line that passes through the interior of a sphere intersects the sphere at two points.

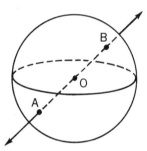

In the diagram above, A and B represent the points of intersection of a sphere with a line passing through the center, O, of the sphere. A line segment that passes through the center of a sphere and whose end points are points on the sphere is called a **diameter** of the sphere. Hence, $\overleftrightarrow{AB}$ is a diameter of the sphere pictured above. A line segment whose end points are a point on a sphere and the center of the sphere is called a **radius** of the sphere. In the sphere pictured above, $\overline{OA}$ and $\overline{OB}$ are radii. A diameter can be thought of as the union of two distinct radii lying on the same line. For example, the diameter $\overline{AB}$ is the union of radii $\overline{OA}$ and $\overline{OB}$; in symbols, $\overline{AB} = \overline{OA} \cup \overline{OB}$.

An important aspect of the study of space figures is the concept of surface area. The **surface area** of a simple closed surface is the total area of the surfaces that form the figure. Consider the right rectangular prism represented below.

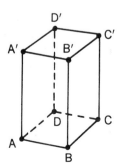

Imagine a physical model of this prism. If we cut the model along edges AA', A'B', B'C', C'D', AB, BC, and CD, and flattened it out, it would look something like this:

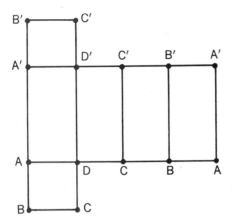

We can see now that the surface area of a prism is the sum of the areas of the sides—in this case, the sum of the areas of the two congruent bases plus the areas of the four lateral faces. How can we calculate the total surface area? Every prism has two congruent bases, so the surface area must contain the area of one base multiplied by 2 (2B, where B stands for the area of a base). It must also contain the area of the lateral faces. In the right rectangular prism pictured above, the area of the lateral faces is calculated as follows: Area = (AB × AA') + (BC × BB') + (CD × CC') + (DA × DD'). In this formula we use AB, AA', BC, and so on, as abbreviations for the longer notation $m(\overset{\longleftrightarrow}{AB})$, $m(\overset{\longleftrightarrow}{AA'})$, $m(\overset{\longleftrightarrow}{BC})$, and so on. Since the prism is a right prism, we know that AA' = BB' = CC' = DD' = h, so Area = (AB × h) + (BC × h) + (CD × h) + (DA × h). By applying the distributive property, we can state

$$\text{Area} = (AB + BC + CD + DA) \times h$$

Then, since (AB + BC + CD + DA) is equal to the perimeter of a base of the prism

$$\text{Area} = \text{perimeter of a base} \times \text{height of the prism}$$
$$= Ph$$

Since we are looking for the total surface area of the prism, we must include the area of the two bases as well as the area of the four vertical sides:

$$\text{Area} = \text{area of two bases} + \text{area of four sides}$$
$$= 2 \times (AB \times BC) + Ph$$
$$= 2B + Ph$$

Now let's calculate the surface area of the following right rectangular prism, in which rectangular regions ABCD and A'B'C'D' are the bases.

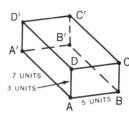

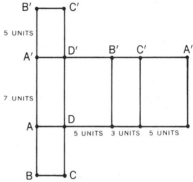

Surface area = (2 × area of a base) + (perimeter of a base × height)

$$SA = 2B + Ph$$
$$= [2 \times (3 \times 5)] + [(3 + 5 + 3 + 5) \times 7]$$
$$= (2 \times 15) + (16 \times 7)$$
$$= 30 + 112$$
$$= 142$$

The surface area is 142 square units.

We can use this same method to determine a formula for finding the surface area of a right triangular prism. Imagine cutting and flattening a physical model of the following right triangular prism.

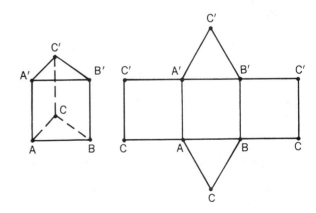

The surface area of this space figure must contain the areas of the two bases—the area of the triangular region ABC plus the area of the triangular region

A'B'C' (ABC is congruent to A'B'C')—which can be represented by 2B, where B stands for the area of either of the two bases. It must also contain the area of the lateral faces, which are rectangular regions.

$$\text{Area} = (AB \times AA') + (BC \times BB') + (CA \times CC')$$

Since AA' = BB' = CC' = h, we can write

$$\begin{aligned}\text{Area} &= (AB \times h) + (BC \times h) + (CA \times h) \\ &= (AB + BC + CA) \times h\end{aligned}$$

And since the perimeter of the base is equal to AB + BC + CA, we can write

$$\text{Area} = Ph$$

Therefore

$$\begin{aligned}\text{Total surface area} &= (2 \times \text{area of a base}) \\ &\quad + (\text{perimeter of a} \\ &\quad\ \text{base} \times \text{height}) \\ &= 2B + Ph\end{aligned}$$

We can generalize from this by saying that the surface area (SA) of any right triangular prism is equal to the sum of the areas of its two bases (2B) and the product of the perimeter of one of the bases and the height of the prism (Ph):

$$SA = 2B + Ph$$

Now let's use this formula to find the surface area of the following right triangular prism.

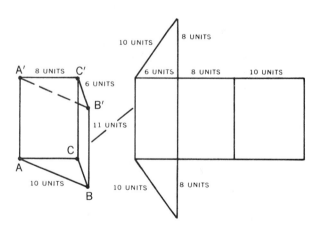

Remember that the area of a triangular region is one-half the product of the base and the height. In either of the triangular regions ABC and A'B'C' of the prism represented above (observing that the sides of these regions form right triangles), we can consider the base and the height 6 units and 8 units respectively.

$$\begin{aligned}SA &= 2B + Ph \\ &= \left[2 \times \left(\frac{1}{2} \times 6 \times 8\right)\right] + [(6 + 8 + 10) \times 11] \\ &= [(2 \times 24)] + [(24 \times 11)] \\ &= 48 + 264 \\ &= 312\end{aligned}$$

The surface area is 312 square units.

Young children need ample opportunity to play with blocks that are cubes, rectangular prisms, pyramids, cones, and spheres. Older children need experiences cutting paper models and pasting them together to make solid space figures. Doyal Nelson has suggested that we use clear plastic for the faces of space figures and use leather glue to fasten Velcro (which can be purchased at a fabric store) along the edges. The pieces then may easily be put together and taken apart. For example, make four equivalent squares out of clear plastic and glue Velcro around each edge.

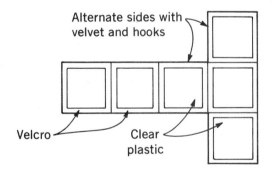

Now fold the squares into a cube.

Terminology, Symbols, and Procedures

Area A measure that expresses the size of a plane region in square units is called the area of that region.

Circle A circle is the set of all points in a plane that are a given (equal) distance from a given point, called the center.

Circular region A circular region is the union of a circle and its interior.

Circumference The distance around a circle is called the circumference.

Cone A cone is a simple closed surface formed by a simple closed region (not a polygon), a point that is not in the plane of this region, and one or more surfaces (at least one of which is curved) formed by the union of those line segments that join the point that is not in the plane of the simple closed region with the points of the curve that bounds the simple closed region.

The simple closed region is called the base of the cone. The surface or surfaces that join the base with the point not in the plane of the base are called lateral faces.

Circular cone A cone with a circular region forming its base is called a circular cone.

Right circular cone If the line segment joining the center of the base with the vertex of the cone is perpendicular to the base, the cone is called a right circular cone.

Cube A cube is a right rectangular prism whose faces are all congruent square regions. All the edges of a cube are also congruent.

Cylinder A cylinder is a simple closed surface formed by two congruent simple closed regions in parallel planes (not polygonal regions) and one or more surfaces (at least one of which is curved) formed by the union of those line segments that join corresponding points of the curves that bound the two congruent regions.

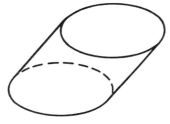

The simple closed regions at the ends of a cylinder are called the bases of the cylinder. The surface or surfaces that join the two bases are called lateral faces.

Circular cylinder   A cylinder with circular regions forming its bases is called a circular cylinder.

Right circular cylinder   If the line segment joining the centers of the bases of a circular cylinder is perpendicular to the bases, then the cylinder is a right circular cylinder.

Right cylinder   If the line segment joining the centers of the bases of a cylinder is perpendicular to the bases, then the cylinder is a right cylinder.

Diameter   A line segment extending from one point on a circle to another point on the circle and passing through the center is called a diameter.

Formula for finding the volume of any right prism   The volume (V) of a right prism is equal to the area of one of its bases (B) times its height (h):

$$V = B \times h \text{ or } V = Bh$$

Formula for finding the volume of a right rectangular prism   The volume (V) of a right rectangular prism is equal to its length (ℓ) times its width (w) times its height (h):

$$V = \ell \times w \times h \text{ or } V = \ell wh$$

Image of a point with respect to a line   If ℓ is any line then the image of a point $P(P \notin \ell)$ is the unique point P' such that ℓ bisects $\overleftrightarrow{PP'}$ and $\ell \perp \overleftrightarrow{PP'}$. If $P \in \ell$, we say that P is its own image.

Line of symmetry   A figure is symmetric with respect to a line ℓ if for any point P of the figure ($P \notin \ell$), there is a corresponding point P' on the figure such that ℓ bisects $\overleftrightarrow{PP'}$ and ℓ is perpendicular to $\overleftrightarrow{PP'}$.

Parallel lines   Parallel lines are lines in the same plane that never intersect.

Parallelogram   A quadrilateral with opposite sides that are congruent and parallel is called a parallelogram.

Parallel planes   Two planes that have no common points are called parallel planes.

Perimeter   The sum of the measures of the line segments that form a polygon is called the perimeter of the polygon.

Pi   The ratio of the circumference of a circle to its diameter is called pi (π). Approximate values of pi are 3.1, 3.14, or $\frac{22}{7}$.

Polygon   A polygon is a simple closed curve formed by the union of three or more line segments (called sides). If the sides of a polygon are all equal (or congruent) and if the angles suggested are all equal in measure, it is called a regular polygon. Otherwise, it is called an irregular polygon.

Prism   A prism is a simple closed surface formed by two congruent polygonal regions in parallel planes and quadrilateral regions joining the two congruent polygonal regions, completely enclosing the space between them.

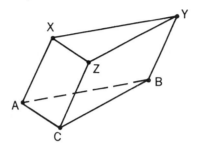

The polygonal regions of the prism pictured (ABC and XYZ) are called the bases of the prism. The quadrilateral regions (ABYX, BCZY, and CAXZ) that join together the two bases are called lateral faces, or sides. The faces of a prism are the polygonal regions that form the prism (ABC, XYZ, ABYX, BCZY, and CAXZ). A line segment formed by the intersection of two sides ($\overline{AB}$, $\overline{BC}$, $\overline{CA}$, $\overline{XY}$, $\overline{YZ}$, $\overline{ZX}$, $\overline{AX}$, $\overline{BY}$, or $\overline{CZ}$) is called an edge. And the point formed by the intersection of three edges or by the intersection of three faces is called a vertex (plural, "vertices"). The vertices in the prism above are A, B, C, X, Y, and Z. Prisms are classified according to the polygonal regions that form the bases. For example, if a prism has rectangular regions forming its two bases, it is called a rectangular prism.

Right prism   If a prism is shaped so that the edges joining the two bases are perpendicular to the bases, then the prism is a right prism.

Right rectangular prism   A rectangular prism that is also a right prism is called a right rectangular prism.

Pyramid   A pyramid is a simple closed surface formed by a simple closed region, a point (vertex) not in the plane of the region, and triangular regions joining the simple closed region and the vertex, completely enclosing the space between them.

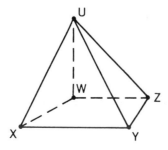

The simple closed region (WXYZ) is called the base of the pyramid. The triangular regions (WXU, XYU, YZU, and ZWU) that join the base with the point, U, not in the plane of the base are called lateral faces. The faces of the pyramid are the polygonal regions that form the prism (WXYZ, WXU, XYU, YZU, and ZWU). A line segment formed by the intersection of two faces ($\overleftrightarrow{\text{WX}}$, $\overleftrightarrow{\text{XY}}$, $\overleftrightarrow{\text{YZ}}$, $\overleftrightarrow{\text{ZW}}$, $\overleftrightarrow{\text{UW}}$, $\overleftrightarrow{\text{UX}}$, $\overleftrightarrow{\text{UY}}$, or $\overleftrightarrow{\text{UZ}}$) is called an edge. A point formed by the intersection of three or more edges, or by the intersection of three or more faces, is a vertex of the pyramid (U, W, X, Y, or Z). Pyramids are classified according to the polygonal region forming the base. For example, if a pyramid has a rectangular region forming its base, it is called a rectangular pyramid.

Pythagorean theorem   The Pythagorean theorem states that in a right triangle the square of the measure of the hypotenuse is equal to the sum of the squares of the measures of the other two sides.

Quadrilateral   A quadrilateral is a polygon with four sides, formed by a simple closed curve of four line segments.

Radius   A line segment extending from the center of a circle to any point on the circle itself is called a radius.

Rectangle   A quadrilateral that has four right angles and opposite sides that are congruent is called a rectangle.

Reflection   A reflection, or flip, is a transformation that carries every point into its image with respect to a given line.

Rhombus   A quadrilateral with all four sides congruent is called a rhombus.

Rotation (turn)   A rotation is a transformation that carries every point A into a point A′ whose distance from a fixed pont O is the same as that of A from O. Under a rotation, every point moves through a given number of degrees around the point O.

Simple closed surface   A simple closed surface is a set of points in space that divides space into three sets of points—the points forming the simple closed surface itself, the points forming the interior of the space figure, and the points forming the exterior of the space figure.

Space region   The union of a simple closed surface and its interior is called a space region.

Sphere   A sphere is a simple closed surface consisting of all points in space that are the same distance from a given point, called the center. A sphere divides space into three sets of points—the points forming the sphere itself, the points forming the interior of the sphere, and the points forming the exterior of the sphere.

Radius of a sphere   A line segment whose end points are a point on a sphere and the center of the sphere is called a radius of the sphere (plural, "radii").

Square   A quadrilateral that has four right angles and four congruent sides is called a square.

Translation (slide)   A translation is a geometric transformation that matches with any point P a point Q that lies at a given distance and in a given direction from P.

Trapezoid   A quadrilateral with exactly two parallel sides is called a trapezoid.

Triangle   A triangle is a polygon with three sides, formed by a simple closed curve of three line segments.

Acute triangle   If all three of the angles of a triangle are acute angles, the triangle is called an acute triangle.

Congruent triangles   Triangles whose corresponding sides and angles are congruent are called congruent triangles.

Equiangular triangle   If the three angles of a triangle are all equal in measure, the triangle is called an equiangular triangle.

Equilateral triangle   If all three sides of a triangle are congruent, the triangle is called an equilateral triangle.

Isosceles triangle   If at least two sides of a triangle are congruent, the triangle is called an isosceles triangle.

Obtuse triangle   If one of the three angles of a triangle is an obtuse angle, the triangle is called an obtuse triangle.

Right triangle   If one of the angles of a triangle is a right angle, the triangle is called a right triangle.

Scalene triangle   If no two sides of a triangle are congruent, the triangle is called a scalene triangle.

Similar triangles   Triangles whose corresponding angles are congruent but whose corresponding sides are not necessarily congruent are called similar triangles.

Volume   Volume is a measure of the space occupied by a space region. Volume is measured in cubic units—for example, cubic inches. One cubic inch of space is the amount of space enclosed by a cube having an edge one inch long.

Practice Exercises

1. Classify each triangular region according to its sides. Classify each according to its angles. Then determine its area and perimeter.

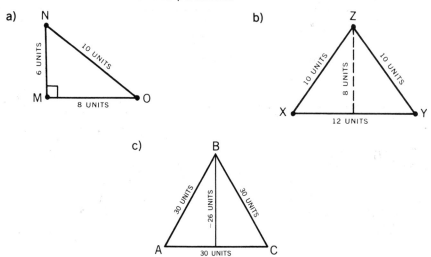

a)

N

6 UNITS

10 UNITS

M   8 UNITS   O

b)

Z

10 UNITS   8 UNITS   10 UNITS

X   12 UNITS   Y

c)

B

30 UNITS   ~26 UNITS   30 UNITS

A   30 UNITS   C

2. Develop a formula for the area of a trapezoid. Use b_1 for the length of the lower base, use b_2 for the length of the upper base (the bases are the parallel sides), and use h for the height of the trapezoid.

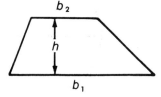

b_2

h

b_1

3. Classify each quadrilateral; then determine its area and perimeter.

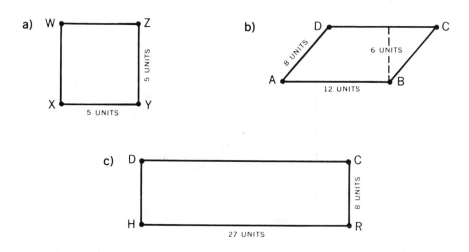

a)

W   Z

5 UNITS

X   5 UNITS   Y

b)

D   C

8 UNITS   6 UNITS

A   12 UNITS   B

c)

D   C

8 UNITS

H   27 UNITS   R

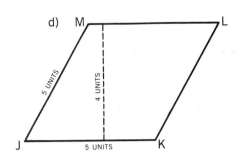

d)

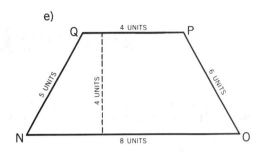

e)

4. Construct a polygon congruent to each figure.

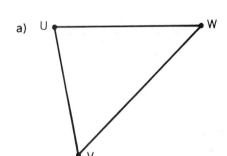

a)

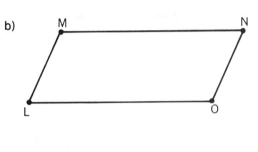

b)

5. Determine the area and circumference of each circle.

a)
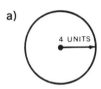

b)
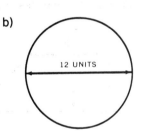

6. Use the Pythagorean theorem to determine the measure of the indicated side in each figure.

a) Find the measure of side *a*.

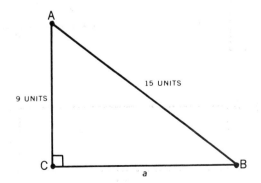

b) Find the measure of side *b*.

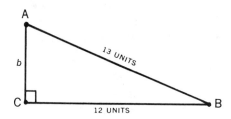

c) Find the measure of side *c*.

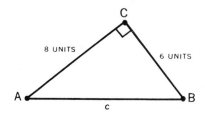

7. Draw a square and use dotted lines to show all the lines with respect to which the square is symmetric.

8. Suppose polygon A′B′C′D′E′ is the image of polygon ABCDE under a translation (slide). What can you say about the following?

   a) the relationship between lines AA′, BB′, CC′, DD′, and EE′
   b) the lengths of line segments AA′, BB′, CC′, DD′, and EE′
   c) the sizes and shapes of ABCDE and A′B′C′D′E′

9. Trace the following figure on a sheet of paper. Then sketch the image of ABCDE under a
$\frac{1}{4}$-turn (that is, a turn of 90°) in a counterclockwise direction with respect to point O.

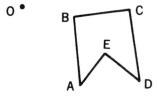

10. The measure of two angles of a triangle are 63° and 46°. What is the measure of the third angle?

11. Draw each figure after a rotation around point P as suggested under each drawing.

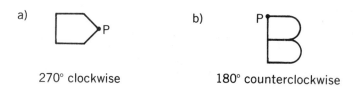

a)   b)

270° clockwise   180° counterclockwise

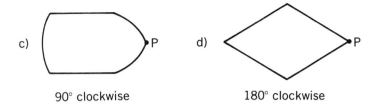

c) 90° clockwise

d) 180° clockwise

12. Draw all the lines of symmetry for each figure.

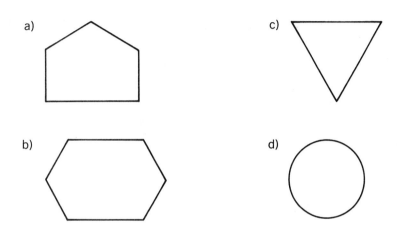

a)

b)

c)

d)

13. Trace each figure on a sheet of paper. Then flip the figure over a line ℓ.

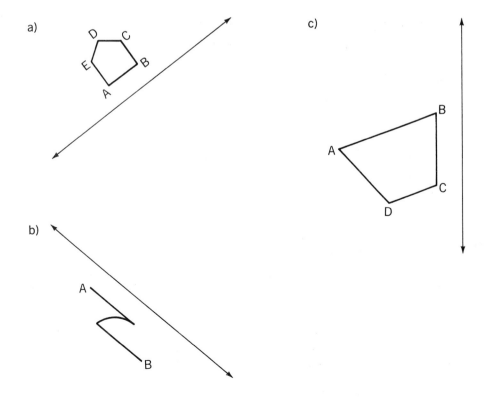

a)

b)

c)

14. Identify each space region, and list the bases, edges, and vertices for each region.

a)

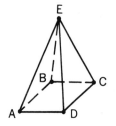

c)

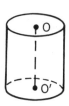

b)

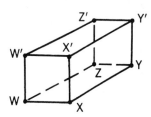

d)

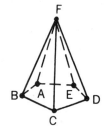

15. Find the volume of each space region represented.

a)

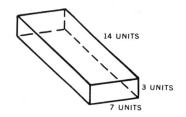

b)

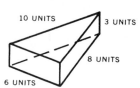

c)

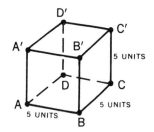

16. Calculate the surface area of each space region represented.

a)

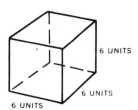

b)

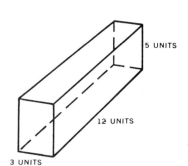

c)
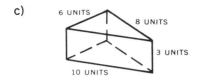

(The bases are right triangles.)

17. For each description listed, match the geometric space figure or figures.

a) The formula for the volume of this
   space figure is $V = Bh$.
b) A space figure with all points
   equally distant from a single point
c) A space figure whose lateral faces
   are rectangles
d) A space figure with four faces
e) A space figure whose lateral faces
   are triangles

Sphere
Pyramid
Prism
Cylinder
Cone

18. If each region were cut out and folded together, what space figure could it make?

a)
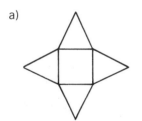

b)
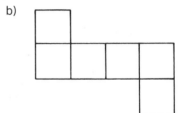

c)
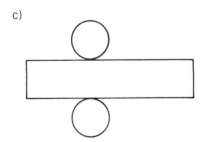

d)
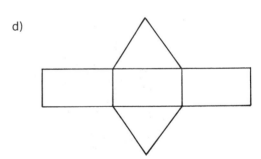

19. Complete the table.

Space Figure	Area of Base	Height	Volume
Cylinder	42 sq. in.	10 in.	
Cube			125 cu. cm.
Triangular prism	37 sq. in.		518 cu. in.
Cylinder	24 sq. m.	50 dm.	
Rectangular prism	27 sq. mm.		243 cu. mm.
Square prism	6 sq. ft.	18 in.	

Discussion Questions

1. Describe the difference between Euclidean geometry and transformational geometry.

2. Discuss the role of formulas in a geometry program. Should formulas be memorized?

3. Discuss how hand-held calculators should be integrated into the elementary school geometry program.

4. Discuss how the extensive technical vocabulary of geometry should be handled in an elementary geometry program.

5. Explain what we mean when we say that all linear measurements are approximate.

6. Discuss the degree of emphasis that should be placed upon geometry in an elementary mathematics program.

7. Locate and discuss the recommendations for teaching geometry in elementary school, reported in *An Agenda for Action* by the National Council of Teachers of Mathematics.

Activities for the Primary Grades

Many geometric topics dealing with plane and space figures are appropriate for children in the elementary school. When children play with blocks they operate in a three-dimensional world; they generally understand space figures and physical models of space figures. By observing space figures, they learn about plane figures. Teaching geometric concepts must begin by having children manipulate concrete objects. Children need help in "seeing" the objects and their properties. The geoboard is a nice device to use on the semiconcrete level for modeling geometric shapes. The Mira can be used on the semi-abstract level where children can begin drawing models. An activity that requires the student to generate an idea is on a much higher level of difficulty than nongenerative activities. String art, straw shapes, Dienes Blocks, and other manipulatives can be used on the more abstract levels, when presenting curves, perimeter, and volume to the class.

Remember that children at the primary level need many experiences with familiar objects and materials. Formal definitions of terms such as triangle, rectangle, or parallelogram mean very little to a first- or second-grade child. Developing visual imagery is vital. One reason to present space figures in elementary mathematics is to develop the children's ability to perceive space relationships on an increasingly abstract level. Perhaps one of the most difficult tasks for a young child is to perceive a three-dimensional figure in a two-dimensional diagram. Children need many experiences observing, drawing, cutting, and folding geometric models.

PLANES AND CURVES ON A PLANE

1. Attribute blocks that are used in the primary grades for patterning and sequencing are an excellent introduction to geometric shapes. Children need many experiences sorting the blocks according to shape, number of corners, and number of sides.

2. Make a set of bingo cards with different shapes in each square. Have the children play bingo: one child holds up a block and the others cover that shape on their cards with a marker. Two sample bingo cards are:

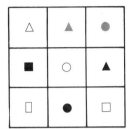   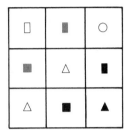

3. Write the numeral that tells the number of sides in each figure.

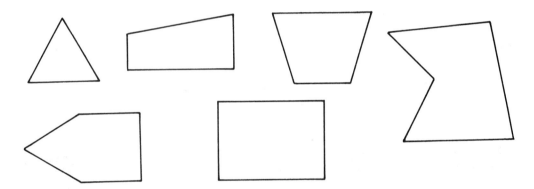

4. Provide the children with cutout shapes that they can paste on worksheets. Start a pattern and have them paste the next shape in place.

Worksheet

5. Give the children sheets of paper to draw pictures of curves. Talk about simple curves, closed curves, and open curves. Transparencies and marking pencils may be used. Project the children's drawings on the screen and discuss.

6. Have the children cut out various shapes (circular, rectangular, square, and triangular). Discuss and compare the shapes of the cutouts. This activity can be extended with activities such as the following.

a) Place several circle cutouts of various sizes on the chalk tray or flannel board. Have children take turns arranging these in order from largest to smallest, or from smallest to largest. This can also be done with cutouts of triangles, rectangles, and squares.

b) Place four or five of these cutouts on the chalk tray or flannel board. Ask one child to examine carefully the order of the shapes. Then have another child scramble the order of the cutouts. Ask the first child to see whether he can replace the cutouts in their original order.

c) Provide heavy cardboard triangles, squares, and circles. Have the children cut copies of these from construction paper and make designs with the copies.

d) Draw an X on the circle.　　　　　　　Draw an X on the triangle.

Draw an X on the rectangle.　　　　　Draw an X on the square.

Mark the smaller rectangle.　　　　　Mark the larger triangle.

Mark the squares that are the same size.

7. Place paper cutouts or drawings of various shapes on the chalktray.

Ask "How many sides does a rectangle (or triangle, and so on) have?" Have the child who answers correctly take the correct picture from the chalktray.

8. Color the interiors of the triangles red, the rectangles green, the circles blue, and the pentagons brown.

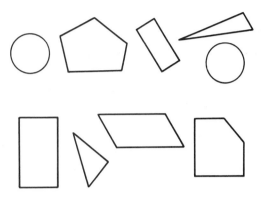

9. Use yellow and red construction paper and make large cutouts of figures such as the following. For each figure you should have a yellow and red cutout that are exactly the same size and shape.

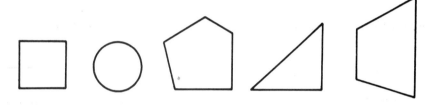

Shuffle the red cutouts and yellow cutouts and place them on a table. Let children take turns matching the figures that have the same size and shape.

RECOGNITION OF SPACE FIGURES

1. Children should be encouraged to verbalize their intuitive understandings of space figures.

    a) Who is inside the playhouse? (Interior, exterior)
    b) What is the shape of the front of your book? (Shape)
    c) How many sides does a cube have? (Space perception)

2. Use attribute blocks and provide opportunities for the children to play, sort, identify, arrange, and discuss the different attributes.

3. Use geoboards and have the children construct simple shapes.

4. Provide each child with a sheet of paper upon which you have pasted or drawn a model of a geometric shape. Have each child look for similar shapes in magazines, cut them out, and paste them on the page. This can be done with both two- and three-dimensional geometric shapes.

5. Cut geometric shapes out of cardboard. Make mobiles on clothes hangers and hang them from the ceiling. For example:

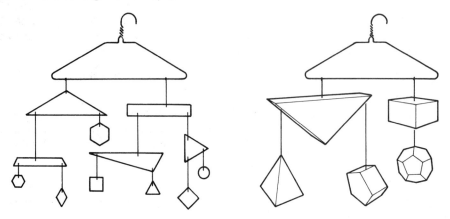

6. Use straws and pipe cleaners or string to make geometric shapes and space figures.

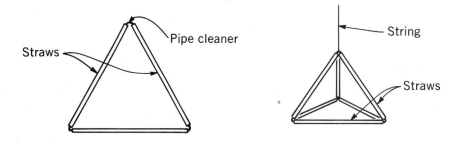

VOLUME

1. Use real objects that have different shapes but the same volume and ask the children to see how many of each shape can be put into a box. Which would be a better shape for a unit of volume—a cube or a sphere?

2. Use cubes of the same size and ask the children to see how many cubes will fit exactly in a cardboard box.

PLANES AND PLANE FIGURES

1. Draw pictures of the following figures on the chalkboard and have children answer the questions.

Is point A inside or outside the triangle?
Is point B inside or outside the circle?

Is point C inside or outside the circle?
Where is line segment DE?

If children have little background in geometric concepts, the teacher should begin with the activities described for first grade. If the children's background is sufficient, use as many similar experiences as are necessary to reinforce and evaluate understanding.

Use questions like the following in a class discussion to determine depth of under-standing.

a) If you drop a rock from an upstairs window to the ground, will it follow a straight path down?
b) Does a rocket ship orbiting the earth follow a straight path or a curved path?
c) Would a bridge over a creek be straight or curved? (This, of course, will depend on the kind of bridge and the size of the creek. Let the children explain their answers.)
d) What are some things you see in the classroom that represent a straight path?
e) How many points are there on a path?

2.

Draw a line segment from point A to point B. A •   • B
A •   W •   • Z
B •   • C   X •   • Y
Draw line segment AB. Draw line segment BC. Draw line segment CA.	Draw line segment WX. Draw line segment XY. Draw line segment YZ. Draw line segment ZW.

3. Look at the following diagram.

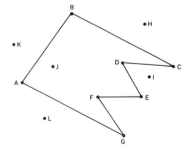

Answer these questions about the diagram.

a) Which points are inside the closed curve?
b) Which points are outside the closed curve?
c) Which points are on the closed curve?

4.

A •   • D

B •   • C

Connect points A and B.
Connect points B and C.
Connect points C and D.
Connect points D and A.
Connect points B and D.
Connect points A and C.
How many line segments did
you draw?

          B •
A •   • C

E •   • D

Connect points A, B, C, D, and E in every
possible way. How many line segments did
you draw?

Mark a point B on the boundary of the figure so that a line
segment connecting A and B
will be inside the figure. Can
you mark a point C on the
boundary of the figure so that
you can draw line segment AC
outside the figure?

Mark a point Y on the boundary so that you
can draw line segment XY outside the figure. Mark a point Z on the boundary of the
figure so that you can draw line segment
XZ inside the figure.

5. Make a shape on the geoboard and turn the board halfway around. Do the shapes still
look alike? Some examples are shown.

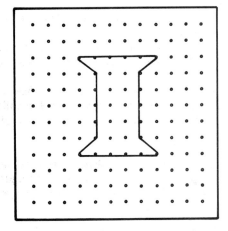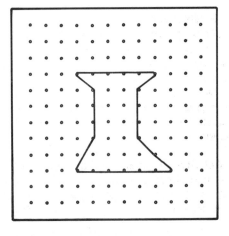

6. The children can use rubber bands to represent different geometric shapes on a geoboard.

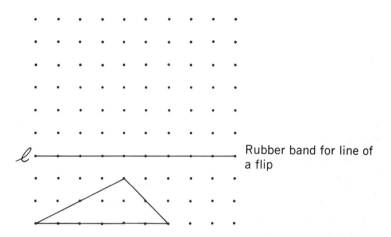

Rubber band for line of a flip

    a) Place a rubber band on the board to show how the figure will look after it is flipped over the line ℓ.

    b) Use a rubber band to make a square. Use more rubber bands to show all of the lines of symmetry.

    c) Make a regular hexagon with a rubber band.

7. Line symmetry can be introduced by folding pieces of paper and having the children cut out familiar shapes. Two examples are shown here:

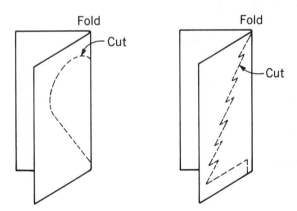

8. On the chalkboard draw a large square, a large rectangle, and a large triangle. These should be drawn so that their areas appear to be equal.

    Ask which figure is smallest and which is largest. Ask for suggestions as to how we could actually determine if one of the figures covers more area than the others. Give children a chance to explain their ideas.

    Draw horizontal and vertical lines over the figures to form equal squares. Ask if this would give us a method that we could use to determine the largest figure. Let the children discuss how they would count only parts of some squares in determining the area of the triangle.

9. Activity: Give each child a set of large paper models of a square, a triangle, and a rectangle. Then provide each child with an acetate grid marked with one-inch squares. Have children measure the area of each shape and record the results in terms of the number of squares. Let them compare their results.

10. Give the children many opportunities to practice tracing figures (not necessarily the common geometric figures). This will help to reinforce the idea that congruent figures are exactly alike in size and shape.

11. Let each child fold sheets of paper and cut out various shapes.

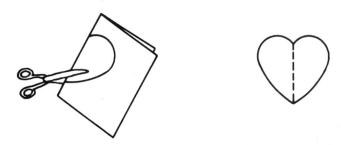

When the paper is unfolded, the child will have a figure symmetric with respect to the line along which the paper is creased.

Fold a sheet of paper into fourths and cut out the various shapes that have two different lines of symmetry.

RECOGNITION OF SPACE FIGURES

At this level, children should be ready to distinguish between many kinds of space figures and give many their proper names. Spheres, cones, cylinders, and pyramids are easy to recognize, but distinguishing between different kinds of prisms and pyramids may be difficult for many children.

1. Children should have the experience of cutting paper or cardboard prisms apart to see what patterns can be folded to form these prisms.

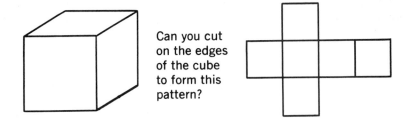

Can you cut on the edges of the cube to form this pattern?

Are there other ways you could cut the cube to form a pattern that can be folded into a cube? How many such patterns are there?

2. Have the children draw pictures using basic three-dimensional figures.

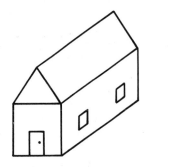

3. Make available to the children paper, plastic, or wooden models of various space figures such as cubes, triangular prisms, and pyramids. Let the children handle and inspect these figures, and have them sketch and identify the flat regions that form the faces of the figures.

Hand-Held Calculator Activities for the Primary Grades

1. When children can add whole numbers on the hand-held calculator, then they can add the numbers to find the perimeter of a figure. Have the children sit on a carpet on the floor, then have one of the children walk along the edge of one side of the carpet, counting the steps. Use this procedure to find the number of steps on each side. Ask the children how we could find the number of steps needed to walk all around the edge of the carpet. Use the calculator to add the number of steps. Have a child walk all around the carpet, following the edge as closely as possible. Check to make sure that the calculated answer is approximately equal to the actual number of steps taken. It is not necessary to use technical language (perimeter) at this point of development.

2. Use masking tape to mark off other figures on the classroom floor. Follow the same procedure as suggested in the preceding exercise for calculating the perimeter of these figures. For example:

3. Use the same procedure again. Mark off large figures on the playground blacktop with chalk. Children need many experiences actually seeing measurements such as 10 meters or 20 feet on the playground. Thus children will begin to develop a foundation for visualizing measurements in the real world. Seeing the actual five meters should mean much more than a short line segment drawn on a chalkboard to represent five meters.

4. Count and record the number of steps taken as children walk. On returning to the classroom, add the recorded numbers to find the total distance traveled in steps. Steps for the length of the hall or the distance to the cafeteria, restroom, and the office can be counted and recorded. Designate certain children to act as recorders (you might want several as a check).

5. Use the hand-held calculator to check simulated practice on worksheets.

6. Use geoboards to calculate perimeters of figures. Remember at this stage of development to use only figures with right angles on the geoboard. Young children cannot calculate the length of diagonals.

Microcomputer Activities for the Primary Grades

All activities suggested for the hand-held calculator can be used with the computer in the immediate mode.

1. Teachers who are proficient in programming graphics could have perimeter activities simulated on the video screen for children to calculate. Remember that, at this stage of development, the children must be ready for semiconcrete and semiabstract levels of functioning.

2. Continue to use the LOGO language to draw geometric shapes on the video screen with the help of the children. Encourage children to experiment by drawing on the video screen.

3. Use programs similar to those suggested in the microcomputer activities for Unit 14; place measurements along the sides of the drawings. Have the children use the computer to determine the perimeters. Remember that the children must be operating at the semiabstract level to do this exercise. With the TRS-80 computer, measurements can be placed on the video screen using a statement in the following format: (line number) Print @ 232, "6 meters".

Activities for the Intermediate Grades

Children at the intermediate level are becoming more adept at using the straightedge, and they should be given opportunities to draw and label polygons. Precision is not to be expected, only reasonable accuracy. At this level, children are capable of understanding quadrilaterals and should be able to use the term freely in their vocabulary.

1. Which of the following are pictures of simple closed curves?

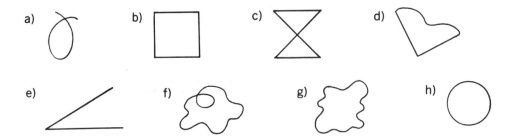

2. Draw a simple closed curve on your paper. Use a blue crayon to draw the curve and a red crayon to color the part of the plane inside the curve. Use a green crayon to color the part of the plane outside the curve.

3. Use a geoboard to model:

    a) geometric shapes
    b) an angle with the least number of degrees
    c) an angle with the greatest number of degrees
    d) a geometric shape with the greatest area
    e) a geometric shape with the least amount of area

Many task cards are commercially available for children to use to discover geometric ideas.

4.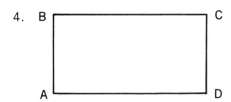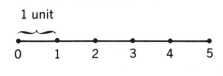

If you could walk around the sides of rectangle ABCD, about how many units of measure would represent the distance you would walk?

5. Mark a point on your paper and label it C. Draw a circle with C as the center.

    a) Mark a point on your circle and label it D.

    b) Draw $\overleftrightarrow{CD}$.

    c) $\overleftrightarrow{CD}$ is a _____ of the circle.

    d) Draw another radius of the circle.

6. Use your ruler to find the perimeter of each polygon (to the nearest inch).

a)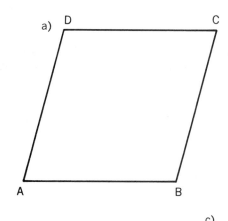

b)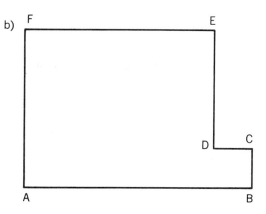

c)

7. Have the children mark large geometric shapes on the schoolyard or other appropriate area with chalk or twine. They can then calculate the areas and perimeters of the shapes.

8. Study the following figure and answer the questions.

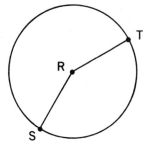

a) Name the center of the circle.
b) Name a radius of the circle.
c) What is true about the lengths of $\overleftrightarrow{RT}$ and $\overleftrightarrow{RS}$?

9. Mark two points approximately two inches apart. Name the points A and B.

a) Draw a circle having its center at point A.
b) Draw a different circle having point A as its center.
c) Draw a third circle having point B as its center.
d) Draw a radius of each circle.

10. Mark two points R and S approximately two inches apart.

a) Draw a circle having its center at point R and passing through point S.
b) Draw a circle having its center at S and passing through point R.
c) Is $\overleftrightarrow{RS}$ a radius of both circles?

11. a) Draw two different circles so that a radius of one has the same length as a radius of the other.
b) Draw two different circles so that one has a radius of different length from the other.
c) Draw two different circles with the same center.

12. Trace points A, B, and C on your paper.

A•

•C

•B

a) Draw $\overleftrightarrow{AB}$.
b) Draw a circle having its center at A and passing through B.

c) Draw a circle having its center at C and a radius equal in length to the length of $\overline{AB}$.
d) Draw a radius of the circle you have just made.
e) Is the length of this radius equal to the length of $\overline{AB}$?

13. Let the children experiment and discover ways to make paper models of cones and pyramids.

Hand-Held Calculator Activities for the Intermediate Grades

1. Use the same type of activities suggested for the hand-held calculator in the primary grades. Use many figures with different shapes, such as:

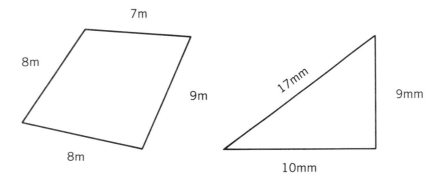

2. Use the hand-held calculator to find the perimeters of geometric figures by adding the lengths of the sides of the figure. Perimeters for regular geometric figures can be calculated using multiplication. Extend this idea: multiply the length of a rectangle by 2, then multiply the width by 2 and add the two products. When children record the measurement on paper, remember that units must be written with the numbers. Also, for a word problem, the measurements must be written in a complete sentence.

3. Use the hand-held calculator to check all geometric calculations.

Microcomputer Activities for the Intermediate Grades

All activities suggested for the hand-held calculator can be used on the microcomputer in the immediate mode.

1. Microcomputer activities suggested for the primary grades can be adapted for the intermediate grades.

2. Encourage children to program graphics on the microcomputer. Each computer has its own unique techniques for producing graphics, so always have a computer manual available for the children; encourage them to locate, read, and study sections of the manual that will help them solve their problems.

3. Children can write simple programs for calculating the area of regular geometric figures. Here we present a general microcomputer program that can easily be made machine-specific:

```
10 PRINT" THIS PROGRAM WILL FIND THE"
20 PRINT "PERIMETER FOR RECTANGLES."
30 PRINT"WHAT IS THE LENGTH OF YOUR RECTANGLE"
40 INPUT L
50 PRINT "WHAT IS THE WIDTH OF YOUR RECTANGLE"
60 INPUT W
70 P=(2*L)+(2*W)
80 PRINT "THE PERIMETER OF A RECTANGLE ";L; " UNITS LONG"
90 PRINT "AND ";W;" UNITS WIDE IS ";P;" UNITS."
```

4. After developing a program similar to the one suggested above, have the children develop programs for the perimeter of

   a) a square
   b) an equilateral triangle
   c) an isosceles triangle
   d) a scalene triangle

Activities for the Upper Elementary Grades

POLYGONS AND CIRCLES

1. Which polygon of each pair below has the interior region with the greater area? (You may make a paper model of one of these regions and cut it to see whether the pieces can be placed on the other region without overlapping.)

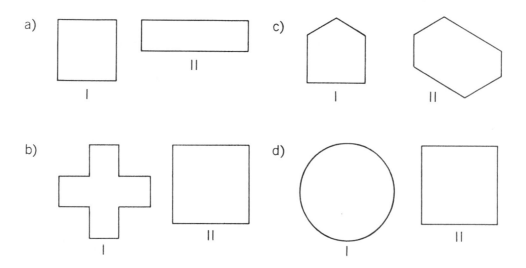

2. Study the diagram and answer the questions.

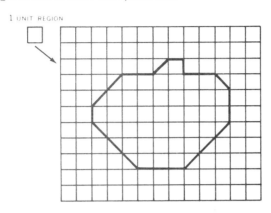

1 UNIT REGION

a) How many unit regions fit entirely within the polygonal region?
b) How many unit regions are necessary to cover the region?
c) The area of the polygonal region is exactly _____ units.

3. Activity:

   a) Draw a rectangle $4\frac{1}{2}$ inches long and $1\frac{1}{2}$ inches wide.

   b) What unit can you use to measure the area of the enclosed region?
   c) Find the area of the region.

4. Again use the geoboard and rubber bands to help develop geometric concepts. Task cards are commercially available and can suggest many more ideas.

5. Find the number of square units in each shaded region.

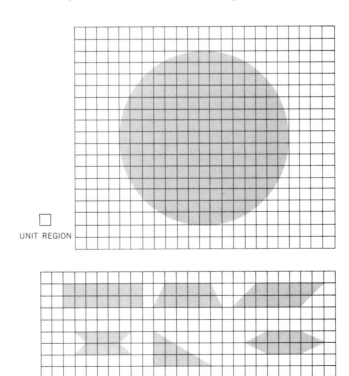

UNIT REGION

6. On one-inch squared paper draw two rectangular regions having a total area of 14 square inches. On the sides of each rectangle write its measure in inches. On the interior of each rectangular region write its measure in square inches.

7. For each of the following exercises, draw rectangles on squared paper and write the measures of the rectangular regions and the measures of their sides as in the last exercise. Use paper marked off in either square inches or square centimeters.

   a) Draw three rectangles such that the measure of each rectangular region is 16 square inches.
   b) Draw three rectangles such that the measure of each rectangular region is 18 square inches.
   c) Draw four rectangles such that the measure of each rectangular region is 24 square inches.

8. Make a chart like the one shown below. Use your drawings in the preceding exercise for the information needed to fill in the chart.

Measures in centimeters of sides of rectangle	Measure in square centimeters of rectangular region

What do you notice about the product of the measures of the sides in each case? What do you notice about the measure of the region in each case?

9. Classify each triangle both according to its angles and its sides.

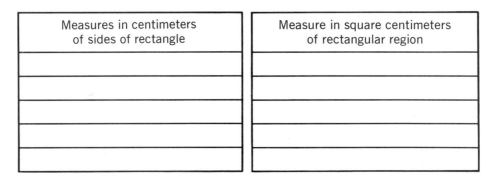

10. Classify each angle according to its measure.

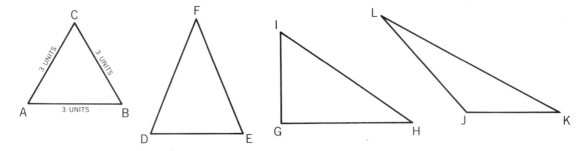

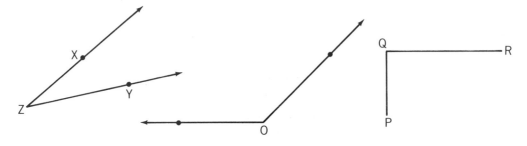

11. In each of the following exercises the given triangle is a right triangle.

a)

T
5 in.
R
8 in.
S

Area of triangular region RST is _____ square inches.

c)

M   9 in.   P
4 in.
Q

Area of triangular region MPQ is _____ square inches.

b)

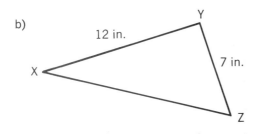

Y
12 in.
7 in.
X
Z

Area of triangular region XYZ is _____ square inches.

d)

B
6 in.   7 in.
A   C

Area of triangular region ABC is _____ square inches.

12. The picture below is a diagram of a kitchen floor, with the lengths of the edges shown. Find the area of the floor.

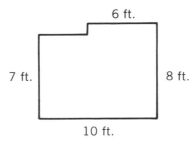

6 ft.

7 ft.   8 ft.

10 ft.

CIRCUMFERENCE OF A CIRCLE

1. Have children measure the diameter and circumference of a circular object with a cloth tape measure. Have them calculate the ratio of circumference to diameter. Have them repeat this process with as many objects as time permits, each time keeping a record of the measurements. If the children make accurate measurements they should obtain a reasonably good approximate value for π. (Use either metric or English units.)

SYMMETRY AND TRANSFORMATIONS

1. Study the following letters of the alphabet.

A B C D E F G H I J

   a) Which of these letters are symmetric with respect to a line?
   b) Do any of the letters shown above have more than one line of symmetry? If so, which ones?
   c) What other letters can you think of that are symmetric with respect to a line?

2. Use your compass to draw a circle (any size) on your paper.

   a) Use your ruler to draw two lines of symmetry for the circle.
   b) Can you draw more lines of symmetry? How many lines of symmetry do you think a circle has?

3. Trace each figure and the line shown with it. After you have done this, draw the flip image of the figure in the line.

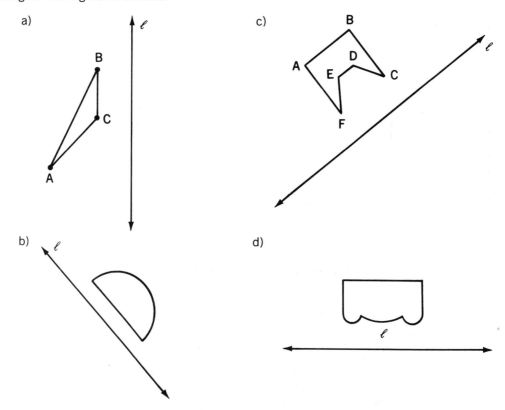

4. Rotations can be conveniently studied using tracings of figures on sheets of acetate. Have students do a number of experiments to sketch the images of various figures under rotations of $\frac{1}{4}$ turn, $\frac{1}{3}$ turn, $\frac{1}{2}$ turn, and so on. Have the students consider questions such as the following.

   a) Does a clockwise rotation through $\frac{1}{2}$ turn give the same image as a counterclockwise rotation through $\frac{1}{2}$ turn? (Assume that the "center of rotation" stays the same.)

b) Around what point can a circle be rotated through a $\frac{1}{2}$ turn clockwise so that the image of the circle is the circle itself?

c) Draw a square. Draw dotted line segments to join both pairs of opposite vertices. Label the point where the segments intersect with the letter C. What is the image of the square under a $\frac{1}{4}$ turn clockwise around point C? Under a $\frac{1}{2}$ turn clockwise around C? Under a $\frac{3}{4}$ turn clockwise around C?

d) Draw other geometric figures that are their own images under $\frac{1}{4}$ turns, $\frac{1}{2}$ turns, and $\frac{3}{4}$ turns.

5. In which cases is the figure labeled ② a slide image (that is, an image under a translation) of the figure labeled ①?

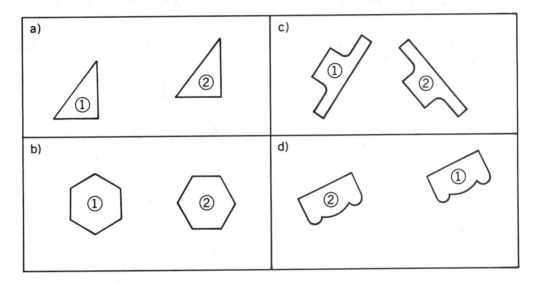

RECOGNITION OF SPACE FIGURES

1. a) Have cutout models of a circle, a rectangle, a square, and a triangle available. Then introduce models of a cube, a sphere, a cone, a cylinder, and a pyramid. Compare the two-dimensional and the three-dimensional models. Ask children to explain the ways in which the figures are alike and the ways in which they are different. (Children should be able to identify the three-dimensional shapes by name.)

   b) Ask one child to think of one of the three-dimensional shapes. Have another child try to identify the shape he is thinking of by asking a series of questions that can be answered only by yes or no. Continue the questions until the object is identified.

2. Ask the children to make patterns that can be folded into cylinders and cones. One way they can discover patterns for these figures is to wrap paper around wooden or plastic models and cut the paper to form the pattern. If the children have trouble with the cone pattern, have them cut ready-made paper cones along the seam.

3. Introduce regular polyhedra by showing the children models of a regular tetrahedron and a cube. Ask the children to make patterns for these figures. Also ask them to try making a pattern for a polyhedron with eight triangular faces.

4. Have the children cut shapes out of cardboard and fold them into space figures. Paste the shapes together. Hang them on wires and place them together to make mobiles. Hang the mobiles from the light fixtures in the classroom.

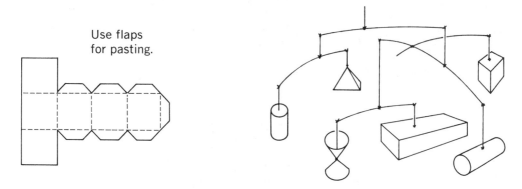

Use flaps
for pasting.

5. Give each child four or five sheets of paper the same size. They should be an even number of inches or centimeters in length or width. Let the children cut four squares out of the paper (one from each corner). Fold the sides up to make a five-sided box. Who can make a box that can hold the most cubes? What size square should be cut from each corner? Who can make a box that holds the least number of cubes? What size square should be cut from each corner?

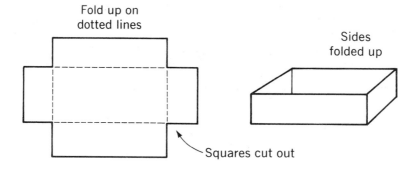

Fold up on
dotted lines

Sides
folded up

Squares cut out

VOLUME

1. Children should be able to determine the volume of a box from a two-dimensional drawing such as the one shown below.

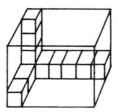

2. Use models of a prism and a pyramid that have equal heights and congruent bases. Ask children to predict which will hold more. If possible, encourage them to guess how much more. Have them experiment by filling the pyramid with sand, then pouring it into the

prism. Have children repeat the experiment enough times to indicate the validity of the test. This same experiment can be done with a cone and a cylinder having equal bases and equal heights.

3. Provide the children with unit cubes (plastic or wooden) and encourage the children to find how many cubes will fit into boxes of various sizes. At this stage, children will begin to discover how many cubes will fill the box by filling one layer and stacking cubes in a column to find how many layers there will be. Some will even do this:

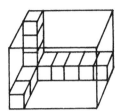

Children who use this method are only a step away from discovering the formula for the volume of a rectangular prism.

Hand-Held Calculator Activities for the Upper Elementary Grades

Use hand-held calculator activities similar to those suggested for the intermediate grades.

1. Perimeters of regular geometric figures can be calculated using multiplication. When children record the measurements on paper, remember that units must be written with the numbers. Also, with word problems, the measurements must be written in a complete sentence.

2. Volume examples can also be calculated on the hand-held calculator. Record the volume using the proper units.

3. Use the hand-held calculator to check all geometric calculations.

4. Measure the circumference and diameters of several cylinders. (This procedure is described in this unit.) Divide the circumference of each cylinder by the diameter, and record the displayed results. Discuss the results with the children.

Microcomputer Activities for the Upper Elementary Grades

All activities suggested for the hand-held calculator at the primary and intermediate levels can be adapted for the microcomputer in the immediate mode.

1. Microcomputer activities suggested for the intermediate grades can be adapted for the upper elementary grades.

2. Encourage children to program graphics on the microcomputer. Each computer has its own unique techniques for producing graphics, so always have a computer manual available for the children; encourage them to locate, read, and study sections of the manuals that will help them solve their problems.

3. Children can write simple computer programs to help them calculate the area of a rectangle. A sample program for the TRS-80 computer is as follows:

```
10  CLS
20  PRINT:PRINT:PRINT"————————THIS PROGRAM WILL FIND"
30  PRINT:PRINT "THE AREA OF A RECTANGLE FOR YOU."
40  PRINT:PRINT:PRINT"WHAT IS THE LENGTH OF YOUR RECTANGLE"
50  INPUT L
60  PRINT:PRINT"WHAT IS THE WIDTH OF YOUR RECTANGLE"
70  INPUT W
80  A = L * W
90  PRINT"THE AREA OF YOUR RECTANGLE IS ";A;" SQUARE UNITS."
100 END
```

4. Children who can write a computer program as suggested in the previous exercise should be permitted to program the computer to solve all practice exercises. Encourage the children to write programs to find the area and perimeter of many types of geometric figures.

5. Teachers can easily prepare practice programs to meet the needs of special children. Using the sample program provided here, the teacher can vary the examples to meet the needs of each child. With each child, the teacher should use only basic multiplication facts that this particular child has memorized. The following program is written for a VIC-20 computer, but it can easily be adapted for other computers, by changing the clear-the-screen command.

```
10  ?"♡"
20  PRINT"YOU WILL BE GIVEN TEN EXAMPLES TO SOLVE BY FINDING THE AREA OF
    A RECTANGLE"
30  ?"A=L*W"
35  IF X=20 THEN END
40  READ L,W,X
50  DATA 2,4,8,5,3,15,6,7,42,4,8,32,9,7,63,
55  DATA 8,7,56,6,3,18,8,6,48,5,7,35,2,10,20
60  ?:?"A RECTANGLE IS ";L;" METERS LONG."
70  ?:?"THE RECTANGLE IS ";W;" METERS WIDE."
80  ?:?"WHAT IS THE AREA OF THE RECTANGLE"
90  INPUT Z
100 IF Z=X THEN?"CORRECT, HERE IS ANOTHER!":GOSUB 500:GOTO 30
110 IF Z<>X THEN?"SORRY, TRY AGAIN!":GOSUB 500:GOTO 60
500 FOR T=1 TO 3000:NEXT T:?"♡":RETURN
```

6. Teachers can adapt the preceding microcomputer program for many other geometric figures.

7. Use IF . . . THEN statements to provide many options for the children.

Suggested Readings

Black, Janet. "Geometry Alive in Primary Classrooms." *The Arithmetic Teacher,* vol. 14, no. 2, February 1967.

Buckeye, David A., and Ginther, John L. *Creative Mathematics.* San Francisco: Canfield, 1971.

Elementary Science Study. *Mirror Cards.* St. Louis: McGraw-Hall, 1975.

Kidd, Kenneth P., and others. *The Laboratory Approach to Mathematics.* Chicago: Science Research Associates, 1970.

Kidder, Richard F. "Euclidean Transformations: Elementary School Spaceometry." *The Arithmetic Teacher,* vol. 24, no. 3, March 1977.

Rea, Robert E., and French, James E. "Fun with Geometry Through Straw Construction." *The Arithmetic Teacher,* vol. 20, no. 7, November 1973.

Young, John E., and Bush, Grace A. *Geometry for Elementary Teachers.* San Francisco: Holden-Day, 1971.

16 Statistics, Probability, and Graphs

Teaching Competencies

Upon completing this unit, you will be able to:

Define the terms *range, median,* and *mode*

Calculate the range, mean, median, and mode for a given collection of data

Determine the possible outcomes in a simple probability problem

Determine the probability that certain events will occur

Construct a graph (frequency polygon, histogram, bar graph, line graph, pictograph, or circle graph) for a given set of data

Use Pascal's triangle to calculate probability

Discussion

Statistics is more widely used today than previously. Statistics has extensive applications in the physical and biological sciences, the social sciences, and business. Microcomputer manufacturers, for example, use statistics to assess and project the buying habits of the population: How many microcomputers should be produced this year to meet public demand? What portion of the population will purchase home computers? What portion of the businesses in the United States will use computers for inventory control? What portion of the microcomputer business can each manufacturer expect to capture this year? These and similar questions are being asked every day. Statistics helps people find answers to such questions by making available intelligent methods for using limited amounts of data to make predictions. **Statistics** is the study of numerical data to determine the relationships that exist among the data (such as central tendencies, dispersion, or scatter).

Teaching problem solving, beginning in kindergarten, helps to develop a foundation upon which basic statistical concepts can be developed.

Children in the elementary grades can benefit from an introduction to some of the basic concepts of statistics. Some acquaintance with the methods of gathering and organizing data should be a part of each child's mathematical experience. Work with elementary statistics can be tied in naturally with activities in science, social studies, sports, and so on, to give insight into the relevance of mathematics in many different areas.

Let's think about a typical elementary classroom. One measure of the classroom is the number of children assigned to the room. As you know, there is no standard number that tells how many children are assigned to an arbitrary classroom. The number varies from one part of the country to another. Suppose we were able to list all the classrooms across the nation as well as the numbers of students assigned to these classrooms. We would then have a collection of information or data. **Data** are collections of numerical facts.

The total **population** for the data we are considering would be enormous. In view of the size of the population, we would do better to work with only a subset or **sample** of the population. In selecting a sample to work with, we must be careful to ensure that the sample will have characteristics similar to those of the total population. Careful selection of the sample is important in any situation where statistics is being used. The sampling technique will vary with the type of study being conducted and the questions to be answered.

Let us return to the example we have been considering. Once we have collected the data we need, we must have some way to put it into a useful form. In other words we must *organize* the data. One way to organize data is to put it into table form. For purposes of discussion, suppose we have obtained data on the 21 classrooms in Wilson School. In this school there are three classrooms at each grade level, K through 6. The data collected are listed below by grade, teacher, and number of students.

K	Mrs. Jones	27
K	Mrs. Carpenter	26
K	Mrs. Fino	29
1	Miss Wear	34
1	Miss Knowlton	33
1	Mrs. Eisenhut	32
2	Miss Bolyard	30
2	Miss Grund	29
2	Mrs. Hilton	31
3	Miss Manson	29
3	Mrs. Whitmire	32
3	Miss Hull	31
4	Miss Brown	36
4	Mrs. Long	34
4	Mrs. Wagner	35
5	Mrs. Young	32
5	Mr. Schmidt	31
5	Mrs. Zimmerman	33
6	Mr. Mills	28
6	Mr. Hrib	29
6	Mr. Hynes	27

Our interest is focused on the number of children in each classroom. So the data in the table above might be further organized as follows.

Children per classroom	Talley	Number of classrooms
36	I	1
35	I	1
34	II	2
33	II	2
32	III	3
31	III	3
30	I	1
29	IIII	4
28	I	1
27	II	2
26	I	1

This table gives the specific number of children found in various classrooms and tells how many classrooms contain that number of children. The number of classrooms containing a given number of students is referred to as the **frequency.** A frequency tells us how many times a particular datum occurs.

Depending on the purpose for collecting the data, we may be interested in the **dispersion** or scattering of the data, or in its **central tendencies.** One measure of dispersion is **range.** The range of the data above is from a low of 26 students per classroom to a high of 36 students per classroom. The range is the difference between the least and the greatest measure. In our example, we would say that the range is 10. The range shows only the difference of the extremes.

The most common measure of central tendency is the **mean.** The mean for the situation we are considering would be the number of students per classroom if the school population were evenly distributed, with the same number of students in each classroom. The mean is also referred to as the **arithmetic mean** or simply as the **average.** What is the average number of students per classroom at Wilson School? The mean can be calculated by adding the measures and dividing by the number of measures.

$$\frac{\text{Sum of measures}}{\text{Number of measures}} = \text{Mean or average}$$

In our example the mean is the sum

$$27 + 26 + 29 + 34 + 33 + 32 + 30 \\ + 29 + 31 + 29 + 32 + 31 + 36 + 34 \\ + 35 + 32 + 31 + 33 + 28 + 29 + 27$$

divided by 21 (the number of classrooms). When we add the above measures, we get a sum of 648.

$$\therefore \text{Average} = \frac{648}{21} \text{ or about 31 children per classroom}$$

As a rule, the mean is an excellent measure for describing the central tendency of a collection of data. It is most reliable when the range of the data is not too great. If the range is great, the mean may be misleading. If one of the classrooms in Wilson School had contained 100 children, the mean would have been almost 34 children per classroom. Actually the figure of 31 would be a better description of the school than the figure 34. To overcome the difficulties that arise from atypically large or small extreme measures, we can use a different measure of central tendency known as the median. The **median** is the middle measure. To find the median class size for Wilson School we can again use the frequency table.

Since the number 11 is halfway between 1 and 21, we can count down from the top (or up from the bottom) to find the middle measure. We find that the 11th measure or median is 31. If we had our earlier hypothetical situation of 100 children in a classroom, the median would still be 31. Note that this one extreme measure has a very great effect upon the mean or average, but very little effect upon the median. This points out that the best measure of central tendency to use in a given situation depends on the distribution of the measures. If the measures are rather close together, with no notably extreme cases, then the mean is probably the best measure of central tendency. If there are one or two scores that are extrememly high or extremely low, the better measure of central tendency to use is probably the median.

A third measure of central tendency is the mode. The **mode** is the measure that occurs most often, that is, with the greatest frequency. The mode at Wilson School is 29 students per classroom, because more classrooms have that number of students than any other. If a sample has two measures that occur with the same frequency (and more than all the others) then the distribution is said to be **bimodal.**

A graph is another convenient device for organizing and presenting data. Let's look at a graph showing the enrollments for the 21 classrooms at Wilson School. The kind of graph shown below is called a **histogram.**

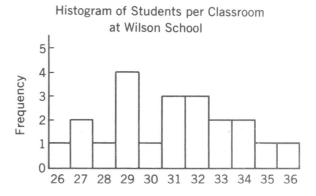

Histogram of Students per Classroom at Wilson School

Number of Students per Classroom

Graphs are essentially pictures designed to show relationships among data so that the reader can easily interpret the data illustrated. A graph must have a title, indicating to the reader what the graph describes. This histogram is only one of several different types of graphs. The type of graph one should select depends upon the data collected and how it can best be presented to the reader.

Let us look at a **frequency polygon,** another type of graph; the following frequency polygon was made by connecting the midpoints of the tops of the bars in the histogram of the students per classroom at Wilson School.

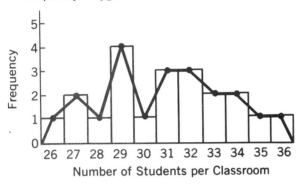

Frequency Polygon of Students per Classroom

Number of Students per Classroom

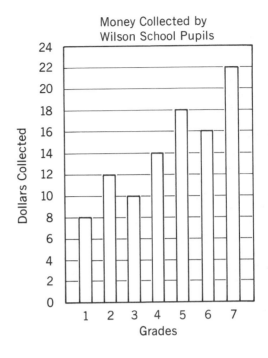

Money Collected by
Wilson School Pupils

Grades

Note the similarities and differences between a histogram and frequency polygon. A histogram is often called a **bar graph,** and a frequency polygon can be called a **line graph.**

Let us look at a bar graph. A bar graph may be drawn horizontally or vertically. The bars must be all the same width. For example, we can compare the amount of money collected by each grade in our school. At a glance you can tell which class collected the most money, which class collected the least, and which classes collected the same amount. Bar graphs are more suited to discrete data, or data that is noncontinuous, distinct and separate from other information.

A line graph can be made by taking the bars off a bar graph and connecting the center point of each bar. A line graph is usually more suited to continuous data. One of the major difficulties in constructing a line graph is the selection of a proper scale. A scale must be able to accommodate the collected data, provide for the variance between greatest and least values to be graphed, and the degree of accuracy required. Let us examine the growth of a seedling. Each morning at 9:00 A.M. a class measures the height of a bean plant. The data is then placed on a graph.

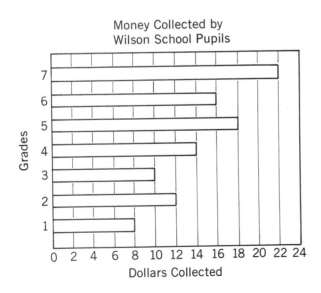

Money Collected by
Wilson School Pupils

Dollars Collected

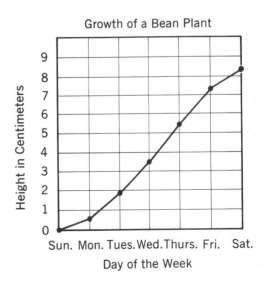

Growth of a Bean Plant

Day of the Week

The horizontal and vertical axes serve as the reference points for the graph. The horizontal axis is the reference line for the days of the week. The vertical axis is the reference line for the height of the plant. Note that the scale is marked in centimeters and that the height is approximated for each day.

A line graph can also show fluctuation, such as the change in temperature.

Daily Average Temperature for a Week in June

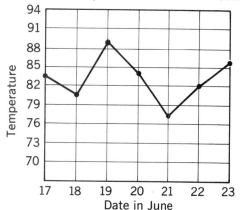

Another type of graph is a **pictograph,** in which pictures represent values; for instance, a picture of a car may represent a certain number of cars sold. Numbers are usually rounded off for convenience: If ⌐☐ represents 100 cars, then ⌐ might represent 50 cars. The pictograph below has a title, a scale, and pictures representing the number of cars sold.

Cars Sold by Jones Agency, 1980–1983

⌐☐ = 100 cars

The first line of the pictograph represents the Jones Agency car sales for 1980. There are $5\frac{1}{4}$ units shown on the line; each unit represents 100 cars. Multiplying $5\frac{1}{4}$ times the scale of 100 indicates that the Jones Agency sold approximately 515 cars dur-

ing the year 1980. The second line of the graph indicates that $6\frac{1}{2}$ 100-car units were sold during 1981. Multiply $6\frac{1}{2}$ by 100; this indicates that the Jones Agency sold approximately 650 cars in 1981. Use the same procedure to interpret the number of cars sold during 1982 and 1983. Approximately 600 cars were sold in 1982 and approximately 800 cars in 1983.

A **circle graph** can be used similarly; sectors of a circle represent percentages of the data being studied. The following circle graph shows the data in the table concerning someone's earnings in a week:

Money Earned by John in a Week			
	Money Earned	Percent of Earnings	Measure of Sector
Lawn mowing	$12.00	40%	40% of 360° = 144°
Weeding garden	7.00	23%	23% of 360° = 83°
Selling vegetables	9.50	32%	32% of 360° = 115°
Collecting trash	1.50	5%	5% of 360° = 18°
Total earned	$30.00		

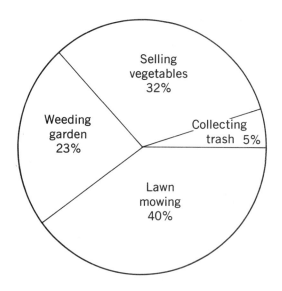

The circle graph is very easy to read, since at a glance one can see the relative value of each item shown; however, in order to construct such a graph students need to understand angular measurement and percentage.

The concept of probability is part of our everyday lives: "I will probably get a C on the test." "The odds are against Oklahoma beating Texas this year."

"Baltimore has a good chance to win the pennant."
"I'll bet two to one it rains tomorrow." Thus children
already use the terminology and ideas of probability;
a modern mathematics program should provide an
opportunity for them to learn more about the subject. The study of probability is becoming a familiar
part of the business world, and children may find it
an important part of their future lives. Much of the
mathematics of probability is extremely complex.
This unit is intended as a basic introduction for
teachers, but fifth or sixth grade pupils should be led
to discover intuitively some of the basic facts of
probability. The topic might be considered enrich-
ment material at these grade levels.

Today many mathematics programs include a
brief examination of probability. To be successful,
such an introduction should be accompanied by experimentation with physical objects. By examining
the results of their experiments and comparing these
results with theoretical data, children can develop a
greater understanding of probability.

We suggest that you also use an experimental
approach to this unit and consider the results in the
light of our discussion of theoretical data. We will
use checkers in our discussion, but you can use any
circular objects (coins, for example) that can be easily flipped and have a different pattern on each side
so that you can easily distinguish which side falls
facing up.

Consider a checker that has a star on one side
and a circle on the other:

If we flip the checker in the air once and let it fall on
a table, will the star or the circle be facing up?
Clearly, there are only two possibilities: either the
star will be up or the circle will be up. (We assume
throughout that the checker or coin does not land on
its edge and that the object used is perfectly balanced, or "honest." Since only one of two possible
results can be obtained by flipping a checker once, a
star or a circle, we can express this by the ratio $\frac{1}{2}$.

This ratio states that there is one chance out of two
possibilities that the star will come up (or, equally
likely, one chance out of two possibilities that the
circle will come up). The ratio $\frac{1}{2}$ is an expression of
the probability that a star (or a circle) will be obtained by flipping the checker once.

Obtaining a star is one "event," and obtaining a
circle is another "event." In one toss of the checker,
only one of these two events can occur, and the two
possible events are equally probable. On one toss—

1. The probability of obtaining a star is $\frac{1}{2}$ (one
   chance out of two possibilities).
2. The probability of obtaining a circle is $\frac{1}{2}$ (one
   chance out of two possibilities).

Note that $\frac{1}{2}$ also means one-half of the total events.

Probability, then, is a numerical measure of the
chance that a particular event will occur, compared
with the total number of events that could possibly
occur. The probability of a particular event occurring
is the ratio of the number of ways the particular
event can occur to the number of possible events.
We can express the ratio mathematically:

$$\text{Probability of a particular event occurring} = \frac{\text{Number of ways the event can occur}}{\text{Total number of possible events}}$$

In flipping a checker once, the total number of possible events is 2. Since the probability of obtaining
a star is $\frac{1}{2}$ and the probability of obtaining a circle is
$\frac{1}{2}$, what else can we say about the nature of probability from our experiment? The sum of the prob-
abilities of all the possible events is $\frac{1}{2} + \frac{1}{2}$, or $\frac{2}{2}$, or 1.
This agrees with our common sense: if we flip a
checker, it must result in one of the possible events
(since we have barred the possibility of the checker
landing on edge). To illustrate another aspect of this
situation, imagine that you have a checker with a
star on both sides. What is the probability of obtaining a circle by flipping the checker?

$$\text{Probability of a particular event occurring} = \frac{\text{Number of ways the event can occur}}{\text{Total number of possible events}} = \frac{0}{2} = 0$$

In short, the event cannot happen.

There are some other facts about probability
that we must know before we can properly interpret
our data. We can obtain theoretical data on probability by computation. For example, we have said that
the probability of obtaining a star by flipping a
checker once is $\frac{1}{2}$ (or 1 out of 2). Suppose we flip the
checker twice in succession. What are the possible

outcomes? Four results are possible, as shown in the table that follows.

FIRST TOSS	SECOND TOSS	POSSIBLE RESULTS
S	S	Star on first toss Star on second toss
C	S	Circle on first toss Star on second toss
S	C	Star on first toss Circle on second toss
C	C	Circle on first toss Circle on second toss

The table shows that the probability of getting a star and a circle is greater than that of getting two stars or two circles. What are the chances that flipping one checker two times will turn up a star both times? One out of four chances, or $\frac{1}{4}$. What are the chances that the two tosses will turn up a circle both times? One out of four chances, or $\frac{1}{4}$. What are the chances that the two tosses will turn up one star and one circle? Two out of four chances, or $\frac{2}{4}$. Three different combinations can be obtained by tossing one checker twice. These combinations are

(1) two stars
(2) two circles
(3) one star and one circle

By performing experiments, we can see whether our theoretical data holds true. However, all experimental data on probability is based on a "long run," that is, a large number of trials. The greater the number of trials we make (the longer the run), the more likely it is that our experimental data will approximate our theoretical data. For example, the familiar expression "fifty-fifty chance" simply means that out of 100 trials (for example, flipping a checker 100 times), the number of stars (or circles) we are likely to flip will be closer to 50 than to 100. However, this is one of the most misunderstood points about probability. It could happen (though it

is unlikely) that a checker would register 99 stars consecutively. What would be the probability of obtaining a star on the next toss? Still one out of two. The probability of obtaining a star is one out of two on *each* flip. But even if we obtain 99 stars and one circle out of 100 tosses, it is likely that in a run of 1000 trials, we would still come closer to 500 stars and 500 circles.

We have examined the possibilities resulting from tossing a checker twice. Note that tossing one checker twice in a row is the same as tossing two checkers at one time. In both situations the same combinations occur.

What are the possible ways the checkers might land? The possibilities are shown in the following tables.

A. One checker tossed twice gives the possible outcomes we have already examined:

FIRST TOSS	SECOND TOSS
star	star
circle	star
star	circle
circle	circle

B. Two checkers tossed at once can come down in only four possible ways:

First	star	star
Second	circle	star
Third	star	circle
Fourth	circle	circle

Now flip three checkers at once. What are the possible ways the checkers might land?

	First Checker	Second Checker	Third Checker
A	circle	circle	circle
B	circle	circle	star
C	circle	star	circle
D	circle	star	star
E	star	circle	circle
F	star	circle	star
G	star	star	circle
H	star	star	star

How many possible ways can the three checkers land? Eight. What are the chances that all three checkers will be circles (Row A)? One out of eight chances, or $\frac{1}{8}$. What are the chances that two will be circles and one will be a star (Rows B, C, and E)? Three out of eight chances, or $\frac{3}{8}$. What are the chances that two will be stars and one will be a circle (Rows D, F, and G)? Three out of eight chances, or $\frac{3}{8}$. What are the chances that all three will be stars (Row H)? One out of eight chances, or $\frac{1}{8}$. Taking three checkers at a time, there are four possible combinations, or ways they can be put together. Notice that again the sum of the ratios is 1 (this will always be true):

$$\frac{1}{8} + \frac{3}{8} + \frac{3}{8} + \frac{1}{8} = \frac{8}{8}, \text{ or } 1$$

Now flip a checker ten times and record the results. Then try twenty times, fifty times, one hundred times. Record your results in a table. (One hundred trials can be considered a long run for this experiment.)

Number of Trials	Circle	Star
1		
2		
3		
.		
.		
.		
100		

What are your experimental results? How many circles did you get? How many stars? Your long-run results should be very close to the theoretical prob-

abilities we have already examined. It would be interesting if each child in the class would flip a checker fifty or a hundred times. You could then combine the results obtained by all the children into one set of data. This would give a long run in the least amount of time.

Tossing the checker twice, you are more likely to get one circle and one star than you are to get 2 circles or 2 stars. If you toss the checker ten times, you are more likely to get 5 circles and 5 stars than you are to get 10 circles or 10 stars. If you toss the checker twenty times, you are more likely to get 10 circles and 10 stars than you are to get 20 circles or 20 stars.

Now that you have experimented with probability, can you begin to define the term? **Probability** is the chance that a particular event will occur in a given set of circumstances, depending on the possible events. The probability that an event will occur is expressed as a ratio between the number of ways a particular event can occur and the number of possible events. Thus if you flip a coin once, the chances of obtaining heads is expressed as $\frac{1}{2}$, or one out of two chances.

Blaise Pascal, a seventeenth-century French mathematician, developed a diagram of probability that is known today as **Pascal's triangle.** To answer some questions for a friend who was a gambler, Pascal spent some time developing the mathematics of gambling (which, of course, is based on probability). Pascal's triangle indicates the probability of occurrence of a particular event.

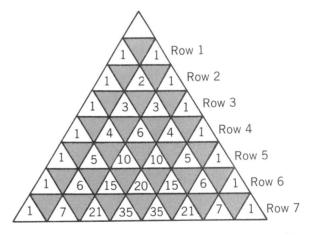

In examining the patterns in the triangle, you will notice that a given number in any row can be found by adding the numbers named in the two adjacent triangles in the row above the given number. For example, look at the numeral 6 in Row 4. The two numbers named in the triangles adjacent to 6 in the preceding row are 3 and 3, and $3 + 3 = 6$. Since the triangle could be continued in the same way, can you name the numbers for the eighth row? (1, 8, 28, 56, 70, 56, 28, 8, 1)

Let's review the information that we obtained from a long run of testing. When flipping two checkers, the probability is that $\frac{1}{4}$ of the total events are circles, $\frac{2}{4}$ (or $\frac{1}{2}$) are 1 circle and 1 star, and $\frac{1}{4}$ are stars. These ratios are read "one out of four," "two out of four," and so on. When three checkers are flipped, $\frac{1}{8}$ of the total events are circles, $\frac{3}{8}$ are two circles and one star, $\frac{3}{8}$ are one circle and two stars, and $\frac{1}{8}$ are stars. In the table below, the center column names the numerator of the probability ratios and the right-hand column names the denominator of the probability ratios. For example, when four checkers are tossed, the probability ratios of the five different ways the checkers could fall are $\frac{1}{16}$, $\frac{4}{16}$, $\frac{6}{16}$, $\frac{4}{16}$, and $\frac{1}{16}$.

Number of Checkers Tossed	Combinations	Number of Combinations
1	1, 1	2
2	1, 2, 1	4
3	1, 3, 3, 1	8
4	1, 4, 6, 4, 1	16
5	1, 5, 10, 10, 5, 1	32
6	1, 6, 15, 20, 15, 6, 1	64
7	1, 7, 21, 35, 35, 21, 7, 1	128
8	1, 8, 28, 56, 70, 56, 28, 8, 1	256

Notice that our table is in the form of Pascal's Triangle. Look at the table and consider the meaning of the rows. Assume that we are tossing a coin. Let's correlate the possible combinations (heads or tails) with the number patterns in the table.

Row 1: 1 coin, 1 toss
2 possible combinations (1 + 1 = 2)

H	T

$\frac{1}{2}$ or 1 out of 2 chances of heads

$\frac{1}{2}$ or 1 out of 2 chances of tails

Row 2: 1 coin, 2 tosses
4 possible combinations
(1 + 2 + 1 = 4)

H H	T H
H T	T T

$\frac{1}{4}$ or 1 out of 4 chances of 2 heads

$\frac{2}{4}$ or 2 out of 4 chances of 1 head and 1 tail

$\frac{1}{4}$ or 1 out of 4 chances of 2 tails

Row 3: 1 coin, 3 tosses
8 possible combinations
(1 + 3 + 3 + 1 = 8)

H H H	T T T
H H T	T T H
H T H	T H H
H T T	T H T

$\frac{1}{8}$ or 1 out of 8 chances of 3 heads

$\frac{3}{8}$ or 3 out of 8 chances of 2 heads and 1 tail

$\frac{3}{8}$ or 3 out of 8 chances of 2 tails and 1 head

$\frac{1}{8}$ or 1 out of 8 chances of 3 tails

Each row can be examined in the same way to determine possible combinations, and the table could be expanded indefinitely.

We have said that flipping two checkers can result in three possible events: both will be stars, both will be circles, or one will be a star and the other a circle. The probability of obtaining a star and a circle is $\frac{2}{4}$.

However, suppose we designated **order** as a part of the event. Suppose we had one red checker and one black checker and then asked, "What is the probability of obtaining a star on the red checker and a circle on the black checker?"

Red Checker	Black Checker
star	star
star	circle
circle	star
circle	circle

Clearly, there is a probability of $\frac{1}{4}$, or 1 out of 4 chances, of obtaining this combination. Notice that when we use one red checker and one black checker, the event of one red star and one black circle is different from the event of one red circle and one black star.

Consider this distinction in terms of dice. A single die has six sides, representing values from 1 through 6. What is the probability of obtaining a 1 if you roll a die once? One chance out of six, or $\frac{1}{6}$.

If you roll two dice, one red die and one blue die, what is the probability that you will roll a 5 on the red die and a 6 on the blue die?

We see from the diagram that there are six possible outcomes for one roll of a single die. But when rolling two dice, we see that there are thirty-six possible outcomes. For example, if we roll a 1 on the red die, there are still six possibilities for the blue die. If we roll a 2 on the red die, there are still six possibilities for the blue die. In other words, for each possible outcome of the red die, there are six possibilities for the blue die. Since there are six possibilities for the red die, there are 6×6, or 36, possibilities for the two dice together.

The dice are independent of each other, so the number that comes up on one die does not affect the number that will come up on the other die. Therefore the probability of a 5 appearing on the red die is $\frac{1}{6}$, and the probability that a 6 will come up on the blue die is also $\frac{1}{6}$. The combined probability that the red die will have a 5 and the blue die a 6 is the product of the two probabilities, or $\frac{1}{6} \times \frac{1}{6} = \frac{1}{36}$. If order does not matter, the probability that on a roll of two dice one die will be 5 and the other die a 6 is $\frac{2}{36}$.

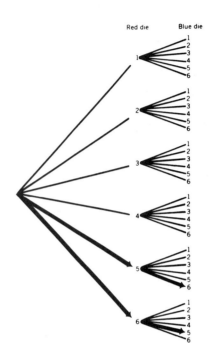

Terminology, Symbols, and Procedures

Circle graph   A graph in which sectors of a circle show proportions of data represented is a circle graph.

Data   Data are collections of numerical facts.

Frequency   In a collection of data, the frequency of a measure is the number of times the measure occurs.

Frequency polygon (or line graph)   A line graph uses line segments to illustrate the change in continuous data.

Graph   Essentially, a graph is a picture designed to show relationships among data in such a way that the reader can easily interpret the data.

Histogram (or bar graph) A bar graph uses either vertical or horizontal bars to indicate relationships among data.

Mean (arithmetic mean or average) The mean for a collection of data is the arithmetic average of the measures. The mean is found by calculating the sum of the measures and dividing by the number of measures.

Median If the measures in a set of data are recorded in order, from greatest to least, the median is the measure listed at the middle.

Mode The mode for a collection of data is the measure that appears with the greatest frequency.

Pictograph A graph in which pictures are used to represent values is called a pictograph.

Probability Probability is the numerical measure of the chance that a particular event will occur, depending on the possible events. The probability that an event will occur is expressed as a ratio between the number of ways a particular event can occur and the number of possible events.

$$\text{Probability of a particular event occuring} = \frac{\text{Number of ways the event can occur}}{\text{Total number of possible events}}$$

Range The range for a collection of data is the difference between the greatest and least measures in the set of data.

Practice Exercises

1. If you flip four pennies at one time, what is the probability that all four coins will show heads? If you flip five pennies, what is the probability that all five pennies show heads? If you flip six pennies, what is the probability that all six pennies show heads? (You may use Pascal's triangle to find the probabilities.)

2. What different combinations are possible for ten pennies flipped at one time? Indicate the ratio for each combination. (Use Pascal's triangle.)

3. Take three slips of paper. On one write the numeral 1, on the second the numeral 2, and on the third the numeral 3. Place all three slips of paper in a hat or box.
   a) What is the probability that you will draw the 1 on the first draw?
   b) On the second draw, what is the probability that you will draw the 2 if you drew the 3 on the first draw?
   c) What is the probability that you will draw the 3 on the first draw, the 2 on the second draw, and the 1 on the third draw?
   d) What is the probability that you will draw an odd number on the first draw?
   e) What is the probability that you will draw an even number on the first draw?

4. a) If you toss a die, what is the probability that you will roll a 6? A 4? A 3?
    b) What is the probability that either a 1 or a 6 will be rolled?
    c) What is the probability that either a 2, 4, or 6 will be rolled?
    d) What is the probability that a 1, 2, 3, or 4 will be rolled?
    e) What is the probability that a 1, 2, 3, 4, or 5 will be rolled?

5. If you place 5 red marbles, 2 blue marbles, and 1 white marble in a bag, what is the probability that on the first draw you will draw a red marble? a blue marble? a white marble?

6. Suppose you toss four pennies 32 times. Each time you record the number of heads. Suppose you obtain the following frequency table.

Number of heads	Tally	Frequency
0	II	2
1	ЖHI II	7
2	ЖHI ЖHI III	13
3	ЖHI I	6
4	IIII	4

   a) What is the mean for this collection of data?
   b) What is the median? the mode? the range?
   c) Make a frequency polygon for this collection of data.

7. Your piggy bank contains 7 quarters, 10 dimes, and 5 nickels. You turn the piggy bank upside down to shake out some coins.

   a) What is the probability of getting a quarter?
   b) What is the probability of getting a dime?
   c) What is the probability of getting a nickel?

8. A regular dodecahedron (a space figure with twelve faces) has a calendar printed so that one month is printed on each face. If you roll the dodecahedron, what are the chances of rolling each of the following?

   a) the month of January
   b) a winter month
   c) a month between January and August

9. Use a deck of 52 regular playing cards without the jokers. What are the chances that if you draw one card it will be one of the following?

   a) the ace of spades   d) a face card
   b) a jack   e) between 3 and 9
   c) a diamond

10. A drawer contains 12 navy blue socks and 12 black socks. You wish to get either a pair of navy blue socks or a pair of black socks. If you are reaching into the drawer without looking, how many socks must you remove in order to be sure you have one matched pair?

11. Draw a circle graph based on the following results of rolling a die 100 times; show proportionately how many times each number was rolled.

Number rolled	Number of times number was rolled
1	14
2	5
3	15
4	32
5	24
6	10

12. Construct a pictogram using the following data concerning the number of years five players of the Kansas City Chiefs played in the National Football League.

Jim Lynch, linebacker	8
Mo Moorman, guard	7
Ed Podolak, running back	6
Willie Lanier, linebacker	8
Elmo Wright, wide receiver	4

Discussion Questions

1. Discuss the type of data appropriate to each type of graph.

2. Discuss the expectations of graphing in kindergarten.

3. Discuss where we might encounter statistics in our daily lives.

4. What statistics should be included in the primary mathematics program?

5. Research the literature to find uses of Pascal's triangle in elementary mathematics. Discuss your findings with the class.

Activities for the Primary Grades

An experimental approach to statistics and probability is perhaps the most beneficial for elementary children. Situations that can be reenacted in the classroom provide motivation and enjoyment. Children should be encouraged to design and perform their own experiments and keep careful records of data. This unit may be coordinated with science or social-studies topics. The uses for statistics and probability are becoming familiar to children through television and newspapers. Space travel has posed new problems in probability. What are the chances that a rocket will achieve a given orbit? What are the chances that the weather will be suitable for lift-off? Industry has used statistics and probability to determine the chances that certain products are defective; the Department of Labor publishes statistics on employment. Many other sources of data are available for interesting class activities. Many activities can be placed on activity cards or prepared for a laboratory approach to mathematics.

Many elementary school mathematics programs begin the study of graphs by teaching children how to read graphs. We suggest that children will develop a better understanding of graphs and graphing if they make graphs first and then learn to read and interpret them.

1. Provide the children in the classroom with wooden cubes for each of their pets. (Note that we are asking the children to function on the semiabstract level, since cubes will be used to represent pets.) Place a chart in front of the children with columns labeled for each type of pet. The chart might look like the one illustrated here.

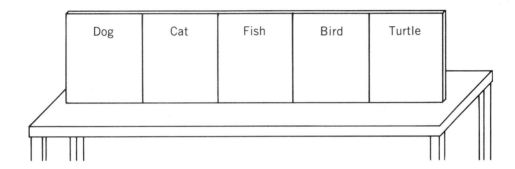

Ask children who have pets to place a cube in the proper column. The children should stack cubes one at a time. Discuss with the children the placement of each cube. The completed activity might be illustrated by the following drawing.

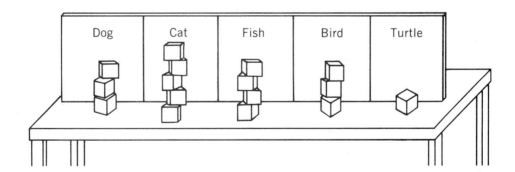

Discuss with the children how the graph shows the number of each type of pet. Ask the children how we might make a picture of the actual graph. Talk about a beginning line (base line) and suggest that we could draw bars to represent the number of cubes in each stack. Draw a picture of the graph and post this graph on the bulletin board. Compare the number of pets with both the actual graph and the drawn graph.

2. Primary grade children can visit other classrooms in the school and record the number of children who have birthdays during each month. Make a bulletin board, using a line graph to show the birthdays of all the children in the school.

3. Young children often wear name tags to help them learn the names of their classmates. Prepare a classroom bulletin with a pretty background; separate it into 12 columns labeled for each month of the year. Ask the children to bring up their name tags one at a time and tell the month of their birthdays. Place the name tags in the proper column and build a bar graph showing the children and their months of birth. A completed bulletin board is pictured here.

Our Birthdays											
Jan	Feb	March	April	May	June	July	Aug	Sept	Oct	Nov	Dec
											Jim
	Kay			Ted							Ole
	Mary			Peg		Leo					Ruth
	Jon			Bill		Ruth	Betty		Sak		Eli
May	Bob	Don	Al	Liz		Carol	Helen	Mike	Ned	Rod	Jake

4. After a few days, gather the children around the bulletin board. Use yarn to connect the center of each bar and then remove the name tags. The bar graph has now been changed into a line graph. Discuss the two types of graphs with the children.

Hand-Held Calculator Activities for the Primary Grades

Use the hand-held calculator to add the number of birthdays for each month in exercise 2 above.

Microcomputer Activities for the Primary Grades

Use the microcomputer in the immediate mode to calculate the number of birthdays in each month in exercise 2. Did you get the same sum using the hand-held calculator and the microcomputer?

Activities for the Intermediate Grades

1. If there are 7 books in one stack, 2 books in the second stack, and 3 books in the third stack, how can I change them so that the same number of books will be in each of the three stacks?

2. Find the average of each collection of numbers.

a)

| 3, 7, 4, 1, 1 |
| 7, 8, 3 |
| 9, 3, 6, 4, 3 |

b)

| 65, 25, 52, 37, 46 |
| 0, 8, 3, 9, 6, 4 |
| 68, 114, 94, 88 |

3. Have the children collect and bring into the classroom graphs from newspapers and magazines to put on a bulletin board.

4. Teachers should provide an opportunity for the children to read their graphs and then discuss and interpret the data with the entire class.

5. Make simple graphs from classroom data. Do not use data that compares children. Have each child make a graph showing his or her own progress. For instance, graph spelling grades of one particular child for each week or the results of memorizing the basic subtraction or multiplication facts.

Hand-Held Calculator Activities for the Intermediate Grades

1. Use books as previously suggested for developing the concept of average. Use the hand-held calculator to check the average.

2. What is the average number of days per month? Discuss with the children what the number 30.416666 means.

3. Roll a die ten times. Record the top number on the die each time, and calculate the average for the ten rolls. Could you tell the average without dividing by ten? How? Could you use the same procedure if the die is rolled 25 times? Explain.

Microcomputer Activities for the Intermediate Grades

1. Teachers can easily write simple programs for children to study and begin to modify. Children will learn how to program by imitation.

```
10   REM—THIS PROGRAM WILL CALCULATE AVERAGES FOR YOU—
20   PRINT"HOW MANY NUMBERS DO YOU WANT TO AVERAGE"
30   INPUT N
40   PRINT"ENTER YOUR ";N;" NUMBERS."
50   FOR X = 1 TO N
60   INPUT Z
65   T=T+Z
70   NEXT X
80   A=T/N
90   PRINT "YOU HAVE ENTERED ";N;" NUMBERS."
100 PRINT"THE TOTAL IS ";T
110 PRINT"THE AVERAGE IS ";A
```

Activities for the Upper Elementary Grades

1. a) If you spin a coin, the chances are 1 out of 2 that the coin will land heads up. What are the chances that it will land tails up? Why? (When we say "What are the chances that a particular event will occur?" we are asking "What is the probability that the event will occur?")

   b) Does the fraction $\frac{1}{2}$ represent this probability?

   c) Can you write 5 more fractions that represent the same probability as $\frac{1}{2}$?

2. Suppose you are blindfolded and a friend places two different pairs of shoes in front of you and tells you to choose one pair. What is the probability that the first two shoes you pick up will be a matched pair? Why?

3. If you were to choose a number at random from the set

$$\{2, 3, 4, 5, 12, 13, 14, 15, 22, 23, 24\}$$

   a) what are the chances that the number would be an even number?
   b) what are the chances that the number would be an odd number?
   c) what are the chances that it would be an even number and a multiple of 5?
   d) what are the chances that it would be an odd number and a multiple of 5?

4. The diagram below is a simple map of three towns and the highways between them.

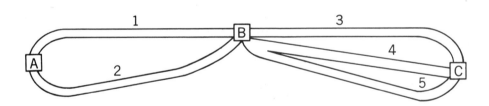

   a) List all the possible routes you could use to get from town A to town C.
   b) How many possible routes did you find?
   c) If we say that taking any one of the routes is equally likely, what is the probability of taking highways 1 and 4?

5. Suppose you have 5 red poker chips, 4 blue chips, and 3 white chips in a bag.

   a) What is the probability of getting a blue chip on the first draw?
   b) What is the probability of getting a white chip on the first draw?
   c) What is the probability of not getting a white chip on the first draw?
   d) Suppose you got a red chip on the first draw. What is the probability of getting another red chip on the next draw?
   e) If you know that the probability of getting a blue chip is zero, what does this tell you about the colors of the chips in the bag?
   f) Write fractions (probability ratios) to represent the probabilities for a, b, c, and d.

6. Flip a coin 25 times and keep a record of the number of times heads appear and the number of times tails appear. From your experiment, what do you think is the probability of getting heads? Now flip the coin 50 times and record the results the same way. How do the two charts compare? Do you think there is any change in the probability of the number of times heads will appear?

7. Many games such as Monopoly or Parcheesi use two dice with a certain number of dots on each face of each die. Usually these dots number from 1 to 6 on each face.

Toss a die 60 times and record the number of times each of the numerals, 1, 2, 3, 4, 5, or 6, appears.

Can you think of a way to record the results of this kind of experiment using two dice at a time? Try it!

Numeral	Occurs
1	I I
2	ᵀᴴᴸ
3	I
4	I I I
5	I I
6	I

8. Make a set of cards with the letters A, B, C, D, and E.

Make 14 **A** cards, 8 **B** cards, 6 **C** cards, 6 **D** cards, and 2 **E** cards.

If you shuffle the cards and draw one card, what are the chances of getting an **A** card? What are the chances of getting an **E** card? Which cards would have equal chances?

Make a simple chart to record this experiment. Guess which type of card you will get. Write it down. Draw a card and write down the letter of the card you actually got. See how many times you win.

9. You have probably played games that have a spinner like the one in this picture. If you do not have one, make one like it with cardboard and a thumbtack. Use stiff flat cardboard and make sure the spinner turns freely.

If you spin the spinner just one time, what are the chances of landing on 6? What are the chances of landing on 3?

Spin the spinner 20 times and keep a record of the results.

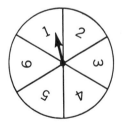

Numeral	1	2	3	4	5	6
Occurs						

Which numeral occurred the greatest number of times?
Which numeral occurred the least number of times?
Which numerals occurred about the same number of times?
According to your experiment, which numeral seems most likely to occur?
Which one seems least likely to occur?

Try this experiment two more times and compare the three records you now have. Have you changed your opinion?

10. Make a chart showing the number of students who are present in class for a 2-week period. What is the average or mean number of students present? What is the median? What is the mode?

11. Last month the temperatures recorded in Blossom City at 5:00 p.m. were 75, 62, 54, 68, 72, 52, 62, 63, 71, 72, 65, 80, 74, 69, 64, 72, 82, 80, 69, 70, 59, 64, 69, 72, 67, 75, 62, 71, 74, and 54.

   a) Make a chart with the above information giving the temperature, the tally, the number of times each temperature was recorded. What is the range?
   b) Find the mean, the median and the mode.
   c) What is the best indicator of the measure of central tendency for this information?

12. The mean age of the people attending a picnic at the fairgrounds was 18. Does this mean that most of the people there were teenagers? Why?

13. I have 5 puppies. These are their weights, in ounces.

Puff	37
Red	45
Ginger	54
Daisie	62
Molly	27

What is the average weight of my dogs?

14. Frank has been keeping a record of the amount of homework he has done each night for 8 nights. About how much time does Frank spend on homework each night?

1st night	30 min.
2nd	45 min.
3rd	10 min.
4th	70 min.
5th	43 min.
6th	21 min.
7th	0 min.
8th	53 min.

15. Check the newspaper each day and graph the maximum and minimum temperatures for a week or a month.

16. Select one or two stocks from those listed in a newspaper and graph the quotations from the paper each day for a month.

17. Children can keep a graph of their own spelling grades or mathematics grades.

18. The children can keep a large graph in the hall for projects undertaken by the entire school or P.T.A. Children should accept responsibility for collecting the data, recording the data, and keeping the graph up to date.

Hand-Held Calculator Activities
for the Upper Elementary Grades

1. Children can use hand-held calculators to calculate an average. If the children know how to add numbers and understand the concept of average, they can add the numbers and then divide the total by the number of numbers involved.

2. Assuming that Americans eat 43,200,000 hot dogs every day, what is the average number of hot dogs eaten every hour? every minute? every second?

3. Bob drove 406 miles in $7\frac{1}{2}$ hours. What is Bob's average driving speed?

Microcomputer Activities
for the Upper Elementary Grades

1. Children in the upper elementary grades should be encouraged to write simple programs for calculating an average. A sample program for calculating averages is as follows:

```
10   REM—A PROGRAM FOR AVERAGES
20   CLS
30   PRINT"GIVE ME SOME NUMBERS AND I WILL GIVE YOU THE AVERAGE."
40   PRINT"ENTER EACH NUMBER ONE AT A TIME."
50   PRINT"WHEN ALL NUMBERS HAVE BEEN ENTERED PRINT →1."
60   PRINT" I WILL GIVE YOU THE AVERAGE."
70   T=0:N=0
80   PRINT"WHAT IS YOUR NUMBER"
90   INPUT Z
100 IF Z = −1 THEN 500
110 T= T+Z:N=N+1
120 GOTO 90
500 PRINT:PRINT"YOU HAVE ";N;" NUMBERS."
510 PRINT "THE TOTAL IS ";T
520 PRINT"THE AVERAGE IS ";T/N
```

Suggested Readings

Baratta-Lorton, Robert. *Mathematics: A Way of Thinking*. Menlo Park, Calif.: Addison-Wesley, 1977.

Biggs, Edith E., and MacLean, James R. *Freedom to Learn: An Active Learning Approach to Mathematics*. Don Mills, Ontario: Addision-Wesley (Canada), 1969.

Billstein, Rick. "A Fun Way to Introduce Probability." *The Arithmetic Teacher*, vol. 24, no. 1, January 1977.

Boyle, Patrick J. *Graph Gallery*. Palo Alto, Calif.: Creative Publications, 1971.

Buckeye, David A., and Ginther, John L. *Creative Mathematics*. San Francisco: Canfield, 1971.

Burns, Marilyn. "Ideas." *The Arithmetic Teacher*, vol. 22, no. 4, April 1975.

Choate, Stuart A. "Activities in Applying Probability Ideas." *The Arithmetic Teacher*, vol. 26, no. 6, February 1979.

Godsave, Bruce F. "Three Games." *The Arithmetic Teacher*, vol. 18, no. 5, May 1971.

National Council of Teachers of Mathematics. *Mathematics Learning in Early Childhood*. 37th Yearbook. Reston, Va.: NCTM, 1975.

National Council of Teachers of Mathematics. *Experiences in Mathematical Discovery: Formulas, Graphs, and Patterns*. Washington, D.C.: NCTM, 1966.

Pereira-Mendoza, Lional. "Graphing and Prediction in the Elementary School." *The Arithmetic Teacher*, vol. 24, no. 2, February 1977.

Pincus, Morris, and Morgenstern, Frances. "Graphs in the Primary Grades." *The Arithmetic Teacher*, vol. 17, no. 6, October 1970.

Shulte, Albert P. "Teaching Statistics and Probability." *1981 National Council of Teachers of Mathematics Yearbook*. Reston, Va.: National Council of Teachers of Mathematics, 1981.

Souviney, Randall. "Probability and Statistics." *Learning*, vol. 5, December 1976.

17 Logic

Teaching Competencies

Upon completing this unit, you will be able to:

Describe the role played by logic and reasoning in a contemporary elementary school mathematics classroom

State examples of both inductive and deductive reasoning that commonly occur in everyday life

Define the terms conjunction, disjunction, and conditional

Read and interpret sentences using the logical connectives $\wedge$, $\vee$, $\rightarrow$, and $\sim$

Tell whether a compound statement is true or false, given what you know about the truth or falsity of its components and what you have learned about connectives

Give examples of both simple and compound statements that primary, intermediate, and upper elementary school children hear frequently

Discussion

We have emphasized in earlier units the central role of structure in today's elementary mathematics curriculum. Concepts that are introduced on an intuitive level in the elementary program are approached in a more abstract manner in work above the elementary level. As the student progresses in mathematics, logic will become increasingly important in his mathematical thinking. He will wonder how one can be sure that this statement or that is always true, and he will become more and more critical of the reasons that are offered as justification for mathematical statements.

As our society evolves, we need more insight and understanding to comprehend, for example, statements made by politicians and advertisers. Knowledge of logic will provide a sound base for children to analyze claims critically. Children and adults must learn to comprehend true-or-false statements and recognize fallacious reasoning.

From an early age, children are exposed to television commercials that use reasoning in their presentations. Consumers must carefully analyze the logic employed in these commercials to ascertain whether logical or fallacious reasoning is being used.

The increased popularity of microcomputers has brought about renewed interest in the study of logic. However, logic is not studied separately in elementary school. Rather, logic is treated like the concept of sets, as a tool for helping children understand other concepts. Symbolic logic is seldom studied in elementary school, but the underlying principles are explored—at a low level of abstraction.

Logic is implicit in the structural approach used in today's elementary programs. Children use logical reasoning more and more as they progress from the primary grades through the intermediate grades. At the intermediate level, children are more conscious of the way in which statements are related to one another, and they become more clearly aware of how they reason their way to solutions of problems. This unit deals with some of the fundamental notions of logic that are commonly used (though often not consciously) in mathematics and everyday life.

In everyday speaking and writing we make constant use of **compound statements.** Compound statements are formed by joining two **simple statements** with a **connective.** Simple statements are statements such as the following:

(1) The sky is clear.
(2) It is cold.
(3) Grass is green.
(4) It is cloudy.
(5) It is raining.

Each of these statements contains a noun phrase and a verb phrase.

We can use connectives such as "and," "or," "if . . ., then . . ." and so on to form compound statements from simple statements. For example, we can use these connectives and the simple statements listed above to form the following compound statements:

> The sky is clear and it is cold.
> It is cold or it is raining.
> If it is cloudy, then it is raining.

These are examples taken from our everyday language. We also have simple statements and compound statements in mathematics. For example, consider these statements:

> $2 < 3$ and $3 < 4$
> $2 < \pi$ or $3 < \pi$
> If $7 > x$, then $8 > x$.

Each statement is composed of two simple statements joined by a connective. The statements used to form a compound statement are often called the **components** of the compound statement.

So far we have introduced three connectives that can be used in forming compound statements. Let's consider how compound statements that use these connectives can be judged true or false.

A compound statement formed by joining two simple sentences with the connective "and" is called a **conjunction.** A conjunction is true if both of its components are true. If either component (or both) is false, the conjunction is considered false.

The symbol $\wedge$ is often used (although not at the elementary school level) for the connective "and."

Consider the compound statement

$$5 + 4 = 9 \quad \wedge \quad 6 - 2 = 5$$
$$\text{(and)}$$

Is this statement true or false? Although the first sentence is true, the entire statement is false; the connective "and" requires *both* of the statements involved to be true in order for the entire statement to be true. What can we say about the following compound statement?

Rectangles have $\wedge$ Triangles have
four sides (and) three angles

This statement is true, since both of its component statements are true. If we use the letters P and Q to represent the component statements, then the conjunction $P \wedge Q$ is true only when both P and Q are true statements. We can show this by using a *truth table*. In the table, T stands for true and F stands for false.

P	Q	P ∧ Q
T	T	T
T	F	F
F	T	F
F	F	F

The first row of the table indicates that, if both components are true, the conjunction is true; the second row indicates that, if the first component is true and the second component is false, the conjunction is false; and so on.

A compound statement formed by joining two simple statements with the connective "or" is called a **disjunction.** In everyday speaking and writing the connective "or" is sometimes used to mean "one or the other, but not both." When "or" is used in this way, it is being used in the **exclusive** sense. In mathematics the word "or" is always used in the **inclusive** sense to mean "either or both." The symbol $\vee$ is used to stand for the connective "or" (used in the inclusive sense). If either (or both) of the components of a disjunction is true, the disjunction is true; otherwise the disjunction is false.

Consider these mathematical statements.

$$6 + 22 = 28 \vee 1 - 1 = 1$$
$$\text{(or)}$$

$$5 > 4 \quad \vee \quad 2 > 2$$
$$\text{(or)}$$

$$\frac{4}{8} = \frac{2}{4} \quad \vee \quad \frac{1}{3} > \frac{1}{5}$$
$$\text{(or)}$$

Each of these disjunctions is true, since in each case one or both of the components is true. The following disjunction is false since neither of its components is true:

Triangles are squares $\vee$ 5 = 6
(or)

The following truth table summarizes what we have said about disjunction and the conditions under which they are true or false.

P	Q	P ∨ Q
T	T	T
T	F	T
F	T	T
F	F	F

The next kind of compound statement we shall consider is the conditional statement. A **conditional** statement is a statement of the form "If P, then Q" where P and Q are used to stand for component statements. In symbols we write "$P \rightarrow Q$," which is read "If P, then Q." Thus "It is cloudy $\rightarrow$ it is raining" would be read "If it is cloudy, then it is raining." Special names are given to the components of a conditional statement. The first component is called the **antecedent** of the conditional statement, and the second component is called the **consequent.** In our last example, the antecedent is the statement "it is cloudy," and the consequent is the statement "it is raining."

To discover how conditional statements are judged true or false, let us consider the following promise that one friend might make to another.

If it rains, then I will drive you home.

Let us think of a promise that is kept as a true statement and of a promise that is broken as a false statement. Let us consider the possible cases. Suppose it does indeed rain and that the person who made the promise does drive his friend home. This case can be expressed in symbols as follows:

P	Q	P → Q
T	T	T

In this case the promise has clearly been kept. Next, suppose it rains and the person does not drive his friend home. Has the promise been kept or broken? Clearly it has been broken. We can represent this case as follows

P	Q	P → Q
T	F	F

Now suppose it does not rain, but the person drives his friend home anyway. Certainly the promise has not been broken, so we may as well say that it was kept. In symbols, this case shows that

P	Q	P → Q
F	T	T

One more possibility remains—the case in which it does not rain and the friend doesn't get driven home. It would not be fair to say that the original promise was broken. Hence we have

P	Q	P → Q
F	F	T

We can summarize our results in the following truth table, which covers all the possibilities:

P	Q	P → Q
T	T	T
T	F	F
F	T	T
F	F	T

Notice that a conditional statement is false in the case where its antecedent is true and its consequent false. In all other cases it is true.

Conditional statements (sometimes called implications) are quite significant; they form the basis for structured reasoning and cause-and-effect arguments. If—then statements also play an important role in the BASIC computer language and understanding how a computer "reasons."

All of the connectives we have examined are used to join two simple statements to give a new, compound statement. The word "not" is also used to obtain one statement from another. When the word "not" is used for this purpose, it is frequently symbolized by the symbol ~ and written in front of the statement it applies to. Thus we could write "It is not raining" as

$$\sim(\text{It is raining})$$

Notice that some familiar mathematical statements could also be written in a different form with this symbol. Thus $3 \not< 2$ could be written as

$$\sim(3 < 2)$$

and $a \not\in \{b,c\}$ could be written as

$$\sim(a \in \{b,c\})$$

If P is a statement, then the statement ~P is called the **negation** or **denial** of P. A statement and its negation obviously have opposite truth values. Thus we have the following truth table

P	~P
T	F
F	T

So far we have been discussing compound statements. Earlier in this book, we agreed to use the term statement to refer to a closed mathematical sentence. (You will recall that this means any statement that is either true or false.) What about compound sentences such as the following?

$$x > 5 \text{ and } x < 10$$

This compound sentence is an open sentence. If we replace x with a numeral, we get a closed statement. Replacing x with '4,' we get the closed statement

$$4 > 5 \text{ and } 4 < 10$$

This is a false conjunction. (What could you replace the variable with to get a true conjunction?)

One way to obtain a statement from an open sentence is to replace the variable with numerals for specific numbers. Another way is to use a **quantifier.** Along with the connectives we have discussed, words called quantifiers are often used in mathematics. We can obtain a true statement from "$x > 5$ and $x < 10$" by writing the quantifier "For some x" in front of the sentence:

$$\text{For some } x, x > 5 \text{ and } x < 10.$$

The meaning of this statement can be expressed in a more natural manner as follows:

Some numbers are greater than 5
and less than 10.

Words such as "some," "all," and "no" are called logical quantifiers. Quantifiers help us express ideas of quantity clearly. The quantifiers "all" and "no" are used to make very sweeping statements to the effect that such and such a thing is true of *every* number or of *every* geometric figure. The quantifier "some" is used when we wish to claim the existence of at least one thing of a given sort. ("Some real number is equal to its own square" is an example of such a statement.)

The main purpose of logic is judging the validity of arguments. By an argument we mean a chain of reasoning designed to show that if certain statements called **premises** are true, then a final statement called the **conclusion** of the argument is necessarily true. We say that an argument is **valid** if there is no way for the premises to be true and the conclusion false. If the truth of the conclusion is not guaranteed by the truth of the premises, the argument is **invalid.**

Consider this argument:

> If it is snowing, then it is cold
> It is snowing
> ─────────────────────
> ∴ It is cold

This argument has two premises (the two statements written above the line). The conclusion of the argument is the statement written below the line. Is it possible for the premises to be true but the conclusion false? No. Therefore the argument is a valid argument. As a matter of fact, every argument similar to this one is valid. Arguments of the form

$$P \to Q$$
$$P$$
$$\therefore Q$$

are valid no matter what statements we may put in place of the letters P and Q. We can prove the validity of this argument form by means of a truth table. Notice that, in the following truth table, every time "T" appears for *both* premises, it also appears for the conclusion.

		Premises		Conclusion
P	Q	P → Q	P	Q
T	T	T	T	T
T	F	F	T	F
F	T	T	F	T
F	F	T	F	F

Since it is impossible for both premises to be true and the conclusion false, this argument is a valid argument.

Now consider this example. Is this a valid argument?

All dogs are animals.
Bambi is an animal.
∴Bambi is a dog.

Our everyday experience refutes this argument. But the argument can be proved invalid by a truth table. This argument has the form

$$P \to Q$$
$$Q$$
$$\therefore P$$

If we make a truth table, we see that it is indeed possible for both premises to be true but the conclusion false. Since the truth of both premises does not guarantee the truth of the conclusion, we know that the argument is invalid.

		Premises		Conclusion
P	Q	P → Q	Q	P
T	T	T	T	T
T	F	F	F	T
F	T	T	T	F
F	F	T	F	F

What role should logic play in the elementary mathematics program? Mathematical logic is a field of study in its own right. It should be obvious that a child of four can speak grammatically correct sentences even though he has not studied English grammar. He will occasionally make mistakes and will need correction. Eventually the child should become familiar with grammar. He will be inventing sentences of his own, some of them rather complex, and he will need to know how to make his communication clear and consistent with standard English usage. The analogy with logic should be easy to see. A careful teacher can do much to develop children's capacities for logical reasoning. The child needs many experiences to discover how to make his thinking sound instead of faulty. The teacher may find that some children in grades 5 or 6 are ready for an elementary discussion of compound sentences and quantifiers. Many children will not be ready to consider these abstract concepts explicitly. As always, it is the teacher's job to assess the needs of individual students and give sensitive guidance based on awareness of these needs.

Terminology, Symbols, and Procedures

Antecedent The first component of a conditional sentence is called the antecedent.

Components The components of a compound statement are the simpler statements that are used to form the compound statement.

Compound statement A compound statement is a statement formed from two or more simpler statements by joining these statements with connectives.

Conditional A sentence of the form P → Q is a conditional sentence.

Conjunction A sentence of the form P ∧ Q is called a conjunction.

Connective A connective is a word (or words) used to form compound statements from simpler statements. The familiar connectives are "and," "or," and "if . . ., then . . . ." The word "not" is sometimes called a connective even though it requires only one statement instead of two. These connectives are also denoted by symbols:

"and" is denoted by the symbol ∧
"or" is denoted by the symbol ∨
"if . . ., then . . ." is denoted by the symbol →
"not" is denoted by the symbol ~

Consequent The second component of a conditional sentence is called the consequent.

Disjunction A sentence of the form P ∨ Q is called a disjunction.

Invalid argument An argument is invalid if the truth of both premises does not guarantee the truth of the conclusion.

Negation or denial A negation is written in the form ~P.

Premise A premise is a statement or assumption.

Quantifier The words "all," "some," and "no" are logical quantifiers. These words are used to indicate whether a given sentence is always true, sometimes true, or never true.

Simple statement A simple statement is a statement that is not composed of other statements. Examples of simple statements are:

The sky is blue.	$6 < 8$
Fire is hot.	$1 \in \{1,2\}$
Ice is cold.	$9 = 18 \div 2$

Truth table A truth table is a table that shows all possible combinations of truth and falsity for the components of a compound statement. The truth tables for conjunctions, disjunctions, conditionals, and negations are shown as follows.

P	Q	P ∧ Q	P ∨ Q	P → Q		P	~P
T	T	T	T	T		T	F
T	F	F	T	F		F	T
F	T	F	T	T			
F	F	F	F	T			

Valid argument   An argument is valid if it is impossible for its conclusion to be false if all of its premises are true.

Practice Exercises

1. Tell whether each statement is simple or compound, and classify each compound statement as a conjunction, disjunction, conditional, or negation.

   a) Jim is tall or Ray is short.
   b) Ice cream melts.
   c) If you stay, then I go.
   d) The hour is late and the air is sweet.
   e) Roses are red.
   f) Smith did it.
   g) $1 \, \epsilon \, \phi$ and $\phi \subset \phi$
   h) If $1 \, \epsilon \, \phi$, then I'm a monkey's uncle.

2. Tell whether each compound statement is true or false.

   a) $(6 < 10) \rightarrow (5 < 10)$
   b) $(6 = 5) \vee (6 > 5)$
   c) $(9 + 1 = 10) \wedge (8 < 7)$
   d) $\sim(7 = 2)$
   e) $(7 < 5) \rightarrow (7 + 1 < 5 + 1)$
   f) $(6^2 = 5) \vee (5^2 = 6)$
   g) $\left(\dfrac{1}{2} = \dfrac{6}{4}\right) \rightarrow (0 \neq 1)$
   h) $(2 < 1) \wedge (1 < 2)$
   i) $(2 < 1) \vee (1 < 2)$
   j) $\sim(1 < 1000)$
   k) $(50 \div 2 = 25) \rightarrow (7 < 3)$
   l) $(8 > 1) \wedge (6 > 1) \wedge (0 > 1)$

3. Rewrite each of the following as a conjunction, a disjunction, or a conditional. (Use words for the connectives.)

   a) Ray and John are good students.
   b) I tried the car, but it wouldn't start.
   c) You will succeed provided you try.
   d) Judy or Susan will call before noon.

4. Assume that P, Q, and R are statements. Assume that P is true, that Q is false, and that R is true. Tell whether the following will be true (T) or false (F).

   a) $P \rightarrow Q$
   b) $(P \rightarrow Q) \rightarrow R$
   c) $P \wedge Q$
   d) $(P \wedge Q) \vee R$
   e) $P \vee R$
   f) $R \vee Q$
   g) $Q \vee R \vee P$
   h) $Q \wedge R \wedge P$
   i) $(Q \wedge R) \rightarrow \sim P$

5. Assume that the universal set is the set of all integers. Tell whether each of the following sentences will be true for all integers x, for some integers x, or for no integers x.

a) $x > 0$ c) $x^2 \geq 0$ e) $x \geq x - {}^{+}1$

b) $x^2 > 0$ d) $x < x + {}^{+}1$ f) $x^4 < {}^{-}1$

6. Which statements are true and which are false?

    a) All isosceles triangles are equilateral triangles.
    b) All squares are rectangles.
    c) Some trapezoids are rectangles.
    d) All squares are quadrilaterals.
    e) All rectangular prisms are cubes.
    f) No triangles are rectangles.
    g) Some right triangles are equilateral triangles.
    h) All quadrilaterals are squares.
    i) No parallelograms are trapezoids. ·
    j) All isosceles triangles are acute triangles.

7. In the following examples assume the conditional is true.

    a) If Figure C is a square, then Figure C has four sides.
    Figure C is a square.
    What can you conclude?

    b) If Bob plays basketball, then he will not have time to do his school work.
    Bob plays basketball.
    What can you conclude?

    c) If it rains, then we will not go on a picnic.
    It does not rain.
    What can you conclude?

    d) If it snows, then we will shovel the sidewalk.
    It is snowing.
    What can you conclude?

8. During class you tell your students, "If we finish the chapter by Wednesday, there will be a test on Friday." In which of the following cases would you have broken your promise?

    a) You finished the chapter and had the test.
    b) You finished the chapter and did not have the test.
    c) You did not finish the chapter but had the test.
    d) You did not finish the chapter and did not have the test.

Discussion Questions

1. Report on the appearance of logic in advertising. Locate several examples of compound statements and determine whether the ads have hidden implications or include fallacious reasoning.

2. Examine at least three elementary school mathematics textbooks, and report on the inclusion of logic—as a separate topic and used within other topics.

3. Find a text that examines converses, inverses, and contrapositives. Report on the advantages and disadvantages of considering these conditionals in an elementary program.

4. Discuss the statement "I always lie." Also, analyze the following situation: A student found a piece of paper. On one side of the paper it read: "The other side is a lie." When the paper was turned over, it read: "The other side is the truth."

5. A certain island has two types of inhabitants. One type always tells the truth, and the other type always lies. As you travel down an unfamiliar path, you come to a fork leading in two different directions. One path leads to the village and the other goes to the caverns. You would like to determine, from the islander standing by the road, which direction leads to the village. Is there ONE (and only one) question that you can ask to be sure of finding your way to the village on the first try?

Activities for the Primary Grades

1. Use a set of attribute blocks and have the children classify the blocks by color. Place all of the red blocks into a box that has been covered with red contact paper, the blue blocks into a blue box, and the yellow blocks into a yellow box. Discuss with the children:

   a) Blocks that are red, blocks that are blue, and blocks that are yellow
   b) Blocks that are not red, or blocks that are not blue, or blocks that are not yellow
   c) Blocks that are not red or blue, blocks that are not blue or yellow, or blocks that are not red or yellow
   d) Blocks that are not red, yellow, or blue

2. Use sorting activities that use other attributes such as shape, size, or thickness. Discuss the different classifications and also examine the items that do not fit the classifications.

3. Introduce the idea of a conjunction to the children by having them select a block that is blue and circular.

4. The quantifiers *all, some, none,* and *one* can be used with young children. If the attribute blocks have been sorted by color and shape the children can be asked questions such as:

   a) Are all of the squares red?
   b) Are all of the red blocks squares?

5. Provide an opportunity for the children to describe certain blocks. For instance, place all of the blocks on the table in front of the children. Have a child describe a block and have another child pick up the block described. The teacher may also want to pick up any other blocks that might also fit the description. For example, one child might say "a block that is blue and square." If another child picks up a large, blue, square block, the teacher might want to pick up a small, blue, square block and then discuss how the two blocks meet the specifications. Children should learn that they will need to be precise in their descriptions.

6. As children become more sophisticated you may want to describe a block by telling what it is not. For example, select a block that is not red, not square, and not thick.

7. Set up simple sequences of three or four blocks and then have a child tell what the next block in the sequence should be. Have the child state the reason for selecting that particular block. What should the next block be in this sequence?

red   yellow   red   yellow

Cubes might also be used. What cube would you place next and why?

red   blue   red   blue   red

8. Children have more difficulty working with disjunctions than they do working with conjunctions. With all of the attribute blocks on the table in front of the children, ask them to select all of the blocks that are yellow or triangular.

9. Place two large loops of yarn on the table or floor. Have the two loops overlap as illustrated in the drawing. Ask children to place attribute blocks into the loops where they belong. In one loop place red blocks. In the other loop place triangles. Discuss the results of the activities. What blocks are in the intersection? Why?

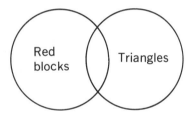

Hand-Held Calculator Activities for the Primary Grades

Children in the primary grades can often be led to discover patterns on the calculator, even when the foundation for those patterns is mathematically beyond their understanding. The children can explore and make simple inferences and even generalizations based on their observations and expectations. Remember that even a very young child is quite capable of formulating generalizations. Consider, for example, a preschooler who inappropriately adds "ed" to every verb used in past tense. The child was not taught to do this but has made a generalization.

1. Have the children explore the calculator to determine which keys will make letters when the calculator is inverted. See whether the children can anticipate before pushing the keys.

2. Have the children push the 1 key, followed by the + key, followed by several presses of the = key. Guide the child to a conditional statement of the form: "If I push . . ., then . . ."

3. Have the children compare and discuss the displays for the following

a)

7	8	9		
4	5	6	⇆	654 − 456 =
1	2	3	⇆	321 − 123 =
7	8	9	⇆	??? − ??? = ???
4	5	6		
1	2	3		

b)

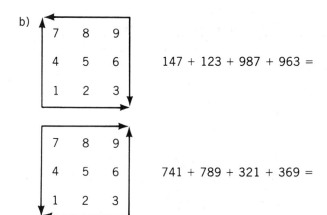

147 + 123 + 987 + 963 =

741 + 789 + 321 + 369 =

Microcomputer Activities for the Primary Grades

Numerous commercial microcomputer programs that focus on distinguishing and discriminating the characteristics of various collections of objects and symbols are available for young children. Following is a simple example written for an Apple computer that can easily be adapted for other microcomputers.

```
10   HOME
20   ?"PUSH THE 'S' KEY IF THE NUMBERS YOU SEE ARE THE SAME."
30   ?"PUSH THE 'D' KEY IF THE NUMBERS YOU SEE ARE DIFFERENT."
40   ?:?:?:?
50   ?"HERE IS A SAMPLE"
60   ?:?:?
70   ?"3","4"
80   ?:?
90   ?"PUSH 'S' OR 'D'";:INPUT A$:?:?
100  IF A$="D" THEN PRINT "GOOD. LET'S GO ON":GOTO 120
110  ?"SORRY, THE NUMBERS ARE DIFFERENT. PUSH 'D' WHEN THEY ARE DIFFER-
     ENT AND PUSH 'S' WHEN THE NUMBERS ARE THE SAME. LET'S TRY SOME
     MORE."
120  ?:?:?:?"WHEN YOU ARE READY, PUSH RETURN":GETR$
130  HOME:READ A,B: IF A=999 THEN PRINT"THAT'S ALL − BYE!!!:END
140  ?A,B:?:?:?:GOTO 90
150  DATA 5,5,7,1,8,3,9,9,33,34,0,0,13,31,4,7,999,999
```

Activities for the Intermediate Grades

Many of the activities suggested for the primary grades can easily be adapted for the intermediate grades and, of course, additional activities appropriate to this age group can be added.

1. Place three large loops of yarn on the floor. Make the loops overlap as illustrated here. Ask the children to place attribute blocks into the appropriate loops.

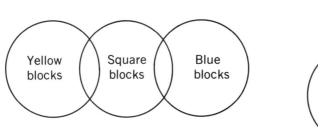
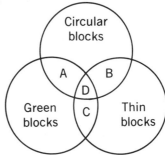

What blocks will be in sections labeled A, B, C, and D? Do you agree with these answers?

- A) Green, circular, thick blocks
- B) Thin, green blocks that are not circular
- C) Circular, thin blocks that are not green
- D) Green, circular, thin blocks

2. Make a pattern that has two or three changes between each pair of blocks in a sequence. Have children take turns selecting a block that could follow in the sequence. Discuss why each block could or could not follow. Study the example below.

Color and shape have changed.

   What block could follow?

3. Let several children create a sequence of blocks that fit a specific pattern. Have other children describe the pattern. Now have one child state a pattern of a sequence and have another child create the pattern.

4. Create a sequence that has a constant changing pattern. Study the example below.

Hand-Held Calculator Activities for the Intermediate Grades

Pattern-searching activities suggested for the primary grades can be expanded and extended for the intermediate grades. You might explore the notion of a valid argument, by discussing the following:

Pushing $16 \div 8 =$ puts 2 in the display
Pushing $6 - 4 =$ puts 2 in the display
So, $16 \div 8$ must equal $6 - 4$
Pushing $4 \times 5 =$ puts 20 in the display
Pushing $3 + 6 =$ doesn't put 20 in the display
So, 4×5 does not equal $3 + 6$

Microcomputer Activities for the Intermediate Grades

Numerous commercial computer programs dealing with elementary notions of logic and reasoning are available. The program listed for the primary grades can easily be adapted for the intermediate grades.

Activities for the Upper Elementary Grades

1. Sally had $6.25 in her school savings account.
   Jeff had $4.98 in his savings account.
   They both withdrew the same amount of money.
   Who has the least money left?

2. Betsy is younger than Paul. Paul is younger than Mark. Is Mark older than Betsy?

3. Set E is the set of numbers divisible by 2.
   Set G is the set of even numbers.
   Set H is the set of whole numbers.
   Set J is the set of odd numbers.
   Mark each statement true or false.

   a) Some members of Set J are members of Set H.
   b) All members of Set H are members of Set J.
   c) No members of Set E are members of Set J.
   d) Some members of Set E are members of Set G.
   e) All members of Set H are members of Set E.
   f) No members of Set G are members of Set J.

4. What new fact can you discover by putting two facts together?
Here is an example: All triangles are polygons.

All polygons are closed curves.

Answer: All triangles are closed curves.

    a) All counting numbers are whole numbers.
       25 is a counting number.
    b) All rectangles are quadrilaterals.
       A square is a rectangle.
    c) All numbers divisible by 6 are divisible by 3.
       24 is divisible by 6.

5. Mark each sentence true or false.

    a) All closed curves are circles.
    b) No quadrilaterals are polygons.
    c) Some polygons are quadrilaterals.
    d) All whole numbers are counting numbers.
    e) No even numbers are odd numbers.

6. Are the following sentences simple or compound?

    a) It is snowing or it is cold.
    b) It is raining.
    c) If it is cold then we will go swimming.
    d) The dog and the cat are eating at the same time.

7. As children use logic to draw conclusions they must be careful not to assume anything that is not specifically stated.

    a) Jim and Mike went swimming.
       Did two children go swimming?
       Did Jim and Mike swim all day?
       Did Jim go swimming?
       Did Mike go swimming?

    b) Susan or her sister plays the piano.
       Does at least one girl play the piano?
       Does Susan's sister play the piano?
       If Susan doesn't play the piano, does her sister play the piano?

    c) Some boys like baseball or all boys like baseball.
       Does at least one boy like baseball?
       Do all boys like baseball?
       If some boys do not like baseball, then do all boys like baseball?

    d) If the record is playing, then you can hear it.
       You cannot hear it.
       What can you conclude?

    e) If the record is playing, then it is rotating.
       Is the conditional true? Is it true that, if the record is playing, then it is rotating? Is the antecedent true? Is the record playing? What can you conclude?

8. Encourage the children to play games that involve logic—games such as chess, Tower of Hanoi, Equations. Other games can be found in *Mathematical Recreations and Essays* by W. W. Rouse Ball.

9. Encourage children to use logic in locating a specific number. As an example, ask the children what is the least number of questions they could ask in order to name a number between 1 and 100 that the teacher is thinking about. Examples of some good questions children could ask are:

Is it an even number?
Is the number greater than 50?
Is the number greater than 75?

Examples of some poor questions children might ask are:

Is it 23?
Is it 78?

With three good questions we have changed the number of possible answers from 100 to 20.

Hand-Held Calculator Activities for the Upper Elementary Grades

Encourage the children to explore patterns and relationships by pushing the keys in a certain sequence. Examine the activities suggested for the primary and intermediate grades and make appropriate modifications for use with older children. A nice variation of the pattern searching mentioned earlier is the game of Nim, adapted for the calculator as a strategy game for two children. Begin with the calculator displaying a two-digit number such as 47 (any reasonable number will do). The children take turns subtracting a single-digit number (except 0) from the number currently in the display. The child who can force another child to display the number 0 at the end of his or her turn is the winner. Help the children to develop a winning strategy, one that will work no matter what the starting number is. (Hint: the strategy depends on who goes first.)

Microcomputer Activities for the Upper Elementary Grades

The activities suggested for the primary and intermediate grades can be easily adapted for the upper elementary grades. One activity that helps to convey how a microcomputer "reasons" and carries out the steps of a program can be used quite successfully with this age group as well as with younger children. Prepare a set of about ten cards, describing some common activity such as washing a car. Each card should describe only one task associated with this activity. In this example, the cards might include: clean the top; get the water; close the windows; get the soap, brush, and bucket; close the doors; etc. Have the children work in groups to determine the overall activity by looking only at their own card. This will be easier for some groups because of context clues. The same situation exists when we examine a computer program: some lines of the program relate directly to the purpose of the program; others are for "cosmetic" purposes, such as clearing the screen or slowing the output.

When the students have determined the overall activity—perhaps after discussion with other groups whose card(s) were not quite as general—then have the children determine the correct order for carrying out the tasks. In our example, should "close the doors" come before or after "close the windows"? You will find that in some cases the order makes little or no difference, while in others the order is critical. This is also an excellent example of how a computer program is structured; some steps could be rearranged without affecting the output but others must appear in certain locations. This activity could help the children realize that there is often more than one way to carry out a task successfully.

Suggested Readings

Baker, Michael. *Syllogisms*. Pacific Grove, Calif.: Midwest Publications, 1981.

Burns, Marilyn. "How to Teach Problem Solving." *The Arithmetic Teacher*, vol. 29, no. 6, February 1982.

Cromie, Robert G. "Logic Puzzles and Piaget's Stage of Formal Operations." *School Science and Mathematics Journal*, vol. 82, no. 7, October 1982.

Greenes, Carol, and Schulman, Linda. "Developing Problem-Solving Ability with Multiple-Condition Problems." *The Arithmetic Teacher*, vol. 30, no. 2, October 1982.

Harnadek, Anita. *Basic Thinking Skills*. Pacific Grove, Calif.: Midwest Publications, 1981.

Harnadek, Anita. *Mind Benders*. Pacific Grove, Calif.: Midwest Publications, 1981.

May, Lola. "One Point of View: Change and Changelessness." *The Arithmetic Teacher*, vol. 27, no. 9, May 1980.

Piaget, Jean, and Inhelder, Barbel. *The Early Growth of Logic in the Child*. New York: W. W. Norton and Co., 1969.

Szetela, Walter. "Analogy and Problem Solving: A Tool for Helping Children to Develop a Better Concept of Capacity." *The Arithmetic Teacher*, vol. 27, no. 7, March 1980.

Appendix A: Answers to Practice Exercises

Unit 2

1. a)　　1407
   b)　　　289
   c)　325296
   d)　　−240
   e)　　　819
   f)　　−2047

2. Set up 〔1〕〔×〕〔3〕〔.〕〔1〕〔4〕〔=〕
   a) 〔1〕〔7〕〔=〕 53.38
   b) 〔4〕〔7〕〔=〕 147.58
   c) 〔2〕〔3〕〔=〕 72.22
   d) 〔8〕〔9〕〔=〕 279.46
   e) 〔4〕〔.〕〔3〕〔=〕 13.502

3. Output on the video screen will vary depending upon the input.

4. Compare your estimates with the answers.
   a)　　12
   b)　　　2.
   c)　　48
   d)　　15
   e)　　　1.9
   f) 4459
   g)　　　0.0126582
   h) 2368
   i)　　　0.44375

5. a)　　12
   b)　　16
   c)　　24
   d) 800

6. a) E.EEEEEEE A whole number cannot be divided by zero. 9 is a product, 0 is a factor, written in multiplication form 0 × □ = 9. There is no number that can be placed in the □ to make this a true sentence.

   b) E.EEEEEEE The product is greater than the number of places that can be displayed on the screen of the calculator.

7. a)　9109
   b) 18218
   c) 27327
   d) 36436
   e) 45545
   f) 54654
   g) 63763
   h) 72872
   i) 81981

8. Answers will be the same as the answers for example 4 above.

9. Constants cannot be set up on the microcomputer in the immediate mode the same way as the set up on a calculator.

The microcomputer does not function the same in the immediate mode as the calculator using a constant.

Microcomputers in the immediate mode function the same as a hand-held calculator when a constant function is not used.

Microcomputers in the immediate mode function differently when a constant is used.

11. Four statements should be changed. In lines 10, 20, 40, and 50 the 7 must be changed to 73.

12. In lines 10, 20, 40, and 50 change the 73 to 9 and change the addition sign (+) to the multiplication sign (*).

13. 10 REM—A multiplication program—
    20 CLS, HOME, or any other signal to your computer to clear the screen.
    30 PRINT "THE FIRST NINE MULTIPLES FOR 9109 ARE: "
    40 FOR X = 1 TO 9
    50 Z = X * 9109
    60 PRINT Z
    70 NEXT X

Unit 3

1. a) Concrete
    b) Semiabstract
    c) Semiconcrete
    d) Concrete
    e) Semiabstract
    f) Abstract

2. Set of seven   X   X   X   X   X   X   X
                    ↕   ↕   ↕   ↕   ↕   ↕   ↕
   Set of nine   X   X   X   X   X   X   X   X   X

3. a) 4   d) 1
    b) 3   e) 70
    c) 0   f) 5

4.

5. a) ● ○ ●

    b) ● ▶ ▮

    c) ■ ▷ ○   Answers may vary

    d) ● ■ ▶

6. a) 4 red rods = 1 Brown rod
    b) 7 white rods = 1 black rod
    c) 3 light green rods = 1 blue rod
    d) $3\frac{1}{2}$ red rods = 1 black rod
    e) 5 red rods = 1 orange rod

7. The answers may vary. Attribute blocks, a set of plastic eating utensils, Dienes Blocks, Cuisenaire rods, Stern rods, etc.

8. The answers will vary.

9.   3 squares, 2 rods, 2 blocks

      (6 rods, 19 blocks)

10. a) $4 < 9$
    b) $8 = 4 + 4$
    c) $7 > 5$

11. $A \subset B$
    $R \not\subset S$
    $M \subset N$
    $D \subset E$
    $T \not\subset V$

12. a) f   b) i   c) f   d) i   e) f   f) f

13. a) {2, 4, 10, 14}   b) {1, 3, 5, 11, 13}
    c) {5, 10, 11, 13, 4}   d) {   }

14. M = {w}   M = {x}   M = {y}   M = {z}
    M = {w,x}   M = {w,y}   M = {w,z}   M = {x,y}
    M = {x,z}   M = {y,z}   M = {w,x,y}   M = {w,y,z}
    M = {x,y,z}   M = {w,x,y,z} M = {   }   M = {w,x,z}

15. a) The elements of Set A are a,b,c,d.
    b) The elements of Set B are c,d,e.
    c) $A \cup B$ = {a,b,c,d,e}
    d) $A \cap B$ = {d,c}

16. a) {8,10,12,14,16}
    b) {   }
    c) {6,8,10}
    d) {1,2,3,4,5,6,7,8}

17. Empty set

18. a) The set of days in a week.
    b) All even numbers between 4 and 14.
    c) The last four letters of the alphabet.
    d) The first five whole numbers.

Unit 4

1. You may desire to use more precision than we have. To the nearest half inch the box would measure $1\frac{1}{2}'' \times 5\frac{1}{2}'' \times 8$. The volume would be 66 cubic inches.

2. There are two rectangles that meet the criteria. A rectangle 4 by 4 and a rectangle 3 by 6. Units are immaterial.

3.

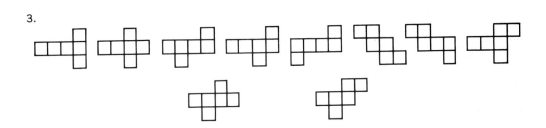

4. a) False statement
    b) Not a sentence
    c) Open sentence
    d) Open sentence
    e) Open sentence
    f) Open sentence
    g) True statement
    h) True statement
    i) False statement
    j) False statement
    k) Open sentence
    l) True statement
    m) Open sentence
    n) Open sentence

5. a) {7}
    b) {96,97,98,99,100}
    c) {1,2,3 . . . 100}
    d) {0,1,2,3,4,5,6}
    e) {0,1,2,3,4}
    f) { } or $\varnothing$

6. a) $\square + 14 = 59$
    b) $42 + 13 = \square$
    c) $2 \times \square = 234$
    d) $130 - 20 = \square$

7. a) $\square = 14$
    b) $\square = 11$
    c) $\square = 4$
    d) $\square = 7$
    e) $\square = 7$
    f) $\square = 6$
    g) $\square = 0$
    h) $\square = 4$

8. $\square + (\square + 3) = 29$
    Lila is age 13 and Mike is age 16.

9. {3,4,5 . . .}

10. Mary is 9 years of age, Tammy is 2 years of age and Kelly is 27.

11. a) Multiplication
    b) Addition
    c) Subtraction
    d) Division

12. The answers will vary. A sample of answers are:

$17 + 26 = 43$	$23 + 20 = 43$
$86 \div 2 = 43$	$97 - 54 = 43$
$21.5 \times 2 = 43$	$43 = 3 \times 14.333 . . .$
$43 = 111 - 68$	$43 = (96 \div 3) + 11$

13. a) $32 \times .25 = \square$ c) $72 \div 29 = \square$
    b) $40 \times 100 = \square$ d) $1.00 - .47 = \square$

Unit 5

1. a) 42 tens, 4 hundreds, 423 ones
   b) 7 tens, 79 ones, 0 hundreds
   c) 38 tens, 3 hundreds, 382 ones
   d) 136 tens, 13 hundreds, 1365 ones
   e) 3 tens, 37 ones, 0 hundreds
   f) 96 tens, 9 hundreds, 963 ones

2. 7 is in the tens place, but there are 57 tens in 578.

3. 4 is in the hundreds place, but there are 24 hundreds in 2481.

4. 6 is in the ones place; there are 386 ones in 386.

5. a) 7 pieces will be necessary: 2 flats, 1 long, 4 cubes.
   b) 21 pieces will be necessary: 2 blocks, 4 flats, 9 longs, 6 cubes.
   c) 9 pieces will be necessary: 6 longs, 3 cubes.
   d) 14 pieces will be necessary: 5 flats, 6 longs, 3 cubes.
   e) 11 pieces will be necessary: 7 flats, 3 longs 1 cube.
   f) 24 pieces will be necessary: 3 blocks, 8 flats, 6 longs, 7 ones.

6. Answers may vary.
   Base ten has ten symbols.
   Each place to the right is ten times greater than the place to its immediate left.
   There is a symbol for the empty set.
   There is decimal point used as a reference point to locate the different places.

7. a) One hundred nine tens seven ones, $(1 \times 10^2) + (9 \times 10^1) + (7 \times 10^0)$, $100 + 90 + 7$
   b) 5 tens 9 ones, $(5 \times 10^1) + (9 \times 10^0)$, $50 + 9$
   c) Seven thousand, five hundred, 2 tens 6 ones, $(7 \times 10^3) + (5 \times 10^2) + (2 \times 10^1) + (6 \times 10^0)$, $7000 + 500 + 20 + 6$
   d) Four hundred 7 tens 6 ones, $(4 \times 10^2) + (7 \times 10^1) + (6 \times 10^0)$, $400 + 70 + 6$
   e) 3 tens 8 ones, $(3 \times 10^1) + (8 \times 10^0)$, $30 + 8$
   f) Three hundred one ten 4 ones, $(3 \times 10^2) + (1 \times 10^1) + (4 \times 10^0)$, $300 + 10 + 4$

8. 123 cubes   11 longs 13 cubes   2 longs 93 cubes
   12 longs 3 cubes   10 longs 23 cubes   2 longs 103 cubes
   1 flat 2 longs 3 cubes   9 longs 33 cubes   1 long 113 cubes
   1 flat 1 long 13 cubes   8 longs 43 cubes
   1 flat 23 cubes   7 longs 53 cubes
                            6 longs 63 cubes
                            5 longs 73 cubes
                            4 longs 83 cubes

9. a) 235   b) 27   c) 4271   d) 1279   e) 134,958   f) 35

10. a) three-five base eight   b) eight-seven base nine   c) four-zero base five

    d) four-three-two base ten (432 could also be read "four hundred thirty-two," although this reading does not emphasize that the numeral is a base-ten numeral.)

        Number names such as twenty, thirteen, forty-five are all base ten names for numbers and cannot be used when discussing bases other than ten. This is why names such as three-five are used in other bases.

11. "One hundred twenty-five base twelve" might be misunderstood as an abbreviated way of saying "One hundred twenty-five in base twelve," which would mean the base-twelve numeral for 125.   "One hundred twenty-five" is so closely connected to our base-ten system, that it would be misleading to use it in reading numerals in other systems.

12. a) 26_{eight} b) $1T_{twelve}$ c) 10110_{two} d) 42_{five} e) 24_{nine} f) 112_{four}

13. a) Sixteen different symbols

    b) Answers will vary. Select the symbols.

A set of symbols could be

Symbol	Value
0	0
1	1
2	2
3	3
4	4
5	5
6	6
7	7
8	8
9	9
t	10
E	11
T	12
N	13
F	14
f	15
10	16
11	17
12	18
13	19
14	20

14. In base ten each place value to the left has a value ten times as great as the value of the place to its immediate right. Each number to the right has a value of one-tenth of the number to its immediate left. In this example we are comparing 40 with 800. $\frac{40}{800}$ can be simplified to $\frac{1}{20}$.

15.

Base 2

2^4	2^3	2^2	2^1	2^0
16	8	4	2	1

Base 3

3^4	3^3	3^2	3^1	3^0
81	27	9	3	1

Base 4

4^4	4^3	4^2	4^1	4^0
256	64	16	4	1

Base 5	5^4	5^3	5^2	5^1	5^0
	625	125	25	5	1

Base 6	6^4	6^3	6^2	6^1	6^0
	1296	216	36	6	1

Base 7	7^4	7^3	7^2	7^1	7^0
	2401	343	49	7	1

Base 8	8^4	8^3	8^2	8^1	8^0
	4096	512	64	8	1

Base 9	9^4	9^3	9^2	9^1	9^0
	6561	729	81	9	1

Base 12	12^4	12^3	12^2	12^1	12^0
	20736	1728	144	12	1

16. b^9, b^8, b^7, b^6, b^5, b^4, b^3, b^2, b^1, b^0

17. a) 22_{nine}, 23_{nine}, 24_{nine}, 25_{nine}, 26_{nine}
  b) 20_{five}, 21_{five}, 22_{five}, 23_{five}, 24_{five}
  c) 110_{two}, 111_{two}, 1000_{two}, 1001_{two}, 1010_{two}
  d) $E0_{twelve}$, $E1_{twelve}$, $E2_{twelve}$, $E3_{twelve}$, $E4_{twelve}$
  e) 1006_{seven}, 1010_{seven}, 1011_{seven}, 1012_{seven}, 1013_{seven}
  f) 536_{eight}, 537_{eight}, 540_{eight}, 541_{eight}, 542_{eight}
  g) 1100_{nine}, 1101_{nine}, 1102_{nine}, 1103_{nine}, 1104_{nine}
  h) 1220_{three}, 1221_{three}, 1222_{three}, 2000_{three}, 2001_{three}
  i) 300_{four}, 301_{four}, 302_{four}, 303_{four}, 310_{four}

18.

Standard Notation	Expanded Notation	Exponential Notation
101101_{two}	$(1 \times 100000)_{two} + (1 \times 1000)_{two}$ $+ (1 \times 100)_{two} + (1 \times 1)_{two}$	$(1 \times 10^5)_{two} + (1 \times 10^3)_{two}$ $+ (1 \times 10^2)_{two} + (1 \times 10^0)_{two}$
1234_{five}	$(1 \times 1000)_{five} + (2 \times 100)_{five}$ $+ (3 \times 10)_{five} + (4 \times 1)_{five}$	$(1 \times 10^3)_{five} + (2 \times 10^2)_{five}$ $+ (3 \times 10^1)_{five} + (4 \times 10^0)_{five}$
3765_{eight}	$(3 \times 1000)_{eight} + (7 \times 100)_{eight}$ $+ (6 \times 10)_{eight} + (5 \times 1)_{eight}$	$(3 \times 10^3)_{eight} + (7 \times 10^2)_{eight}$ $+ (6 \times 10^1)_{eight} + (5 \times 10^0)_{eight}$
212_{three}	$(2 \times 100)_{three} + (1 \times 10)_{three}$ $+ (2 \times 1)_{three}$	$(2 \times 10^2)_{three} + (1 \times 10^1)_{three}$ $+ (2 \times 10^0)_{three}$

6045_{seven}	$(6 \times 1000)_{seven} + (4 \times 10)_{seven} + (5 \times 1)_{seven}$	$(6 \times 10^3)_{seven} + (4 \times 10^1)_{seven} + (5 \times 10^0)_{seven}$
5214_{six}	$(5 \times 1000)_{six} + (2 \times 100)_{six} + (1 \times 10)_{six} + (4 \times 1)_{six}$	$(5 \times 10^3)_{six} + (2 \times 10^2)_{six} (1 \times 10^1)_{six} + (4 \times 10^0)_{six}$
212_{four}	$(2 \times 100)_{four} + (1 \times 10)_{four} + (2 \times 1)_{four}$	$(2 \times 10^2)_{four} + (1 \times 10^1)_{four} + (2 \times 10^0)_{four}$
$12TE_{twelve}$	$(1 \times 1000)_{twelve} + (2 \times 100)_{twelve} + (T \times 10)_{twelve} + (E \times 1)_{twelve}$	$(1 \times 10^3)_{twelve} + (2 \times 10^2)_{twelve} + (T \times 10^1)_{twelve} + (E \times 10^0)_{twelve}$
8640_{nine}	$(8 \times 1000)_{nine} + (6 \times 100)_{nine} + (4 \times 10)_{nine}$	$(8 \times 10^3)_{nine} + (6 \times 10^2)_{nine} + (4 \times 10^1)_{nine}$

19.

Base 10	Base 9	Base 8	Base 7	Base 6	Base 5	Base 4	Base 3	Base 2
1	1	1	1	1	1	1	1	1
2	2	2	2	2	2	2	2	10
3	3	3	3	3	3	3	10	11
4	4	4	4	4	4	10	11	100
5	5	5	5	5	10	11	12	101
6	6	6	6	10	11	12	20	110
7	7	7	10	11	12	13	21	111
8	8	10	11	12	13	20	22	1000
9	10	11	12	13	14	21	100	1001
10	11	12	13	14	20	22	101	1010
11	12	13	14	15	21	23	102	1011
12	13	14	15	20	22	30	110	1100
13	14	15	16	21	23	31	111	1101
14	15	16	20	22	24	32	112	1110
15	16	17	21	23	30	33	120	1111
16	17	20	22	24	31	100	121	10000
17	18	21	23	25	32	101	122	10001
18	20	22	24	30	33	102	200	10010
19	21	23	25	31	34	103	201	10011
20	22	24	26	32	40	110	202	10100
21	23	25	30	33	41	111	210	10101
22	24	26	31	34	42	112	211	10110
23	25	27	32	35	43	113	212	10111
24	26	30	33	40	44	120	220	11000
25	27	31	34	41	100	121	221	11001

20. a) Place-value
   b) Base
   c) One
   d) Standard notation, expanded notation, exponential notation
   e) Digits

21. a) Three hundred forty-five million, seven hundred sixty-eight thousand, two hundred thirty-one.
   b) Eight hundred billion, one hundred seventy-two million, four hundred thirty-eight thousand, four hundred ten.
   c) Twenty-one million, four hundred seventy-eight thousand.
   d) Seven billion, four hundred two thousand, eight.

e) Four hundred three billion, three million, five hundred thousand, ten.

f) One quadrillion, one trillion, one billion, one million, one thousand, one.

g) Seventy-three trillion, four hundred three billion, two hundred one million, one hundred thousand, nine hundred seven.

h) Two hundred forty-three quadrillion, six hundred fifty-seven million, two hundred thousand, four hundred.

i) Fifty-six sextillion, twenty quintillion, forty quadrillion, sixty trillion, fifty billion, forty million, thirty thousand, twenty.

j) Seven hundred quintillion, seven hundred.

22. Each place in the base-nine numeral occupies two places in the base-three numeral. Each digit in the base-nine numeral is then connected to its respective base-three representation, thus providing the quick conversion.

Unit 6

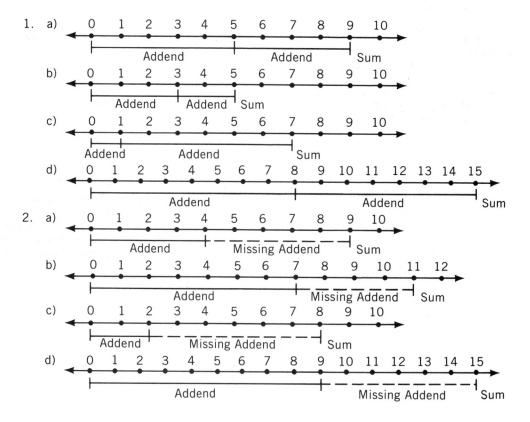

3. a) $4 + 7 = 11, 7 + 4 = 11, 11 - 4 = 7, 11 - 7 = 4$
   b) $2 + 7 = 9, 7 + 2 = 9, 9 - 7 = 2, 9 - 2 = 7$
   c) $6 + 7 = 13, 7 + 6 = 13, 13 - 7 = 6, 13 - 6 = 7$
   d) $31 + 44 = 75, 44 + 31 = 75, 75 - 44 = 31, 75 - 31 = 44$

4. a) $\Box - 9 = 8, \Box - 8 = 9$
   b) $\Box - 4 = 9, \Box - 9 = 4$
   c) $\Box - 53 = 39, \Box - 39 = 53$
   d) $\Box - 7 = 6, \Box - 6 = 7$

5. a) $8 + 1 = 9$, $1 + 3 = 4$, $10 + 30 = 40$
    b) $6 + 1 = 7$, $2 + 3 = 5$, $20 + 30 = 50$
    c) $3 + 5 = 8$, $7 + 1 = 8$, $70 + 10 = 80$
    d) $2 + 5 = 7$, $5 + 4 = 9$, $50 + 40 = 90$
    e) $7 + 2 = 9$, $4 + 2 = 6$, $40 + 20 = 60$
    f) $8 + 1 = 9$, $6 + 2 = 8$, $60 + 20 = 80$

6. a)
    ```
        1 ten  8 ones
      +4 tens 1 one
        5 tens 9 ones = 59
    ```
    b)
    ```
        2 hundreds 4 tens 7 ones
      +5 hundreds 3 tens 2 ones
        7 hundreds 7 tens 9 ones = 779
    ```
    c)
    ```
        7 tens 3 ones
      +2 tens 5 ones
        9 tens 8 ones = 98
    ```
    d)
    ```
        3 hundreds 6 tens 4 ones
      +2 hundreds 1 ten  3 ones
        5 hundreds 7 tens 7 ones = 577
    ```
    e)
    ```
        4 tens 8 ones
      −1 ten  7 ones
        3 tens 1 one  = 31
    ```
    f)
    ```
        7 hundreds 6 tens 5 ones
      −2 hundreds 1 ten  3 ones
        5 hundreds 5 tens 2 ones = 552
    ```
    g)
    ```
        8 tens 7 ones
      −6 tens 4 ones
        2 tens 3 ones = 23
    ```
    h)
    ```
        5 hundreds 9 tens 7 ones
      −1 hundred   5 tens 6 ones
        4 hundreds 4 tens 1 one  = 441
    ```

7. There are several different methods for recording the steps. Your method may be different from the one shown.

    a)
    ```
        37 =   3 tens  7 ones
      + 49 = + 4 tens  9 ones
               7 tens 16 ones
               7 tens (1 ten 6 ones)
              (7 tens 1 ten) 6 ones
               8 tens 6 ones = 86
    ```
    b)
    ```
        61 =   6 tens 1 one
      + 54 = + 5 tens 4 ones
              11 tens 5 ones
               1 hundred 1 ten 5 ones = 115
    ```
    c)
    ```
        73 =   7 tens  3 ones
      + 88 = + 8 tens  8 ones
              15 tens 11 ones
              15 tens (1 ten 1 one)
             (15 tens 1 ten) 1 one
              16 tens 1 one
               1 hundred 6 tens 1 one = 161
    ```
    d)
    ```
        219 =   2 hundreds 1 ten   9 ones
      + 466 = + 4 hundreds 6 tens  6 ones
                6 hundreds 7 tens 15 ones
                6 hundreds 7 tens (1 ten 5 ones)
                6 hundreds (7 tens 1 ten) 5 ones
                6 hundreds 8 tens 5 ones = 685
    ```
    e)
    ```
        378 =   3 hundreds  7 tens  8 ones
      + 154 = + 1 hundred   5 tens  4 ones
                4 hundreds 12 tens 12 ones
                4 hundreds 12 tens (1 ten 2 ones)
                4 hundreds (12 tens 1 ten) 2 ones
                4 hundreds (13 tens) 2 ones
                4 hundreds (1 hundred 3 tens) 2 ones
               (4 hundreds 1 hundred) 3 tens 2 ones
                5 hundreds 3 tens 2 ones = 532
    ```
    f)
    ```
        56 =   5 tens 6 ones =   4 tens 16 ones
      − 29 = − 2 tens 9 ones = − 2 tens  9 ones
                                 2 tens  7 ones = 27
    ```

g) $346 =$ 3 hundreds 4 tens 6 ones =   2 hundreds 14 tens 6 ones
     $-\ 83 = -$ _____ 8 tens 3 ones $= -$ _____ 8 tens 3 ones
                                                2 hundreds   6 tens 3 ones $= 263$

h) $459 =$ 4 hundreds 5 tens 9 ones =   3 hundreds 15 tens 9 ones
     $-\ 272 = -$ 2 hundreds 7 tens 2 ones $= -$ 2 hundreds   7 tens 2 ones
                                                1 hundred   8 tens 7 ones $= 187$

i) $521 =$ 5 hundreds 2 tens 1 one =   4 hundreds 11 tens 11 ones
     $-\ 146 = -$ 1 hundred 4 tens 6 ones $= -$ 1 hundred   4 tens   6 ones
                                                3 hundreds   7 tens   5 ones $= 375$

j) $832 =$ 8 hundreds 3 tens 2 ones =   7 hundreds 12 tens 12 ones
     $-\ 398 = -$ 3 hundreds 9 tens 8 ones $= -$ 3 hundreds   9 tens   8 ones
                                                4 hundreds   3 tens   4 ones $= 434$

8. a) $37 + 28 = (30 + 7) + (20 + 8)$ Renaming
                $= 30 + (7 + 20) + 8$ Associative property
                $= 30 + (20 + 7) + 8$ Commutative property
                $= (30 + 20) + (7 + 8)$ Associative property
                $= 50 + 15$ Addition
                $= 50 + (10 + 5)$ Renaming
                $= (50 + 10) + 5$ Associative property
                $= 60 + 5$ Addition
                $= 65$ Renaming

    b) $276 + 49 = (200 + 70 + 6) + (40 + 9)$ Renaming
                 $= 200 + 70 + (6 + 40) + 9$ Associative property
                 $= 200 + 70 + (40 + 6) + 9$ Commutative property
                 $= 200 + (70 + 40) + (6 + 9)$ Associative property
                 $= 200 + 110 + 15$ Addition
                 $= 200 + (100 + 10) + (10 + 5)$ Renaming
                 $= (200 + 100) + (10 + 10) + 5$ Associative
                 $= 300 + 20 + 5$ Addition
                 $= 325$ Renaming

    c) $48 + 75 = (40 + 8) + (70 + 5)$ Renaming
                $= 40 + (8 + 70) + 5$ Associative property
                $= 40 + (70 + 8) + 5$ Commutative property
                $= (40 + 70) + (8 + 5)$ Associative property
                $= 110 + 13$ Addition
                $= (100 + 10) + (10 + 3)$ Renaming
                $= 100 + (10 + 10) + 3$ Associative property
                $= 100 + 20 + 3$ Addition
                $= 123$ Renaming

9. a) $500 =$ 50 tens 0 ones =   49 tens 10 ones
         $-\ 273 = -$ 27 tens 3 ones $= -$ 27 tens   3 ones
                                      22 tens   7 ones $= 227$

    b) $802 =$ 80 tens 2 ones =   79 tens 12 ones
         $-\ 367 = -$ 36 tens 7 ones $= -$ 36 tens   7 ones
                                      43 tens   5 ones $= 435$

    c) $900 =$ 90 tens 0 ones =   89 tens 10 ones
         $-\ 258 = -$ 25 tens 8 ones $= -$ 25 tens   8 ones
                                      64 tens   2 ones $= 642$

10. **Addend + Addend = Sum**   Sum = Addend + Addend
     Sum − Addend = Addend   Addend = Sum − Addend

Unit 7

1. a)

Three sets of four triangles equals twelve triangles; thus $3 \times 4 = 12$.

b) ● ● ● ●   Three rows of four dots
   ● ● ● ●   is twelve dots; thus
   ● ● ● ● $3 \times 4 = 12$.

c)

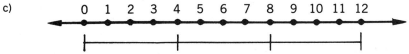

Three segments of four units each equals twelve units; thus $3 \times 4 = 12$.

d)

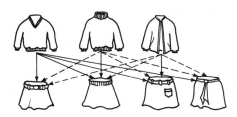

The set of ordered pairs of three sweaters and four skirts equals twelve outfits; thus $3 \times 4 = 12$.

2. a) ● ●   b) ● ● ● ● ● ●   c) ● ● ●   d) ● ● ●
   ● ●   ● ● ● ● ● ●   ● ● ●   ● ● ●
   ● ●   ● ● ● ● ● ●   ● ● ●
   ● ●   ● ● ●
                                  ● ● ●

3. The array on the left is a 3-by-6 array and the one on the right is a 6-by-3 array.

Since both arrays contain 18 objects, we can see that $3 \times 6 = 6 \times 3$.

4. a) $5 \times 4 = 20$ b) $3 \times 7 = 21$ c) $3 \times 12 = 36$

5.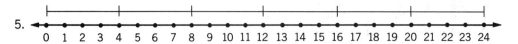

6. 5
   + 5
   ___
   10
   + 5
   ___
   15   Four fives are added to make 20.
   + 5
   ___
   20

7. a) A × B = {(x, e), (x, f), (x, g), (x, h), (y, e), (y, f), (y, g), (y, h), (z, e), (z, f), (z, g), (z, h)}

   b) B × A = {(e, x), (e, y), (e, z), (f, x), (f, y), (f, z), (g, x), (g, y), (g, z), (h, x), (h, y), (h, z)}

   c) With each ordered pair in Set A × B, match the pair in Set B × A that has the same elements in reverse order. That is, with (x, e) match (e, x), with (x, f) match (f, x), and so on. The matching that results is a one-to-one correspondence between A × B and B × A. Therefore A × B and B × A are equivalent sets.

   d) Yes, R × S ↔ S × R for all finite Sets R and S. Since the cardinal numbers of equivalent sets are the same, n(R × S) = n(S × R) for all finite Sets R and S; but n(R × S) = n(R) × n(S) and n(S × R) = n(S) × n(R). Hence from the equivalence of R × S and S × R we can deduce the commutative property of multiplication of whole numbers.

8. a) 3 × 7 = 21   b) 4 × 8 = 32
      21 ÷ 3 = 7 or 21 ÷ 7 = 3   32 ÷ 4 = 8 or 32 ÷ 8 = 4

9. a)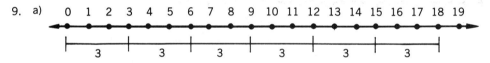
   There are 6 sets of 3 in 18.

   b)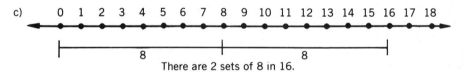
   There are 3 sets of 4 in 12.

   c)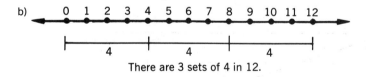
   There are 2 sets of 8 in 16.

   d)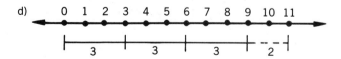
   There are 3 sets of 3 in 11, with 2 left over.

10. a)   □ ÷ 8 = 7   and   □ ÷ 7 = 8
    b)   9 × □ = 72   and   □ × 9 = 72
    c)   □ ÷ 6 = 18   and   □ ÷ 18 = 6
    d) 184 ÷ 8 = 23   and   184 ÷ 23 = 8

e) $168 \div 12 = 14$ and $168 \div 14 = 12$
f) $9 \times 12 = 108$ and $12 \times 9 = 108$
g) $13 \times 17 = 221$ and $17 \times 13 = 221$
h) $1116 \div 9 = 124$ and $1116 \div 124 = 9$

11. a)

$$
\begin{array}{ccc}
3 & 30 & 4 \\
2\overline{)6} & 2\overline{)60} & 2\overline{)8} \\
\underline{6} & \underline{60} & \underline{8}
\end{array}
$$

$$
\begin{array}{c}
34 \\
2\overline{)68} \\
\underline{60} \\
8 \\
\underline{8}
\end{array}
$$

b)

$$
\begin{array}{ccc}
4 & 40 & 6 \\
\times\ 3 & \times\ 3 & \times\ 3 \\
\hline
12 & 120 & 18
\end{array}
$$

$$
\begin{array}{c}
46 \\
\times\ 3 \\
\hline
18 \\
\underline{120} \\
138
\end{array}
$$

12. a) $6 \times 97 = 6 \times (100 - 3) = (6 \times 100) - (6 \times 3) = 600 - 18 = 582$
    b) $7 \times 48 = 7 \times (50 - 2) = (7 \times 50) - (7 \times 2) = 350 - 14 = 336$
    c) $4 \times 98 = 4 \times (100 - 2) = (4 \times 100) - (4 \times 2) = 400 - 8 = 392$
    d) $3 \times 1998 = 3 \times (2000 - 2) = (3 \times 2000) - (3 \times 2) = 6000 - 6 = 5994$

13. $48 - 6 = 42, 42 - 6 = 36, 36 - 6 = 30, 30 - 6 = 24, 24 - 6 = 18$
     $18 - 6 = 12, 12 - 6 = 6, 6 - 6 = 0$
     6 has been subtracted from 48 eight times, thus $48 - 6 = 8$

14.

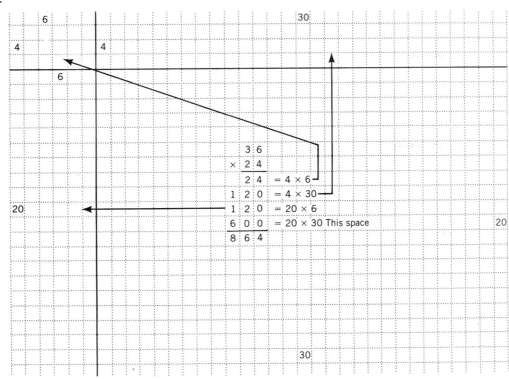

15.

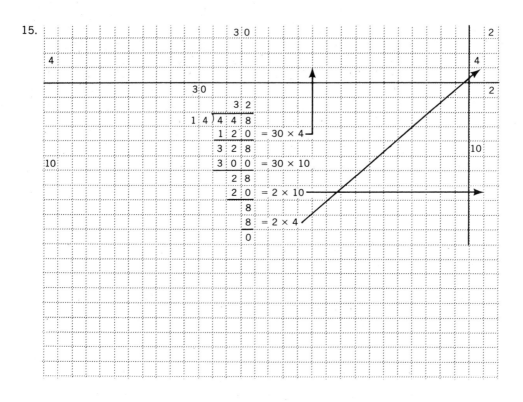

Unit 8

1. a) {1, 2, 4, 8}
   b) {1, 17}
   c) {1, 2, 3, 4, 6, 8, 12, 24}
   d) {1, 2, 4, 5, 10, 20, 25, 50, 100}
   e) {1, 2, 5, 10}

2. a) $1 \times 12, 2 \times 6, 3 \times 4, 12 \times 1, 6 \times 2, 4 \times 3$
   b) $1 \times 27, 3 \times 9, 27 \times 1, 9 \times 3$
   c) $1 \times 48, 2 \times 24, 3 \times 16, 4 \times 12, 6 \times 8, 48 \times 1, 24 \times 2, 16 \times 3, 12 \times 4, 8 \times 6$
   d) $1 \times 100, 2 \times 50, 4 \times 25, 5 \times 20, 10 \times 10, 100 \times 1, 50 \times 2, 25 \times 4, 20 \times 5$
   e) $1 \times 10, 2 \times 5, 10 \times 1, 5 \times 2$

3. Your answers should show the following kinds of arrays.

   a) 9-by-1, 3-by-3, and 1-by-9
   b) 1-by-11, and 11-by-1
   c) 1-by-10, 2-by-5, 5-by-2, and 10-by-1
   d) 1-by-4, 2-by-2, and 4-by-1

4. a) {2}   b) {2, 7}   c) {2, 3}   d) {2, 5}   e) {41}

5. a) $2 \times 2 \times 7$ b) $2 \times 3 \times 13$ c) 2×19 d) $2 \times 2 \times 23$ e) $2 \times 5 \times 11$

6. a) Divisible by 3
   b) Divisible by 3
   c) Divisible by 3 and 5
   d) Divisible by 2 and 3 and 5
   e) Divisible by 2

7. If the sum of the digits is divisible by 9, then the original number is divisible by 9.

8. 5 and 7, 11 and 13, 17 and 19, 29 and 31, 41 and 43, 59 and 61, 71 and 73

9. a) 6
    b) 42
    c) 10
    d) 4

10. a) $2 \times 2 \times 3 \times 3 \times 5 = 180$
    b) $2^2 \times 3 \times 5 \times 7 \quad = 420$
    c) $2 \times 2 \times 2 \times 7 \quad = 56$
    d) $3 \times 3 \times 5 \quad\quad = 45$

11. Composite. Yes. The conjecture that the data was suggesting was first formulated by Goldbach in 1742. He hypothesized that all even numbers greater than two can be written as the sum of a pair of prime numbers.

12. 1, 13, 169. Any number that can be expressed as a prime number squared has exactly three divisors: one, the number itself, and its positive square root.

13. $28 = 1 + 2 + 4 + 7 + 14$

Unit 9

1. Answers may vary.

a) 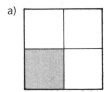 b) 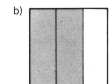 c) 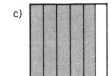 d)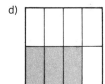

2.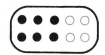

3. Answers may vary

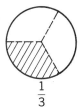 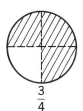 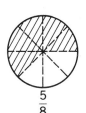 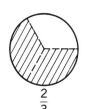 

$\dfrac{1}{3}$ $\dfrac{3}{4}$ $\dfrac{5}{8}$ $\dfrac{2}{3}$ $\dfrac{7}{8}$

4.

A number line showing:

0 $\quad$ 1 $\quad$ $1\frac{1}{3}$ $\quad$ $1\frac{1}{2}$ $\quad$ $1\frac{2}{3}$ $\quad$ 2

$\frac{1}{2}$ $\quad$ $\frac{2}{2}$ $\quad$ $\frac{4}{2}$

$\frac{1}{3}$ $\quad$ $\frac{2}{3}$ $\quad$ $\frac{3}{3}$ $\quad$ $\frac{4}{3}$ $\quad$ $\frac{5}{3}$

$\frac{1}{4}$ $\quad$ $\frac{2}{4}$ $\quad$ $\frac{3}{4}$

$\frac{1}{6}$ $\quad$ $\frac{2}{6}$ $\quad$ $\frac{3}{6}$ $\quad$ $\frac{4}{6}$ $\quad$ $\frac{5}{6}$ $\quad$ $\frac{6}{6}$

5. a) $\frac{1}{9}, \frac{1}{8}, \frac{1}{7}, \frac{1}{6}, \frac{1}{5}, \frac{1}{4}, \frac{1}{3}, \frac{1}{2}$ $\qquad$ c) $\frac{1}{6}, \frac{1}{3}, \frac{3}{6}, \frac{4}{6}, \frac{5}{6}, \frac{3}{3}$

   b) $\frac{1}{5}, \frac{2}{5}, \frac{3}{5}, \frac{4}{5}, \frac{5}{5}, \frac{6}{5}$ $\qquad$ d) $\frac{1}{8}, \frac{1}{4}, \frac{1}{3}, \frac{3}{8}, \frac{5}{8}, \frac{2}{3}, \frac{3}{4}, \frac{4}{4}$

6. a) $\frac{1}{10} = \frac{2}{20}$ $\quad$ c) $\frac{3}{8} < \frac{2}{3}$ $\quad$ e) $\frac{2}{3} < \frac{5}{6}$ $\quad$ g) $\frac{5}{8} < \frac{3}{4}$

   b) $\frac{3}{4} > \frac{3}{8}$ $\quad$ d) $\frac{1}{2} > \frac{5}{12}$ $\quad$ f) $\frac{11}{8} > \frac{5}{4}$ $\quad$ h) $\frac{3}{14} = \frac{6}{28}$

7. a) $\frac{2}{3}$ $\quad$ c) $\frac{9}{16}$ $\quad$ e) $\frac{2}{3}$ $\quad$ g) 25

   b) $\frac{1}{4}$ $\quad$ d) $\frac{5}{6}$ $\quad$ f) $\frac{13}{23}$ $\quad$ h) $\frac{2}{3}$

8. a) $\frac{18}{5}$ $\quad$ c) $\frac{15}{8}$ $\quad$ e) $\frac{9}{2}$ $\quad$ g) $\frac{27}{5}$

   b) $\frac{53}{10}$ $\quad$ d) $\frac{22}{7}$ $\quad$ f) $\frac{131}{8}$ $\quad$ h) $\frac{50}{7}$

9. a) $\frac{1}{2}, \frac{2}{4}, \frac{3}{6}, \frac{4}{8}, \frac{5}{10}, \frac{6}{12}, \frac{7}{14}$ $\quad$ c) $\frac{5}{7}, \frac{10}{14}, \frac{15}{21}, \frac{20}{28}, \frac{25}{35}, \frac{30}{42}, \frac{35}{49}$

   b) $\frac{3}{8}, \frac{6}{16}, \frac{9}{24}, \frac{12}{32}, \frac{15}{40}, \frac{18}{48}, \frac{21}{56}$

10. $3; 5 \times 7; 3 \times 7; \frac{3 \times 7}{5 \times 7}$; equivalent

11. If a rectangular region is divided into 7 regions of the same size, then we can represent $\frac{4}{7}$ by shading 4 of these regions. If each of the 7 regions into which the original was divided is itself divided into 100 smaller regions (all the same size), then the original region will have been divided into 7×100 or 700 equivalent regions. Since each shaded region will also get divided into 100 smaller regions (all the same size), the shaded portion of the original rectangular region will consist of 4×100 or 400 small regions. Thus the portion of the original rectangular region that is shaded can be represented by $\frac{4 \times 100}{7 \times 100}$ or $\frac{400}{700}$. Therefore $\frac{4}{7} = \frac{400}{700}$.

12. a) $5\frac{4}{5}$ $\quad$ c) $5\frac{2}{7}$ $\quad$ e) $3\frac{7}{12}$ $\quad$ g) $8\frac{1}{6}$ $\quad$ i) $1\frac{12}{13}$

   b) $4\frac{1}{4}$ $\quad$ d) $2\frac{2}{3}$ $\quad$ f) $7\frac{3}{4}$ $\quad$ h) $3\frac{4}{5}$ $\quad$ j) $4\frac{8}{9}$

13. a) false   c) true   e) false   g) true
      b) false   d) true   f) false   h) true

Unit 10

1. a) $\dfrac{5}{7} + \dfrac{4}{7} = \dfrac{9}{7} = 1\dfrac{2}{7}$ b) $\dfrac{7}{5} + \dfrac{11}{5} = \dfrac{18}{5} = 3\dfrac{3}{5}$ c) $\dfrac{5}{4} + \dfrac{3}{4} = \dfrac{8}{4} = 2$

2.

Addends

+	$\dfrac{5}{12}$	$\dfrac{1}{12}$	$\dfrac{7}{12}$	$\dfrac{11}{12}$	$\dfrac{1}{4}$	$\dfrac{17}{12}$	$\dfrac{2}{3}$	$\dfrac{5}{6}$	$\dfrac{2}{5}$	$\dfrac{1}{2}$	$\dfrac{1}{3}$	$\dfrac{3}{4}$	$\dfrac{1}{7}$
Addends $\dfrac{3}{12}$	$\dfrac{2}{3}$	$\dfrac{1}{3}$	$\dfrac{5}{6}$	$1\dfrac{1}{6}$	$\dfrac{1}{2}$	$1\dfrac{2}{3}$	$\dfrac{11}{12}$	$1\dfrac{1}{12}$	$\dfrac{13}{20}$	$\dfrac{3}{4}$	$\dfrac{7}{12}$	1	$\dfrac{11}{28}$
Addends $\dfrac{3}{4}$	$1\dfrac{1}{6}$	$\dfrac{5}{6}$	$1\dfrac{1}{3}$	$1\dfrac{2}{3}$	1	$2\dfrac{1}{6}$	$1\dfrac{5}{12}$	$1\dfrac{7}{12}$	$1\dfrac{3}{20}$	$1\dfrac{1}{4}$	$1\dfrac{1}{12}$	$1\dfrac{1}{2}$	$\dfrac{25}{28}$

3. a) $\dfrac{3}{16} + \dfrac{7}{16} = \dfrac{10}{16} = \dfrac{10 \div 2}{16 \div 2} = \dfrac{5}{8}$

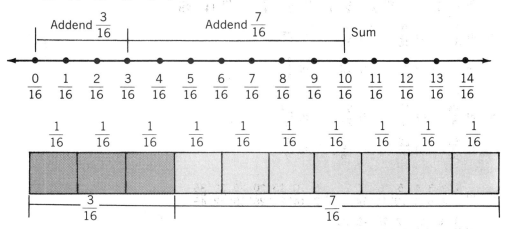

b) $\dfrac{6}{7} + \dfrac{5}{7} = \dfrac{11}{7} = \dfrac{7}{7} + \dfrac{4}{7} = 1\dfrac{4}{7}$

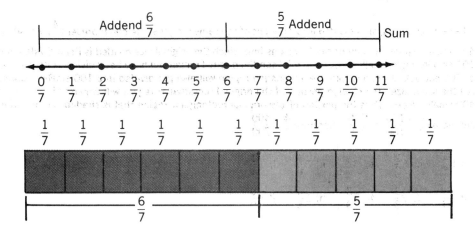

c) $\frac{7}{8} + \frac{3}{8} = \frac{10}{8} = \frac{8}{8} + \frac{2}{8} = 1 + \frac{2}{8} = 1\frac{1}{4}$

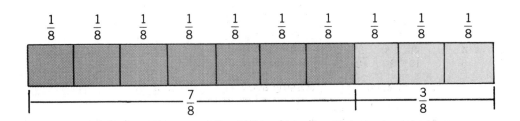

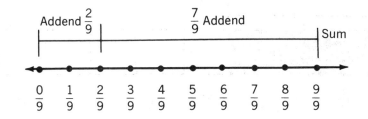

d) $\frac{2}{9} + \frac{7}{9} = \frac{9}{9} = 1$

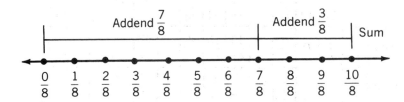

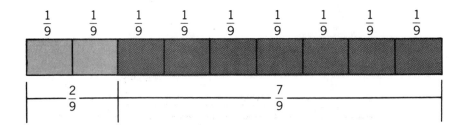

4. a) 12   b) 60   c) 24   d) 45   e) 30

5. a) $1\frac{2}{5} - \frac{4}{5} = \frac{7}{5} - \frac{4}{5} = \frac{3}{5}$

   b) $1 - \frac{1}{6} = \frac{6}{6} - \frac{1}{6} = \frac{5}{6}$

   c) $\frac{5}{3} - \frac{5}{9} = \frac{15}{9} - \frac{5}{9} = \frac{10}{9} = 1\frac{1}{9}$ or

   $1\frac{2}{3} - \frac{5}{9} = \frac{15}{9} - \frac{5}{9} = \frac{10}{9} = 1\frac{1}{9}$

6.

	Sums												
—	$\frac{7}{12}$	$\frac{5}{12}$	$\frac{11}{12}$	$\frac{3}{4}$	$\frac{13}{16}$	$\frac{23}{24}$	$\frac{31}{36}$	$\frac{4}{5}$	$\frac{6}{7}$	$\frac{1}{2}$	$\frac{5}{6}$	$\frac{7}{8}$	$\frac{9}{10}$
Addend $\frac{5}{12}$	$\frac{1}{6}$	0	$\frac{1}{2}$	$\frac{1}{3}$	$\frac{19}{48}$	$\frac{13}{24}$	$\frac{4}{9}$	$\frac{23}{60}$	$\frac{37}{84}$	$\frac{1}{12}$	$\frac{5}{12}$	$\frac{11}{24}$	$\frac{29}{60}$
Addend $\frac{3}{4}$			$\frac{1}{6}$	0	$\frac{1}{16}$	$\frac{5}{24}$	$\frac{1}{9}$	$\frac{1}{20}$	$\frac{3}{28}$		$\frac{1}{12}$	$\frac{1}{8}$	$\frac{3}{20}$

7. a) $\frac{4}{5} - \frac{3}{10} = \frac{8}{10} - \frac{3}{10} = \frac{5}{10} = \frac{1}{2}$

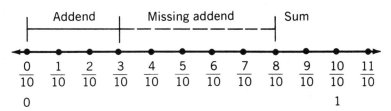

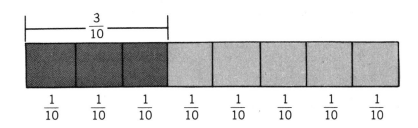

b) $\frac{7}{8} - \frac{3}{4} = \frac{7}{8} - \frac{6}{8} = \frac{1}{8}$

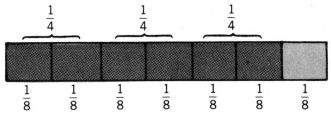

c) $\frac{5}{6} - \frac{1}{3} = \frac{5}{6} - \frac{2}{6} = \frac{3}{6} = \frac{1}{2}$

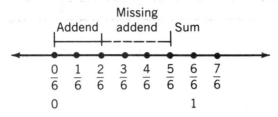

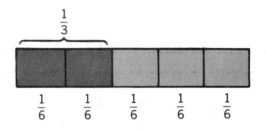

d) $\frac{2}{3} - \frac{1}{4} = \frac{8}{12} - \frac{3}{12} = \frac{5}{12}$

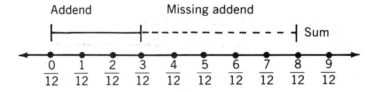

Note that circular regions could be used instead of rectangular ones.

8. a)

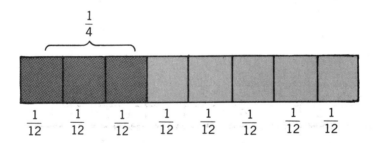

$\therefore 3 \times \frac{1}{4} = \frac{3}{4}$

b)

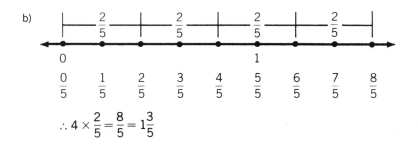

$$\therefore 4 \times \frac{2}{5} = \frac{8}{5} = 1\frac{3}{5}$$

c)

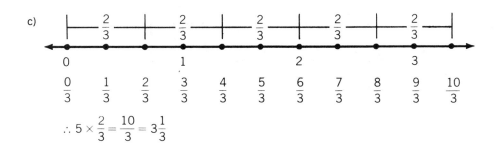

$$\therefore 5 \times \frac{2}{3} = \frac{10}{3} = 3\frac{1}{3}$$

d)

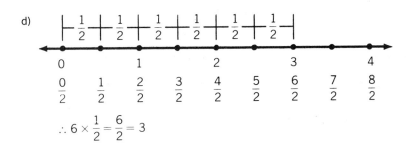

$$\therefore 6 \times \frac{1}{2} = \frac{6}{2} = 3$$

e)

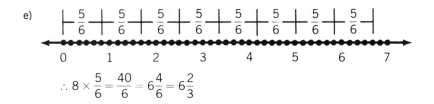

$$\therefore 8 \times \frac{5}{6} = \frac{40}{6} = 6\frac{4}{6} = 6\frac{2}{3}$$

f)

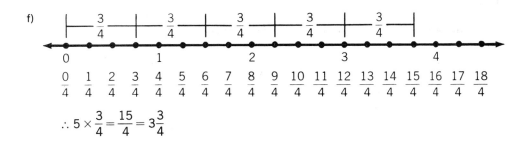

$$\therefore 5 \times \frac{3}{4} = \frac{15}{4} = 3\frac{3}{4}$$

9. a) $\frac{1}{2} \times \frac{3}{4} =$

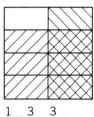

$$\frac{1}{2} \times \frac{3}{4} = \frac{3}{8}$$

b) $\frac{2}{3} \times \frac{1}{4} =$

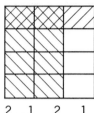

$$\frac{2}{3} \times \frac{1}{4} = \frac{2}{12} = \frac{1}{6}$$

c) $\frac{2}{5} \times \frac{1}{6} =$

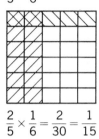

$$\frac{2}{5} \times \frac{1}{6} = \frac{2}{30} = \frac{1}{15}$$

d) $\frac{5}{6} \times \frac{1}{8} =$

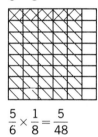

$$\frac{5}{6} \times \frac{1}{8} = \frac{5}{48}$$

e) $\frac{3}{8} \times \frac{4}{5} =$

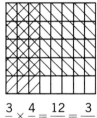

$$\frac{3}{8} \times \frac{4}{5} = \frac{12}{40} = \frac{3}{10}$$

f) $\frac{2}{3} \times \frac{4}{5} =$

$$\frac{2}{3} \times \frac{4}{5} = \frac{8}{15}$$

10. a)

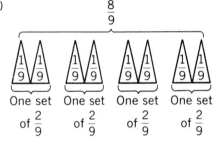

$$\frac{2}{9} \overline{)\frac{8}{9}} \quad \begin{array}{r} 4 \\ \hline -\frac{8}{9} \\ \hline \end{array}$$

b)

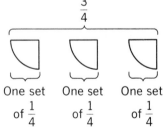

$$\frac{1}{4} \overline{)\frac{3}{4}} \quad \begin{array}{r} 3 \\ \hline -\frac{3}{4} \\ \hline \end{array}$$

c)

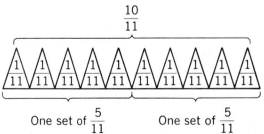

$$\frac{5}{11} \overline{)\frac{10}{11}} \quad \begin{array}{r} 2 \\ \hline -\frac{10}{11} \\ \hline \end{array}$$

d)

$$\frac{3}{8}$$

One set of $\frac{1}{4}$ or $\frac{2}{8}$ $\frac{1}{2}$ set of $\frac{1}{4}$

$$\frac{1}{4}\overline{)\frac{3}{8}} \qquad 2\frac{1}{8}\overline{)\frac{3}{8}}$$

$$\begin{array}{r} 1\frac{1}{2} \\ 2\frac{1}{8}\overline{)\frac{3}{8}} \\ -\frac{2}{8} \\ \hline \frac{1}{8} \end{array}$$

e)

$$\frac{5}{6}$$

One set of $\frac{2}{3}$ or $\frac{4}{6}$ One $\frac{1}{4}$ set of $\frac{2}{3}$

$$\frac{2}{3}\overline{)\frac{5}{6}} = 4\frac{1}{6}\overline{)\frac{5}{6}}$$

$$\begin{array}{r} 1\frac{1}{4} \\ 4\frac{1}{6}\overline{)\frac{5}{6}} \\ -\frac{4}{6} \\ \hline \frac{1}{6} \end{array}$$

f)

$$\frac{4}{3} \text{ or } \frac{20}{15}$$

One set of $\frac{4}{5}$ or $\frac{12}{15}$ $\qquad$ $\frac{8}{12}$

$$1\frac{8}{12}$$

$$1\frac{2}{3}$$

$$\frac{4}{5}\overline{)\frac{4}{3}} = 12\frac{}{15}\overline{)\frac{20}{15}}$$

$$\begin{array}{r} 1\frac{8}{12} = 1\frac{2}{3} \\ 12\frac{}{15}\overline{)\frac{20}{15}} \\ -\frac{12}{15} \\ \hline \frac{8}{15} \end{array}$$

11. a) $\frac{5}{3}$ d) $\frac{8}{7}$ g) $\frac{1}{17}$

   b) 4 or $\frac{4}{1}$ e) $\frac{5}{9}$ h) $\frac{9}{31}$

   c) $\frac{6}{5}$ f) $\frac{4}{9}$ i) $\frac{8}{55}$

12. a) $\dfrac{\frac{2}{9}}{\frac{8}{9}} = \dfrac{\frac{2}{9}\times\frac{9}{8}}{\frac{8}{9}\times\frac{9}{8}} = \dfrac{\frac{2}{9}\times\frac{9}{8}}{1} = \dfrac{18}{72} = \dfrac{2}{8} = \dfrac{1}{4}$

   b) $\dfrac{\frac{3}{4}}{\frac{1}{4}} = \dfrac{\frac{3}{4}\times\frac{4}{1}}{\frac{1}{4}\times\frac{4}{1}} = \dfrac{\frac{12}{4}}{1} = \dfrac{12}{4} = 3$

c) $\dfrac{\frac{10}{11}}{\frac{5}{11}} = \dfrac{\frac{10}{11} \times \frac{11}{5}}{\frac{5}{11} \times \frac{11}{5}} = \dfrac{\frac{110}{55}}{1} = 2$

h) $\dfrac{\frac{3}{7}}{\frac{2}{3}} = \dfrac{\frac{3}{7} \times \frac{3}{2}}{\frac{2}{3} \times \frac{3}{2}} = \dfrac{\frac{9}{14}}{1} = \dfrac{9}{14}$

d) $\dfrac{\frac{3}{8}}{\frac{1}{4}} = \dfrac{\frac{3}{8} \times \frac{4}{1}}{\frac{1}{4} \times \frac{4}{1}} = \dfrac{\frac{12}{8}}{1} = \dfrac{12}{8} = 1\dfrac{4}{8} = 1\dfrac{1}{2}$

i) $\dfrac{\frac{4}{5}}{\frac{6}{7}} = \dfrac{\frac{4}{5} \times \frac{7}{6}}{\frac{6}{7} \times \frac{7}{6}} = \dfrac{\frac{28}{30}}{1} = \dfrac{28}{30} = \dfrac{14}{15}$

e) $\dfrac{\frac{5}{6}}{\frac{2}{3}} = \dfrac{\frac{5}{6} \times \frac{3}{2}}{\frac{2}{3} \times \frac{3}{2}} = \dfrac{\frac{15}{12}}{1} = 1\dfrac{3}{12} = 1\dfrac{1}{4}$

j) $\dfrac{\frac{5}{9}}{\frac{3}{5}} = \dfrac{\frac{5}{9} \times \frac{5}{3}}{\frac{3}{5} \times \frac{5}{3}} = \dfrac{\frac{25}{27}}{1} = \dfrac{25}{27}$

f) $\dfrac{\frac{4}{3}}{\frac{4}{5}} = \dfrac{\frac{4}{3} \times \frac{5}{4}}{\frac{4}{5} \times \frac{5}{4}} = \dfrac{\frac{20}{12}}{1} = \dfrac{5}{3} = 1\dfrac{2}{3}$

k) $\dfrac{\frac{1}{3}}{\frac{7}{8}} = \dfrac{\frac{1}{3} \times \frac{8}{7}}{\frac{7}{8} \times \frac{8}{7}} = \dfrac{\frac{8}{21}}{1} = \dfrac{8}{21}$

g) $\dfrac{\frac{2}{3}}{\frac{1}{4}} = \dfrac{\frac{2}{3} \times \frac{4}{1}}{\frac{1}{4} \times \frac{4}{1}} = \dfrac{\frac{8}{3}}{1} = 2\dfrac{2}{3}$

l) $\dfrac{\frac{5}{6}}{\frac{3}{4}} = \dfrac{\frac{5}{6} \times \frac{4}{3}}{\frac{3}{4} \times \frac{4}{3}} = \dfrac{\frac{20}{18}}{1} = \dfrac{20}{18} = \dfrac{10}{9} = 1\dfrac{1}{9}$

13. a) $<$ b) $=$ c) $>$

14. a) $\dfrac{13}{27} < \dfrac{27}{55}$ b) $\dfrac{18}{21} < \dfrac{71}{81}$ c) $\dfrac{23}{67} < \dfrac{6}{17}$

15. a) $\left(\dfrac{3}{4} \times \dfrac{5}{6}\right) \div \dfrac{2}{3} = \dfrac{15}{24} \div \dfrac{2}{3}$

$= \dfrac{15}{\overset{}{\underset{8}{24}}} \times \dfrac{\overset{1}{3}}{2}$

$= \dfrac{15}{16}$

c) $\dfrac{2}{5} \times \left(\dfrac{2}{3} \div \dfrac{3}{4}\right) = \dfrac{2}{5} \times \left(\dfrac{2}{3} \times \dfrac{4}{3}\right)$

$= \dfrac{2}{5} \times \dfrac{8}{9}$

$= \dfrac{16}{45}$

b) $\left(\dfrac{7}{8} \div \dfrac{4}{5}\right) \times \dfrac{1}{2} = \left(\dfrac{7}{8} \times \dfrac{5}{4}\right) \times \dfrac{1}{2}$

$= \dfrac{35}{32} \times \dfrac{1}{2}$

$= \dfrac{35}{64}$

d) $\dfrac{5}{7} \div \left(\dfrac{4}{9} \times \dfrac{2}{5}\right) = \dfrac{5}{7} \div \dfrac{8}{45}$

$= \dfrac{5}{7} \times \dfrac{45}{8}$

$= \dfrac{225}{56}$

$= 4\dfrac{1}{56}$

16. a) $\dfrac{7}{\overset{}{\underset{3}{9}}} \times \dfrac{\overset{1}{3}}{8} = \dfrac{7 \times 1}{3 \times 8} = \dfrac{7}{24}$

e) $\dfrac{5}{6} \div \dfrac{20}{21} = \dfrac{\overset{1}{5}}{\underset{2}{6}} \times \dfrac{\overset{7}{21}}{\underset{4}{20}} = \dfrac{1 \times 7}{2 \times 4} = \dfrac{7}{8}$

b) $\dfrac{\overset{1}{4}}{\underset{1}{8}} \times \dfrac{\overset{3}{15}}{\underset{7}{28}} = \dfrac{1 \times 3}{1 \times 7} = \dfrac{3}{7}$

f) $\dfrac{3}{11} \times 2\dfrac{4}{9} = \dfrac{\overset{1}{3}}{\underset{1}{11}} \times \dfrac{\overset{2}{22}}{\underset{3}{9}} = \dfrac{1 \times 2}{1 \times 3} = \dfrac{2}{3}$

c) $\dfrac{6}{7} \div \dfrac{4}{5} = \dfrac{\overset{3}{6}}{7} \times \dfrac{5}{\underset{2}{4}} = \dfrac{15}{14} = 1\dfrac{1}{14}$

g) $2\dfrac{5}{6} \div 3\dfrac{1}{4} = \dfrac{17}{6} \div \dfrac{13}{4} = \dfrac{17}{\underset{3}{6}} \times \dfrac{\overset{2}{4}}{13} = \dfrac{34}{39}$

d) $\dfrac{8}{9} \div \dfrac{4}{18} = \dfrac{\overset{2}{8}}{\underset{1}{9}} \times \dfrac{\overset{2}{18}}{\underset{1}{4}} = \dfrac{2 \times 2}{1 \times 1} = \dfrac{4}{1} = 4$

h) $1\dfrac{3}{8} \times 4\dfrac{2}{3} = \dfrac{11}{\underset{4}{8}} \times \dfrac{\overset{7}{14}}{3} = \dfrac{77}{12} = 6\dfrac{5}{12}$

17. $12\frac{1}{2} \times 11\frac{3}{4} = \frac{25}{2} \times \frac{47}{4} = \frac{1175}{8} = 146\frac{7}{8}$ square feet

$146\frac{7}{8}$ square feet must be changed to square yards by dividing by 9 because there are 9 square feet in one square yard. It will require $12\frac{23}{72}$ square yards.

Unit 11

1. $300 + 40 + 6 + .1 + .02 + .008$ or
$(3 \times 100) + (4 \times 10) + (6 \times 1) + \left(1 \times \frac{1}{10}\right) + \left(2 \times \frac{1}{100}\right) + \left(8 \times \frac{1}{1000}\right)$

2.   a) $2\frac{1896}{10,000}$ c) $\frac{12}{99} = \frac{4}{33}$ e) $\frac{8}{9}$ g) $\frac{71}{198}$

   b) $\frac{3201}{1,000,000}$ d) $\frac{46}{99}$ f) $\frac{1}{4}$ h) $\frac{72}{999} = \frac{8}{111}$

3.   a) $.\overline{571428}$ b) $1.\overline{923076}$ c) $.7\overline{272}$ d) $.91\overline{6}$ e) $.3\overline{3}$ f) $.6\overline{6}$

4. No. Every fractional number can be written as a terminating decimal or as a repeating decimal. Suppose $\frac{a}{b}$ is any fraction with a whole-number numerator and a counting-number denominator. To rewrite $\frac{a}{b}$ as a decimal, we can go through the usual division process after rewriting $\frac{a}{b}$ in the form $b\overline{)a}$. Suppose we are going through the division algorithm. Each time we go through the subtraction stage, one of two things could happen: We get a difference of zero or we get a difference not equal to zero. If we ever get a difference of zero, the division algorithm is at an end, and the quotient we have obtained is a terminating decimal. What happens if we never do get a difference of zero? Because of the way the division algorithm operates, there are only a limited number of possible differences one can obtain at the subtraction stage (these differences are 0, 1, 2, 3, ..., and $b-1$). If the division algorithm never yields a difference of zero, then at some point one of the other possible differences occurs a second time. If we are already to the right of the decimal point when this occurs, then we will soon come once again to this same difference. Once these differences begin to repeat, the digits in the quotient repeat also.

5.   a)   2.34
          17.1
          .0234
      $+$ .123
      ⎯⎯⎯⎯⎯⎯⎯
          19.5864

   b)   43.7 $=$ 43.700
      $-$ 12.684 $=$ $-$ 12.684
      ⎯⎯⎯⎯⎯⎯⎯⎯⎯⎯⎯⎯⎯⎯⎯⎯⎯
                     31.016

   c)   7.43
      $\times$ 2.1
      ⎯⎯⎯⎯⎯⎯⎯
          .743
          14.86
      ⎯⎯⎯⎯⎯⎯⎯
          15.603

   d) $6.2\overline{)8.928}$
      Multiply both divisor and dividend by 10.

              1.44
      $62\overline{)89.28}$
          62.00 ⟵(1 × 62)
          27.28
          24.80 ⟵(.4 × 62)
           2.48
           2.48 ⟵(.04 × 62)
              0

6. a) $\frac{3}{39} = \frac{12}{\square}$

Since $3 \times 4 = 12$ $39 \times 4 = 156$
therefore $\square = 156$, and 12 cans of tomato juice cost 156 cents, or $1.56.

  b) $\frac{5}{1} = \frac{35}{\square}$ $\square = 7$ Seven cars are needed.

  c) $\frac{100}{1} = \frac{\square}{3}$ $\square = 300$ Three hundred centimeters are needed.

  d) $\frac{1}{.6} = \frac{\square}{1}$ $\square = 1.66\overline{6}$ Approximately 1.67 kilometers measure the same length as one mile.

7. a) $\frac{\square}{100} = \frac{50}{150}$ $\square = 33\frac{1}{3}$ The chair has been discounted or marked down $33\frac{1}{3}$%.

  b) $\frac{\square}{100} = \frac{37}{61.9}$ $\square = 59.7$ Gasoline has increased at the rate of 59.7%

  c) $\frac{10}{100} = \frac{33}{\square}$ $\square = 330$ The test was taken by 330 children.

  d) $\frac{56}{100} = \frac{\square}{500}$ $\square = 280$ Two hundred eighty children walk to school.

  e) $\frac{17}{100} = \frac{391}{\square}$ $\square = 2300$ The total number of children is 2300.

8. a) $r \times b = p$
     $\square \times \$150 = \$50$
     $\square = \frac{50}{150} = \frac{1}{3}$
     $\square = 33\frac{1}{3}$% discount

  b) $r \times b = p$
     $\square \times 61.9 = 37$
     $\square = \frac{37}{61.9}$
     $\square = 59.7$% or about 60% increase

  c) $r \times b = p$
     $.10 \times \square = 33$
     $\square = \frac{33}{.10}$
     $\square = 330$
     330 students took the test

  d) $r \times b = p$
     $.56 \times 500 = \square$
     $280 = \square$
     280 students walk to school

  e) $r \times b = p$
     $.17 \times \square = 391$
     $\square = \frac{391}{.17}$
     $\square = 2300$
     2300 children attend Greenfield

9. a) 938,000   c) 4,660,000,000   e) .0831   g) .0022
   b) 23,700   d) 5,300,000   f) .000003641   h) .00004681

10. a) 7.3×10^3 c) 8.9×10^9 e) 1.6432×10^4
    b) 2.4×10^7 d) 1.23×10^2 f) 4.3756×10^2

11. $\frac{1}{3} = .3333 \ldots$ repeats beginning after the first decimal place.

   $\frac{5}{7} = .71428571428 \ldots$ repeats beginning after the sixth decimal place.

   $\frac{6}{13} = .4615384615384 \ldots$ repeats beginning after the sixth decimal place.

12. $\frac{1}{2}$ can be represented by shading 50 of the 100 squares. Since 1% is $\frac{1}{100}$, one square out of the 100 might be shaded. Clearly $\frac{1}{2}$% would be a shading of the square representing 1%.

Unit 12

1. a)

Addend

+	⁻5	⁻4	⁻3	⁻2	⁻1	0	⁺1	⁺2	⁺3	⁺4	⁺5
⁺5	0	⁺1	⁺2	⁺3	⁺4	⁺5	⁺6	⁺7	⁺8	⁺9	⁺10
⁺4	⁻1	0	⁺1	⁺2	⁺3	⁺4	⁺5	⁺6	⁺7	⁺8	⁺9
⁺3	⁻2	⁻1	0	⁺1	⁺2	⁺3	⁺4	⁺5	⁺6	⁺7	⁺8
⁺2	⁻3	⁻2	⁻1	0	⁺1	⁺2	⁺3	⁺4	⁺5	⁺6	⁺7
⁺1	⁻4	⁻3	⁻2	⁻1	0	⁺1	⁺2	⁺3	⁺4	⁺5	⁺6
0	⁻5	⁻4	⁻3	⁻2	⁻1	0	⁺1	⁺2	⁺3	⁺4	⁺5
⁻1	⁻6	⁻5	⁻4	⁻3	⁻2	⁻1	0	⁺1	⁺2	⁺3	⁺4
⁻2	⁻7	⁻6	⁻5	⁻4	⁻3	⁻2	⁻1	0	⁺1	⁺2	⁺3
⁻3	⁻8	⁻7	⁻6	⁻5	⁻4	⁻3	⁻2	⁻1	0	⁺1	⁺2
⁻4	⁻9	⁻8	⁻7	⁻6	⁻5	⁻4	⁻3	⁻2	⁻1	0	⁺1
⁻5	⁻10	⁻9	⁻8	⁻7	⁻6	⁻5	⁻4	⁻3	⁻2	⁻1	0

(left label: Addend)

b)

Factor

×	⁻5	⁻4	⁻3	⁻2	⁻1	0	⁺1	⁺2	⁺3	⁺4	⁺5
⁺5	⁻25	⁻20	⁻15	⁻10	⁻5	0	⁺5	⁺10	⁺15	⁺20	⁺25
⁺4	⁻20	⁻16	⁻12	⁻8	⁻4	0	⁺4	⁺8	⁺12	⁺16	⁺20
⁺3	⁻15	⁻12	⁻9	⁻6	⁻3	0	⁺3	⁺6	⁺9	⁺12	⁺15
⁺2	⁻10	⁻8	⁻6	⁻4	⁻2	0	⁺2	⁺4	⁺6	⁺8	⁺10
⁺1	⁻5	⁻4	⁻3	⁻2	⁻1	0	⁺1	⁺2	⁺3	⁺4	⁺5
0	0	0	0	0	0	0	0	0	0	0	0
⁻1	⁺5	⁺4	⁺3	⁺2	⁺1	0	⁻1	⁻2	⁻3	⁻4	⁻5
⁻2	⁺10	⁺8	⁺6	⁺4	⁺2	0	⁻2	⁻4	⁻6	⁻8	⁻10
⁻3	⁺15	⁺12	⁺9	⁺6	⁺3	0	⁻3	⁻6	⁻9	⁻12	⁻15
⁻4	⁺20	⁺16	⁺12	⁺8	⁺4	0	⁻4	⁻8	⁻12	⁻16	⁻20
⁻5	⁺25	⁺20	⁺15	⁺10	⁺5	0	⁻5	⁻10	⁻15	⁻20	⁻25

(left label: Factor)

2.

Number System	Subsets
Counting numbers	Counting numbers
Whole numbers	Counting numbers, whole numbers
Rational numbers	Integers, whole numbers, counting numbers, rational numbers
Irrational numbers	Irrational numbers
Real numbers	Rational numbers, irrational numbers, integers, whole numbers, counting numbers, real numbers
Integers	Whole numbers, counting numbers, integers

3. a) $^-2$ e) $\frac{^+2}{3}$ i) $^-73$

b) $^+3$ f) $^-217$ j) $^+49$

c) 0 g) $^+43$ k) $\frac{^-7}{8}$

d) $\frac{^-1}{4}$ h) $^+47$ l) $\frac{^+14}{23}$

4. a)

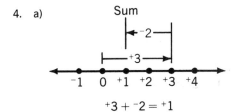

$$^+3 + {}^-2 = {}^+1$$

b)

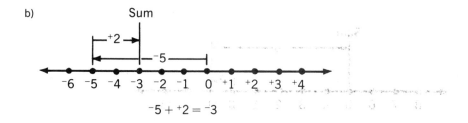

$$^-5 + {}^+2 = {}^-3$$

c)

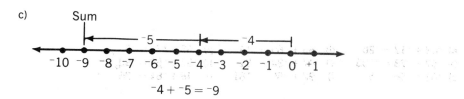

$$^-4 + {}^-5 = {}^-9$$

d)

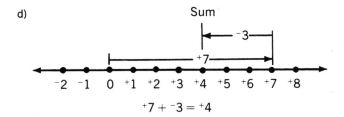

$^+7 + {}^-3 = {}^+4$

e)

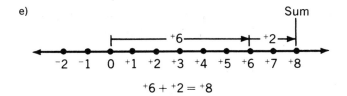

$^+6 + {}^+2 = {}^+8$

f)

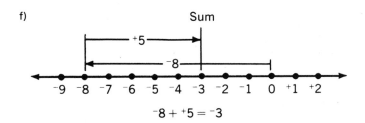

$^-8 + {}^+5 = {}^-3$

g)

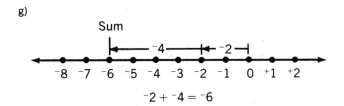

$^-2 + {}^-4 = {}^-6$

h)

$^+1 + {}^-6 = {}^-5$

5. a) $^-43 + {}^+17 = {}^-26$ d) $^-83 + {}^+69 = {}^-14$ g) $^-68 + {}^+73 = {}^+5$
    b) $^-57 + {}^-78 = {}^-135$ e) $^+47 + {}^+34 = {}^+81$ h) $^-37 + {}^-53 = {}^-90$
    c) $^+61 + {}^-56 = {}^+5$ f) $^-92 + {}^-89 = {}^-181$ i) $^+48 + {}^-84 = {}^-36$

6. a) $\square + {}^-8 = {}^+7$

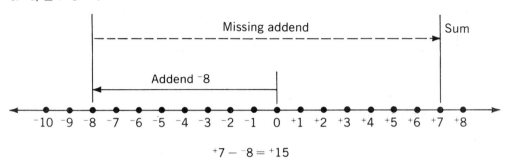

$${}^+7 - {}^-8 = {}^+15$$

b) ${}^-3 + \square = {}^-4$

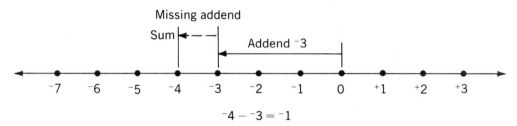

$${}^-4 - {}^-3 = {}^-1$$

c) ${}^+2 + \square = {}^+6$

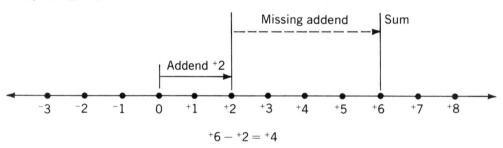

$${}^+6 - {}^+2 = {}^+4$$

d) ${}^+3 + \square = {}^-9$

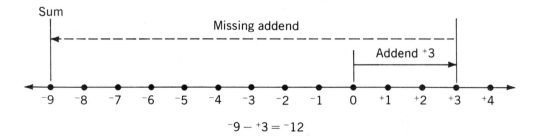

$${}^-9 - {}^+3 = {}^-12$$

e) $^-8 + \square = {}^-1$

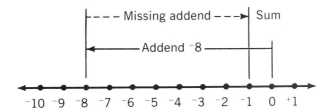

$$^-1 - {}^-8 = {}^+7$$

f) $^-7 + \square = {}^+4$

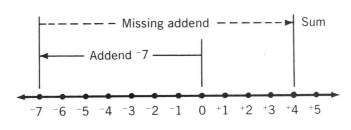

$$^+4 - {}^-7 = {}^+11$$

7. a) $^-24 - {}^-42 = {}^+18$ d) $^-73 - {}^+91 = {}^-164$
   b) $^-51 - {}^+68 = {}^-119$ e) $^+86 - {}^-27 = {}^+113$
   c) $^+23 - {}^-19 = {}^+42$ f) $^+39 - {}^+93 = {}^-54$

8. a) $^+7 \times {}^-9 \ = {}^-63$ e) $^+32 \times {}^-23 = {}^-736$ i) $^-85 \times {}^-19 = {}^+1615$
   b) $^-8 \times {}^+6 \ = {}^-48$ f) $^-47 \times {}^-18 = {}^+846$ j) $^-39 \times {}^+17 = {}^-663$
   c) $^-9 \times {}^-6 \ = {}^+54$ g) $^-68 \times {}^+42 = {}^-2856$ k) $^+74 \times {}^-51 = {}^-3774$
   d) $^-43 \times {}^-17 = {}^+731$ h) $^+53 \times {}^+65 = {}^+3445$ l) $^-67 \times {}^+37 = {}^-2479$

9. a) $^-48 \div {}^+6 = {}^-8$ e) $^-69 \div {}^-3 \ = {}^+23$ i) $^+98 \div {}^-14 \ = {}^-7$
   b) $^+72 \div {}^+9 = {}^+8$ f) $^-144 \div {}^+6 = {}^-24$ j) $^-204 \div {}^-34 = {}^+6$
   c) $^-63 \div {}^-7 = {}^+9$ g) $^-72 \div {}^-4 \ = {}^+18$ k) $^-208 \div {}^+26 = {}^-8$
   d) $^-42 \div {}^-7 = {}^+6$ h) $^+84 \div {}^-12 = {}^-7$ l) $^+378 \div {}^-42 = {}^-9$

10. a) $\dfrac{^+3}{4} \times \dfrac{^-7}{8} = \dfrac{^-21}{32}$ e) $\dfrac{^-3}{5} + \dfrac{^-5}{9} = \dfrac{^-52}{45} = {}^-1\dfrac{7}{45}$ i) $\dfrac{^-5}{8} \times \dfrac{^-4}{15} = \dfrac{^+1}{6}$

   b) $\dfrac{^-5}{6} \div \dfrac{^-2}{3} = \dfrac{^+5}{4} = {}^+1\dfrac{1}{4}$ f) $^+7.8 - {}^-.21 = {}^+8.01$ j) $^-1.84 \div {}^+2.3 = {}^-.8$

   c) $^+.8 \times {}^-.06 = {}^-.048$ g) $\dfrac{^+7}{8} - \dfrac{^+2}{3} = \dfrac{^+5}{24}$ k) $^+2.03 - {}^+1.45 = {}^+.58$

   d) $^-.96 \div {}^+1.2 = {}^-.8$ h) $^-3.41 + {}^+2.9 = {}^-.51$ l) $\dfrac{^+9}{13} + \dfrac{^-2}{7} = \dfrac{^+37}{91}$

11. a) G b) F c) G (and E, since every set contains itself as a subset) d) A, B, C, D, and E
    e) E, D, and G f) none

Unit 13

1. a) $m(\overset{\bullet\;\;\bullet}{AB})$ ≈ 3 inches

    ≈ $2\frac{1}{2}$ inches

    ≈ $2\frac{2}{4}$ inches

    ≈ $2\frac{5}{8}$ inches

    ≈ $2\frac{10}{16}$ inches

    ≈ 1 decimeter

    ≈ 7 centimeters

    ≈ 67 millimeters

    c) $m(\overset{\bullet\;\;\bullet}{XY})$ ≈ 2 inches

    ≈ $1\frac{1}{2}$ inches

    ≈ $1\frac{2}{4}$ inches

    ≈ $1\frac{4}{8}$ inches

    ≈ $1\frac{9}{16}$ inches

    ≈ 0 decimeters

    ≈ 4 centimeters

    ≈ 39 millimeters

    b) $m(\overset{\bullet\;\;\bullet}{MN})$ ≈ 4 inches

    ≈ $4\frac{1}{2}$ inches

    ≈ $4\frac{2}{4}$ inches

    ≈ $4\frac{4}{8}$ inches

    ≈ $4\frac{7}{16}$ inches

    ≈ 1 decimeter

    ≈ 11 centimeters

    ≈ 114 millimeters

    d) $m(\overset{\bullet\;\;\bullet}{CD})$ ≈ 2 inches

    ≈ 2 inches

    ≈ $2\frac{1}{4}$ inches

    ≈ $2\frac{2}{8}$ inches

    ≈ $2\frac{3}{16}$ inches

    ≈ 1 decimeter

    ≈ 6 centimeters

    ≈ 56 millimeters

2. a) 5 centimeters < 52 millimeters
    b) 1 meter > 99 centimeters
    c) 1 yard < 36 feet
    d) 4 liters > 401 milliliters
    e) 1 mile = 5280 feet
    f) 4 kilograms > 453.6 grams
    g) 23 centimeters > 2.3 millimeters
    h) 7 decimeters < 1 meter
    i) 1 bushel > 2 pecks
    j) 8 pints = 1 gallon
    k) 9 pounds > 140 ounces
    l) 2 feet > 0.5 yards
    m) 3 meters = 300 centimeters

3. a) 7.2 meters
    b) 410 meters
    c) 50 meters
    d) 6.72 meters
    e) .08 meters
    f) 4 meters
    g) .92 meters
    h) 1.241 meters
    i) 82,400 meters

4. a) .72 liters   c) 7.2 deciliters   e) .0072 hectoliters
    b) 72 centiliters   d) .072 dekaliters   f) .00072 kiloliters

5. a) False   d) False
    b) True   e) True
    c) True   f) True

6. a) 540 centimeters   e) 72,000,000 microliters
    b) 81,000 meters   f) 5.24 deciliters
    c) 10^{12} (or 1,000,000,000,000 microliters) g) .002473
    d) 5.497 kilograms   h) 70 decimeters

7. a) 16 ft. 18 in. or 17 ft. 6 in. or $17\frac{1}{2}$ ft.   f) 3 m 56 cm or 356 cm
    b) 10 hrs. 22 min.   g) 4 yds. 31 in. or 4 yds. 2 ft. 7 in.
    c) 1 m 52 cm or 152 cm   h) 11 cm 4 mm or 114 cm
    d) 12 rd. 54 ft. or 15 rd. $4\frac{1}{2}$ ft.   i) 2 gal. $3\frac{4}{5}$ pt.
    e) 10 ft. 10 in.   j) 22 m 6 cm or 2206 cm

8. a) $5\frac{2}{3}$ yards   f) 36,960 feet
    b) 63 inches   g) $\frac{3}{8}$ acres
    c) $2\frac{1}{2}$ gallons   h) $21\frac{1}{2}$ pints
    d) 22 ounces   i) 441 sq. feet
    e) 48 tablespoons   j) 48 cups

9. 2 quarters; 1 quarter, 5 nickels; 1 quarter, 1 dime, 3 nickels; 1 quarter, 2 dimes, 1 nickel; 5 dimes;
4 dimes, 2 nickels; 3 dimes, 4 nickels; 2 dimes, 6 nickels; 1 dime, 8 nickels; 10 nickels.

10. Approximately 27 pennies measure about 4 cm, therefore one penny is about .148 mm in thickness.

11. Quarters	Dimes	Nickels	Quarters	Dimes	Nickels
4	0	0	1	2	11
3	2	1	1	1	13
3	1	3	1	0	15
3	0	5	0	10	0
2	5	0	0	9	2
2	4	2	0	8	4
2	3	4	0	7	6
2	2	6	0	6	8
2	1	8	0	5	10
2	0	10	0	4	12
1	7	1	0	3	14
1	6	3	0	2	16
1	5	5	0	1	18
1	4	7	0	0	20
1	3	9			

12. Approximately 8 dimes measure about one cm, thus one dime is about .125 mm in thickness.

Unit 14

Answers to the examples that relate to the geoboard will vary. Some possible answers are given.

1.
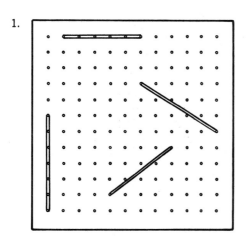

2.
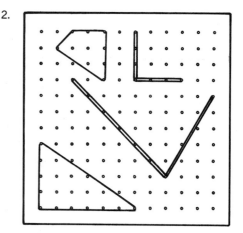

a)

b)

3.
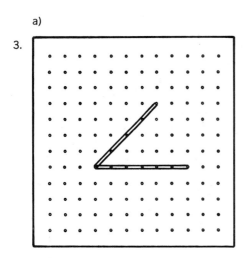

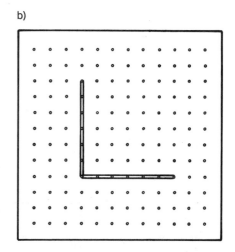

c)

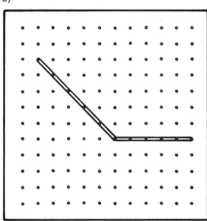

d)

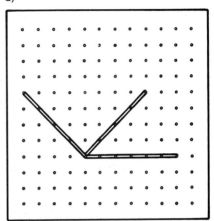

e)

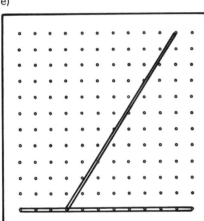

4.

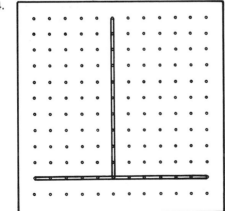

5. A   B

a) an infinite number of lines
b) one line segment

6. a) congruent   b) acute

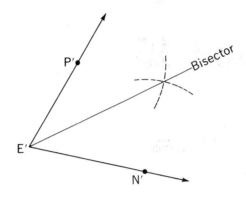

7. a) 65°   b) 45°   c) 10°   d) 17°   e) 87°   f) 4°

8. a) 140°   b) 90°   c) 30°   d) 10°   e) 135°   f) 71°

9. Answers will vary, depending on the given figure. But the results should appear this way:

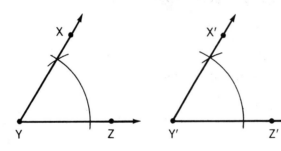

10. a) point   (A)
    b) ray   ($\overrightarrow{FG}$)
    c) line   ($\overleftrightarrow{HK}$ or $\overleftrightarrow{KH}$)
    d) acute angle   (∠ZXY or ∠YXZ)
    e) right angle   (∠NOM or ∠MON)
    f) line segment   ($\overline{ST}$ or $\overline{TS}$)
    g) obtuse angle   (∠PQR or ∠RQP)
    h) adjacent angles, or complementary angles [$m(\angle LRM) + m(\angle MRN) = 90°$]
    i) adjacent angles, or supplementary angles [$m(\angle AED) + m(\angle DEB) = 180°$]

11. a) True   c) False   e) True   g) False
    b) True   d) False   f) False

12. $\overline{AB}$ $\overline{AC}$ $\overline{AD}$ $\overline{AE}$ $\overline{AF}$
    $\overline{BC}$ $\overline{BD}$ $\overline{BE}$ $\overline{BF}$
    $\overline{CD}$ $\overline{CE}$ $\overline{CF}$
    $\overline{DE}$ $\overline{DF}$
    $\overline{EF}$

Unit 15

1. a) scalene triangle
    right triangle

    $A = \frac{1}{2}bh$ $\qquad\qquad\qquad$ $P = m(\overleftrightarrow{MO}) + m(\overleftrightarrow{ON}) + m(\overleftrightarrow{NM})$

    $A = \frac{1}{2} \times 8 \times 6$ $\qquad\qquad$ $P = 8 + 10 + 6$

    $A = \left(\frac{1}{2} \times 8\right) \times 6$ $\qquad$ $P = 24$

    $A = 4 \times 6$ $\qquad\qquad\qquad$ The perimeter is 24 units.

    $A = 24$

    The area is 24 square units.

    b) isosceles triangle
    acute triangle

    $A = \frac{1}{2}bh$ $\qquad\qquad\qquad$ $P = m(\overleftrightarrow{XY}) + m(\overleftrightarrow{YZ}) + m(\overleftrightarrow{ZX})$

    $A = \frac{1}{2} \times 12 \times 8$ $\qquad\quad$ $P = 12 + 10 + 10$

    $A = \left(\frac{1}{2} \times 12\right) \times 8$ $\quad$ $P = 32$

    $A = 6 \times 8$ $\qquad\qquad\qquad$ The perimeter is 32 units.

    $A = 48$

    The area is 48 square units.

    c) equilateral triangle
    equiangular triangle

    $A = \frac{1}{2}bh$ $\qquad\qquad\qquad$ $P = 3s$

    $A = \frac{1}{2} \times 30 \times 26$ $\qquad\quad$ $P = 3 \times 30$

    $A = \left(\frac{1}{2} \times 30\right) \times 26$ $\quad$ $P = 90$

    $A = 15 \times 26$ $\qquad\qquad\qquad$ The perimeter is 90 units.

    $A = 390$

    The area is 390 square units.

2. If we cut out two copies of the trapezoid shown on the left, we can place the pieces together to form the figure shown on the right.

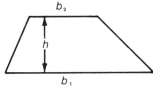
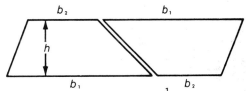

The figure on the right has area $h(b_1 + b_2)$, so the trapezoid has area $\frac{1}{2}h(b_1 + b_2)$.

3. a) square

$A = s^2$

$A = 5 \times 5$
$A = 25$
The area is 25 square units.
$P = m(\overleftrightarrow{WX}) + m(\overleftrightarrow{XY}) + m(\overleftrightarrow{YZ}) + m(\overleftrightarrow{ZW})$
$P = 4s$
$P = 4 \times 5$ The perimeter is 20 units.
$P = 20$

b) parallelogram

$A = bh$	$P = 2\ell + 2w$
$A = 12 \times 6$	$P = (2 \times 12) + (2 \times 8)$
$A = 72$	$P = 24 + 16$
The area is 72	$P = 40$
square units.	The perimeter is 40 units.

c) rectangle

$A = \ell w$	$P = 2\ell + 2w$
$A = 27 \times 8$	$P = (2 \times 27) + (2 \times 8)$
$A = 216$	$P = 54 + 16$
The area is 216	$P = 70$
square units.	The perimeter is 70 units.

d) rhombus

$A = bh$	$P = 4s$
$A = 5 \times 4$	$P = 4 \times 5$
$A = 20$	$P = 20$
The area is 20 square units.	The perimeter is 20 units.

e) trapezoid

$A = \frac{1}{2}(b + b')h$	$P = a + b + c + d$
$A = \frac{1}{2}(8 + 4) \times 4$	$P = (8 + 6) + (4 + 5)$
$A = 6 \times 4$	$P = 14 + 9$
$A = 24$	$P = 23$
The area is 24 square units.	The perimeter is 23 units.

4. a) 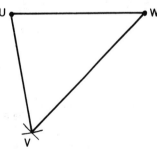   b)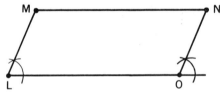

5. a) $A = \pi r^2$ $C = \pi d$
        $= 3.1 \times (4 \times 4)$ $= 3.1 \times (4 + 4)$
        $= 3.1 \times 16$ $= 3.1 \times 8$
        $= 49.6$ $= 24.8$
   The area of the circle is   The circumference is
   approximately 49.6 square   approximately 24.8 units.
   units.

b) $A = \pi r^2$
$= 3.1 \times (6 \times 6)$
$= 3.1 \times 36$
$= 111.6$
The area is approximately 111.6 square units.

$C = \pi d$
$= 3.1 \times 12$
$= 37.2$
The circumference is approximately 37.2 units.

6. a) $c^2 = a^2 + b^2$
$225 = a^2 + 81$
$a^2 = 144$
$a = 12$
Side a is 12 units long.

b) $c^2 = a^2 + b^2$
$169 = 144 + b^2$
$b^2 = 25$
$b = 5$
Side b is 5 units long.

c) $c^2 = a^2 + b^2$
$c^2 = 36 + 64$
$c^2 = 100$
$c = 10$
Side c is 10 units long.

7. Every square has four lines of symmetry.

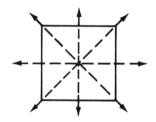

8. a) Each line coincides with or is parallel to each of the others.
   b) They are all the same length.
   c) Polygon ABCDE is the same size and shape as polygon A'B'C'D'E'; in other words, the two polygons are congruent.

9.

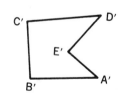

10. Since the sum of the measures of the angles of any triangle is 180°, the measure of the third angle must be 71°.

11. a)

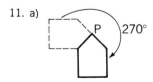

b)

c)

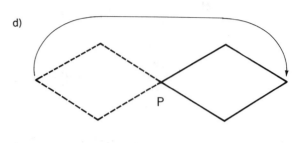

d)

12. a)

b)

c)

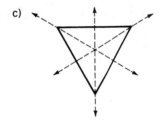

d)

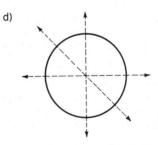

A circle has an infinite number of lines of symmetry and they cannot all be drawn.

13. a)

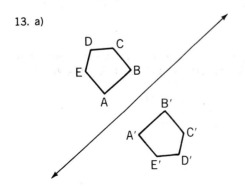

b)

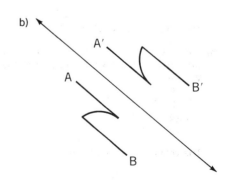

c)

14. a) rectangular pyramid
    base: the rectangular region ABCD
    edges: $\overleftrightarrow{AB}$, $\overleftrightarrow{BC}$, $\overleftrightarrow{CD}$, $\overleftrightarrow{DA}$, $\overleftrightarrow{AE}$, $\overleftrightarrow{BE}$, $\overleftrightarrow{CE}$, $\overleftrightarrow{DE}$
    vertices: A, B, C, D, E

   b) rectangular prism
    bases: any one of the following pairs of rectangular regions — WXYZ and W'X'Y'Z', and XX'Y'Y and WW'Z'Z, WW'X'X and ZZ'Y'Y
    edges: $\overleftrightarrow{WW'}$, $\overleftrightarrow{XX'}$, $\overleftrightarrow{YY'}$, $\overleftrightarrow{ZZ'}$, $\overleftrightarrow{WX}$, $\overleftrightarrow{XY}$, $\overleftrightarrow{YZ}$, $\overleftrightarrow{ZW}$, $\overleftrightarrow{W'X'}$, $\overleftrightarrow{X'Y'}$, $\overleftrightarrow{Y'Z'}$, $\overleftrightarrow{Z'W'}$
    vertices: W, X, Y, Z, W', X', Y', Z'

   c) right circular cylinder
    bases: the two circular regions with centers O and O'
    edges: (We haven't defined the edges of a cylinder.)
    vertices: (We haven't defined the vertices of a cylinder.)

   d) pentagonal pyramid
    base: the pentagonal region ABCDE
    edges: $\overleftrightarrow{AB}$, $\overleftrightarrow{BC}$, $\overleftrightarrow{CD}$, $\overleftrightarrow{DE}$, $\overleftrightarrow{EA}$, $\overleftrightarrow{AF}$, $\overleftrightarrow{BF}$, $\overleftrightarrow{CF}$, $\overleftrightarrow{DF}$, $\overleftrightarrow{EF}$
    vertices: A, B, C, D, E, F

15. a) $V = \ell wh$ $V = Bh$
      $= 14 \times 7 \times 3$ or $= (14 \times 7) \times 3$
      $= 294$ $= 98 \times 3$
              $= 294$

    The volume is 294 cubic units.

   b) The polygons forming the bases of this prism are right triangles. The area of each base is therefore equal to one-half the product of the legs of the right triangle bounding the base.
      $V = Bh$
      $= \left(\frac{1}{2} \times 6 \times 8\right) \times 3$
      $= 24 \times 3$
      $= 72$

    The volume is 72 cubic units.

c) $V = \ell wh$ $V = Bh$
  $= 5 \times 5 \times 5$ or $= (5 \times 5) \times 5$
  $= 125$ $= 25 \times 5$
        $= 125$

The volume is 125 cubic units.

16. a) $SA = 2B + Ph$
  $SA = [2 \times (6 \times 6)] + [(6 + 6 + 6 + 6) \times 6]$
  $SA = [2 \times 36] + [24 \times 6]$
  $SA = 72 + 144$
  $SA = 216$
  The surface area is 216 square units.

b) $SA = 2B + Ph$
  $SA = [2 \times (3 \times 12)] + [(12 + 3 + 12 + 3) \times 5]$
  $SA = [2 \times 36] + [30 \times 5]$
  $SA = 72 + 150$
  $SA = 222$
  The surface area is 222 square units.

c) The polygons forming the bases of this prism are right triangles. The area of each base is there-fore equal to one-half the product of the legs of the right triangle bounding the bases.

  $SA = 2B + Ph$
  $SA = \left[2 \times \left(\frac{1}{2} \times 6 \times 8 \right) \right] + [(6 + 8 + 10) \times 3]$
  $SA = [2 \times 24] + [24 \times 3]$
  $SA = 48 + 72$
  $SA = 120$
  The surface area is 120 square units.

17. a) prism, cylinder
    b) sphere
    c) cylinder, prism
    d) triangular pyramid
    e) pyramid

18. a) rectangular pyramid
    b) cube
    c) cylinder
    d) triangular prism

19.

Space Figure	Area of Base	Height	Volume
Cylinder	42 sq. in.	10 in.	420 cu. in.
Cube	25 sq. cm	5 cm	125 cu. cm
Triangular prism	37 sq. in.	14 in.	518 cu. in.
Cylinder	24 sq. m	50 dm	120 cu. m
Rectangular prism	27 sq. mm	9 mm	243 cu. mm
Square prism	6 sq. ft.	18 in.	9 cu. ft.

Unit 16

1. $\frac{1}{16}, \frac{1}{32}, \frac{1}{64}$

2. There are eleven possible combinations.

   a) all tails   1/1024   g) 6 heads and 4 tails   105/512
   b) 1 head and 9 tails   5/512   h) 7 heads and 3 tails   15/128
   c) 2 heads and 8 tails   45/1024   i) 8 heads and 2 tails   45/1024
   d) 3 heads and 7 tails   15/128   j) 9 heads and 1 tail   5/512
   e) 4 heads and 6 tails   105/512   k) all heads   1/1024
   f) 5 heads and 5 tails   63/256

3. a) $\frac{1}{3}$ b) $\frac{1}{2}$ c) $\frac{1}{6}$ d) $\frac{2}{3}$ e) $\frac{1}{3}$

4. a) $\frac{1}{6}, \frac{1}{6}, \frac{1}{6}$ b) $\frac{1}{3}$ c) $\frac{1}{2}$ d) $\frac{2}{3}$ e) $\frac{5}{6}$

5. red marble $\frac{5}{8}$, blue marble $\frac{2}{8}$ or $\frac{1}{4}$, white marble $\frac{1}{8}$

6. a) Mean $= \frac{67}{32}$ or about 2 heads per toss   b) Median $= 2$; mode $= 2$; range $= 4$

   c)

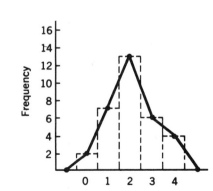

7. a) $\frac{7}{22}$ b) $\frac{10}{22}$ or $\frac{5}{11}$ c) $\frac{5}{22}$

8. a) $\frac{1}{12}$ b) $\frac{3}{12}$ or $\frac{1}{4}$ c) $\frac{6}{12}$ or $\frac{1}{2}$

9. a) $\frac{1}{52}$ b) $\frac{4}{52}$ or $\frac{1}{13}$ c) $\frac{13}{52}$ or $\frac{1}{4}$ d) $\frac{12}{52}$ or $\frac{3}{13}$ e) $\frac{20}{52}$ or $\frac{5}{13}$

10. 3 socks

11. Results of 100 rolls of a die:

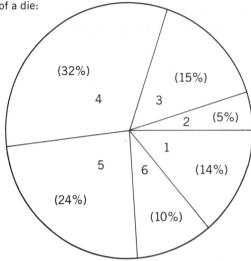

12. Number of years five Kansas City Chiefs played in N.F.L.

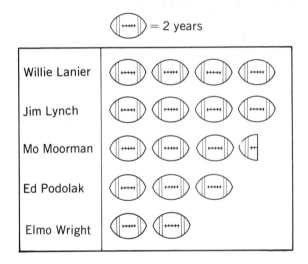

Unit 17

1. a) compound, disjunction
   b) simple
   c) compound, conditional
   d) compound, conjunction
   e) simple
   f) simple
   g) compound, conjunction
   h) compound, conditional

2. a) T   c) F   e) T   g) T   i) T   k) F
   b) T   d) T   f) F   h) F   j) F   l) F

3. a) Ray is a good student and John is a good student.
   b) I tried the car and it wouldn't start.
   c) If you try, then you will succeed.
   d) Judy will call before noon or Susan will call before noon.

4. a) F   c) F   e) T   g) T   i) T
   b) T   d) T   f) T   h) F

5. a) some   c) all   e) some
   b) some   d) all   f) no

6. a) false   f) true
   b) true   g) false
   c) true   h) false
   d) true   i) true
   e) false   j) false

7. a) You can conclude that Figure C has four sides.
   b) You can conclude that Bob does not do his homework.
   c) You can conclude that we might have gone on a picnic.
   d) You can conclude that we shoveled the sidewalk.

8. a) truth   b) lie   c) truth   d) truth

Appendix B

Checklist of Mathematical Concepts

Developed and Compiled by the Mathematics Education Team
Department of Elementary-Secondary Education
Kent State University
September 1983 Revision by James W. Heddens

This checklist is a summary of mathematical concepts organized under subheadings named *Concept Clusters*. The items on the checklist have been sequenced in a logical order within each concept cluster; however, a pupil does not learn all the concepts in a given concept cluster before he/she begins to study another concept cluster—for example, the concept cluster *Place Value* and *Addition and Subtraction of Whole Numbers*. Teachers have the responsibility of arranging concepts from different concept clusters into a program that meets the mathematical needs of their children.

Since children do not learn mathematics in a linear fashion, concepts as listed on the checklist should be introduced, developed, and continually reinforced through a spiral curriculum. Mastery of basic skills should always follow concept development. Understanding (concept development) and skill (mastery of basic facts and algorithms) constitute power.

The checklist should be continuously updated. In the appropriate space at the right of each concept, record the date (month and year) in *pencil*.

TABLE OF CONTENTS

A. RELATIONSHIPS

	INTRODUCTION	IN PROCESS	MASTERY

1. Size and Quantity (single object)
   a. big—little
   b. long—short
   c. tall—short
   d. large—small
   e. many—few
   f. high—low
   g. all—none
   h. heavy—light
   i. thick—thin

2. Position
   a. under—over
   b. first—last
   c. middle
   d. high—low
   e. far—near
   f. bottom—top
   g. above—below
   h. in front of—behind—on top of
   i. beside—by—next to
   j. between
   k. around
   l. inside—outside
   m. right—left

3. Comparison of Two or More Quantities
   a. younger(est)—older(est)
   b. fewer(est)
   c. more(most)—less(least): referring to sets
   d. greater than—less than: referring to sets
   e. larger(est)—smaller(est)
   f. longer(est)—shorter(est)
   g. straight—crooked
   h. bigger(est)—littler(est)
   i. heavier(est)—lighter(est)
   j. taller(est)—shorter(est)
   k. thicker(est)—thinner(est)

4. Measurement
   a. Capacity
      (1) empty—full
      (2) pair
      (3) cupful
      (4) spoonful
      (5) pint
      (6) quart
      (7) liter
      (8) gallon
   b. Linear
      (1) ruler
      (2) meterstick
      (3) yardstick
   c. Temperature
      (1) hot—cold
      (2) thermometer
      (3) degree
   d. Weight
      (1) metric units: gram, kilogram
      (2) customary units: ounce, pound

	INTRODUCTION	IN PROCESS	MASTERY

e. Time
 (1) early—late
 (2) yesterday—tomorrow
 (3) today
 (4) morning—afternoon
 (5) noon—midnight
 (6) night—day
 (7) evening
 (8) minute
 (9) hour
 (10) week
 (11) month
 (12) year
 (13) fast—slow
f. Money
 (1) penny
 (2) nickel
 (3) dime
 (4) quarter
 (5) buy—sell
 (6) spend—save
 (7) pay
 (8) cost

5. Geometric Figures and Shapes
(sorting activities and recognition)
 a. square
 b. rectangle
 c. circle
 d. triangle
 e. cube
 f. sphere (globe or ball)

6. Awareness of Similarities and Differences
(sorting activities according to one or more characteristics listed below)
 a. categories: animals, boys, girls, etc.
 b. shape
 c. size
 d. color
 e. thickness

7. Patterns: Begin with two objects then increase the number of objects to three or more.
 a. observing patterns
 b. orally describing patterns
 c. duplicating and then extending patterns
 d. completing patterns
 e. creating patterns

B. **CONCEPT CLUSTER—READINESS ACTIVITIES FOR OPERATIONS WITH COUNTING NUMBERS AND WHOLE NUMBERS**
 1. Numberness
  a. recognizing a set as a collection of distinguishable objects
  b. viewing a model of a set and verbally stating its cardinality (0—9)
  c. matching a set model of cardinal numbers (0—9) with the appropriate numeral
  d. matching the appropriate numeral with a set model of cardinal numbers (0—9)

	INTRODUCTION	IN PROCESS	MASTERY

e. recognizing one-to-one correspondence between the elements of two equivalent sets (0–9)

f. demonstrating one-to-one correspondence between the elements of two equivalent sets (0–9)

g. using one-to-one correspondence to determine whether two sets (0–9) are equivalent or non-equivalent

h. recognizing, by visual inspection, whether two sets (0–9) are equivalent or non-equivalent

i. constructing two or more disjoint sets that model the same cardinal number (0–9)

j. constructing a disjoint set that contains one element more (or less) than a given set (0–9)

k. , ordering numbers (0–9) on a number line

l. writing numerals (0–9)

m. recognizing odd and even numbers (0–9)

n. recognizing a written word name for a number (0–9)

o. associating a written word name with the appropriate numeral (0–9)

p. writing a word name for a number when shown a given numeral (0–9)

q. writing numerals 10–20

r. writing numerals 21–99

s. associating a Roman numeral with a given number (1–100)

t. writing a Roman numeral for a given number (1–100)

2. Counting

   a. rational counting by 1's to
     (1) 10
     (2) 20
     (3) 50
     (4) 100

   b. rational counting by 2's to
     (1) 20, starting with two
     (2) 19, starting with one
     (3) 50 or more, starting with any one-place number

   c. rational counting by 5's

   d. rational counting by 10's

   e. identifying the number of objects in a set (0–9) by
     (1) counting each object
     (2) grouping the objects into subsets
     (3) visual inspection

   f. identifying equalities and inequalities

   g. relating the words "greater than," "less than," and "equal to" to *part of*

   h. recognizing the symbols >, <, and =

   i. relating the words "greater than" to the symbol > when comparing two numbers

   j. relating the words "less than" to the symbol < when comparing two numbers

   k. relating the words "equal to" to the symbol = when comparing two numbers

   l. identifying greatest/least, given three or more numbers

	INTRODUCTION	IN PROCESS	MASTERY

m. recognizing ordinal numbers, first through tenth

n. modeling counting on the number line

o. naming the number that is one greater than or one less than a given one- or two-place number

p. supplying the missing numerals when several are missing in a sequence (0–100)

q. writing the word names for numbers (10–100)

r. writing the numeral, given the word names for numbers (10–100)

3. Place Value

a. recognizing another way of modeling ten "ones" as one "ten"

b. modeling any two-place number as ones and tens (expanded notation)

c. interpreting the place-value model of any two-place number in standard notation

d. rewriting a numeral in expanded notation relating the word name for place value with the numeral (e.g., 34 = 3 tens 4 ones)

e. extending b, c, d through the hundreds' place

f. renaming numerals in several different ways (e.g., 273 can be renamed as 273 ones, 27 tens 3 ones, or 2 hundreds 7 tens 3 ones)

g. renaming numerals with zeros as place holders in several different ways (e.g., 300 can be renamed as 300 ones, 30 tens 0 ones, or 3 hundreds 0 tens 0 ones)

h. extending the concepts *b* through *g* to the thousands' place and beyond

i. rounding numbers to the nearest
    (1) ten
    (2) hundred
    (3) thousand
    (4) any place value greater than thousands' place

j. expressing place value in exponential form
    (1) positive integral exponents
    (2) zero as an exponent
    (3) negative integral exponents

REMARK

At this time in the program, numeration systems without place value could be contrasted with numeration systems having place value.

C. CONCEPT CLUSTER—ADDITION AND SUBTRACTION OF WHOLE NUMBERS

1. recognizing the union of two disjoint sets as a model for addition

2. modeling the union of two disjoint sets

3. associating the + sign as the appropriate symbol for addition

4. modeling addition of two one-place numbers, using manipulative materials

5. modeling the commutative property of addition

6. interpreting set models for addition as addition sentences

7. modeling an addition sentence, given a basic addition fact

8. modeling addition on a number line

	INTRODUCTION	IN PROCESS	MASTERY

9. recognizing the words "addend" and "sum"
10. organizing the 100 basic addition facts according to a given sum (0 through 18)
11. memorizing the basic addition facts with
    a. zero as *one* of the addends and the commutative property
    b. one as *one* of the addends and the commutative property
    c. two as *one* of the addends and the commutative property
    d. "doubles" and "doubles plus one" and the commutative property
    e. facts related to tenness (by the associative property) and the commutative property
    f. the four remaining facts that were not included in the above organization (*a* through *e*)
12. comparing the sums of two basic addition facts using the sysmbols > <, or =
13. extending and expanding the basic addition facts; example: (2 + 3) to (20 + 30)

REMARK

Throughout this portion of the checklist, the word "regrouping" is used in place of "carrying" and "borrowing"; the latter terms are not mathematically meaningful.

	INTRODUCTION	IN PROCESS	MASTERY

14. naming the sum of a two-place whole number and a one-place whole number (no regrouping)
15. naming the sum of a two-place whole number and a two-place whole number (no regrouping)
16. naming the sum of a three-place whole number and a two-place whole number (no regrouping)
17. naming the sum of a three-place whole number and a three-place whole number (no regrouping)
18. naming the sum of a many-place whole number and a many-place whole number (no regrouping)
19. naming the sum of three or more one-place whole numbers in *column addition* (no regrouping)
20. naming the sum of three or more two-place whole numbers in *column addition* (no regrouping)
21. naming the sum of three or more one-place and many-place numbers (no regrouping)
22. generalizing the sum of two even numbers
23. generalizing the sum of an even number and an odd number (and vice versa)
24. generalizing the sum of two odd numbers
25. naming the sum of a two-place whole number and a one-place whole number with a single regrouping
26. naming the sum of a two-place whole number and a two-place whole number with regrouping (ones to tens)
27. naming the sum of a many-place whole number and a many-place whole number with regrouping (ones to tens or tens to hundreds)
28. naming the sum of a two-place whole number and a two-place whole number with two regroupings
29. naming the sum of a three-place whole number and a two-place whole number with two regroupings

	INTRODUCTION	IN PROCESS	MASTERY
30. naming the sum of a three-place whole number and a three-place whole number with two regroupings			
31. naming the sum of a many-place whole number and a many-place whole number with several regroupings			
32. estimating sums			
33. problem solving that requires addition of whole numbers			
34. finding missing addends (readiness for subtraction)			
35. understanding subtraction as the inverse of addition			
36. understanding the minus sign			
37. using set separation as a model for subtraction			
38. expressing a related addition sentence in subtraction form: (addend + addend = sum ↔ sum − addend = addend)			
39. modeling subtraction on the number line			
40. memorizing the basic subtraction facts			
41. extend and expand the basic subtraction facts: example, $(5 - 3)$ to $(50 - 30)$			
42. naming the difference between a two-place whole number and a one-place whole number (not a basic fact and no regrouping)			
43. naming the difference between two, two-place whole numbers (no regrouping)			
44. naming the difference between a three-place whole number and a two-place whole number (no regrouping)			
45. naming the difference between two, three-place whole numbers (no regrouping)			
46. naming the difference between two, many-place whole numbers (no regrouping)			
47. naming the difference between a two-place whole number and a one-place whole number (not a basic fact) with regrouping			
48. naming the difference between two, two-place whole numbers with regrouping from tens to ones			
49. naming the difference between a three-place whole number and a two-place whole number with regrouping from tens to ones			
50. naming the difference between a three-place whole number and a two-place whole number with regrouping from hundreds to tens			
51. naming the difference between a three-place whole number and a two-place whole number with double regrouping			
52. naming the difference between two, three-place whole numbers with a single regrouping			
53. naming the difference between two, three-place whole numbers with double regrouping			
54. naming the difference between two, many-place whole numbers with several regroupings			
55. naming the difference when a zero appears in a single place of the minuend			
56. naming the difference when zeros appear in the tens and ones place of the minuend			
57. estimating differences			
58. problem solving that requires subtraction of whole numbers			

REMARK

The words "minuend", "subtrahend", "difference", should be meaningfully related to "sum", "given addend", "missing addend" respectively.

D. CONCEPT CLUSTER—MULTIPLICATION AND DIVISION OF WHOLE NUMBERS

INTRODUCTION	IN PROCESS	MASTERY

1. using sets as a model for multiplication of whole numbers
    a. recognizing the number of sets
    b. recognizing the number of objects in each set
2. associating the $\times$ sign as the appropriate symbol for multiplication
3. interpreting set models as basic multiplication facts
4. verifying the commutative property for multiplication
5. using set models to illustrate several basic facts
6. using arrays as a model for multiplication
7. modeling multiplication of two, one-place whole numbers on the number line
8. using successive addition as a model for multiplication
9. recognizing the words "factor" and "product"
10. memorizing the basic multiplication facts using
    a. zero as a factor
    b. one as a factor
    c. two, three as a factor
    d. four, five as a factor
    e. six, seven as a factor
    f. eight, nine as a factor

REMARK

Attention should be given to "one" as the identity element for multiplication. From this point on, consider writing 6×6 and 7×7 as 6^2 and 7^2 introducing the words "exponent" and "base of the exponent."

11. naming the product if one factor is a multiple of 10, 100, etc.
12. expanding the basic multiplication facts (for example, 2×3 to 2×30)
13. modeling the distributive property of multiplication over addition (Caution: Begin with a one-place whole number times a two-place whole number)
14. naming the product of a one-place whole number and two-place whole number by using the distributive property of multiplication over addition (two partial products)
15. naming the product of a one-place whole number and a three-place whole number by using the distributive property of multiplication over addition (three partial products)
16. naming the product of two, two-place whole numbers by using the distributive property of multiplication over addition (four partial products)
17. naming the product of a one-place whole number and a two-place whole number by using the standard algorithm
18. naming the product of a one-place whole number and a three-place whole number by using the standard algorithm

	INTRODUCTION	IN PROCESS	MASTERY
19. naming the product of two, two-place whole numbers by using the standard algorithm			
20. naming the product of two, three-place whole numbers by using the standard algorithm			
21. naming the product of two, many-place whole numbers by using the standard algorithm			
22. estimating products			
23. problem solving that requires multiplication of whole numbers			
24. finding the missing factor			
25. using objects to model division (measurement and partitive interpretations of division)			
26. using symbols that indicate division ($2\overline{)6}$, $6 \div 2$, $\frac{6}{2}$)			
27. expressing a related multiplication sentence as a division sentence (product ÷ factor = factor)			
28. using the number line to model division			
29. using arrays as a model for multiplication			
30. using successive subtraction as a model for multiplication			
31. memorizing the basic division facts for whole numbers			
32. understanding division by one			
33. understanding division of a nonzero number by itself			
34. developing the terms dividend, divisor, and quotient			
35. naming the quotient of a one-place or two-place dividend and a one-place divisor with a remainder other than zero			
36. expanding basic division facts $2\overline{)8}$ $2\overline{)80}$ $2\overline{)800}$			
37. naming the quotient of a two-place dividend and a one-place divisor (not a basic fact)			
38. naming the quotient of a three-place dividend and a one-place divisor			
39. introduce uneven division (example: $2\overline{)7}$)			
40. naming the quotient of a many-place dividend and a one-place divisor			
41. developing standard division algorithm			
42. naming the quotient of a three-place dividend and a two-place divisor (where the divisor is a multiple of ten)			
43. naming the quotient when the divisor is 100, 1000, etc.			
44. naming the quotient of a three-place dividend and a two-place divisor (other than multiple of ten)			
45. estimating dividend and divisor as an aid in establishing the quotient a. place value b. numerical value			
46. naming the quotient of a many-place dividend and a many-place divisor			
47. problem solving requiring division of whole numbers with emphasis on meaningful interpretation of a remainder			
48. understanding why division by zero is undefined			
49. examining the divisibility rules for 2, 3, 5, 10			
50. differentiating between division and factoring			
51. factoring one-place or two-place products			

	INTRODUCTION	IN PROCESS	MASTERY

52. defining prime numbers and composite numbers
53. naming the prime factors of any whole number greater than one

E. CONCEPT CLUSTER—INTEGERS

1. Readiness Activities for Operations with Integers
   a. eliciting situations in which pupils need numbers other than whole numbers to communicate some measure of distance, temperature, and time (Explore some everyday, familiar uses of directed numbers.)
   b. using a number line to model magnitude and direction from zero
   c. recognizing that the symbols + and − take on new meanings (When these symbols are written to the upper left of the numeral, the numeral names an integer other than zero.)
   d. recognizing that zero has no sign of direction even though zero is an integer
   e. using the number line (both horizontal and vertical positions) to model the set of integers
   f. listing the set of integers using set notation $\{\ldots,\ ^-3,\ ^-2,\ ^-1,\ 0,\ ^+1,\ ^+2,\ ^+3,\ \ldots\}$
   g. investigating the law of trichotomy
   h. using the number line to model positive and negative movement from integers other than zero
   i. guiding the discovery of "opposites"
   j. discussing the isomorphic relationship between the counting numbers and the positive integers
   k. defining integers
2. Addition and Subtraction of Integers
   a. modeling, on the number line, the sum of two integers with the same sign of direction (two positive integers or two negative integers)
   b. naming the sum of two integers with the same signs of direction (two positive integers or two negative integers)
   c. modeling, on the number line, the sum of two integers with different signs of direction
   d. naming the sum of two integers with different signs of direction
   e. defining and using additive inverse elements
   f. naming the sum of one-, two-, and three-place integers (two addends with both like and unlike signs of direction)
   g. naming the sum of more than two integers
   h. summarizing the basic properties under the operation of addition of integers
   i. establishing generalizations for addition of integers
   j. finding the missing addend
   k. understanding subtraction of integers as the inverse operation of addition
   l. modeling, on the number line, subtraction of integers as the difference between two integers
   m. naming the difference between two integers
   n. establishing a generalization for subtraction of integers
   o. problem solving that requires addition or subtraction of integers

	INTRODUCTION	IN PROCESS	MASTERY

3. Multiplication and Division of Integers
   a. modeling on the number line, the product of two positive integers
   b. naming the product of two positive integers
   c. modeling, on the number line, the product of a positive integer and a negative integer
   d. modeling, on the number line, the product of a negative integer and a positive integer (use the commutative property)
   e. naming the product of two integers with unlike signs
   f. discovering the product of two negative integers using "properties" and "patterns" approaches
   g. naming the product of two negative integers
   h. naming the product of more than two integers
   i. summarizing the basic properties under the operation of multiplication
   j. establishing generalizations for multiplication of integers
   k. finding the missing factor
   l. understanding division of integers as the inverse operation of multiplication of integers
   m. naming the quotient of any two integers
   n. establishing generalizations for division of integers
   o. problem solving that requires multiplication or division of integers

F. CONCEPT CLUSTER—THE SET OF RATIONAL NUMBERS

Caution: The pupil should demonstrate power with all four operations on the *positive* rational numbers and zero. Once these competencies are achieved, the four operations on all rational numbers (positive, negative, zero) should be investigated.

1. Rational Numbers Expressed as Decimals
   a. Readiness Activities for Operations with Decimals
      (1) understanding tenths place value, using manipulative models and the number line
      (2) generalizing that ten tenths can be written as 1.0
      (3) writing the word name for a number in tenths' place
      (4) writing a symbol given the word name for a number in tenths' place
      (5) understanding hundredths' place value, using manipulative models and the number line
      (6) generalizing that ten hundredths can be written as 0.1
      (7) writing the word name for a numeral in hundredths' place
      (8) writing a symbol given the word name for a number in hundredths' place
      (9) understanding thousandths' place value

	INTRODUCTION	IN PROCESS	MASTERY
(10) generalizing that ten thousandths can be written as 0.01			
(11) writing the word name for a number in thousandths' place			
(12) writing a symbol given the word name for a number in the thousandths' place			
(13) extending place value beyond thousandths' place			
(14) using the law of trichotomy in comparing two or more decimals			
(15) modeling decimals on the number line			
(16) generating equivalent decimals by appending zeros			
(17) recognizing place-value symmetry with respect to the ones' place			
b. Addition and Subtraction of Rational Numbers Expressed as Decimals (1) naming the sum of two rational numbers expressed as decimals having the same place value			
(2) naming the sum of two rational numbers expressed as decimals having different place values			
(3) naming the sum of more than two rational numbers expressed as decimals having different place values			
(4) verifying the basic properties for addition of rational numbers expressed as decimals			
(5) problem solving requiring addition of rational numbers expressed as decimals			
(6) naming the difference between two rational numbers expressed as decimals having the same place value (with regrouping and without regrouping)			
(7) naming the difference between two rational numbers expressed as decimals having different place values (with regrouping and without regrouping)			
(8) problem solving requiring subtraction of rational numbers expressed as decimals			
c. Multiplication and Division of Rational Numbers Expressed as Decimals (1) generalizing the placement of the decimal point in the product			
(2) naming the product of two rational numbers expressed as decimals when it is necessary to append zeros to the left of a nonzero digit as decimal holders			
(3) naming the product of more than two rational numbers expressed as decimals			
(4) verifying the basic properties for multiplication of rational numbers expressed as decimals			
(5) solving word problems requiring multiplication of rational numbers expressed as decimals			
(6) naming the quotient of rational numbers expressed as decimals when the divisor is a whole number			

	INTRODUCTION	IN PROCESS	MASTERY

(7) generalizing the placement of the decimal point in the quotient of rational numbers expressed as decimals when the divisor is not a whole number (using the multiplicative identity element)

(8) naming the quotient of any two rational numbers expressed as decimals by using the division algorithm

(9) problem solving requiring division of rational numbers expressed as decimals

2. Rational Numbers Expressed as Fractions
   a. Readiness Activities
      (1) separating regions into equivalent sub-regions (circular and rectangular)
      (2) expressing one many different ways
      (3) developing terms: fraction, fraction bar, denominator, numerator, equivalent fractions, etc.
      (4) using the number line to model rational numbers
      (5) modeling equivalent fractions using the number line
      (6) generating sets of equivalent fractions when
         (a) the first element of a set is a proper fraction
         (b) the first element of a set is an improper fraction
         (c) the first element of a set is a mixed numeral
      (7) renaming fractions in simplest form
      (8) rewriting improper fractions as mixed numerals
      (9) rewriting mixed numerals as improper fractions
     (10) developing the concept of least common denominator by using the concept of least common multiple
     (11) comparing fractional numbers
     (12) determining the least common denominator by using the concept of greatest common factor
   b. Addition and Subtraction of Rational Numbers Expressed as Fractions
      (1) modeling addition of rational numbers expressed as fractions with *like* denominators
      (2) naming the sum of two rational numbers expressed as fractions with *like* denominators
      (3) modeling addition of rational numbers expressed as fractions with *unlike but related* denominators
      (4) naming the sum of two rational numbers expressed as fractions with *unlike but related* denominators
      (5) modeling addition of rational numbers expressed as fractions with *unlike and unrelated* denominators
      (6) naming the sum of two rational numbers expressed as fractions with *unlike and unrelated* denominators

	INTRODUCTION	IN PROCESS	MASTERY

(7) naming the sum of more than two rational numbers expressed as fractions

(8) solving word problems requiring addition of rational numbers expressed as fractions

(9) verifying the basic properties for addition of rational numbers expressed as fractions

(10) modeling subtraction of rational numbers expressed as fractions

(11) naming the difference between two rational numbers expressed as fractions with *like* denominators (with and without regrouping)

(12) naming the difference between two rational numbers expressed as fractions with *unlike but related* denominators (with and without regrouping)

(13) naming the difference between two rational numbers expressed as fractions with *unlike and unrelated* denominators (with and without regrouping)

(14) problem solving requiring subtraction of rational numbers expressed as fractions

c. Multiplication and Division of Rational Numbers Expressed as Fractions

   (1) modeling multiplication of two rational numbers expressed as fractions, using superimposed regions

   (2) naming the product of two rational numbers expressed as proper or improper fractions (using examples where no internal simplification is possible)

   (3) simplifying the example by using the multiplicative identity before naming the product of two rational numbers expressed as proper or improper fractions

   (4) naming the product of two rational numbers expressed as mixed numerals (rewritten as improper fractions)

   (5) naming the product of more than two rational numbers expressed in various forms (stress the use of internal simplification)

   (6) verifying the basic properties of multiplication of rational numbers expressed as fractions

   (7) naming the product of two rational numbers expressed as mixed numerals (using the distributive property of multiplication over addition)

   (8) problem solving requiring multiplication of rational numbers expressed as fractions

   (9) modeling division of rational numbers expressed as fractions (when the quotient has a remainder of zero)

   (10) modeling division of rational numbers expressed as fractions (when the quotient has a remainder *other than* zero)

	INTRODUCTION	IN PROCESS	MASTERY
(11) naming the quotient of two rational numbers expressed as fractions using the division frame			
(12) generalizing the algorithm for naming the quotient of two rational numbers expressed as fractions (using the complex fraction form)			
(13) naming the quotient of two rational numbers expressed as fractions (using the algorithm)			
3. Interrelating the Decimal Symbol with the Fraction Symbol for Rational Numbers			
a. defining rational numbers			
b. rewriting fractions as decimals			
c. generalizing the types of decimals that represent rational numbers			
d. rewriting terminating decimals and decimals that have a repeating pattern of digits as fractions			
4. Rational Numbers Expressed as Percents			
a. interpreting the symbol for percent (%) as a fraction and as a decimal			
b. rewriting percents as decimals and fractions			
(1) percents less than 100%			
(2) percents equal to or greater than 100%			
c. rewriting fractions or decimals as percents			
d. problem solving requiring percents			

G. CONCEPT CLUSTER—RATIO AND PROPORTION

	INTRODUCTION	IN PROCESS	MASTERY
1. defining ratio			
2. writing a ratio in two different forms			
3. defining proportion			
4. writing a proportion in two different forms			
5. developing vocabulary: means and extremes			
6. discovering the relationship between the product of the means and the product of the extremes			
7. naming the missing term in a proportion by using			
a. the concept of equivalent fractions			
b. the relationship between the product of the means and the product of the extremes (sometimes called means—extremes property)			
8. problem solving requiring proportions			

H. CONCEPT CLUSTER—MEASUREMENT

	INTRODUCTION	IN PROCESS	MASTERY
1. Money			
a. identifying the following coins:			
(1) penny			
(2) nickel			
(3) dime			
(4) quarter			
(5) half dollar			
b. recognizing relationships between and relative values of:			
(1) penny			
(2) nickel			
(3) dime			
(4) quarter			
(5) half dollar			

	INTRODUCTION	IN PROCESS	MASTERY
c. recognizing various combinations of coins equivalent to the value of a:			
(1) nickel			
(2) dime			
(3) quarter			
(4) half dollar			
d. making change for amounts up to one dollar			
e. recognizing and using money notation (¢, $)			
f. recognizing currency and making change for currency			
g. solving examples and word problems involving money			
2. Time (reading a clock)			
a. relating the face of the clock with the number line through 12 for hours			
b. relating the face of the clock with the number line through 60 for minutes			
c. telling time by the hour			
d. telling time by the minute			
e. translating time from the clock face to a digital clock			
f. understanding the difference between A.M. and P.M.			
g. solving examples and word problems involving time			
h. extending time to the 24-hour clock			
3. Length (metric units and customary units)			
a. recognizing metric units and their symbols and interrelating them to each other			
(1) meter (m)			
(2) decimeter (dm)			
(3) centimeter (cm)			
(4) millimeter (mm)			
(5) dekameter (dam)			
(6) hectometer (hm)			
(7) kilometer (km)			
b. changing one metric unit to another			
c. measuring lengths, using a metric ruler or trundle wheel			
d. problem solving involving metric measures of length			
e. recognizing customary units and their abbreviations and interrelating them to each other			
(1) inch (in.)			
(2) foot (ft.)			
(3) yard (yd.)			
(4) mile (mi.)			
f. changing one customary unit to another			
g. measuring lengths, using a foot ruler or a yardstick			
h. comparing centimeter to inch, meter to yard, and kilometer to mile			
4. Volume or Capacity (metric units and customary units)			
a. recognizing metric units and their symbols and interrelating them to each other			
(1) liter (L)			
(2) kiloliter (kL)			
(3) milliliter (mL)			
b. changing one metric unit to another			

	INTRODUCTION	IN PROCESS	MASTERY

c. measuring volume (capacity), using a liter container
d. problem solving involving metric measures of volume (capacity)
e. recognizing customary units and their abbreviations and interrelating them to each other
    (1) cup (c.)
    (2) pint (pt.)
    (3) quart (qt.)
    (4) gallon (gal.)
f. changing one customary unit to another
g. measuring volume (capacity), using a cup, pint container, etc.
h. comparing a liter to a quart, liter to a gallon, etc.
5. Weight or Mass (metric units and customary units)
    a. recognizing metric units and their symbols and interrelating them to each other
        (1) gram (g)
        (2) kilogram (kg)
    b. changing one metric unit to another
    c. measuring weight (mass), using gram and kilogram weights
    d. problem solving involving metric measures of weight (mass)
    e. recognizing customary units and their abbreviations and interrelating them to each other
        (1) ounce (oz.)
        (2) pound (lb.)
        (3) ton (T.)
    f. changing one customary unit to another
    g. measuring weight (mass), using ounces and pounds
    h. comparing kilograms to pounds
6. Temperature (metric units and customary units)
    a. recognizing the metric unit for temperature, namely, Celsius
    b. measuring temperatures, using a Celsius thermometer
    c. problem solving involving the metric measure of temperature
    d. recognizing the customary unit for temperature, namely, Fahrenheit
    e. measuring temperatures, using a Fahrenheit thermometer
    f. comparing Celsius to Fahrenheit

I. **CONCEPT CLUSTER—GEOMETRY**
    1. Basic notions
        a. distinguishing between the concept of and model for
            (1) point
            (2) line
            (3) plane
        b. recognizing the "betweenness" relationship of points
    2. Identifying shapes
        a. closed curves
            (1) simple polygons
            (2) circles and other elliptical shapes

	INTRODUCTION	IN PROCESS	MASTERY

	INTRODUCTION	IN PROCESS	MASTERY
b. regions			
(1) polygonal			
(2) circular and other elliptical regions			
3. Modeling shapes			
a. closed curves			
(1) simple polygons			
(2) circles and other elliptical shapes			
b. regions			
(1) polygonal			
(2) circular and other elliptical shapes			
4. Concept of a definition			
a. recognizing the necessity of definitions			
b. recognizing the characteristics of a definition			
(1) reversibility			
(2) unique characterization			
c. recognizing the necessity of undefined terms			
5. Using definitions to identify a(n)			
a. line segment			
b. half-line			
c. ray			
d. angle			
(1) vertex			
(2) sides			
e. angle degree			
6. Modeling a(n)			
a. line segment			
b. half-line			
c. ray			
d. angle			
7. Measuring angles with a protractor and classifying them as			
a. right angles			
b. acute angles			
c. obtuse angles			
8. Distinguishing between "equal measure" and "equal" pertaining to geometric figures			
9. Developing the meaning of "congruence"			
10. Classifying pairs of angles by			
a. measure			
(1) complementary			
(2) supplementary			
b. location			
(1) adjacent			
(2) nonadjacent			
(3) vertical			
11. Recognizing the concept of "parallel to" for			
a. lines			
b. segments			
c. rays			
d. planes			
12. Modeling parallel			
a. lines			
b. segments			
c. rays			
d. planes			
13. Using definition to identify simple two-dimensional closed figures			
a. polygons			
(1) triangles			
(a) according to angle measure			

	INTRODUCTION	IN PROCESS	MASTERY
(b) according to side measure			
(2) quadrilaterals			
(a) trapezoid			
(b) parallelogram			
(c) rectangle			
(d) square			
(e) rhombus			
(f) rhomboid			
(g) trapezium			
b. circles			
14. Recognizing terms related to simple, two-dimensional			
a. polygons			
(1) side			
(2) altitude			
(3) median			
(4) diagonal			
(5) vertex			
b. circles			
(1) center			
(2) radius			
(3) diameter			
(4) arc			
(5) chord			
(6) tangent			
(7) secant			
15. Recognizing the concept of symmetry			
a. with respect to a point			
b. with respect to a line			
c. with respect to a plane			
16. Distinguishing between exterior and interior			
a. with respect to an angle			
b. with respect to a simple closed curve			
17. Using compasses and straightedge for basic constructions			
a. copying a segment			
b. copying an angle			
c. bisecting a line segment			
d. constructing a perpendicular to a line from			
(1) a point on the line			
(2) a point not on the line			
e. bisecting an angle			
f. constructing a parallel to a line through a point			
g. constructing simple, two-dimensional closed figures			
18. Developing the concept of perimeter			
a. understanding the meaning of perimeter			
b. applying the meaning of perimeter to problems involving plane figures			
c. developing formulas for the perimeter of polygons			
19. Developing the concept of circumference			
a. understanding the meaning of circumference			
b. developing the formula for the circumference of a circle			
20. Developing the concept of area			
a. understanding the meaning of area			
b. developing formulas for the area of simple, two-dimensional, closed figures			
c. using formulas to compute the area of			
(1) triangles			

	INTRODUCTION	IN PROCESS	MASTERY

      (2) quadrilaterals
      (3) circles
21. Identifying space figures
    a. prisms
      (1) triangular
      (2) rectangular (including cubes)
    b. pyramid
      (1) triangular
      (2) rectangular
    c. cylinder
    d. cone
    e. sphere
22. Developing the concept of volume
    a. understanding the meaning of volume
    b. developing formulas for space figures
    c. using formulas to compute the volume of
      (1) prisms
      (2) cylinders
      (3) pyramids
      (4) cones
      (5) spheres

J. CONCEPT CLUSTER—EXPONENTIAL NOTATION

REMARK
Begin all work with positive integral exponents. When children achieve power with those concepts, introduce nonpositive integral exponents.

1. expressing repeated factors as numerals using exponential form
2. rewriting numbers expressed in exponential form as repeated factors
3. understanding the terms exponent, base of an exponent, exponential form, and power
4. representing counting numbers as numerals in exponential form
5. understanding that any nonzero number raised to the zero power is one
6. writing a number in expanded form using exponents
7. multiplying numbers written in exponential form and expressing the product in exponential form
8. dividing numbers written in exponential form and representing the quotient in exponential form
9. understand that for any nonzero number a and any positive number x, that

$$a^{-x} = \frac{1}{a^x} \text{ and } a^x = \frac{1}{a^{-x}}$$

10. multiplying numbers expressed in exponential form (using any integral exponent) and expressing the product in exponential form
11. dividing numbers expressed in exponential form (using any integral exponent) and expressing the quotient in exponential form

K. CONCEPT CLUSTER—SCIENTIFIC NOTATION
1. defining scientific notation
2. understanding the purpose of expressing numbers in scientific notation

	INTRODUCTION	IN PROCESS	MASTERY

3. expressing numbers in scientific notation
4. writing numbers expressed in scientific notation as numbers written in standard form
5. determining the number of significant digits in a number expressed in scientific notation
6. naming products and quotients of numbers written in scientific notation
7. rewriting factors, dividends, and divisors in scientific notation as a means of approximating products and quotients
8. applying scientific notation to problem solving

L. CONCEPT CLUSTER—PROBABILITY

1. discovering the meaning of probability
2. investigating the social and economic significance of probability
3. identifying a sample space (all possible outcomes)
4. establishing the meaning of theoretical probability
5. establishing the meaning of experimental probability (includes such terms as "randomness," and "trial")
6. recognizing an event as a subset of a particular sample space
7. stating a formal definition for the theoretical probability of an event as the ratio of the number of favorable outcomes to the total number of outcomes
8. expressing theoretical probability as a fraction, decimal or percent
9. understanding that the theoretical probability of an event, $P(E)$, is greater than or equal to zero and less than or equal to one ($0 \leq P(E) \leq 1$)
10. determining a sample space for a particular experiment
11. recognizing an event as a subset of a particular calculated sample space
12. stating a formal definition for the experimental probability of an event as the ratio of the number of favorable outcomes to the total number of outcomes of the experience
13. expressing experimental probability as a fraction, decimal, or percent
14. recognizing the essential difference between theoretical and experimental probability
15. computing theoretical probability of events
16. practicing the computation of experimental probability of events
17. understanding that, as the number of trials increase, the experimental probability for an event approaches the theoretical probability

REMARK

Throughout the previous discussion we have assumed the presence of equally likely simple events.

18. investigating experimental probability
    a. recognizing that the total set of outcomes for successive trials, each of which has exactly two outcomes, is a sample space

	INTRODUCTION	IN PROCESS	MASTERY

b. drawing tree diagrams to illustrate the arrangement of total outcomes when the results of successive trials, each having exactly two outcomes, are recorded

c. determining the theoretical probability of an event resulting from successive trials, each with exactly two outcomes

d. generating Pascal's triangle

e. comparing Pascal's triangle to the set of total outcomes yielded by the tree diagrams for two successive trials, each of which has exactly two outcomes

f. comparing Pascal's triangle to the set of total outcomes yielded by the tree diagram for three successive trials

g. generalizing that Pascal's triangle can illustrate the number of ways that events can occur after a given number of trials

M. CONCEPT CLUSTER—STATISTICS
1. finding the mean
2. finding the median
3. finding the mode
4. finding the range
5. collecting data
6. organizing data
7. picturing data by drawing graphs
8. reading graphs
9. interpreting information from graphs

N. CONCEPT CLUSTER—GRAPHS (NON-ALGEBRAIC)
1. observing and collecting data
2. recording data
   a. experiences involving recording by placing physical objects in appropriate rows or columns according to a particular trait
   b. experience with recording by making tallies
3. constructing graphs from materials
   a. block charts: using unlined paper, then using paper ruled in squares
   b. pictographs
4. interpreting data from tallies
5. developing graphic skills
   a. choosing an appropriate type of graph
   b. choosing appropriate labels
   c. choosing appropriate scales
   d. converting a record or tally to a graph
   e. writing or verbalizing a summary of the graph

REMARK
Provide opportunities for children to become aware of incomplete information on graphs.

6. interpreting different types of graphs
   a. number lines
   b. graphs using concrete objects
   c. block charts
   d. pictographs
   e. bar graphs

	INTRODUCTION	IN PROCESS	MASTERY

f.   line graphs
g.   histograms
h.   frequency polygons
i.   smooth curves
j.   circle graphs
k.   percentile curves
7.   experiences in constructing different types of graphs (see #6)

O.   CONCEPT CLUSTER—RECTANGULAR COORDINATE GRAPHS

1.   understanding the need for "order" in an ordered pair
2.   finding the position corresponding to a given ordered pair in a coordinate system
3.   naming the ordered pair corresponding to a given position in a coordinate system
4.   understanding the $1-1$ correspondence between points on a rectangular graph and the ordered pairs associated with these points
5.   naming points located *on* horizontal or vertical axes:
     $(-3,0)$, $(0,6)$, $(0,0)$
6.   associating the first number of an ordered pair with the horizontal axis and the second number of the ordered pair with the vertical axis
7.   finding solutions to open sentences with two variables:
     $\triangle + \square = 8$; $3\square + 2\triangle = 12$
8.   plotting solutions to linear equations on a coordinate graph as in #7
9.   writing simple open sentences given several ordered pairs
10. finding solutions to inequalities of the form
     $\triangle + \square \leq 7$; $2\triangle + \square > 8$
11. plotting solutions to inequalities of #10

Appendix C

Some Microcomputer Terms

ADDRESS A numbered location in computer memory used to store data.

ALPHANUMERIC A character set that includes numbers, letters, symbols, and punctuation marks or a combination of these.

BREAK A key on a microcomputer that causes a computer to interrupt the program that is running. Some computers use a STOP key rather than a BREAK key. Some computers use a combination of keys.

CLEAR Some microcomputers have a key marked CLEAR that will clear the screen. This key does not clear the memory. All microcomputers have techniques for placing a clear statement into a program.

DATA Numbers, facts, letters, symbols, names, or strings used in a microcomputer.

DIM A dimension command telling the computer to reserve memory space for numeric arrays and string variables.

END A command that causes a computer program to halt. This statement ends program execution.

ERROR A computer statement usually indicating deviation from a correct form.

FOR The beginning part of a FOR—NEXT loop that repeats a set of program lines until a certain incremented value is attained.

GOSUB A command that causes a program to branch to an indicated line (beginning of a subroutine within the program).

GOTO A command that causes a computer program to branch to a specified line.

IF As the beginning part of an IF—THEN statement, causes the computer to execute a specific instruction under certain conditions.

INPUT Causes the computer to wait for character entry from the keyboard and assigns the entered value to a variable.

LIST Displays on the video screen all or part of a computer program that is currently in memory.

LOAD Causes a stored computer program to be transferred from storage to the computer memory.

NEXT The command that terminates a FOR—NEXT loop.

NEW Causes the computer to delete the present program from memory.

PRINT Outputs characters that are placed within quotation marks on the video screen. The question mark (?) can be used instead of the word "PRINT."

RANDOM A number selected from an orderless set of numbers.

READ Causes the computer to transmit data from one location to another.

REM Permits the programmer to place explanatory comments in the program that have no effect upon program execution.

RETURN A command that causes the computer to branch back to the statement following a GOSUB statement.

RETURN or ENTER key Causes the computer to place the line just typed into the memory of the computer.

RND A computer command for a random number selection.

RUN Causes a computer to execute a program that is stored in memory.

SHIFT A key (similar to the shift key on a typewriter keyboard) that causes the computer to print the character on the upper part of a key.

STEP A command indicating to the computer to count by a specified increment.

THEN The second part of an IF—THEN statement instructing the computer to execute a specific instruction under certain circumstances.

Index

7323